Child Development

Child Development

Fergus P. Hughes
University of Wisconsin, Green Bay

Lloyd D. Noppe
University of Wisconsin, Green Bay

Illene C. Noppe
University of Wisconsin, Green Bay

West Publishing Company
St. Paul   New York   Los Angeles   San Francisco

Photo Credits

ii Jeff Smith, The Image Bank

1 Click/Chicago; **5** Walter Hodges, Click/Chicago; **9** Jeff Persons, Stock, Boston; **10** The Bettmann Archive, Inc.; **13** Meg Gerken, Click/Chicago; Michael Nichols, Magnum Photos; **18** The Bettmann Archive, Inc.; **20** Erika Stone, Peter Arnold, Inc.; **21** The Bettmann Archive;

31 Eve Arnold, Magnum Photos, Inc.; **35** Charles Gupton, Stock, Boston; **39** Rick Kopstein, Monkmeyer Press; **47** Mimi Forsyth, Monkmeyer Press; **50** Natalie Leimkuhler;

61 Petit Format/Nestle, Photo Researchers, Inc.; **63** Martin M. Rotker, Taurus Photos; **66** Sybil Shelton, Peter Arnold, Inc.; **70** © David Scharf, Peter Arnold, Inc.; **72** Petit Format/Nestle, Photo Researchers, Inc.; **73** Petit Format/Nestle, Photo Researchers, Inc.; **75** (top) Petit Format/ Nestle, Photo Researchers, Inc.; **7.5** (bottom) Petit Format, Photo Researchers, Inc.; **81** © Nancy Durrell McKenna, Photo Researchers, Inc.; **85** Joseph Nettis, Photo Researchers, Inc.; **88** (Top l, r) Ellis Herwig, Stock, Boston; Elizabeth Crews, Stock, Boston; (Bottom l, r) Ed Lettau, Photo Researchers, Inc.; Lew Merrim, Monkmeyer Press;

101 Joseph Schuler, Stock, Boston; **105** © Biophoto Assoc., Photo Researchers, Inc.; **113** Vivienne, Photo Researchers, Inc.; **114** Peter Vandermark, Stock, Boston; **117** Rick Kopstein, Monkmeyer Press; **118** Elizabeth Crews, Stock, Boston; **121** Paul Conklin, Monkmeyer Press; **124** © F. Scianna, Magnum Photos, Inc.; **126** © Daemmrick, Stock, Boston;

137 Elizabeth Walk Robbins; **140** Helmut Gritsher, Peter Arnold, Inc.; **145** Diana Rasche, Click/ Chicago; **148** Erika Stone, Peter Arnold, Inc.; **151** © Richard Fukuhara, Click/Chicago; **158** Michal Heron, Monkmeyer Press;

167 Mimi Forsyth, Monkmeyer Press; **173** (a, b) Hazel Hankin, Stock, Boston; **175** © Costa Manos, Magnum Photos, Inc.; **177** Peter Vandermark, Stock, Boston; **179** © Bruce Roberts, Photo Researchers, Inc.; **183** Mike Mazzschi, Stock, Boston; **186** © Royce L. Bair, Monkmeyer Press;

Photo credits continued after Subject Index

Copyediting: Judith Peacock
Text Design: John Edeen
Artwork: Rolin Graphics
Composition: Graphic World
Cover Photograph: Jeff Smith, The Image Bank
Cover Designer: Paula Schlosser

COPYRIGHT © 1988 By WEST PUBLISHING
COMPANY
50 W. Kellogg Boulevard
P.O. Box 64526
St. Paul, MN 55164-1003

Library of Congress Cataloging-in-Publication Data

Hughes, Fergus P.
   Child development/Fergus Hughes, Lloyd Noppe,
      Illene Noppe. p. cm.

   Includes bibliographies and index.
   ISBN 0-314-64017-7
   1. Child development. I. Noppe, Lloyd D.
II. Noppe, Illene C. III. Title.
RJ131.H84 1988   87-21283
155.4—dc19   CIP

To the memory of my parents, James and Alice Hughes,
who gave me life and taught me much about it.

To the memory of my father and to my mother,
Alexander and Adele Noppe, who knew the meaning
of childhood and shared it with me.

To my parents, Morris and Fanny Cupit, who
inspired me with their love of education and knowledge.

About the Authors

Fergus Hughes is an Associate Professor of Human Development at the University of Wisconsin-Green Bay, where he has been teaching courses of child, adolescent, and adult development since 1972. Born in Dublin, Ireland, and raised there, in Toronto, and in the New York City area, he earned his B.A. from St. John's University and his M.A. and Ph.D. in Developmental Psychology from Syracuse University.

Professor Hughes is an active scholar and writer. He co-authored the book *Human Development: Across the Life Span*, has had articles published in such journals as *Developmental Psychology, Journal of Genetic Psychology* and the *Academic Psychology Bulletin*, and recently co-authored a chapter in the *Annual Review of Psychology*. He maintains a strong commitment to undergraduate teaching, however, with classes ranging in size from twenty to three hundred, and he has been honored for teaching excellence by his faculty colleagues.

Lloyd D. Noppe is an Associate Professor of Human Development and Psychology at the University of Wisconsin-Green Bay, where he has taught since 1980. Born in Forest Hills, New York, he earned his B.A. from Lake Forest College and his Ph.D. from Temple University. He presently teaches courses in life span development, tests and measurements, child and adolescent development, and educational psychology.

Professor Noppe has co-authored *Human Development: Across the Life Span*, has published articles in the *Journal of Creative Behavior*, the *Journal of Personality Assessment*, the *Journal of Genetic Psychology*, and has made contributions to other books and at progressional symposia. He also has consulted on a variety of educational evaluation programs and frequently presents workshops for teachers and other school personnel.

Illene C. Noppe is an Assistant Professor of Human Development and Psychology at the University of Wisconsin-Green Bay, where she has taught since 1984. She has taught courses in infancy and early childhood, educational psychology, gender roles, cognitive development, and death and dying. Prior to coming to the University of Wisconsin, she taught courses covering the entire human lifespan for the Psychology Department at Lawrence University. Professor Noppe was born in the Bronx, N.Y., and earned her B.A. from Lake Forest College and her Ph.D. from Temple University.

Among Professor Noppe's scholarly works are chapters for *Human Development: Across the Lifespan*, a publication in the *Journal of Early Adolescence*, and articles for the *Women Studies Encyclopedia*. She is currently studing how parental expectations prior to the birth of their first baby affect parent-infant interaction styles and levels of parental stress after the birth of the baby.

Contents

7 Learning and Information Processing   199

8 Intelligence   237

9 Language   269

10 Personality and the Self   305

11 Family Relationships   341

14 Gender Development   447

Preface

Child development is an active, dynamic, continuous process. More accurately, it is the interaction of many processes, because development occurs simultaneously in a number of areas: the physical, the intellectual, the social, and the emotional. The goal of this book is to familiarize students with the complex, often interrelated, processes involved in a child's development from conception through adolescence, by offering comprehensive, up-to-date coverage of relevant theory and research in as appealing a manner as possible.

Topical Arrangement

This book is not about childhood or adolescence as stages of life, but about child and adolescent development. Therefore, it uses a topical arrangement. The topical approach provides students with the most complete understanding of the developmental process itself. The theory and research emphasized are developmental theory and research. Rather than teaching the reader how many words a 2-year-old can understand, the text describes the continuous process of language development; rather than listing the reasons given by 6-year-olds for choosing friends, the text traces the development of social awareness throughout childhood and adolescence. The milestones in each area are included, of course, as illustrations of development in the various topical areas, but the emphasis is on processes rather than on specific behaviors.

While the topical areas within child development are fairly well established, the field of study grows continuously, with some areas receiving greater emphasis than others. In addition to providing balance among the topics covered, this book reflects current trends in child development research. For example, there is extensive treatment of topics that until recently have received little attention in college textbooks: infant perception, so-

cial cognition, the development of the self-concept, children's play and its relationship to creativity, gender roles and gender differences, biological influences on personality, the sibling relationship, the father's role in parenting, and development in nontraditional families.

Furthermore, information on the environmental settings in which development occurs (the school, the home, the particular culture, etc.) is integrated into the various topical areas. As an example, school-related issues are covered in the chapters on physical growth, perception, cognition, learning, intelligence, language, gender, and play and creativity.

Finally, material on atypical development is incorporated into the appropriate topical areas rather than treating developmental abnormalities as separate topics. For example, shyness is discussed in the chapter on social interaction, mental retardation in the chapter on intelligence, and attention deficit disorder in the chapter on learning and information processing.

Interdisciplinary Approach

Child development is by definition an interdisciplinary process. Most of the research in the area would fall under the discipline of psychology, but knowledge of development in childhood and adolescence has been considerably enhanced by the research of biologists, sociologists, and cultural anthropologists as well. Consequently, this book integrates research and theory from a number of disciplines into each topical area. For example, the chapter on physical growth focuses not only on biological aspects of development, but also on social and psychological correlates of physical attractiveness. The chapter on family relationships presents sociological research on the changing American family, as well as psychological studies on the impact of various child-rearing approaches and the development of attachment. Cross-cultural research is integrated throughout the text, but most particularly in the chapters on social interaction, cognition, and language. The gender-roles chapter especially illustrates the interdisciplinary emphasis, since psychological, sociological, anthropological, and biological perspectives on gender roles and differences are examined in depth.

Integration of Theory and Research

The field of child development contains many intriguing theories about how human beings grow and develop. These theories, in turn, have stimulated a wealth of research efforts. By presenting significant theoretical and research contributions to the field, this textbook provides an exciting combination of facts and ideas.

Theories

The major theoretical perspectives on child development are introduced in the first chapter. Then, these theories—such as the behavioral, the cognitive developmental, and the psychoanalytic—are referred to repeatedly in chapters dealing with relevant topical areas. For example, the basic tenets of cognitive developmental theory are introduced in the opening chapter, but individual cognitive theories are discussed in greater depth in the chapters on perception, cognition, social interaction, gender, and play.

Research

Students in a child development course need to be familiar with the research in the field, and to understand how studies are conducted. This book exposes students to child development research in several ways. First, it includes a chapter on the basic principles of research methodology, with numerous illustrations of research procedures and designs. Second, it frequently describes studies in detail in the body of the text. Third, many chapters contain a feature called "Research Close-up,"

which describes a particular study in detail. Finally, at the end of each chapter a section entitled "Readings from the Literature" reprints a relevant research article in its entirety.

Readability

Child development is an inherently appealing field of study for most college students, but its appeal is enhanced if the material is presented in an interesting way. This book attempts to be scholarly and challenging to the undergraduate, while at the same time maintaining a "reader friendliness" that should engage and maintain the student's interest. The material is presented in such a way that students should do more than learn a set of facts about child and adolescent development; they should also be stimulated to think about what they are learning, and perhaps someday to seek their own answers to the many unanswered questions in the field.

Pedagogical Aids

This text contains a number of features designed to enrich the student's learning experience by focusing on examples of developmental research and theory in child development. *Issues in Child Development* focuses on a controversy or unanswered question in the field of child development (e.g., "Are there sex differences in moral reasoning?" or "What happens when mother goes to work?"). *Problems in Child Development* deals with abnormalities of development in the various topical areas (e.g., shyness, mental retardation, deafness).

Research Close-up describes a particular study in some detail. In addition to illustrating various research strategies, this feature shows students how individual studies attempt to answer general questions about the developmental process. *Applying Our Knowledge* illustrates practical applications of developmental principles, and helps the student to realize that theory and research in child development are relevant to problem solving in the everyday world.

Readings from the Literature

One of the most important features this book offers is *Readings from the Literature*. As mentioned earlier, this feature reprints a research article from a journal in the child development field. These readings describe recent studies, although occasionally a classic study from the past is included. The purposes of the readings are to encourage students to become familiar with original sources in the field, to provide examples of the various forms of research methodology, and to reinforce points about child development made in the preceding chapter.

Acknowledgements

We would like to thank Mary Schiller, our editor at West Publishing Company, for stimulating our interest in writing this book, for encouraging us throughout all phases of the project, and for making numerous helpful suggestions along the way. We also wish to thank our production editor, Beth Wickum, for assuming responsibility for this project so late in its development and for working so efficiently and cheerfully to see that we met our production deadline.

We would like to thank our reviewers for their constructive and useful comments. Good reviewing is both a skill and an art. It is easy to be critical but not easy to suggest improvements; it is easy to be positive but not easy to explain the reasons why. Our reviewers never took the easy way out. As a result, they helped us considerably, and we are very grateful to them. They are N.J. Austin, Thomas Berndt, Theodore Bosack, Keith Carlson, Debra Clark, R. Daniel DiSalvi, Sandra Rappaport Fiske, Robert Haaf, Susan Hegland, Bruce Hinrichs, Elizabeth Hogeland, Paul Jose, Melvyn King, Janet Malone, Betty Marrs, Dennis Molfese, Charles Nelson, Robert O'Neill, M.C. Pugmire-Stoy, Gregory Reichhart, Theresa Roberts, Frederick Schwantes, Robert Stewart, and M. Virginia Wyly.

Finally, we would like to thank our typists, Hope Mercier and Barbara Delforge, for the speed, efficiency, and reliability of their work. A project as massive as writing a textbook is much easier to handle if authors can trust the skills of their typists, and we certainly could.

Fergus Hughes
Lloyd Noppe
Illene Noppe

Introduction: Concepts and Theories

What is a child? How do children develop? Whether we realize it or not, most of us have definite theoretical beliefs about children's development. These beliefs influence the way we relate to children, as well as the way we understand ourselves. For example, parents who see themselves as responsible for all that their children grow to be probably believe that children's development is heavily influenced by environmental forces. By contrast, parents whose child-rearing attitude is that "you work with the raw material nature has provided" are likely to believe that internal forces are influential in the development of the child. What is more, such philosophical views of childhood are hardly new. As you will see in this chapter, differing attitudes about the importance of environmental or biological influences on the child have had a long history in philosophy and psychology.

For thousands of years human beings have contemplated the nature of developmental change. Why then, after so many centuries of discussion, do we not have a single, widely accepted theory of development? The issues of most significance to understanding child development are often very controversial. No field of study, from nuclear physics to art history, is without some degree of intellectual conflict. When humans try to understand their own children's developmental changes, the task becomes especially complex and subjective. Furthermore, the factors contributing to patterns of development have themselves not remained constant during the course of history. Yale psychologist William Kessen (1979) suggested that the child is a cultural invention, defined by broad social forces that also affect those who study children in ways they may only dimly recognize.

This chapter, therefore, introduces the perspectives that underlie contemporary theory and research in child development. It deals, first of all, with a number of the themes, or issues, most critical to an understanding of the developmental process. Then it briefly traces the historical roots of this field from ancient Greece to modern times. Finally, the chapter examines three theoretical perspectives that encompass all modern views on children's development and that were forged out of centuries of philosophical speculation.

Examining the origins of modern theories will show the diversity of views that make up current understanding of child development. It will also show the magnitude of change across the centuries and the relationship between philosophical positions and the kinds of theories formulated. You should realize that the questions asked today about the nature of childhood have been asked before, and many have been asked for hundreds—and even thousands—of years. We like to think, however, that we are closer now to providing answers, since in this century researchers have added the techniques of scientific research to what has been a long history of philosophical speculation.

Themes of Child Development

A number of issues must be kept in mind by anyone studying child development. These "themes," as they will be called here, are characteristics of the developmental process itself. Even though they will be discussed separately, they overlap to a certain extent. The themes to keep in mind as you begin your course of study are that child development (1) is an individual process; (2) involves both hereditary and environmental factors; (3) is a process of change, although all changes are not genuine developments; (4) is a continuous process that cannot be described only by ages and stages; and (5) is an interdisciplinary study.

Norms and Individual Differences

Anxious parents often ask a child psychologist what their children *should* be doing at certain ages: "Jimmy is 14 months old and hasn't started walking yet. Is this normal?" or "Mary is 5 and doesn't share her toys well with other children. Shouldn't she be better at sharing by now?" The experts generally reassure the parents that child development is an individual process, with no two children developing in exactly the same way. Norms, or averages, are useful guidelines, but individual variations within norms must be accepted and perhaps even appreciated. Relying too heavily on norms and making comparisons between one child and another can often have disastrous results.

The individuality of children's development does not mean, of course, that the process cannot be studied scientifically. All scientific research involves the study of individual instances of a given physical or psychological phenomenon and generalization from those instances to related phenomena. For example, a physicist discovers that when solid objects are released and allowed to fall freely to the ground, their falling speed accelerates at a consistent and predictable rate. The physicist then makes a generalization by applying the newfound information to the acceleration rate of all falling bodies in the atmosphere, even though only a small number of instances of the phenomenon actually have been observed.

The same approach—generalization from a small but representative number of examples—is used in the social sciences as well. Because of the complexity of human behavior, however, the social scientist generalizes with a lesser degree of confidence than does the physicist. The rate of falling bodies may be highly predictable, but children provide numerous exceptions to every rule. Since each child's development is a unique experience, behavioral norms do not uniformly apply. To be sure, there are similarities in children's developmental patterns. They are all members of the same species, and most of them are raised in similar social settings. Nevertheless, the infinite complexity of the individual, the complexity of the environment in which development occurs, and the complex nature of the child's interaction with the environment virtually guarantee that no two children will develop in precisely the same way.

Therefore, when generalizations about development are presented in this textbook or in any other source, caution in interpreting such information is needed. Murphy, Heider, and Small (1986) suggested that an overview of typical ages and sequences of development offers an important window to what can be generally expected from a child, but excessive anxiety or rigid adherence to norms can blind us to the needs of specific children. Developmental researchers and theorists must constantly shift between the larger picture of universal patterns of change and the extensive variety of individual differences which operate within these general milestones.

Heredity and Environment

One of the oldest controversies in the history of philosophy, and eventually in child development as well, is the nature-nurture controversy: is behavior primarily determined by biological or genetic factors within the organism (nature) or by experience in the external world (nurture)? The extreme of the nature side of the question was represented by the maturation theorists at the turn of the century, while the extreme advocates of the opposite stress on nurture were the early behaviorists. Both types of theory will be discussed in greater detail later in this chapter. The argument between the behaviorists and the maturation theorists was never really resolved. Instead, the nature-nurture controversy as an either-or proposition simply died by the 1950s as theorists came to realize that neither side could offer a complete explanation of the child's behavior (Anastasi 1958).

The approach to the nature-nurture question most frequently taken today is the interactionist approach: behavior is the product of the **interaction** of both hereditary and environmental factors. This interaction is not a simple additive process. Heredity and environment do not merely combine as the ingredients in a recipe are combined. In other words, the percentage contributed by either heredity or environment to the overall process of development cannot be determined easily. Instead, interaction is multiplicative, with the contribution of each element continuously influencing and being influenced by the contributions of the other.

Interaction is a dynamic two-directional process, as illustrated by the following example. Many adults have had the experience of trying to calm a crying baby. They may have found that the more the baby cried, the more tense they became, and the more tense they became, the more the baby cried. Can we determine how much of the infant's distress was caused by the adult and how much by the baby? Of course not. The additive approach is unworkable in an interactive situation. All we can reasonably conclude is that both infant and adult simultaneously influenced one another in a back-and-forth fashion.

Despite the difficulty of precisely accounting for all the inherited and environmental factors in human behavior, the nature-nurture question should not be ignored, nor should the interaction concept be considered an easy solution to the question because it seems to cover all possibilities. Efforts at separating out the inherited and environmental factors in child development continue today, many of them employing imaginative research strategies and some of them raising fascinating questions. McCall (1981), for example, proposed an interactive model of early mental development, labeled the "scoop" approach, that will be described in Chapter 3.

In reading the chapters of this text, remember that a child's characteristics may never be determined totally by inherited factors or totally by environmental influences. Both elements combine in an interactive fashion, and it is difficult—but at least theoretically possible—to separate them for purposes of study. The controversy over the relative importance of nature and nurture is still a crucial issue for the field of child development.

Development and Change

All development involves change, but not every change represents a genuine development. To develop means to grow out of, to evolve from. In the literal sense of the word, to develop is to unwrap. Indeed, a definite sense of unwrapping is present in the developmental process—a sense of one state of affairs not only following but also emerging directly from that which preceded it. Nondevelopmental change, in contrast, is a transition requiring no evolution, no unwrapping. A girl, for example, might change her clothing, the arrangement of the furniture in her room, or the record on her turntable. In each of these instances, one situation merely folllows another without the necessity of any connection between the current state of events and the preceding state. It would be absurd to suggest that the first record on the turntable developed into the present record, when in fact there is no relationship between the two records at all.

Child development, then, is an orderly process dealing with the emergence of one state from another, and those who investigate this process engage in little analysis of nondevelopmental

change. For this reason, the study of child development involves much more than a mere cataloging of events occurring in children's lives as they grow older. It would be difficult and pointless to list all of the changes observed during childhood, or even over the span of a single year.

As a practical example of the difference between a developmental and a nondevelopmental change, consider the case of John, a high school sophomore preparing for a psychology exam by memorizing the definitions at the end of each chapter in his textbook. Knowing that he would not be able to memorize all the definitions in one sitting, he begins his studying early and sets a goal of memorizing only five terms a day. There certainly will be a change from day to day in what John is studying, as well as a gradual increase in the total number of definitions he has learned. However, these are nondevelopmental changes. Why? Because what John studies in any given day is unrelated to what he studied the day before.

It is possible, however, that John's situation might illustrate a developmental as well as a nondevelopmental change. Suppose that John discovers that each day he learns new lists of words more quickly and efficiently than he did the day before. He finds that he is becoming skilled at absorbing new information; there are changes in the quality of his approach to the material, as well as quantitative changes in the total amount of material learned. Now the changes in his study habits and in his approaches to learning are truly developmental changes. Each day's activity builds upon and emerges from the previous day's activity. The experience of studying the first chapter definitely affected the experience of studying the second, and so on. In summary, whereas the changes in the content of John's knowledge—the sum total of what he knows—may be nondevelopmental changes, the changes in the way he learns are genuine developments.

Developmental psychologists are interested in the patterns created when children integrate each new experience into their already existing reservoir of experiences while simultaneously drawing on that reservoir to interpret the experience at hand. It is not the life experiences themselves that are of interest; it is the ways in which the child interacts with those experiences and the ways in

This three-generation family illustrates the fact that human development is a continuous unfolding beginning at conception and ending at the moment of death.

which the interactions lead to increasingly more sophisticated interactions. To use the concrete terms of the earlier example, it is not what the student has learned that is of interest, but how his approaches to learning have changed because of his exposure to the learning process and how the changes in his approaches will allow him to function more effectively when he encounters a new learning situation.

Ages, Stages, and Continuity

The development of an individual child is a process of constant integration of current experiences into previously formed structures. It is a continuous unfolding, beginning at conception and ending when the child enters adulthood, however that term may be defined. The developmental pro-

cess is often described in terms of ages ("You're old enough to pick up after yourself.") or stages ("Adolescence is a stressful time of life"). However, any parent knows that ages or stages often reveal little about the developmental level of a particular child. Jane may be able to pick up after herself at 4, but 6-year-old Katie never seems to remember to clean up her room. Steve may have had major difficulties adjusting to the changes in his body at puberty, while Michael's life hardly changed at all when he became a teenager.

What is the relationship between chronological age and child development? William Kessen (1960) proposed that a characteristic may be considered development if it can be related to age in an orderly way. He argued that age in itself is not the equivalent of development, however, because development is affected by many factors in addition to age and because there are wide individual variations in the rate of human growth. In other words, child development occurs over a definite period of time, but time alone is not a sufficient condition for development to occur.

Age is a convenient reference point for development, and we frequently generalize from age norms as when we say that children begin to use logic at age 6 or that adolescents begin to date at age 14. However, we should always remember that it is not the age we are describing, but the developmental process; we should not expect all human beings to develop at the same rate, even though we all measure our chronological ages in the same units of time.

If age and development should not be viewed as equivalent, what can be said of the concept of stages? For explanatory purposes, the span of childhood is often divided into developmental stages: infancy, early childhood, middle childhood, adolescence. A **developmental stage** can be thought of as a time period within the life cycle that is characterized by a particular cluster of physical, emotional, intellectual, or social characteristics. In other words, there should be some consistency within stages in the characteristic that is studied, as when we say that the infant's ways of solving problems, of expressing needs, or of interacting with peers differ from the ways of the preschool child.

Convenient as the stage concept is for academic purposes, it may foster serious misconceptions. One common misconception is that stages of development are discrete entities. In reality, they are not separate at all, but evolve from one another constantly. The stage concept may also lead to the false impression that stages in children are static. However, stages are anything but static, since they all include continuous development within them. For example, babies do not simply remain suspended in the stage of infancy until they are ready to spring forward into early childhood; constant change occurs within the phase of infancy, as within all life stages. Adolescence not only follows middle childhood but also gradually evolves from it. Much of who we are during any life stage is an outgrowth of who we were during the preceding stages. Although developmental stages or

phases—and their associated chronological ages—are valuable reference points, individual variation is the predominant characteristic of children's development.

An Interdisciplinary Study

No single discipline is broad enough to describe all of the biological, social, intellectual, and emotional changes that children experience as they mature. How, for example, can we discuss the physical changes of puberty without at the same time discussing the psychological effects of physical maturation? How can we examine the psychological effects of divorce on a young child without also examining recent changes in one of our major social institutions, the family unit? Can we paint an accurate picture of the development of the child if we study only our own culture and no others? The perspectives of scholars from many disciplines must be considered, not in isolation from one another, but in an integrated fashion (Charlesworth 1972). This issue is repeatedly discussed in the newsletters of the Society for Research in Child Development (e.g., McCall 1983), the major professional organization in the field.

The major contributions to child development come from the social science disciplines of anthropology, sociology, and psychology, as well as from the natural science discipline of biology. The contributions have not been of equal weight, however. The vast majority of scholars in the field of child development are psychologists, and most of the research discussed in this text is psychological research. The contributions of the specific disciplines will be introduced only when such reference is appropriate. For example, in some areas—such as sensory, physical, and reproductive development—most of the work has been contributed by biologists. In other areas—such as learning, cognition, intelligence, and perception—psychologists have contributed the greatest amount. Finally, although there is much to learn from cross-cultural comparisons about virtually any aspect of child development, this text will focus primarily on development in American society. Cross-cultural references will be made only when a comparison of cultures will serve to illustrate a point about our culture or when such comparisons provide a test of the universality of developmental principles.

The field of anthropology focuses on human culture and examines cultural variations throughout the world. The value of an anthropological perspective on child development becomes apparent when we realize that most of what we know about childhood comes from the work of researchers studying development in the United States and Western Europe (Munroe, Munroe & Whiting 1981). Therefore, what we consider "normal development" may be normal only in these cultures, whereas totally different developmental progressions might be observed in other parts of the world. Only by making cross-cultural comparisons can we avoid the serious error of generalizing too freely from data collected in our own society. Furthermore, if we fail to make cross-cultural comparisons, we may never know which qualities of children are primarily of biological (nature) origin and which are learned (nurture). For these reasons, anthropology is an essential component of the interdisciplinary study of child development.

Sociology is the branch of social science that analyzes group relationships and social institutions (Goodman & Marx 1982). Child development cannot be studied in a vacuum. We must constantly be attuned to the social forces influencing the lives of children—to the changes in values as well as institutions. For example, a sociologist might study the American family unit and how it has been changing in recent generations. (See Issues in Child Development "Do We Really Value Children?" for an interesting viewpoint.) Other important factors examined by sociologists are shifts in population (according to age or geography, for instance), variations among the socioeconomic classes in the United States today, participation in organized religion by teenagers, elementary schools as educational institutions for children, and the rates of delinquency in urban versus rural communities. Each of these topics suggests that the interdisciplinary study of child development must include contributions from the field of sociology.

Psychology may be defined broadly as the study of individual consciousness and behavior (Gleitman 1986). The field is divided into at least a dozen areas of specialization in order to explore emotions, thoughts, body language, sensations, learning, memory, perceptions, morals, treatment of problems, complex organizations, small-group functioning, differences between boys and girls, and numerous other aspects of the mind and its resulting activities. Developmental psychologists, in particular, are heavily identified with the field of child development. They are interested in the intellectual, social, and emotional changes that occur over time, and in the underlying mechanisms responsible for such developments. In addition, their concern with physical growth, neurophysiology, genetics, or endocrinology is an attempt to make a connection between biology and psychology.

Although it is clear that developmental psychology provides the core of the interdisciplinary study of child development, the field of human biology offers an equally extensive tradition of describing the processes of life. Children are obviously biological organisms who are partly controlled by genetic factors. Indeed, the interaction of psychology and biology is frequently incorporated into models of development from G. Stanley Hall and Sigmund Freud to Jean Piaget and Erik Erikson.

Nevertheless, many behavioral scientists believe that the biological components in child development have been either totally ignored or at least downplayed far too long. Psychologist David Lykken, director of a project involving hundreds of twins at the Minnesota Center for Twin and Adoption Research, believes that an astonishing number of intellectual and personality characteristics may have biological rather than psychological origins. These include extroversion, conformity, a tendency to worry, creativity, optimism, and cautiousness. As Lykken (1987) points out, "The evidence is so compelling that it is hard to understand how people could *not* believe in the strong influence of genetics on behavior" (p. 59).

The extent to which biological factors influence child development has yet to be determined, but explanations of behavior that focus on the biological rather than the environmental seem to be

Issues in Child Development

Do We Really Value Children?

As a society we cherish, protect, and value our children. Much of our television programming is geared to a child's mentality. Restaurants have special menus for them. New toys and electronic gadgets are manufactured every year just to keep children entertained. Amusement parks exist to indulge childhood fantasies. However, disturbing signs suggest that children are increasingly seen as an undesirable element in American society. Reported incidents of child abuse are on the rise, child pornography has become a thriving enterprise, family size is decreasing, and owners of apartment complexes freely practice age discrimination by refusing to rent to people with children.

Cross-cultural psychologist Richard Logan (1977) suggested that, with increasing frequency, children are seen as burdens in our society. In simpler, preindustrial cultures—those with a rich, continuing tradition—children were seen as continuers of the cultural values. Futhermore, they were actually needed by their parents to perform the tasks necessary for their society's subsistence. These children worked alongside their elders and felt responsible for themselves as well as for others. They had a strong sense of belonging to and being committed to the cultural group.

In the United States today, according to Logan, cultural change is so rapid that parents no longer see their children as continuing a cultural tradition. The expectation is that the future will be different from (and probably better than) the life parents have experienced. In addition, modern American families do not rely on their children's economic contributions. The result is that children are seen as qualitatively different from adults. They are rarely expected to work or to assume any meaningful responsibility, and they are seen as consumers rather than producers of the economy. The children themselves no longer experience a feeling of being needed by or being committed to the cultural group.

Few Americans would want their children to be forced into the world of work, and most parents emphasize individual initiative and achievement in their offspring rather than group loyalty and dependence. However, Logan observed that many adults may at some level resent the privileged status of children and may see them as irresponsible, lazy time-wasters who have little else to do than spend their parent's hard-earned money. In other words, the same society that extends a privilege to children may secretly resent them for accepting it.

At the same time that the pressures of contemporary life lead adults to envy the freedom of their offspring, other writers have noted that parents may be unknowingly inflicting their own forms of stress on children (Elkind 1981b; Postman 1982). For example, increasing competition in schools; media portrayals of sexuality, crime, and "good life"; major alterations of family styles; and early professionalism in art, music, and sports may be creating a generation of excessively pressured children. Their worries about the nuclear age and "needs" for designer clothing may rival adult stress.

Are parents' best intentions to help their children succeed resulting instead in high levels of juvenile delinquency, drug and alcohol abuse, eating disorders, moral confusion, intellectual burnout, and sexual promiscuity? Zigler and Lang (1986) are concerned that this trend may begin even during infancy:

> Nine-month-old Eric is typical of a phenomenon that has come to be known in the popular media as the "gourmet baby." He has two educated, professional parents who have delayed childrearing until their early thirties. He has all the best equipment that money can buy—the right furniture, the right stroller, and a genuine shearling cover for his car seat. Eric has swimming lessons, looks at flash cards of famous paintings and simple words, plays with the best "developmentally engineered" toys and will begin the study of the violin in a year or two. He also has enough stimulation in the course of a day to make even a college student want to take a nap and shut it all out—which is just what Eric does. (P. 8)

Whether or not Logan is correct in his assertion that children are less valued today than we may realize, his thesis—along with the observations of Elkind, Postman, and Zigler and Lang—makes a significant point about the influence of culture, and of cultural change, on the process of child development.

*Psychologists suggest that children today may be expected to grow up too fast—
that they are hurried into adulthood before childhood is done.*

increasing (Leiderman 1987). For now, we can only conclude that it is unreasonable to exclude biological components from our search for a complete understanding of child development.

The History of Developmental Theory

Children themselves may have changed very little throughout the centuries, but adult interest in childhood and attitudes towards the young have certainly changed. This section briefly examines historical changes in society's view of children, beginning with the writings of early Greek philosophers and ending at the present day.

Early Greek Conceptions

One of the earliest stage theories of child development was outlined by the Greek philosopher Plato (ca. 427–347 B.C.). Plato suggested that the human soul is made up of three elements: appetites, spirit, and reason. The appetites, which appeared at birth and dominated the infant and early childhood years, were the basic physical and emotional needs of a child. The spirit—representing assertiveness, courage, and convictions—developed during later childhood and early adolescence. Finally, with maturity, the rational and intelligent component of the soul might become the most influential.

According to Plato's philosophy of **idealism,** human beings never come to know the world as it really exists. They only acquire images filtered through and possibly distorted by their senses.

Throughout most of our history, children were seen as small versions of adults. However, in the eighteenth century there emerged the idea of childhood innocence. Notice that the children in this picture have their pet and some toys with them.

Thus, any two people might have different perceptions of reality, since the world is filtered through their individual thought processes. As you will discover in Chapter 5, such ancient ideas are remarkably similar to those of modern child psychologists who advocate "enrichment" theories of perception.

In contrast to Plato, Aristotle (ca. 384–323 B.C.) did not believe that the fundamental meaning of the world could be discovered in images or predetermined ideals in the mind. Instead, he felt that children could learn to comprehend reality by critically examining their sensory impressions to discover universal patterns in the environment. Aristotle felt that a child's experiences (especially careful observations) could help to clarify reality rather than introduce distortions or misrepresentations of truth, as Plato had contended. Thus, reality can be known directly. In this philosophy, known as **realism,** the truth of any knowledge can be demonstrated to the mutual consent of critical thinkers everywhere.

The Middle Ages

During the Middle Ages in Europe (A.D. 1000–1500), issues concerning child development were basically neglected. People's thoughts were preoccupied with death, as they struggled to survive war and disease and the chaos of a feudal political system. Most adults had little or no education, and their lives were easily dominated by narrowly defined religious dogma. Thus, there was little recognition of the special needs of children or adolescents. In fact, infants were frequently abandoned (Watson 1978).

The pessimism of medieval Europe was partially grounded in the theological doctrine of original sin. Many related ideas about child development were similarly derived from literal interpretations of the Bible. Development, therefore, was to follow a strict path of religious education to counteract original sin and to permit the revelation of God's universal laws to all children (Muuss 1982). Unquestioning obedience was expected of a child, with very stern disciplinary measures following any sign of misbehavior. Children were required to work at an early age. Toys, fairy tales, and make-believe were not known. In paintings, children resembled miniature adults; their clothing was merely a smaller version of adult garments. In sum, the special treatment of children that is taken for granted today was not in evidence during the Middle Ages (Aries 1962).

The Reawakening of Humanity

Between the Middle Ages and the eighteenth century, the early Greeks' philosophical ideas and their consequences for child development gradually returned. The period known as the Renaissance was a time of cultural advance for much of the European world, and it led to renewed study of child development (Watson 1978).

In sharp contrast to the uniformity and insensitivity of the medieval period, the 1600s emphasized individual differences as well as developmental stages. John Amos Comenius (1592–1670), for example, proposed four 6-year stages with corresponding educational goals. These stages focused on perception (birth to 6 years), imagination (6 to 12 years), rationality (12 to 18 years), and ambition (18 to 24 years), respectively (Muuss 1982)

The Enlightenment

The eighteenth-century period known as the Enlightenment introduced a more optimistic view of human freedom and potential. The Enlightenment can be characterized as a period of greater interest in children by society. Rather than viewing children as depraved, parents began to see childhood as a time of innocence (Kessen 1965). Children were not incomplete adults, but were special individuals worthy of attention and study. Thus, toward the close of the eighteenth century in Europe, a number of philosophers, educators, and scientists turned their attention to describing the course of child development. For instance, the first careful, systematic observations of children were presented in published diaries. Dietrich Tiedemann's (1748—1803) biography of his infant son described motor skills, language, thinking capacities, and socioemotional behaviors. Heinrich Pestalozzi's (1746–1827) data are based upon his 4-year-old son's learning, but he also contributed numerous suggestions to assist parents and teachers in their observations of children.

The Age of Science

As the nineteenth century began, increasing access to education promoted a technological revolution that ultimately altered views about childhood and affected the structure of the family. Although philosophic writings on the nature of thought continued to influence educational theory and other practical areas, the principal impetus for understanding child development shifted to the realm of science.

Charles Darwin (1809–1882), the leading advocate of the theory of evolution, maintained that the human being should be viewed as a part of nature, the highest of a long chain of life forms beginning with one-celled organisms. His concepts of natural selection and survival of the fittest were major influences on understanding the developmental process: individuals of any species who are better equipped to adapt to their changing environment—for social, emotional, physical, or intellectual reasons—will survive to reproduce. Therefore, adaptability might be thought of as one of the child's most valuable characteristics.

Perhaps Darwin's most developmentally oriented contribution was to suggest a relationship between the evolution of the species and the growth of the child. This speculation made respectable the value of studying individual change. Indeed, the notion of seeking the origins of adult behaviors and attributes in childhood experiences is still widely accepted. The diary Darwin published about his infant son's activities demonstrated his commitment to the importance of individual development for understanding human evolution. Darwin's **baby biography** was not the only published account of early development, as noted earlier, but it was the most influential because of his substantial scientific reputation (Kessen 1965; Watson 1978).

As illustrated by Darwin's work, the nineteenth century witnessed a revolution in ideas about child development. The scientific method began to replace philosophical discussion and religious dogma. The requirements of developing children, for example, were documented and made available to parents in the form of child-rearing manuals. Books were written specifically for children, clothing was designed for their activities, discipline became less severe, and restrictions were placed on the ages and hours of child workers. Compulsory public education was introduced, separating many children from the domain of work, and the family became the cradle of development (with men and women adopting distinctly different roles). A major effort was underway to seek effective ways to understand the complex patterns of change in children.

The Twentieth Century

With the nineteenth century drawing to a close, a field of study specifically concerned with the ways in which children developed started to come together. From the mid-1880s to the early 1920s theorists in the United States were developing a legitimate scientific tradition, and developmental researchers began to be recognized as legitimate scientists. Somehow it seemed possible that with a great enough effort, the process of rearing children might be fully understood and perfected. The study of child development was no longer regarded as a set of philosophical problems, but rather as a part of the scientific enterprise.

After World War I, there was, particularly in the United States, a great deal of interest in accumulating the details of children's healthy learning and growth. Perhaps this was because viewing children as the hope of the future coincided with the American spirit of optimism. This position was furthered by actions of the government (the passage of strict legislation to protect and promote children's welfare, along with the establishment and funding of institutes for child study), private philanthropy (the creation of charitable organizations for children, and the support of extensive longitudinal research), and the universities. Furthermore, as the work of anthropologists became known, American researchers developed an interest in comparing the child-rearing practices in the United States with those of other cultures.

*In the middle of the twentieth century much of the research in child development
has focused on the relatively neglected periods of infancy and adolescence.*

As the twentieth century progressed, several trends in the study of child development became apparent. First, rather than concentrating only on "what" children are like at particular ages, developmentalists became concerned with explaining "how" or "why" changes take place. A second trend has been greater emphasis on different phases of the lifespan. By the 1960s, concentration on early and middle childhood development was gradually balanced with new attention to prenatal and infant development at one extreme and, more recently, to adolescence at the other. Finally, a third trend, which will become apparent throughout the remaining chapters, has been the blending of various theories and disciplines. It became obvious

that no one theory or discipline could explain a process as complex as child development (Charlesworth 1972).

In summary, the past two thousand years of Western history have seen (1) an increased interest in the study of children, (2) an increased effort to use scientific methodology in the study of child development, (3) an increased concern with the underlying processes of development rather than only on the outcomes, and (4) an increased recognition that no one theory or academic discipline is broad enough to explain fully the development of the child.

Perspectives in Child Development

Although individual theories of child development may seem too numerous to comprehend, considerable cohesiveness does exist among them. In fact, they may be grouped into three general perspectives. These perspectives differ in their assessments of the relative importance of inherited and environmental factors on children's development (nature versus nurture). They differ also in another way: the first two perspectives—environ-

mentalist and organismic theories—view the human being as essentially rational, while the third—the psychoanalytic theory—sees human beings as creatures of appetite and emotion rather than of reason (see Table 1.1).

Environmentalism

The first major perspective on child development will be referred to as **environmentalism,** emphasizing the view that children grow to be what they are because of their environments (Langer 1969). Rejecting inborn tendencies and the con-

Table 1.1 Perspectives in Child Development

Perspective	Representative Theories	Basic Belief about Child Development
Environmentalist	British empiricism (John Locke) Behaviorism (John Watson, B.F. Skinner, Albert Bandura, Howard and Tracey Kendler) Cultural anthropology (Margaret Mead, Ruth Benedict, B. Malinowski)	The child is an empty organism at birth. The child is passive. Development is determined by experience with the environment. The adult's role is to shape the child according to socially accepted standards of behavior.
Organismic	Naturalism (Jean-Jacques Rousseau) Maturationism (G. Stanley Hall, Arnold Gesell) Cognitive developmental theory (Jean Piaget) Humanism (Abraham Maslow) Ethology (John Bowlby)	The child is active in determining his or her course of development. There is an interaction between organism and environment so that both are involved in varying degrees in the process of development.
Psychoanalytic	Psychoanalytic (Sigmund Freud, Anna Freud, Erik Erikson)	The child is not rational but is a creature governed by emotion, or appetite. Development is a process of constant compromise between the individual's needs and society's expectations.

cept of freedom of choice, environmentalist theorists see the human organism as being almost completely determined by external forces, much as a piece of clay is molded in a sculptor's hands.

British Empiricism

The origins of modern environmentalist perspectives can be traced to the ideas of John Locke (1632–1704). Locke's philosophy of British **empiricism** illustrated a new concept of human nature that changed the direction of scientific thought.

Locke believed that the human mind is a blank slate at birth, and that all knowledge of the world comes through the senses. Empty at birth, the growing human organism is basically passive, and simply receives and responds to elementary sense impressions. Complex ideas are nothing more than combinations of simple ideas that have become associated, or connected, in the mind, just

as, in the world of art, a mosaic is a picture formed from hundreds of individually meaningless bits of colored tile. The ultimate extension of Locke's theory is that children are uncivilized creatures who need the strong hand of adults to shape them into everything they are eventually to become. They are incomplete versions of adult human beings, and society's role is to civilize them.

Behaviorism

The twentieth-century equivalent of Locke's ideas can be found in the writings of John B. Watson (1878–1958). Watson believed that the only way to understand the child is through the objective observation of behaviors. He rejected the methods of subjective introspection or analysis of the unconscious, as well as explanations that relied on instincts or other interpretations that could not be scientifically proven.

According to behaviorists, parents like this exasperated mother play a crucial role in shaping children into the kind of persons they eventually become.

Watson's **behaviorism** was inspired not only by the empiricist philosophy of Locke, but also by the animal learning experiments that were taking place in the late 1800s and early 1900s. He agreed with Locke that the human mind is a blank slate at birth, and that the child is molded by environmental experience. However, it was the new technology of learning researchers that explained for Watson how environmental experience imposes itself on the child: through principles of conditioning and reinforcement. (A prominent example of such principles, which will be discussed at length in Chapter 7, is the view that rewarded behaviors are more likely to appear in the future while punished behaviors are likely to diminish.) Thus, Watson believed that the only behavior worth studying is learned behavior. Psychology's goal is not the understanding of the mind, but the prediction and control of behavior.

Since children's pattern of development is determined by what they learn, and not by any instinctive or inherited tendencies, parents play a crucial role in shaping children into the kind of persons they will become. Indeed, Watson believed that children can be formed into virtually anything adults want them to be. "Give me a dozen healthy infants," he said, "and my own specified world to bring them up in and I'll guarantee to take any one at random and train him to become any type of specialist I might select—doctor, lawyer, artist, merchant, chief, and yes, even beggarman and thief, regardless of his talents, penchants, tendencies, abilities, vocations, and race of his ancestors. There is no such thing as an inheritance of capacity, talent, temperament, mental constitution, and behavioral characteristics" (Watson 1925, 82).

A complete acceptance of Watson's point of view certainly makes parenting sound like an awesome and frightening responsibility. Behaviorists today, however, are not nearly so extreme in believing that inborn tendencies are of no consequence in the process of child development, that principles of animal learning can be applied unthinkingly to human beings, or that human learning can be so completely attributed to the experiences of reward and punishment. In fact, behaviorism has been constantly expanded and modified throughout the twentieth century.

One modification of Watson's behaviorism involved the extension of learning principles from the animal laboratory to the real world. The work of conditioning researchers such as B.F. Skinner (b. 1904) was based on the responses of rats and pigeons to schedules of material reinforcements (such as food). Even so, it was fairly easy to generalize these concepts to children's behavior. Skinner initiated discussion by describing an ideal society that he felt would insure healthy child development by adherence to reinforcement principles. As a result, conditioning techniques were applied to everything from programmed instruction in the classroom to the modification of undesirable behaviors in schizophrenics, retardates, and delinquents.

A second variation on behaviorism was stimulated by the work of Albert Bandura (b. 1925) beginning in the 1960s. This perspective is known as social learning. The key concept is that development is guided by the imitation or avoidance of behavior modeled by other people (see Chapter 7). By observing the consequences of someone else's actions, for example, children can learn how to brush their teeth, how not to ride a bicycle, how to solve a puzzle, or how not to irritate their teacher. The major significance of the social-learning approach is that it describes learning as taking place without the presence of any obvious reward or punishment. For instance, children use adults as models and imitate their behaviors without ever being rewarded for doing so. In fact, they often pick up parental behaviors, mannerisms, and speech patterns that parents actively try to discourage.

A third variation on Watson's behaviorism was inspired by the work of Howard Kendler (b. 1919) and Tracey Kendler (b. 1918). In the 1950s and 1960s, the Kendlers discovered developmental differences in the ways children learn and solve problems in laboratory settings. Young children seem to respond to a learning task exactly as Watson predicted, and as animals do: they repeat rewarded behaviors and delete behaviors that are not rewarded. Older children, perhaps as a result of their greater verbal skills, seem to develop mental strategies when solving problems and to verbalize these strategies to themselves. Simply stated, older children and adults do not always repeat rewarded behaviors and often repeat those that are punished or ignored as part of a long-range strategy for maximizing reward.

Cultural Anthropology

Watson's behaviorism, with its emphasis on principles of learning and conditioning, was not the only type of theory to stress the overwhelming significance of the environment (nurture instead of nature) in child development. Sharing Watson's views, but for different reasons, were cultural anthropologists such as Margaret Mead (1901–1978) and Ruth Benedict (1887–1948). Like the behaviorists, these cultural anthropologists emphasized experiential factors in development and were eager to demonstrate how different patterns of child rearing reflected variations in culture. They tended to downplay developmental stages and hereditary mechanisms.

Bronislaw Malinowski's (1884–1942) field work in the Trobriand islands is a useful example. He wanted to test the inevitability of conflict that Sigmund Freud suggested would occur between parents and their preschool children, but observations of Pacific Ocean island culture indicated no support for this aspect of Freud's theory. Such cross-cultural research suggested that child development is influenced not only by inner biological mechanisms, but also by environmental factors.

Organismic Theories

The second perspective on child development puts considerably less emphasis than the first on environmental influences. Instead, organismically oriented theorists stress the importance of factors within the organism itself. Thus, children grow to be what they make themselves to be rather than what the environment makes them (Langer 1969).

Some organismic theorists almost totally ignored environmental influences on children, believing that the entire plan for development is innate. Advocates of this extreme and no longer fashionable position were the maturation theorists G. Stanley Hall and Arnold Gesell. The prevailing trend in **organismic theory** today is to stress the organism-environment interaction, with each side simultaneously and continuously influencing the other.

Naturalism

The philosophical viewpoint that best exemplifies the organismic perspective was the one expressed by the eighteenth-century philosopher Jean-Jacques Rousseau (1712–1778). According to Rousseau's philosophy of **naturalism,** children are innately good unless corrupted by the evils of society. They come into the world equipped by God with a plan for their development, and no harm will come to them if they are allowed to grow with a minimum of supervision. Development, from Rousseau's perspective, consisted of five stages that correspond to the evolution of human culture: animal feelings of pleasure and pain (birth to 5 years), savage sensory awareness (5 to 12 years), rational functioning and exploration (12 to 15 years), emotional and social interests (15 to 20 years), and a spiritual maturity during adulthood.

Maturationism

Early in the twentieth century, Rousseau's ideas about nature's plan for the child's development surfaced again in the writings of those who advocated the perspective of **maturationism.** Although there has been a variety of maturational theories, they all had in common a belief that the plan of development is innate, and that the environment is a distant secondary influence. As an example, G. Stanley Hall (1844–1924) believed that the individual development of the child repeats, in brief, the phases of human evolution. Thus, a 6-year-old child playing cops-and-robbers might actually be reliving a prehistoric period when humans were primarily hunters and food-gatherers, living in caves. Hall described adolescence as a period of "storm and stress" corresponding to a turbulent state of Western civilization prior to the modern era. The extreme positions Hall adopted, as might be supposed, were quickly challenged by cross-culturally and environmentally oriented theorists (Muuss 1982).

Another prominent maturation theorist was Arnold Gesell (1880–1961), a student of G. Stanley

Jean Piaget (1896-1980) maintained that children constructed their own understanding of the world around them and that intellectual development is an active, dynamic process.

Hall. Like his famous teacher, Gesell regarded behaviorism with suspicion and emphasized internal biological factors in development while virtually ignoring the role of the environment. Gesell, an extremely careful observer of child development who depended on extensive data collection, devoted his career to counteracting the environmental trend that was sweeping the social sciences throughout the middle of the twentieth century (Senn 1975).

Gesell advocated the **normative** tradition of developmental data analysis, which was a widely used approach from the 1920s until the 1950s. This involved establishing developmental norms for behavior, with little interest in the analysis of deviations from those norms. For example, the notion of the "terrible twos" suggests that parents should expect problems during their child's second year of life. In reality, of course, there is much variation among 2-year-olds, and many parents report that age 2 was a delightful time for their children while age 3 was an absolute nightmare. Nevertheless, Gesell's belief that there are typical behaviors for every age during childhood and adolescence became very popular with the general public in the 1920s and is still widely circulated today.

Cognitive Developmental Theory

The most significant organismic perspective to emerge in the last half century has been cognitive developmental theory. As opposed to focusing on learned behaviors, cognitive developmentalists attempt to explain how the individual thinks and the way in which thought processes vary during childhood. The perspective is organismic in that the emphasis is on internal mental processes and their interactions with the environment rather than on the influence of the environment itself. Intellectual development is seen as an active, dynamic, constructive process.

The most influential of the cognitive developmental theorists was Jean Piaget (1896–1980). Piaget believed that intellectual development is not merely a continuous stream of associations or learned events, but a universal sequence of qualitatively different stages of interpreting the world. He suggested that we do not simply react to our environment; we each construct our own understanding of it according to an interaction of our experiences and inherent characteristics (Senn 1975). As will be pointed out in Chapter 6, many of Piaget's specific conclusions about children's development are questioned today. However, his influence has been considerable, and many of his basic assumptions are widely accepted. For example, today it is taken for granted that any point in a given child's cognitive development represents more than, or at least something different from, the sum of accumulated bits of learning.

Humanism

Rather than being a particular theory, **humanism** focuses on the dignity and freedom of all individuals in response to political, religious, or scientific authority that has become narrow and repressive. Humanists, such as Abraham Maslow

(1908–1970), reject the view of human nature that emphasizes environmental control and observable action. Instead, they stress internal factors and self-perceptions. While they do not believe that scientific standards of objectivity are useless, they point out that it is necessary to consider as well the phenomenological perspective (an immediate, personal intuition) of the individual. Similarly, humanists feel that it is important for children to choose their own destinies and by their own actions to achieve their creative potentials. Thus, the humanists share with other organismic theorists an interest in the internal workings of the human organism and a belief in the active role of children in determining their own path of development.

Ethology

Ethology is the study of animal behavior in its natural contexts. Ethologists generally maintain that much animal behavior is genetically linked—the result of a long evolutionary process (Gould 1982). For example, the newborn offspring of animals that constantly move about (such as cattle, sheep, chickens) must quickly recognize and learn to follow their parents in order to survive. The newborn offspring will therefore *imprint* on the parent, automatically following when the parent—emitting a species-specific call—moves away.

As applied to the study of child development, ethology suggests that human as well as lower animal behavior may have biological origins. For example, John Bowlby (b. 1907) suggested that biological mechanisms are responsible for parent-child attachment in human beings. These resemble behaviors that occur in lower animals. When infants are threatened or fear separation from their mothers, an automatic attachment system is activated. The child displays behaviors such as calling, crying, reaching, and following that trigger maternal reactions such as approaching, smiling, and touching.

The merits of Bowlby's point of view will be discussed further in Chapter 11. The ethological perspective that certain behaviors are "wired into" the organism by virtue of its being human presents a challenge to the environmentalist view that human beings are "empty" at birth and gradually shaped by their cultural experiences.

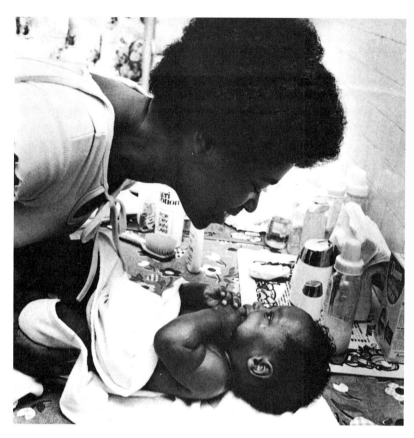

Ethologists argue that there are biological mechanisms responsible for the process of parent-child attachment in human beings.

The Psychoanalytic Perspective

Environmentalists and organismic theorists differed in their perceptions about the roles of nature and nurture in the development of the child. Both shared a common assumption, however, that humans are basically rational, and that human development proceeds by a set of orderly principles. In marked contrast is the third major perspective on child development—the **psychoanalytic theory** of Sigmund Freud (1856–1939).

Freud contended that rationality and conscious understanding of behavior played only a secondary role in motivation and development. The human being is a creature of appetite rather than reason. Development is a process whereby the person tries to resolve inner conflicts while attempting to compromise between his or her own inner needs and society's expectations (Langer,

1969). Emotional energy, derived from powerful instincts and shaped by early social interactions, defines daily conflicts. Freud's pessimistic view of the developmental process—focusing not on behaviors or thoughts, but on coping with uncomfortable feelings—was not destined for immediate popularity. Nevertheless, his contributions to **psychoanalysis** and the questions they have created remain a cornerstone of child development (Kessen 1965).

Trained as a medical doctor specializing in nervous conditions, Freud's belief that some physical disorders were caused by emotional problems was a revolutionary synthesis. He combined various concepts—an energy model from nineteenth-century physics, instinctual drives from evolutionary biology, and literary and philosophical references to the unconscious and sexuality—with

Sigmund Freud (1856-1939) suggested that human beings are creatures of passion and appetite rather than reason.

methods that were intended to elicit the dynamics of personality functioning. These methods included free association to verbal suggestions, interpretation of dreams, discussion of childhood memories, relaxation techniques, analysis of family relationships, and the release of emotional tensions.

During the 1920s and 1930s, psychoanalytic theory played an increasingly greater role in advancing knowledge of children's development. Psychoanalysis was broadened to explore patterns of childhood growth for their own sake instead of merely for laying the foundations of adult neurosis. Although several neoanalysts (modifiers of psychoanalytic theory) substantially extended Freud's

work, his own daughter, Anna, provided the most developmentally oriented modifications.

Anna Freud (1895–1982) was an important leader in helping psychoanalysis to move away from adult therapy and to become involved in research with children and adolescents. Her writings are especially detailed about the process of adolescent development, an area that was relatively neglected by her father. She indicated how the balanced personality of later childhood is upset by the changes of puberty and described the ways in which adolescents often react to the resulting anxiety. Thus, the credibility of psychoanalysis improved as its promoters grew less isolated from other influences, as both theory and method became more flexible, and as the scope of interest directly incorporated the development of children (Muuss 1982).

Perhaps the most influential advocate of psychoanalytic theory in the mid-to-late twentieth century has been Erik Erikson (b. 1902). Like many other European scholars, Erikson was forced to escape the terror of Nazi Germany, where he had been studying with Anna Freud. Erikson's career, unlike that of Sigmund Freud, provided him with a broad cultural outlook on child development. Prior to his psychoanalytic training, Erikson had been an artist and a teacher. In the United States, he worked with children as well as with adult patients, studied normal as well as deviant development, worked with lower- as well as with upper-class individuals, and experienced a variety of ethnic settings. These interactions led Erikson away from a sexual orientation in favor of a balance between biological and social factors.

Erikson's writings often focus on the unique history of the individual. However, he also suggested a universal lifespan sequence of eight stages—each represented by a special conflict between the needs of the self (the ego) and society's demands. In doing so, he created a psychosocial approach to the study of personality development that has provoked further theory and empirical research, particularly with respect to adolescent development (Muuss 1982).

The three major developmental perspectives—the environmentalist, the organismic, and the psychoanalytic—will be referred to repeatedly throughout this book. Many of the areas to be covered are discussed by theorists within each of the perspectives. There is, for example, an environmentalist view of morality emphasizing the role of reinforcement and punishment in teaching a child appropriate behaviors, an organismic view focusing on the active role of the individual in constructing a set of moral values, and a psychoanalytic view linking moral development to the unconscious process of identification with the same-sex parent.

The appropriateness of the various perspectives in explaining children's development depends on the particular aspect of development being considered. For example, in the area of language acquisition, the organismic view is the most widely accepted today, the environmentalist view has lost favor since the 1950s, and a psychoanalytic view is virtually nonexistent.

Finally, it is likely that in most cases no one theory provides a complete answer to the complex questions of how a child develops. In many situations, the best answer involves a synthesis of all three points of view.

Summary

1. Child development is an individual and continuous process which is influenced by a complex interaction of hereditary and environmental factors.
2. The study of child development is interdisciplinary and includes contributions from psychologists, sociologists, biologists, and anthropologists, as well as from professionals in other fields.
3. The early Greek philosophers Plato and Aristotle offered perceptive ideas about the nature of development. Their disagreements on how human beings perceive the world can be found in more modern theoretical positions.
4. Little consideration for the individual or the study of child development was found during the Middle Ages. Rigid theological doctrine provided the only guidance for interpreting behavior.
5. Between the Middle Ages and the eighteenth century, concern about philosophical ideas and their consequences for child development gradually returned.
6. By the late nineteenth century, the optimism of American scholars led to the formation of the developmental field. Theories of development and the scientific method did not always work smoothly together; however, valuable insights did emerge.
7. The early twentieth century was characterized by a strong belief in the importance of environmental influences on children's development. This perspective is typified by the work of John Watson, the founder of behaviorism.
8. Early twentieth-century contrasts to Watson's behaviorism were Freud's psychoanalytic theory, with its emphasis on underlying emotional forces, and the maturationism of Hall and Gesell, with its suggestion that developmental patterns are innate.
9. The middle of the twentieth century has seen an emphasis on the "how" and "why" rather than on the "what" of child development, increased attention to infant development and to adolescence, and a growing effort to integrate a variety of theories and disciplines in the study of child development.

Key Terms

interaction	organismic theory
developmental stage	naturalism
idealism	maturationism
realism	normative
baby biography	humanism
environmentalism	ethology
empiricism	psychoanalytic theory
behaviorism	psychoanalysis

Suggested Readings

Borstelmann, L.J. (1983). Children before psychology: Ideas about children from antiquity to the late 1800s. In P.H. Mussen (Ed.), *Handbook of child psychology* (4th ed., vol. 1). New York: Wiley.

An excellent chapter that culls diverse information from a variety of sources. The historical data are fascinating and the analysis is insightful.

Cairns, R.B. (1983). The emergence of developmental psychology. In P.H. Mussen (Ed.), *Handbook of child psychology* (4th ed, vol 1). New York: Wiley.

An informative chapter that provides an illuminating review of developmental psychology within the past century or so.

Crain, W.C. (1985). *Theories of development: Concepts and applications* (2nd ed.). Englewood Cliffs, NJ: Prentice-Hall.

A well-written appraisal of many twentieth-century developmental theories that includes the practical implications of each position described.

Kessen, W. (1965). *The child.* New York: Wiley.

A classic collection of extensive excerpts and perceptive commentary on the nature of infants and children during the past few centuries.

Langer, J. (1969). *Theories of development.* New York: Holt, Rinehart & Winston.

An excellent overview of perspectives in child development. Langer groups all developmental theories into three general categories and explains clearly and precisely how they differ from one another, how they are similar, and where they overlap.

Readings from the Literature

William Kessen (1979), a renowned observer of and contributor to the field of child development, presents an insightful essay on children in historical context. More uniquely, however, he suggests that those who study children are equally affected by cultural and historical forces that influence their work. Although many researchers now have a reasonable grasp of the roots of their field, it is difficult to perceive the current impact of society on the study of children. A brief discussion of earlier themes in child development is followed by Kessen's analysis of three persisting beliefs that have implicitly guided our views of children. Bear in mind the questions below when you read Kessen's article:

- *How has the American fascination with technology and science resulted in unrealistic expectations for the field of child development?*

- *What are the consequences of assuming that mothers are responsible for successful child development, particularly during the first few years of life?*

- *Why does the exploration of child development as an individual phenomenon (the child as a self-contained unit) prevent us from getting a complete picture of the processes of change?*

The American Child and Other Cultural Inventions

William Kessen
Yale University

The theme of the child as a cultural invention can be recognized in several intellectual and social occasions. Ariès' (1962) commentary on the discovery and transformation of childhood has become common knowledge; there is an agitated sense that American children are being redefined by the present times (Lasch, 1978); there is a renewed appreciation of the complexity of all our children (Keniston, 1977); and ethnographic and journalistic reports tell us of the marvelous departures from our own ways of seeing children that exist in other lands (Kessen, 1975). In simple fact, we have recently seen a shower of books on childish variety across cultures and across the hierarchies of class and race.

We could have just as readily discovered commanding evidence of the shifting nature of childhood by a close look at our own history. Consider just three passages drawn haphazardly from the American past. To the parents of the late 18th century:

> The first duties of Children are in great measure mechanical: an obedient Child makes a Bow, comes and goes, speaks, or is silent, just as he is bid, before he knows any other Reason for so doing than that he is bid. (Nelson, 1753)

Or to our parents and grandparents:

> The rule that parents should not play with their children may seem hard but it is without doubt a safe one. (West, 1914)

Or hear a parent of the 1970s speak of her 6-year-old:

> LuAnn liked the school in California best—the only rules were no chemical additives in the food and no balling in the hallways. (Rothchild & Wolf, 1976)

And we cannot escape the implications of an unstable portrait of the child by moving from folk psychology to the professional sort. On the contrary, a clear-eyed

study of what experts have said about the young—
from Locke to Skinner, from Rousseau to Piaget, from
Comenius to Erikson—will expose as bewildering a
taxonomy as the one provided by preachers, parents,
and poets. No other animal species has been cata-
loged by responsible scholars in so many wildly dis-
crepant forms, forms that a perceptive extraterrestrial
could never see as reflecting the same beast.

To be sure, most expert students of children continue
to assert the truth of the positivistic dream—that we
have not yet found the underlying structural simplicities
that will reveal the child entire, that we have not yet
cut nature at the joints—but it may be wise for us child
psychologists in the International Year of the Child
to peer into the abyss of the positivistic nightmare—
that the child is essentially and eternally a cultural
invention and that the variety of the child's definition is
not the removable error of an incomplete science.

For not only are American *children* shaped and marked
by the larger cultural forces of political maneuverings,
practical economics, and implicit ideological commitments (a new enough recognition), *child psychology* is
itself a peculiar cultural invention that moves with the
tidal sweeps of the larger culture in ways that we
understand at best dimly and often ignore.

To accept the ambiguity of our task to give up debates
about the fundamental nature of the child—is not, however, a defeatist or unscientific move. Rather, when
we seriously confront the proposition that we, like the
children we study, are cultural inventions, we can
go on to ask questions about the sources of our diversity
and, perhaps more tellingly, about the sources of our
agreements. It is surely remarkable that against the
background of disarray in our definition of the child, a
number of ideas are so widely shared that few
scholars question their provenance and warrant. Para-
doxically, the unexamined communalities of our
commitment may turn out to be more revealing than our
disagreements. Within the compass of the next
several pages, I point toward disagreements that were
present at the beginnings of systematic child study,
and then turn in more detail to the pervasive and shared
themes of American childhood in our time, themes
that may require a more critical review than we have
usually given them.

Present at the Birth

When child psychology was born, in a longish parturition
that ran roughly from Hall's first questionary studies
of 1880 (Hall, 1883) to Binet's test of construction of
1905 (Binet & Simon, 1916), there were five determining spirits present. Four of them are familiar to us
all; the fifth and least visible spirit may turn out to be the
most significant. One of the familiars was in the line
of Locke and Bain, and it appeared later for Americans
as John Broadus Watson; the line has, then and now,
represented behavior, restraint, clarity, simplicity,
and good news. Paired in philosophical and theoretical
opposition was the spirit that derived from Rousseau,
Nietzsche, and Freud, the line that represented mind,
impulse, ambiguity, complexity, and bad news. The
great duel between the two lines has occupied students
of children for just under 300 years.

The third magus at the beginning was the most fully
American; William James can stand as the representative
of the psychologists whose central concern was with
sensation, perception, language, thought, and will—the
solid, sensible folk who hid out in the years between
the World Wars but who have returned in glory. It is of
at least passing interest to note that the cognitivists
participated lightly in the early development of child
study; James and, even more, Munsterberg and,
past all measure, Titchener found results from the study
of children too messy for the precision they wanted
from their methods.

The godfather of child psychology, the solidest spirit of
them all, was Charles Darwin, foreshadowing his
advocates and his exaggerators. His contemporary
stand-in, G. Stanley Hall, was the first in a long and
continuing line that has preached from animal ana-
logues, has called attention to the biological in the child,
and has produced a remarkably diverse progeny that
includes Galton, Gesell, and the ethologists.

I rehearse (and oversimplify) the story of our professional
beginnings to call attention to how persistent the lines
have been, how little they have interpenetrated and
modified one another, and how much their contributions

to our understanding of the child rest on a network of largely implicit and undefended assumptions about the basis of human knowledge, social structures, and ethical ascriptions. The lines of the onlooking spirits are themselves historical and cultural constructions that grew, in ways that have rarely been studied analytically or biographically, from the matrix of the larger contemporaneous culture.[1]

And so to the fifth and circumnatal spirit, the one that knew no technical psychology. In the middle 50 years of the 19th century, the years that prepared the United States for child psychology, dramatic and persistent changes took place in American society. I could sing the familiar litany of urbanization, industrialization, the arrival of the first millions of European immigrants (another strand of diversity among children that requires a closer look). We know that the Civil War transformed the lives of most American families, white and black (although we still know remarkably little about the daily lives of children during and after the war). The United States developed, and *developed* is the word of choice, from an isolated agricultural dependency to an aggressive and powerful state. Technology and science joined the industrial entrepreneurs to persuade the new Americans, from abroad and from the farm, that poverty was an escapable condition if one worked hard enough and was aggressively independent. But there were other changes that bore more immediately on the lives of American children; let me, as an example of cultural influences on children and child psychology rather than as a worked-through demonstration of my thesis, extract three interwoven strands of the changes that touched children.

The first, and the earliest, was the evolving separation of the domain of work from the domain of the home. When women left or were excluded from the industrial work force in the 1830s and 1840s, the boundary marked by the walls of home became less and less

penetrable. First for the white, the urban, the middle-class, the northeastern American, but enlisting other parts of the community as time went on, work (or *real work* as contrasted with *homework,* the activity of women and schoolchildren) was carried on in specialized spaces by specialized people, and home became the place where one (i.e., men) did not work (Cott, 1977; Lasch, 1977).

The second and entailed change was the radical separation of what a man was from what a woman was. Colonial and early Federal society, like all other cultures, had stable and divergent visions of the proper sphere of male and female. But in the half century under our present consideration, something of a moral metamorphosis occurred in the United States (and in large measure, in England, too) and one of modern history's most eccentric arrangements of human beings was put in place. The public world of men was seen as ugly, aggressive, corrupting, chaotic, sinful (not an altogether regretted characteristic), and irreligious. The increasingly private world of women was, in inevitable antithesis, sweet, chaste, calm, cultured, loving, protective, and godly. The muscular Christianity of the Mathers and Edwardses became the feminized Christianity of matrons and pastors; the caretaking of culture became the task of women's groups (Douglas, 1978). So dramatic a statement of the contrast is hardly an exaggeration of the facts. And the full story remains to be told; historians of medical practice, for example, are just beginning to reveal the systematic attempt to desex American and British women in the 19th century with methods that ranged from sermons to surgery (Barker-Benfield, 1977).

The third change in American life that set the cultural context for child psychology followed on the first two. Children continued to be cared for by women at home, and in consequence, they took on the coloration of mother, hearth, and heaven. The early American child, who was told, "consider that you may perish as young as you are; there are small Chips as well as great Logs, in the Fire of Hell" (18th-century primer, quoted by Johnson, 1904), became Little Eva, Huckleberry Finn, and eventually Peter Pan. The sentimentalization of children—caught for tombstones and psychology books best by Wordsworth's "Heaven lies about us in our infancy!"—had implications for family

---

[1] It has become a cliché to speak of psychoanalysis as an outgrowth of Jewish intellectual culture in turn-of-the-century Vienna (a shallow summary at best), but no corresponding common saying exists for, say, Watson's growing up in postwar Carolina, or Hall's curious combination of *odium sexicum* and *odium theologicum* in Victorian times, or Binet's history as an apostate continental associationist.

structure, education, and the definition of the child in expert writings that we have not yet, nearing the end of the 20th century, fully understood or confronted.

Thus it was that American child psychology began not only under the conflicting attention of Locke, Rousseau, James, and Darwin, but with the progressivist, sexist, and sentimental expectation of the larger culture standing by.

The Common Themes of American Child Psychology

Are we now free of our origins? It would be both unhistorical and undevelopmental to believe so, in spite of all we have learned about research and about children over the last 100 years. The positivist promise of pure objectivity and eternal science has been withdrawn. Therefore, it may be methodologically thera-peutic to glance, however briefly, at several common themes of our field that seem dependent, in the usually complicated way of human history, on the story I have sketched thus far. All of the themes may be ready for a thoughtful new evaluation.

The Commitment to Science and Technology

The notable success of the physical sciences in the 19th century, the elation that followed on the Darwinian revolution, and the culture's high hopes for a techno-logical utopia joined at the end of the 19th century to define child psychology as scientific and rational.

The vagaries of casual stories about children, the eccentricities of folk knowledge, and the superstitions of grandmothers were all to be cleansed by the mighty brush of scientific method (Jacoby, 1914; Watson, 1928). The conviction that we are scientists remains one of the heart beliefs of child psychology, and in its humane and sensible forms, the commitment to a systematic analytic examination of the lives of children and their worlds is still the unique and continuing contribution of child psychology to American culture.

But some less obvious and perhaps less defensible consequences of the rational scientific commitment were pulled along into child psychology by the high hopes

of its founders. Perhaps the one that we have had the most difficulty in handling as a profession is the implication *in all theories of the child* that lay folk, particularly parents, are in need of expert guidance. Critical examination and study of parental practices and child behavior almost inevitably slipped subtly over to advice about parental practices and child behavior. The scientific statement became an ethical imperative, the descriptive account became normative. And along the way, there have been unsettling occasions in which scraps of knowledge, gathered by whatever procedures were held to be proper science at the time, were given inordinate weight against poor old defense-less folk knowledge. Rigorously scheduled feedings of infants, separation of new mothers from their babies, and Mrs. West's injunction against playing with children can stand as examples of scientism that are far enough away not to embarrass us enlightened moderns.

More, I risk the guess that the sentimental view of the child that prevailed at the beginnings of child psychol-ogy—a vision which, let it be said, made possible humane and appropriate reforms in the treatment of children—was strongly influential in what can only be called a salvationist view of children. Child psycholo-gists, again whatever their theoretical stripe, have taken the Romantic notion of childish innocence and open-ness a long way toward the several forms of "If only we could make matters right with the child, the world would be a better place." The child became the carrier of political progressivism and the optimism of reform-ers. From agitation for child labor reform in the 1890s to Head Start, American children have been saviors of the nation. The romantic inheritance of purity and per-fectibility may, in fact, have misled us about the proper unit of developmental study and about the major forces influencing human growth and change. I will return to the consideration of our unit of study shortly.

There has often also been a socially hierarchical message in our scientific-normative interactions with the larger culture. Tolstoy said that there is no proletarian literature; there has been no proletarian child psychology either, and the ethically imperative forms of child psychology, our messages to practice, have ranged from pleas for equitable treatment of all children to recipes for forced assimilation to the expected forms of child behavior. Once a descriptive norm has been established, it is an antique cultural principle to urge adherence to it.

Finally, for some eras of child study, there has been an enthusiastic anticipation that all problems are reducible by the science of the moment; intellectual technology can succeed (and imitate) the 19th century's commercial and industrial technology in the progressive and ultimate betterment of humankind. The optimism of the founders of child study and their immediate successors is dimmer today—"The sky's the limit" may be replaced by "You win a few, you lose a few"—and serious questions have been posed even for the basic assumptions underlying the scientific analysis of human behavior (Barrett, 1978). Child psychology may soon have to face anew the question of whether or not a scientific account of human development can be given without bringing in its wake the false claims of scientism and the arrogance of an ethic based on current findings.

The Importance of Mothers, Early Experience, and Personal Responsibility

Strangely at odds with the theme of rational scientific inquiry has been the persistence of the commitment to home and mother in otherwise varying portraits of the child. Some child psychologists have been less than laudatory about the effectiveness of particular mothering procedures (Watson dedicated his directive book on child rearing to the first mother who raises a child successfully), but critics and praisers alike have rarely doubted the basic principle that children need home and mother to grow as they should grow (again, the normative injunction enters). I do not mean to dispute the assumption here; I want only to suggest its connection with the mid-19th-century ideology that long preceded systematic child psychology and to point out several riders on the assumption that have, in the past, been less vividly visible.

Two riders on the home-and-mother position are under active debate and study nowadays—the irrelevance of fathers and the critical role of early experience. The cases represent with the starkness of a line drawing the influence of contemporaneous cultural forces on the definition of psychology's child. It would be difficult to defend the proposition that the recent interest in the

place of fathers or the possibilities of out-of-home child rearing grew either from a new theory of development or from striking new empirical discoveries. Rather, for reasons too elaborate to explore here, fewer and fewer American women have been willing or able to devote all of their work time to the rearing of children. It will be instructive to see how much the tasks assigned fathers and daycare centers reflect the old ascriptions to essential maternity. Psychology follows culture, but often at a discreet distance.

The blending of new social requirements into old ideology is precisely demonstrated by the incorporation of fathers and day-care workers into the premise that what happens to the child in the first hours, weeks, months of life holds an especially determining position in human development. Proclaimed on epistemological grounds by Locke, gathered into the American ethos in part because it so well fit the perfectionist argument, elevated to scientific status by evolutionary theory, the doctrine of the primacy of early experience has been an uncontested part of American culture and American child psychology throughout the history of both. Only in the last several years has the premise been called seriously into question (Kagan, Kearsley, & Zelazo, 1978) and, even then, at a time when ever more extravagant claims are being made about the practical necessity of safeguarding the child's first hours (Klaus & Kennell, 1976).

The assumption of essential maturity and the assumption of the determining role of early experience join to support yet another underdebated postulate of child psychology. If something goes wrong in the course of a child's development, it is the primary responsibility of the mother (or whoever behaves as mother), and once more in echo of the salvationist view, if a social problem is not repaired by modification of the child's first years, the problem is beyond repair. The working of the postulate has produced ways of blaming mothers that appear in all theoretical shapes and, more generally, ways of blaming other victims of social injustice because they are not readily transformed by the ministrations of the professionals (Ryan, 1971).

The tendency to assign personal responsibility for the successes and failures of development is an amalgam of the positivistic search for causes, of the older Western tradition of personal moral responsibility, and of the conviction that personal mastery and consequent personal responsibility are first among the goals of child rearing. It is difficult to imagine an American child psychology without a core commitment to the proposition that *someone* is responsible for what happens in the course of development.

The Belief in the Individual and Self-Contained Child

Hovering over each of the traditional beliefs mentioned thus far is the most general and, in my view, the most fundamental entanglement of technical child psychology with the implicit commitments of American culture. The child—like the Pilgrim, the cowboy, and the detective on television—is invariably seen as a free-standing isolable being who moves through development as a self-contained and complete individual. Other similarly self-contained people—parents and teachers—may influence the development of children, to be sure, but the proper unit of cultural analysis and the proper unit of developmental study is the child alone. The ubiquity of such radical individualism in our lives makes the consideration of alternative images of childhood extraordinarily difficult. We have never taken fully seriously the notion that development is, in large measure, a social construction, the child modulated and modulating component in a shifting network of influences (Berger & Luckmann, 1966). The seminal thinkers about children over the past century have, in fact, been almost undeviating in their postulation of the child as container of self and of psychology. Impulses are in the child; traits are in the child; thoughts are in the child; attachments are in the child. In short, almost every major theory of development accepts the premises of individualism and takes the child as the basic unit of study, with all consequences the choice has for decisions that range from selecting a method of research to selecting a therapeutic maneuver. Uniform agreement on the isolable child as the proper measure of development led to the research paradigms that have dominated child psychology during most of its history; basically, we have observed those parts of development that the child could readily transport to our laboratories or to our testing sites. The use of isolated preparations for the study of development has,

happily, been productive of remarkable advances in our knowledge of children, but with the usual cost of uniform dogma, the commitment to the isolable child has occasionally led child psychology into exaggerations and significant omissions.

There are signals now aloft that the dogma of individualism, both in its claim of lifelong stability of personality and in its claim that human action can be understood without consideration of context or history, is under severe stress. The story that Vygotsky (1978) told 50 years ago, the story of the embeddedness of the developing mind in society, has finally been heard. The image of the child as an epigenetic and continuous creation of social and biological contexts is far more ambiguous and more difficult to paint than the relative simplicities of the traditional and culturally justified self-contained child; it may also illuminate our understanding of children and of our science.

The Present Moment

The cultural epigenesis that created the American child of the late 20th century continues, and so does the epigenesis that created child psychology. Necessarily, there is no end of the road, no equilibrium. Rather, the transformations of the past 100 years in both children and child psychology are a startling reminder of the eternal call on us to be scrupulous observers and imaginative researchers; they may also serve to force our self-critical recognition that we are both creators and performers in the cultural invention of the child.

References

Ariès, P. [*Centuries of childhood: A social history of family life*] (R. Baldick, Trans.). New York: Knopf, 1962.

Barker-Benfield, G. J. *Horrors of the half-known life.* New York: Harper & Row, 1977.

Barrett, W. *The illusion of technique.* Garden City, N.Y.: Doubleday, 1978.

Berger, P. L., & Luckmann, T. *The social construction of reality: A treatise in the sociology of knowledge.* Garden City, N.Y.: Doubleday, 1966.

Binet, A., & Simon, T. [Upon the necessity of establishing a scientific diagnosis of inferior states of intelligence] (E. S. Kite, Trans.). In A. Binet & T. Simon, *The development of intelligence in children.* Baltimore, Md., Williams & Wilkins, 1916. (Originally published, 1905).

Cott, N F. *Bonds of womanhood; Women's sphere in New England, 1780—1835.* New Haven, Conn.: Yale University Press, 1977.

Douglas, A. *The feminization of American culture.* New York: Avon Books, 1978.

Hall, G. S. The contents of children's minds. *Princeton Review,* 1883, *11,* 249-272.

Jacoby, G. W. *Child training as an exact science: A treatise based upon the principles of modern psychology, normal and abnormal.* New York: Funk & Wagnalls, 1914.

Johnson, C. *Old-time schools and school-books.* New York: Macmillan, 1904.

Kagan, J., Kearsely, R. B., & Zelazo, P. R. (With the assistance of C. Minton). *Infancy: Its place in human development.* Cambridge, Mass.: Harvard University Press, 1978.

Keniston, K., & Carnegie Council on Children. *All our children: The American family under pressure.* New York: Harcourt Brace Jovanovich, 1977.

Kessen, W. (Ed.). *Childhood in China.* New Haven, Conn.: Yale University Press, 1975.

Klaus, M. H., & Kennell, J. H. *Maternal-infant bonding.* Saint Louis: Mosby, 1976.

Lasch, C. *Haven in a heartless world: The family besieged.* New York: Basic Books, 1977.

Lasch, C. *The culture of narcissism: American life in an age of diminishing expectations.* New York: Norton, 1978.

Nelson, J. *An essay on the government of children under three general heads: Viz., health, manners, and education,* London: (no publisher), 1753.

Rothchild, J., & Wolf, S. B. *The children of the counterculture.* Garden City, N.Y.: Doubleday, 1976.

Ryan, W. *Blaming the victim.* New York: Random House, 1971.

Vygotsky, L. S. *Mind in society: The development of higher psychological processes* (M. Cole, V. John-Steiner, S. Scribner, & E. Souberman, Eds.). Cambridge, Mass.: Harvard University Press, 1978.

Watson, J. B. *Psychological care of infant and child.* New York: Norton, 1928.

West, M. *Infant care* (Publication No. 8). Washington, D.C.: U.S. Children's Bureau, 1914.

The first form of this article was read as an invited address to Division 7 (Developmental Psychology) of the American Psychological Association during the annual meeting, Toronto, August 1978.

Source: Kessen, W. (1979) The American child and other cultural inventions. *American Psychologist 34 (10),* 815-820. Copyright 1979 by the American Psychological Association. Reprinted by permission of the publisher and author.

Methodological Approaches

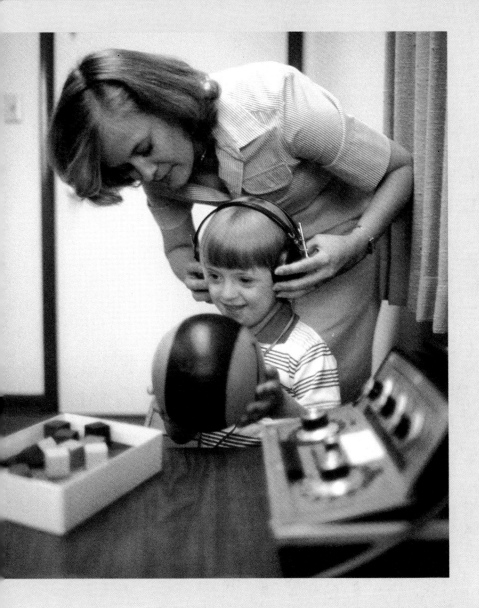

John is reading his local newspaper one Monday morning before leaving for his office. He comes across a headline that proclaims "Freud's Theory of Child Development Disproved." Recalling his undergraduate course in introductory psychology, John is intrigued and somewhat confused. His psychology professor did point out flaws in Freud's approach to child development, but the value of this theory was clearly stated. In reading the brief newspaper article, John learns that the researchers could not find any evidence to support the connection between oral behaviors in adults and the weaning process in babies.

Perhaps John would be able to interpret the validity of the dramatic headline more effectively if he knew some of the details about how the researchers carried out their study. Did they work in a laboratory or in a natural setting? Were the participants in the research aware of the investigators' purposes? How was the information about infant weaning or adult behavior obtained? Research on children is often based on a theoretical framework about the problem—for instance, were the researchers sympathetic to Freud's theory or another view of child development? John could not expect to properly evaluate the research without knowing what methods were selected for the study and why they were chosen.

This chapter discusses the scientific method, various research strategies, procedures for data collection, and developmental designs. As you read, ask yourself how each approach offers another small window into a very complex structure. How do we know if a theory about child development is useful for understanding change across the early portion of the lifespan? Where do we get information concerning perceptions in infants, adolescent sexual attitudes, or friendship among children? To answer such questions, the developmental researcher follows a loosely organized set of principles that guide the research process from problem formation to the final report.

The Scientific Method

Most professionals who study children follow the steps in the basic scientific method. Not all knowledge of child development has been ob-

tained in this manner. However, since the scientific approach is more systematic and permits broader verification than do limited personal experience or unchallenged faith, the majority of research reported in this textbook has followed the scientific method.

Establishing the Problem

Scientific research begins with extensive consideration of a significant problem yet to be fully resolved. Then researchers narrow the issues to a manageable few by selecting certain variables that can be practically defined and examined. A **variable** is a concept that varies in at least two ways—in other words, it can be categorized or measured. Sex, for instance, can be categorized as male or female. It is a *dichotomous*, or two-part, *variable*. Intelligence can be measured by the number of intelligence quotient (IQ) points attained on a continuous scale of, for example, 0 to 200. Therefore, intelligence is a *continuous-scale variable*. Developmental researchers study problems that essentially establish relationships among variables of consequence to change in children. They must also be careful to frame the problem within the context of appropriate theory and previous research on the topic.

In the Research Close-up "Prematurity and the Scientific Method," one of the variables Holmes and Nagy (1982) employed was the status of the newborn infants: preterm, sick full-term, healthy full-term with prolonged hospitalization because of maternal postnatal complications, and healthy full-term. Frequently, researchers distinguish between *independent (causal)* and *dependent (resultant)* variables. The infants' status was classified as an independent variable since it was presumed to be a potential cause of their problem behaviors. Note that some independent variables—such as neonatal status, sex, or gestational age—cannot be readily manipulated by researchers. Other independent variables, such as the type of therapeutic intervention or the amount of praise provided by a teacher, can be controlled by the researcher. This distinction is crucial for establishing genuine cause-and-effect relationships.

The various scores Holmes and Nagy used for evaluating the infants' behaviors are classified

Research Close-up

Prematurity and the Scientific Method

A practical issue that has received much recent and deserved attention concerns the negative effects of prematurity on infant development. Much evidence has been obtained that indicates significant differences between full-term and preterm babies with respect to physical, social, and emotional characteristics (see Chapter 3 for a detailed discussion of prematurity and its consequences). Researchers interested in examining this problem have several important steps to climb prior to collecting data. First, they must read past research relating to the topic to explore the nature of the problem, the exact procedures used to study it, the results of the investigations, and the limitations of any conclusions presented.

Deborah Holmes and Jill Nagy (1982) and their associates at Loyola University and the Evanston Hospital—apparently were concerned that previous findings on the subject of prematurity were not clear. In particular, they noted (1) previous studies often failed to examine infants from the first days of life, (2) comparisons between healthy full-term and all preterm infants were inappropriate, and (3) there was a lack of sensitive assessment techniques for documenting conditions during the neonatal (newborn) period. Therefore, Holmes and Nagy were prepared to undertake the next step in planning their own work. They decided to attempt to clarify the confusion

in the literature by examining infants very thoroughly during the early weeks after birth and by sampling from the following four groups: (1) eleven preterms who were in the intensive care unit, (2) twelve sick full-terms who were in the intensive care unit, (3) eight healthy full-terms who were in the neonatal nursery for prolonged periods because their mothers had postnatal complications, and (4) thirteen healthy full-terms who were in the neonatal nursery for the usual three or four days.

According to the researchers, the infants were all from two-parent, middle-class families; received good prenatal care; were of birthweights that corresponded to gestational age; and did not evidence central nervous system damage. The infants were evaluated forty-eight hours prior to hospital discharge for qualities such as alertness, social responsivity, and motoric activity using the Brazelton Neonatal Behavioral Assessment Scale—Kansas modification. In addition, birthweights and gestational ages were recorded for each infant, and they were administered the Obstetrical Complications Scale and the Postnatal Complications Scale developed by Littman and Parmelee.

After collecting their data, Holmes and Nagy statistically analyzed the information to compare the effects of prematurity, the effects of illness, and the effects of extended hospitalization. The statistical techniques used were varied in order to effectively disentangle the influences of the different factors mentioned on the infant's development. In the Holmes and Nagy sample,

results did confirm that preterm infants exhibit more immaturity and less optimal behaviors than their full-term counterparts. However, the researchers were led to conclude "that these deficits in early behavior may not be due to preterm birth per se but to other factors associated with preterm birth" (Holmes and Nagy 1982, 748).

Indeed, the groups most similar in tested performance patterns were the preterm infants and the full-terms who were also in the intensive care unit. It is important to note that these full-term infants were, on the average, normal gestational age and birthweight, and had mothers with no major obstetrical problems, but that they did spend a prolonged period of time in the hospital (two weeks compared with three weeks for the preterm infants). Neither illness nor hospitalization may be entirely responsible for behavioral differences in newborn babies, however, because on some measures the full-terms with sick mothers performed similarly to the preterms, while the sick full-terms with normal mothers had patterns similar to those of the healthy full-terms. The researchers suggest that perhaps perinatal (around the time of birth) stress, evidenced by the Obstetrical Complications Scale, might explain some of the difficulties. In sum, Holmes and Nagy claim that preterm delivery may only lead to problems for infant development when complicated by some combination of severe postnatal illness, the environment of an extended hospital stay, and the amount of stress during labor, rather than simply being due to immaturity itself.

as dependent variables, since they are presumed to be the result of variations in the independent variable. The researcher's task is to provide an **operational definition** for each variable studied. The operational definition assigns specific meaning in quantitative or categorical terms to the use of a variable. For Holmes and Nagy, the independent variable was operationally defined by classifying the infants into the four categories previously stated on the basis of gestational age, infant health, and maternal health. The dependent variables, which might be affected by the health and gestational status the infant exhibited, were operationally defined by the scores on the Brazelton Neonatal Behavioral Assessment Scale.

Based on knowledge of past research and relevant theory, researchers often attempt to predict the outcome of their investigations before collecting data. This "educated guess" about how two or more variables are related is known as a **hypothesis**. Sometimes no hypotheses are formulated; instead, the researcher offers one or several questions derived from the research problem. This is usually the case in exploratory studies in which the relationships among the variables have yet to be clearly defined. Holmes and Nagy did not state a formal hypothesis in their report, although the tone of their introduction implies that they did not expect to find that gestational age was the major factor in the behavioral problems of newborns.

Methodology for the Study

In addition to establishing the problem, some of the most important decisions facing the researcher are the various aspects of methodology. Selecting an appropriate **sample** is often the first step in the method for conducting research. The sample consists of those children, or subjects, who participate in the research project and are assumed generally to reflect the characteristics of similar children of concern to the researcher.

The larger group from which the sample is drawn is known as the *population*. Since it is rarely possible for a researcher to investigate a total population, an attempt is made to obtain a representative sample in order to generalize the results beyond the sample to that larger population (large

samples are usually more representative than small ones).

If researchers choose limited or inadequate samples, the results cannot be validly generalized to other samples. For example, Holmes and Nagy had difficulty obtaining an equal number of infants, balanced for males and females, in each of the four status groups. In addition, since equating infants for severity of illness, extent of hospital stay, and maternal complications was beyond their control, they expressed caution in the interpretation of their study.

Other aspects of methodology facing the developmental researcher are the overall strategy, procedures, and design of the study. These features must be explicit and unambiguous so that others can attempt to confirm the results independently. Subsequent sections of this chapter, therefore, will describe in greater detail research strategies, data collection procedures, and those designs of particular interest for the study of development.

Analysis of the Results

Analysis of research results need not provoke fear among students new to the study of child development. Statistics are merely efficient numerical tools designed to simplify the researcher's task of drawing conclusions from the data obtained. The methods for analyzing data can be classified according to three questions that reflect the formulation and design of the research problem.

1. Does the researcher wish to summarize data or to estimate the likelihood of chance findings?
2. Does the researcher wish to focus on differences between groups or on the relationship among variables?
3. Does the researcher wish to examine only one dependent variable or more than one simultaneously?

Descriptive and Inferential Statistics

Summarizing data succinctly involves the use of familiar concepts, such as percentages and averages (mean, median, mode). These procedures and other related ones are known as **descriptive statistics**. In contrast, statistics which determine the probability of obtaining similar results with a

Statistical analysis, which helps reduce the complexity of data collected, takes many forms. Computers have greatly increased the efficiency with which researchers can understand statistical information.

different sample from the same population are called **inferential statistics.** The results of inferential analysis are always reported in terms of probability, because the researcher, without studying every member of the population, never can be completely certain that chance factors have been eliminated.

Furthermore, a statistically significant finding (a result where the researcher is fairly confident that chance is not involved) does not necessarily imply practical or important results. These findings are probably not a fluke, but their meaning may be open to various interpretations. For example, Holmes and Nagy, by providing the average scores for each of the independent and dependent variables, and by calculating a statistic for determining the likelihood of finding differences among the groups again, used both descriptive and inferential statistics, respectively.

Correlational and Group Differences Statistics

Since Holmes and Nagy were primarily interested in comparing the behavioral characteristics of infants in the four neonatal statuses, their research first employed the group differences approach. When an investigation deals with attributes or performances of two or more groups, the data will be analyzed with **group differences statistics** (these usually are also inferential statistics).

However, Holmes and Nagy were also interested in the relative contribution made by each independent variable used to create the four groups. It was possible, therefore, to focus on the degree of relationship among variables instead of on the differences between groups. For example, what is the relationship between gestational age or birthweight or length of hospital stay or maternal complication level and the behavioral characteristics of the infants? The analysis of data relating the degree and direction of relationship among two or more variables requires the use of **correlational statistics.**

Correlations may vary in strength from low (indicating little relationship) to high (indicating a strong relationship). In a sample of children, for instance, the correlation between their height and weight is likely to be high (.79), but the correlation between their height and their IQ scores is likely to be low (.13). Correlation statistics may be both descriptive and inferential. The higher the correlation between variables, the better is our ability to predict one by knowing the other. If the amount of infant babbling correlates highly with verbal skill at age 3, for example, we might expect a vocal infant to be a talkative toddler. This type of relationship, know as a *positive correlation,* occurs when scoring high on one variable suggests scoring high on the second variable. However, the direction of a relationship can also be reversed. For example, suppose research demonstrated that the more time adolescents spend studying, the fewer juvenile delinquent acts they would commit. A relationship in which scores on one variable increase while scores on the other one decrease is called a *negative correlation.*

Even high positive or negative correlations cannot provide perfectly accurate predictions for a given individual, however. Statistics are usually procedures for describing general tendencies exhibited by a total sample. Correlation statistics, therefore, are expressed in terms of both strength and direction, and they describe the nature of relationships, as well as the probability of their existence in similar samples from the same population. Furthermore, correlations do not imply that one variable causes changes in another, merely that the two are somehow related. The interpretation of correlation statistics requires the utmost caution and a continued search for causal factors, as the Holmes and Nagy research demonstrates.

Univariate and Multivariate Statistics

In the Holmes and Nagy study, the combined influence of the independent variables was examined with respect to the scores on the Brazelton Scale (the dependent variable) for the infants. Statistics that are used to analyze more than one dependent and independent variable at a time are

known as **multivariate statistics.** There has been a substantial increase in multivariate analyses in recent years as development theorists have come to recognize that a child's behavior is difficult to understand without considering the simultaneous effects of several variables.

Univariate statistics involve the analysis of only one dependent variable at a time. Although easier to calculate as well as to interpret, they may not accurately reflect developmental complexity. Holmes and Nagy also used univariate statistics to analyze the overall differences among the four neonatal groups.

Interpretation of the Research

The researcher who has subjected data to statistical analysis is ready to begin the concluding phase of the project. This may take the form of a report to fellow professionals (and possibly to the

Table 2.1 Structure of the Scientific Method

I. Establishing the problem
  A. Significance and overview of the topic
  B. Theoretical background and past research
  C. Operational definition of variables
  D. Hypotheses and research questions
II. Methodology for the study
  A. Characteristics of the sample
  B. Research strategies
  C. Procedures for data collection
  D. Developmental designs
III. Analysis of the results
  A. Descriptive and inferential statistics
  B. Correlational and group differences statistics
  C. Univariate and multivariate statistics
IV. Interpretation of the research
  A. Relating results to hypotheses
  B. Limitations of the findings
  C. Implications of the study
  D. Suggestions for the future

public as well), if the researcher feels the contribution would be valuable. Research reports describe the type of information outlined thus far in this chapter, including a discussion of the value of the results. The discussion entails a review of all findings with respect to the researcher's hypotheses, other relevant research and theory, limitations of the methodology, potential applications of the results, and appropriate directives for additional investigations. Several points concerning Holmes and Nagy's discussion of their results have been mentioned briefly. Perhaps, to the consumer of research, this final phase of the project is the most exciting, because it links the past with the future of the problem. It permits the researcher to offer some interresting speculation that creatively may extend the original ideas and details presented. Table 2.1 summarizes the research process according to the scientific method.

Research Strategies

Three nonstatistical questions, determined partially by the purposes of the study and partially by practical considerations, also confront the researcher.

1. Can or should the researcher actively manipulate one or more variables of interest?
2. Can or should the researcher examine a single individual or a group?
3. Can or should the research be conducted in a natural or a laboratory setting?

The answers to these questions guide the overall methodology of the investigation. Most of the following discussion, however, deals with aspects of the first question.

Experimental Approach

The primary goal of an **experimental strategy** is to isolate a particular variable hypothesized to affect development and to manipulate its influence within part of the sample. Ultimately, the researcher compares the effects of the manipulation and its absence among different groups in the sample to determine if that variable causes developmental change.

A recurring controversy in developmental methodology involves the significance of the experimental strategy for illuminating the nature of change. Borrowed from the physical sciences, the method of experimental research, according to Appelbaum and McCall (1983) and other critics, has become excessively worshipped. The problems of the experimental strategy will be discussed after the strategy is explained more fully. The research of Steuer, Applefield, and Smith (1971) will be used as an example.

Key factors in experimental research are (1) identifying a causal, or independent, variable that can be manipulated and (2) applying the manipulation or treatment to one part of a sample (experimental group), but not to another (control group) for comparative purposes. Steuer and her colleagues were interested in the effects of aggressive television programming on preschool children. They hypothesized that exposure to such hostile behaviors (independent variable) causes increased interpersonal aggression (dependent variable). Two small groups of 4- to 5-year-old children were then shown approximately two hours of either aggressive (experimental group) or nonaggressive (control group) programming over a period of eleven days.

These groups of children previously had been matched on their typical amount of aggression displayed and frequency of television watching. The matching procedure was used to be certain that both groups were similar prior to application of the treatment. Sometimes the equivalence of groups in large samples can be assumed if the subjects are randomly assigned to the experimental or the control condition. Another possibility would be for the researcher to have used only one group to compare the amount of interpersonal aggression before and after the treatment (watching aggressive programming) began. However, this strategy has several statistical flaws that need not concern us here.

In the Steuer, Applefield, and Smith study, several observers behind one-way mirrors were trained to record the amount of aggression displayed during free play by each child in both the experimental and control groups. The results of these observations clearly indicated that those children who viewed aggressive television programming (experimental group) displayed significantly more aggressive acts toward others in the free play situation than did the children who viewed non-aggressive programs (control group). Therefore, the researchers suggested that watching televised hostility caused the children to behave more aggressively since they appeared to behave similarly before viewing the programs.

If this conclusion appears reasonable, why do some developmental researchers question the value of the experimental strategy? Every study has its limitations. Research evidence should be accepted only after analyzing the results of many investigations of the same problem that used different approaches. In the experiment just discussed, the authors themselves point out a possible weakness: "that one or two subjects were influenced directly by the television manipulation and that other subjects began to display more hostility in retaliation, independently of the televised stimuli" (Steuer et al. 1971, 447). Although experimenters try to control for such difficulties by careful planning, being able to predict every potential confounding factor is rare.

The experimental strategy has other weaknesses, too. As mentioned, developmental change may be influenced simultaneously by several variables. It is unlikely, however, that a researcher would be able to manipulate more than one or two variables in any given experiment. In addition, many of the factors that concern child development are either impractical or unethical for a researcher to manipulate. Holmes and Nagy's research on prematurity provides an example. Although it may be important to determine if infants are negatively affected by limited gestational age, no experimenter would seriously consider research that deliberately induces premature labor and delivery. Therefore, Holmes and Nagy's research had to be nonexperimental. Even Steuer's study borders on the violation of ethical research principles (see Issues in Child Development, "The Ethics of Research"), because children were asked to view television programs that had a potentially negative impact on behavior. However, the treatment was of short duration (two hours) and included programs the children would have viewed at home on Saturday mornings anyway.

Nonexperimental Methods

Wohlwill (1973), among others, has suggested that nonexperimental methods, especially if designed from a multivariate perspective, are most appropriate for developmental research. The nonexperimental strategy largely consists of (1) comparisons of group differences in which no researcher manipulations occur (such as the study by Holmes and Nagy), and (2) correlational approaches in which relationships between nonmanipulated factors are evaluated (also found in the Holmes and Nagy study). Common variables in nonexperimental group comparisons—which are of significance to child development researchers but cannot be manipulated—include sex, age, race, and socioeconomic status. Correlational research (analyzed using correlation statistics, as described previously) focuses on the apparent influence of any one measureable variable on another.

The major flaw of nonexperimental research, however, concerns the apparent relationship between variables or the apparent differences between groups. Since the researcher has not actually manipulated any of the variables, it is impossible to draw causal conclusions. Consider, for example, a study of adolescent boys that demonstrates a positive relationship between the number of good friends a boy has and a lack of concern about grades in school. Does having many friends cause a boy to think about other things besides grades? Or does not caring about his grades allow him the time to be with his friends? Perhaps high self-esteem causes him to think positively about school, as well as to relate honestly and cheerfully to other boys. Caution is necessary regarding the nature and direction of cause-and-effect relationships despite variables that seem to "go together." Complex correlation procedures, which indicate more effectively the likelihood of causal links in nonexperimental research, are increasingly being used, but this is beyond the scope of this chapter.

Studying Individuals

As Chapter 1 mentioned, most of the research in child development is based on the analysis of groups of children. Generalizations about how these findings can be applied to a particular child

Research in child development is often nonexperimental since manipulation of critical variables by a scientist might be unethical. Would these adolescent boys behave naturally if studied in a controlled setting?

entail some degree of uncertainty. The difficulties of translating group data to the individual level occasionally have encouraged researchers to study only one subject or family in greater detail. Intensive examinations of a single child also point out questions or topics that should be more widely investigated through group research. In other words, the process of alternating between group and individual research strategies provides the study of child development with an appropriate balance.

Since many elements of group research have already been considered, this section will briefly describe a few variations of the individual strategy. The earliest type is merely an extension of the baby biography discussed previously. This strategy was elevated to a new plateau of respect by Jean Piaget's exhaustive studies of the cognitive development of his own three infants (1963). Piaget's observations—originally termed the **clinical method**—

were largely nonexperimental. However, he frequently intervened to demonstrate developmental change convincingly. For example, consider the following excerpt from *The Origins of Intelligence in Children* in which Piaget (1963) discusses the behavior of his daughter Lucienne (4½ months old), who

> looks at a rattle with desire, but without extending her hand. I place the rattle near her right hand. As soon as Lucienne sees rattle and hand together, she moves her hand closer to the rattle and finally grasps it. A moment later she is engaged in looking at her hand. I then put the rattle aside; Lucienne looks at it, then directs her eyes to her hand, then to the rattle again, after which she slowly moves her hand toward the rattle. As soon as she touches it, there is an attempt to grasp it and finally, success. (P. 111)

Issues in Child Development

The Ethics of Research

The aspects of methodology considered in this chapter pose issues of secondary importance in contrast to the rights of participants in child development research. Neither statistics nor research strategy is relevant if the dignity of the subject is not protected. It is often quite difficult, however, to determine where to draw the line between research that is ethical and a study that violates human dignity. Developmental research is not morally neutral. Researchers must accept responsibility for articulating ethical hypotheses, conducting safe investigations, alleviating the concerns of participants, reaching justifiable conclusions, and properly disseminating the information of colleagues and the public.

Although few formal restrictions are placed on the research process, a widely recognized set of guidelines is described in the American Psychological Association's booklet *Ethical Principals in the Conduct of Research with Human Participants* (1982). While thinking about some of the basic principles and controversial decisions the booklet raises, perhaps it is also useful to consider whether it is unethical *not* to do research that may ultimately contribute to the improvement of human welfare (Achenbach 1978). Once the choice has been made to pursue the research, however, attention should be devoted to the details of the study that balance the rights of participants with the legitimate goals of the researcher.

Several principles appear to be so simple and straightforward that no honest researcher would hesitate to comply:

- Participants should be fully informed about the nature of the research.

- Subjects must volunteer without any coercion (consent should be ob-tained from participating children, as well as their parents).

- No treatment should be physically or mentally harmful.

- Confidentiality of the data must be preserved.

- There should be no restrictions on subject withdrawal at any time.

- Participants are entitled to knowledge about the results.

There may be more to these ideals than meets the eye. For example, how can a researcher obtain the informed consent of a subject if the goal of a study is to compare the effects of cognitive development on racial prejudice? Most children would attempt to behave according to socially acceptable standards unless the researcher disguised the true purpose of the investigation. In this case, after collecting the data, subjects could be debriefed (the entire process could be carefully explained). Although this is clearly not informed

---

Perhaps more common than Piaget's approach is the **case-study method**. This strategy, primarily derived from the psychoanalytic perspective, carefully follows and documents the therapeutic progress of an individual. Excerpts from case studies may be used to highlight patterns of change, as well as developmental problems. The major advantages of case studies are that they permit a great deal of flexibility in procedure, require no sophisticated statistical analyses, and yield rich and often fascinating accounts of individual development. What the case study lacks in representativeness and comparability, it makes up for in vivid details that may suggest the course of future developmental research.

As a final example of the individual strategy, consider the single-subject experimental design. In this research strategy, the behavior of only one child, or a few children, is manipulated over time. Single-subject experimental design is used to demonstrate the principles forwarded by the behaviorist perspective. When these principles are discussed in Chapter 7, bear in mind that they often are based upon one child rather than a group. In general, such mini-experiments show the processes of behavioral learning under relatively controlled conditions and the ways in which they may

consent, is it an unethical procedure?

A researcher is observing certain behaviors in a preschool and notices one of the children stealing another child's watch. Should the action be quietly coded and then ignored? If so, is the researcher accountable for assisting in a crime? Must the confidentiality and privacy of the children be respected? Perhaps a casual warning to the thief would suffice. Or perhaps the incident should be reported to the teacher.

The establishment of a program to improve the memory skills of high school students may involve a different dilemma. If a control group is not also given the opportunity to learn from the treatment, is the researcher indirectly discriminating against this group? Does the researcher have an obligation to make potential benefits of the study available to all participants

as compensation for their time and effort?

The reactions of participants to the mere presence of the researcher may itself be a surprising and important phenomenon. This was the case, for example, in Milgram's (1963) use of a phony electric-shocking device that subjects were operating to encourage learners (actually research assistants) in the next room. The subjects were clearly upset by the nature of their task. However, despite volunteering and knowing they could leave at any time, few of the adult subjects disobeyed the instruction to "shock" the "learners" or decided to withdraw from the anxiety-provoking situation. It is apparent that the status or implied authority of a researcher must be wielded very cautiously, especially for participants who may be less able to make "free" choices (infants and young children, the mentally retarded, the mentally ill, incarcerated juveniles, and even animals).

As we continue to work toward understanding socially sensitive issues in child development, what constitutes ethically defensible research will become increasingly difficult to define. There can be no easy, step-by-step cookbook of ethical guidelines that will enable researchers to eliminate all risks from their investigations. Each plan must be evaluated on its own merits and modified or abandoned if necessary so that the gains in knowledge are perceived to far outweigh the likelihood of problems. Researchers must design valuable studies that will inspire the confidence of participants in a joint venture to explore child development.

alleviate certain problems. A 7-year-old boy who is afraid of dogs, for instance, might be systematically rewarded for behaving in a relaxed manner. Overall, single-subject experiments share with clinical, or case, studies the narrow focus on individual change. They do, however, emphasize observable behaviors and more controlled conditions instead of underlying cognitive or personality structures.

The Laboratory or the Field?

A major criticism of methodology in child development has been the tendency to avoid the natural settings of behavior in favor of the laboratory environment (McCall 1977a). Although investigations in a highly controlled and standardized setting have made valuable contributions, the artificiality of laboratory research has limited a more complete understanding of change. The trend in recent years, therefore, has been a revival of the role of naturalistic research that was once the prevalent developmental methodology. Impetus for this shift in perspective has been provided by such diverse disciplines as ethology, cultural anthropology, and environmental psychology. A provocative synthesis by Bronfenbrenner (1979), *The Ecology of Human Development*, suggests the need for developmentalists to address the interaction of people within their natural settings.

The laboratory versus naturalistic setting should not be confused with the experimental versus the nonexperimental strategy controversy. Even though laboratory research has typically been experimental and naturalistic research usually has been nonexperimental, either strategy can be used in either setting. Bronfenbrenner (1979) stressed the importance of the "ecological validity" of the setting; that is, the experiment should be conducted in a setting that seems natural to children. Day-care centers, hospitals, restaurants, homes, schools, shopping malls, parks and playgrounds, skating rinks, and libraries are just a few of the locations that offer researchers an opportunity to examine behavior in a natural context. Furthermore, unobtrusive manipulation can be introduced into natural settings; this strategy is termed a **field experiment** (e.g., a small change in a classroom teaching technique).

Researchers who worry that important variables cannot be manipulated easily in settings outside of the laboratory also must wonder how results obtained in strange situations can be generalized to the real world. Of course, the laboratory can be a most useful setting for examining how children behave in unfamiliar environments.

Sometimes a researcher may be able to take advantage of a **natural experiment**—one in which crucial changes may be investigated without deliberate intervention—by simply being in the right place at the right time. For example, if a bowling alley is planning to make some changes in the rules, researchers could observe certain adolescent behaviors prior to the changes and again after the changes had been instituted. Thus, the researchers would be able to take advantage of a naturally occurring treatment without distorting the reality of the surroundings or events.

Problems in Doing Research

Regardless of the research strategy selected, there are several other problems beyond those previously mentioned. The details of the research design may produce biases that severely influence the data collected.

Some of these biases are referred to as **demand characteristics**, or the cues about the research to which subjects may unknowingly react. For instance, participation in the research itself may stimulate some children to improve their performance or to change their attitudes. This is quite similar to the concept of a placebo drug: people think taking a pill (really only sugar) will make them better, and it does. Subjects may try to please the researcher, purposely resist the research, or attempt to figure out exactly what the researcher wants to explore. These behaviors may be a function of the attractiveness of the materials, where the research is conducted, the nature of the instructions or procedures, or the characteristics of the researchers themselves (such as age, sex, race, physical qualities, and personality).

Another type of bias is known as a **response set**, or the tendency to respond continually in a similar manner despite any variation in the source of stimulation. Children, for example, often try to do what they believe will be considered socially good or conventionally correct, despite what the researcher says or does. Researchers, however, are also likely to be guilty of reacting according to response sets. One tendency of observers, for example, is to rate the present behavior of a child according to previous ratings. When researchers allow their judgment to be affected by the past behavior of the child, the halo effect is said to be operating. A final instance of researcher bias is the *expectancy effect*, in which children pick up subtle clues as to what the researcher hopes will occur.

Researchers must take all possible precautions so as to minimize these different sources of bias. For example, they may choose procedures that do not create extreme reactions or hire assistants unfamiliar with the goals of the research to interact with their subjects.

This survey of research strategies clearly indicates the diversity of choices available to the investigator of child development. Figure 2.1 summarizes these principal research strategies according to the questions formulated earlier. This chapter has pointed out the limitations, as well as the benefits, of the various strategies. Unfortunately, because researchers can employ no more than a few of these approaches in any given study, the

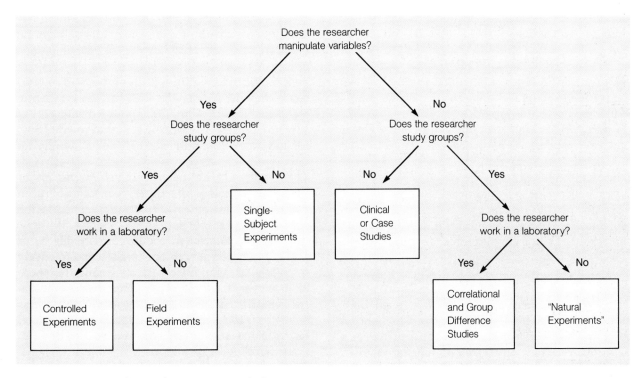

Figure 2.1   Flow chart of Basic Research Strategies

acquisition of useful data is a gradual, time-consuming process. As the following sections will show, researchers, having determined their basic strategy, then must select an appropriate data collection procedure and choose a suitable developmental design.

Procedures for Collecting Data

Whatever strategy researchers select for testing hypotheses or answering research questions, another critical decision they face is precisely how to operationalize the variables that are to be manipulated or measured. Thousands of somewhat different methods have been used for collecting data throughout the history of developmental research. However, these variations can be summarized in three basic ways: (1) surveying subjects directly, (2) obviously or unobtrusively observing subjects' behavior, and (3) providing subjects with certain tasks or tests to complete. Although each of these methods will be described separately, remember that researchers do not necessarily employ

any one of them exclusively, even within the same investigation.

Survey Method

Perhaps the most obvious method of obtaining information from children is to request it in a straightforward manner. This **survey approach** can take several forms. *Interviews* (often called interview schedules) are personal surveys administered face-to-face or, occasionally, by telephone. *Questionnaires*, in contrast, are self-administered surveys that may be distributed individually or initiated through the mail. Surveys by mail or by telephone are plagued by lack of cooperation and have not been found to be cost-effective for gathering detailed and sensitive types of data (Kerlinger 1973).

The personal interview and, to a lesser extent, the carefully constructed questionnaire can be useful methods to study child development. Respondents may be asked two extreme types of questions: structured and unstructured. If the interview is structured, the question sequence will be rigidly prepared and provoke fairly simple responses. Although structured questions may make interpretation easier, the unstructured interview offers the opportunity for the respondent to provide more detailed information. Furthermore, the interviewer is able to introduce follow-up questions for clarification and generally to establish greater rapport with the respondent.

A potential danger of the interview method is that questions of interest to the researcher may be too delicate for the child to react to comfortably. This may lead to resistance, dishonesty, or a general tendency to respond in a fashion presumed by the child to be socially desirable. In such cases, a self-administered questionnaire—especially if returned anonymously—would provide a more advantageous approach.

Why is the face-to-face interview used, considering the weaknesses suggested (not to mention the time and expense involved)? The answer lies in the weaknesses of the self-administered questionnaire. The self-administered questionnaire is based upon possibly erroneous assumptions: that questions are interpreted the same way by all children and that all children are equally capable of expressing their ideas in writing. These assumptions are particularly doubtful for research with young children. Different survey methods, as well as various observational or testing approaches, are chosen according to the kind of information desired and the developmental level of the sample.

In sum, the survey method can be an important tool for the developmental researcher. Although a fairly costly procedure (except for relatively small samples), the flexibility of a personal interview is an attractive feature. The most difficult aspect of using an interview approach is being certain the interviewers are carefully trained and sensitive to the feelings of children.

Observational Method

Instead of directly confronting children, researchers often decide simply to observe them and draw conclusions from their behavior. Sometimes researchers elect to use observations made for them by others who are familiar with the children (e.g., parents, friends, or teachers).

Unlike survey methods, **observational research** is very appropriate for infants and young children, who are less likely to be as self-conscious as adolescents or adults. Of course, some types of observation may be unnoticed by the subjects because they occur after the fact (such as evaluating children's artwork) or they involve disguised observers (disguised as passengers on a crowded bus, for example). Sometimes subjects will simply ignore observers after sufficient time has elapsed. The use of observational methods, however, places the entire burden of interpretative responsibility on the researchers' observations rather than on the subjects' own responses.

Just as survey methods vary in degree of structure, there are both open-ended and relatively restricted forms of observation. Among the open, or narrative, forms are the subject's personal diaries, anecdotal accounts, and records of continuous behavioral sequences. Although rarely available, diaries are relatively regular, retrospective descriptions that provide developmentally interesting documentation of change. Anecdotal records offer more sporadic, yet disinterested, accounts of unusual or characteristic behaviors. Continuous narrative methods, called **running records** or **specimen descriptions**, involve richly detailed notes of behavior as it occurs. Specimen descriptions are the more extensive and formal variation of the running records that have been used frequently by teachers since the turn of the century to evaluate classroom interactions (Irwin & Bushnell 1980).

The use of unstructured observational methods need not be restricted to studying behavior in school settings. Many other kinds of research reports offer illustrative anecdotes, and many others would benefit from incorporating narrative methods. A primary advantage of these techniques is the permanent availability of extensive descriptions of behavior in a natural context. Unfortunately, on-the-spot narrative methods require expensive and time-consuming recording, in contrast to diaries and anecdotes, which can be examined after the event. The researcher thus is asked to compromise between detailed sequences and an informal flexibility. It would be a serious mistake, however, to dismiss the value of casual observation methods. Piaget's descriptions, for instance, changed the course of research in infant development.

CHILD ___WALTER LEONARD___   DATE __9/24/79__

TASK	YES	NO	IF "NO," DATE FIRST SEEN
1. Can pick out the following shapes as they are named			
circle	✓		
square	✓		
triangle	✓		
rectangle	✓		
1. Can count from 1 to 10	✓		
3. Can name properly the following shapes			
circle	✓		
square	✓		
triangle	✓		
rectangle		✓	10/2
4. Demonstrates understanding of the following relational concepts			
bigger	✓		
smaller	✓		
longer		✓	10/19
shorter		✓	10/26
5. Can do one-to-one correspondence for			
two objects	✓		
three objects	✓		
five objects	✓		
ten objects		✓	11/9
more than ten objects		✓	11/9
6. Can follow directions involving the following concepts			
first	✓		
middle		✓	11/16
last		✓	12/13
7. Demonstrates understanding of			
more than		✓	3/7
less than		✓	4/2

Figure 2.2   A Sample Observation Checklist

Source: From *Observational Strategies for Child Study,* by D. Michelle Irwin and M. Margaret Bushnell, p. 202. Copyright © 1980 by Holt, Rinehart and Winston, CBS College Publishing.

Structured observational approaches are typically less detailed samples of behavior that provide the dual benefits of efficiency and reliability. These techniques include time and event sampling, checklists, and rating scales. The time-sampling method is used to examine the frequency of predetermined categories of behavior (such as physically aggressive acts) for a specific interval (such as thirty minutes) at a selected period of the day (such as 2:00-2:30 P.M.). In event sampling, the observer waits for an anticipated behavior to occur and then notes the duration and other details relevant to that behavior. For instance, the observer watches four minutes of consecutive physical aggression between Roger and Jim over a toy truck. The scuffle began when Roger started punching Jim to obtain the truck.

Checklists are carefully planned observation forms that allow little variation or elaboration from the fairly simple target behaviors selected in advance. Although such descriptions provide no time reference, they are extremely simple to use for many kinds of observations (see Figure 2.2). The rating scale is similarly efficient, but requires a judgment by the rater as to the quantitative extent of the subject's behavior. An observer, for example, might be asked to rate the aggressiveness of Roger's behavior on a scale from 1 to 10, or to indicate how frequently Roger engages in aggressive behavior (often, occasionally, seldom, never).

Most observational research in child development has used structured techniques rather than unstructured ones. There are several reasons for this pattern: ease of recording or coding behaviors, greater efficiency in terms of time and money, more control over behavior to be observed, ability to obtain larger samples, and simplicity of scoring and statistical analysis. Even structured methods, however, are not without certain important weaknesses. Time sampling may miss the continuity of behavior; event sampling may miss the behavior altogether; checklists can be superficial; and rating scales are easily affected by observer bias (such as the halo effect described earlier).

Any type of observational data collection has the advantage of obtaining information in a relatively natural manner, especially if the observer makes an effort to remain in the background. The main weakness of this approach, however, is that the inferences the observer makes about a child's behavior are colored by the observer's perspective. To minimize this difficulty, it is essential to compare the independent ratings of at least two observers. Agreement among observers tends to insure the value of conclusions drawn from the observations. In recent years, observational methods have become more reliable tools for understanding child development because of technological advances in portable videotape equipment, electronic event recorders, and sophisticated computer programs. These improvements permit researchers to place increasing confidence in the use of observational techniques.

Testing Method

The data collection most widely used in developmental research is the presentation of **standardized tasks and tests** to children. These methods are more challenging to the children than surveys and more intrusive than observation.

However, they are able to provide large amounts of reliable (consistent) data that help researchers avoid the effects of their own biases and possibly those of the subjects in the study. Interpretations of the data are usually carefully defined by having all children respond to an identical set of stimuli or directions; researchers then score the responses according to a predetermined set of criteria. Since the children are not informed in advance of the "correct" responses, they are presumably less likely to be aware of the researcher's hypotheses.

Standardized tests or tasks can be defined as systematic methods for obtaining samples of categorical or numerical information. The samples are inferred to represent a child's characteristics. A child's responses typically are compared with those of an appropriate representative sample (called a norm group) for interpretation.

Hundreds of commercially distributed tests and innumerable unpublished ones are available. They may be divided into tests that attempt to measure:

- achievement (mastery of specifically learned kinds of information)
- intelligence (several types, depending on the definition of intelligence accepted)
- special aptitudes (for example, motoric, linguistic, or musical)
- personality (attributes such as depression, femininity, and dominance)
- attitudes and values (religious, political, aesthetic)
- interest or vocational orientations (career leanings such as artistic, social, or practical).

Clearly, the above list is not exhaustive, and there are other reasonable ways to classify the multitude of tasks and tests.

Despite the popularity of standardized tests in child development research, certain disadvantages accompany this method. These weaknesses should be considered above and beyond factors such as the qualifications of the test interpreter, rapport between test-taker and test administrator, and any distracting conditions during the testing session. Tests, for example, can be considered artificial and limited samples of behaviors, thoughts, and feelings. Particularly in the realm of personality assessment, tests are not immune to deliberate distortions by children who wish to appear socially

This young girl is being administered one of the many items from the Bayley Scales of Infant Development. Standard tests like this may provide valuable information to both researchers and clinicians.

"normal" or who fear being labeled as somehow maladjusted. There are also aspects of development that may not be amenable to contrived measurement techniques and would be better assessed through surveys or observational methods. Furthermore, many tests cannot be interpreted any more objectively than other methods to draw inferences about development. The underlying question for test users, then, concerns the validity of a test for its intended purpose.

Testing, however, has been unfairly portrayed as a villainous approach for assessing human behavior. There certainly have been abuses of the testing process in both research and actual practice. For instance, it can be unfair or misleading to label permanently a child's intelligence according to the results of one imperfect testing procedure. However, such individually disturbing situations should not be permitted to diminish the contributions of tests. When carefully constructed and employed, they are efficient tools in such diverse areas as evaluation of academic performances, selection for special programs, and counseling of troubled individuals. Optimism concerning the future of testing is warranted because of improved technical training, recent statistical advances, and an increasing awareness of the complex relationships between developmental theory and test construction.

This discussion of data collection methods has only begun to suggest the variety of resources from which the inventive researcher can either select or modify. These examples indicate the basis for most of the conclusions discussed in later chapters. Most of the important biological types of data frequently used in developmental research have not yet been mentioned. Many of these procedures may be familiar: measuring height and weight, heart rate, respiration rate, galvanic skin response, reaction time, brain wave patterns, visual acuity, auditory discrimination, and others. Exciting new biofeedback techniques demonstrating voluntary control over bodily processes also offer the possibility of integrating psychological and physiological data for a broader understanding of child development.

Developmental Designs

The strategies and procedures discussed up to this point would be familiar to all researchers in the social sciences and education. Additional considerations confront researchers in child development because they are primarily interested in examining patterns of change or stability across the early portion of the lifespan. Important variables in developmental research, therefore, are time and the factors with which it interacts to produce developmental change.

Time, an elusive concept, presents special difficulties for the researcher, depending on how it is defined. In other words, time could refer to the interval between birth and the present (chronological age), to the period when an individual was born (generation or age cohort), or to the particular occasion when the research was conducted (time of measurement).

This section explores some of the designs and issues that relate to the meaning of time for the study of child development. Remember, however, that not every study is directly concerned with time itself. Much research, such as the Holmes and Nagy study, is only peripherally concerned with time (gestational age and future development). Other investigations use events that have occurred in the past but do not measure changes. Such retrospective, or historical, designs are actually quite common in developmental research.

Cross-sectional Research

The **cross-sectional design** focuses on the simultaneous comparison of children of different chronological ages (see Figure 2.3). Developmental change and chronological age are not synonymous, as was pointed out earlier; therefore, such research

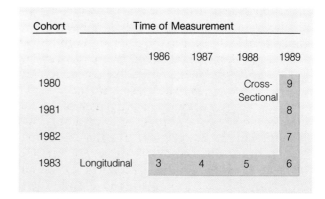

Figure 2.3 Comparison of the Classic Developmental Designs (Ages of the Samples within the Table)

provides specific details of age differences, from which we tend to infer developmental change. Researchers need to exercise caution in making inferences based on cross-sectional data, since they have not manipulated their subjects' age, cohort (year of birth), or development history. In other words, are age differences found due to universal processes of development or to the different experiences to which subjects of particular cohorts have been exposed?

Consider, for example, a study to examine the gender role development of females. Suppose the sample consisted of 6-year-olds, 14-year-olds, and 22-year-olds. Each female was interviewed during June 1986 concerning her personal conceptions of masculinity and femininity. If the results indicated that 22-year-olds express the most feminine characteristics and 6-year-olds the most masculine characteristics, would a researcher be able to justify the conclusion that girls become more feminine as they develop? Since the subjects were not followed continuously from the age of 6 to the age of 22, the only way we could confidently assume such a developmental pattern is if each cohort studied was quite similar. This assumption, however, might be seriously questioned. It is likely that the experiences which have influenced the gender role conception of females born in the 1980, 1972, and 1964 cohorts were vastly different.

Cross-sectional research is not without some significant advantages, particularly if relevant cultural variables appear to be minimal. It can be conducted in a short period of time; therefore, funding is not a major problem, nor is extensive cooperation required from either subjects or research associates. Many investigations of children's intellectual development have compared the abilities of one age to another. The value of this research for establishing challenging educational curricula, creating appropriate television programs or reading materials, designing interesting toys and games, and provoking further study of continuous individual development has been unparalleled. Nevertheless, interpretations of cross-sectional data should be evaluated cautiously in light of the possible confusion between age differences due to particular environmental variations and age differences due to genuine developmental processes.

Longitudinal Research

In contrast to the flaws of cross-sectional research, the **longitudinal design**, at first glance, may appear to be far more useful. This approach allows the researcher to study the same group of children over an extended period of months, years, or even longer (see Figure 2.3). Using a longitudinal design eliminates the two basic weaknesses of cross-sectional research: lack of comparability between different age groups and the absence of continuity in individual development. Although the longitudinal approach truly addresses age changes from one point in time to another, there are numerous practical disadvantages as well as one major conceptual dilemma. That is, because only one group is being evaluated, the findings at different ages may be a function of cultural conditions *when* the data were collected rather than the *age* of the sample. In other words, the time of measurement is a very critical variable that could be confused with developmental change. Research on vocational development in adolescents during an economic recession, for instance, would be strongly influenced by a time-of-measurement component.

Since it often may be reasonable to rule out time of measurement as a problem, however, why are longitudinal studies employed relatively infre-

quently in developmental research? Unfortunately, they are costly ventures that require the long-term cooperation of subjects and researchers. The longitudinal approach also demands careful and foresighted planning to avoid the obsolescence of research strategy or data collection procedures. For example, if a researcher discovers in 1986 that an intelligence test used at the start of the investigation in 1978 is no longer valid, how can the results of comparisons with a revised form of the test be meaningful? Once the methodology has been established and the early data collected, the researchers are constricted by the original theory and procedures of the study.

In addition to the financial, intellectual, and practical problems of maintaining extended commitments by researchers to the project, the difficulties of retaining and continually relocating a representative sample are considerable. Our mobile society leads to the "disappearance" of subjects; some become ill or even die, and others merely lose interest in the research. How can the researcher be sure that what remains of the sample near the conclusion of the study is comparable on relevant characteristics to the original sample? For example, a longitudinal study of achievement motivation in college students could be conducted over a four-year period. What could we conclude about the development of achievement motivation by comparing the senior class with themselves as freshmen? It is likely that those students lacking high-achievement motivation would have dropped out, transferred to an easier school, or taken some time off from college. In any event, the seniors are clearly not the same sample they were four years earlier. There are not only fewer of them, but also they possess different characteristics.

Furthermore, researchers must consider what effects participating in the study itself will have on the sample. Would adolescents tested on aspects of physical development react to the measurement process by intensively trying to improve their skills and coordination before retesting the following year? Similarly, researchers cannot control the individual experiences of subjects over the course of the investigation. How would we evaluate the results of a study on the personality development of

Longitudinal designs enable researchers to follow the same children across different stages of development. However, cultural changes over time and numerous practical problems can compromise this type of research.

girls between the ages of 4 and 14 who may encounter varied life situations that will influence personality development (e.g., failing school, losing a parent, moving to another part of the country, getting a sibling, having a serious illness or accident, winning a million-dollar lottery)? Lastly, the longitudinal approach involves only one cohort. Cultural factors that may affect patterns of development, therefore, are ignored. In other words, can the results of longitudinal research be attributed to universal developmental change or to the history of a particular cohort?

Sequential Research

One approach to resolving the dilemmas posed by the previously discussed developmental designs involves a complex convergence of methods. Although the concept is not new, relatively little attention had been paid to the use of **sequential design** until the past decade. Sequential designs have been proposed in a variety of forms; however, the basic task is to link modifications of cross-sectional and longitudinal designs within a more comprehensive investigation. Sequential designs retain the advantages of the simpler designs while reducing their disadvantages. Thus, descriptions of developmental change can more accurately reflect the intricacies of the child or adolescent.

Perhaps the most effective means of illustrating the value of sequential designs is to discuss part of the work by Nesselroade and Baltes (1974) with adolescents. Their research focused on personality and ability changes over a two-year period among four cohorts who ranged in age from 13 to 16 initially and from 15 to 18 at the conclusion of the study (see Figure 2.4). One of their findings, derived from nearly three thousand subjects tested on forty variables, concerned a decrease in socioemotional anxiety between 1970 and 1972. If only one cohort had been studied in a simple longitudinal design—say those born in 1956—Nesselroade and Baltes might have assumed that between the ages of 14 and 16 adolescents become less anxious. However, they noted that anxiety similarly decreased for the 1954, 1955, and 1957 cohorts (three additional longitudinal studies), suggesting instead that cultural influences during the research

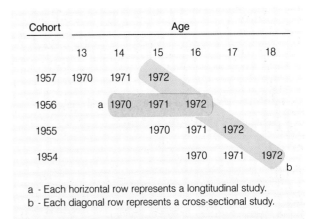

Figure 2.4 Sequential Design of Nesselroade & Baltes (1974) (Years of Measurement within the Table)

Source: From Nesselroade, J.R. and Baltes, P.B. (1974) Adolescent personality development and historical change: 1970-1972. *Monographs of the Society for Research in Child Development* 39 (1, Serial No. 54). Copyright 1974 by the Society for Research in Child Development, Inc.

interval were responsible for the change. Any single cross-sectional study (in 1970, 1971, or 1972) would have resulted in age differences in anxiety without indicating a possible source for the apparent developmental change.

Therefore, sequential designs may be employed to limit the confusion regarding the relative importance of cultural versus developmental factors in age differences. These designs also provide the researcher with a compromise between the desire to examine individual continuity over an extended period and the practical aspects of more abbreviated research. For example, Nesselroade and Baltes (1974) spent only two years obtaining data on a five-year interval (ages 13 through 18) of adolescent development. In addition to saving time and money, insuring the cooperation of subjects, and eliminating the obsolescence of procedures, they were able to lessen the effects of repeated testing and unusual personal experiences during the study. Sequential designs, in sum, may well be worth the additional planning and sophisticated statistical analyses they require.

Applying Our Knowledge

The Use of Developmental Theory and Research

From ancient philosophers to contemporary developmentalists, the path of a happy childhood leading to a successful life has long been ·sought. The public appetite for consuming unending quantities of information, advice, and support concerning nearly every aspect of development has reached staggering proportions in recent years. There are books, magazines, tapes, newsletters, organizations, workshops, pamphlets, college courses, and a host of other materials available dealing with caring for our babies, extending an adolescent's creativity, coping with failure, maximizing our child's learning, pulling our family together after a divorce, and so forth. It does not seem likely that this quest is a passing fad, since the trend has been accelerating for decades. Our interest in advice on child development reflects the history of attempts to share such knowledge, as well as the current status of developmental theory and research evidence.

Consider the following suggestions from a 1930 government pamphlet on how to train a child to be happy:

> Begin when he is born.
> Feed him at exactly the same hours every day.

Do not feed him just because he cries.
Let him wait until the right time.
If you make him wait, his stomach will learn to wait.
His mind will learn that he cannot get things by crying.
You do two things for your baby at the same time. You teach his body good habits and you teach his mind good habits. (Weill 1930, 1)

The spirit of these remarks was stimulated by J. B. Watson's ideas on the crucial role of the parent in controlling the infant's environment. Watson staunchly believed that establishing an early, "scientific" routine for child care would promote the development of a well-adjusted and self-disciplined adult. Despite the fact that little, if any, research has been able to demonstrate the type of relationship which Watson hypothesized would exist, many parents have continued to practice very rigid methods of infant caretaking. Ironically, the results of Bell and Ainsworth's (1972) research on coping with crying infants, for example, indicates that immediate attention to their needs is the most effective approach for having a baby that cries less frequently.

Many similar instances could be cited whereby premature recommendations were publicly adopted, conclusions drawn by developmentalists were widely misinterpreted, or generalizations from limited evidence were grossly exaggerated. These all-too-frequent distortions do not, and should not, diminish the importance of deriving practical applications from devel-

opmental theory and research. Instead, they should caution both professional and layperson alike about the need to examine the implications of developmental work very carefully. It would be prudent to bear in mind that definitive conclusions are not based on a single investigation; that every piece of research or strand of theory has limitations; that each child's development is an extremely complex interaction of many factors; and that our observations may be biased by the values of our culture, our training, and our personal histories.

Although we may never be in the position to offer perfect predictability about the course of child development, the techniques and knowledge of the present and the future offer an invaluable, practical awareness of the issues involved in understanding children.

The discussion of alternative designs demonstrates the avenues available to further the understanding of child development. There is no one best approach for developmental research. Each question or hypothesis presents its own special set of circumstances that must be individually evaluated. Despite the relatively recent improvement in developmental design principles, we are increasingly planning our investigations by fruitfully integrating long-established canons of the scientific method with research strategies and data collection procedures appropriate for exploring the nature of development (see Applying Our Knowledge "The Use of Developmental Theory and Research" for a related note of caution).

Summary

1. Most developmental research is conducted in accord with the traditional scientific method. This organizes the process into a series of logical steps—from clarifying the problem to interpreting results.
2. The initial task of the researcher is to define a problem carefully by focusing on a limited number of variables that can be provided with very specific meanings.
3. Hypotheses of research questions about the relationships among the selected variables are developed. A sample, or representative group of research participants, is chosen to be studied.
4. After the data have been collected, researchers analyze the results using statistical techniques. The various statistics available are quantitative tools for understanding information.
5. Research findings are then summarized and communicated to other interested people.
6. The experimental approach manipulates and controls variables in order to provide comparisons for establishing the causes of developmental change.
7. Since not all variables in child development can be manipulated realistically or ethically, nonexperimental strategies are employed to suggest the reasons for group differences or relationships among variables.
8. Some researchers use clinical or case studies and single-subject experiments to obtain detailed assessments of individuals rather than broad generalizations about groups.
9. There has been a resurgence of interest in moving from extensive laboratory research toward developmental studies conducted in their natural settings.

10. Any research strategy has limitations—particularly demand characteristics and response sets—that must be considered seriously in designing a study.
11. Survey methods such as interviews and written questionnaires yield important data when carefully constructed and sensitively administered.
12. A wide variety of observational methods affords the researcher a more unobtrusive approach. However, it is the observer, rather than the subjects, who may exhibit a biased perspective.
13. Testing, which offers considerable advantages and disadvantages to the developmental researcher, probably has been the most widespread data collection procedure.
14. Cross-sectional research frequently is used to compare groups of different chronological ages at the same time.
15. Longitudinal research allows one sample to be followed over an extended time period to trace the patterns of development.
16. In response to the weaknesses of classic developmental research, sequential designs are becoming accepted as the best method for studying complex developmental processes.

Key Terms

variable	case-study method
operational definition	field experiment
hypothesis	natural experiment
sample	demand characteristics
descriptive statistics	response set
inferential statistics	survey approach
group differences	observational research
statistics	standardized tests or
correlational statistics	tasks
multivariate statistics	cross-sectional design
univariate statistics	longitudinal design
experimental strategy	sequential design
clinical method	

Suggested Readings

Achenbach, T.M. (1978). *Research in developmental psychology: Concepts, strategies, methods.* New York: Free Press.

    An excellent integration of various aspects of research methodology presented with style, insight, and frequent examples.

Appelbaum, M.I. & McCall, R.B. (1983). Design and analysis in developmental psychology. In P.H. Mussen (Ed.), *Handbook of child psychology* (4th ed., vol. 1). New York: Wiley.

A very authoritative, contemporary, and concise overview of research methods and statistical analysis relevant to child development.

Baltes, P.B., Reese, H.W. & Nesselroade, J.R. (1977). *Life-span developmental psychology: Introduction to research methods.* Monterey, CA: Brooks/Cole.

Another volume that offers a good deal of information on research methods. However, it is not quite as interesting as Achenbach's presentation.

Bronfenbrenner, U. (1979). *The ecology of human development: Experiments by nature and design.* Cambridge, MA: Harvard University Press.

A thoughtful discussion combined with a plea for developmental researchers to devote more attention to studying behavior in natural settings.

Nesselroade, J.R. & Reese, H.W. (Eds.). (1973). *Life-span developmental psychology: Methodological issues.* New York: Academic Press.

An important volume containing a number of difficult chapters by different authors. The chapters address most of the significant aspects of developmental methods.

Wolman, B.B. (Ed). (1982). *Handbook of developmental psychology.* Englewood Cliffs, NJ: Prentice-Hall.

A massive book with several chapters dealing with cross-cultural research, longitudinal methods, and ethical issues.

Readings from the Literature

The following study by Steven Beck and his associates is an unusual example of research on the process of doing research. Beck, Collins, Overholser, and Terry (1984) devised a fairly simple methodology that was equally straightforward to analyze statistically. In addition, their work touches on the critical issues of ethics in conducting research and the representativeness of volunteer samples. These researchers concluded that their study met a reasonable definition of ethical safeguards. Furthermore, they believe their study demonstrated that children who did not receive parental permission to participate were significantly different on a crucial variable from those children whose parents allowed them to participate. The questions below should help you to focus on the major points of the article:

- Do you believe that the procedures used in this study to assess children's social competence were justified in light of the benefits attained for understanding child development?

- If you were a parent who received the letter and consent form presented in the article, would you permit your child to participate in the research? Why or why not?

- What suggestions do you have for helping developmental researchers to improve the rate of cooperation in studies requiring child participation?

A Comparison of Children Who Receive and Who Do Not Receive Permission to Participate in Research

Steven Beck, Lynn Collins, James Overholser, and Karen Terry
Ohio State University

In a study examining children's social competence in elementary school settings, the authors had the opportunity to compare children who received parental permission to participate to children who did not receive permission. Results indicated that children who were not involved in the study were more likely to be viewed by teachers as having unsatisfactory relationships with peers than children who were in the study. The present results suggest that investigators begin reporting the number of children who do not participate in a given study and begin examining whether minors who receive parental permission differ on important dimensions from minors who do not receive such permission. Ethical considerations of the present study are discussed.

The obligation to obtain informed consent from research participants is the keystone of the protective safeguard of ethical research. According to the National Commission for the Protection of Human Subjects of Biomedical and Behavioral Research (1977), studies involving children must obtain the assent of each prospective minor as well as the permission of the child's parent prior to participation. Parent permission is necessary for a minor to participate in a research investigation.

The most recent requirements for obtaining informed consent from human research participants are derived from the 1981 guidelines issued by the Department of Health, Education and Welfare. These guidelines closely parallel those recommended by the American Psychological Association (Ad Hoc Committee on

Ethical Standards in Psychological Research, 1983). The basic elements of these guidelines for experimental research are complete and understandable information about the research, a description of discomforts and risks and benefits that may be expected to occur, disclosure of any appropriate alternative procedure that may be available, an offer to answer any inquires, and an understanding that the person is free to withdraw consent at any time (Keith-Spiegel, 1983).

In short, informed assent for children and their parents is considered necessary to authorize children's participation in research. While such guidelines are essential, a problem faced by many investigators conducting research with children, particularly in schools, is the difficulty in securing permission from parents of potential child subjects. In school settings, children are usually recruited to participate in a research project and letters are sent home with children explaining the nature and purpose of the project to the parents. Often, however, such letters may never reach the parents or they become misplaced at home, or parents may refuse to allow their child to participate. Consequently, a proportion of children do not receive permission to participate in research. The number of minors who have been unable to participate in research due to the lack of consent varies from 10% of the sample (Ford, 1982) to as high as 70% of the potential subject pool in longitudinal studies (McCarthy & Hodge, 1982). This raises the question of whether children who receive consent to participate differ systematically from children who, for whatever reasons, do not receive such consent. The present study uses teacher judgment to compare children who did receive consent to those who did not receive consent to participate in a research project. To the best of our knowledge, the present analysis is the first direct comparison of these two populations, addressing whether research conducted in elementary school settings may be investigating a biased sample of children—namely, children who give assent and receive parental permission to participate.

Method and Results

In a cross-sectional investigation examining the relationships between multiple measures of first- and sixth-grade children's social competence (i.e., classroom behavioral observations, teacher ratings of classroom behaviors, children's self-report ratings of interpersonal behavior, and academic achievement scores) and peer friendship and likability (which was obtained using peer nominations and peer ratings), the present investigators obtained written consent from the children and parental proxy consent. The study was conducted in four first-grade and four sixth-grade classrooms in two predominantly white middle-class schools located in the suburbs of a large midwest city. After discussing the project with each class and explaining what type of information would be collected, we gave letters to each child to take home that provided information about the project to parents. The parent consent form read as follows:

> We (Steven Beck, Ph.D., and his associates from the Department of Psychology, Ohio State University) are interested in children's social development. By finding out more about children's social development and specifically children's friendships, it may be possible to help children who have few friends or who lack friendship skills. We are asking your permission to allow your child to participate in a project that will be conducted at his/her school with first and sixth grade children.
>
> The project will involve your child rating children in his/her class who s/he prefers to play with and does not prefer to play with. At the same time, your child will be rated by his/her classmates determining how your child is viewed (in terms of being a playmate) by children in the class. This information will, of course, remain confidential (that is, this information will not be made known to his or her teacher nor to the children in the class). However, your child may experience some mild discomfort identifying children as poor playmates.
>
> Your child will also be asked to fill out a questionnaire telling the investigators how they would respond in various interpersonal situations. Finally, your child, along with other participating children, will be observed in class by one or two undergraduate students to see how they interact with others.
>
> The possible benefits of this project are to eventually begin to help children who have few friends. Furthermore, the investigators will have a discussion with your child's class about ways of developing and maintaining friends.
>
> If you agree to allow your child to participate, please sign the attached form and have your child give it to his/her teacher. Please note your child will not be rewarded or

penalized in any way for participating or not participating. Also note that if you agree to allow your child to participate in this project, your child will also be asked permission to participate and your child can withdraw from the project at anytime.

Thank you for your cooperation. If you have any questions or would like further information regarding this project, please feel free to contact Dr. Steven Beck at - - -.

Attached to the letter was a standard form from the university for consent for participation in social and behavioral research, which included the title of the study, issues of confidentiality, information about freedom to withdraw consent at any time, acknowledgment that the form had been read and understood, the investigator's signature, and lines for parental and child signatures.

To obtain consent to participate, the child had to return the letter signed by both the parent and the child. After a few days a second copy was sent home with those children who did not return the original consent form. Attached to this copy was a short note that read:

Parents:

This is a short reminder to read the attached consent form to determine if your child can participate in the project that is described.

If you could return the attached consent form tomorrow it would be greatly appreciated.

Thank you

In all, 115 children from a potential sample of 177 eventually returned signed parental and child consent forms. Thus, 65% of the children and their parents consented to participate. Each letter returned granted permission to participate. By grades, 52 to 77 first-grade children (68%) and 63 of 100 sixth-grade children (63%) consented.

Since the study was examining children's peer relationships, we attempted to determine if children with poor relationships were underrepresented in the sample of children who gave assent and received parental permission to participate. To assure confidentiality for those children and parents who had not consented, the eight teachers whose classes were involved in the project were asked to indicate the number of children in the class (without giving names) who appeared to be either aggressive or withdrawn from peers. To standardize this procedure, written descriptions of aggressive and withdrawn children were given to each teacher. Green, Beck, Forehand, and Vosk (1980) have found that teachers could accurately identify children who were having peer problems using the same written descriptions. Teachers were then asked to indicate the number of children they had listed who were on the roster of children who received permission to participate in the project. In this way, we were able to ascertain the number of children (without identifying them) not participating in the project who were viewed by teachers as having problematic peer relationships. It is important to recognize the nonintrusiveness of this procedure and the fact that the procedure safeguarded against the identification of children not participating in the study; thus, we believe these children's privacy had not been invaded and our procedures comply with new regulations on the use of subjects in behavioral science research.

Twenty children were identified by teachers as having problematic peer relationships. Twelve children, 7 first-graders and 5 sixth-graders, were nominated as being aggressive with peers. Eight children, 4 first-graders and 4 sixth-graders, were identified as being withdrawn from peers. Only 8 (40%) of the 20 children gave and received parental consent to participate in the study (6 first-graders, 4 who were identified as aggressive and 2 as withdrawn, and 2 sixth-graders, both identified as aggressive). A chi-square analysis indicated that more children who did not receive permission to participate in the study were perceived by teachers as having unsatisfactory peer relationships than children allowed to participate ($X^2 = 6.18$, df, 1, $p < .05$.)

Discussion

The first issue that needs to be addressed in the present study involves the ethical considerations of collecting information about children not participating in the larger study. The three-step procedure of giving teachers a brief description of aggressive or withdrawn children, having teachers recollect the number of children in their classes who fit such descriptions, and finally having teachers indicate the number of children who fit one of the descriptions from the roster of children participating in the larger project (thus being able to derive the number of children in each class who had problematic peer relationships who were not on the roster) was nonintrusive and ensured complete anonymity of the children not involved in the larger study. This procedure appears to comply with federal and American Psychological Association guidelines for conducting research and was carefully reviewed by our Human Subject Review Committee. Informed consent requirements were exempted since the investigators and the Human Subject Committee determined that the expected benefits of this research outweighed the potential minimal risks.

The reader should be aware, however, of the potential ethical problems inherent in the present study. Deception could be constructed since children whose parents did not give permission to participate in the larger study were involved in a project (with the rest of the children who did participate in the larger study) that required teacher "ratings" or "labeling" of children. One could argue that children were involved in a project that required teachers to perform a task for the investigators that teachers may not have done otherwise. Before one may conduct a study involving deception, principles outlined in the Ethical Principles of Psychologists state that the investigator has a responsibility to (1) determine whether the use of deception is justified by the study's scientific value, (2) determine whether alternative procedures are available, and (3) ensure that participants are provided with sufficient explanation as soon as possible.

The critical ethical question is: Are the risks involved in this project minimal when weighed against the potential benefits of the study (i.e., documenting a possible sampling bias in children who do not receive parental permission in school-conducted research and alerting investigators to this phenomenon)? We believe that the procedure employed of teachers identifying (to themselves, ensuring anonymity) children who have problematic peer relationships provided minimal, if any, risk for the identified children when weighed against the potential advancement of knowledge through this

procedure. We reasoned that new information was not being supplied to the teachers about their pupils. We also assumed that prior to the present study teachers were already cognizant of those children in their classroom who had poor peer relationships; hence, it is difficult to see how having teachers recollect the actual number of children in their classroom would pose a risk for these children.

In the present study the procedure for identifying children was employed only after it was determined that alternative procedures were not available. For example, archival records, such as previous teachers' ratings or past records of children's peer relationships, would have been an even more nonintrusive procedure for retrieving information relevant for the present study. Unfortunately, previous school records did not include sociometric or peer relationship information. In addition, the study was conducted in one school that experienced a sizable influx of new students since it was located in a rapidly growing neighborhood, so that a significant number of children were new to the school and securing previous kindergarten or fifth-grade teacher rating was not feasible. For future investigators, archival records or previous teacher ratings or recollections appear to be a preferable alternative for collecting sensitive information about school-age children.

The first author held evening discussion meetings with parents of children from both schools who were involved in the larger and present study. Since the current study was considered by the investigators and the Human Subject Committee as minimal risk research, it was viewed not necessary to inform parents individually of the present study.

Although the present data are based on a limited sample examining children's peer relationships, and a rather simple statistical procedure was employed, the results nonetheless suggest the discomforting finding that elementary-age children who do not participate in research may differ on important dimensions from children who agree to participate. The present findings suggest that more problematic children (i.e., children whom teachers viewed as being either aggressive or withdrawn with peers) may not be allowed to participate in research conducted in schools. Given this finding, a more relevant question, which was not examined in the present study, is why children and parents do not participate in psychological research conducted in schools. The present study did find that all of the children who returned letters to the experimenters agreed to participate in the study. No parent or child provided information explaining why they refused to participate.

It is important that investigators begin reporting the proportion of children nor given permission to participate in future studies, and if possible, assess if these children differ from participating subjects. Surprisingly, an examination of empirical studies using infants, children, and adolescent subjects published in 1982 in *Child Development, Developmental Psychology, and Journal of Consulting and Clinical Psychology* found that only 14% of the articles reported the number of children and parents who had not given consent to participate. This finding suggests that investigators either are not following recommended human protection guidelines or, more likely, are failing to report the loss of potential subjects because they assume that nonparticipating subjects do not differ from consenting subjects.

Investigators conducting research in school settings using mailed consent forms to parents as a means of securing proxy consent should begin to examine why children and parents comply or do not comply to research proposals. Interestingly, the investigators in the present study informally observed when they came to the classrooms to interview or observe children that many children who were not eligible to participate since they did not return parental consent forms often eagerly requested to be involved in the study. This rather informal observation suggests that parents are primarily responsible for not allowing their children to participate. Well-intentioned parents may not give voluntary consent for their children to participate in research due to a lack of a research background or to their fear that participation might somehow embarrass themselves or embarrass or harm their child. Such information could be collected by requesting that parents return consent forms to school even if they do not want their child to participate in a study and by allowing parents the opportunity to indicate, by checking one or more boxes, rationales for refusing participation. Besides collecting a valuable data bank of the refusal rate of specific types of proposals, such information may allow investigators of children's research to better allay concerns or fears that children or parents may have regarding psychological research. One problem with this approach is that some dropout would be expected, given that some parents or children would never return the form indicating why they refused permission.

Given the recent interest in minor consent issues (cf. Melton, Koocher, & Saks, 1983), further research is needed to determine if minors who receive permission and minors who do not receive permission to participate in research vary on potentially important psychological characteristics. Until such data are collected, investigators conducting research on children in school settings may unknowingly be examining a biased sample of children. Finally, the present study is unusual since the ethical issues of collecting information about children without parental permission was resolved only after it was determined that the study provided minimal risk to the children and that the potential findings from this study outweighed the risks. Investigators should not deviate from basic ethical guidelines until all the advantages and disadvantages and additional safeguards of each exemption or alteration are carefully considered.

References

American Psychological Association. (1983). *Ethical principles in the conduct of research with human participants*. Washington, D.C.: Author.

Department of Health, Education and Welfare. (1981). *Institutional guide to DHEW policy on the production of human subjects* NIH Publications No. 72-101). Washington, D.C.: U.S. Government Printing Office.

Ford, M.E. (1982). Social cognition and social competence in adolescence. *Developmental Psychology, 18,* 323-340.

Green, K., Beck, S., Forehand, R., & Vosk, B. (1980). Validity of teacher nominations of child behavior problems. *Journal of Abnormal Child Psychology, 8,* 397-404.

Keith-Spiegel, P. (1983). Children and consent to participate in research. In G.P. Melton, M.J. Koocher, & M.J. Saks (Eds.), *Children's competence to consent*. New York: Plenum Press.

MacCarthy, J.D., & Hodge, D.R. (1982). Analysis of age effects in longitudinal studies of adolescent self-esteem. *Developmental Psychology, 18,* 373-379.

Melton, G.P., Koocher, M.J., & Saks, M.J. (Eds.). (1983). *Children's competence to consent.* New York: Plenum Press.

National Commission for the Protection of Human Subjects of Biomedical and Behavioral Research (1977). *Report and recommendation: Research involving children* (DHEW Publication No. [OS] 77-004). Washington, D.C.: U.S. Government Printing Office.

Manuscript received in final form January 5, 1984.

Source: Beck, S.J., Collins, L., Overholser, J., and Terry, K. (1984) A comparison of children who receive and who do not receive permission to participate in research. *Journal of Abnormal Child Psychology, 12 (4),* 573-580. Plenum Publishing Corp. Reprinted by permission of the publisher and author.

Prenatal Development, Birth, and the Newborn

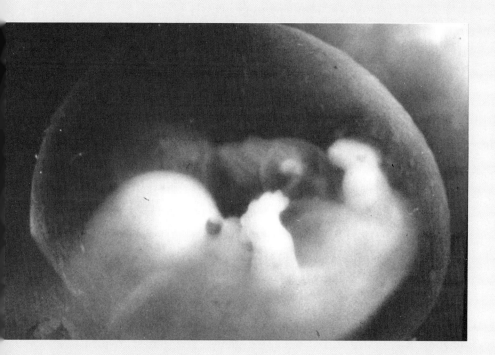

What is your prenatal and newborn quotient? Here are a few true-false questions designed to test your knowledge of development before and after birth.

1. It takes approximately nine weeks after conception for the developing baby to resemble a tiny human being.   T F
2. While in the womb, babies are protected against potentially harmful agents such as drugs and viruses.   T F
3. It is highly improbable that parents with brown eyes can give birth to a blue-eyed child.   T F
4. The older a woman gets, the greater the risk of giving birth to a child with Down's syndrome.   T F
5. Throughout the pregnancy, the baby's and mother's blood systems intermingle in order to provide nutrients to the baby.   T F
6. The ideal age for a woman to conceive and give birth is between 15 and 23 years.   T F
7. Presently, the amount of alcohol that may be safely consumed during pregnancy is undetermined.   T F
8. Premature births are always a result of poor prenatal care.   T F
9. The infant's reflexes first become noticeable at about two months after birth.   T F
10. The best way to soothe a crying infant is to place the baby up on your shoulder and gently rock him or her up and down.   T F

You will find the answers to these questions as you read this chapter.

This chapter discusses the series of complex changes that begin with conception and culminate in the appearance of a completely new and unique person. The chapter starts with an examination of how the mechanisms of inheritance help to determine the traits and characteristics that make individuals unique. The discussion will proceed through the stages of pregnancy, from fertilization to the moment of birth. The typical developmental characteristics of the embryo will be described, as well as the development of the fetus as the pregnancy comes to term.

The chapter will then discuss the stages of the birth process—labor, delivery, and afterbirth—and consider some of the problems, such as prematurity, that are associated with the birth process. Finally, the characteristic features of newborns will

be highlighted—such as their behaviors for adaptation (reflexes), cycles of arousal, and alertness and sleepiness. Assessment techniques designed to determine the status of the newborn will be presented.

Determiners of Growth

The formation of a brand-new individual is guided by the genetic blueprint laid down at conception. The environmental medium provided by the uterus also plays a significant role in prenatal development. This section takes a closer look at these determiners of growth.

The Genetic Plan

Expectant parents often wonder what their baby will be like. Probably the question uppermost in their minds is the sex of the baby. This is often followed by, "What color hair will he or she have? What color eyes? Who will the baby look like?" After birth, numerous behavioral traits are attributed to one side of the family or the other ("When he gets angry, doesn't he act just like they all do on his mother's side?"). The answers to questions about physical and behavioral traits can be found in the study of the human genetic makeup.

Cell Division
With the notable exception of the sperm and egg cells, there are twenty-three pairs of **chromosomes** in the nucleus of every cell in the human body. Chromosomes are microscopic, threadlike structures containing **genes.** The genes, in turn, are composed of a chemical substance known as deoxyribonucleic acid (DNA). They carry coded information that influences inherited characteristics such as eye color, hair color, height, and skin pigmentation. There are many variations of each characteristic. For example, variations in eye color would include blue eyes, brown eyes, and gray eyes. Each of these variations is referred to as an inherited trait. Thus, we might speak of blue eyes as a trait that runs in a certain family.

The twenty-three pairs of chromosomes in each nucleus consist of twenty-two pairs of auto-

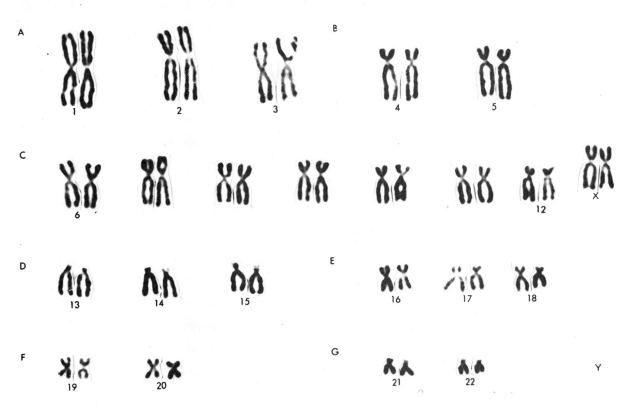

Karyotype of a human cell.

somes and one pair of sex chromosomes. Each pair of *autosomes* is identical in size and shape in both sexes. The *sex chromosomes*, however, are identical in a female (who has two X chromosomes) but are clearly different in a male (who has an X and a Y sex chromosome). The chromosomes of a cell can be stained and arranged in an ordered series of pairs. The resulting picture, the **karyotype,** makes it possible to study the genetic makeup of an individual.

Body cells reproduce through a process of cell division known as mitosis. During **mitosis,** the DNA replicates itself, enabling the chromosomes to make carbon copies of themselves. Half of the duplicated chromosomes migrate to one side of the dividing cell; the other chromosomes to the other side. When the cell divides, two cells, with exactly the same genetic material, result from the original single cell (see Figure 3.1).

Inherited characteristics are transmitted from parent to child in the reproductive process when the sperm (the sex cell of the male) and the egg (the sex cell of the female) unite. Unlike all other cells, sex cells do not have forty-six chromosomes; each sex cell has only twenty-three chromosomes. An egg cell has twenty-two autosomes and one sex chromosome, which is always an X; a sperm cell has twenty-two autosomes and one sex chromosome, which may be either an X or a Y.

How can we start at conception with a forty-six chromosome cell and eventually develop sex cells containing only half that number? There is another process by which body cells divide: **meiosis.** Meiosis is similar to mitosis (although the arrangement of the chromosomes prior to cell division differs between meiosis and mitosis). However, meiosis also involves a *second* division, which

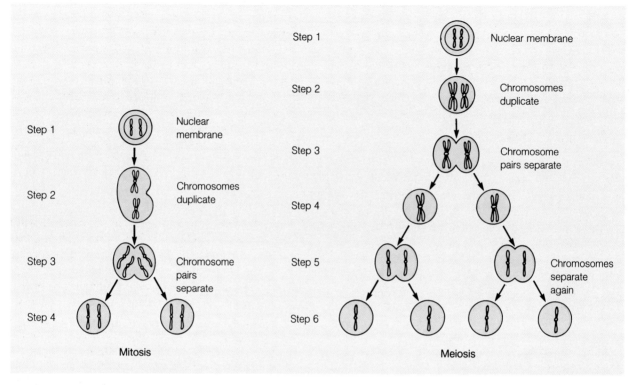

Figure 3.1   Mitosis and Meiosis

results in sex cells with only twenty-three chromosomes from the parent body cell (see Figure 3.1)

When egg and sperm unite, the result is a new forty-six chromosome cell containing twenty-three chromosomes from the mother and twenty-three from the father. Thus, each parent contributes equally to the genetic makeup of the child, although the new cell is a unique combination of genetic material that has never before existed.

Inherited Traits

Inherited traits depend on at least two genes, one from each pair of chromosomes. The actual genetic makeup of the individual is referred to as the **genotype.** The actual physical appearance of the individual is known as the **phenotype.** The phenotype may match the genotype. For example, if a child inherited a gene for brown eyes from his mother, and a gene for brown eyes from his father,

then his genotype for eye color contains two genes for brown eyes. Because they are the same, his genotype for eye color is referred to as **homozygous,** and he will have brown eyes (the phenotype).

However, consider the case of a little girl who has inherited a gene for brown eyes from one parent, and a gene for blue eyes from the other. This child's genotype is **heterozygous** for eye color—she has two different genes for the same trait.

Despite the fact that the little girl has a gene for blue eyes, phenotypically she is brown-eyed. How can that be? Some variations of a trait tend to take precedence over others. The genes for these traits are considered to be dominant; the genes for brown eyes are *dominant* over the genes for blue eyes, which are considered to be *recessive*. Recessive genes usually are expressed in the phenotype when the gene pair is homozygous. In the eye color example, this means that blue-eyed persons have two genes for blue eyes in their genotype.

While a number of human traits primarily depend on one pair of genes, some physical and behavioral characteristics such as height and intelligence are **polygenic;** that is, they are determined by a number of interacting gene pairs. Such traits are quite complex and are very much influenced by environmental factors.

Genetic Disorders

Genetic disorders, or diseases, have many origins. A number of these result from defective autosomal recessive genes. Tay-Sachs disease, for example, is an inherited enzymatic disorder in which the nervous system is gradually destroyed, with inevitable death by 4 to 6 years of age. Tay-Sachs disease is relatively more common in Jewish people of eastern European descent; it affects 1 in 25,000 Jews in the United States (Benirschke et al. 1976).

Sickle-cell anemia is a disorder in which blood cells are shaped like sickles. These blood cells can clump together and block the blood vessels. People suffering from sickle-cell anemia may experience delayed growth and delayed puberty, problems with their nervous systems, and blindness. Blacks are victimized by this disease more than whites; 1 in 500 U.S. blacks has the disease.

Phenylketonuria (PKU), also inherited as an autosomal recessive characteristic, results in an inability to produce an enzyme that is necessary for the digestion of phenylalanine, a substance found in many proteins. PKU infants are at risk for becoming mentally retarded and developing other behavioral problems, because the unmetabolized phenylalanine affects the central nervous system. A diet that contains minimal amounts of phenylalanine can control the effects of the disorder. PKU has been found in 1 in 10,000 births for northern Europeans (Benirschke et al. 1976).

Cystic fibrosis is yet another autosomal recessive disorder, affecting 1 in 3,700 births in the United States (Benirschke et al. 1976). The disease usually appears in infancy or early childhood, and leads to a mucous buildup in the respiratory system and malfunctioning of the sweat glands. Children with cystic fibrosis are very susceptible to respiratory infections; often death occurs in late childhood or adolescence.

In addition to autosomal genetic disorders, a number of recessive disorders are linked to the X chromosome. Examples of sex-linked genetic disorders are hemophilia, color blindness, and baldness. The Y chromosome does not have the genetic material to mask the effects of the recessive gene, and it will therefore be expressed in the phenotype of the male. The mother, who is a carrier, may not show any signs of the characteristic if (and most likely) she also has the dominant trait (e.g., blood-clotting factor, normal color vision, hair) on her other X chromosome.

Down's Syndrome

Another group of genetic disorders results from some sort of chromosomal abnormality. Often these abnormalities are the result of errors in meiosis, where one pair of chromosomes fails to separate (called *nondisjunction*). **Down's syndrome,** the leading recognizable cause of mental retardation, typically occurs when chromosome pair 21 does not separate. At fertilization, an additional chromosome 21 is added, leading to extra genetic material in the condition called *Trisomy 21.*

What is the cause of the meiotic error leading to Down's syndrome? It has been estimated that Trisomy 21 occurs in 1 out of 200 conceptions; 75 to 85 percent of these conceptions are spontaneously aborted (Pueschel & Thuline 1983). Most striking is the fact that Trisomy 21 is linked to maternal age. For a woman younger than 30, the risk is 1 in 1,500, and even less if she is between the ages of 15 and 19. At ages 30 to 34 the risk is 1 in 750; at ages 35 to 39 the risk is 1 in 300. A woman who is 40 years old has a risk of about 1 in 100; and, by the time she is 45, it is 1 in 25 (Menolascino & Egger 1978; Pueschel & Goldstein 1983).

It is not known why maternal age is so directly linked to Trisomy 21. Since a woman carries her ova from her prenatal period, the eggs may deteriorate upon exposure to a number of environmental agents. Pueschel and Goldstein (1983) also mention the possibility that older women may not have as effective a biological mechanism for rejecting abnormal fetuses as do younger women. Fathers may contribute the extra chromosome in about 25 percent of Trisomy 21 cases, although paternal age does not seem to be the causative factor (Pueschel & Thuline 1983).

The mental retardation associated with Down's Syndrome need not be severe. Intervention programs and the stimulation of the home environment have helped many Down's syndrome youngsters to engage in complex mental activities such as reading.

Trisomy 21 is not the only cause of Down's syndrome. A more rarely occurring form (4 to 6 percent) occurs in a Down's child who has the normal pair of chromosome 21 plus an extra piece of chromosome 21 attached to another chromosome. This form of Down's syndrome, known as *translocation*, may be inherited from a phenotypically normal parent. *Mosaicism* is yet another form of Down's syndrome, where the individual has cells with the normal number of chromosomes and cells with the extra chromosomal material. Mosaicism results in fewer Down's syndrome features and occurs in 1 to 2 percent of all Down's syndrome cases.

Down's syndrome children usually are easily identifiable; they have flat faces, slanting eyes, and a fold in the eyelid. To some people, these features look Asian, which led to the term *mongolism*—a term that is avoided today. The degree of retardation can range from mild to severe. However because of counseling with parents, early intervention, and special education programs, most Down's children are in the mild to moderate range of IQ (Pueschel & Thuline 1983). Down's syndrome is also associated with congenital heart disease and a number of serious metabolic problems, which in the past have severely limited life expectancy.

Because Down's syndrome children typically have very pleasant and affectionate dispositions, families may try to avoid institutionalization for as long as possible. There is no doubt that the home environment is more stimulating than an institution. Home-reared Down's syndrome children have IQs that on the average are fifteen points (one standard deviation) higher than the IQs of institutionalized children (Rosenblith & Sims-Knight 1985). However, institutionalized children may be more severely retarded than home-reared children in the first place. Even in cases of mild retardation, however, a Down's syndrome child may overtax the resources of a family and an alternate living environment may be considered.

Other Chromosomal Abnormalities

Quite a few chromosomal abnormalities result from nondisjunctive failures of either the X or Y chromosome, leading to a possibility of up to six combinations of X and Y chromosomes in a single individual. In general, the more X chromosomes present, the more retarded the person. Because the Y chromosome carries less genetic material, it does not affect IQ as significantly (Vandenberg & Vogler 1985). In addition, an individual with a Y chromosome is phenotypically male, no matter what the number of X chromosomes, and the absence of the Y chromosome leads to a phenotypic female.

Turner's syndrome refers to a female with only one X chromosome (XO). She tends to be physically underdeveloped (no ovaries or breasts) and short and squat. But typically she is of normal intelligence. Turner's syndrome girls may have psychological problems resulting from the reactions of others to their strange appearance, or because they have difficulty inferring underlying emotions from facial expressions (McCauley et al. 1987).

A male who has one or more X chromosomes (XXY, XXXY, XXYY, XXXYY) has Klinefelter's syndrome. These males typically have small genitalia and little facial or pubic hair and are sterile. About 20 percent of children with Klinefelter's syndrome are mentally retarded; the more X chromosomes, the greater the IQ deficit (Pueschel & Thuline 1983).

One of the most interesting anomalies of the sex chromosomes is XYY syndrome. These males are unusually tall and may have low-average to borderline IQs. XYY syndrome was originally observed in inmates in maximum security prisons, and it was believed that the extra chromosome genetically predisposed these men toward aggression. However, more carefully conducted research has found that the incidence of XYY among prison inmates is not disproportionately greater than the incidence of the syndrome in the general population; thus, the hypothesis that criminality is linked to the Y chromosome is unfounded (Vandenberg & Vogler 1985). However, being abnormally tall and less intelligent may lead an individual into potentially aggressive situations.

The Joining of Nature and Nurture

Looking at development in terms of what is due to the environment and what is due to heredity has occupied researchers for many years. A popular strategy was to examine identical and fraternal twins on some given trait, such as intelligence or temperament. Identical, or monozygotic, twins were originally one fertilized egg; the egg split into two separate cells, ultimately leading to two individuals with the same genetic makeup. Fraternal, or dizygotic, twins result when two eggs are fertilized at exactly the same time. Despite the fact that fraternals share the same birthday, they do not have the same genetic makeup; the overlap of genetic material is no different than it is for other siblings. Thus, if identical twins are reared apart (as in the case of being placed into two different homes for adoption), but are similar on a psychological trait, one could argue in favor of nature. The similarity between fraternal twins could be argued as due to nurture.

While such efforts have turned up some interesting results about the inheritance of intelligence and schizophrenia, too many questions about the relative contributions of nature and nurture remain. Could the high correlations between identical twins, especially when reared together, result from being treated similarly by parents, teachers, and friends? How can schizophrenic genes be separated from the environment a schizophrenic parent creates? How can intellectual potential be determined when there is only deprivation in an environment?

These identical twins were originally from one fertilized egg that divided and separated to form two individuals with the same genotype.

Contemporary views have moved away from the formula that behavior is one part genes, another part heredity. Rather, they focus upon the *interaction* of the genes and the environment. Consider, for example, what your IQ would be like had you been reared in a war-torn community. You may have been malnourished prenatally. Your parents wouldn't have had the energy or resources to provide you with stimulating materials. Your schooling may have been disrupted or nonexistent. Because of your genetic makeup, your IQ could reach some bottom limit under such conditions (say, 80 IQ points), and probably be nowhere near the upper limit (say, 140 IQ points). The hypothetical genetic parameters placed upon the range of possible IQ scores is known as the **reaction range** (Gottesman 1963). As Figure 3.2 illustrates, the role of a favorable environment is to allow expression of your genetic potential.

A useful model of gene-environment interaction is the **scoop model** proposed by McCall (1981). McCall advised that the development of a behavior (mental development, in particular) be viewed as if it were a scoop (see Figure 3.3). Visualize an individual as a ball placed at the left end of the scoop. Because the sides of the scoop are steep, a wind (an environmental factor) may temporarily push the ball off course, but the ball will right itself in its path. Borrowing on the work of biologist Conrad Waddington (1957), McCall claimed that such behavior at the beginning of the scoop is **canalized;** during infancy individuals follow the same developmental path that has been species-specific for thousands of years. With development, the scoop broadens out, the slope declines, and individuals can take a number of developmental paths (the grooves in Figure 3.3). Now

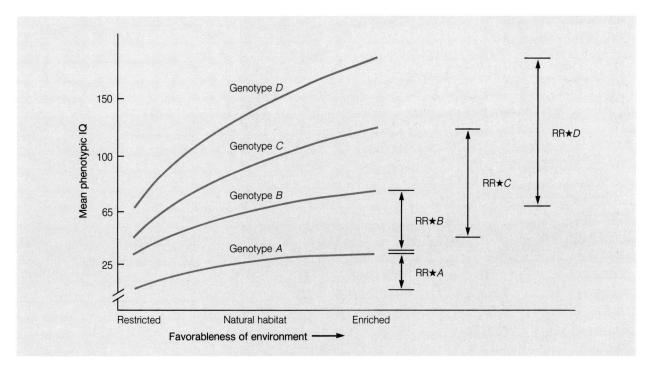

Figure 3.2 Reaction Ranges of IQs in Favorable and Unfavorable Environments

RR refers to reaction range. Notice that individuals C and D, for example, can have the same IQ score despite different reaction ranges and exposure to different environments.
Source: From *The Handbook of Mental Deficiency: Psychological Theory and Research,* edited by Norman R. Ellis. New York: McGraw-Hill, 1963. Reprinted by permission of editor.

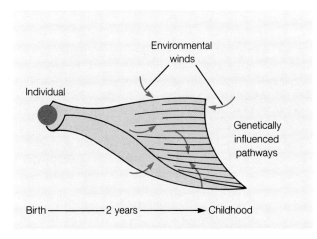

Figure 3.3 The Scoop Approach to Thinking About Development

Source: From McCall, R.B. (1981) Nature-nurture and the two realms of development: a proposed interaction with respect to mental development. *Child Development, 52,* 1–12. Copyright 1981 by the Society for Research in Child Development, Inc. Reprinted by permission of the author and publisher.

there is a greater variety of genetically determined options, plus a greater opportunity for the environment to steer individuals away from the original course. Thus, later behaviors are less canalized.

The concept of reaction range and the scoop model to reflect an approach to development that incorporates genetic and environmental factors

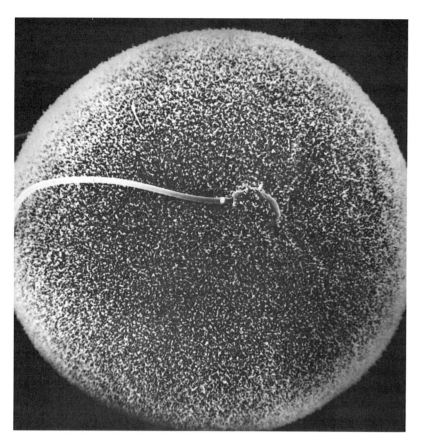

Sperm on an egg.

within a developmental time line. As you continue to read about prenatal development, infancy, and beyond, consider the resiliency of certain behaviors despite environmental variations and the incredible capacity for change and adaptability.

Conception and Birth

A man can ejaculate through his penis a small amount of fluid that contains between 50 million to 100 million sperm cells per cubic centimeter of semen. Each microscopic cell is composed of an oval-shaped head and a long, whiplike tail that propels the cell forward as it "swims" in the seminal fluid. When sperm cells are deposited in a woman's vagina during intercourse, they embark on a journey of about six inches: up through the cervix into the uterus and from the uterus into the fallopian tube, the pathway leading from the ovary

to the uterus. The journey is hazardous and most sperm cells do not survive it; less than one thousand of them ever reach the fallopian tube, or oviduct.

Conception, or fertilization, typically occurs in the oviduct—if an egg cell is available to be fertilized, of course. In actuality, fertilization is an improbable occurrence. Only one mature egg cell is released from a woman's ovary every month, a process known as *ovulation*. Optimally, the egg cell must be fertilized within twenty-four to forty-eight hours after ovulation, because beyond that point it is already beginning to deteriorate. Sperm cells ordinarily maintain their ability to fertilize an egg for only seventy-two hours after ejaculation. Therefore, fertilization is possible, although by no means inevitable, only if insemination occurs within a period beginning seventy-two hours before ovulation and ending twenty-four to forty-eight hours afterward. There are exceptions, however; sperm cells

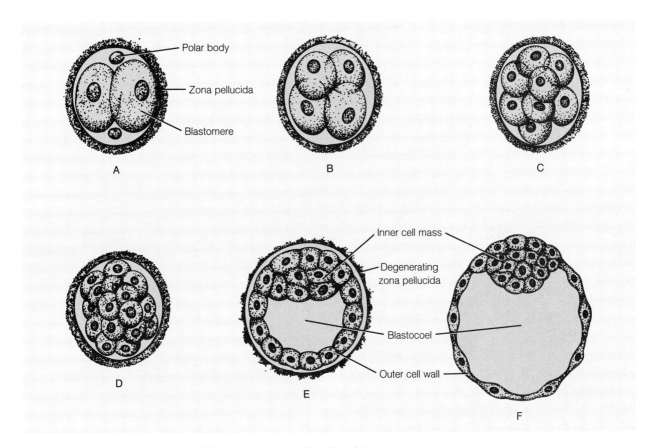

Labels in figure:
- Polar body
- Zona pellucida
- Blastomere
- A
- B
- C
- Inner cell mass
- Degenerating zona pellucida
- Blastocoel
- Outer cell wall
- D
- E
- F

Figure 3.4 Early Stages of Cell Division in the Fertilized Egg

have been known to have remarkably long lives (Jones 1984).

The egg cell is surrounded by several layers of follicle cells through which the sperm must pass. Once the nucleus of one sperm cell has penetrated these barriers, a chemical reaction occurs in the egg cell wall that prevents penetration by any of the other sperm cells in the oviduct. Fertilization has now taken place, and the newly fertilized egg cell is referred to as a **zygote.**

Stages of Prenatal Development

The average length of a pregnancy is thirty-eight weeks from ovulation, with variations of two weeks before and two weeks after for a full-term baby. During this period of *gestation,* a single-celled organism becomes a fully formed baby, with all major organ systems established and functional.

Germinal Stage (0 to 2 Weeks)

After fertilization, the zygote continues its journey down the oviduct to the uterus. The 12-hour-old zygote divides into two cells through mitosis. Cell division continues to occur approximately every twelve hours. By the time the developing organism reaches the uterus—on the fourth or fifth day after fertilization—it has become a cluster of about five hundred cells and is referred to as a **blastocyst.**

Although the blastocyst resembles a solid ball, it actually consists of a fluid-filled center (blastocoel), a layer of cells that forms its outer wall, and a cluster of cells attached to the inner wall (the inner cell mass). The inner cell mass eventually will become the **embryo,** the name given to the developing organism from the second to the eighth week after conception. The outer cell wall, referred to as the chorion, will eventually become the placenta, amniotic sac, and other structures that support the pregnancy (see Figure 3.4).

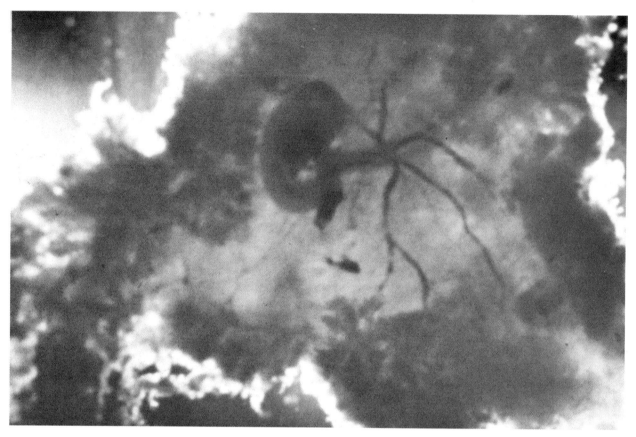

Human embryo between the fourth and fifth week.

On approximately the eighth day after fertilization, the blastocyst adheres to the uterine wall and begins to implant itself by digesting the surface cells of the uterine lining. By approximately the twelfth day, the egg is firmly implanted; and, by the end of the second week after fertilization, the uterine tissue completely surrounds the newly developing organism in a cozy nest. When implantation is complete, the organism is referred to as an embryo.

Embryonic Stage (2 to 8 Weeks)

The embryonic stage is often referred to as the *critical period* of prenatal development. The risk of spontaneous abortion, because of genetic abnormalities is high. Since all of the major organ systems are forming (organogenesis), an injury to the rapidly differentiating tissue may cause defects in the heart, eyes, brain, and other organs. At the beginning of this stage, the embryo is simply a two-layered organism; by the end, it is 1¼ inches long and has the appearance of a human baby.

After implantation, tiny, threadlike projections of cells—the chorionic villi—begin to extend from the outer wall of the blastocyst (or chorion) into the surrounding uterine tissue. In a sense, the organism is beginning to tap the mother's blood vessels as a means of feeding itself, and it does so by absorbing vitamins, minerals, carbohydrates, fats, and proteins through the chorionic villi.

The area in which the chorion is attached to the uterine wall becomes the **placenta,** a disklike membrane that eventually covers over half of the inner surface of the uterus. The placenta is a highly vascular membrane, meaning that it is rich in blood vessels; toward the end of the pregnancy, seventy-five gallons of blood will come in contact with the

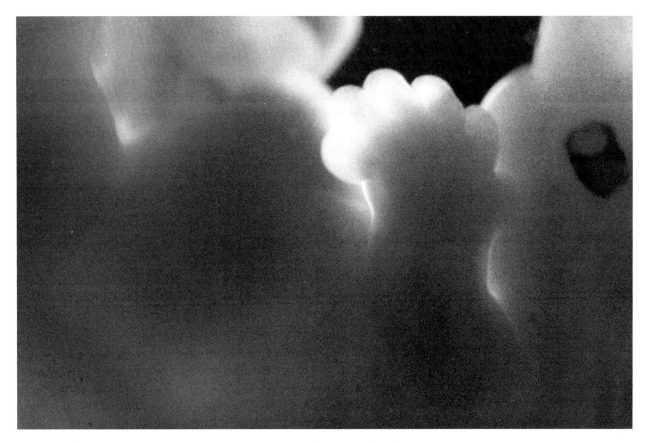

Human embryo at seven weeks; most organs and appendages are formed.

placenta every day. The blood volume is significant, because from the mother's bloodstream the child will draw needed nutrients, including oxygen; and into the mother's bloodstream the child will discharge waste products, such as carbon dioxide. Thus, the placenta serves as the exchange filter between mother and unborn child, although the circulatory systems of both remain independent.

While the outer cell wall (chorion) is busy transforming itself into structures related to the nurturing of the growing organism, the inner cell mass becomes the embryo and a membrane referred to as the *amnion*. The amnion grows over the embryo and later becomes the fluid-filled **amniotic sac.** This sac will be the organism's home for the duration of the pregnancy. Initially, the amniotic sac is quite distinct from the chorion. However, as the sac enlarges, the amnion and chorion eventually fuse.

The embryo is directly connected to the chorion wall and the placenta by the umbilical cord, which contains two arteries to transport the embryo's deoxygenated blood to the placenta and one vein to bring oxygen-rich blood back to the embryo.

A good deal occurs during the embryonic period of development. Early in this stage, the embryo itself has differentiated into three layers: the **ectoderm** (outer layer) which will give rise to the skin, sensory organs, brain, and spinal cord; the **mesoderm** (middle layer) which will form the muscles, blood, and circulatory system; and the **endoderm** (inner layer) which will give rise to the digestive system, respiratory system, and lining of the internal organs.

By the end of the third week after conception, the foundations for the brain, spinal column, and nervous system have been established, and a primitive heart has been formed that already beats. The

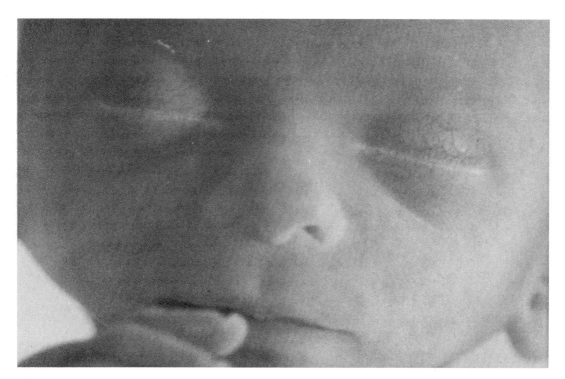

A human fetus at 4 months.

A human fetus near the fifth month.

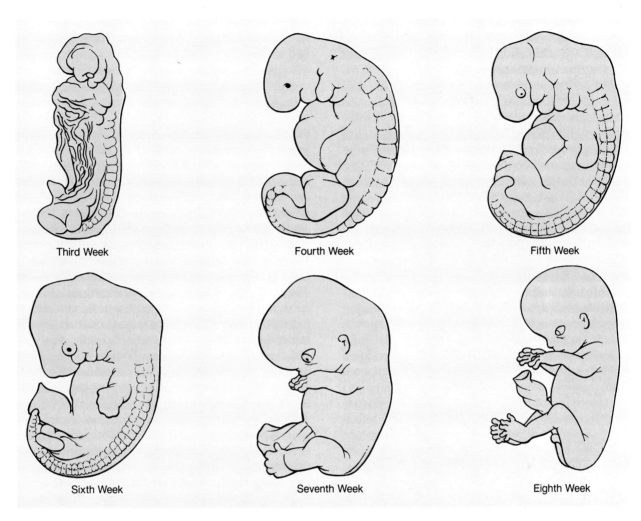

Third Week   Fourth Week   Fifth Week

Sixth Week   Seventh Week   Eighth Week

Figure 3.5 Development of the Human Embryo from the Third Week
Through the Eighth Week After Conception

neural tube, forming the spinal column, closes during the fourth week. If it does not, a serious abnormality—spina bifida—could result. Infants born with an open spine have impaired functioning of the legs, poor bowel and bladder control, and possible brain damage. The top of the neural tube forms three swellings that become the early structures of the brain. Also by fourth week, the head is forming, and small buds appear that will later develop into arms and legs. By the time the embryonic period ends, arms and legs are well formed, and the blood vessels and all major inter-

nal organs also are formed. Bone cells begin to appear, which marks the end of the embryonic period.

The 8-week-old embryo is a top-heavy creature. The size of the head looks rather disproportionate to the rest of the body because of the rapid development of the brain (see Figure 3.5).

Fetal Stage (8 Weeks to Birth)

When bone cells make their appearance in X rays, the developing organism·is referred to as a **fetus,** and it is called this until birth. The basic human structure now has been formed; the mechanisms by which it receives the nurturing necessary for development have been well established. During the fetal stage, routine blood tests may detect certain genetic disorders. (See Applying Our Knowledge "Testing For Genetic Disorders in the Fetus.")

Cell differentiation slows down, but the fetal period still involves quite a few refinements in organs and systems. For example, during the third prenatal month, the unique patterns on toes, fingers, and palms are fairly developed; the veins develop and begin to nourish cells; and a complex network of muscles evolves. During the fetal period many of the physiological systems link up with one another, leading to a more integrated organism. For example, during the fourth month the brain becomes more compact, and the beginnings of interconnections between the brain, spinal column, and limbs are evident. Because of these links, behaviors such as swallowing, sucking, squinting, and frowning appear early in the fetal period. Also by the fourth month the fetus is moving limbs and body in utero, actions that are felt by the mother and may bring home the reality of the pregnancy. At 5 months, sleep and wake cycles are observable. A 6-month-old fetus is capable of breathing movements and crying; fetal respiration involves the taking in of amniotic fluid and exhaling it through the mouth. These behaviors are significant because they indicate increasing maturity and intercoordination of the central nervous system. These behaviors may also be a rehearsal of the systems before they become fully operational at birth.

Several other aspects of the fetal period are noteworthy. During the fourth month, the fetus develops a fine, downy protective layer of hair—lanugo—that covers much of the face, portions of the back, and other areas of the body. Much of it is usually shed at birth, but sometimes parents of newborns are shocked by the hairy appearance of their baby. In the last trimester of pregnancy, a waxy, cheeselike substance—the vernix caseosa—is secreted to protect the skin from continual exposure to the fluid and minerals in the amniotic sac. The respiratory system is not sufficiently developed to sustain life outside the uterus until the seventh month of pregnancy. Week 28, therefore, is often referred to as the age of viability. Medical

support systems are able to help infants born earlier than week 28. However, prior to week 24, the lungs do not have any air sacs and heroic acts to save the baby are at this time probably futile.

The last trimester is a time of rapid growth in height and weight. The fetus gains about 5½ pounds through the deposit of subcutaneous fat, which helps nourish and insulate the infant's body. The brain's structure more closely resembles that of an adult, with its distinctive layers, convolutions, and indentations. Additionally, the brain shows evidence that rudimentary sensory and motoric systems are in place. Table 3.1 summarizes the major changes that occur throughout fetal development, as well as lists the approximate size of the fetus at the end of each month of prenatal life.

Factors Affecting Fetal Development

The suspicion that environmental events have an impact on embryonic and fetal development has been present for a long time. The Bible cautions women not to drink wine while pregnant. An old wives' tale states that if a pregnant woman is startled by a rabbit, her baby will have a harelip. There has also been an awareness that certain illnesses contracted by the mother during pregnancy (e.g., German measles) are related to defects in the newborn. However, the prevailing attitude was that the placenta served as a highly effective screen for toxic agents—what was bad for the baby would not filter through.

This belief was dispelled during the early 1960s when severe physical deformities in children were linked to maternal ingestion of a mild sedative, thalidomide (Lenz 1962). Thalidomide was prescribed by European physicians (particularly in West Germany) for pregnant women who were suffering from morning sickness and/or anxiety. When taken during day 20 through day 35 after conception, the infant may have been born without arms or legs, or with flipperlike appendages. In addition, many thalidomide babies suffered from defects in the eyes, ears, heart, intestines, or urogenital tract. Ironically, the drug has no toxic effects on adults, or on infants exposed to the drug before or after the sensitive period.

Table 3.1 Characteristics of Prenatal Development

End of Month	Approximate Size and Weight	Representative Changes
1	0.6 cm (³⁄₁₈ in.)	Eyes, nose, and ears not yet visible. Backbone and vertebral canal form. Small buds that will develop into arms and legs form. Heart forms and starts beating. Body systems begin to form.
2	3 cm (1¼ in.) 1 g (¹⁄₃₈ oz)	Eyes far apart, eyelids fused, nose flat. Ossification begins. Limbs become distinct as arms and legs. Digits are well formed. Major blood vessels form. Many internal organs continue to develop.
3	7. 5 cm (3 in.) 28 g (1 oz)	Eyes almost fully developed but eyelids still fused; nose develops bridge; and external ears are present. Ossification continues. Appendages are fully formed, and nails develop. Heartbeat can be detected. Body systems continue to develop.
4	18 cm (6½-7 in.) 113 g (4 oz)	Head large in proportion to rest of body. Face takes on human features, and hair appears on head. Skin bright pink. Many bones ossified, and joints begin to form. Continued development of body systems.
5	25-30 cm (10-12 in.) 227-454 g (½-1 lb)	Head is less disproportionate to rest of body. Fine hair (lanugo hair) covers body. Skin still bright pink. Rapid development of body systems.
6	27-35 cm (11-14 in.) 567-681 g (1¼-1½ lb)	Head becomes less disproportionate to rest of body. Eyelids separate and eyelashes form. Skin wrinkled and pink.
7	325-425 cm (13-17 in.) 1135-1362 g (2½-3 lb)	Head and body become more proportionate. Skin wrinkled and pink. Seven-month fetus (premature baby) is capable of survival.
8	40-45 cm (16½-18 in.)	Subcutaneous fat deposited. Skin less wrinkled. Testes descend into scrotum. Bones of head are soft. Chances of survival much greater at end of eighth month.
9	50 cm (20 in.) 3178-3405 g (7-7½ lb)	Additional subcutaneous fat accumulates. Lanugo hair shed. Nails extend to tips of fingers and maybe even beyond.

Source: Exhibit 29-2, "Changes Associated with Fetal Growth" (p. 746) from *Principles of Anatomy and Physiology*, 4th ed., by Gerard T. Tortora and Nicholas P. Anagnostakos. Copyright © 1984 by Biological Sciences Textbooks, Inc.: A and P Textbooks, Inc.; and Elia-Sparta, Inc. Reprinted with permission of Harper & Row.

Since the thalidomide tragedy, a number of environmental factors (that is, external to the embryo or fetus) have been identified that can cause developmental malformations. These are referred to collectively as **teratogens.** Agents that have been identified as teratogens are drugs, chemicals, maternal diseases, maternal chronic conditions, malnutrition, radiation, oxygen deprivation, and maternal stress.

There are four major negative outcomes of teratogenic exposure. First, teratogens may be the cause of spontaneous abortions in early pregnancy, miscarriage or stillborn death during later pregnancy, and death during the neonatal period. Second, teratogens can lead to a number of physical malformations. These defects typically result from exposure during a period in which rapid growth is taking place. The central nervous system is particularly vulnerable because of its continuous development throughout the entire prenatal period. Third, teratogens may lead to low birthweight and/or prematurity in infants. This, in turn, can lead to a number of developmental problems during the perinatal period. Finally, teratogens may be related either directly, or indirectly, to a variety of negative behavioral outcomes. For example, teratogens are suspected as being the cause of such problems as hyperactivity, lowered intelligence socres, and irritability during infancy. Physical defects may hamper the socialization of the child; a number of psychological problems could stem from peer group and/or parental rejection.

In examining some teratogens, keep in mind that environmental agents may account for a rather small percentage of birth defects. Aproximately 60 percent of birth defects are due to unknown causes (Kalter & Warkany 1983). With early detection and appropriate treatment, or with careful supervision of the pregnancy, the actual risk to the developing organism can be minimized.

Teratogens do not affect developing organisms in exactly the same way. Some infants, because of a genetic vulnerability to a teratogen, may be more severely affected than others. Even in the thalidomide tragedy, not every embryo that was exposed to the drug during the sensitive period was adversely affected. The physical condition of the mother, both prior to her pregnancy, and during her pregnancy, may also play a significant role in the developmental outcome of teratogenic exposure. A woman who has had a poor medical record or a history of poor nutrition or a woman who is in a chronic state of stress may be more at risk than a healthy woman. Additionally, it is important to learn if teratogens were taken singly or together with other potentially toxic agents. For example, the combined effect of smoking and drinking on birthweight is much greater than the effects of exposure to either toxic agents by itself (Sokol, Miller & Reed 1980). Finally, what is and what is not a teratogen is somewhat a matter of opinion. A broader definition of teratogens would include any factor that can potentially produce congenital malformations (including maternal and paternal age). A narrower definition may look at only those agents having a sustained record of dem-

Table 3.2 Known Human Teratogens

Alcohol

Androgenic hormones (testosterone, progestins)

Antimetabolites (aminopterin, methotrexate)

Anticonvulsants (phenytoin, trimethadione)

Alkylating agents (busulfan, cyclophosphamide)

Chlorobiphenyls (causes "Yusho" disease)

Coumarin

Diethylstilbestrol

Organic mercury (causes Minamata disease)

Thalidomide

13-*cis*-Retinoic acid

Source: From Hoar, R.M. (1986) *Biology of Reproduction* Champaign, IL: Society for the Study of Reproduction. Reprinted by permission of the publisher.

onstrated effects on the embryo and fetus. For example, Hoar (1986) reported that the list of proven teratogenic agents is relatively small (see Table 3.2); approximately 15 drugs or chemicals have been demonstrated to produce birth defects in humans. There are many other *suspected* teratogens, but unequivocal proof is hard to find. This is because much of the research is conducted on animals, or prenatal histories are taken after a birth defect is observed (that is, retrospectively).

Maternal and Paternal Age

The ideal age for a woman to conceive and give birth is within the range of 18 to 35. Mothers under the age of 18 are considerably more likely to deliver prematurely, perhaps because they are less apt to receive adequate prenatal care and because of the immaturity of their reproductive systems. Mothers past the age of 35 are more likely to give birth to children with chromosomal abnormalities (e.g., Down's syndrome). Furthermore, the likelihood of neonatal mortality increases considerably for infants whose mothers are age 40 or older (Smith 1978). The typical age of new mothers in the United States is in the range of 20 to 24.

The father's age at the time of conception is less important than the mother's age. Nevertheless, the likelihood of genetic disorders in the child increases tenfold from the time the new father is 30 to the time he is 60, although such paternally linked disorders are rare.

Maternal Nutrition

A pregnant woman needs additional protein, calcium, iron, folic acid, and vitamin B_6 in her diet. Protein deficiencies in pregnant rats have resulted in smaller offspring, increased infant mortality, and lowered intelligence, as evidenced in maze-learning ability; in humans there is some evidence that maternal protein deficiencies produce similar effects in the newborn. In particular, malnutrition may be related to a decrease in the number of cells in children's brains (Winick & Russo 1969).

Research examining individuals who were conceived during a Nazi-imposed famine in western Holland during World War II has revealed that when malnutrition is short-lived, the effects on subsequent development are minimal. However, the rate of infertility, spontaneous abortions, and miscarriages was exceptionally high during the Dutch famine (Stein et al. 1975).

A pregnant woman typically is advised to gain about twenty-five pounds, eleven pounds of which is additional body fat, two pounds for the placenta, three pounds for the increase in breast and uterine size, one pound each of amniotic fluid and increased maternal blood volume, and seven pounds for the fetus itself (Jones 1984).

Maternal Sensitization

Approximately 90 percent of people in the United States have an inherited substance in their bloodstreams called the *Rh factor*. Those who have this substance are Rh-positive; those lacking it are Rh-negative.

If an Rh-negative woman is pregnant with an Rh-positive baby, a condition known as **maternal sensitization** might occur if the Rh-positive blood enters the mother's body. The mother's body will reject the Rh factor as a foreign substance, and chemical substances called *antibodies* will be created to attack and destroy blood cells containing the Rh factor. Thus, the antibodies may destroy the red blood cells of her Rh-positive fetus. In rare cases the fetus will die, but more typically the child will be born suffering from anemia, a condition curable

by means of blood transfusions (Guttmacher 1973). Currently, Rh-negative women are given injections of rhogam within seventy-two hours after the birth of their first child. The rhogam injections prevent the buildup of Rh-positive antibodies in the mother, reducing the risk of Rh incompatibility in subsequent births.

Maternal Diseases

Infectious diseases such as syphilis, gonorhea, or rubella (German measles) can seriously affect the developing organism. Untreated venereal diseases in the mother will result in the child's being born with the same diseases or may result in the death of the fetus. Rubella is a viral infection that, if contracted by the mother during the first trimester of pregnancy, may result in miscarriage, stillbirth, or various forms of damage to the child's sensory and internal organs.

Some diseases, such as those of the herpes simplex virus family, are transmitted when the infant passes through the cervix during delivery. Another disease, toxoplasmosis, is caused by a simple organism that lives in improperly cooked meats and cat feces. The disease is barely noticeable in adults; in infants it has been linked to unusually small head size, and defects in the eyes, brain, lungs, and liver.

Of greater concern is the finding that the virus causing acquired immune deficiency syndrome (AIDS) can be transmitted in utero (Di Maria et al. 1986; Marion et al. 1986). Presently, the mechanisms of fetal transmission are unknown. For example, researchers examining 18-month-old identical twins were puzzled when one twin tested positive for the AIDS virus and the other twin tested negative (Menez-Bautista et al. 1986). Some evidence suggests that the fetus may be most adversely affected by the virus at a sensitive period of the pregnancy (Di Maria et al. 1986). Marion and others (1986) reported that children suspected of having contracted the AIDS virus in utero manifested problems in addition to those of the immune system. These children had growth failures, small heads, and facial abnormalities distinguishable from other congenital defects, such as those occurring from prenatal exposure to alcohol.

Chronic noninfectious diseases in the mother also may affect the developing fetus. For example,

Applying our Knowledge

Testing for Genetic Disorders in the Fetus

One of the most prevalent fears of expectant parents is that their child will be born with a tragic or even fatal disease, such as cystic fibrosis, Down's syndrome, hemophilia, Tay-Sachs disease, sickle-cell anemia, or a defect in the neural tube. Each of these so-called genetic disorders is extremely rare in the general population, and their probability of occurrence can be estimated by a genetic counselor who extensively examines the family history of the prospective parents.

Many of these genetic disorders can now be detected in the fetus by the middle of the pregnancy. For example, women routinely undergo blood tests early in their pregnancies to measure the maternal blood level of alpha-fetoprotein, or AFP. This substance is manufactured in the liver of the fetus; when the fetus urinates, it enters the amniotic fluid and eventually crosses into the mother's bloodstream. If a blood test indicates that the pregnant woman has abnormally high-AFP levels, her fetus may have a neural tube disorder known as spina bifida—an "exposed" spinal cord not covered by the backbone. Such a condition can result in only minor physical

impairment, but it also can lead to paralysis of the lower body and, in its extreme form, can result in death within the first two years of life. High-AFP levels also may indicate severe underdevelopment of the fetal brain. However—and this is a crucial point to remember—high-AFP levels may mean nothing at all as far as the health of the fetus is concerned (Chedd 1981). For this reason, no decision is made about the future of the pregnancy based on a high-AFP level until follow-up tests are performed.

Ultrasound involves analysis of high-frequency sound waves that are bounced off the fetus and then analyzed by a computer. It can be used to view fetal behaviors, as well as the physical development of the fetus. Ultrasound is a commonly used technique, although there is concern that some side effects may be difficult to detect and may show up later in the child's life (Bases 1985).

Another method of detecting genetic disorders in a fetus is amniocentesis. A three-inch-long needle is inserted through the mother's abdominal wall during the fourteenth or fifteenth week of pregnancy, and less than an ounce of fluid is withdrawn from the amniotic sac. Fetal cells contained in the fluid then can be tested to diagnose the presence of genetic disorders such as Down's syndrome or Tay-Sachs disease (a nervous system disorder). The procedure also is used as a follow-up when high-AFP levels indicate

the possibility of neural tube defects. Finally, amniocentesis is successful in ruling out the presence of genetic disorders in 95 to 98 percent of all cases (Fuchs 1980).

A more recently developed genetic screening test is chorion villi sampling, which involves the removal of a small piece of the chorion for testing. The advantage of this procedure is that it can be done during the first trimester of pregnancy (which is earlier than amniocentesis). It is also relatively painless, since the tissue is removed through the vagina and the puncturing of the abdominal wall is not required (Fogel 1984).

The possibility of screening for genetic disorders is a dramatic advance in medical technology, yet it raises a number of troublesome legal and moral issues. Few would argue against genetic screening if the disorder were treatable in utero; the screening then would be seen as preventive medicine. However, if disorders cannot be treated, awesome dilemmas arise. Should a child be brought into the world who may be physically handicapped, mentally handicapped, or both; who may have a limited life expectancy in any case; or who may place severe emotional or economic hardships on the parents? Which pregnancies should come to term and which should be terminated? Who should make the decision?

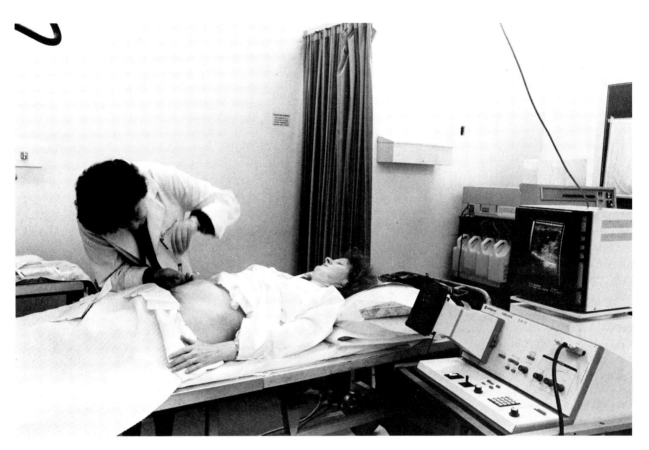

A woman undergoing amniocentesis.

diabetes may result in fetal death within a few weeks prior to the delivery. Hypertension (high blood pressure) may result in a maternal condition known as *toxemia,* characterized by excessive water in the tissues and protein in the urine. In extreme cases, toxemia may result in the death of the mother.

Maternal Stress

A number of studies have demonstrated a relationship between high levels of maternal stress and pregnancy and labor complications (Ferreira 1960), low birthweight in infants, infant irritability (Ottinger & Simmons 1964), and even behavioral problems of later childhood (Stott & Latchford 1976). When a pregnant woman is under stress, the blood flow in her body is temporarily diverted from the uterus to various other organs; the result

is a temporary oxygen deficiency in the fetus (Stechler & Halton 1982). In many of these cases in which there were poor developmental outcomes, the stress was long-term and accompanied by low-socioeconomic conditions or an unfavorable environment (Rosenblith & Sims-Knight 1985).

However, remember that a relation between maternal stress and birth complications, infant irritability, and so forth does not demonstrate that stress actually causes pregnancy problems. In fact, stress may be the result rather than the cause of such difficulties. Perhaps a woman is more likely to feel stress if she is carrying a very active fetus or if she is experiencing a particularly difficult pregnancy. In any case, there is no link between minor everyday stress levels and the condition of the fetus.

Smoking

Whereas smoking is typically included under drugs in discussions of teratogens, it is unclear as to whether or not the observed effects are due to the drug nicotine, or to other potentially harmful substances such as carcinogens, lead, arsenic, and cyanide. The major known effect of smoking on the fetus is oxygen deprivation (Stechler & Halton 1982). This occurs in two ways: first, nicotine causes the blood vessels to constrict, reducing the flow of oxygen from mother to fetus; second, the increased levels of carbon monoxide (CO) from the cigarette smoke reduce the capacity of the fetal blood to carry oxygen to cells of the body (Stevens 1979).

Studies have commonly found that the incidence of prematurity, low birthweight, spontaneous abortion, and death rate during the perinatal period is higher for those infants whose mothers smoked during their pregnancy, than for those infants whose mothers did not smoke (Naeye 1978). The magnitude of the effects seems to increase directly with the number of cigarettes smoked. Even more frightening is the finding that the risk of an infant's dying from **sudden infant death syndrome** (SIDS, commonly known as "crib death") is increased by 52 percent for those infants whose mothers smoked during the pregnancy (Naeye, Ladis & Drage 1976).

Alcohol

As a result of extensive research on the effects of alcohol on the developing fetus, alcohol is now widely recognized as a teratogen. The combined effects, which have been labeled **fetal alcohol syndrome** (FAS), produce four basic congenital problems (Clarren & Smith 1978):

1. Defects of the central nervous system leading to mental retardation, a small head, or irritability in infancy.
2. Low birthweight and overall poor growth in height and weight postnatally.
3. Distinctive facial appearance, including a narrow forehead, small nose and midface, and a wide space between the upper lip and nose.
4. A variety of other congenital defects, such as cardiac murmurs, malformations of the eyes and ears, and problems with joints in the skeleton.

It is unclear, at present, how the alcohol produces the characteristics of FAS. Evidence derived from experiments with mice suggests that the facial anomalies are caused by early exposure to alcohol, corresponding to the third week of a human pregnancy (Sulik, Johnston & Webb 1981). Apparently, exposure to alcohol late in the pregnancy also has harmful effects on the fetus. It is believed that the fetal brain is particularly susceptible to alcohol in the second and third trimester.

Finally, it is unclear what are safe amounts of alcohol to consume during pregnancy. Any amount of alcohol may be harmful to the embryo and the fetus, but the effects may not be readily observable. Much of the research on FAS has focused on babies born of chronic alcoholics or heavy drinkers. Some evidence suggests that moderate drinking is related to low birthweight (Streissguth et al. 1981) or milder versions of FAS (Hanson et al. 1978). In all probability, some fetuses will be more sensitive to the teratogenic effects of alcohol than others. But, research has also found that 4-year-old children who had been exposed to alcohol in utero, but who did not manifest any overt signs of FAS, had poorer scores in a task designed to assess ability to attend to visual stimulation, and they had poorer reaction times (Streissguth et al. 1984).

Drugs

Narcotics such as heroin will cross the placenta and result in fetal addiction. Marijuana smoking has been linked to spontaneous abortion of the fetus, and hallucinogenic drugs such as lysergic acid diethylamide (LSD) may damage fetal chromosomes (Jones 1984). Cocaine use has been related to a significantly higher rate of spontaneous abortions and infant death (Chasnoff et al. 1985).

Obstetric medications of any sort will cross the placenta and influence the fetus in a variety of ways. For example, anesthetics and analgesics administered to a woman during the birth process have been known to depress the neonate and cause respiratory difficulty. Some researchers in this area (e.g., Steinschneider 1970) have concluded that before any drug is considered safe, it must be studied carefully in terms of both its immediate and long-term effects on the child. For example, diethylstilbestrol (DES), a synthetic form of estrogen, was taken by women between 1945 and 1970 to prevent miscarriage. The harmful effects of this hormone were not noticeable until the offspring reached reproductive maturity: the risk of cervical cancer and problem pregnancies in females and deformities in the reproductive organs of males are statistically greater for those exposed to DES prenatally (Stechler & Halton 1982).

Environmental Toxins

Several chemicals commonly found in the environment have been linked to a number of developmental problems. For example, women who ate large quantities of fish contaminated with polychlorinated biphenyls (PCBs)—as found in Lake Michigan salmon and trout—had infants who exhibited weak reflexes, were motorically immature, and showed disorganized behavior (Jacobson et al. 1985). PCB-exposed infants also had poor visual recognition memory (Jacobson et al. 1985). Depending upon when it was ingested, lead may be related to children's poorer performance on language and visual spatial tasks (Shaheen 1984). Organic mercury (methyl mercury), found in contaminated fish, has been clearly implicated in abnormal neurological development (Kalter & Warkany 1983). Finally, radiation exposure to the ovum, embryo, or fetus has clearly been demonstrated to be teratogenic. Most of the effects involve the central nervous system, resulting in increased risks of microcephaly (small head), brain and skull malformations, and Down's syndrome. Such birth defects were made painfully apparent in studies of women who were pregnant when exposed to the radiation from the atomic bombs dropped on Hiroshima and Nagasaki during World War II (Blot & Miller 1973).

Birth

In the human being, the term of pregnancy is 266 days after conception, or 280 days after the mother's last menstrual period. The overwhelming majority of pregnancies come to term within two weeks in either direction from the due date.

The birth process occurs in three stages. The first is the opening, or **labor,** stage, which is also the longest of the three. The average labor time for a first pregnancy is thirteen hours and just over eight hours for later pregnancies (Guttmacher 1973). Averages may mean little, however, because the duration of labor varies considerably, depending on the particular woman and the particular pregnancy.

Labor is defined by hormonally triggered contractions of the long muscles in the uterine wall, which eventually propel the fetus downward from the uterus through the cervix (the area connecting the uterus and vagina) and into the birth canal. While there are many variations in the timing of labor, the general parameters are as follows: At the beginning of labor the contractions come at intervals between five and twenty minutes apart, they last for less than a minute, and they are minor in their intensity; women in early labor can move about freely and continue their everyday activities. Gradually, however, the contractions increase in frequency, duration, and intensity. Toward the end of the labor stage there may be one minute between contractions; they may last for a minute to a minute and a half and cause great pain. Furthermore, toward the end of labor many women experience nausea, chills, hyperventilation, loss of feeling in their hands and feet, and great emotional turmoil. It is little wonder that Lamaze instructors refer to the end of labor as the "hurricane phase."

During labor the contractions cause the normally closed cervix to open to a diameter of ten centimeters (four inches). The cervix is first stretched as the fetal head presses downward and the uterine wall thins out, a process known as *effacement* of the cervix. Gradually the opening enlarges to permit the child to pass through the birth canal. When the cervical opening is of sufficient width, the labor stage is said to come to an end.

The second stage of childbirth is the delivery, or expulsion, stage, which can last from a half hour to two hours. The contractions now serve to expel the child from the uterus rather than to dilate the cervix. The appearance of the head is known as *crowning.* The head normally emerges in the face-down position. Then the infant rotates so that the shoulders are on a vertical axis (that is, on a line perpendicular to the floor if the woman is lying on her back) to permit easy passage through the birth canal.

Research Close-up

A Test of the "Gentle Birth" Hypothesis

A child is born out of the dark, warm, soothing environment of the womb and enters a world of unaccustomed light and sound. The child is held upside down, handled, weighed, and measured, and later bathed, combed, powdered, and injected with a needle. French obstetrician Frederick Leboyer (1975, 15) referred to the birth experience of the child as a "tidal wave of sensation, surpassing everything we can imagine"; he argued that we must minimize the trauma of separation from the womb by giving birth in darkened rooms with as little sensory stimulation as possible. The newborn should be placed immediately on the mother's abdomen, the severing of the umbilical cord should be delayed, and the child should later be gently massaged and placed in a warm bath. Such

actions could make birth a joy rather than a shock and should contribute to the child's healthy development.

In contrast to the cold, sterile, and impersonal operating-room delivery supposedly performed in most hospitals, the Leboyer approach was widely heralded in the 1970s as a more humane way of bringing children into the world. However, genuine evidence in support of the Leboyer technique was lacking. No one had scientifically analyzed the effects of "gentle birth" on children's later development until 1980, when Nancy Nelson and her associates at McMaster University Medical Centre carried out such a study.

Fifty-six pregnant women who had no initial delivery preference were randomly assigned either to a traditional delivery group or to a group that used Leboyer's techniques. There were no differences in the amount of crying exhibited by the newborns for whom birth was a "shock" and those for whom birth was a "joy." The warm, sooth-

ing Leboyer bath did not calm the infants. The groups of newborns did not differ in their scores on development assessment at twenty-four and at seventy-two hours. Furthermore, no developmental differences were found between the two infant groups when they were 8 months of age.

The Nelson study suggests that the normal stresses of childbirth are not too much for an infant to handle. Furthermore, the traditional delivery, with its cold, impersonal attention to procedure rather than to the people involved, may be somewhat of an exaggeration, at least in today's hospitals.

The widespread use of the Lamaze method in U.S. hospitals (involving education about the anatomy and physiology of pregnancy and delivery, respiration techniques, conditioned relaxation, redirection of attention, and social support) has led to a reduction in anxiety and pain and has had a positive effect on maternal attitudes (Wideman & Singer 1984).

In 96 percent of the cases, the fetus is positioned for delivery with the head downward. In the other 4 percent, the fetus presents buttocks first (a breech presentation) or, very rarely, the fetus is positioned sideways on a horizontal plane (a transverse presentation) (Guttmacher 1973). The latter presentations often necessitate a cesarean delivery, in which an incision is made in the lower abdomen, and the fetus is removed surgically.

Cesarean deliveries have been increasing in recent years. The nationwide average was 15.2 per-

cent in 1978 (National Institute of Child Health 1980) and may be higher in specific locales. They are required in the case of many breech presentations, in the presence of fetal distress, or when the fetus is simply too large to pass through the birth canal (National Institute of Child Health 1980). Concern over **anoxia,** a lack of oxygen, may also account for the increased frequency of cesarean births. When oxygen deprivation continues for a few minutes, permanent loss of brain cells, and

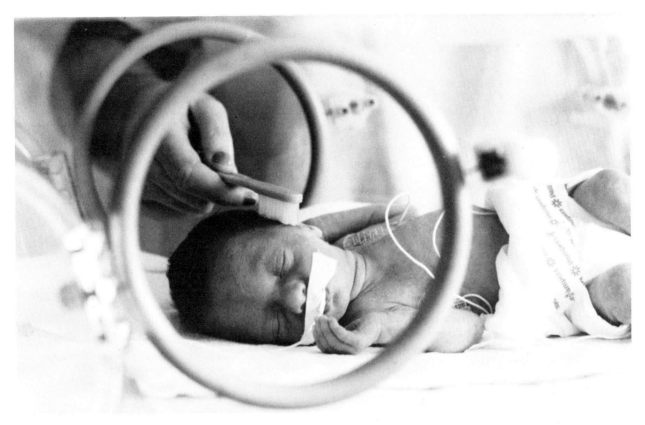

This premature infant is having his or her hair combed while laying in its isolette.

bleeding within the skull, may lead to cerebral palsy and poor motor and cognitive development.

After the child has been expelled, the third stage of birth begins. This is known as the **afterbirth,** and it consists of the expulsion of the placenta and amniotic sac by means of uterine contractions. The afterbirth lasts about thirty minutes and is by far the easiest stage of birth, because the delivery passage already has been widened during the expulsion stage. The uterus contracts after birth, and the placenta tears away from the uterine wall. Some bleeding is to be expected as the placenta tears free, but as the uterus shrinks, the blood flow is stemmed. The placenta and fetal membranes then are expelled from the uterus by means of the contractions and perhaps a gentle tugging on the umbilical cord by those assisting at the birth.

Some observers believe that typical delivery-room procedures are too shocking for newborns. The Research Close-up "A Test of the 'Gentle Birth' Hypothesis" presents an alternate procedure.

Prematurity

Approximately 5 to 7 percent of all births in the United States are preterm (Goldberg & DiVitto 1983). These infants are born before week 37 of gestation, and they weigh less than a full-term infant (usually less than 2,000 grams or 5½ pounds). Obviously, the older the premature infant, the heavier he or she will probably be, and the better the chances of survival. In the early 1980s premature infants who weighed 1,000 to 1,500 grams (2¼ to 3¼ pounds) at birth had a 80 to 85 percent survival rate, whereas babies who weighed 750 to 1,000 grams at birth (1½ to 2¼ pounds) had a 50 to 60 percent survival rate (Goldberg & DiVitto 1983). Full-term infants who are small for their gestational age (weighed less than 2,500 grams, or 5½ pounds) may also be at risk.

Why are premature infants so at risk? Because of the immaturity of their physical systems, they lack the basic mechanisms necessary for survival. Their greatest handicap is the immaturity of their lungs, which often lack the surfactin (a secretion that maintains the elasticity of the lungs) necessary for the exchange of oxygen from the air. Prematures lack subcutaneous fat, so their skin has a transparent, wrinkled appearance; they also lack brown fat, which surrounds the internal organs. Because of this lack of fat, these infants have difficulty maintaining their body temperature. Digestive problems are also common to premature infants. Because of a weak sucking reflex, they may have to be fed by a hollow tube that is inserted down their throats for the first few weeks of life. Additionally, premature infants have less developed central nervous systems than full-terms. This can make them physically irritable, and certain behaviors, such as the smile, may be late in development.

Most premature infants are placed in isolettes for a period of time after their birth. The isolette provides an environment that controls temperature, humidity, and oxygen. Lacking muscle tone, premature infants can only lie limply in the isolette, looking lost in all of the equipment designed to save their lives. It is no wonder that parents of these children are intimidated by their babies and may find them hard to care for. Of course, the long-term separation between parents and child can also contribute to possible problems in parent-infant relationships. Generally, premature infants will remain hospitalized until at least the time when they would have been full-term—usually the stay is longer.

What are the causes of prematurity? According to Goldberg and DiVitto (1983), premature birth can be caused by maternal health problems, abnormalities in the mother's reproductive system, or multiple births. Prematurity also results from chronic illnesses (e.g., diabetes), severe stress, and poor living conditions; women who are of lower-socioeconomic classes are more likely to have premature infants. Particularly at risk are adolescents under 15 years of age because of the immaturity of their reproductive systems. However, it is important to recognize that about 50 percent of preterm births are due to unknown causes—they are born of women who have had normal pregnancies and who were healthy and under good medical care.

As can be imagined, there has been concern over the immediate and long-term consequences of prematurity. Goldberg (1979) found that a number of the typical characteristics of the preterm infant can put stress on the parent-infant interaction system, although the majority of families do make successful adaptations over time. In addition, it has been proposed that the prolonged period in the isolette leads to a situation of sensory deprivation, which could damage both intellectual and social development. Hospital personnel today make a concerted effort to encourage parents to come to the hospital and handle their baby. Stimulating preterm infants by rocking; using patterned crib sheets; playing recorded heartbeats; and stroking, massaging, and flexing the body have also been beneficial—particularly after thirty-six gestational weeks, when the infant becomes more responsive to the environment.

The research findings on long-term outcomes for prematures are controversial. There is some evidence of language delays among school-aged children who were prematurely born. Perhaps most encouraging is the finding that by age 5, many preterms do not significantly differ from full-terms on measures of intellectual development (Goldberg 1983; Siegel 1983). Thus, developmental delays apparent in preterms during infancy eventually are compensated. Indeed, it appears that the home environment becomes a more significant predictor of later outcomes than does prematurity.

The Newborn

The average newborn is about twenty inches in length and weighs about 7½ pounds, with males slightly longer and heavier than females. Typically, the eyes of the neonate are smoky blue, the head is disproportionately large, and there is practically no voluntary control over the head or the legs. The newborn's legs may be bowed, the neck is short, and he or she may have no chin and a flattened nose. Sometimes the head is misshapen because of the passage through the narrow birth canal.

Most newborns are given the Apgar Screening Test (Apgar, 1953) at one minute—and possibly three, five, and ten minutes—after birth. The Ap-

Table 3.3 Criteria and Scoring of the Apgar Test

Score	A Appearance (color)	P Pulse (heart rate)	G Grimace (reflex irritability)	A Activity (muscle tone)	R Respiration (respiratory effort)
0	blue, pale	absent	no response	limp	absent
1	body pink, extremities blue	slow (below 100)	grimace	some flexion of extremities	slow, irregular
2	completely pink	rapid (over 100)	cry	active motion	good, strong cry

gar is a quick assessment of the status of the newborn. The Apgar score, ranging from 0 to 10, is based upon five signs: heart rate, respiratory effort, reflex irritability (determined by stimulation of the soles of the feet), muscle tone, and color. Each of these signs can be given a score of 0, 1, or 2, with a score of 2 being the best possible condition. Generally, newborns with low-Apgar scores (0 to 3) must be closely monitored; Apgars of 7 to 10 are signs of a robust infant (see Table 3.3).

Another neonatal assessment that is becoming increasingly popular is the Dubowitz Scoring System (Dubowitz, Dubowitz & Goldberg 1970). This scoring system measures the neurological and physical characteristics of the newborn and is useful in determining the gestational age of a newborn. It is particularly helpful in assessing the condition of small-for-gestational-age and preterm infants.

A test that has become increasingly popular in neonatal assessment is the Brazelton Neonatal Behavioral Assessment Scale, or NBAS (Brazelton 1984). The NBAS contains twenty neurological items that measure reflexes and movements such as grasping, sucking, and crawling. In addition twenty-seven items measure behaviors such as levels of wakefulness, sleeping and crying, responses to a variety of stimuli, cuddliness, and irritability. The NBAS is designed to be used with the normal newborn; it has been useful in a number of investigations on a variety of factors that can influence neonatal behavior. For example, a popular use of the NBAS involves relating infant scores to mother-infant interactions. The scale may be useful in determining how easily parents can adapt

to the needs of their infant (Linn & Horowitz 1983). Some researchers have even trained new mothers to give the Brazelton to their infants during their hospital stay, in an effort to sensitize the women to the behavioral capabilities of their newborn babies.

Reflexes

Much of the preceding discussion on neonatal assessment involved an examination of the newborn's reflexes. When infants come into the world, they are already equipped with the ability to perform a large number of automatic behavioral reactions, or **reflexes.** Some of these reflexes, such as sucking and rooting, are clearly related to the survival of the newborn, whereas others are not. All are significant because they reflect the maturation and development of the nervous system (Taft & Cohen 1967). Reflex testing in infants, therefore, is helpful in localizing abnormalities in the central nervous system and the integrity of the peripheral nerves.

Reflexes actually develop in utero: the sucking reflex develops between the second and third fetal month; the stepping reflex between eight and nine fetal months. Many reflexes do not persist indefinitely, but disappear within the first six months of life, as they are replaced by more complex adaptations to the environment. Grasping, for example, is an involuntary response to an object placed in the hand and is replaced by deliberate grasping at about 4 months of age.

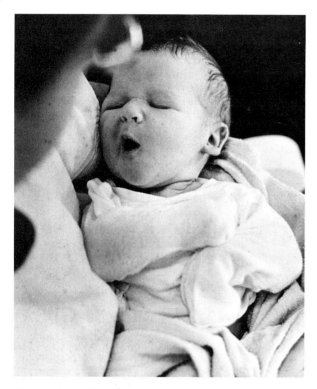

The rooting reflex.

The tonic neck reflex.

The plantar (foot grasp) reflex.

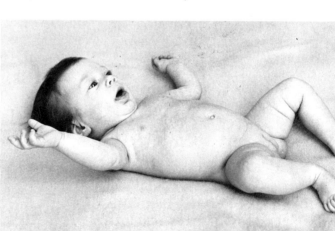

The Moro reflex.

In the psychological sense, reflexes are significant because they indicate that the human baby is by no means an "empty organism," but has at his or her disposal a number of wired-in responses to the environment. They are significant, too, in the sense that they appear to form the foundations for later, more complex learned behaviors. Piaget, for example, viewed neonatal reflexes as the roots of sensorimotor intelligence during the period of infancy.

Infant States

For harried parents of newborn babies, the ideal newborn would immediately adjust to the adult day-night cycle of wakefulness and sleep. However, this sort of pattern is many weeks (or months) away. Rather, it often seems as if the infant's behaviors are random and disorganized; the baby appears to sleep and wake up, sometimes moving quite actively while asleep, sometimes lying still, sometimes fussing or looking about—with no apparent pattern to the behavior. (See Problems in Child Development "Sudden Infant Death Syndrome" for a discussion of SIDS in relation to infant states.)

It is now known that neonatal behavior is organized around different levels of sleep and wakefulness, called **states**. These states are presumed to reflect the maturity of the central nervous system. By painstakingly observing neonatal behavior for hours, researchers have been able to categorize different types of sleep and wakefulness in infants. A number of such classification systems exist, but Wolff's (1966) is one of the most accepted. Table 3.4 provides Wolff's definitions of seven infant states.

Young infants spend about sixteen to seventeen hours per day asleep, with the rest of the time in various states of wakefulness (Parmelee et al. 1964). However, the actual percentage of time in each state can vary greatly from one child to the next. During the newborn period, these periods of sleep and wakefulness alternate during the day and night until about the age of 1 month, when the time spent in stretches of being asleep or awake increases.

Infant states provide an important window on both neurological organization and responsiveness of infants. For example, the slow, regular, or nonrapid eye movement (NREM) sleep seems to demand the most organization of the infant's central nervous system (Beckwith & Parmelee 1986). A particular brain wave pattern during this form of sleep has predicted scores on intelligence tests up to 8 years of age for children who were born prematurely (Beckwith & Parmelee 1986).

The rapid eye movements (REM) and diffuse motor activity associated with irregular sleep may actually serve as stimulation for the central nervous

Table 3.4 Wolff's Classification of Infant States

Regular Sleep or Nonrapid Eye Movement Sleep (NREM Sleep)	Full rest; low muscle tone and motor activity; eyelids closed and eyes still; regular breathing (about thirty-six times per minute)
Irregular Sleep or Rapid Eye Movement Sleep (REM Sleep)	Increased muscle tone and motor activity; facial grimaces and smiles; occasional eye movements; irregular breathing (about forty-eight times per minute)
Periodic Sleep	Intermediate between REM and NREM sleep—bursts of deep, slow breathing alternating with bouts of rapid, shallow breathing
Drowsiness	More active than NREM sleep but less active than REM or periodic sleep; eyes open and close; eyes glazed when open; breathing variable but more rapid than in NREM sleep
Alert Inactivity	Slight activity; face relaxed; eyes open and bright; breathing regular and more rapid than in NREM sleep, eyes moving together
Active Alert	Frequent diffuse motor activity; vocalizations; skin flushed; irregular breathing
Distress	Vigorous diffuse motor activity; facial grimaces; red skin; crying

Source: Adapted from Wolff, P.H. (1966) The causes, controls, and organization of behavior in the neonate. *Psychological Issues, 5 (1),* 7–11. Reprinted by permission of International Universities Press, Inc.

system as the baby sleeps; it is uncertain if young babies dream as do adults. Interestingly, the amount of REM sleep declines as the infant ages and as more time is spent being awake. Also, newborns tend to go immediately into REM sleep, whereas adults first go through a series of NREM stages before reaching the REM sleep state. The

Problems in Child Development

Sudden Infant Death Syndrome

In the United States, about 10,000 infant deaths per year are attributed to sudden infant death syndrome (SIDS). It is the most frequent cause of death among infants from 1 week to 1 year of age (Schiffman et al. 1980). Death typically occurs when the infant presumably has been asleep (hence the term *crib death*)—only to be discovered dead in the early morning or after naptime by horrified parents or babysitters. Until the early 1970s, there was little formal recognition of such deaths as due to a clinically defined syndrome.

Since then, much has been learned about the patterns of SIDS victims, and many hypotheses have been examined. According to Naeye (1980), SIDS is the sudden, unexpected death of an infant who appeared to be healthy and for whom no discernible cause of death can be identified by an autopsy. It first appears in infants who are 2 to 3 weeks old. The incidence of SIDS peaks at 3 months and then decreases to the point where it is rarely seen after the first year of life. In Naeye's research, the majority of SIDS victims were nonwhite males, had a premature birth and/or an infection in the amniotic fluid, were born into low-socioeconomic-class homes, and tended to die during the winter months (Naeye 1980). Additionally, the SIDS rate for babies of adolescent mothers is five times that of babies of older mothers (Babson & Clarke 1983). Infants whose mothers were on methodone maintenance programs during pregnancy or who smoked are also at greater risk of succumbing to SIDS. Factors such as these, however, account for less than half of all SIDS deaths; many others occur in families that do not fit these patterns.

The leading hypothesis about the cause of SIDS implicates some aspect of the respiratory system of the infant. All infants and adults have periods of *apnea,* or interruption of breathing. A small neurovascular organ in the neck monitors the oxygen content in the blood and restarts breathing. Naeye (1980) presented evidence that this organ is underdeveloped in infants who have died of SIDS. Thus SIDS may be caused by a subtle form of brain damage.

Another interesting hypothesis has been offered by Lipsitt (1979). Lipsitt noted that between 2 to 4 months of age, learned behaviors supplant many reflexive behaviors crucial for the infant's survival. Some infants may not respond to the threat of respiratory failure with either a strong reflexive response or a learned response to restart breathing. In a sense, SIDS victims may suffer from a learning disability that causes them to be ineffective in making an appropriate operant response to restart breathing.

In addition to the above theories, SIDS has been linked to infant botulism (Marx 1978) and to heat stroke, caused by excessive clothing and coverings at the time of death (Stanton, Scott & Downhan 1980). There are many other explanations, and it is possible that SIDS may be caused by a number of factors, not just a single agent or defect.

Presently, the only prevention is to place an infant who is at risk on a home apnea monitor, which sounds an alarm if the infant stops breathing. There is no cure for SIDS, but better identification of at-risk infants should help to reduce the death rate.

changeover to the adult pattern occurs during the first six months of life.

Another very significant state is alert inactivity. Although newborns do not spend very much time in this state, it is the time that they are most responsive to the environment. Babies in alert inactivity will actively scan their visual world, and their behavior often encourages interactions with their parents. Byrne and Horowitz (1979) found that placing a crying infant up on an adult's shoulder and intermittently rocking the baby has a calming effect. Putting the infant to an adult's shoulder is also an effective way of bringing the baby to alert inactivity. Infants who are carried about with their heads peeking over a parent's shoulder may have more opportunities for visual and social experiences.

After considering all of the changes involved in the development of a new human being—from the moment of conception until after the child's birth—it is easy to forget that this is just the beginning. The drama of prenatal development, birth, and early infancy sets the stage for many other wondrous changes in child development.

Summary

1. The answers to the true-false questions at the beginning of this chapter are as follows: 1. T; 2. F; 3. F; 4. T; 5. F; 6. F; 7. T; 8. F; 9. F; 10. T.
2. The plan of human physical growth is determined by the genetic material in the cells. Cell division takes place by mitosis. The sex cells, however, undergo a second division known as meiosis.
3. A number of genetic disorders, such as Down's syndrome, occur during meiosis. A failure in chromosomal separation could lead to a number of birth defects.
4. Reaction range and the scoop model are concepts for understanding the interaction between genetic makeup and environmental factors. The scoop model emphasizes that biological inheritance is more influential early in development, whereas environmental factors play a more significant role in shaping the individual later in development.
5. Pregnancy is divided into three stages. The germinal stage includes the first two weeks after fertilization; the embryonic stage covers the next six weeks; and the fetal stage goes from the eighth week until the moment of birth.
6. Teratogens are factors that can cause developmental malformations. They have their highest impact upon the developing organism during periods in which cell division is most rapid.
7. Fetal alcohol syndrome refers to the cluster of symptoms associated with exposure to alcohol in utero. The syndrome includes central nervous system problems, low prenatal and postnatal weight, facial anomalies, and other congenital defects.
8. Birth is a three-stage process consisting of the opening stage (labor), the expulsion stage (delivery), and the afterbirth stage.
9. Infants born before week 37 of gestation are considered premature and are at risk because of the immaturity of their respiratory systems.
10. Neonatal assessments such as the Apgar Screening Test, the Dubowitz Scoring System, and the Neonatal Behavioral Assessment Scale are designed to determine physical and behavioral capabilities of the newborn.
11. Automatic behavioral reactions, or reflexes, are important indices of the functioning of the central nervous system. Reflexes are vital to the survival of the infant and provide the first behaviors for learning about the world.
12. The levels of sleep and wakefulness that have been observed in infants are known as states. States regulate the extent to which the young infant interacts with the world.

Key Terms

chromosomes	embryo
genes	placenta
karyotype	amniotic sac
mitosis	ecotoderm
meiosis	mesoderm
genotype	endoderm
phenotype	fetus
homozygous	teratogens
heterozygous	maternal sensitization
polygenic	sudden infant death
Down's syndrome	syndrome
reaction range	fetal alcohol syndrome
scoop model	labor
canalized	anoxia
zygote	afterbirth
blastocyst	reflexes
	infant states

Suggested Readings

Goldberg, S. & DiVitto, B.A. (1983). *Born too soon: Preterm birth and early development*. San Francisco: Freeman.

A carefully written book about premature infants by authors who have done extensive research with preterm infants and their families. Included are discussions of intensive care, major developmental milestones, perceptual development, personality, and parenting and intervention programs for the premature infant.

Leboyer, F. (1975). *Birth without violence.* New York: Knopf.

A well-illustrated discussion of the "gentle birth" hypothesis in which the author argues for a more humane way of bringing babies into the world.

Nilsson, L. (1976). *A child is born.* New York: Delacorte Press.

A vivid visual diary of life before birth. Lennart Nilsson is one of the world's best-known photographers of the prenatal world.

Readings from the Literature

This chapter presented information about the characteristics of premature infants which often render them "at risk." The following article describes a treatment for enhancing the development of premature infants. As you read, consider these questions:

- *How may the neonatal intensive care unit be problematic for the development of premature infants?*

- *What measures did the researchers use to assess the outcome of their treatment program? What additional variables would you have included to assess the effectiveness of the program?*

- *How successful was the program in light of the results found by the authors?*

Use of Oscillating Waterbeds and Rhythmic Sounds for Premature Infant Stimulation

**Kayreen A. Burns, Ruth B. Deddish,
William J. Burns, and Roger P. Hatcher**
Northwestern University Medical School

Twenty-two healthy infants born at gestational ages of 28–32 weeks were randomly assigned to experimental or control groups within the first 4 days following birth. Experimental infants were placed in incubators equipped with oscillating waterbeds and rhythmic sounds. Control infants were placed in traditional incubators. All infants remained in their respective environment for 4 weeks. Measures of treatment effects included weight gain, head measurement, weekly 2-hour observations of state organization, and the Brazelton Neonatal Behavioral Assessment Scale (NBAS). No significant differences were obtained between the two groups on any of the physical measures. A priori cluster scores on the BNBAS showed significantly greater developmental progress in motoric and state organization processes for the experimental group. A statistically significant interaction effect was found between the two groups for the amount of time they spent in active sleep during the treatment period and at the time of discharge. These results suggest that general developmental progress was enhanced in the experimental group by the stimulation procedure.

The application of stimulation procedures to human infants for the purpose of enriching developmental progress has borrowed some of its principles from the animal studies that investigated the effects of deprivation and enrichment on newborn animals (Denenberg, 1967; Harlow, 1958; Levine, 1960). The general finding that a deprived environment hinders development in animals and that stimulation enriches development has led to the hypothesis that similar effects might be found when stimulation is applied to the human newborn, especially to infants born prematurely. In a recent review of the literature on prematurity and infant stimulation, Schaefer, Hatcher, and Barglow (1980) have noted that the use of rhythmic sounds such as heartbeat and the use of tactile and vestibular-proprioceptive stimulation have all been researched at length. These authors conclude that although stimulation studies have suffered methodological flaws, there is strong evidence in support of the efficacy of stimulation for the preterm infant.

More recent research has shown that long-term developmental prognosis for infants born at very early gestational ages is improving, and yet these infants still remain at higher than average risk for developmental delay (Schaefer et al., 1980). The concern about environmental factors contributing to this risk begins in the nursery. There has been some agreement that the usual environment of the neonatal intensive care unit is deficient in normal developmental experience. Lawson, Daum, and Turkewitz (1977) studied the quality and quantity of the stimulation that preterm infants received in the intensive care unit and concluded that it is inappropriate in both its extreme intensity and in its lack of rhythmicity and contingency. Therefore, later developmental deficiences in these infants may be due to a combination of the medical complications of prematurity, the degree of central nervous system abnormalities at birth, and the developmentally deficient environment of the intensive care nursery.

However, the opinion that preterm infants may be positively or negatively affected by environmental factors is a point of controversy in the current literature. Cornell and Gottfried (1976) note that there is no firm support for the assumption that preterm infants in the intensive care setting experience sensory deprivation. Parmelee (1981) disagrees with the hypothesis that preterm sensory experiences alter developmental progress. He believes that the preterm maturation of the human nervous system is for the most part genetically rather than environmentally controlled.

An account of the formulation of the stimulation procedures used in the present study may be found in the writings of Barnard (1972, 1974, Note 1), Korner (Note 2, Note 3), Korner, Kraemer, Haffner, and Cosper

(1975), and Kramer and Pierpont (1976). Korner (Note 3) hypothesized that prematurely born infants have been deprived of an essential period of intrauterine stimulation. She placed infants on oscillating waterbeds as a compensatory vestibular-proprioceptive stimulation similar in kind to that which she hypothesized would occur in utero. Barnard (Note 1) has suggested that the rhythmic stimulation that occurs naturally in utero is intended to enhance neurological maturation in the developing fetus and that this maturing process in turn aids the development of state behavior organization. Barnard placed premature infants in incubators equipped with a rocking mechanism and heartbeat sounds. She found that these babies developed more quiet sleep during the immediate neonatal period and had better weight gain than the control group. Kramer and Pierpont (1976) provided oscillating waterbeds and auditory sounds to a group of preterm infants and found that their weight gain and biparietal head diameters were significantly greater than a group of control infants; however, they found no neonatal behavioral differences.

The population, methodology, and dependent variables of the present study are similar to those of Kramer and Pierpont (1976), but several important changes were made. Unlike Kramer and Pierpont's study in which the duration of the experimental treatment was allowed to vary, depending on how long the infant was kept in the incubator, in the present investigation the duration of treatment was held constant for all infants in order to establish experimental control. Also, in the Kramer and Pierpont (1976) study, the mechanical rocking took place for only 1 hour prior to each feeding, whereas in the present study, the waterbed oscillation and auditory sounds were continuous during the 4 weeks of treatment. This increased amount of stimulation in the present study was designed to produce a greater experimental effect. Premature infants in this study were of earlier gestational age than those studied by Kramer and Pierpont. Drillien (1964, 1970) has shown that the earlier the prematurity, the greater the risk for developmental problems. Thus, it seems reasonable that the greater the potential deficits, the more potential for demonstrating the effectiveness of intervention.

As in the Kramer and Pierpont study, the Brazelton Neonatal Behavioral Assessment Scale (BNBAS) was used in the present study as a measure of the infant's interactive behavior. The literature on the BNBAS is very broad and complete (Sameroff, 1978), and recent advances in statistical analysis of the scores (Als, 1978) have made its results interpretable and, therefore, meaningful. Sell, Luick, Poisson, and Hill (1980) have successfully used the BNBAS with preterm infants as early as 36 weeks conceptual age and have used the a priori clusters (Als, Tronick, Lester, & Brazelton, 1977) to analyze BNBAS results. Sostek, Quinn, and Davitt (1979) also used the BNBAS with preterm infants at 36 weeks conceptual age and interpreted scores using cluster scores.

To provide a complementary measure with the BNBAS, state observations were added as an additional dependent variable. Although the BNBAS assesses many sets of behaviors at one point in time, state observations recorded one set (state) over many points in time. Head circumference, biparietal head diameter, and body weight measures were also collected for group comparisons.

The purpose of the present study was to demonstrate that special stimulation in the form of oscillating waterbeds and rhythmic sounds provided for preterm infants would enhance their development, as measured by physical parameters, BNBAS, and state behavior observations.

Method

Subjects

Twenty-two infants between 28 and 32 weeks gestational age, determined by the mother's last menstrual period, were randomly assigned to treatment and control groups. Random assignment to groups was accomplished, with each new subject using a blind card system derived from a table of random digits. Every infant who entered the Special Care Nursery at Prentice Women's Hospital during the 10 months of the study and who fit subject criteria was enlisted in the study. Infants were excluded from the study if they required mechanical ventilation beyond 5 days of life, if they were born to drug-addicted mothers, or if they had major

Table 1 Subject Characteristics

Characteristic	Experimental	Control
Sex		
Male	4	5
Female	7	6
Race		
Black	3	5
White	6	4
Spanish	2	2
Gestational age at birth (weeks)		
M	29.7	29.8
SD	1.6	1.5
Days of hospitalization		
M	50.5	49.0
SD	17.1	15.5
Conceptual age at discharge (weeks)		
M	36.3	36.2
SD	1.7	1.8
Weight at birth (g)		
M	1,240	1,201
SD	193	236
Weight at end of treatment (g)		
M	1,604	1,601
SD	238	314
Biparietal diameter (cm)		
Beginning of treatment	6.5	6.3
End of treatment	7.2	6.8

central nervous system, gastrointestinal, or cardiac anomalies. The physical and background characteristics of the samples are listed in Table 1.

Procedure

A Classics Product waterbed filled with 22 lb. of warm water and covered with a ½-inch layer of foam insulation was placed in the infant's incubator. A 500 cc Penlon anesthesia bag connected to a Bird Mark 7 Intermittent Positive Pressure Breathing (IPPB) machine was placed under the waterbed, and the inflation and deflation of this bag produced an oscillation motion at a frequency of 16 oscillations per minute. The anesthesia bag was placed under the foot of the water mattress so that the wave motion was from foot to head, with a wave amplitude of no greater than ¼ inch when the infant was lying on the mattress. A 2½-inch speaker was placed at the head of the waterbed in each incubator. It was connected to a continuous loop cassette which played a recording of the intrauterine sounds of a pregnant woman (Murooko, Capitol Records, 1974) that was judged to be approximately 65–80 db by a biologic check. Each experimental infant was placed in this environment by the 4th day of life and remained there for 4 weeks. Control infants were given routine care in a standard incubator for a similar period. All 22 infants were given the same medical and nursing care, and all parents were allowed equal access to their infants. Daily weight was recorded as was weekly head circumference and biparietal diameters. Weekly state organization observations of 2 hours' duration were collected during the 4 weeks of the experimental procedures and again at discharge. Observations were begun between 10:30 A.M. and 2 P.M. Nurses generously scheduled interventions so that nonemergency interruptions would not occur during observations. However, when major intrusive interruptions occurred, the observation was discontinued for ½ hour. Eight state categories, adapted from Thoman (1975), were defined as follows: quiet sleep, active sleep, REM sleep, drowsy, cognitive alert, motoric alert, fussing, and crying. For each 10 sec sampling interval, a single coding of the predominant state was recorded. A single observer who had 90% reliability with two outside observers completed all of the state observations. The BNBAS was administered just prior to discharge from the hospital by a trained examiner who was blind to the subject group assignment.

Results

No significant differences between experimental and control groups were found on weight, head circumference, or biparietal measures either at the beginning of the study or on the gain scores obtained at the end of the 4 weeks of experimental treatment. Since the discharge weight of each infant in the study was the same (4½ lbs.), there were by design no weight differences at discharge; no significant differences were

Table 2 Dimensions of the Brazelton Examination

Dimension	Experimental		Control		
	M	SD	M	SD	t
Interaction Organization	2.72	.47	2.60	.52	.54
Motoric Organization	2.09	.30	2.55	.52	2.50†
State Control Organization	1.55	.53	2.00	.63	1.84*
Physiological Organization	1.18	.60	1.45	.82	.89

Note. For each group, $N = 11$.
*$p < .05$, one-tailed.
†$p < .05$, two-tailed.

found between the experimental and control groups in number of days required to reach the criterion weight for discharge (Table 1).

A priori clusters developed by Als (1978) were used to analyze the BNBAS scores. This analysis integrates the 47 scores of the BNBAS into four dimensional scores that provide summary descriptions of the quality of the infant's functioning. Each of the dimensional scores is expressed on a 3-point scale, (1 = well organized, 2 = average, and 3 = worrisome). Therefore, the closer the dimension score is to 1, the more organized is the infant. As shown in Table 2, both the motoric organization cluster and the state organization cluster score were significantly better for the experimental group than for when a one-tailed t test analysis was performed. If a more conservative two-tailed analysis were used, the motoric organization cluster would remain fairly firm, whereas the state organization cluster would be of only marginal significance ($p < .08$).

The percentage of time spent in each of the eight state categories was used to compare the two groups at the end of the 1st week of the study and again at the time of discharge. The only category that demonstrated significant relationship was that of active sleep. The percentage of time spent in active sleep was analyzed as a 2 × 2 factorial, with measures repeated at Week

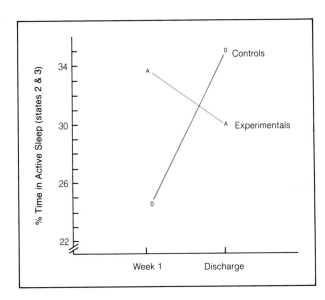

Figure 1 Interaction between groups and weeks for time spent in active sleep.

1 and discharge. Although significant main effect differences were not obtained between groups, a significant interaction was obtained between experimental and control groups for the time spent in active sleep at Week 1 and discharge, $F(1, 16) = 4.53$, $p < .05$. This interaction is illustrated in Figure 1.

Discussion

Based on the findings of previous studies, it was hypothesized that the gentle rolling movements of the oscillating waterbed and the rhythmic sound would provide a beneficial climate for the enhancement of physical growth parameters, developmental progress, and state organization. Contrary to the findings of Kramer and Pierpont (1976), no significant differences were found between the two groups in any of the physical parameters measured. Although Kramer and Pierpont (1976) were unable to obtain indications of differences on the BNBAS, positive findings were obtained in the present study on two dimensions of this scale. The experimental group received significantly higher scores than did the control group on the motoric

organization dimension and marginally significant scores on the state organization dimension of the BNBAS. The finding of advanced motoric development for the experimental infants is of special importance because motor organization is frequently delayed in preterm infants (Parmelee, 1981).

In regard to the finding on the BNBAS of enhanced organization of state control, researchers have repeatedly found that the effects of rhythmic movement and sound have a soothing effect on the state of infants (Barnard, 1972; Hasselmeyer, 1964; McNichol, 1974; Scarr-Salapatek and Williams, 1973). Thus, it was not surprising that both BNBAS and state observation findings suggested that state control was enhanced by the waterbed treatment in this study. Experimental and control groups differed significantly in whether percentages of active sleep time increased or decreased from treatment to discharge, with experimental infants decreasing and control infants increasing the percentage of time in active sleep. This reduction in active sleep for the experimental group was part of an 8.4% decrease in total sleep time. The control group, on the other hand, increased the total sleep time by 6.8% between Week 1 and discharge. State control findings on the BNBAS were notable, since the mean age of the infants at the time of testing was 36 weeks, whereas the exam is designed to assess infants at 40 weeks. It appears that the experimental procedure applied to these preterm infants influenced their development enough to provide differences measurable even at this early age.

The findings in this study suggest that the use of rhythmic vestibular-proprioceptive and auditory stimulation in the case of very preterm infants may enhance their development. Since rhythmic sounds and oscillating movements were combined in the treatment phase, there is no way of knowing the unique contributions of each. One limitation of the present investigation was the very small sample size. Although further study is needed with a larger sample, the instrumentation available at the present time is very cumbersome and expensive, making it very difficult to collect this data. Progress, however, is being made to fill this technological gap.

Reference Notes

1. Barnard, K. *Effect of stimulation on sleep organization and motor development in prematures*. Paper presented at the conference on Follow-up of the High-Risk Newborn: A Practical Approach, Tucson, April 1978.
2. Korner, A. *Reduction in sleep apnea in preterm infants on oscillating waterbeds*. Paper presented at the International Conference of Infant Studies, Providence, April 1978.
3. Korner, A. *Intervention with preterm infants: Why, to what end, and by what means?* Paper presented at a meeting on Early Experience and the High-Risk Infant, Chicago, May 1979.

References

Als, H. Assessing an assessment: Conceptual, considerations, methodological issues, and perspective on the future of the Neonatal Behavioral Assessment Scale. In A. Sameroff (Ed.), *Monographs of the Society for Research in Child Development*, 1978, *43* (5–6, Serial No. 177).

Als, H., Tronick, E., Lester, B., & Brazelton, T. B. The Brazelton Neonatal Assessment Scale (BNBAS). *Journal of Abnormal Child Psychology*, 1977, *5*, 215–231.

Barnard, K. The effects of stimulation on the duration and amount of sleep and wakefulness in the premature infant (Doctoral dissertation, University of Washington, 1972). *Dissertation Abstracts International*, 1972, *33* (5-B), 2167. (University Microfilms No. 72-28,573)

Barnard, K. The effect of stimulation on the sleep behavior of the premature infant. *Communicating Nursing Research*, 1974, *6*, 12–33.

Cornell, E., & Gottfried, A. Intervention with premature human infants. *Child Development*, 1976, *47*, 32–37.

Denenberg, V. Stimulation in infancy, emotional reactivity, and exploratory behavior. In D. Glass (Ed.), *Neurophysiology and emotion*. New York: Rockefeller University Press, 1967.

Drillien, C. *The growth and development of the prematurely born infant*. Baltimore, Md.: Williams & Wilkins, 1964.

Drillien, C. The small-for-date infant; Etiology and prognosis, *Pediatric Clinics of North America*. 1970, *17*, 9–24.

Harlow, H. The nature of love. *American Psychologist*, 1958, *13*, 673–685.

Hasselmeyer, E. The premature neonate's response to handling. *American Nurses Association*, 1964, *11*, 15–24.

Korner, A., Kraemer, H., Haffner, E., & Cosper, L. Effects of waterbed flotation on premature infants: A pilot study. *Pediatrics*, 1975, *56*, 361–367.

Kramer, L., & Pierpont, M. Rocking waterbeds and auditory stimuli to enhance growth of preterm infants: Preliminary report. *Journal of Pediatrics*, 1976, *88*, 297–299.

Lawson, K., Daum, C., & Turkewitz, G. Environmental characteristics of a neonatal intensive care unit. *Child Development*, 1977, *48*, 1633–1639.

Levine, S. Stimulation in infancy. *Scientific American*, 1960, *202*, 81–85.

McNichol, T. Some effects of different programs of enrichment on the development of premature infants in the hospital nursery (Doctoral dissertation, Purdue University, 1973). *Dissertation Abstracts International*, 1974, *34*(9-B), 4707–08. (University Microfilms No. 74-5013)

Parmelee, A. Auditory function and neurological maturation in preterm infants. In S. Friedman & M. Sigman (Eds.), *Preterm birth and psychological development*. New York: Academic Press, 1981.

Sameroff, A. (Ed.). Organization and stability of newborn behavior: A commentary on the Brazelton Neonatal Assessment Scale, *Monographs of the Society for Research in Child Development*, 1978, *43*(5–6, Serial No. 177).

Scarr-Salapatek, S., & Williams, M. The effects of early stimulation on low birth weight infants. *Child Development*, 1973, *44*, 94–104.

Schaefer, M., Hatcher, R., & Barglow, P. Prematurity and infant stimulation: A review of research. *Child Psychiatry and Human Development*, 1980, *10*, 199–212.

Sell, E., Luick, A., Poisson, S., & Hill, S. Outcome of very low birth weight (VLBW) infants. 1. Neonatal behavior of 188 infants. *Journal of Developmental and Behavioral Pediatrics*, 1980, *1*, 78–85.

Sostek, A., Quinn, P., & Davitt, M. Behavior, developmental and neurological status of premature and full-term infants with varying medical complications. In T. Field (Ed.), *Infants born at risk*. New York: SP Medical & Scientific Books, 1979.

Thoman, E. Early development of sleeping behaviors in infants. In N. Ellis (Ed.), *Aberrant development in infancy*. Hillside, N.J.: Erlbaum, 1975.

Received January 1, 1982
Revision received May 14, 1982

Patterns of Physical Growth

4

Certainly the most noticeable aspect of human development is the development of the body. We see our bodies every day; we observe carefully every detail and we note the changes, sometimes proudly and sometimes with a sense of foreboding. We notice, too, the bodies of those around us. We comment on how big the neighbor's children are getting, how much older Uncle John has been looking lately, or how much weight Cousin Mary has gained or lost. When we see our own children growing up, we are reminded that we, too, are getting older; for many people, the reminder is not a pleasant one.

Physical development is in itself an important aspect of the process of child development, but it is important also because of its impact on the psychological development of the individual. As will become apparent, self-image and body image are inevitably correlated. Our bodies are, after all, not just things we possess or inhabit; our bodies also define who we are.

This chapter discusses the process of physical development from conception to adolescence. It includes normal growth patterns; individual differences within the population; the relationship between physical development and personality development; and, finally, the role of environmental factors on growth.

Patterns of Growth

Physical development is not a random process. In fact, it is highly directional. Development of the body proceeds in two directions simultaneously. The first is **cephalocaudal growth** (literally meaning "from the head to the tail"). Cephalocaudal development is exemplified by the way in which infants can control the muscles of the head and neck before they can control the muscles of the trunk. In terms of physical growth, the head region of the infant is more developed than the trunk region, a phenomenon that is particularly striking during prenatal developmnent (see Chapter 3). The second direction of growth is proximodistal (from the areas nearest the center of the body out to the extremities). **Proximodistal growth** can be seen in the way in which prehension develops from the clumsy clamping of objects at 4

months to neatly picking up small objects at 9 months (pincer grasp).

Physical and behavioral development has also been observed to proceed from relative globality to increasing differentiation and integration. This growth pattern is considered by a number of developmentalists to be the defining feature of any type of development; Heinz Werner (1957) referred to it as the **orthogenetic principle.** During the course of development, different functions and structures of the body become increasingly specialized. This growth pattern is particularly significant during the prenatal period (see Chapter 3), but also is observable in postnatal behavioral development. Because development proceeds in the direction of increasing differentiation and integration, behavior becomes increasingly refined and coordinated. For example, neonates move their bodies in a very diffuse manner. When one part of the body moves, many other parts of the body follow suit. Thus, motoric movements initially are global. With development, specific hand, feet, head, and torso movements separate out from the global movement—these movements are increasingly differentiated. Eventually, such movements also become integrated, one with another, so that the child can do such complex skills as pick up a marble and drop it into a hole, or scribble with a crayon.

Additional patterns of growth are illustrated by the normal growth curves for the various parts of the human body (see Figure 4.1). The graph shows that the brain and head develop earliest in life. In fact, most of the development takes place prenatally or in early infancy. The curve for general body growth (which includes body dimensions, musculature, and internal organs) is somewhat different. It is relatively rapid during the first four years of life, slows down during the elementary school years, and then spurts again at puberty before leveling off. Reproductive growth (including the testes, ovaries, prostate gland, uterus, fallopian tubes, penis, and vagina) is a significant indice of the growth spurt of early adolescence. The curve for reproductive growth follows a different course. There is very little development of these organs until puberty, at which point they develop rapidly until they reach their adult level of functioning.

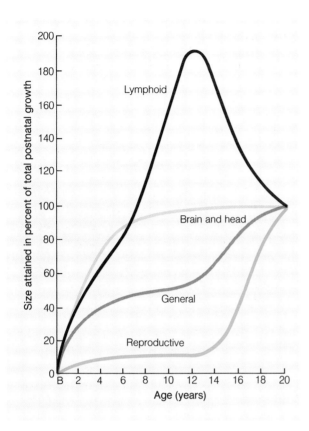

Figure 4.1 Growth Curves of Different Parts of the Human Body

Source: Redrawn from Harris, J.A., Jackson, C.M., Patterson, D.G., and Scammon, R.E. (1930) *The measurement of man.* Minneapolis: University of Minnesota Press.

Each of these patterns of growth (cephalo-caudal-proximodistal, global to differentiated, differential growth rates for different parts of the body) provides models to follow as the patterns of physical growth unfold in this chapter. This section of the chapter discusses brain development, the influence of hormones on physical development, body growth, and motor development.

Brain Development

The part of the human brain responsible for the sophisticated psychological functioning that distinguishes human beings from lower animals is the **cerebral cortex.** *Cortex* means "covering," and the cerebral cortex forms the outer surface of the brain. Weighing approximately half of the weight of the entire nervous system, the cerebral cortex is marked by indentations or grooves called **sulci** and the ridges between them called **gyri.** The cortex is divided into two symmetrical halves, or hemispheres, by a fissure running from front to back. The hemispheres are connected by tracts of nerve fibers (Tanner 1978).

The adult cerebral cortex can be divided into several areas that have specialized functions. The map in Figure 4.2 shows, for example, that certain areas of the cortex are concerned with motor activity, and other areas are concerned with sensory activity. These areas are called the *primary motor areas* and *primary sensory areas*, respectively. There is an area for vision; one for hearing; one for movement of the hands, mouth, legs, lips, and tongue; and other areas for receiving sensation in these parts of the body. There is a motor speech area and a sensory speech area. There are also "association" areas, in which mental activity is integrated.

Three months after birth the primary areas of the cortex are fairly mature, particularly the motor area. Development continues to spread out from the primary areas until the cell structures are well developed throughout the cerebral cortex. A clear and direct connection exists between an infant's ability to move the arms and the development of a specific portion of the primary motor area of the cortex. However, the connection between a child's ability to solve a mental problem and the development of a specific area of the cortex is not so clear. The older people get, the more difficult it becomes to make direct connections between cortical structure and psychological functions. This does not mean, of course, that such connections do not exist.

A number of researchers (e.g., Gardner 1982b; Geschwind 1968; Tanner 1970) have proposed that at about ages 5 through 7, the primary areas of the cortex that link up with sites on the brain associated with language mature. These associative areas (or cross-model zones, according to Gardner 1982) receive environmental input via the primary areas and integrate the information. Children who experience a soft, cold, and sweet object can then conceptualize it as ice cream; they also are able to

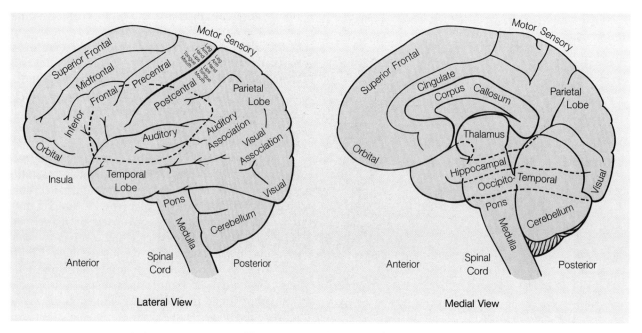

Figure 4.2   Areas of the Human Brain Showing Localization of Function

associate the sound of the words *ice cream* with the qualities of the substance the words denote. Furthermore, sights become associated with smells; sounds with sights; and so forth. The relatively late, but extensive, growth of the cross-model zones is probably related to the tremendous surge of symbolic activity (such as in reading and writing) during the preschool and early elementary school years. Additionally, Tanner (1978) suggested that the development of higher intellectual abilities, even in adolescents and adults, is connected to the maturation of certain structures or cell assemblies in the cortex, and that the stages of intellectual development suggested by Piaget and others (see Chapter 6) probably are connected to levels of cortical maturation.

Thus, there is an increase in "association" fibers connecting the various areas of the cortex and laying the groundwork for higher-order thinking. Brain development in infancy and childhood is also characterized by an increase in the size and number of nerve cell fibers in the cerebral cortex and an increase in the number of nerve fibers connecting the cortex to the lower portions of the brain. These latter fibers conduct sensory impulses to the brain

and motor impulses from the brain to the rest of the body.

The Nerve Cell

The most revealing evidence of brain development in childhood and adolescence comes from studies on the process of **myelination.** To understand this process, it is necessary first to discuss the structure and function of the nerve cell itself. The nerve cell, or **neuron,** consists of a cell body, which is the main portion, and a number of fine, threadline projections extending from the cell body. These projections, which resemble the branches of a tree, are called **dendrites;** the dendrites in the cerebral cortex increase in number as people mature. In addition to the dendrites, each neuron has one extremely long projection called an **axon.** The axon and the dendrites are referred to as the nerve fibers of the cell.

The adult human brain contains approximately 100 billion neurons, all of which are formed during the prenatal period. Chapter 3 described how the central nervous system arises from the outermost layer, the ectoderm, during the embryonic period. Neurons multiply rapidly during the embryonic and fetal periods. They grow in size and

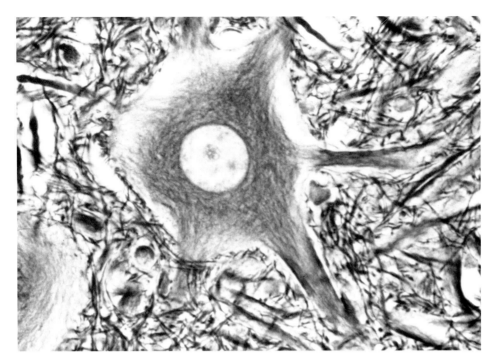

Human neurons with their synapses visible.

then migrate to specific sites of the brain. The migratory routes are helped by supportive cells, called *glial* cells, and pathways taken by the neurons seem to be genetically predetermined. Once the neurons are established in their specific locale, interconnections with other neurons are formed through the growth of axons and dendrites. It is truly amazing that neuron development, growth, and migration all take place prenatally.

When a neuron is stimulated, a nerve impulse is conducted electrochemically. The speed of the impulse actually can be measured and depends on the thickness of the axon. The thicker the axon, the faster the impulse is conducted. An increase in the speed of nerve impulse transmission indicates an increase in the efficiency of the system. Presumably, organisms with thicker nerve fibers would be more responsive to stimulation from the environment and more efficient in their overall functioning. Interestingly enough, human beings have relatively thin nerve fibers compared with those of many other organisms. How, then, can the advanced and complex nervous system of humans be explained? The efficiency of nerve fibers does not depend on thickness alone.

Myelination

As humans develop through childhood and adolescence, their nerve fibers are increasingly surrounded by a fatty layer called a *myelin sheath*. This sheath, or cover, serves as an insulator to the nerve fiber—the sheath apparently protects the fiber and allows it to conduct a nerve impulse much more rapidly than if the sheath were not present. In a sense, the myelin compensates for the relative thinness of the nerve fibers.

From a developmental standpoint, the level of brain and nervous system maturity is linked to the level of myelination of nerve fibers. The process is by no means complete at the time of birth, and it occurs at different times for different nerves. For example, the optic nerve is myelinated very shortly after birth, whereas the nerve fibers necessary for small-muscle control are not myelinated until about the age of 4. Obviously, a child has some small-muscle control before the age of 4, since nerve fibers can function before they are myelinated; the most efficient functioning however, does not appear until myelination is complete. Some of the favorite play activities of 4- and 5-year-olds—drawing, painting, working with a pair of scissors, cutting and pasting—illustrate the effects of myelination of nerve fibers; 2- and 3-year-olds are not yet capable of such activities.

Myelination in some areas is not complete until adolescence or beyond. Is there a relationship during adolescence between neural maturation and specific forms of complex thinking? This is extremely difficult to determine. In fact, considering the magnitude of the intellectual growth that occurs around the time of puberty, it is almost surprising that the brain does not show a corresponding significant growth at that time. Figure 4.1 showed that most growth in brain size takes place in early infancy, and that brain changes during development are apparently changes in complexity. The increasing myelination and the increasing number of dendrites in the cerebral cortex are probably responsible for the vast cognitive changes that can be observed. The complex associations among the various nerve cells may be necessary for abstract thinking.

The Message of the Hormones

Human beings end up at different final points in their growth and grow at different rates because their genes transmit different messages. However, the mechanisms for translating these messages into growth patterns are the same for everyone. These mechanisms, known as the *endocrine glands,* are located in various parts of the body. The endocrine glands most important in the process of physical growth are the **pituitary gland,** located at the base of the brain; the thyroid gland, with two lobes located on opposite sides of the windpipe; the cortex of the adrenal gland, located on the kidneys; and the gonads, or sex glands, located in the ovaries of a woman or the testes of a man (Katchadourian 1977; Tanner 1970, 1978; Tortora & Anagnostakos 1984).

Each of these glands is capable of secreting into the bloodstream a chemical substance called a *hormone,* a word derived from a Greek word meaning "to excite" or "to arouse." In a sense, this is what the hormones do: they arouse or stimulate the body to grow and develop in prescribed ways. However, the glands do not secrete hormones indiscriminately. If they did, growth would be a cha-

otic process indeed. There has to be a control mechanism in the brain to inform the glands when and how much of their hormones they should secrete, and this is the function of the **hypothalamus** in the lower-central portion of the brain.

The hypothalamus regulates the body's internal environment. For example, it controls body temperature, blood pressure, and blood distribution to the brain, as well as regulating the endocrine system. A stalk of nerve fibers connects the hypothalamus to the pituitary gland, which is located directly beneath it. The hypothalamus transmits its messages to the pituitary. In turn, the pituitary gland stimulates and controls all of the other glands in the endocrine system. For this reason, the pituitary is often referred to as the master gland of the body.

How does the pituitary control all of the other glands? Obviously, it is not connected to them directly. Rather, it secretes into the bloodstream certain hormones whose sole function is to stimulate the other glands to secrete their special hormones. These "messenger" hormones are called *trophins.* As an example, the pituitary secretes a hormone called thyroid-stimulating hormone (TSH); this hormone, in turn, stimulates the thyroid gland to secrete thyroid hormone (thyroxine). In a sense, the pituitary sends out TSH to tell the thyroid gland when and how much thyroid hormone to secrete. The hormones most directly connected to the growth process are described in the following sections.

Human Growth Hormone

Secreted by the pituitary gland itself, human growth hormone (HGH) was once thought to be the most important determinant of physical growth; indeed, it is related to overall body size, to the synthesis of protein, and to carbohydrate and fat metabolism. However, it is now recognized that this hormone is not solely responsible for the regulation of physical growth. In fact, the levels of human growth hormone in the bloodstream will vary depending on such environmental factors as physical exercise and stress. Human growth can be influenced by environmental factors to some extent, but variations in the process do not correspond to variations in the level of HGH.

Thyroid Hormone (Thyroxine)

Thyroxine is secreted by the thyroid gland at the instigation of the pituitary gland's thyroid-stimulating hormone (TSH). The major functions of thyroxine are the regulation of the body's metabolism and the development of the brain and nervous system. It first appears in the fetal bloodstream about halfway through the mother's pregnancy. The level of thyroxine is relatively high in the fetus and young infant, declining gradually until about the age of 2. The brain and nervous system develop most rapidly from the mid-prenatal period to about the age of 2; as the brain approaches maturity, the thyroxine level declines. Thyroxine also regulates the body's growth in both size and skeletal proportion; it is responsible for converting cartilage to bone tissue; and it is responsible for the development of the teeth.

Adrenal Hormones

The hormones of the adrenal cortex are usually released in response to adrenocorticotrophic hormone (ACTH), which is secreted by the pituitary gland. The most important hormones secreted by the adrenal cortex are cortisol, which affects cellular metabolism; aldosterone, which is necessary for life because it maintains sodium in tissue fluids; and adrenal androgens, which are male sex hormones responsible in part for the sex-related changes of puberty. The cortisol and aldosterone levels per unit of body weight are fairly constant throughout life, but there is a dramatic increase in adrenal androgen secretion at puberty. The higher level is maintained, with a gradual decline throughout adulthood.

Sex Hormones

Male sex hormones are referred to as **androgens.** The most important of these is testosterone, which is produced by the male sex glands located in the testicles. Testosterone can be found in the bloodstream of children, but it increases dramatically at puberty and then declines very gradually throughout adulthood. Its major effect is to masculinize the body; the hormone is responsible for a number of masculinizing changes that occur at puberty (Jones 1984).

The major female sex hormone is **estrogen,** which is secreted by sex glands located in the ova-ries. Just as its male counterpart is responsible for the development of masculine characteristics at puberty, estrogen is responsible for dramatic feminizing changes at puberty. Estrogen, like testosterone, is present in young children, but there is a dramatic increase in the hormone level during adolescence. Another major female sex hormone is progesterone, which is secreted from the ovaries in the middle and latter part of each menstrual cycle. Its primary responsibility is to prepare the uterus for possible pregnancy.

Female hormones and androgens are present in people of both sexes, but the proportions differ. For males, androgens are predominant, and for females, estrogen is predominant. However, both masculine and feminine physical characteristics can be found to some extent in persons of either gender (Jones 1984).

All of the hormones previously mentioned—individually and in combination—directly influence every aspect of physical growth as predetermined by the genes. Thus, the body has a very sensitive and sophisticated system for regulating its own growth. For most people, growth proceeds in a regular and orderly fashion following instructions from the hypothalamus. (Issues in Human Development "Are Children Growing Up Faster Than Their Parents Did?" discusses the phenomenon of advanced timing of physical growth among contemporary adolescents.)

Growth of the Body

A summary of height and weight changes from the prenatal period through adolescence is contained in Table 4.1.

Growth in both areas is extremely rapid during prenatal development, gradually slows down throughout the years of childhood, and spurts during early adolescence.

In addition to developmental height and weight changes, there is a change from infancy to adolescence in the proportions of the various parts of the body. The most noticeable change is that the head of the infant is much larger in proportion to overall body length than is the head of an adult. The head of a newborn takes up about 25 percent of overall body length. If the proportions were the

Table 4.1 Milestones of Height and Weight Growth Across the Lifespan

	Prenatal	Infancy B to 1 year	Early Childhood 1 to 4 years	Middle Childhood 5 to 12 years	Adolescence 12 to 18 years	Adulthood 18 years +
Height	One month after conception: 1 inch in length 3 mo.: 3 in. 4 mo.: 6 in. 5 mo.: 12 in. 6 mo.: 14 in. 7 mo.: 16 in.	Birth: 21 inches Increase by .10 inch in first year	Increase by 5 inches in second year; 2½ inches in third year, etc.	Increase by 5 percent to 6 percent per year	Increase by 10 to 12 percent per year during early adolescence Males complete 98 percent of growth in height by age 16, females by age 14	Maximum height attained by age 20 Slight decrease in height (½ to 1 inch) in late 50s and 60s
Weight	3 mo.: 1 oz. 4 mo.: 4 oz. 5 mo.: 1 lb. 6 mo.: 2 lb. 7 mo.: 3 lb.	Birth: 7½ pound Weight doubles by 5 months; triples by end of first year	Age 2: 7- to 8-pound increase Age 3: 3- to 4-pound increase	Increase by 10 percent per year	Increase by 20 percent per year during early adolescence	Weight gain slows down in early adulthood Slight but steady increase from age 18 to age 65 followed by a gradual decrease

Source: Bischof 1976; Hamill, Drizd, Johnson, Reed & Roche 1977; Kent 1976; Tanner 1970, 1978; Tortora & Anagnostakos 1984; Troll 1982.

same in an adult who was six feet tall, that person's head would measure approximately eighteen inches in length (about twice the normal size). Not only is the head of an infant proportionately larger than that of an adult, but the arms and legs are proportionately shorter, and the legs have more of a curved appearance. Interestingly, the disproportionate physical features of young infants may make them attractive to older members of their species. Konrad Lorenz (1970), the noted ethologist, proposed that the young of a species manifest *babyishness*—a large head with large forehead, large and widely spaced eyes, small nose, small chin, and round face (see Figure 4.3). These features are appealing to adults and elicit from them desires to cuddle and nurture the baby (Nash & Feldman 1981).

A typical 2-year-old has a disproportionately large head; short arms; and short, bowed legs. The shoulders are sloped rather than squared, the waistline does not seem to exist, and the abdomen protrudes. The same child at age 6 has changed dramatically to the point of resembling a small adult. The legs have stretched considerably, and—compared with the child's overall height—they are both longer and straighter. When 6-year-olds sit in adult chairs, their feet may not touch the floor yet, but they no longer stick out as a toddler's do. The arms are longer, too, and the 6-year-old may reach and climb more efficiently than a younger child. The abdomen is flat, the waistline has made its appearance, and the ribs may have begun to show. The shoulders are now more square than round, and the height increase is a result of growth in the legs and trunk more than of growth in the head (Lowrey 1973).

Finally, look at the same child at puberty. Much of the gawky appearance of many adolescents stems from differential growth spurts of various parts of the body. There has been growth in

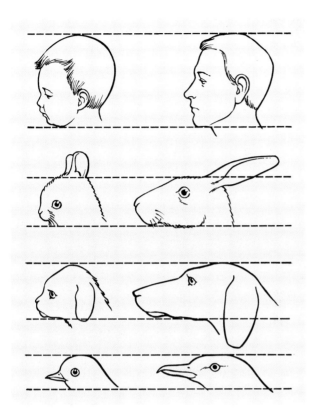

Figure 4.3 Babyishness

The babyishness features of the young have common features across species and are appealing to older members of the same species (or across species).
Source: From Lorenz, K. (1935) *Studies in Animal Behavior* (translated by R. Martin) London: Methuen Press. Reprinted by permission of the publisher.

all parts of the body since age 6, but proportionately more in the legs than in the torso or head. During the adolescent growth spurt, the hands and the feet undergo rapid growth, which leads—for a time—to disproportionately large hands and feet. The shoulders have widened in proportion to the rest of the body, and in the female there is disproportionate widening of the hips. The face has changed in appearance, too. More growth has occurred in the lower part of the face than in the upper. The jawbone has lengthened and thickened, and it protrudes forward more than it did in childhood. The chin is more prominent; the nose larger proportionately; and the profile straighter (Katchadourian 1977).

Motor Development

Many of the earliest developmental milestones involve aspects of motor development—the development of the ability to move the body. The first attempts to sit up, crawl, and walk are memorable events for parents, for they present concrete evidence that their baby is becoming independent, and is following a normal course of developmental events. For these reasons motor development was the focal point of some of the early developmental research that was carried out in the 1930s by Arnold Gesell, Myrtle McGraw, and Mary Shirley (see Chapter 1). One of the most important findings of such research was that motor development follows a cephalocaudal-proximodistal pattern.

Motor development typically is broken into gross-motor development (involving behaviors such as sitting, crawling, standing, and walking) and fine-motor development (involving the ability to grasp objects with the hands and to smoothly move the fingers for prehension and manipulation). Milestones for motor development appear in Table 4.2. This section examines in detail the ontogeny of one gross-motor milestone (walking) and one fine-motor developmental milestone (prehension).

Walking

In a symbolic sense, children reflect human history when they go from walking on all fours to walking erect on two legs (Thelen 1984). The onset of walking indicates the soundness of the central nervous system and has a significant impact upon the social and cognitive development of the infant. McGraw (1945) believed that the development of locomotion served as a model of the maturation of the motor cortex. In her pioneering research, McGraw proposed seven major phases in the achievement of erect locomotion (see Figure 4.4). Each progressive phase in this cephalocaudal progression reflects further neuromuscular maturation:

• *Phase A: The Newborn or Reflex Stepping:* When supported by an adult, the infant will make rhythmical stepping movements that are independent of head and body movements.

Table 4.2   Locomotor Development in Infancy

Age	Head Control	Prehension	Sitting	Walking
Newborn	Head balanced (.1 mo.) Head erect, vertical for 3 seconds or more (.8 mo.)			
1 month	Head erect and steady for 15 seconds (1.6 mo.)			
2 months	Head erect and steady when infant is carried around (2.5 mo.)		Sits with support (2.3 mo.)	
3 months		Fingers in opposition to palm; thumb not used (3.7 mo.)	Sits with only slight support (3.8 mo.)	
4 months	Head balanced (4.2 mo.)	Partial opposition of thumb and fingers (4.9 mo.)		
5 months			Sits alone momentarily (5.3 mo.)	
6 months		Complete thumb opposition (6.9 mo.)	Sits alone 30 seconds or more (6 mo.) Sits alone steadily (6.6 mo.) Sits alone; good coordination (6.9 mo.)	
7 months		Poorly developed pincer grasp—thumb and index finger (7.4 mo.)		Makes early stepping movements (7.4 mo.)
8 months		Neat pincer grasp (8.9 mo.)		Makes stepping movements (8.8 mo.)
9 months				Walks with help (9.6 mo.)
10 months				Sits down (9.6 mo.)
11 months				Walks alone (11.7 mo.)
12 months				
13 months				
14 months +				Walks backward (14.5 mo.) Walks upstairs with help (16 mo.)

(Norms from Bayley, N. (1969). *The Bayley scales of infant development.* New York: The Psychological Corporation.

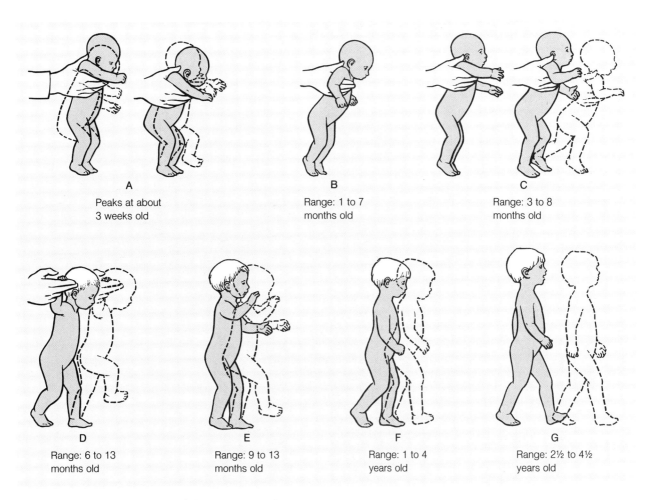

A
Peaks at about
3 weeks old

B
Range: 1 to 7
months old

C
Range: 3 to 8
months old

D
Range: 6 to 13
months old

E
Range: 9 to 13
months old

F
Range: 1 to 4
years old

G
Range: 2½ to 4½
years old

Figure 4.4   Seven Phases of Erect Locomotion

Source: From McGraw, M. (1945) *The neuromuscular maturation of the human infant.*
New York: Columbia University Press. Reprinted by permission of the publisher.

- *Phase B: Inhibition:* The stepping reflex ceases at this time. The feet appear as if they are "glued to the floor." However, the baby's posture and head control are greatly improved.
- *Phase C: Transition:* The baby's activity increases. He or she will often bounce up and down, or stand in place and stamp, as if to practice the stepping movements without propelling the body forward.
- *Phase D: Deliberate Stepping:* The baby will engage in deliberate stepping actions when supported by an adult.
- *Phase E: Independent Stepping:* The baby takes the first independent steps. This early toddling is characterized by a large distance between the feet, arms extended for balance, legs lifted high with each step, and jumpy and isolated movements.

- *Phase F: Heel-Toe Progression:* The toddler's gait becomes better coordinated, as the legs move closer together, the steps are less exaggerated, and the feet move from heel-to-toe.
- *Phase G: Integration:* Finally, the child walks more like an adult, with arms moving in synchrony with the legs.

The inhibition phase of walking presents a particularly challenging problem to the study of motor development. Is the disappearance of co-ordinated stepping a sign of regression? Or, as McGraw suggested, does it reflect maturation and reorganization of cortical centers of the brain? If

Issues in Child Development

Are Children Growing Up Faster Than Their Parents Did?

A U.S. girl in 1985 probably had her first menstrual period between the ages of 12½ and 13. A U.S. female born in 1910 first experienced menstruation at age 14, and data from several European countries indicate that girls in the nineteenth century did not begin to menstruate until they were 15½ to 17½ (Malina 1979; Tanner 1962). A similar pattern has been observed in the timing of puberty among boys.

Not only do children reach puberty faster than they did 150 years ago, but also each generation has tended to be taller by approximately an inch and heavier than the generation that preceded it. This phenomenon of advanced development is known as the **secular trend** (Roche 1979; Tanner 1962, 1978).

Two observations should be made about the secular trend. First, it has not been occurring throughout recorded history: as far as can be determined, children from ancient times up through the Middle Ages matured at the same rate as children do today and potentially could reach the same adult stature; puberty appears to have been delayed only in the nineteenth century (Malina 1979). It is in the past 150 years that an acceleration in rate of maturation has been no-

ticed. Furthermore, the increase in *rate* is more pronounced than final adult measurement. Second, the trend appears to be slowing down in recent generations, or even coming to a complete stop. Fortunately, children are not getting indefinitely taller and reaching puberty indefinitely earlier.

What are the reasons for the secular trend across the last 150 years? A number of reasons have been cited: improved nutrition, improved environmental circumstances, reduced family size, urbanization, and the fact that genes for height seem to be dominant over genes for shortness. When a person from a tall family marries a person from a short one, the children tend slightly toward the taller side rather than being halfway in between (Malina 1979; Tanner 1978).

---

the inhibition phase of walking is necessary for the achievement of erect locomotion, any interference with this phase may be an impediment to walking. But, Zelazo (1976) found that when infants were given daily practice in the stepping reflex, they increased the number of steps per minute and actually walked earlier than control groups. Additionally, the work of Thelen (1984, 1986) suggests that the stepping reflex does not really disappear. Rather, the kicking movements that infants make when on their backs are strikingly similar to their stepping movements. Infants find it easier to "walk" lying on their backs because fat is rapidly depositing in their legs, making them too heavy for the infants to lift. Thus, when Thelen (1986) supported 7-month-old infants on a treadmill, they immediately made alternating stepping movements closely resembling mature walking. When

infants are continually given practice in stepping, the exercise increases muscular strength so that their legs can support and balance their bodies when walking. Perhaps the next step in this research is to determine whether or not babies who are vigorous and frequent kickers also are early walkers.

Prehension

Fine-motor coordination also follows a regular developmental pattern. A newborn infant moves both arms and both legs when stimulated, but gradually the movements become more localized: the forearm moves independently; then the wrist is rotated; and, eventually, the individual fingers are separately controlled. The grasp reflex is

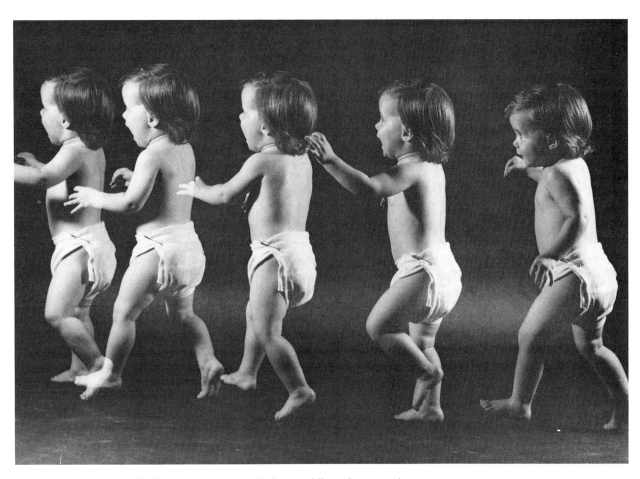

A sequential photograph of the movement made by a toddler when running.

present at birth (see Chapter 3). Using their power-ful neonatal grip, newborns can support their own weight by hanging from a rod with both hands. The grasp reflex is replaced by voluntary prehen-sion. By the age of just under 4 months, on the average, an infant can grasp an object by "clamp-ing" it between the palm and the four fingers, which seem to function as one unit (the thumb is not yet used effectively). By 7 months there is com-plete opposition between the thumb and the other fingers (when the infant grasps) and by 9 months the fingers seem to operate independently, as when the infant uses the thumb and forefinger (the pincer grasp) to pick up small objects (Bayley 1969).

Also significant to prehension is the devel-opment of visually guided reading, or the ability

to grasp what is seen. As in walking, reaching and grasping have significant implications for the evo-lution of human life. The reaching for an object occurs during the newborn period when the in-fant's eyes are fixated on the object. Such reaching usually takes the form of a crude hand swipe that is in the general direction of the object; rarely is the neonate successful at grasping (Rosenblith & Sims-Knight 1985). Because the newborn appar-ently does not adjust reaching and grasping to the properties of the object, this movement is called **visually initiated reaching.** Such reaching has an automatic quality, suggesting that it is biologically triggered by a visual stimulus.

Parallel to other motoric milestones, this new-born form of reaching ceases at about 2 to 3 months of age. It is replaced by a more intentional form of

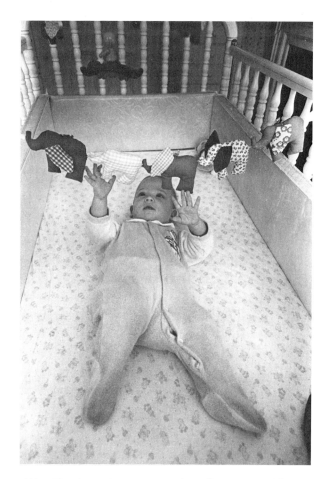

Attractive toys strung across the crib encourage the infant to grasp the object that he sees. This movement is known as visually guided reaching.

reaching that uses the feedback obtained from the object. This behavior, known as **visually guided reaching,** is assumed to reflect maturation of the motor cortex, but can be affected by practice and experience. When babies are given opportunities to practice reaching and grasping, visually initiated reaching persists and forms the basis of the behaviors seen in visually guided reaching (Bower 1982). Additionally, institutionalized babies who were moderately deprived of social and visual stimulation made rapid progress in visually guided reaching when they were given the opportunity to swipe at objects attached to the sides of their cribs (White 1971).

Later Motor Development

Motor development does not end with infancy and toddlerhood. During the preschool period a number of gross-motor skills become central to social play. For example, skills with playground balls—throwing, catching, and kicking—appear during the preschool years and continue to gain in importance in the play of elementary school children. Climbing, jumping, and running are favorite activities of 4- and 5-year-olds. Hopping is a slower achievement, although by age 6 or 7 most children are fairly adept at this activity (Cratty 1974). Skipping—the ability to step and hop in sustained tempo, using one side of the body, and then the other—is optimally acquired by age 6. All of these behaviors signify further neurological maturation and integration during childhood. Their onset may indicate that the child is ready to handle some of the cognitive and social demands expected of school-aged children. Thus, the appearance of skipping in kindergarten has been positively related to school achievement in first grade (Robeck 1978).

Motor development in children from the ages of 6 to 12 has been described by Cratty (1970). Selected behaviors described by Cratty can be found in Table 4.3. Drawing and writing are two fine-motor skills developed during childhood. Manual dexterity—such as that required for typing, playing the piano, or tying a knot—is not maximized until adolescence. With respect to gross-motor development, boys are superior to girls in forceful acts of the hands and arms (such as throwing a ball) and in acts of the legs (such as running or jumping). Girls, in contrast, are superior to boys in motor activities requiring rhythm and accuracy, such as hopscotch and ball-bouncing games. Significantly, during these years both sexes can learn how to swim, ski, and skate—motor activities not typically acquired through spontaneous locomotion.

Adolescence brings with it an increase in body movement speed, as well as an increase in motor coordination.

There is gradual improvement in balance and agility, and in motor skills such as running and jumping. Reaction time (the time required to respond to unexpected stimuli) improves until approximately the ages of 18 to 20. Sex differences

Table 4.3 Selected Locomotor Behaviors in Elementary School Children

Age	Selected Behaviors
6 years	Girls superior in movement accuracy; boys superior in forceful, less complex acts Skipping acquired Throwing with proper weight shift and step
7 years	One-footed balancing without vision possible Can walk 2 inch-wide balance beams Can hop and jump accurately into small squares Can execute accurate jumping-jack exercise
8 years	12-pound pressure on grip strength by both sexes Number of games participated in by both sexes greatest at this age Can engage in alternate rhythmical hopping in 2-2, 2-3, or 3-3 pattern
9 years	Girls can throw a small ball 40 feet Girls can vertical jump 8½ inches and boys 10 inches over their standing height-plus-reach Boys can run 16½ feet per second
10 years	Boys can throw a small ball 70 feet Can judge and intercept pathways of small balls thrown from a distance Girls can run 17 feet per second
11 years	Standing broad jump of 5 feet possible for boys—6 inches less for girls
12 years	Standing high jump of 3 feet possible.

Source: Cratty, B.J. *Perceptual and motor development in infants and children* (1st ed.). New York: Macmillan, 1970, pp. 212–13. Reprinted by permission.

are found in motor performances and in motor coordination, with boys superior to girls, but there are no noticeable sex differences in reaction time (Tanner 1962).

The study of motor development provides many examples of how all spheres of development are influenced by the movement of the body. Social development is affected by the ability to crawl after people, or to bounce a ball with peers. Cognitive development is enhanced by the ability to reach out for objects and to manipulate, combine, and rearrange them. Finally, the sheer exuberance of having mastery over the body has profound implications for the budding of an integrated personality, or the sense of autonomy, initiative, and industry (Erikson 1968). In the Problems in Child Development feature, observations on how blind babies respond to increased opportunities for movement underscore these points.

Individual Variation in Growth

The major focus of this chapter has been on the regularities of physical development, such as those observed in the typical patterns of growth. However, dramatic individual differences occur both in the rate of growth and in overall physical appearance—differences accounted for by hereditary factors and by variations in the environment (Tanner 1978). This section will first examine the numerous physical changes that occur during adolescence. It will then focus on the differences in the rate of human growth and the psychological impact of these differences, which is particularly apparent during adolescence. Finally, the section looks at body satisfaction and body image—the reaction of individuals to the recognition that their bodies are different from those of other people.

The Physical Changes of Puberty

For the most part, growth is fairly steady during the childhood years. For example, most children have lost the "baby fat" of infancy, the heart and lungs increase steadily, the calcium deposits in bone tissue increase, and the digestive system stabilizes so that the number of upset stomaches decrease.

During puberty, however, the physical changes are so profound that virtually every tissue in the body is affected (Katchadourian 1977). For example, there is a remarkable acceleration in the growth of the skeletal system, leading to what is known as the adolescent growth spurt. The dramatic growth observed in adolescents is due to the rate at which adult height is attained. For boys, at the time of their peak growth rate, 3 to 5 inches are added to their height in one year; for girls, 2½ to 4½ inches (Tanner 1970). This rate of growth approximates the growth rate of a 2-year-old. The skeletal structure also changes so that boys acquire

Problems in Child Development

How Sonic Aids Facilitate Motor Development in Blind Children

Blind children raise their heads and chests, sit, roll over, and stand at about the same time as do sighted children. However, several motor milestones, such as reaching and walking, are significantly delayed because the sight of attractive objects (a major incentive for walking) is absent for blind children (Fraiberg 1977).

For several years, T.G.R. Bower and his associates have been experimenting with a sonic device based upon the principles of echolocation observed in bats.

Worn about the head, the device emits sounds that are reflected back by objects in the environment. Besides locating objects, the echoes transmit information about objects in the environment. For example, a loud sound indicates the object is large; a quiet sound indicates the object is small. A low pitch indicates an object is near; a high pitch indicates it is further away.

When such devices are worn by blind adults, it takes months, or even years, of intense training to learn how to effectively translate the signals. However, infants make rapid progress; the youngest infants in a study by Aitken and Bower (1982) began to immediately transpose the auditory signals into information about the visual world, a feat of rapid intersensory coordination that apparently is lost in adulthood.

Equally impressive was the impact of the sonic device upon the motoric development of the children. The youngest subject in Aitken and Bower's study, AN, was given the aid at 6 months of age. AN began reaching with both hands at 7 months, crawling at 14 months, and walking at 16 months. Thus, her motor milestones were on a sighted, rather than on a blind, schedule. Whereas older infants did not make as rapid progress as AN, the reactions described in Bower's research are noteworthy:

> They begin reaching for objects; they become fascinated with moving their own hands in front of them (a behavior analogous to the visual-hand regard seen so commonly in sighted infants); and older ones even go through doorways without mistakes. All of this is accompanied by great joy—as if the infants themselves were grasping the miraculous nature of it all. (Acredelo & Hake 1982, 276).

a more or less V-shaped physique, with broad shoulders and narrower hips. A girl's hips develop more rapidly than other areas so that she acquires the typical female shape, with hips wider than shoulders (Tanner 1978).

Another pubertal change is in the composition of muscle and body fat. Males are more muscular and stronger than females at all ages, but the differences are hardly noticeable until puberty, when the increase in testosterone leads to a more dramatic spurt in muscle development for boys than for girls. Additionally, as puberty approaches, a spurt in fat growth occurs approximately one year after the beginning of the height spurt. Because of the influence of the female sex hormone estrogen,

the fat layer continues to grow rapidly in girls, but not in boys. Thus, boys actually show a decrease in thickness of the fat layer and are likely to consider themselves as "too thin"; girls during puberty worry that they are "too heavy" (Clifford 1971; Frazier & Lisonbee 1950).

The physical changes during adolescence also involve the internal organs. During the adolescent years the heart doubles in size, and in young adulthood the circulatory system is at its peak efficiency. There is an increase in the size of the lungs and *vital capacity* (the amount of air exhaled from the lungs after a person has taken the deepest breath possible). Such changes lead to increased strength

With adolescence comes an increase in the trainability of the muscles. Lifting weights can dramatically effect muscle size and strength after puberty.

and endurance, particularly for adolescent males. For both sexes, puberty brings an increase in physical prowess; movement of the body brings with it an exuberance and effortlessness that many adults, with great effort, strive to attain.

Without a doubt, the most dramatic changes of puberty involve the development of the reproductive organs and the appearance of secondary sex characteristics. The internal reproductive organs enlarge and change shape for both boys and girls. Girls experience a surge in hormones (such as *follicle-stimulating hormone*) that leads to the first

menstrual bleeding, called the **menarche**. For boys, the increase in testosterone leads to sperm production; the first ejaculation is experienced during puberty.

The increase in hormone production leads to a variety of changes for males and females. For girls, puberty is accompanied by breast development, pubic hair, smooth and hairless skin, and widening of the hips. For boys, the shoulders widen, facial and body hair appears, the voice deepens, and muscles enlarge.

The great number of physical changes have immense psychological consequences (Katchadourian 1977). For one, the child is transformed into an adult, both in terms of physical appearance and reproductive capacity. Additionally, physical differences between males and females are greatly enhanced. Finally, as will be discussed in the following sections, the *timing* of all of these pubertal events is most significant for the socioemotional development of the adolescent.

Diversity in Childhood and Adolescence

Nowhere is the difference in the rate of human growth more evident than in the junior high school classroom. A group of 12- or 13-year-olds will contain some children who have reached puberty and look like full-grown adults, as well as some children who are small and childlike in every respect. When the physical changes of puberty were discussed earlier, the age at which these changes occur was not mentioned. There is a good reason for this: the age of puberty varies from one child to the next.

For boys, the height spurt may begin as early as age 10½ or as late as age 16; it may end by age 13 or as late as age 17½. A boy's testes may begin to enlarge as early as 9½ or as late as 13½, with penile growth occurring a year later. The other changes of puberty occur in a fairly regular progression after the initial growth of testes and scrotum. What, then, does a particular boy of 14 look like? On the one hand, he may resemble a child. His testes may have begun to develop, but there may be no other signs of puberty. On the other hand, he may have completed his height spurt,

What is the age range of these children? They are all eleven years old, despite the considerable variation in size.

and his genitals may resemble those of an adult. His voice may have changed, he may be shaving daily, and his strength and stamina may be closer to that of an adult than of a child. Figure 4.5 contains drawings of three 14-year-old boys, all of whom are at different levels of maturity.

A girl can have her first period as early as 10½ or as late as 15½. Her breasts may begin to develop as early as age 8 or as late as age 13. A similar range of five years marks the beginning of the height spurt. As is the case with boys, there is a time in the development of girls when some may not have

reached puberty and others have already completed the process. Figure 4.5 also shows three girls of exactly the same age (12 years) but at very different points in the process of physical maturation. Figure 4.5 also illustrates the gender differences in growth rate referred to in this chapter. Girls reach puberty 1½ to 2 years earlier than boys.

Virtually everyone reaches puberty within the ranges outlined in the diagram, and most people are somewhere in the middle of the range. However, within the total population, some people mature very early—at the beginning of the range—and some mature at the very end.

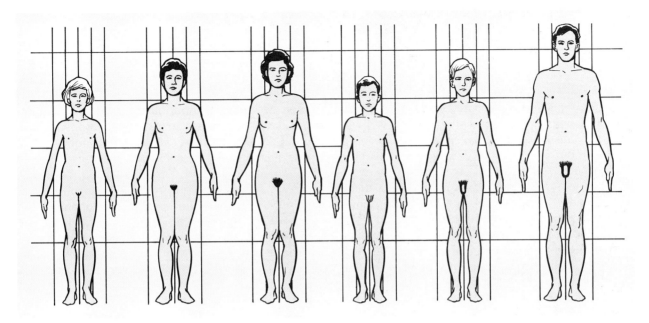

Figure 4.5   Three 14-Year-Old Boys and Three 12-Year-Old Girls at Different Stages of Puberty.

Source: From "Growing Up" by J.M. Tanner. Copyright by *Scientific American, Inc.* All rights reserved.

Early Versus Late Maturation

There are advantages and disadvantages associated with the extremes of early and late maturity. These will be discussed first for early maturers and then for those who reach puberty late. Most of these findings are taken from an extensive longitudinal study of adolescents carried out at the University of California from the late 1930s to the late 1950s (Jones 1938; Jones 1957; Jones & Bayley 1950; Jones & Mussen 1958).

The early-maturing girl is in a singular position. She is taller, heavier, and more womanly in appearance than her peers, so she is more conspicuous. She has an athletic advantage over the other girls in her class, and this may be beneficial if involvement in sports is valued for girls in her class or in her social circle. She will have a stronger sense of her own femininity than does the girl who has not yet reached puberty (Rierdan & Koff 1980). Because she looks older and more attractive than her peers, she is more likely to be approached for

dates. She may not actually begin dating earlier than other girls, because chronological age is a better predictor of the beginning of dating than is level of sexual maturity (Dornbusch et al. 1981). However, she may date more often, have earlier sexual experiences, have more sexual partners, and marry earlier than the late-maturing girl.

The early-maturing boy will have an even greater athletic advantage over his peers than does the early-maturing girl, because the pubertal change in strength and stamina is more dramatic for boys than for girls. Besides being bigger and stronger than he was, the postpubescent boy can also run faster, jump higher, and play harder and longer than he could before. Like the early-maturing girl, the early-maturing boy will be more attractive to the opposite sex. He, too, will have more dating opportunities, earlier sexual experiences, and more partners than the late maturer. Despite such advantages, there is some evidence linking early maturity in males to deviant behavior (Duncan et al. 1985).

The early maturer of both sexes is more likely than the late maturer to have social experiences that encourage emotional maturity. For example, because they look older, early maturers might be entrusted with more responsibility by adults and be regarded as more competent by peers. Thus, they might become more assertive in social situations (Steinberg 1981).

In some ways, however, the early-developing female in our culture is not nearly as fortunate as the early-developing male. The womanly figure of a young adolescent girl may be an embarrassment to her; indeed, early-developing girls often have poor self-concepts and body images (Peskin 1973; Tobin-Richards, Boxer & Petersen 1984). By contrast, the early-developing boy usually is blessed with the ideal male physique. We might also wonder if the natural athletic advantage of the early developer is as valued a feature in a girl as it is in a boy, since boys are more likely than girls to link athletics with social success (Eitzen 1975; Rice 1984). Finally, the sexual advantage of the early developer may elevate a boy in the esteem of his peers but may only tarnish a girl's reputation in a society still uncertain about the value of female sexuality (Faunce & Phipps-Yonas 1979).

The late-maturing girl is likely to suffer anxiety about her appearance. Boys will not swarm around her as they might her early-maturing classmate, and she may worry that she is not feminine enough. She is generally less mature in her heterosexual interests. Dating, dancing, wearing makeup, and dressing to attract boys may appeal to her less than these activities appeal to her age-mates. Indeed, the late-maturing girl may still be playing children's games and cherishing her dolls while many of her classmates are preparing for their first dates.

The late-maturing boy is less physically attractive than other boys, less well groomed, less athletic, and less likely to be a leader. He has a great need for attention and approval from others, and he may try hard to get that attention in socially unacceptable ways. For example, he may become disruptive in school, or he may become the class clown. He may have difficulty dealing with authority figures such as parents and teachers, and he may be rebellious and hostile, perhaps directing toward other people the hostility he feels toward himself.

It is difficult to say, when comparing early- and late-maturing girls, which of them is in the advantaged position. Many women looking back on their adolescent years are grateful for their lack of beauty and lack of popularity because—not having dates to occupy their lives—they developed other interests. Many adolescent beauties grow into women who feel that their physical charms did them more harm than good when they were young. Indeed, the girl in the ideal position may be neither the early nor the late developer, but the one who is right "on time." In a recent study, the girl whose development was in step with that of her age-mates had the most positive self-concept; the late developer was second; and the early developer last (Tobin-Richards, Boxer & Petersen 1984).

There is no doubt that early-maturing boys have a tremendous advantage over late maturers. It is interesting, and perhaps not surprising, to note that the effects of late maturity—the feeling of inadequacy, the need for approval, and the dependency—can still be found in males of college age (Weatherly 1964) and even in men approaching middle adulthood (Jones 1957). For women, any personality differences all but disappear by the end of adolescence.

It is important to recognize that many variables—other than pubertal timing—affect adolescent adjustment. The results of some studies depend on how timing of puberty is measured. For example, many pubertal changes occur over a period of time. The adolescent growth spurt, often used as an index of pubertal status, is not a discrete stage, but rather a continuous event (Brooks-Gunn, Petersen & Eichorn 1985). Judgment on early versus late maturity may differ depending on whether the determination of pubertal status involves bone X rays, onset of menarche, growth of pubic hair, or penile or breast development (Brooks-Gunn, Petersen & Eichorn 1985). Finally, a number of measures in such research have found no effects due to pubertal status. School truancy, adjustment, popularity, need for discipline, and grade repetition were not related to pubertal status in one recent study (Duncan et al. 1985); grade effects were

How we view our bodies—our body image—has significant consequences for our self-esteem. Adolescence is a time at which body image is of central concern.

more apparent in school achievement, family relations, peer relations, body image, and psychopathology in another (Petersen & Crockett 1985).

Psychological Impact of Growth

As the earlier discussion of the timing of sexual maturation illustrated, it is difficult to discuss physical development without also examining the psychological correlates of growth. In fact, a definite relationship exists between the perception people have of their bodies—the **body image**—and the perception they have of themselves as a

whole. (See Applying Our Knowledge "Learning to Value One's Body" for suggestions on how educators can help adolescents develop a healthy body image.) Our body image is strongly influenced by cultural standards of what is considered to be the ideal body. For example, U.S. males generally want to be tall (about six feet in height), with a large frame, large muscles, and an ideal weight of about 180 to 200 pounds (Gunderson 1965).

Females place facial attractiveness much higher on their list of desired physical characteristics than men do. In addition, women would like to have relatively small frames. Research with adolescents (Frazier & Lisonbee 1950) and adults (Berscheid, Walster & Bohrnstedt 1973) indicates that females worry more about being overweight than males do, and that women are more likely to be dissatisfied with the (large) size of their abdomen, hips, buttocks, and thighs than men are.

As early as 1890, a link between body image and self-esteem was observed (James 1968). People with a positive body image are more likely than those with average or poor body images to see themselves as above average in likeability, intelligence, and assertiveness (Berscheid, Walster & Bohrnstedt 1973; Jourard & Secord 1955). Consider the comments made by respondents to a body-image survey: "If I had been plain instead of pretty, I would be a much weaker and sadder person" and "My body gets more and more pleasing as I grow more self-assured and begin to like myself more" (Berscheid, Walster & Bohrnstedt 1973, 126).

Other indications of a link between body image and self-esteem can be found in the previously mentioned studies of early- and late-maturing adolescents. Late-maturing adolescent boys, who generally are lower in body satisfaction than their earlier-maturing peers, also have been found to be less emotionally and heterosexually mature, more restless, more anxious, higher in need of attention and approval from others, lower in self-confidence, less likely to be assertive or to take leadership positions, more dependent, and more rebellious (Dwyer & Mayer 1968–1969; Mussen & Bouterline-Young 1964; Weatherly 1964). Recent evidence suggests that early-maturing boys are most satisfied with their height and weight and early-maturing girls are most dissatisfied with their weight (Duncan et al. 1985).

Applying Our Knowledge

Learning to Value One's Body

One of the major developmental tasks of adolescents according to psychologist Robert Havighurst (1972), is to accept their own physique and to learn to use their bodies effectively. For many adolescents—especially those whose bodies deviate significantly from the "ideal" physique—such acceptance may be difficult to achieve. For this reason, Havighurst and others have suggested that schools might assist the adolescent who has a poorly developed body image. Educators might incorporate some of the following suggestions into their curricula:

• In grouping students for physical education classes, use criteria of physical development rather than chronological age. Late developers would then compete with other late developers and would have an opportunity to experience success in athletic competition instead of failing constantly or merely keeping the bench warm.

• In biology classes, teach children about human physical development, with particular emphasis on physical variation.

• Encourage children to understand and appreciate the capabilities of the human body by offering coursework in body movement (for example, dancing and pantomime) as well as in drawing, with emphasis on the human form. Body movement can be incorporated into virtually every academic subject, from the arts to the natural sciences to the social sciences (Werner & Burton 1979).

• Become the kind of teacher from whom students will seek information and advice with respect to their own physical development. Perhaps this role is a difficult one for many adults to assume; a student will seek advice from teachers who are sensitive, knowledgeable, and respectful of the seriousness of the child's feelings. Responses such as "What are you worried about? You'll grow out of it" may indicate a lack of awareness of how deeply disturbing children's anxieties about their physical development can be. It is also important that teachers not permit nicknames based on physical traits to be used in their classrooms (Woolfolk 1987).

• Accept the inevitable (Woolfolk 1987). Adolescents will spend what adults consider to be a disproportionate amount of time on their appearance. By allowing students to spend a few minutes at the end of class to adjust their appearance or by incorporating issues of appearance into curriculum-related materials, educators will show that they understand their students' concerns about body image.

Physical Attractiveness and Social Desirability

To what extent does physical attractiveness influence our choice of friends? It is unlikely that we consciously exclude unattractive people from our circle of friends and instead actively seek out the best-looking physical specimens. However, whether we are aware of it or not, we do rely on physical criteria to some degree, as suggested in the literature on the characteristics required for popularity. At all age levels,

• in childhood (Cavior & Dokecki 1969, 1970; Dion 1977; Kleck, Richardson & Ronald 1974; Krieger & Wells 1969),

• in adolescence (Cavior & Dokecki 1973; Coleman 1961; Gronlund & Anderson 1957), and

• in adulthood (Byrne, Ervin & Lamberth 1970; Coombs & Kenkel 1966; Goldman & Lewis 1977; Smits & Cherhoniak 1976)

physically attractive people have a better chance at being popular than do unattractive people. Physical attractiveness—or in males, athletic prowess—is close to the top of every list of socially desirable characteristics.

Adult standards of physical attractiveness are established very early in childhood. When asked to select the most attractive individuals from among a group of facial photographs, children between the ages of 3 and 5 adhered closely to adult choices (Dion 1973). Children also view the mesomorphic (muscular) body build as more desirable than the ectomorphic (thin) or endomorphic (rounded) body builds (Staffieri 1967). In fact, children seem to avoid obese peers (Asher, Oden & Gottman 1977).

It has been found that physically attractive children, in addition to being popular with peers, score significantly higher than others in school achievement, as indicated by report card grades (Salvia, Algozyne & Sheare 1977) and teacher ratings (Clifford 1975). In one study (Rich 1975) teachers saw physically attractive children as having more desirable personality traits than unattractive children, and the less attractive child was criticized more for misbehavior than was the attractive one. Furthermore, the evidence suggests that physically attractive children actually have more positive interactions with their teachers than do unattractive children (Algozzine 1977).

Various studies show that good-looking children are perceived as more pleasant, more approachable, more achievement-oriented, and more desirable as friends than are unattractive children. How can this be interpreted? On the one hand, we might conclude that people in our society choose their friends and acquaintances for very superficial reasons and that we care more about physical characteristics than we do about personality. However, another explanation is possible.

It may be that because attractive people grow up with more attention from others and more social interaction than do unattractive people, the pretty and the handsome develop more sophisticated social skills. Parents of attractive babies have more positive attitudes toward their newborns than parents of unattractive babies, and such positive attitudes and high expectations persist during childhood (Hartup 1983). The expectation of "beauty-as-good" may lead to a self-fulfilling prophecy. Then, to complete the cycle, attractive children are not preferred for their beauty alone, but because they really *are* more personable. Perhaps they are more self-confident and more secure in dealing with others, as well as being more experienced, and this gives them social skills that less attractive people do not have.

The link between body image and overall self-concept is correlational and not necessarily causal.

That is, although we know there is a relationship between body image and self-esteem, we do not know which one causes the other. Does having an attractive body raise a person to self-esteem and self-confidence? Or does having a self-confident outlook on life cause a person to feel that his or her body is attractive, no matter what it really looks like? Clearly, it is difficult for us to form a truly objective opinion about our physical appearance, and our opinion is probably influenced to some extent by our overall self-esteem.

Environmental Influences on Physical Development

Thus far the role of biological timetables in physical development has been emphasized. Our genetic code sets the upper limit for the expression of physical (and, possibly, psychological) characteristics, as well as the schedules for their appearance and/or disappearance. Early research in physical development assumed that the biological timetable was the dominant factor in motor development. To support this hypothesis, Myrtle McGraw (1935) used the co-twin method. In McGraw's research, one identical twin would receive training in a skill such as stair climbing, while the other twin would not. McGraw found that practice was not the significant factor in acquiring a motor skill; the identical twin eventually caught up to his or her sibling.

Since McGraw's early work, it has become apparent that physical and motoric maturation is not entirely determined by biological factors. The environment is now also acknowledged as a significant factor in physical growth and development. Biological predispositions either flourish or fail to approach their potential within an environmental context. Nutrition and exercise, which will be considered in this final section, are examples of environmental factors that influence the growth process.

Nutrition

Everybody needs protein, carbohydrates, fats, water, minerals, and vitamins to maintain health. Proper nutrition ensures that the body has

Ethiopian victims of famine.

the material to sustain life as well as to repair injuries. The proportions of nutrients, however, vary across the life cycle. In periods of peak growth—infancy, adolescence, and during pregnancy—nutritional demands are greatest.

Infants, of course, receive their initial nutritional requirements through breast milk or formula. With maturity of the digestive system, eruption of teeth, and greater caloric requirements, infants gradually are introduced to solid foods. Milk consumption declines as solids are introduced, but it remains a significant source of calcium and protein throughout the early childhood years.

Caloric requirements continue to increase throughout the childhood years. Good nutrition continues to mean a daily sampling from each of the basic food groups.

Anyone who has ever witnessed the overflowing shopping carts of families with adolescent children knows that the need for food increases even more during adolescence. In fact, in absolute terms, the need for food is greatest during puberty (Katchadourian 1977). These caloric requirements exceed those needed by infants and nursing mothers. For girls, the greatest need for food occurs between the ages of 12 and 15 (around menarche). For boys, the peak caloric requirements occur between 14 and 17 years, coinciding with the male growth spurt (Katchadourian 1977).

The Effects of Malnutrition

Severe malnutrition in children is relatively rare in the United States. In poor and underdeveloped countries of Africa, Asia, and Latin America, inadequate diets are more common. One severe form of malnutrition is due to an insufficient amount of protein and calories in the diet (Ricciuti 1980). Two conditions may result from severe protein-calorie deprivation. The first is **nutritional marasmus,** literally meaning "wasting away," or starvation. Marasmus typically begins during the first few months of life and continues for an indefinite time. It can lead to serious retardation in physical growth and motor development and poor performance on intelligence and perceptual/cognitive tasks. At 5 or 6 months of age, such children may have body weights not much different from their birthweights, and at 10 months they may weigh as little as a normal 1-month-old (Ricciuti 1980).

Kwashiorkor is another form of severe malnutrition that results from a diet lacking in protein, but not in calories. In developing countries, kwashiorkor becomes more of a problem after babies are weaned, because the babies lose the valuable source of protein found in breast milk. This has also become a problem in developing countries where women, in their attempt to be modern, choose bottle feeding, but dilute the formula so much that it is nutritionally inadequate. Children suffering from kwashiorkor have thinning hair and swollen faces, legs, and abdomens; they may develop severe skin lesions. Given a supportive environment, children suffering from kwashiorkor may be able to overcome some of their physical and intellectual handicaps (Ricciuti 1980).

Malnutrition need not be severe to have adverse consequences for children. In many poor countries, malnutrition is of a mild-to-moderate variety, but it is also long-term. These children may experience some growth retardation—particularly in height, weight, and head circumference. Mild-to-moderate malnutrition may result in impaired ability to attend to cognitive tasks. However, this impairment may also be due to the unfavorable social conditions in which many of these children live (Ricciuti 1980).

The Current Status of Nutrition in the United States

Along with increasing awareness of the special dietary needs of children, concern has grown over children's eating habits in a fast-food culture. However, national surveys of the nutritional status of preschoolers have found little evidence of serious nutritional deficits in children, although there are various deficiencies in vitamins and minerals (particularly iron) that vary across ethnic groups and socioeconomic status (Eichorn 1979).

Relatively little is known about the eating habits of children in their middle childhood and adolescent years. Existing data suggest that children are consuming too much food high in salt, fat, and sugar, despite the fact that by kindergarten children know the difference between "good" and "bad" food (Shonkoff 1984).

Perhaps the greatest concern with eating patterns during childhood and adolescence lies with obesity, a condition in which an individual is at least 20 percent above the ideal weight for height, age, and sex (Shonkoff 1984). Obese children are subject to a number of health-related problems, as well as to being ostracized by peers. Excessive caloric intake and lack of exercise are the two major determinants of childhood obesity (Shonkoff 1984). Whether or not obese children become obese adults is presently unclear. Obese children can become lean adults by reducing caloric intake and by increasing physical activity. The converse is also true; skinny children who fail to exercise and who eat excessively can become overweight adults. Because obese children also are growing children, faddish diets could lead to serious nutritional deficiencies. Thus, the preferred approach is to encourage the obese child to become more physically active and to discourage snacking.

Exercise

Along with good nutrition, exercise and practice in motor skills are essential to wellness during infancy and childhood. Children who lack opportunities to move their bodies may experience a number of problems. As already mentioned, lack of exercise has been implicated as a major cause of childhood obesity. A more drastic example comes from the work of Wayne Dennis (1960), who observed children reared in two orphanages in Iran. Because of a large child-to-caretaker ratio and impoverished conditions, the institutionalized infants were given little opportunity to move their bodies. They were rarely taken out of their cribs, so their mattresses developed depressions that made it very difficult for them to roll over. The babies were given no toys to play with, little opportunity to sit up, and little stimulation from their caretakers. Most of the time, these children lay on their backs in their cribs. As a result of such deprivation, only 42 percent of infants aged 1 to 2 could sit alone; none could walk. Of the older children observed by Dennis, only 8 percent of the 2- to 3-year-olds and 15 percent of the 3- to 4-year-olds could walk alone.

In more normal circumstances, young children will express their sheer exuberance for life by moving their bodies. Getting a preschooler to exercise is not a difficult task. Providing an environment for large- and small-muscle activity—as well as channeling body movements in skilled actions such as dancing, throwing, catching, tricycle riding, and swimming—can enhance the physical development of young children.

Most children in the middle years also enjoy physical exercise. Organized sports have become increasingly popular over the past ten years, although many children still do not regularly engage in physical exercise (Shonkoff 1984). With age, participation in physical activity steadily declines. Because the types of physical activities popular during childhood are not pursued in adulthood (e.g., baseball, basketball, and football), it has been suggested that schools teach and encourage those car-

Organized sports are increasingly popular during middle childhood. It is related both to physical and psychological well-being. Optimally, exercise should persist throughout the lifespan.

diovascular skills that can be continued in adulthood (Shonkoff 1984).

Throughout the entire life cycle, the changes in an individual's body have profound implications for his or her social, emotional, and psychological life. This is especially highlighted by the numerous physical changes of puberty and their relationship to adolescent psychological development. This chapter has shown how brain development links up with the child's increasing neurological and cognitive sophistication, how hormones direct reproductive functioning and the changes of puberty, how the child increases in stature with age, and how motor development expands the limits of the world for the child.

Your knowledge of physical development should have followed a path akin to the orthogenetic principle. In other words, your knowledge at

the beginning of this chapter was relatively global, but now it has become more differentiated and integrated within your overall understanding of child development.

Summary

1. In general, growth proceeds in two directions: the cephalocaudal direction (from the head downwards into the trunk) and the proximodistal direction (from the center of the body to the extremities).
2. The orthogenetic principle states that development always proceeds from relative globality to increasing differentiation and integration.
3. The brain and nervous system are the areas of the body that develop the fastest. They are well developed early in life.
4. The function of hormones—chemical substances secreted into the bloodstream by the various glands of

the body—is to stimulate the growth patterns established in the genetic code.

5. Growth in height and weight proceeds at a rapid pace during infancy and early childhood, slows down during middle childhood, and accelerates again during early adolescence.

6. Children in our society tend to be both taller and heavier than the generation that preceded them, a phenomenon known as the secular trend.

7. Motor development is typically divided into gross-motor development (involving behaviors such as sitting, crawling, standing, and walking) and fine-motor development (involving the use of fingers and hands for manipulation and prehension).

8. Puberty is initiated when a hormonal signal from the pituitary gland stimulates the sex glands (ovaries or testes) to secrete sex hormones. These sex hormones are responsible for the development of primary and secondary sex characteristics.

9. Wide individual variations exist in the rate of growth, with some adolescents reaching puberty significantly earlier than, and some significantly later than, their peers.

10. There is a strong positive relationship between body image and self-esteem.

11. In contrast to physically unattractive people, good-looking people have been found to be more popular and more socially desirable at all age levels studied.

12. Protein, carbohydrates, fats, water, minerals, and vitamins are essential throughout the life cycle, although quantities and proportions vary as a function of age.

13. Severe malnutrition not only affects the physiological status of the child, but also leads to serious retardation or attentional deficits.

14. Exercise is critical to physical growth. The task is to teach children skills that will lead to lifelong pursuits of physical activity.

Key Terms

cephalocaudal growth	hypothalamus
proximodistal growth	androgens
orthogenetic principle	estrogen
cerebral cortex	secular trend
sulci	visually initiated reaching
gyri	visually guided reaching
myelination	menarche
neuron	body image
dendrites	nutritional marasmus
axon	kwashiorkor
pituitary gland	

Suggested Readings

Hofer, M.A. (1981). *The roots of human behavior.* San Francisco: Freeman.

A vivid illustration of the interdisciplinary approach to human development. This book discusses the field of developmental psychobiology—the study of the relationship between biology and behavior. Included is an interesting discussion of hereditary-environment questions. The link between biology and psychology is well established.

Katchadourian, H. (1977). *The biology of adolescence.* San Francisco: Freeman.

A book dealing not only with biology, but also with related behavioral issues, such as body satisfaction, sexual attitudes and feelings, drug use, and eating disorders. It is well illustrated and contains a number of interesting case histories and first-person accounts pertaining to adolescent physical growth.

McGraw, M.B. (1935). *Growth: A study of Johnny and Jimmy.* New York: Appleton.

A classic study of motor development that establishes the basis for much of our contemporary understanding of the maturational approach toward physical growth. McGraw presents a detailed analysis of her co-twin experiments in which she trained one twin in a motor skill and then observed the differences and similarities between both twins in their motor development.

Tanner, J.M. (1978). *Fetus into man: Physical growth from conception to maturity.* Cambridge, MA: Harvard University Press.

A well-written summary of Tanner's work on physical development during childhood and adolescence. It includes a discussion of growth patterns, gender differences, standards of normal growth, growth disorders, and psychological consequences of growth variations.

Readings from the Literature

During the elementary school years, motor development plays a significant role in peer-group relations, children's self-esteem, and the ways in which children spend their free time. Because of these factors, greater emphasis is being placed upon physical education than was true of the past. The following article addresses the question of whether or not motor development during the elementary school years differs for boys and girls.

As you read, consider these questions:

- *After puberty, what differences are there between boys and girls in their motor proficiency?*

- *What differences did the authors find in motor skills between boys and girls in third grade through fifth grade?*

- *What are the educational and social implications of the authors' findings?*

Sex Differences in Motor Performance of Young Children: Fact or Fiction?

Evelyn G. Hall and Amelia M. Lee
Louisiana State University

Prepubescent boys and girls who had participated for one or more years in a coeducational physical education program were classified by grade (3, 4, and 5) and year (1977, 1978, and 1979). Scores from the AAHPER Youth Fitness Test were analyzed for differences. Results indicated that females at prepubescent ages may be expected to perform at similar levels to boys of the same age on most test items. While differences were not significant, girls in 1979 were actually better than boys of the same age from the two previous years.

The literature has focused considerable attention on the development of physical and motor proficiency in young children. Available research suggests a linear progression on performance of most tasks for both sexes from age 7 to age 12, with the performance of boys exceeding that of girls in tests of running speed, jumping ability, throwing, and strength. (Corbin, 1973; DiNucci, 1976; Espenschade & Eckert, 1967; Johnson, 1962; Keogh, 1973; Milne, Seefeld, & Reuschlein, 1976; Singer, 1969).

After 12 years of age an even greater sex difference is evident; males show a sharp increase in performance of most physical activities, while females plateau or even decline. A comprehensive study by Hunsicker and Reiff (1977) compared males and females aged 10 to 18 years on the items of the AAHPER (American Association for Health, Physical Education, and Recreation) physical fitness test in 1958, 1965, and 1975. In all cases, males were superior to females—with marked differences after age 13. There was significant improvement for both sexes between 1958 and 1965 and slight improvement between 1965 and 1975.

Astrand (1952) studied the maximal oxygen uptake for subjects from 4 to 18 years of age and found a gradual improvement with age for both sexes. Males in Astrand's study increased at a greater rate over age than did females. After the onset of puberty, this difference usually becomes more pronounced. Postpubescent females are adversely affected in endurance events because increased body weight has a negative effect on oxygen uptake. Although Corbin (1973) has provided evidence that females of all ages have a lower work capacity than do males, it should be noted that in the past only the exceptional girl participated in vigorous sports demanding top physical conditioning. There is no reason to believe that differences between prepubescent males and females reported in many early studies reflect true physiological differences.

Innate physiological differences between the sexes which result in differential physical performance after puberty are not challenged. At puberty, the pituitary gland of the male begins to secrete the male sex hormone, testosterone, which is a growth stimulant. Thus, the postpubescent male grows taller in stature and acquires greater muscle mass than his female counterpart. Again, it must be reemphasized that greater testosterone levels do not persist in males between birth and the onset of puberty. Moreover, it is very important to consider that the maturation rate of the prepubescent female is greater than that of her male counterpart.

The absence of physiologically based explanations for sex differences in physical performance and the presence of an accelerated rate of female maturation suggest a performance advantage for females prior to the onset of puberty. Historically, females have neither been encouraged nor expected to excel in physical feats. Thus, the most reasonable explanation for observed sex differences in earlier research is failure to account for social-cultural factors which have limited the performance of young females.

With the advent of Title IX and increased opportunities for coeducational experiences for both sexes, society is now more ready to accept the benefits of participation in physical activities, regardless of gender. There is certainly no evidence that such experiences have caused any detrimental effects to motivation of either sex to participate. Ensuing changes in cultural expectations may be expected to enhance early reinforcement patterns for developing physical prowess in young females. Parents, teachers, and significant others, through providing positive reinforcement and expectations, may aid all children in becoming equally competent in the realm of physical performance capabilities prior to puberty.

Physiological data provide evidence that young females possess physical capacities at least equal to those of young males. In a recent study (Bunker 1975) explored the effects of coeducational testing on performance of school children on the AAHPER physical fitness test. Results indicated that while males performed essentially the same in coeducational and noncoeducational situations, females improved considerably in coeducational groups. To date, there are no longitudinal studies on the effects of long-range coeducational programs on performance by both sexes. Therefore, the main concern of the present study was to investigate the effect over a three-year period of an existing coeducational program of instruction in a school setting. Physical performance was assessed by the AAHPER test on physical performance of all children in grades 3, 4, and 5 over three years (1977, 1978, and 1979).

The objective of the present research was twofold: (1) to compare scores of equal numbers of males and females in grades 3, 4, and 5 on specific physical tests over a three-year period (1977, 1978, and 1979); (2) to compare the most recent set of female scores (1979–1980) at all three grade levels to male scores from the previous two years (1977–1978 and 1978–1979). The comparison of 1979–1980 female fitness scores to male scores in 1977–1978 and 1978–1979 was made to test the hypothesis that performance of females with greater coeducational experience (three years) would equal or even surpass males with less coeducational experience (one or two years).

Method

Subjects

Subjects for this study were prepubescent males and females ($N = 540$) from a suburban residential area who

Table 1 Mean Performance on the Five AAHPER Fitness Tests by Year, Sex, and Grade

	Situps (no.)	Shuttle (sec.)	Broad Jump (in.)	Dash (sec.)	Walk-run (sec.)
1977–1978					
Males					
Grade 3	17.4	12.1	50.8	9.7	185.9
Grade 4	24.1	11.2	59.5	8.6	157.9
Grade 5	29.8	10.8	58.9	8.3	163.8
Females					
Grade 3	17.7	12.2	48.8	9.5	198.8
Grade 4	23.9	11.6	53.2	9.2	183.1
Grade 5	27.0	11.4	58.3	8.6	166.8
1978–1979					
Males					
Grade 3	26.4	11.6	53.2	9.0	163.6
Grade 4	30.8	11.4	55.3	8.3	150.2
Grade 5	39.9	10.7	61.9	7.8	136.0
Females					
Grade 3	28.2	12.1	50.6	9.3	177.8
Grade 4	33.7	11.5	55.5	8.5	158.2
Grade 5	38.4	11.1	59.0	8.1	151.9
1979–1980					
Males					
Grade 3	35.1	11.6	52.9	8.8	167.0
Grade 4	44.9	10.8	59.4	8.0	146.3
Grade 5	47.0	10.3	64.2	7.7	136.1
Females					
Grade 3	39.7	11.6	55.7	8.8	172.5
Grade 4	44.1	11.1	59.0	8.2	162.0
Grade 5	48.0	10.5	64.7	8.0	153.2

participated in a daily coeducational physical education class of at least 30 minutes duration. Subjects were divided equally by grade (grades 3, 4, and 5) and by year (1977–1978, 1978–1979, and 1979–1980). The school selected for participation in the study introduced coeducational instruction in 1976 and currently emphasizes development of skill and physical proficiency equally for both sexes. Children in this school have been exposed to excellent instruction, which includes a daily session of at least 10 minutes of conditioning exercises. During each session vigorous cardiovascular, muscular strength, and muscular endurance exercises are stressed for all children. The mean age for the subjects was 9.1 years. Scores from the AAHPER fitness test were randomly selected from the total student population. Scores for 30 males and 30 females were selected from grades 3, 4, and 5 for a three-year period (1977–1978; 1978–1979; 1979–1980) and utilized in the data analysis.

Materials

Scores were taken from the three-year period on five of the AAHPER physical fitness tests: situps, shuttle run, 50-yard dash, broad jump, and the 600-yard walk-run. Testing was completed each year during the month of November by the male elementary school physical education teacher. Subjects were tested in a coeducational setting with an identical protocol for all grades and all years.

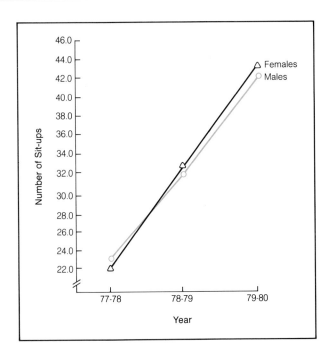

Figure 1 Performance on situps by sex and year.

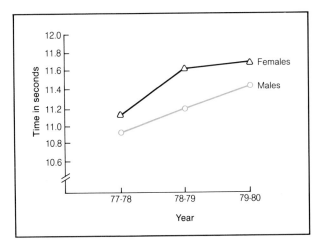

Figure 2 Performance on the shuttle run by sex and year.

Procedure

A sex × grade × year (2 × 3 × 3) factorial analysis of variance was used to analyze the data. Separate ANOVAS were employed on each of the five fitness measures. The five scores were not treated as correlated measures. The Newman-Keuls method of post hoc comparisons was applied whenever significant differences were present for main effects or interactions.

Results

The means for all children in all grades for all three years are shown in Table 1. The ANOVA results for situps, shuttle run, 50-yard dash, broad jump, and 600-yard walk-run are presented in Table II. Significant main effects were found for sex on the 50-yard dash ($p < .01$), the shuttle run ($p < .01$), the 600-yard walk-run ($p < .01$), and the broad jump ($p < .05$). Moreover, presented in Table II are significant main effects for year and grade on all five fitness events ($p < .01$).

There was a significant interaction for sex by year on the standing broad jump ($p < .01$). Since boys' scores were much better than girls' scores in 1977–1978, it was more meaningful to utilize post hoc Newman-Keuls tests to determine meaningful trends for both sexes.

The results of the sex × year interactions are shown in Figures 1-5. Each sex improved steadily over the three-year period on these tests. Newman-Keuls analysis showed significant gains for both sexes from 1977–1978 to 1978–1979 and from 1978–1979 to 1979–1980 ($p < .01$).

On situps, girls actually performed better than boys in 1979–1980 (see Figure 1). On the standing broad jump and 600-yard walk-run, which are power and endurance tests respectively, boys demonstrated significant performance advantages. However, according to Newman-Keuls post hoc analyses boys performed significantly better than girls on the broad jump only in 1977–1978, not the latter two years ($p < .01$). Moreover, females made significant gains on the broad jump from 1977–1978 to 1979–1980 and from 1978–1979 to 1979–1980 ($p < .01$). As shown in Figure 4, girls were actually better on broad jump performance than boys in 1979–1980. On the 600-yard walk-run, males clearly demonstrated superiority over females for all three years ($p < .01$). While there were few significant sex differences, the gap in performance favoring

131

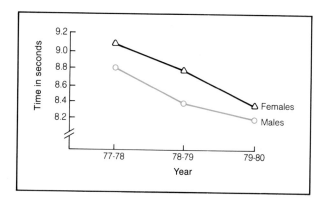

Figure 3 Performance on the 50-yard dash by sex and year.

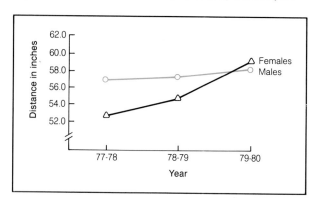

Figure 4 Performance on the broad jump by sex and year.

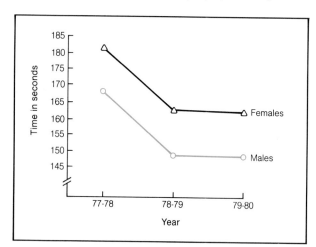

Figure 5 Performance on the 600-yard walk-run by sex and year.

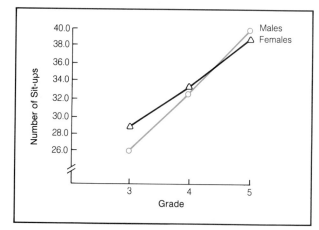

Figure 6 Performance on situps by sex and grade.

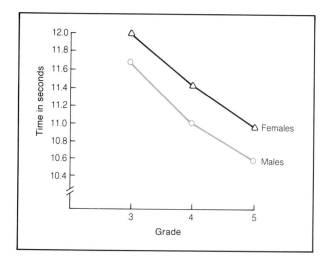

Figure 7 Performance on the shuttle run by sex and grade.

males was greatest in 1977–1978, but closed progressively in 1978–1979, and 1979–1980.

Results of the grade × sex interactions are shown in Figures 6-10 for the purpose of comparing the sexes developmentally. There were no significant sex differences for any of the five test items. On situps and the standing broad jump, both sexes showed significant improvement over the three grades ($p < .01$). On the

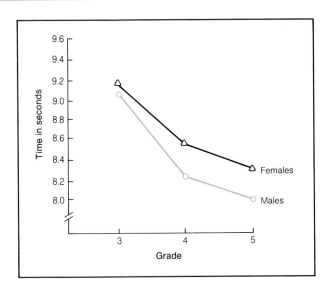

Figure 8 Performance on the 50 yard dash by sex and grade.

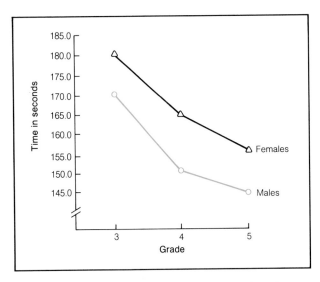

Figure 10 Performance on the walk-run by sex and grade.

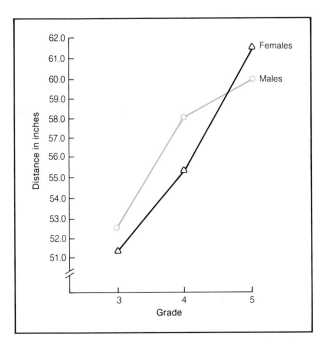

Figure 9 Performance on the broad jump by sex and grade.

shuttle run and 50-yard dash, no significant developmental gains were shown. On the 600-yard walk-run, fourth and fifth grades of each sex performed significantly better than third graders ($p < .01$).

Table 3 shows mean comparisons of girls in 1979–1980 to boys in 1977–1978 and 1978–1979 on the five test items. The following results were found: Girls, at all grade levels, in 1979–1980 performed significantly better on situps than boys from the two previous years ($p < .01$). While the differences were not significant, girls in 1979–1980 also performed better than the boys from 1977–1978 and 1978–1979 on the 50-yard dash, shuttle run, and broad jump in all cases except two (see Table 2). However, on the walk-run, boys were consistently better than girls in all grade levels.

Discussion

The importance of adequate experiences for all children to aid them in developing skill and physical fitness must not be neglected in our schools. The results of the present study showed that a program of excellent coeducational instruction benefited children of both

133

Table 2 F Ratios from ANOVAs for Sex × Year × Grade Analysis on the Five Separate Fitness Tests

Source	df	Situps	50-yard Dash	Shuttle Run	Broad Jump	Walk-run
Sex	1	.44	12.11^b	22.83^b	4.56^a	52.95
Year	2	131.05^b	43.35^b	28.58^b	20.17^b	48.63
Sex × Year	2	.58	.57	.76	4.16^b	.09
Grade	2	40.53^b	101.88^b	85.42^b	80.04^b	71.02
Sex × grade	2	.93	2.14	.45	.59	.08
Year × grade	4	.46	.57	1.16	1.26	.44
Sex × year × grade	4	.43	1.63	1.32	2.02	2.57

^{a}p <.05.
^{b}p <.01.

sexes in grades 3, 4, and 5 on the AAHPER physical fitness tests. Moreover, there were no apparent motivational problems in this study, since boys and girls showed continual improvement from 1977–1978 to 1978–1979 to 1979–1980 on situps, shuttle run, standing broad jump, 50-yard dash, and 600-yard walk-run.

The present data support Bunker's (1975) earlier research, which reported that girls from ages 10 to 17 performed significantly better on the AAHPER tests when tested in coeducational groups than when tested in all female groups. Boys in Bunker's (1975) study performed at similar levels whether tested in coed or all-male groups. Although no same-sex groups were tested in the present study, there was continued improvement for both sexes over the three-year period. The present data provide evidence that there are no true physiological sex differences in performance at the third- fourth-, or fifth-grade level. Differences reported in earlier studies are more likely related to sociocultural expectations and not to real physiological differences. In the past sociocultural milieu, expectations for performance by females were much lower than for males. The present data reveal a closing of the performance gap between the sexes shown in 1977–1978. In the present situation—with equal opportunity to learn skills and become physically fit—girls have actually progressed to an equal level of performance. Girls in 1979–1980 were actually better than boys of the same age from the two previous years on most AAHPER tests. Moreover, girls in 1979–1980 performed

Table 3 Mean Comparisons of Scores from Girls in 1979 to Boys in 1977 and 1978 for Three Grade Levels and Five Fitness Tests

	Girls 1979–1980	Boys 1977–1978	Boys 1978–1979
Situps			
Grade 3	39.7	17.4^a	26.4^a
Grade 4	44.1	24.1^a	30.8^a
Grade 5	48.0	29.8^a	39.9
50-yard Dash (sec)			
Grade 3	8.8	9.0	9.7
Grade 4	8.2	8.6	8.3
Grade 5	8.0	8.3	7.8^b
Shuttle Run (sec)			
Grade 3	11.6	12.1	11.6
Grade 4	11.1	11.2	11.4
Grade 5	10.5	10.8	10.7
Broad Jump (in.)			
Grade 3	55.7	50.8	53.2
Grade 4	59.0	59.5^b	55.3
Grade 5	64.7	58.9	61.9
Walk-run (sec)			
Grade 3	172.5	185.9	163.6^b
Grade 4	162.0	157.9^b	150.2^b
Grade 5	153.2	163.8	136.0^b

^{a}Girls scores in 1979 were significantly better, $p < .01$.
^{b}Boys' scores in 1977 and 1978 were better than girls scores in 1979.

better than boys in 1979–1980 on situps and broad jump at the fifth-grade level.

Developmentally, all children improved as age increased. This finding supports several earlier studies which have shown that general physical proficiency in children increases with age (Corbin, 1973; Espenschade & Eckert, 1967; Singer, 1969).

In conclusion, data reported in the present research provide evidence that females at prepubescent ages may be expected to perform at similar levels to boys at that age. The provision of equal opportunities in a coeducational situation served in this case as an effective program for the development of fitness in all children.

References

Astrand, P. O. *Experimental studies of physical working capacity in relation to sex and age.* Copenhagen: Munksgaard, 1952.

Bunker, L. K. *Social factors affecting performance on the AAHPER Youth Fitness Test.* Unpublished research, Motor Learning Laboratory, University of Virginia, 1975.

Corbin, C. A. *A textbook of motor development.* Dubuque, Iowa: William C. Brown, 1973.

DiNucci, J.M. Gross motor performance: A comprehensive analysis of age and sex differences between boys and girls ages six to nine years. In J. Brockhoff (Ed.), *Physical education, sports and the sciences.* Eugene: Microform Publications, University of Oregon, 1976.

Espenschade, A. S., & Eckert, H. M. *Motor development.* Columbus, Ohio: Charles E. Merrill, 1967.

Hunsicke•, P., & Reiff, C. Youth Fitness Report: 1958 1965 1975. *Journal of Physical Education and Recreation,* 1977, *48*(1), 31–33.

Johnson, R. D. Measurements of achievement in fundamental skills of elementary school children. *Research Quarterly,* 1962, *33,* 94–103.

Keogh, J. Fundamental motor tasks. In C. Corbin (Ed.), *A textbook of motor development.* Dubuque, Iowa: William C. Brown, 1973.

Milne, C., Seefeldt, V., & Reuschlein, P. Relationship between grade, sex, race, and motor performance in young children. *Research Quarterly,* 1976, *47,* 726–730.

Singer, R. N. Physical characteristics, perceptual motor, and intelligence differences between third and sixth grade children. *Research Quarterly,* 1969, *40,* 803–811.

Source: Hall, E.G. and Lee, A.M. (1984) Sex differences in motor performance of young children: fact or fiction? *Sex Roles, 10,* 217–229. New York: Plenum Publishing Corporation. Reprinted by permission of the publisher and author.

Sensation and Perception

As she held her 2-week-old infant in her arms, Jeanne found herself wondering, "What do you see when you look at me? What do you hear when I sing to you? Do you like it when I stroke your back with my hand, or do you feel it at all? Would you even know the difference if someone else was holding you? Does the world make any sense to you at all, or is it just an overwhelming mass of stimulation?"

Friends had different opinions. Some said that a young infant is too confused by the newness of the world to perceive anything meaningful. Others argued that, while they may not show it, newborns are keenly aware of their surroundings. One friend observed that human infants are not even able to see when they first come into the world. Unfortunately, Jeanne's new daughter was unable to resolve the controversy because she didn't provide much feedback about the way she was perceiving the world. Had she been able to describe what she was then perceiving, or to remember it later on, Jeanne and many of her friends would probably have been surprised. Although the sensory and perceptual capacities of the young infant are immature, they are better developed than most people realize.

This chapter focuses on the remarkable sensory capacities of the newborn child. It discusses the five major senses—vision, audition, taste, smell, and touch—and traces their development from infancy through adolescence. The senses will not be given equal coverage, however. Considerably greater emphasis will be placed on vision, and more emphasis on audition than on the remaining three. This imbalance is due to the fact that more research has been done on vision than on the other senses. Research on touch, taste, and smell has been limited in both quantity and scope.

This chapter will also discuss factors that direct and focus human sensation and either limit or elaborate upon sensory input. The first topic to be covered will be the influence of culture on perception. The recognition that cultural differences exist in perceptual areas, such as the ability to perceive depth in pictures, leads psychologists to believe that a child's perception of the world can be heavily influenced by life experiences. This topic will be followed by an examination of two major theoretical perspectives on perceptual learning and development and their implications for child development in general.

Sensory Processes

The five human senses are the channels through which we acquire information about the world. If these channels, or even any one of them, are not working to capacity, then our ability to gather information is significantly reduced, and physical, intellectual, social, and emotional functioning will be impaired.

This section of the chapter details the development of the five senses, with particular attention to the period of infancy, when the child begins to interact with the outside world. Two points will be emphasized. First, the senses are all well developed at birth or soon thereafter. Second, the sensory capacities of the young infant facilitate the parent-child attachment process and form a basis for later cognitive functioning, as will be seen in Chapter 6.

Vision

Vision is not the best developed of the senses at birth; hearing is. Nevertheless, the infant's ability to see clearly and to perceive form, patterns, depth, and color has generated more research than has the study of any of the other senses. (For information on how researchers are able to gather data from infants, see Issues in Child Development "How Can Infant Perception Be Studied?")

Structure and Function of the Eye
To understand developmental changes in the visual system, it is necessary to examine briefly the structure and function of the human eye.

The *cornea* is the curved transparent outer surface at the front of the eye, through which light is admitted. The *iris* is the colored surface behind the cornea, which, like the lens of a camera, adjusts to control the amount of light admitted through the opening at its center. The opening itself is known as the *pupil.* Behind the iris is the curved *lens,* which

Issues in Child Development

How Can Infant Perception Be Studied?

Because babies are unable to tell us about their sensory experience of the world, we must rely on nonverbal measures to study infant perceptual development. Of course, we could simply observe their everyday physical reactions (e.g., crying, blinking their eyes, pulling their feet back) to environmental stimulation, but, as Rosenblith and Sims-Knight (1985) pointed out, such naturalistic observations are not very scientific. Why? Because observers watching the same infant often disagree in their descriptions of the child's behavior, because naturalistic observations are difficult to quantify in terms of the intensity of the child's reaction, and because in a natural setting it is difficult to know exactly what the baby is reacting to. If infants turn their heads when offered a musical toy, is the reaction caused by the shape, color, smell, sound, or feel of the object, or even by the presence of the adult who approaches with the toy in hand?

Physical and physiological reactions are indeed used to gather data in research on infant perception. However, they are used in laboratory settings where guidelines for observation are established in advance, infant behaviors are carefully quantified, and efforts are made to determine exactly what features of the stimuli the infant is reacting to. The techniques most often used in research of this type are **habituation** and *paired comparisons*.

Habituation

A novel stimulus, such as a sudden loud noise or bright light, will cause a person to react physiologically (e.g., changes in brain wave patterns, slowing of heart rate) and possibly also physically (e.g., head turning, jumping up from a chair). This reaction is called an "orienting reflex." After a while, however, the person gets used to the stimulus, so that it is no longer seen as novel, and it no longer triggers the orienting reflex. The person is now said to have habituated to the stimulus.

The habituation technique is often used to test the ability of infants to discriminate among various stimuli presented to their senses. The child is first exposed to one stimulus (e.g., a tone, an odor, a colored light) until habituation has occurred, and this first stimulus no longer produces an orienting reflex. Then a second stimulus is presented, similar but not identical to the first. If an orienting response occurs—a physiological reaction such as a change in heart rate or a physical reaction such as turning the head—the infant is responding to the second stimulus as if it were completely new. Thus, the infant can discriminate between the two tones, odors, or colors. If no orienting response occurs to the second stimulus, then the infant does not perceive a difference between the new stimulus and the habituated stimulus.

Paired Comparisons

Used primarily to assess infant visual perception, the paired-comparisons technique involves presenting two stimuli side by side and observing the child's preference for one or the other. For example, the child might be placed in an infant seat and shown two visual displays on adjacent screens. A schematic drawing of a human face might appear on one screen and a bull's-eye pattern on the other (as in the Fantz research discussed in the section "Pattern Preferences").

Using sophisticated photographic techniques, researchers can determine exactly what the infant is looking at at any given moment. Thus, if infants spend considerably more time looking at one of the two slides, it can be concluded that (1) they recognize the difference between them and (2) they appear to have preferences for some stimuli over others.

Despite the limits on infants' visual acuity, they see more clearly than is often realized and they appreciate complex and interesting visual displays.

focuses images that enter the eye. If the object of vision is close to the face, the lens bulges at the center; if the object is distant, the lens flattens out. The muscles in the eye that cause the lens to bulge or to flatten out are called the accommodatory muscles, or *ciliary muscles.*

The inner-rear surface of the eye upon which the visual image is focused in known as the *retina.* The grainy surface of the retina is made up of a mosaic of light-sensitive nerve cells. Among these receptor cells are *rods,* which are sensitive only to dim light, and *cones,* which are stimulated by brighter light and are sensitive to color. Finally, the

center of the retina, the point at which an image is focused, is known as the *fovea.*

Visual Acuity

Visual acuity is the ability to recognize all of the individual components in a visual display. If a slide projected on a screen is out of focus, the viewer sees only a blur; the individual elements in the picture appear to run together. As the picture is brought into focus, however, the individual elements become increasingly distinct. The viewer reports seeing the picture more clearly. Visual acuity is this clarity of vision.

The newborn infant does not see the world as clearly as does the adult—for a variety of reasons. For one thing, the distance from an infant's lens to the retina is proportionally shorter than in the adult eye—the "short eyeball" phenomenon—and as a result the visual image projected on the infant retina is less clearly focused. In addition, the retina itself is immature at birth. Rods and cones are functional in the newborn, but the cones are not as densely packed in the foveal area as occurs in the adult eye. The retina matures rapidly during infancy but is structurally unlike an adult retina until approximately 11 months of age (Banks & Salapatek 1983). What is more, the ciliary muscles are immature at birth although they will mature rapidly during the first two months of life. During the first month of life, infants make efforts to accommodate to the distance of objects when they focus on them, but their efforts are often unsuccessful (Banks 1980). Particularly during that first month, and even up until 3 months of age, infants misjudge distances and often over- or underaccommodate (Banks & Salapatek 1983).

Finally, visual acuity is also influenced by the contrast between the object being viewed and the background against which it is presented. Most tests of visual acuity use a high degree of contrast between object and background, as when a child is asked to identify a row of black letters on a white chart in a doctor's office. In reality, however, the world consists of visual stimuli that vary considerably in their contrast levels. Consider the difficulty a person might have in reading an eye chart if both letters and background were presented in different shades of gray!

The range of contrast to which infants are sensitive is quite limited during the first six months of life, and adultlike **contrast sensitivity** will not be attained until late in the first year. However, the limits on their contrast sensitivity do not put young infants totally at a loss when they view the world. Many objects in their everyday environments are well within their contrast sensitivity range (e.g., the contrast between skin and hair at the hairline of a human face), and contrasts become easier to detect as objects are brought closer to the face and thus take up a larger portion of the visual field. The young infant derives the greatest amount of visual information, therefore, from high-contrast stimuli presented at close range (Banks & Salapatek 1981, 1983).

Estimates of infant visual acuity for high-contrast stimuli are approximately 20/450 at 1 to 2 months and 20/150 at 3 to 4 months. This means that an infant can see an object at a distance of twenty feet as well as an adult with perfect vision can see it at 450 or at 150 feet respectively. Visual acuity of 20/20 is attained by the age of 6 months or shortly thereafter.

In summary, even a very young infant already sees the world with reasonable clarity, and current estimates of infant visual acuity are probably conservative (Banks & Salapatek 1983). The infant definitely sees more than light and shadow. Many adults could instantly experience the visual acuity of a newborn infant simply by removing their glasses.

Form Perception

When human infants enter the world from out of the darkness of the womb, they are already able to see an environment of various shapes and contours. In fact, even newborns will notice the contours of a form and will move their eyes in order to fixate the contour in the center of their fields of vision (Banks & Salapatek 1983). According to Haith (1979), human beings appear to come into the world equipped with a number of looking "rules." They use these rules to find the interesting visual features of the environment:

- If you are awake and alert, and the light is not too bright, open your eyes.
- If opening your eyes reveals darkness, scan the environment intensively.
- If opening your eyes reveals light, scan the environment broadly.
- If you find an edge, stop scanning broadly and continue scanning around the edge.
- When scanning near an edge, reduce the range of fixations perpendicular to the edge if there are many contours in the area.

As infants mature, their visual-scanning strategies change considerably in two ways. First, the breadth of their scans across the visual field increases (Banks & Salapatek 1983). Second, there is an increasing tendency to go from scanning just

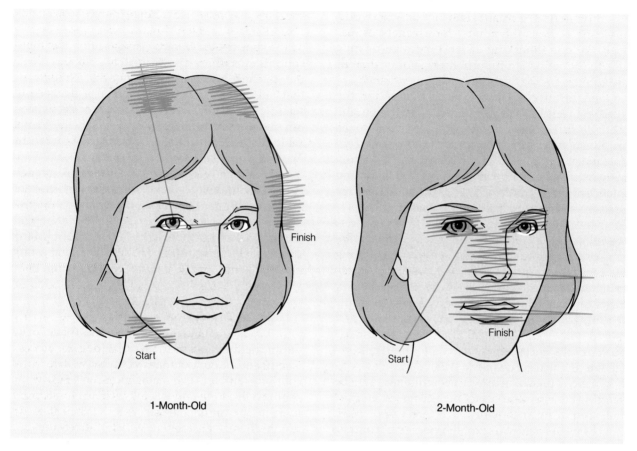

Figure 5.1   Scanning Patterns of a Human Face by 1- and 2-Month-Olds

the outer edges of forms to examining the internal features as well. Consider the difference between the ways in which 1-and 2-month-olds scan a human face (see Figure 5.1). The 1-month-old looks primarily at the contours of the face and spends little time examining the internal features, whereas the 2-month-old seems particularly drawn to the eyes and mouth while almost ignoring the external contours. In addition, the younger infant engages in repeated short-range fixations in areas of interest, while there is a greater sweep across the visual display in the scanning pattern of the older child (Haith, Bergman & Moore 1977; Salapatek 1975).

Focusing on the edges rather than on the internal features of perceived forms may actually cause the very young infant to miss much visual information (Siegler 1986). As an illustration of what may be missed, consider the results of studies by Milewski (1976, 1978). Milewski first familiarized 1- to 4-month-old babies with a compound figure (a circle within a square) and then altered the figure in one or more ways to see if the babies would notice the difference. The alterations consisted of a change in the internal figure only, a change in the external figure only, or a change in both figures; a control group saw the original figure again with no alterations. Four-month-olds were likely to notice all of the alterations equally. One-month-olds, on the other hand, noticed that something was different only if the external figure had been changed from a square to a circle or triangle. Changes only in the internal figure were not apparent to them, presumably because they confined their visual scanning to the outer contours of the compound figure.

Reasons for the very young infant's tendency to scan the edges rather than the internal features of forms are not entirely clear. One possibility is that larger forms have more appeal than smaller ones, and the outer form is always larger than those contained within it (Milewski 1978). Another explanation centers not on the size of the form itself, but on its innate appeal for the infant; if the internal features of an object are not especially interesting, then the outer contours will be scanned. However, if the internal features are particularly appealing to them, they will notice these features instead of looking primarily at the contours (Banks & Salapatek 1983). Ganon and Swartz (1980) demonstrated this phenomenon, using Milewski's (1978) research design but substituting high-interest patterns (checkerboards, bull's-eyes) for simple geometric shapes as the internal figures in the display; now even the 1-month-old infants noticed internal changes in the figures as readily as they attended to external changes. Similarly, in the Salapatek (1975) study of infants' scanning of human faces, the 1-month-olds did in fact spend some time looking at the eyes and mouth, although they concentrated on the outer edges of the display.

In summary, it seems clear that human beings perceive forms in their environments at a very young age, that initially they are more taken with the edges of forms than with their internal features—unless the internal features are particularly stimulating—and that between 1 and 2 months of age they become quite capable of and especially interested in exploring internal features as well as contours.

Pattern Preferences

In light of the sophistication of their visual acuities and their tendencies at an early age to selectively scan their environments, it seems that even young infants are able to see a world rich in varied patterns. A good deal of research on infant visual perception has focused on the question of what kinds of patterns the young infant prefers to look at. Newborns seem to prefer patterns that are neither too simple nor too complex, perhaps because of sensory limitations that make it difficult for them to appreciate complexity (Banks & Salapatek 1983; Olson & Sherman 1983). As the infant

develops, however, complexity in patterns is increasingly appreciated. Robert Fantz, a pioneer in pattern perception research, found that infants beyond the age of 1½ months typically prefer to look at bull's-eye patterns rather than at stripes, at checkerboard patterns rather than at simple squares, and at facelike patterns rather than at anything else (Fantz 1958, 1961, 1963; Fantz & Nevis 1967; Fantz, Fagan & Miranda 1975). (See Figure 5.2.)

In addition to complexity, young infants prefer to look at curved lines rather than at straight lines, at irregular over regular patterns, at concentric over nonconcentric patterns, and at symmetrical over asymmetrical stimuli. They also prefer patterns of high-contour density, with contour density being determined by dividing the total length of the stimulus edge by the surface area of the stimulus (Olson & Sherman 1983).

Although even newborn babies show pattern preferences and pattern preferences change with age, it cannot be concluded that pattern preferences improve, or why they do or do not improve with age. This is because, as Banks and Salapatek (1983) pointed out, the stimuli used in the various studies have differed considerably, and no specific guidelines have been developed that all researchers can agree on. For example, what does it mean to say that infants prefer complex stimuli over simple stimuli when there is no clear, easily understood definition of complexity in a pattern? Does complexity refer to the number of elements in a display, the number of angles, the arrangement of elements, or some other variable? Until this and other such questions can be answered, little more can be said about the developmental aspects of pattern perception.

The Perception of Faces

The work of Robert Fantz and his associates indicated that young infants have a particular preference for the pattern of a human face. What is the reason for this fascination with faces or facelike patterns? While a 1-month-old infant typically scans the external contours of a face, the gaze of the 2-month-old is drawn to the internal features, such as the eyes and mouth (Haith, Bergman &

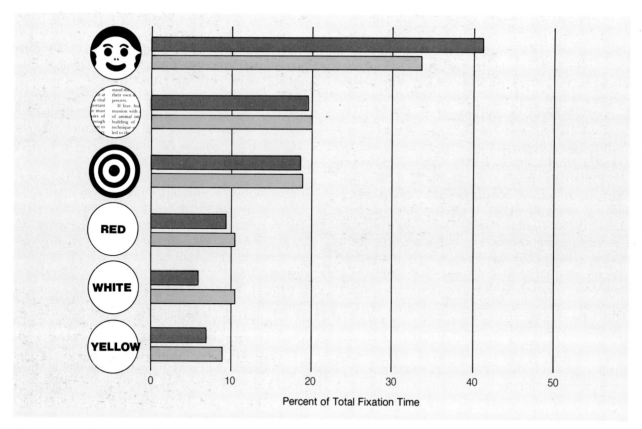

Figure 5.2   Pattern Preferences in Young Infants

Importance of pattern rather than color or brightness was illustrated by the response
of infants to a face, a piece of printed matter, a bull's-eye, and plain red, white,
and yellow disks. Even the youngest infants preferred patterns. Black bars show the
results for infants from 2 to 3 months old; gray bars, for infants more than 3
months old.
Source: Illustration by Alex Semenoick from "The Origin of form Perception" by
R.L. Fantz (p. 72). Copyright 1981 by *Scientific American,* Inc. All rights reserved.

Moore 1977). The 2-month-old is also able to differentiate between normally arranged facial displays and those that are scrambled—that is,
schematic drawings containing the correct facial
features but in the wrong places (Maurer & Barrera
1981; Olson 1981; Olson & Sherman 1983). By the
age of 3 months, infants' eyes are sensitive enough
to distinguish between photographs of two different faces. Infants can also tell the difference between a smile and a frown (Barrera & Maurer 1981).
The 5-month-old seems to perceive a face as an
overall pattern rather than as a collection of indi-

vidual features; infants of this age are quick to notice when a feature is missing or misplaced in a
schematic face they have become accustomed to
looking at (Caron et al. 1973). At 6 months the
infant prefers real to schematic faces, familiar to
unfamiliar ones, correctly drawn to scrambled
ones, and moving ones to those that are immobile
(Sherrod 1981). And by 7 months of age, the role
of facial perception in parent-child communication
becomes particularly clear because now the infant
can generalize facial expressions, such as happi-
ness and fear, from one face to another (Nelson &
Dolgin 1985).

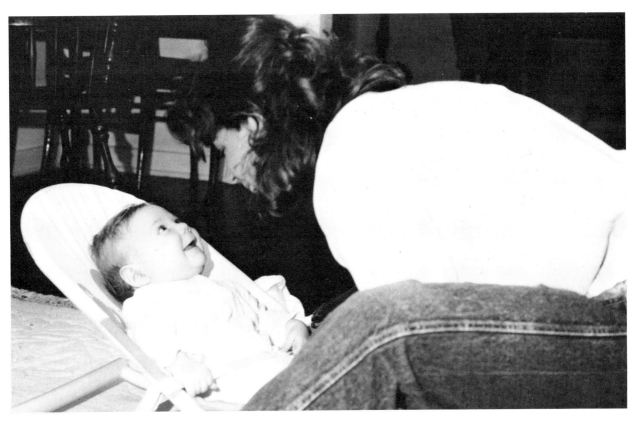

Whether it is seen as a socially significant stimulus or merely as an interesting pattern, the human face is particularly appealing to the young infant.

The special appeal of faces for an infant has never been completely explained. On the one hand, sensitivity to faces could have adaptive significance for a child, and by the middle of the first year this sensitivity probably has an important role in preverbal communication (Nelson & Dolgin 1985). However, for the infant younger than 4 months, the face may be appealing only because it is an interesting and complex pattern and not because of its particular social significance (Siegler 1986).

Depth Perception

Human beings see the world in three, rather than in two, dimensions. A number of cues indicate that objects in our visual fields vary in their distance from us. Two general categories of depth cues have been identified. *Monocular cues* need only one eye. This category can be further divided into *static* cues and *kinetic* cues, or cues dependent upon movement. Since artists use static monocular cues to create the illusion of depth in a painting, they are often referred to as pictorial cues. These include partial overlap, shadow, relative and familiar size, blurring of background objects, and linear perspective. Kinetic monocular cues are provided when there is a change over time in the retinal image, as when the image enlarges as the object approaches the face. *Binocular cues* to depth require the use of two eyes. They result from the fact that each eye sees a slightly different image, a characteristic of vision known as **binocular disparity.** The depth perception that results in known as **stereopsis;** it involves the convergence of the eyes on a single target and the fusion of the two slightly different visual images into one.

Table 5.1   The Development of Depth Cues in the Human Infant

Type of Cue	Description	Development
Monocular		
Static	*Pictorial cues* such as those used by artists to create the illusion of depth in a painting. They include partial overlap, shadow, relative and familiar size, blurring of background objects, linear perspective.	5 to 7 months*
Kinetic	Cues produced by changes over time in the retinal image. When an object draws closer, it is gradually enlarged.	1 month**
Binocular		
Stereopsis	Cues resulting from *binocular disparity,* meaning that the eyes see slightly different images since they view the world from different vantage points. Stereopsis involves (1) the convergence inward of the two eyes as they fixate on the same point and (2) the fusion of the slightly different images seen by the two eyes.	2 to 4 months***

Data Sources:
*Kaufmann, Maland & Yonas 1981; Yonas, Cleaves & Pettersen 1978; Yonas, Pettersen & Granrud 1982.
**Carroll & Gibson 1981; Yonas et al. 1977; Yonas et al 1980.
***Bechtold & Hutz 1979; Gordon & Yonas 1976; Yonas et al 1978.

As can be seen in Table 5.1, young infants are sensitive to all three types of information about depth. However, the information becomes available in a developmental sequence: kinetic monocular cues appear first, then binocular cues, and finally static monocular cues. (For an interesting experiment in infant depth perception, see Research Close-up "The Visual Cliff.")

Is the ability to perceive depth innate in human beings or is it acquired? Little attention has been given to the role of experience in infant depth perception (Banks & Salapatek 1983). The role of experience may vary depending on the depth cue under discussion. A later section of this chapter discusses sociocultural influences on perception. At that point cultural variations in the use of pictorial cues will be examined.

Size and Shape Constancy

A person stands near a railroad track and watches a train approach from a distance, pass by, and disappear across the horizon in the opposite direction. Throughout this experience, the visual image of the train projected on the viewer's retina is in constant change. The image increases in size and then decreases, and the shape of the image changes as the train is viewed from different angles. Nevertheless, the viewer knows that, despite the changing size and shape of the retinal image, the train itself does not change in size or shape. This is because the viewer possesses what are known as perceptual constancies.

Size constancy is the realization that the actual size of an object stays the same despite changes in the size of the visual image. In a sense, the viewer compensates for differences in size by figuring the element of distance into the equation. **Shape constancy** is the realization that the shape of an object remains the same regardless of the angle from which it is viewed. A clock on the wall is seen as round by a person standing directly in front of it. As seen from underneath, the retinal image of the clock is not round at all, but elliptical; however, the viewer takes account of the viewing angle and still sees the clock as being round.

As far as can be determined, size and shape constancy are not present at birth but are acquired sometime during the first year of life. Size constancy is definitely present by the age of 6 months; whether it can be found earlier is open to debate. Some research indicates that even 4-month-olds

Research Close-up

The Visual Cliff

One of the more interesting classic techniques devised to study depth perception in infancy was the visual cliff (Gibson & Walk 1960). The visual cliff consisted of a board located at the center of and spanning the width of a piece of heavy glass. The glass was raised a foot or more above the floor. On one side of the board, a checkerboard-patterned material lined the underside of the glass, while on the other side, the checkerboard-patterned material lined the floor some distance below. In other words, there was a "deep" and a "shallow" side of the cliff on opposite sides of the center board. (The visual cliff is illustrated by the photograph at the beginning of this chapter.)

In the Gibson and Walk experiment, thirty-six babies, ranging in age from 6 to 14 months, were placed on the center board and called by their mothers to come across either the deep or the shallow side. A preference for the shallow, or safer, side was thought to indicate that the subject could perceive depth. Most of the babies were willing to cross the shallow side; only a few would venture out across the deep side of the cliff. Many of the infants sat on the board, crying and reaching for their mother; but they would not approach her on the deep side, and some even crawled away from her onto the shallow side. Therefore, Gibson and Walk succeeded in demonstrating that babies as young as 6 months can perceive depth.

In a later study, Campos, Langer, and Crowitz (1970) found that being placed on the deep side produced consistently greater heart rate deceleration in 2-month-olds than did being placed on the shallow side. Heart rate deceleration is an indicator of attention. Thus, even very young infants can differentiate between the deep and the shallow side.

show evidence of size constancy while other research indicates that they do not (Banks & Salapatek 1983; Day & McKenzie 1981; McKenzie, Tootell & Day 1980). In one early study, size constancy was found even in infants between 1 and 2 months of age, but no one has been able to replicate that finding (Bower 1964). Banks and Salapatek (1983) suggested that size constancy may indeed be present at 4 months of age or even earlier, but its presence is difficult to demonstrate. They noted also that considerable development may occur in size constancy between 4 and 6 months of age, perhaps because during this time the infant begins to engage in visually guided reaching. Infants reach for what they look at, picking up objects within reach and moving them closer to their faces. This type of hands-on experience may be important for the development of perceptual constancies.

Shape constancy can be demonstrated at an earlier age than size constancy and is definitely found even as early as 3 months of age (Banks & Salapatek 1983; Caron, Caron & Carlson 1979). The specific experiences that bring about the development of shape constancy, or size constancy for that matter, are not known. It seems likely that the experience of the world need not be extensive, however, since 3-month-olds are not yet able to get around by themselves or to coordinate the activities of looking or reaching.

Color Vision

Human beings, as well as many lower animals, see the world in color. As anyone knows who replaces a black-and-white television set with a color television set, color not only makes the world more attractive, but also aids in visual perception. Color heightens the contrast among the elements in a visual display, making individual elements stand out more clearly against the background (Bornstein 1978; Siegler 1986).

Color is perceived because the light waves reflected off objects in the environment are of different lengths, ranging approximately from 400 to

700 nanometers. The colors of the spectrum—red, orange, yellow, green, blue, indigo, and violet—are arranged in order from the longest to the shortest wavelength. Thus, a person perceives an object as green instead of blue because the light waves reflected off that object are longer than those reflected off an object seen as blue.

Despite the popular belief that infants see the world only in fuzzy shades of gray, even very young infants respond differently to light waves of different lengths (Banks & Salapatek 1983; Siegler 1986). Three-month-old infants who have habituated to a particular light wave do dishabituate when presented with substantially longer or shorter waves. That is, they react to different wavelengths as novel stimuli, and thus can be said to perceive the differences. Does this mean that infants psychologically perceive color just as an adult does? It appears that they do, as indicated by the work of Bornstein (1976).

Bornstein first habituated 3- and 4-month-olds to a particular light wave and then exposed them to two other waves equally different in length from the first but in opposite directions. Most importantly, one of the new waves crossed a color boundary while the other one did not. For example, if the original wave were 510 nanometers in length, it would be seen as green; a light wave that is 30 nanometers shorter is clearly seen as blue while a wave that is 30 nanometers longer is still seen as green but of a different shade than the original stimulus. If the infant can discriminate between wavelengths but does not actually perceive color as adults do, then each of the new light waves would be equally novel and would produce equal responses in the infant. What actually happened, however, was that the reaction to the blue light was considerably different from the response to the different shade of green. Although equally different in length from the first wave, the new stimuli were not equally novel to the infants, meaning that not just wavelength differences were being responded to. Infants really do react to color differences; indeed, such reactions have been found as early as the first week after birth (Adams & Maurer 1984; Adams, Maurer & Davis 1986), indicating that color vision is well established very early in life.

The sense of hearing, well developed since early infancy, allows us to detect the slightest whisper and to withstand the sounds of loud rock music.

Audition

The human ear is a remarkably sensitive and highly efficient organ. It can detect the slightest whisper of a sound, even in atmospheres not particularly conducive to effective hearing. Consider the case of a parent who, in the midst of a busy, noisy party, suddenly hears the cries of a troubled infant coming from an upstairs bedroom. What is interesting is that the same sensitive organ that can hear a baby's slightest whimper in another part of the house can also tolerate the overwhelming roar of jet engines, city traffic, and rock music, provided that these are only occasional occurrences.

From a structural standpoint, the ear is almost completely developed by the time of birth and is free of mucus and amniotic fluid within a few hours after birth (Keith 1975). Thus, the newborn infant is already quite capable of hearing; in fact, as will be pointed out later in this section, the sense of hearing is well developed even before birth.

Intensity and Frequency

Studies of the hearing ability of newborns typically have used either physiological measures—such as heart rate (which accelerates when a newborn hears something)—or behavioral measures—such as blinking, a startle response, or the cessation of sucking (Acredolo & Hake 1982). Results of these studies indicate that the newborn's hearing is actually quite well developed in relation to that of an adult, but a few minor deficiencies in newborn hearing should be mentioned.

Differences in **intensity** of sound waves are perceived by human beings as differences in loudness of sound; intensity is calculated according to units of sound referred to as *decibels* (db). The louder the perceived sound, the higher is the number of decibels. The *auditory threshold* is the number of decibels at which sound becomes audible. Below this threshold, sound will not be heard.

Newborn infants can hear sounds, but their auditory thresholds are approximately 20 db higher than those of adults (Aslin, Pisoni & Jusczyck, 1983; Trehub & Schneider, 1985) thus an infant might have trouble hearing a soft whisper but can easily hear sounds within the normal range of human conversation. The amount of difference between an infant's and an adult's auditory threshold depends on the technique used to assess neonatal hearing (electroencephalogram [EEG] data indicate lower thresholds than data on heart rate), on the characteristics of the particular infant being tested (there appears to be considerable individual variation), and on the **frequency** of the sound presented. Frequency is the characteristic of sound waves experienced by the perceiver as *pitch,* and the measure of frequency is a unit known as the *hertz* (Hz).

Pitch as well as loudness is involved in determining auditory thresholds because, although able to hear sounds within a broad frequency range of 20 to 20,000 Hz, human beings are most sensitive to sounds within a more limited range of 100 to 4,000 Hz. The greater the deviation in pitch from the maximum sensitivity range, the louder the sound must be in order for it to be heard.

Infants are able to hear sounds throughout the normal human frequency range, but they are more sensitive to those at the higher than at the lower end (Lamb & Bornstein 1987; Olsho 1984). For low-frequency sounds an infant's auditory threshold is higher than that of an adult; in other words, sounds that an average adult can hear will not be loud enough to be heard by an infant. At high frequencies, however, there is little difference between the auditory threshold of an adult and that of a young infant (Schneider, Trehub & Bull 1980; Trehub, Schneider & Endman 1980).

The greater responsiveness of infants to higher-pitched tones can be demonstrated by their behavior when exposed to several tones that vary in pitch. Newborns are more likely to turn their heads toward the source of sound when a higher-frequency tone is presented than when they are exposed to a lower one (Morrongiello & Clifton 1984; Morrongiello, Clifton & Kulig 1982).

Research on the ability to detect minor frequency differences during infancy is rare. When infants in the first six months of life are studied, frequency discrimination has been found in some cases (Spears & Hohle 1967; Wormith, Pankhurst & Moffitt 1975), but not in others (Leventhal & Lipsitt 1964; Trehub 1973); for now the only safe conclusion to draw about this age period is that more research is needed in the area (Aslin, Pisoni & Jusczyck 1983). On the other hand, evidence of frequency discrimination after 6 months of age is more impressive. It appears that the older infant can discriminate among tones of different frequency nearly as well as an adult can (Olsho 1984; Olsho et al 1982).

Speech Perception

In real life, of course, infants are rarely exposed to pure tones. What they hear instead are complex sounds consisting of tones of various frequencies—usually ranging between 100 and 4,000 Hz. They are most likely to hear the sounds they are especially responsive to—the sounds of human speech!

The fact that newborn infants respond more readily to sounds at higher than at lower frequencies does not mean that they prefer high-pitched sounds. In fact, they are easily distressed by sounds in the higher-frequency range (above 4,000 Hz), whereas complex sounds of lower frequencies (between 200 and 2,000 Hz) are soothing and relaxing to them. Perhaps it is more than coincidence that this preferred range is precisely the range in which normal human speech occurs (Rosenblith & Sims-Knight 1985). Thus human infants seem particularly keyed into the vocalizations of members of their own species, a finding which, in theory at least could have adaptive significance for the survival of the offspring.

Even within their preferred frequency range of 200 to 2,000 Hz, infants are still more responsive to higher- than to lower-pitched sounds. Perhaps this is why adults automatically raise the pitch of their voices when speaking to a baby (Fogel 1984). Indeed, adults may find it difficult *not* to raise the pitch of their voices when addressing an infant! This higher-pitched way of speaking to infants, accompanied by exaggerated intonations, has been referred to as **motherese** (Siegler 1986). Almost 80 percent of the vocalizations of mothers to infants in the first six months of life fall into this category of speech (Stern, Spieker & MacKain 1982).

Even by the time they are 1 or 2 months of age, infants can perceive differences between similar speech sounds: *pah* and *bah*, *ma* and *na*, *s* and *z* (Eimas et al 1971; Siegler 1986). By 4 months of age they can readily distinguish among the various consonant and vowel sounds of their language (Aslin, Pisoni & Jusczyck 1983; Fogel 1984; Kuhl & Miller 1982; Trehub 1973). Considering their preference for sounds in the frequency range of human speech and their early sophistication at discriminating between similar speech sounds, infants seem to come into the world with a natural predisposition for attending to, and later understanding, human speech (Eimas 1985).

Not only is general speech perception apparent quite early in life, but also very young infants can recognize specific adult voices—most typically the voices of their mothers (DeCasper & Fifer 1980; Mehler et al. 1978; Mills & Melhuish 1974). De-Casper and Fifer (1980) found that 3-day-old infants would regularly vary their normal patterns of sucking in order to be rewarded by the sound of their mothers' voices reading a story; the same babies would not alter their sucking patterns in order to hear the voice of another woman reading the same story. Considering how young the babies were at the time of testing, it is unlikely that they had thoroughly familiarized themselves with their mothers' voices in the short time since birth; therefore, this study is thought to provide evidence that even a fetus can hear and distinguish among sounds from the outside world (Aslin, Pisoni & Juscyck 1983). Apparently there may be some truth in the popular wisdom that a mother's voice is more soothing to a crying newborn than is the voice of a stranger. Interestingly enough, newborn infants show no preference for their fathers' voices over that of a male stranger (DeCasper & Prescott 1984).

In summary, the sense of hearing is remarkably well developed in human infants. They hear particularly well at higher frequencies, and they can differentiate between one human voice and another. There is little to be said about further development during childhood and adolescence, except that hearing continues to improve slightly as a child grows up.

Taste

Considering the number of items they attempt to put in their mouths, infants would seem to obtain much of their knowledge of the world through this sensory organ. An extremely sensitive area of the human body, the mouth is highly receptive to pressure, to pain, to temperature, and—uniquely—to taste. *Taste buds,* which are tiny cells located on small raised surfaces known as *papillae,* are found throughout the mouth but particularly on the upper surface of the tongue. They allow human beings to distinguish among the four primary taste qualities of sweetness, sourness, saltiness, and bitterness.

The taste buds are present and apparently capable of functioning in the fourth intrauterine month (Bradley & Stearn 1967). In fact, they are far more widely distributed in the mouth of a fetus or an infant than they are in the mouth of an adult. Whether the taste buds actually function, however, depends on the stimulation they receive. Since the

The earliest taste preference in childhood is for that of sweetness, but this preference is usually outgrown by adolescence.

fetus opens its mouth by 9½ weeks after conception and begins to swallow amniotic fluid soon thereafter (Humphrey 1978), and since the fluid undergoes continual chemical changes throughout pregnancy, the taste buds may be stimulated prenatally; thus, the sense of taste is present even before birth (Acredolo & Hake 1982).

The most frequently used measures of a new baby's taste discrimination have been sucking frequency and the amount of liquid swallowed. It has been found that infants ranging from 1 day old to 4 months old suck faster and swallow more when presented with sweet solutions than with any others (Desor, Maller & Turner 1973; Engen, Lipsitt & Peck 1974; Desor, Maller & Greene 1977). Engen, Lipsitt, and Peck (1974) even found a preference in newborns for a slightly sweeter sucrose solution over a glucose solution. It would seem that the first

tooth to make its appearance in the human infant is the "sweet tooth"—and, for some unknown reason, the preference for sweetness is more noticeable in heavier newborns than in lighter ones and more noticeable in girls than in boys (Nisbett & Gurwitz 1970).

Newborn babies clearly do not like sour or bitter solutions. Steiner (1979) observed facial reactions of infants to a variety of different-tasting liquids and noted that sour and bitter solutions caused grimacing and pursing of the lips even in the youngest children, whereas sweet solutions resulted in facial relaxation, and what resembled a look of contentment.

Interestingly enough, newborn babies seem to be fairly indifferent to the taste of salt, and are equally likely to drink water salted or unsalted (Desor, Maller & Andrews 1975). By the time they are 4 months of age, however, they actually show a preference for salted over unsalted water, and this preference continues until they are approximately 2 years old (Beauchamp, Cowart & Moran 1986).

Even the newborn, then, is a discriminating taster, but do tastes change as children get older? Eating patterns certainly do. As Walk (1981) pointed out, children's preference for sweetness is usually outgrown by adolescence or adulthood. What is more, as children develop, taste preferences are increasingly affected by the context in which they are experienced. For example, children beyond the age of 2 will reject sweetened or salted water, but they will accept sweetness or saltiness in appropriate foods; salt adds to the flavor of soup but makes water undrinkable (Beauchamp & Moran 1985; Cowart & Beauchamp 1986).

A reasonable interpretation of these findings is that, while the basic sensory apparatus for taste is present from birth, actual taste preferences are heavily influenced by experience, even at a very young age. While most 2-year-olds will not drink sweetened water, some will do so, and these are children whose mothers routinely fed them sweetened water during infancy (Beauchamp & Moran 1985).

In reviewing the literature on developmental changes in taste, Engen (1977) noted that adults can differentiate among similar tasting solutions with greater accuracy than children can. It is not known why these age differences are found. Is there some physiological change in the organism that brings about a greater refinement in taste discrimination, or do the changes occur because of experience? Walk (1981) prefers the experiential explanation: the experience they have with eating allows people to discriminate more accurately between one food and another, and to educate their taste buds by exposing them to a wider variety of foods. By tasting only a spoonful of soup, an experienced chef should be able to determine precisely what its ingredients are and in precisely what proportions they were added.

Smell

About the seventh month after conception, the nostrils open. The human fetus should, theoretically at least, begin to respond to odors (Acre-

dolo & Hake 1982). It is a theoretical question, of course, because testing the sense of smell in a fetus is not possible, although Sarnat (1978) found that even premature infants as young as 28 weeks gestational age respond to strong odors.

The research on olfaction—the sense of smell—during infancy has been somewhat limited, especially in comparison with studies of vision and audition. Existing research does indicate that infants are capable of detecting odors, and that olfactory sensitivity increases considerably even during the first week of life (Acredolo & Hake 1982; Lamb & Bornstein 1987).

Evidence of the increasing sensitivity of the olfactory system has been demonstrated in a number of studies of young infants' sensitivity to parental odors (Cernoch & Porter 1985; MacFarlane 1975; Schaal et al. 1980). For example, MacFarlane (1975) tested infants' head-turing reactions to their mothers' breast pads. At 2 days of age, infants were no more likely to turn toward a breast pad used by their own mothers than they were to turn toward one used by a stranger. However, by 6 days a definite preference was emerging, and the preference became stronger with each passing day. Young infants clearly favored the breast pad that gave off an odor characteristic of their own mothers.

In a study by Cernoch and Porter (1985), 2-week-old infants were more likely to turn their heads toward a pad that had been worn under their mothers' arms than toward a similar pad worn by a stranger. Interestingly enough, this effect was demonstrated only for breast-fed infants; bottle-fed infants did not show similar signs of odor recognition. Neither group of infants displayed any recognition of their fathers' underarm pads. Reasons for the greater olfactory sensitivity of breast-fed infants are unclear. Among the possibilities suggested by Cernoch and Porter (1985) are that the process of nursing causes a mother's body to produce chemical substances whose odors are particularly appealing to a nursing child, or that a nursing infant simply has more prolonged contact with mother's skin than does a bottle-fed baby and so her odor becomes more familiar. Whatever the reason, it seems that human olfaction is well developed in early infancy, and also that the sense of smell may play a role in early mother-child socialization. Not only do infants recognize and respond to their mothers' odors, but mothers can recognize their own 2-day-old infants by their characteristic odors alone (Porter, Cernoch & McLaughlin 1983; Russell, Mendelson & Peeke 1983)!

As additional support for the view that olfaction is well developed early in life, Steiner (1979) found that infants on the day they were born made positive or negative facial responses to a variety of odors—despite the fact that they could have had no previous experience with the odors in question. Apparently, as in the case of the sense of taste, the sense of smell is present at a very early point in a child's development.

There is little to report about the development of olfaction throughout the childhood years because little research has been done on the topic. The sense of smell seems to reach a peak of sophistication by the age of 10, with slight change throughout the remainder of the lifespan (Rovee, Cohen & Shlapack 1975).

Touch

The sense of touch is already well developed in newborn infants, and even in fetuses a few months before birth (Spears & Hohle 1967; Acredolo & Hake 1982). The early sophistication of the tactile system is evident in the newborn's reflexive responses. For example, pressing slightly on the palm will cause the infant to grasp the pressure stimulus and to begin sucking, and stroking the infant's cheek will also produce a sucking and a rooting response.

As infants develop, the sense of touch is used more frequently and more efficiently as a means of exploring the environment. Illustrating these trends are findings by Ruff (1984), who studied the techniques used by 6- to 12-month-old infants in manipulating and exploring objects. Seated on their mothers' laps, the babies were given objects one at a time to handle, and their behaviors were recorded on tape. Ruff discovered that mouthing objects decreased with age, as did simply looking at them and transferring them between hand and mouth. Fingering objects increased significantly with age from 6 to 12 months; older infants were more likely than younger ones to move their fin-

gertips across the surfaces of objects. Thus, the sense of touch was used increasingly as a means of exploring the world. In addition, touch was used more efficiently with increasing age. When objects differed in texture, fingering increased; when they varied in shape, infants were more likely to rotate them and to pass them from one hand to the other. Fingering objects seems to provide the most information about texture, while rotating objects and looking at them from different angles seem to tell more about shape. The infant, therefore, touches and handles materials in ways that are increasingly appropriate for getting as much information as possible from the environment.

Tactile sensitivity changes little throughout the childhood years, or for that matter throughout the remainder of the lifespan. While some studies indicate a decrease in tactile stimulation after age 50, others do not. This leads to the conclusion that age decreases in tactile sensitivity are certainly not inevitable; such changes occur in a minority of individuals (Kenshalo 1977).

Integration of the Senses

Up to this point in the chapter the various senses have been discussed separately, almost as if they function in isolation from one another; but, of course, this is not the case at all. Each of the senses can be thought of as a subsystem within the overall human perceptual system. Each subsystem is integrated with, or coordinated with, all of the others (Mendelson & Haith 1976). Six-month-old infants will turn their heads to see a ringing bell, will reach to touch it, and—if possible—will bring it immediately to their mouths for tasting. The ability of a person of any age to enjoy a meal depends not only upon the taste, but also upon the food's appearance, aroma, and texture. More generally, perception of the world depends upon the coordination of information simultaneously processed by the various sensory subsystems.

There is little disagreement on the necessity of sensory integration, but there is controversy as to how and when this integration first occurs. One view is that the sensory systems first develop independently, and slowly, as a result of interaction with the environment, and become coordinated during the first year of life. Jean Piaget, for example, spoke of action sequences such as looking, listening, sucking, and grasping as developing individually at first and gradually becoming coordinated; thus, looking and listening become coordinated between the ages of 2 and 4 months (e.g., the child turns his or her head and eyes in the direction of a sound), as do looking and grasping, and grasping and sucking (Flavell 1985).

The opposite side of the argument, and the one more widely accepted today, maintains that the sensory systems do not develop individually, but that some degree of sensory integration is present even from birth. A number of studies within the past ten years point to evidence of sensory integration at a very young age (Gibson & Spelke 1983; Siegler 1986; Spelke 1979, 1981, 1985). For example, babies within the first month of life seem to turn their heads toward a variety of sounds, such as a click, a rattle, or a human voice saying "baby" (Alegria & Noirot 1978; Crassini & Broerse 1980; Field et al. 1980; Wertheimer 1961). Even newborn babies display a primitive form of eye-hand coordination! That is, they recognize a relationship between looking at and touching. Von Hofsten (1982) found that newborns will extend their arms slightly forward when they look at a slowly moving object, as if aiming their hands at the object. Reaching and hearing also seem to be coordinated in early infancy; young babies who hear a noise-making toy in a dark room seem to extend their arms in the general direction of the toy (Wishart, Bower & Dunkeld 1978).

Slightly older babies display signs of even more sophisticated sensory integration. For example, Spelke (1985) reported that 5-month-olds prefer to look at a film with a visually appropriate sound track rather than at one with an inappropriate sound track. The infants in her study saw films of a stuffed animal—a yellow kangaroo—bouncing up and down on a grassy surface. In one film they heard a "thump" each time the kangaroo landed on the grass; in another film the "thump" and the landings were not coordinated. The babies actually preferred to look at the film in which action and sound were matched. Even at this young age, their perception of events involves a blending of auditory and visual information, and the mismatch between the two was clearly noticeable to them—although they perhaps were not as annoyed as adults watching a film with a sound track out of sync!

A similar preference for coordinated information from the different senses was found by Schiff, Benasich, and Bornstein (1986), who studied infants' perceptions of approach and recession. When a sound-producing object comes closer, it looks larger and sounds louder; when it moves away from the viewer, it appears smaller and sounds softer. If auditory information and visual information are being coordinated, a person would naturally expect the pattern of larger-louder during approach and smaller-softer during recession. In fact, even 5-month-old infants display adequate auditory-visual coordination to expect such a pattern, and they appear confused when the pattern is altered. That is, if an approaching object becomes quieter instead of louder, they seem to have more difficulty making sense out of the experience.

In summary, not only are the individual senses quite well developed at birth or soon thereafter, but also the young human infant is already skilled at coordinating input from the various senses into meaningful perceptions. That is not to say that experience is unimportant in sensory development, but only that infants begin life with an innate capacity to organize their sensory input (Lamb & Bornstein 1987).

Cognitive Aspects of Perception

Thus far this chapter has emphasized the basic sensory channels through which information from the outside world is relayed to the human organism. But human beings are also capable of the active cognitive process that directs and translates sensory input. The adequate functioning of the sense organs determines what *can* be seen, heard, smelled, touched, or tasted, but what is actually perceived at any particular time is influenced by a host of psychological and sociocultural factors: attitudes, expectations, interests, needs, and prior experiences.

Sociocultural Factors in Perception

Despite the fact that all human beings are equipped with the same sensory equipment, there are marked cultural differences in the ways in which the world is perceived. Cross-cultural research on perception has dealt mostly with the sense of vision and has emphasized two particular areas of study: three-dimensional perception and optical illusions.

Perceiving Three Dimensions in Two

Human beings perceive in three dimensions, and some depth cues (e.g., kinetic cues, stereopsis) appear either to be innate or to depend on physiological maturation. Other depth cues such as size, shadowing, and the partial overlapping of figures appear to be learned, and it is these "pictorial" cues that are susceptible to the influence of culture.

Pictorial depth cues make it possible to perceive depth where none actually exists—on a two-dimensional surface such as a painting or a photograph. An artist suggests depth in a painting by making figures in the foreground larger than those in the background, by making "closer" figures overlap those "farther away," by using shadow, by blurring the figures in the background, and by using perspective (as when the buildings on two sides of a street seem to come closer to one another when viewed from an increasing distance). When looking at a painting or a photograph, people perceive depth only because they have learned to associate certain cues with depth. The sensory information provided by binocular cues clearly indicates that no depth really exists. In a sense, people learn to perceive depth in pictures despite sensory evidence to the contrary.

Pictorial depth perception is found in American children as young as 5 months of age (Yonas, Cleaves & Pettersen 1978; Yonas & Granrud 1985), and a relationship exists between the age of the child and sophistication in using pictorial depth cues. The performance of older children is more accurate and more consistent than that of younger ones (Gibson & Spelke 1983). It is difficult to know, however, whether the age differences result from the maturing of the sense organs or from children's experience in looking at pictures, since age and experience can never be completely separated. The

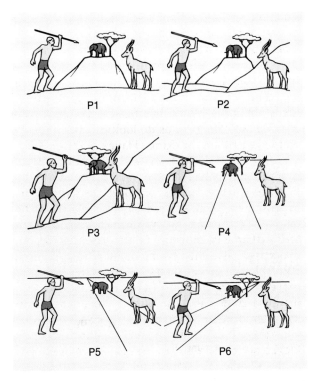

Figure 5.3 Line Drawings Used to Study Cultural Differences in Depth Perception

Source: Journal of Social Psychology, 52, p. 186, 1960. Reprinted with permission of the Helen Dwight Reid Educational Foundation. Published by Heldref Publications, 4000 Albemarle St., N.W., Washington, D.C. 20016. Copyright 1960.

prevailing belief among psychologists is that learning is significantly involved in pictorial depth perception; people develop habits of attending selectively to certain types of information, such as pictorial depth cues, and ignoring others (Gibson 1969). Such perceptual habits seem to depend upon the characteristics of the culture in which the child is raised.

Hudson (1960) carried out one of the better-known studies of cultural differences in three-dimensional perception. In this study, South African children—and some adults—were tested. Some subjects were black, some white, some educated, and some uneducated. All were shown a group of line drawings containing a variety of depth cues (see Figure 5.3). The drawings contained depth cues of size (e.g., the man and the antelope are larger than the elephant and the tree), partial overlap (e.g., the overlapping hills, the antelope overlapping the elephant), and perspective (e.g., the sides of the road come together in the upper half of P-4).

Hudson questioned the participants in his study about the relative nearness of the figures. An answer indicating that the man and the antelope were nearer than the elephant was characteristic of a three-dimensional perceiver, whereas a two-dimensional perceiver saw no difference in the nearness of the figures. Hudson discovered that three-dimensional perception was related to the degree of schooling the child had experienced, and to the degree of exposure to pictures in books and magazines. Unschooled children, who apparently had little opportunity to view drawings and photographs, were more likely to miss the depth cues in the stimulus drawings than were school-educated children and teachers.

Hagen and Johnson (1977) found further evidence of the influence of experience on depth perception in pictures. They tested American children and adults using Hudson's materials and an Americanized version of his test. In the Americanized version, familiar-looking drawings of children were used instead of a hunter and wild animals. Hagen and Johnson found that adults performed better than children when the original Hudson stimulus materials were used, and that adults and children performed equally well when the American version was used. In other words, developmental differences in the ability to perceive pictorial depth disappeared when the stimulus materials were made more familiar, making it clear that the factor of prior experience is highly significant in studies of this type.

Optical Illusions

An optical illusion occurs when a viewer consistently misperceives information in a visual display. Illustrative of optical illusions referred to extensively in cross-cultural research are the following:

• *The Sander Parallelogram.* When looking at the diagonal lines within the parallelogram in Figure 5.4, most people in Western societies see line A as being longer than line B. In fact, the lines are identical in length.

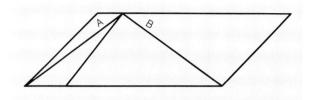

Figure 5.4   The Sander Parallelogram

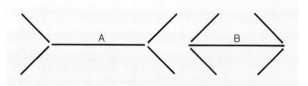

Figure 5.5   The Müller-Lyer Illusion

• *The Müller-Lyer Illusion.* Figure 5.5 contains two horizontal lines, with diagonal lines at the ends of each pointing either away from (A) or toward (B) the midpoint of the horizontal line. Westerners typically see the horizontal lines as being different in length, with A the longer of the two. In fact, the horizontal lines are identical in length.
• *The Horizontal-Vertical Illusion.* Figure 5.6 presents two variations of this illusion. In each case, the horizontal and vertical lines are identical in length. Nevertheless, most Westerners see the horizontal line, particularly in the case of the inverted T, as being shorter than the vertical.

The current thinking about optical illusions is that illusions are learned rather than innate and that they result from a set of inferences made about the world. The fact that these inferences vary from one culture to another explains cultural differences in susceptibility to illusions (Deregowski 1980; Segall, Campbell & Herskovits 1966).

Segall, Campbell and Herskovits (1966) attributed to various cultural groups three specific sets of perceptual inferences. These inferences are not made by persons in all cultures, and as a result cultural differences exist in susceptibility to illusions. The three sets of inferences are:

1. *The Carpentered World.* Westerners live in a world of straight lines, squares, and rectangles—configurations that do not usually occur in nature. Conse-

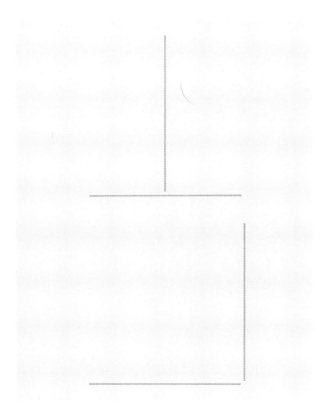

Figure 5.6   The Horizontal-Vertical Illusion

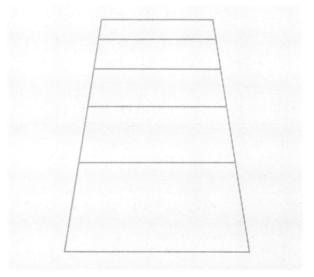

Figure 5.7   The Foreshortening of Receding Horizontals Effect

quently, Westerners tend to perceive "carpentered" images more readily than non-Westerners do.

Consider an example of how carpentered-world inferences might enhance susceptibility to illusions. In the Sander parallelogram (Figure 5.4), Westerners typically see the internal diagonal line on the left (A) as longer than the one on the right (B); non-Westerners do not. Segall suggested that people living in a carpentered world see the Sander parallelogram as three dimensional; the left diagonal (A) connects opposite corners of the *front* of the figure, while the right diagonal (B) connects opposite corners of its *side*. Since the front is seen as a larger surface than the side, the left diagonal is seen as longer than the right.

2. *The Foreshortening of Receding Horizontals.* Imagine a person standing in the center of an empty room on a floor covered by squares of tile. If the person visually follows a line of tiles as they recede into the distance, he or she will notice that the shape of the tiles appears to change, from square to increasingly trapezoidal (see Figure 5.7). The sides of the tile that are parallel to the viewer's line of vision appear to shorten more than those that run from side to side across the line of vision.

People who live in primarily vertical worlds, such as modern cities, dense forests, or at the bottom of steep canyons, are less likely to notice the proportionately greater shortening of lines parallel to their line of vision than are people who live in vast open spaces—farmers, plains dwellers, desert peoples.

In terms of susceptibility to illusions, a Kansas farmer might be more susceptible to the horizontal-vertical illusion (Figure 5.6) than is the forest dweller. The vertical line may appear to be longer than the horizontal line because of the farmer's tendency to see the line as extending backward into space, with the vertical representing a line parallel to the line of vision. Experience indicates that such lines are subject to a distorted shortening relative to horizontal lines, and so the farmer compensates for the distortion by imagining a perceptual increase of the vertical but not of the horizontal line. As a result, the vertical is perceived as the longer of the two lines, even though the lines are actually identical in length. Presumably, a forest dweller would make no such compensation and would be less susceptible to the horizontal-vertical illusion.

3. *Symbolizing Three Dimensions in Two.* As was noted in the previous section of this chapter, the habit

The ability to read involves differentiating among written symbols, decoding letters to sounds, and using higher order units of meaning.

of representing the world in drawings is culture-specific. Familiarity with two-dimensional representations of the three-dimensional world may influence susceptibility or resistance to a variety of optical illusions contained in line drawings.

Theories of Perceptual Development

The findings of cross-cultural research on selected aspects of visual perception indicate significant cultural differences in the ways human beings perceive the world. It seems that many of these differences can be attributed to acquired inferences rather than to biological factors. While few of these studies involved developmental comparisons, and many used adult participants rather than children, the implications for the field of child development are considerable. It appears that experience is largely responsible for children's perceptual development. The sense organs, as noted earlier in this chapter, are remarkably sophisticated at birth

or shortly afterwards. Thus, the changes in the ways children perceive the world as they grow up are influenced by the particular experiences, attitudes, values, and biases of the cultures they live in.

But how are these experiences acquired? To answer that question, this section discusses two major theories of perceptual development. The first theory emphasizes the child's developing ability to differentiate among the distinctive features of objects in the environment. The second theory stresses the child's tendency to enrich sensory input by bringing to it a set of prior experiences, attitudes, and values. (Applying Our Knowledge "Learning to Read" discusses a major perceptual task in our culture.)

Differentiation Theory
According to **differentiation theory** (Gibson 1979; Gibson & Spelke 1983), perception is an *active, purposeful,* and *meaningful* process of seeking out the invariant abstract properties of events, objects,

Applying Our Knowledge

Learning to Read

One of the most dramatic illustrations of perceptual development in the young child is the emergence of the ability to read. Ultimately the sophistication of a child's reading skills is influenced by a variety of psychological and social factors, such as motivation, interest, the presence of direct reinforcement, and exposure to adult models who enjoy reading. However, the basic ability to make sense of the written word initially depends upon a number of underlying perceptual processes.

What does a child need to do in order to derive meaning from written symbols? According to Gibson and Levin (1975; Gibson 1969), reading occurs in three different phases. First is *the ability to differentiate among written symbols*. The child must recognize differences among the letters of the alphabet by attending to the distinctive features of each letter, and noticing how a particular letter differs from others. For example, the features of a capital *A* include a horizontal line (−), a diagonal line (╱), a diagonal line in the reverse direction (╲), an intersection of lines, and symmetry between the right and left halves of the letter. Unlike a *B*, an *A* contains no vertical line (|), and no curved lines of any sort. An *A* and a *B*, therefore, are relatively easy to differentiate between. A *P* and an *R*, however, share a number of common features (e.g., vertical lines, closed curves, intersections) and differ only on the diagonal line contained in the *R*. Letters that contain similar features are harder to differentiate between than are letters with radically different features. What is more, some differences are easier to detect than others (Gibson et al. 1962). Letters that differ only in the fact that one is a closed figure and the other is an open figure (an *O* and a *U*) are easier to differentiate between than are letters differing only in rotation or reversal (a *b* and a *d*).

A second phase in the reading process according to Gibson (1969; Gibson & Levin 1975) is *the ability to decode letters to sounds*. This is not, however, a simple one-to-one association process. Simple association can explain how a child learns to name the letters of the alphabet, but it does not explain how a child learns to read. In the English language, there is often little resemblance between the sound of a word and the sounds of the individual letters contained within it; for example, the spoken word *brought* does not include the sounds of the letters *o, u, g* or *h*. A knowledge of the sounds of the individual letters will not always prepare a child to correctly pronounce the entire word.

What, then, does a child do when decoding letters to sounds? Gibson (1969) described the child's gradual recognition of "spelling patterns"—clusters of letters pronounced the same way in all words in which they appear. In a sense, the child acquires invariant rules for pronunciation that may be used when letters are combined in certain ways. As an illustration of the use of spelling pattern rules, consider the letter combinations *CABE* and *CIPE*. While these are not real words, anyone who can read English can pronounce them correctly. The reader knows, first of all, that a *C* followed by an *A* is pronounced as a *K*, while a *C* followed by an *I* is pronounced as an *S*. The reader also knows that the *E* at the end of each word gives the initial vowel a long rather than a short sound. If the *E* were not present, as in *CIP*, the word would have a different sound. The ability to correctly pronounce such patterns in nonsense words improves with age from early elementary school to adulthood, and children characterized as "good readers" are better able to pronounce nonsense words than are "poor readers" (Calfee, Venezky & Chapman 1969).

Invariant spelling patterns can be entire one-syllable words (e.g., *cat, bed*) or merely letter combinations, such as *BL, SH,* or *CK,* that can be combined into words. The child who knows how to pronounce *BL* and *CK,* as well as the letter *A,* can pronounce the word *black*. In time the child can pronounce words of any length as he or she recognizes the patterns contained within them.

A final stage in learning to read is *the ability to use higher-order units*. As Gibson and Levin (1975)

(continued next page)

Applying Our Knowledge (continued)

pointed out, an effective reader goes beyond the word to derive meaning from sentences or paragraphs. Indeed, some children are able to read words very well but treat the words as single units and therefore have little understanding of what they are reading (Cromer 1979). To help children go beyond mere word recognition to meaningful reading, Gibson and Levin concluded that written material presented to

children should be of high-intrinsic interest and should contain sentences that vary in length and complexity. Many children's books contain short and overly simplified sentences, perhaps in the belief that complexity will confuse a beginning reader. However, in a number of studies it has been found that comprehension is best when written material most closely resembles the child's own manner of speaking (Gammon 1970).

Even a kindergartner uses sentences that are lengthy and contain a rich variety of parts of speech, phrases, and clauses (Gibson & Levin 1975). Underestimating a child's ability to handle complexity and variety on the printed page may actually inhibit the child's reading progress. A sentence such as *See Spot run* is rarely found in human speech, even during early childhood!

and places. The sense organs pick up stimulation from the environment, but it is not the stimulation that we perceive; instead, we perceive events and objects in an organized unified way.

To illustrate the active and meaningful nature of perception, Gibson (1979) speaks of **affordances,** meaning those things that the environment offers or provides to the perceiver: the sun affords warmth; a roof affords shelter from the rain. Affordances are possibilities for action. Thus, perception must be thought of as an active process rather than as a mere receiving of environmental stimulation. The meaningfulness of perception is illustrated by the fact that from the constant flow of available information, people select what is most meaningful to them. They perceive that which has the most important affordances for them. This principle was illustrated earlier in this chapter when it was noted that newborn infants are particularly attentive to their mothers' voices and to the odors of their bodies. The mother is an object that offers more important affordances, or possibilities for action, than are offered by various other objects in the environment.

Advocates of differentiation theory argue that there are five general trends in perceptual development:

1. Exploration of the world becomes more systematic and orderly.
2. The child continues to discover new affordances as he or she grows.
3. Perception increases in specificity, and more subtle invariants and affordances are discovered.
4. Perception becomes more efficient.
5. Perceived affordances become less narrowly focused and are easier to generalize to new situations.

Enrichment Theory

Differentiation theorists believe that perceptual development means perceiving the world with increasing accuracy. **Enrichment** theorists represent an opposite point of view. They argue that as people develop, their perception is increasingly influenced by what they bring of themselves to the act of perceiving. Illustrating this point of view, cognitive psychologist Jerome Bruner (1973) discussed the concept of going "beyond the information given" in the act of knowing, by which he meant that people bring to any cognitive act a good deal of their own previous cognitive history. Two individuals with different experiences of life, different theoretical biases, and different mental categories may view an identical object or event but have totally different perceptions of it. For example, some spectators at a basketball game never see the fouls committed by the home team but constantly see imagined fouls committed by the opponents.

Much of Bruner's early perceptual research dealt with the effects of values, needs, and personality factors in the process of perception. He found, for example, that poor children consistently overestimated the size of coins while richer children did not—presumably because the coins were most significant for those who needed them the most (Bruner & Goodman 1947). He observed that people recognize certain words more easily than others from a rapidly presented word list; and that people recognize most easily the words which have particular positive significance in their lives (Postman, Bruner & McGinnies 1948). In contrast, certain threatening words are specifically not seen in a visual display—a phenomenon described as perceptual defense (McGinnies 1949). Bruner remarked that such findings resemble what occurs in the case of lovers (who) "either for defense or enhancement, see only the good and beautiful in their chosen ones" (1973, 97).

Summary

1. Human visual acuity develops rapidly during the first six months of life. The young infant's acuity is limited for a variety of reasons.
2. Even newborn infants are sensitive to the contours of forms; the earliest scanning strategies focus on the edges of forms while later strategies emphasize the internal features.
3. Young infants show definite preference for complex patterns over simple ones, and they seem to have a particular interest in the patterns of a human face.
4. Depth is perceived through the use of various cues. Kinetic monocular cues develop first, followed by binocular cues and then static monocular cues. All three types of cues are present by the age of 7 months.
5. Size constancy is definitely present by the age of 4 to 6 months, while shape constancy is found as early as 3 months.
6. Human infants see the world in color, and current evidence indicates that color vision is present from birth.
7. Newborns' hearing is well developed but their intensity thresholds are higher and their frequency discrimination poorer than those of adults. In other words, infants have more difficulty than adults in hearing soft noises and in distinguishing between tones of similar pitch.
8. Infants are particularly tuned in to human speech and can distinguish among various speech sounds by the time they are 1 to 2 months of age.
9. The senses of taste, smell, and touch are well developed even before birth. There is little evidence of age decline in any of these senses.
10. The senses can be thought of as systems that do not develop in isolation, but are integrated with one another very early in life.
11. There are noticeable cross-cultural differences in visual perception, and even differences within cultures, that are related to the amount of schooling received. These differences, often observed in studies on three-dimensional perception of pictures, strongly suggest that perception has a significant experiential component.
12. The differentiation theory of perceptual development suggests that as people develop, they become increasingly attuned to the distinctive features of the environment they live in.
13. The enrichment theory of perception is that perceivers bring more of themselves to the act of perception as they develop. It becomes increasingly difficult to distinguish between the mental state of the perceiver and the reality that he or she is perceiving.

Key Terms

habituation
visual acuity
contrast sensitivity
binocular disparity
stereopsis
size constancy
shape constancy
intensity
frequency
motherese
differentiation theory
affordances
enrichment theory

Suggested Readings

Gibson, E.J. (1969). *Principles of perceptual learning and development*. New York: Appleton-Century-Crofts.

The most concise and comprehensive overview of the work of James and Eleanor Gibson, pioneers in the study of human perception. The book presents a thorough discussion of differentiation theory, and a comparison and contrast of the theory with cognitive and "response-oriented" theories.

Perception: Mechanisms and models: Readings from Scientific American. (1972). San Francisco: Freeman.

A collection of *Scientific American* reprints spanning approximately thirty years. Many of them have already become classic articles in the field. Areas covered include the sensory systems, illusions, and development of specific perceptual functions. There are many excellent illustrations throughout.

Walk, R.D. (1981). *Perceptual development.* Monterey, CA: Brooks/Cole.

A relatively short but concise summary of theory and research in the area of perceptual development across the life span. Written with enthusiasm and humor, the book covers sensory development, attention, the effects of sensory deprivation, perception in special populations (e.g., the elderly, the blind, the deaf), and a number of theoretical issues related to human perception.

Readings from the Literature

The following article deals with the recognition of facial expressions in 7-month-old infants. As you read the article, keep in mind these questions:

- What do the authors mean when they conclude that the 7-month-old infant seems to respond to facial expressions in a categorical fashion?

- What are the possible reasons for the preference of the infants in this study for fear faces rather than happy ones?

- What does this study, and related studies discussed in the article and in the previous chapter, tell us about the role of sensory and perceptual development in the infant's social interactions?

The Generalized Discrimination of Facial Expressions by Seven-Month-Old Infants

Charles A. Nelson
Purdue University

Kim G. Dolgin
University of Minnesota

Two experiments were conducted to examine 7-month-old infant's perception of the facial expressions happy and fear. Using a paired-comparison procedure, infants in the first experiment were able to generalize their discrimination of these 2 expressions across the faces of 4 male and female models if they were first presented with the set of happy faces, but not if they were first presented with the set of fear faces. A second experiment was conducted to examine the source of the stimulus presentation order effect. Here a second group of 7-month-old infants was presented with a single male or female face posing both the happy and fear expressions simultaneously. The results revealed significantly longer looking to the fear face. This preference to look at fear faces is discussed, as are its implications for studies of expression recognition in general.

The human face plays a central role in parent-infant communication prior to the onset of language; for example, the face may serve as the primary medium through which the infant learns about the caretaker's feelings and intentions. Therefore, it is not surprising that a great deal of attention recently has been directed toward understanding the infant's ability to perceive facial expressions (for recent reviews of this literature, see Dolgin & Azmitia, in press; Field & Walden, 1982; Nelson, in press; Oster, 1981). With few exceptions (e.g., Caron, Caron, & Myers, 1982; Nelson, Morse, & Leavitt, 1979), the studies designed to examine this ability have tested infants with expressions posed by a single model. Accordingly, it is difficult to determine if infants were discriminating changes in facial expression per se, or discriminating changes in the features of the face that might in fact be specific to that individual's face (e.g., some portion of the mouth or eyes). A more robust test of this ability, then, might be to determine if infants can generalize their discrimination of facial expressions across the faces of several individuals. By "generalized discrimination" it is meant that discrimination along one dimension (e.g., facial expression) persists despite changes along some other dimension (e.g., the model's face). Thus, to claim that infants are able to discriminate changes in facial expressions per se, rather than changes in isolated features of the face, it would seem necessary to demonstrate that infants are able to recognize the arrangement of certain features of the face (i.e., those signifying expressions) as being invariant across the faces of several individuals.

There have been two recent studies that have examined the infant's ability to generalize his/her discrimination of facial expressions across multiple models' faces. Nelson et al. (1979) reported that 7-month-old infants could generalize their discrimination of happy and fear expressions across the faces of three different female models. This discrimination was constrained, however, by the order in which the stimuli were presented. That is, infants could discriminate the two expressions if they were first familiarized to happy faces, but not if they were first familiarized to fear. More recently, Caron et al. (1982) reported that 7-month-olds could fully generalize their discrimination of happy and surprise expressions across six different female models' faces, although at 5½ months such discrimination only obtained when infants were habituated to the set of happy faces.

On the basis of these two studies, it appears that by 7 months infants are responding to facial expressions in a somewhat categorical fashion, although their doing so may depend in part on the order in which the stimuli are presented. There were unfortunately two limitations of both studies, however, First, the findings were specific only to female faces. Second, no attempt was made to determine why discrimination was constrained by the order in which the stimuli were presented. One goal of the present study was to ascertain whether such generalized discrimination would persist across faces of both sexes. A second goal

was to shed light on the nature of infants' differential responding to happy and fear faces.

Experiment 1

The primary goal of the first experiment was to establish whether 7-month-old infants could generalize their discrimination of happy and fear expressions across four different male and female models' faces. A secondary goal was to determine if the stimulus presentation order effect originally reported by Nelson et al. (1979) could be replicated.

Method

Using a paired-comparison procedure, 32 7-month-old infants (M = 210.53 days, range = 198–233 days, SD = 9.14 days) were presented with three 30-sec familiarization trials. Each familiarization trial consisted of identical color photographs of either a male or female model posing the same happy or fear expression on both the left and right sides of the screen. Following the familiarization phase infants were presented with two 10-sec test trials, in which a fourth male or female model's face was seen posing the familiar expression on one side and the novel expression on the other; the position of the faces was reversed during the second test trial. Evidence of discrimination would be inferred if infants looked significantly longer at the novel stimulus than the familiar stimulus at test. Two male and two female faces were used in all. These faces were selected from a set of seven that had been photographed by the authors and then judged by 12 adults (using a seven-point scale) as being most prototypical of happy and fear expressions. Half the infants were familiarized to happy faces and tested on fear, while the other half were familiarized to fear and tested on happy. The order in which the four models were shown to the infants and the order in which the novel test stimulus was presented on the left and right sides on the two test trials were counterbalanced across subjects. Approximately 3 sec intervened between trials. Testing took place in a darkened room. The infant was positioned on the parent's lap facing a screen onto which an investigator could project slides of the two stimuli (each stimulus subtended approximately 16 degrees) using two Kodak carousel slide projectors (Model 800). Trained and reliable observers (M = 96%), blind to condition, recorded when the infant looked at either of the stimuli (on the basis of corneal reflections). These looking times were recorded directly onto an Esterline Angus event recorder and subsequently scored blind by another investigator.

Results

To analyze the discrimination findings, the data from the two test trials were pooled, yielding one score for novelty and one for familiarity. The looking times were then incorporated into an ANOVA, comparing the two groups (familiarize to happy, test on fear or familiarize to fear, test on happy) and the novel versus familiar stimulus. The results revealed a significant group × novel/familiar looking time interaction, $F(1,30) = 7.82, p < .01$. Duncan's multiple-range test (Keppel, 1973) was used to analyze the source of this interaction and revealed that only infants familiarized to happy and tested on fear evidenced a significant novelty preference (M familiar = 7.31 sec vs. M novel = 9.69 sec; crit $t(30) = 2.15, p < .05$).

Further inspection of the data indicated that there was no statistically reliable decline in looking over the three familiarization trials to either the happy or fear faces. In addition, on each trial infants familiarized to happy looked as long as those familiarized to fear.

Discussion

The primary finding of interest was that infants could generalize their discrimination of happy and fear expressions across both male and female models' faces if they were first familiarized to the set of happy faces. However, generalized discrimination was not obtained when fear served as the familiarization stimulus. There was no evidence in the present study (as was speculated by Nelson et al. [1979]) that such differential responding to happy and fear resulted from different rates of habituation to the set of happy and fear faces. Nevertheless, it is possible that the failure of infants to prefer the novel happy expression after having been familiarized to the set of fear faces could have resulted from an initial tendency of infants to look longer, or "prefer," fear faces. Such preferences might persist through the test trials and thus preclude infants from attending to the novel (happy) stimulus. While there appeared to be no absolute looking preference for happy faces as compared with fear faces between

groups (i.e., when the looking times of infants familiarized to happy were compared with the looking times of these familiarized to fear), it is possible that such preferences would emerge when tested *within* groups (such as occurs during the test trials). The goal of the second experiment was to test for such within-group preferences.

Experiment 2

Method

In the second experiment another group of 32 7-month-old infants ($M = 216.34$ days, range = 206–229 days, SD = 6.39) was tested, using the same four models as before. Each infant was presented with two 45-sec trials of a happy versus fear expression posed by one of the four models used in Experiment 1. The left and right positions were reversed from trial 1 to trial 2, and infants were randomly assigned to view one of the four models (e.g., trial 1 = model A happy and model A fear; trial 2 = model A fear and model A happy). The same apparatus, setting, and procedure were used as before.

Results

Looking times were incorporated into an ANOVA, and comparisons were made among the four groups (i.e., infants who had seen model A, B, C, or D), whether infants looked longer to happy or fear, and the two trials. The results revealed a significant main effect of the happy vs. fear component, $F(1,28) = 5.79, p < .025$, and of the trials component, $F(1,28) = 6.33, p < .025$. Inspection of the data indicated that infants looked longer to the fear than the happy stimulus (collapsing over trials 1 and 2, M fear = 17.57 sec and M happy = 15.05 sec) and looked more on trial 1 than on trial 2 (collapsing over happy vs. fear, M trial 1 = 17.1 sec and M trial 2 = 15.52 sec). In addition, a significant group × trial interaction was found, $F(3,28) = 5.49, p < .005$. When Duncan's multiple-range test was used to examine this interaction, the overall finding of interest was that model D recruited more looking than models B or C. It should be noted, however, that this preference to look at model D did not affect the fact that overall infants looked longest to the fear face independent of which face was posing the expression, and that more time was spent looking on the first trial than on the second.

General Discussion

The results of the second experiment suggested that infants tended to look longer at fear faces than at happy faces and that this preferential responding was not specific to any one individual's face.

What is most intriguing about this finding is that infants in the first experiment familiarized to fear faces looked no longer than infants familiarized to happy faces on any of the three familiarization trials. However, when infants in the second experiment had the option to look at one or the other expression, they preferred to look most at the fear face. Given this finding, one is tempted to speculate that the informational value of these two expressions is perceived as equivalent when seen one at a time, but as unequivalent when seen together. Why the distribution of looking is in favor of fear is not clear. It may simply be that fear is considerably more novel to the infant because of how infrequently it is encountered in the natural environment at this age (e.g., Malatesta & Haviland, 1982), but that this novelty only manifests itself when fear is seen simultaneously with some other expression. Alternatively, it may be, as some ethologists have suggested (e.g., W. R. Charlesworth, personal communication, February 1983), that it is more important for an infant to attend to fear than to happy, as the former may signal that the infant is in danger. However appealing this latter explanation appears, it unfortunately fails to account for why fear is looked at longer than happy only when the two are seen together.

Overall, the present set of findings suggests that 7-month-old infants perceive happy and fear facial expressions in a categorical fashion, although this ability depends on the order in which the stimuli are presented. Furthermore, it appears that when infants have a choice, they tend to look longer at fear faces than at happy faces. It is the subject of future work to determine whether this tendency to look more at fear relative to happy can be attributed to the relative novelty of fear expressions in the infant's environment, to some psycholphysical difference that makes fear more salient, or to some sort of species-specific predisposi-

tion to "prefer" fear faces. It is also the subject of future work to determine whether such expression preferences have any bearing on infants' social development (e.g., are some expressions posed by the caretaker more successful than others in recruiting and sustaining the infant's attention?). Independent of such suggestions for future research, the present results collectively suggest that happy and fear facial expressions are perceived as categorically distinct by at least 7 months of age.

References

Caron, R.F., Caron, A.J., & Myers, R.S. (1982). Abstraction of invariant face expressions in infancy. *Child Development*, 53, 1008-1015.

Dolgin, K., & Azmitia, M. (in press). The development of the ability to interpret emotional signals: What is and is not known. In G. Zivin (Ed.), *From state through expression: Biology-environment interactions in the development of expressive behavior*. New York: Academic Press.

Field, T.M., & Walden, T.A. (1982). Production and perception of facial expressions in infancy and early childhood. In H.W. Reese & L.P. Lipsitt (Eds.), *Advances in child development and behavior* (Vol. **16**, pp. 169-221). New York: Academic Press.

Keppel, G. (1973). *Design and analysis*. Englewood Cliffs, NJ: Prentice-Hall.

Malatesta C.Z., & Haviland, J.M. (1982). Learning display rules: The socialization of emotion expression in infancy. *Child Development*, **53**, 991-1003.

Nelson, C.A. (in press). The perception and recognition of facial expressions in infancy. In T.M. Field & N.A. Fox (Eds.), *Social perception in infancy*. Norwood, NJ: Ablex.

Nelson, C.A., Morse, P.A., & Leavitt, L.A. (1979). Recognition of facial expressions by seven-month-old infants. *Child Development*, **50**, 1239-1242.

Oster, H. (1981). "Recognition" of emotional expression in infancy? In M.E. Lamb & L.R. Sherrod (Eds.), *Infant social cognition: Empirical and theoretical considerations* (pp. 85-125). Hillsdale, NJ: Erlbaum.

Source; Nelson, C.A. and Dolgin, K.G. (1985)
The generalized discrimination of facial expressions by seven-month-old infants. *Child Development*, **56**, 58-61. © 1985 by the Society for Research in Child Development, Inc.

Cognitive Development

6

What makes a sailboat move? Jane, age 3½ answers that it moves because the sky is blue. Obviously, the child does not understand the principles of sailing. But what are we to think if we ask twenty preschool children the same question, and we receive twenty remarkably similar but incorrect answers? What if seven or eight of the children actually respond that the color of the sky is what makes a sailboat move? That the children give wrong answers obviously means that they are less knowledgeable than we are; that they give similar or even identical wrong answers seems to indicate that they are not even thinking the way adults do. In the case of the sailboat, they may be interpreting the question in a different way than it was intended, or their understanding of cause-and-effect relationships may not be the same as that of an adult.

This chapter asks a number of questions about how children think: Are there developmental changes in thinking processes during childhood and adolescence? At what point in development do children begin to analyze their own thought processes? What is the highest level of human intellectual functioning? When is this level reached, and is it reached by everyone? All of these are questions about the nature of human cognition; while none have simple answers, researchers in the field of cognitive psychology have been able to provide a number of interesting insights into them.

The purposes of this chapter are to discuss theory and research in the area of human cognition, to provide an understanding of the issues, and to suggest at least partial answers to some of the major questions. More importantly, the chapter focuses on cognitive development—the differences in problem-solving abilities that occur as the child progresses from infancy through adolescence. The emphasis will not be on the mere accumulation of knowledge as a child grows from infancy through adolescence. In other words, instead of focusing on "what" is learned, the chapter deals more often with the "how" and the "why"—the process rather than the product.

The chapter will emphasize the work of Jean Piaget. This is neither because Piaget was completely correct in his assertions nor because his views are accepted unanimously. In fact, they are constantly challenged by researchers in the field of human cognition (e.g., Gelman & Baillargeon 1983). Piaget's work will be emphasized because he offered a model by which psychologists and educators can attempt to understand cognitive development. Few would dispute the fact that it is the most comprehensive model available, that it has generated the greatest amount of research, and that it has been the model most widely applied in recent years, particularly in the field of education. Few would deny that Piaget's descriptions of children's behaviors were remarkably accurate, although serious questions have risen in recent years about his interpretations of those behaviors. Besides describing Piaget's theory of cognitive development, this chapter will present some opposing points of view.

The final section of the chapter discusses environmental influences on human cognition. The influence of culture, as revealed in cross-cultural comparisons, will be examined. An analysis of educational and child-rearing influences is included, along with the significance of nutrition in cognitive growth.

The Theory of Jean Piaget

The most comprehensive of all theories of human intellectual development is the one developed by the Swiss biologist-philosopher Jean Piaget (1896–1980). Piaget was originally trained as a biologist, and he began his career studying shellfish. He published his first paper at the age of 11; this remarkable accomplishment marked the beginning of a long career that spanned nearly three quarters of a century.

Piaget's theory of intellectual growth is based on the belief that there are strong parallels between biological and psychological functioning. Intelligence is a particular instance of biological adaptation to the environment. Human beings do not have furry coats to protect them from the cold; they do not have the speed to outrun most predatory animals, nor the skill to climb trees. They do, however, have the intelligence to produce clothing and vehicles of transportation. As you read this page, you are probably seated in an environment that has been carefully designed for your comfort and protection. The air temperature, the humidity, and the lighting may all be regulated. It is a natural environment only in the sense that it indicates natural human adaptation—intelligence.

Intelligence can be considered from three different perspectives: the *content*, the *structure*, and the *function* (Piaget 1983). All are important, but Piaget placed the greatest emphasis on the latter two.

The Content of Intelligence

The *content* of intelligence is the raw material; put simply, it is what is known. For example, if a group of people are asked to explain the working of an automobile engine, many different answers might be given. One person might describe the four-stage operation of each cylinder in the engine block: the intake, the compression, the combustion, and the exhaust. Another might discuss the little horses under the hood of the car that produce the horsepower to make the wheels turn. Each of these answers has very different *content*.

What is there about a person's thinking that would lead him or her to believe in the existence of horses under the hood? This is precisely what Piaget was interested in. He felt that if he was to understand the nature of human intelligence, he needed to know more than whether or not people gave right or wrong answers to a question. He needed to know why they gave the answers they gave. What is there about the process of human thinking that leads a person to put forth a certain product? To describe the underlying processes of human thinking, Piaget introduced the concept of the *structure* of intelligence.

The Structure of Intelligence

Intellectual or cognitive structures are developed because of the interaction between the human being and the environment. These structures determine the way in which people can deal with ideas or issues. They provide an outlook on life (Flavell 1982). A cognitive structure is not a tangible object; it cannot be seen or touched. There-

fore, the concept may be difficult to understand at first unless it is illustrated by a concrete example:

A child and an adolescent watch an identical film on television, and yet their cognitive experiences while viewing the film are very different. The child sees a story filled with action and adventure, with several boring scenes in between; the boring scenes are those in which the characters speak to one another but do little else. The adolescent sees a story about the nature of human love or ambition or greed that has many action scenes used to convey the filmmaker's message. The child is not less intelligent than the adolescent, but simply has a different world view because the child's cognitive structures are not as well developed as those of the adolescent.

Cognitive structures originate in early infancy; they begin to develop as soon as the child begins to have environmental experiences. But what of the newborn, who has not yet had any environmental experiences? According to Piaget, even completely inexperienced infants have built-in structures that program them to interact with the environment. These are the *physical structures*, such as the human brain and nervous system, the specific sensory organs, and the reflexes—or, as Piaget referred to them, the automatic behavioral reactions. The infant exercises these structures in interacting with the environment and, by doing so, begins immediately to develop **cognitive structures.**

The Function of Intelligence

All living organisms, in interacting with their environments, function by the twofold process of *organization* and *adaptation*. Organization involves the tendency to integrate the self and the world into meaningful patterns of parts within a whole in order to reduce complexity. Thus, Piaget described the increasing organization of the developing embryo and fetus, and the impressive organization of the reproductive system. The same tendency toward increasing organization can be found in the realm of thought.

Adaptation to the environment is the second aspect of functioning in the organism. The living organism adapts to the demands of the environment in two ways. On the one hand, it manipulates the outside world in such a way as to make it more similar to the organism itself. On the other hand, the organism modifies itself so that it becomes more like the environment. The first of these tendencies is referred to as **assimilation,** and the second as **accommodation** (Piaget 1983).

To assimilate something means to make it similar to one's self. Assimilation involves taking something from the outside world and fitting it into a structure that already exists. Human beings assimilate food by breaking it down into nutritional components; the food they eat becomes a part of themselves.

When people accommodate to something, they change themselves in some way to meet external demands. To continue with the food example, the body not only assimilates food, but also accommodates to it by secreting gastric juices to break it down and by producing stomach contractions to digest it. Similar physical adaptations occur when the body accommodates to heat by perspiring and to cold by shivering.

Piaget maintained that assimilation and accommodation apply to intellectual processes as well as to physical processes. The child assimilates new ideas—new "food for thought"—by fitting them into already existing cognitive structures, and accommodates to these ideas by changing his or her cognitive structures in response to them. If an idea is new, and the cognitive structures necessary to make sense out of it are present, children will make it a part of their thought processes and will change their ways of thinking in response to it. Intellectual development will not occur, of course, if the ideas the child is exposed to are familiar (i.e., have already been assimilated), or if they are too advanced for the structures to assimilate.

The Motivation for Growth

Intellectual structures organize the environment and adapt to it, but why do they do so? As discussed earlier, the organism seeks order and organization. It seeks to avoid imbalance, or **disequilibrium,** between itself and external reality. Therefore, the motivation for intellectual growth comes from an internal need for order, harmony, or balance. People need to feel that their way of thinking about the world is consistent with perceived reality.

The internal motivation for intellectual development is a highly significant concept in Piaget's theory. Theoretically, at least, children should not need to be coaxed or tricked into learning about the world. They need only be exposed to it in a manner they are capable of appreciating. They seek knowledge because they have an inner drive toward that knowledge. When some new intellectual "food" comes their way, they reach out for it spontaneously.

Piaget's Stages of Development

Piaget believed that intellectual development passes through a series of qualitatively different stages, each building upon and evolving from those which preceded it (Piaget 1983). This section examines the stages through which individuals pass as they move from infancy to adolescence, beginning with **sensorimotor intelligence.**

Sensorimotor Development (Birth to 1½ Years)

A key concept in Piaget's theory is that thought begins in activity. Thus, the earliest forms of thinking and problem solving are of a sensory and of a physical nature. Piaget stressed that intelligence can be physical as well as mental, as can be seen in his observations of his daughter Lucienne: When Lucienne was approximately 1 year old, her father showed her the chain of his watch, and then placed it into a matchbox; he partially closed the box so that the chain could be seen through an open slit that was too small to admit the child's fingers. Lucienne approached the problem of recovering the chain on a physical, or sensorimotor, level. She shook the box, struck it with her hand, and banged it against the edge of her crib, until finally the chain slipped out. Lucienne had solved her problem, but she had done so physically rather than mentally; the solution *was* the motor activity.

Schemes

If cognitive structures develop because of their interaction with the environment by means of organization and adaptation, what can be said of the neonate who has had little or no chance for environmental interaction? The newborn baby possesses only physical structures, including the human nervous system, the sense organs, and the reflexes. However, during the sensorimotor stage basic physical structures are modified as a result of environmental interaction, and the infant is capable of increasingly sophisticated interactions with the world. For example, newborn infants will suck indiscriminately on anything placed against their mouths. Gradually, however, they become more selective, and sucking becomes increasingly limited to the times when it is appropriate to do so, as when the nipple is presented. This selectivity indicates the infants' tendency to organize the world; some things are to be sucked on, while others are not. It also indicates adaptation to the environment; infants assimilate new experiences and their future behavior is accommodated accordingly.

During the sensorimotor period, consistent action sequences—classes of acts that have regular common features—emerge from the basic physical structures. Piaget called these action sequences **schemes,** which are the sensorimotor equivalent of concepts. Included among the infant's schemes are sucking, grasping, vocalizing, and looking—action patterns exercised by the infant on a variety of objects.

Substages of Sensorimotor Intelligence

In describing the development of schemes and, more generally, the transition from a primarily reflexive interaction with the world to a more sophisticated sensorimotor intelligence, Piaget divided the sensorimotor stage into six substages.

Substage 1 (birth to 1 month). The primary activity in this substage is the exercise of reflexes. Minor variations in reflexive behavior may occur because of environmental interaction. For example, as mentioned in the previous section, there might be increased selectivity of sucking.

Substage 2 (1 to 4 months). Individual schemes continue to develop, but towards the end of this substage there is evidence of coordination of schemes. For example, sucking-grasping is one of the most well-established schemes in substage 2; parents often notice that everything their baby grasps is brought to his or her mouth for sucking, and the baby will attempt to grasp whatever is placed in his or her mouth.

A key feature of substage 2 is the *primary circular reaction:* the infant accidentally discovers an interesting sensory or motor experience related to his or her own body and continues to repeat it. Consider the behavior of Piaget's son at 2 months of age:

> (Laurent) scratches and tries to grasp, lets go, scratches and grasps again, etc. (At first) . . . this can only be observed during the feeding. Laurent gently scratches his mother's bare shoulder. (The next day) . . . Laurent scratches the sheet which is folded over the blankets, then grasps and holds it a moment, then lets it go, scratches it again, and recommences without interruption. (Piaget 1963, 191)

Substage 3 (4 to 8 months). Coordination of schemes continues, and the circular reaction seen at substage 2 takes on a new dimension. Up through the second substage, the activities repeated as ends in themselves are somewhat oriented toward the infant's own body. As young infants exercise their sensorimotor schemes, they appear more interested in their own actions than in the materials upon which the actions are performed; thus, they are more interested in the experience of grasping than in the object grasped.

In substage 3, however, infants are definitely interested in the effects of their actions on the outside world. In an effort to prolong interesting experiences resulting from their own actions, infants perform *secondary circular reactions*—repeated behaviors with pleasing effects on the environment. Again, consider the behavior of Laurent Piaget, now 4 months old. Lying in his bassinet, Laurent looks up at some rattles that have been attached with a string to the hood; his father attaches a watch chain to the rattles:

> (Laurent) pulls . . . the chain or the string in order to shake the rattle and make it sound: the intention is clear. I now attach a paper knife

to the string. The same day I attach a new toy half as high as the string . . . Laurent begins by shaking himself while looking at it, then waves his arms in the air and finally takes hold of the rubber doll which he shakes while looking at the toy. (Piaget 1963, 164)

Substage 4 (8 to 12 months).   In the previous substage, Laurent definitely intended to pull the string, resulting in shaking the rattle. However, Piaget was unwilling to see his son's actions as clearly goal-directed. Instead he suggested that Laurent did not differentiate between his own actions and their results. In other words, he did not pull the string *in order to* shake the rattle, but he saw the pulling of the string and the shaking of the rattle as contained within the same activity.

In substage 4 there is planned, goal-directed activity. In fact, infants will now activate one scheme for the specific purpose of producing another, as when they push aside an object for the purpose of grasping what is behind it. In a sense, substage 4 involves the deliberate bringing together or coordination of secondary circular reactions.

Substage 5 (12 to 18 months).   In the second year of life, the child now goes a step beyond clearly intentional behavior and the deliberate coordination of unrelated schemes. Now there is also intentional variation of interesting events. The substage 3 infant repeats an action in an attempt to prolong an interesting environmental result. At substage 5 there is repetition but also an attempt to vary the activity, instead of simply repeating it precisely. This behavior is referred to as a *tertiary circular reaction*. Furthermore, the child seems to enjoy novelty and looks for new ways of producing interesting experiences. Consider the experimental approach of Piaget's 13-month-old daughter Jacqueline in her bath:

Jacqueline engages in many experiments with celluloid toys floating on the water . . . Not only does she drop her toys from a height to see the water splash or displace them with her hand in order to make them swim, but she pushes them halfway down in order to see them rise to the surface. Between the ages of a year and a year and a half, she amuses herself by filling with

water pails, flasks, watering cans, etc . . . by filling her sponge with water and pressing it against her chest, by running water from the faucet . . . along her arm, etc. (Piaget 1963, 273)

Substage 6 (18 to 24 months).   In some ways, substage 5 marks the end of the sensorimotor stage because beyond the age of 1½ years children begin to engage in representational thinking (Flavell 1985). That is, they become capable of using symbols—of letting one thing stand for another—and are no longer limited in intelligence to sensorimotor activity on the world. Substage 6, then, can be thought of as a transitional period between sensorimotor and preoperational intelligence, a discussion of which will begin on page 174.

The Object Concept

One of the most significant developments of the sensorimotor stage is the acquisition of the *object concept*. As described by Flavell (1985), this involves the realization that objects exist independently of our awareness of or interaction with them. A person reading a book knows, for example, that the book has an existence independent of the reader; its existence is equally obvious whether it is being read at the moment or whether it sits on the back shelf of a library.

Piaget (1964) maintained that young infants do not have the object concept and must gradually acquire it through experience with the world. While parents rarely define it as such, they often notice the lack of an object concept in their baby: a 4-month-old drops a spoon while seated in a high chair, but instead of looking for it, the baby proceeds to ignore it. Being out of sight, the spoon no longer exists in the baby's mind.

Piaget believed that the object concept is acquired gradually during the sensorimotor stage. From birth to 4 months (sensorimotor substages 1 and 2), there is no recognition that objects exist independently of the infant's sensory and motor knowledge of them. Out of sight means out of mind. Thus, if infants are tracking a moving object with their eyes and the object disappears behind a screen they will almost immediately lose interest in it (Flavell 1985). However, between the ages of 4 and 8 months (substage 3), infants begin to dif-

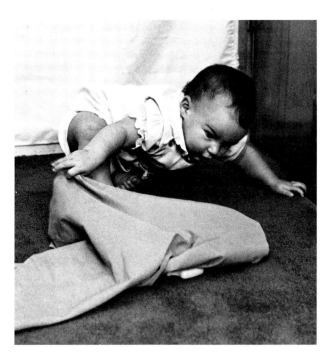 

Now you see it. Now you don't. A key feature of sensorimotor development is the development of the object concept—the realization that objects exist even when we are unable to perceive them.

ferentiate between object and self. Now infants will attempt to look for the dropped spoon. If they watch an electric train disappearing into a tunnel, they will turn their attention to the other end of the tunnel in anticipation of the train's return (Nelson 1971; Flavell 1985). They will also attempt to uncover an object that is partially covered, apparently realizing that the hidden part of the object still exists although it cannot be seen. On the other hand, the 4- to 8-month-old will not search for something that has been completely covered even as they watch; if the child is shown a toy and begins to reach for it and the toy is then covered by a cloth, the child will stop in mid-reach, as if the toy has magically ceased to exist!

Between 8 and 12 months (substage 4), infants will now remove a cover to find an object that they have seen being covered, indicating recognition that an object exists although it is not directly perceived. The object concept is still immature at this point, however, and babies can be easily

tricked. If the baby has become accustomed to retrieving an object hidden under cover A, and the adult then moves the object from cover A to adjacent cover B, the child will continue to seek the hidden object under cover A. The child is unable to form a mental representation of the movement of the object from A to B and is dominated by the sensorimotor habit of going to cover A, even though such an action is no longer appropriate. This behavior is referred to as the AB, or substage 4, error.

From 12 to 18 months (substage 5), the concept of the object existing independently of the child's actions becomes more firmly established. Now the child will look for an object in the last place it was seen. Thus, if a toy is first placed under cover A and then moved under cover B, the child will go directly to cover B when looking for it. In Piaget's terminology, the child in substage 5 can cope with *visible displacements* of objects. Not until substage 6, however, from 18 to 24 months, is the object concept firmly established as the child learns to cope with *invisible displacements*. While successfully handling visible displacements, the substage 5 child cannot deal with displacements that are not seen and must be imagined. For example, a toy is placed in a cup, and the cup is placed first under cover A and then under cover B where the toy is dropped out; the empty cup is then set aside and the child asked to find the toy. Since the cup was empty when removed from cover B, a reasonable assumption is that the toy was deposited under cover B, even though this displacement was not seen. Unable to deal with such an invisible displacement, the substage 5 child looks for the toy where last seen—in the cup. The substage 6 child, by contrast, notices that the cup is empty, mentally represents the displacement of the toy from cup to cover B, and quickly locates the hidden object.

For Piaget, the object concept illustrated the infant's movement from action-oriented sensory and motor intelligence to the more mature representational intelligence of the toddler. It also illustrated a decreasing egocentrism, as the child slowly learns to separate self from the external world. In illustrating these points about infant development, the value of Piaget's object concept research is unchallenged. Furthermore, there is general agreement today that Piaget's descriptions of infant behavior were quite accurate. However, it should also be pointed out that there are valid criticisms of the object concept research.

Questions have recently arisen about Piaget's interpretations of infant's difficulties with displacement problems. In particular, much controversy surrounds the AB, or substage 4, error. In the first place, many 8- to 12-month-olds do not commit the error of looking only under cover A when a hidden object is moved from A to B. In addition, many children well into the second year of life *do* commit the AB error, making it difficult to argue that committing the AB error illustrates a genuine substage development (Flavell 1985). Finally, when an AB error is committed, does it necessarily mean that infants are locked into sensorimotor habits and unable to mentally represent the movement of objects from A to B? Critics of Piaget's interpretation suggest that the infant's deficiency may be one of memory rather than of representational skill. Perhaps the infant who sees an object moved from one hiding place to another gets confused and sim-

ply cannot remember where the object was last seen. In fact, the longer the delay between hiding time and search, the greater is the likelihood of AB error (Fox, Kagan & Weiskopf 1979), and, in general, 8- to 10-month-old infants perform less well on delayed search tasks than do 14- to 16-month-olds (Schacter & Moscovitch 1984).

In one of the more intriguing studies of the AB error, Schacter and his associates (1986) found that adults with organic memory disorders are likely to perform like 8- to 12-month-old infants on a hidden object task. The participants in the Schacter study developed the habit of finding an object (e.g., a paper clip, a rubber band) in one of four drawers of a plastic container; when a new object was hidden in a different drawer, most of the amnesic adults were unable to find it, and returned to their earlier habit of looking in the drawer initially used as a hiding place. The researchers concluded that memory deficiencies should be considered as possible contributors to AB errors. In fact, a study by Baillargeon, Spelke, and Wasserman (1985) indicates that when the memory component is removed from measures of the object concept, even 5-month-old children display evidence of knowing that out of sight does not mean out of mind.

In summary, the sensorimotor stage involves intelligent activity on a sensory and on a motor level. It provides the basis for all future intellectual development. Physical structures are modified because of the infant's interaction with the environment. During the sensorimotor stage the infant develops behavioral sequences called schemes. The infant exercises these schemes on the materials in the environment and eventually coordinates the schemes with one another, leading to increasingly complex forms of behavior. Finally, the sensorimotor stage involves the development of the object concept—the recognition that the world has an existence independent of a child's psychological contact with it.

Preoperational Development (1½ Years to 6 Years)

The end of the sensorimotor stage of development is marked by the emergence of an ability

An empty cardboard box becomes a car. The ability to represent reality to yourself and to engage in make-believe play appears during the preoperational stage of development.

to represent experiences mentally rather than to interact with them directly and physically. It is the ability to let one thing stand for another and to think about things without physically acting upon them. This representational ability marks the appearance of **preoperational intelligence.**

Representation occurs in many forms. A mental image is a representation of reality; an image of an isolated beach on a sunny day—with blue water, white sand, and swaying palm trees—in a sense makes those objects present in the mind of the knower without the actual physical experience of the scene. Representation is also found in symbolic play. The child pretends that a wooden box is a car, that an empty plate has food on it, or that a broom handle is a gun. Perhaps the most obvious indication of the emergence of the ability to use symbols is the child's use of language in the second and third years of life. Clearly, the newfound ability to use language—to let a word stand for an object or person—indicates a dramatic change in the child's intellectual functioning.

To illustrate the emergence of representational ability, Piaget again presented Lucienne with the chain-in-the-matchbox problem when she was 1½ years old—at the beginning of the preoperational stage. This time she looked at the box, silently opened and closed her mouth several times, then reached over directly, slid the box open, and removed the chain. Apparently she was able to represent the activity to herself mentally, and then proceed to solve the problem directly. Actually, the problem had been solved in her mind before she even touched the box, whereas when she was younger she did not begin the problem-solving procedure until she took the box in her hands.

Preoperational children share with adults the ability to represent reality to themselves by means of signs and symbols; like those of the adult, the young child's thought processes are internal. Nevertheless, compared with the older child and adult, the young child is still at a great disadvantage cognitively because preoperational thought is unsystematic, inconsistent, and illogical. A look at some of the characteristics of preoperational thought will illustrate its unsystematic nature.

A major characteristic of preoperational thought is **transductive reasoning.** The logical reasoning of the adult may be inductive, as when general rules are induced based on a series of particular observations: the sun always rises in the east. Adults also use deductive reasoning, which involves making a judgment about a particular instance based on a general rule: since cows in general give milk, any particular cow will give milk. Transductive reasoning, on the other hand, is reasoning neither from the particular to the general nor from the general to the particular, but from particular instance to particular instance. For example, a child might reason that since dogs have four legs and horses have four legs, dogs are horses, a conclusion both illogical and incorrect. What the child has done is to relate two particular instances of the general class of four-legged animals. This is transductive reasoning.

Another characteristic of preoperational thought is confusion about *cause-and-effect* relationships. The young child will often see a cause-and-effect relationship where none exists, while failing to see a true cause-and-effect relationship. For example, a little boy who falls and hurts himself while playing indoors during a thunderstorm may blame the thunderstorm and develop a fear of such weather conditions. Or, more sadly, a little girl may not be able to understand that she did not cause her father to leave home after a divorce settlement.

Preoperational children exhibit **animism** in their thinking: because they have life, thoughts, and feelings, all things are seen as having life. Rock gardens exist because the rocks "like each other," chairs are hurt when big people sit on them, and dolls get lonely if not played with often enough.

Preoperational thought demonstrates **artificialism.** For everything that exists there must be a psychological reason, just as children have psychological reasons for the things they do. Leaves fall off trees because they want to keep the ground warm, the moon shines to give us light at night, and flowers grow to make us happy. Young children are not capable of understanding things in terms of physical reasons. When they ask why the sky is blue, they are not asking for a discussion of refracted sunlight in the atmosphere. They may want to know why the person who painted the sky chose the color blue!

Preoperational thought is *perceptually bound.* That is, children judge the world by the way it looks to them. Nickels may be more valuable than dimes because nickels are bigger. Two halves of a cookie might look like more than a whole cookie, so the child prefers the halves to the whole. Geometric shapes are grouped together, not according to logical categories of size and shape, but according to pattern; they are arranged so they look nice.

Preoperational thought is inflexible and irreversible. In what Piaget called a *mental experiment,* young children run off thoughts in their heads in the sequence in which they might act them out. The child's thinking resembles a film in a projector that cannot be stopped, rewound, reversed, or edited. The ability to reconstruct thought processes and the ability to reverse them mentally are essential in the development of logical thought.

Preoperational thought possesses the characteristic of **centration.** The child centers on the most noticeable features of the environment and ignores other features. For example, a young child may believe that the taller of two glasses always contains more water than the shorter one regardless of the width of the glasses in question. In actuality, a shorter glass might contain more water than a taller one if the shorter glass is wider. However, the young child may center on height and fail to attend to the width of the glasses at all.

Finally, preoperational thought is extremely *egocentric.* Children see the world from their own points of view. Piaget presented children with a task in which they were required to point to a picture representing the view of a landscape seen not by them, but by a doll placed opposite them. Most young children choose the scene they see rather than what the doll might see, apparently unaware of the fact that viewpoints other than their own exist (Piaget & Inhelder 1956).

The characteristics of preoperational thought will gradually disappear as children move from

This little boy interrupting his mother's telephone conversation displays the egocentrism typical of toddlers. He is unable to see the world from any point of view other than his own.

toddlerhood through early childhood. By the time they are ready to enter middle childhood, at about the age of 6 or 7, the first signs of operational thinking are beginning to emerge and a new and different stage of thought is about to be entered.

The Stage of Concrete Operations (6 Years to 12 Years)

Thinking in the stage of **concrete operations** no longer consists of disjointed representational acts. Now these acts, which previously lacked or-

der and consistency, become parts of whole systems of related acts. They become *operations*. Operations may be logical, such as those dealing with principles of formal logic or those dealing with mathematical concepts. They may also be what Piaget termed "sublogical," and these deal with concepts of space and time.

A course in mathematics or in formal logic provides a student with a fairly good idea of what it means to use a mental operation. For example, the principles of algebra are the same regardless of the numbers entered into the algebraic formulas.

Similarly, formal logic does not seek to determine whether statements are true or false, but whether they derive from a logically consistent system. For example, the statements that "All Irishmen have red hair" and "John is an Irishman" lead to the logically correct conclusion that "John has red hair." Logically correct as it is, the conclusion may not be true, of course, because the major premise is false. All Irishmen do not have red hair.

The development of concrete operations allows the child to deal with the concepts of classes, of relations, and of quantity.

Classification

To understand the concepts involved in **classification,** the child must perceive the logical similarity among a group of objects and must be able to sort them according to their common features. Preoperational children tend to rely on perception when they classify; they make judgments on the basis of what things look like. When shown an assortment of objects and asked to group the ones that go together, they frequently construct what Inhelder and Piaget (1964) referred to as *graphic collections,* or interesting arrangements of the figures. For example, when given a group of circles, triangles, and squares and asked to sort them according to their defining properties, young children might place the triangle on top of the square and say they have made a house. (See Figure 6.1.)

By the age of 5 or 6, when they are moving into the stage of concrete operations, children begin to sort objects by their logically defining properties. Thus, in the example of the geometric shapes mentioned above, they are now likely to group the objects according to shape, size, or color, rather than to make an interesting pattern.

A mature notion of classification begins to appear after the age of 7, and in some children considerably later (Winer 1980). This is what Piaget termed *class inclusion*—the relationship between classes and subclasses. An adult can readily understand that classes can be contained within classes. However, the young child's appreciation of class inclusion is somewhat limited. Consider what happens when a 6-year-old is shown a group of dogs—six collies and two poodles—and asked, "Are there more dogs or more collies?" Since the child has trouble understanding the concept of

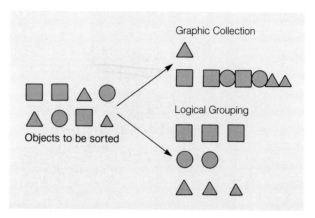

Figure 6.1 Graphic Collections
Graphic collections are arrangements of figures into perceptually pleasing patterns rather than arrangements of figures by logically defining properties. Below are the responses to a classification task by a preoperational child.

"Buc (5;3) . . . makes a collective object (Three large squares in a line and together forming a rectangle, but with an additional smaller square laid against three of its sides); then a complex object made up of squares and triangles." Inhelder, B. & Piaget, J. (1964) *The Early Growth of Logic in the Child.* New York: Norton, p. 28.

class inclusion, he or she relies on a less sophisticated perceptual solution to the problem. The child sees more collies than poodles, and so responds that there are more collies than dogs. Instead of seeing the subclasses (e.g., collie) in relation to the supraordinate class (dog), the child compares the subclasses to one another and therefore fails to solve the problem (Ahr & Youniss 1970)

By the age of 8 or 9, the child has an understanding of *multiple classification* and can classify on two dimensions at once. Piaget (1964) presented children with a row of green objects (e.g., a pear, a hat, a tree), which intersected with a column of different-colored leaves. At the point of intersection there was a blank space, and the child was asked to determine what should appear in this space. The corect answer is a figure that shares the common feature of the row (green) and the column (leaf), and so the child should choose a green leaf. Multiple classification appears only after simple

Arranging objects according to size is difficult for preoperational children because they must keep in mind that the same object is simultaneously "bigger than" some and "smaller than" others.

classification and class inclusion have been mastered.

Seriation

A second major development indicating the transition to operational thought is the development of a mature understanding of relations. This understanding will allow the child to see the world in an orderly manner, to detect and understand consistencies and patterns as the adult does.

The understanding of relations is illustrated by the following example: Suppose a child were asked to choose ten people at random and order them according to height, a relatively simple task for an adult. A preoperational child could not complete the ordering successfully. Young children do have a basic understanding of concepts such as "greater than" and "less than," but in an ordering

task, the child is required to know not only that John is taller than Mary, but also that John is, at the same time, shorter than Jim. Thus, the task becomes more difficult because it requires the ability to decenter—to attend simultaneously to more than one feature of the situation. As noted in the previous section, preoperational thought is characterized by centration, the tendency to focus on one dimension and to ignore others. The young child focuses on the fact that John is taller than Mary but cannot hold in his or her mind at the same time the thought that John is shorter than Jim.

The task used to test the child's skill at ordinal relations is referred to as **seriation.** Typically, Piaget presented children with a group of sticks of different sizes and asked them to order the sticks from the smallest to the biggest. Preoperational children do not seem to be capable of seriating because seriation involves the ability to view the world as an orderly place with systematic rules for relating objects or events. Seriation requires the use of concrete operations.

Conservation

An understanding of quantity involves an awareness that, regardless of changes in physical appearance, quantity remains the same unless material is added or subtracted. A cookie broken in half may look different as two pieces than it did as one; but, since nothing was added or subtracted, the actual quantity must still be the same. A little boy, however, may decide that he has more cookie to eat than he did before because two pieces look like more than one piece. In contrast, the older child and the adult make judgments on the basis of a genuine understanding of quantity. The appearance may be different; but, since nothing was added or subtracted, the total amount has not changed.

A person who uses logical operations is said to *conserve* the amount—to recognize that the amount does not change regardless of any number of changes in the physical appearance of the material. Thus, the task used to determine one's understanding of quantity is referred to as **conservation.**

Conservation experiments have been carried out using a variety of materials. Piaget maintained that conservation does not occur suddenly but appears gradually, and that different forms of conservation emerge at different times in the child's life.

Conservation of number (5 to 6 years). The child is presented with two rows of objects, one containing five objects and one containing four. Then the row containing the four objects is spread out, as the child watches, so that the objects at the ends of the row are farther apart from one another than the end objects in the row of five. The child is asked again which row has more. The nonconserver will say that the spread-out row has more because, in fact, it looks longer. The older child and the adult would answer correctly; because the

number has not changed, the row with five objects still has more, regardless of how the objects are arranged.

Conservation of liquid (7 to 8 years). The child is shown two identical glasses of liquid. The liquid from one glass is then poured, in the child's presence, into a much taller but thinner glass, and the child is asked if the amount of liquid in the glasses is still equal (see Figure 6.2). The nonconserver will now say the tall glass has more because it looks bigger. The conserving older child and adult will say that the amount of liquid is still the same because nothing has been added and nothing subtracted; the new glass is taller, but it is also narrower.

Conservation of length (7 to 8 years). The child is presented with two identical "roads" made of long blocks. One of the roads is subsequently arranged in a zigzag rather than a linear fashion. The child is asked if the two roads are still the same length. The conserver will answer correctly that they are. The length of an object remains the same regardless of how the segments of the object are arranged.

Conservation of mass (7 to 8 years). If two balls of clay are identical, and one of them is then flattened out, is the amount of clay in each ball still the same, regardless of the shape? (See Figure 6.3.) The conserver says yes; the nonconserver says no.

Conservation of weight (7 to 8 years). If two balls of clay are weighted and found to be identical in weight, will they still be identical if one of the balls is flattened out, or will one weigh more than the other? The conserver will say they are still the same because nothing has been added to or subtracted from either one. The nonconserving child will say that they are now different because they look different.

Conservation of area (7 to 8 years) A number of blocks representing houses are placed on a flat surface representing a field. If the houses are rearranged—spread all over the field instead of lined up along the edge—do they still cover the same area? The conserver says yes. The percep-

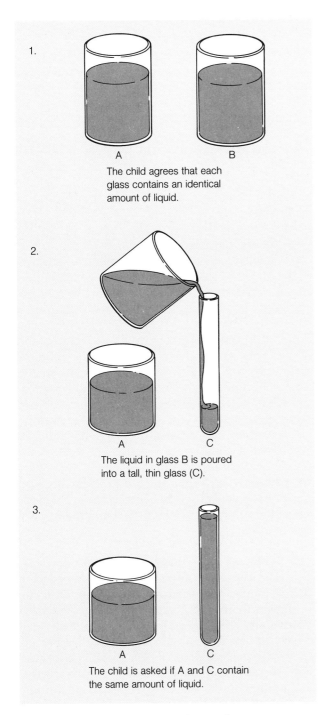

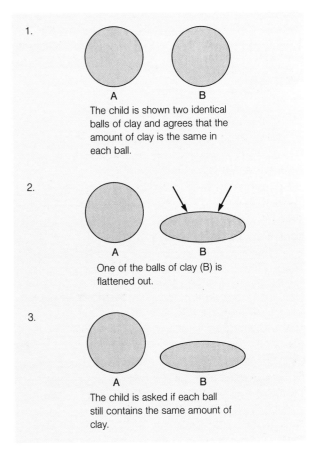

1. The child is shown two identical balls of clay and agrees that the amount of clay is the same in each ball.

2. One of the balls of clay (B) is flattened out.

3. The child is asked if each ball still contains the same amount of clay.

Figure 6.3   Conservation of Mass

The *nonconserver* answers that the amount of clay in the balls is now different because the balls no longer resemble one another.

The *conserver* answers that the amount of clay in each ball is still the same because no clay was added to or subtracted from either side.

1. The child agrees that each glass contains an identical amount of liquid.

2. The liquid in glass B is poured into a tall, thin glass (C).

3. The child is asked if A and C contain the same amount of liquid.

Figure 6.2   Conservation of Liquid

The *nonconserver* answers that C now contains more liquid than A because the appearance of the liquid in the glasses is different.

The *conserver* answers that A and C are the same because no liquid has been added or taken away from the original amount in B.

tually bound nonconserver says no; they look like they cover more space.

   Conservation of volume (11 to 12 years).   A child might be presented with a tower that is two cubes long, two cubes wide, and three cubes high, so that each of the three layers has four cubes. Then the top layer is removed, and two of its cubes are added to each of the other two layers so that the structure is now three cubes long, two cubes wide, and two cubes high. The child is asked if the structure still takes up the same amount of space as before, or putting the question another way, is the volume the same as it was originally? To conserve volume, the child must pay attention simultaneously to length, width, and height. Conservation of volume usually does not appear before early adolescence.

Cognitive Conceit

In addition to an understanding of classes, relations, and quantity, Piaget described a huge number of changes in thinking that occur with the emergence of concrete operations. There is a mature understanding of the concepts of time, concepts of space, and concepts of causality. Inductive reasoning also emerges to replace the transductive reasoning of the preoperational child.

Furthermore, as might be expected, these dramatic changes in the quality of children's thinking are reflected in their personalities. Elkind (1981a) described the phenomenon of **cognitive conceit.** Children, delighting in their newfound logical cognitive structures, develop too much faith in them and are overwhelmed by their own cleverness. Realizing that adults do not know everything, they may decide that adults do not know anything. Such children find pleasure in attempting to trap adults in their own logical inconsistencies, and parents find themselves presured to give logical reasons for all of their "house rules." They may be faced with statements such as, "The other night you let me stay up until 9:30. Why can't I stay up tonight?" The hapless parents may be forced into an awareness of the fact that they are not consistent or logical in their disciplinary practices.

The Stage of Formal Operations (12 Years to Adult)

In Piaget's theory, the final stage in the development of thought is the stage of **formal operations.** As stated previously, the child develops from reliance on a sensorimotor form of intelligence to a stage of unsystematic mental representation to a stage of systematic mental representation. However, the child's thinking is still considerably more limited than that of the adolescent or adult, because the child lacks essential characteristics of formal operational thought.

The Hypothetico-Deductive Cognitive Strategy

Formal operational thinkers deal with a problem by first considering all possible solutions and mentally examining the outcome of each solution. They set up hypotheses—if-then statements—and systematically test them out, and they are able to speculate on which of their hypotheses are most likely to be correct. The concrete operational thinker, on the other hand, does not employ a planned approach to problem solving, but usually resorts to a more time-consuming trial-and-error technique.

Combinatorial Analysis

Related to the hypothetico-deductive strategy is the ability to generate all possible combinations of a set of elements, an ability lacking in concrete thinkers but characteristic of formula reasoning. The best example of such differences in reasoning is found in the experiment in which children and adolescents were given five flasks of colorless chemicals and asked to combine them in such a way as to produce a yellow liquid (Inhelder & Piaget 1958). Before they began to solve the problem, adolescents usually considered all of the twenty-six possible ways in which the liquids could be combined, including combinations of three, four, and five as well as two. Children tended to combine the liquids two at a time, and often needed prompting to even consider other possibilities. Their approach to the problem was unsystematic and even disorganized.

Abstract Reasoning

The reasoning of concrete operational children is limited to the concrete. They have difficulty dealing with abstract concepts such as democracy, charity, and religion and typically define them concretely. If asked for an explanation of democracy, they may say only that it means that all people can vote. Religion may mean attending church services and nothing more. The formal operational thinker, on the other hand, may define religion as a state of mind, or as an attitude toward the self or toward others, or as an abstract feeling.

Abstract reasoning allows adolescents to contemplate the meaning of their own lives, to question their social and moral values and those of

The adolescent who first acquires formal operational skills often spends much time "lost in thought" as reality is dominated by the realm of possibility.

others, to analyze human relationships, to try to understand the symbolism contained in art and literature, and to see beneath their own superficial behavior and that of other people. One of the most significant features of adolescents' ability to reason about abstract issues is that for the first time they are capable of thinking about their own thought processes. They can, in a sense, perform operations on their own operations; they can deal with their thought processes as objects of thought, and this greatly enhances their cognitive flexibility.

Contrary-to-Fact Reasoning

The child can reason about situations that have happened or are happening, but not about those that only might happen or have never happened. The adolescent and the adult can also reason about the hypothetical and the contrary-to-fact.

For example, what might be the current status of U.S.-Soviet arms limitation talks if Walter Mondale had been elected president in 1984 instead of Ronald Reagan?

In summary, the use of formal operations includes the ability to reason about the hypothetical and the contrary-to-fact, the ability to understand abstract concepts, and the ability to consider a wide range of possibilities instead of only a few. When adolescents first acquire these abilities, they become absorbed in them. In many ways their minds are dominated by possibility instead of reality, and they may spend more time in a world that might have been rather than the world which is. As a consequence, the adolescent is often seen as an idealist, as a nonconformist, as a daydreamer, and—in the minds of some people—as a troublemaker. Adults who feel threatened by the questioning attitudes of adolescents should realize that such questioning is often a sign of healthy, intellectual growth.

Piaget's Theory in Perspective

Piaget's theory has had a dramatic impact on the field of child development. It explains much about the thinking and behavior of children and adolescents, and it has generated a considerable amount of research. Nevertheless, few psychologists would assert that Piaget's theory, or any one theory, offers a complete picture of the complexity of child development. In fact, a number of researchers in recent years have challenged Piaget's interpretations of young children's thinking, and have questioned many of the assumptions on which his entire theory is based.

Did Piaget Underestimate the Preschool Mind?

In Piaget's theory, the mind of the preschool child is characterized less by what it can do than by what it is not yet able to do. *Pre*operational thinking is thinking without benefit of mental operations. The preschooler's mind is disorganized, confused, and devoid of an understanding of cause and effect, logical groupings, relationships, and the concept of quantity. Thus, the world preschoolers perceive lacks stability, consistency, and order. What is more, Piaget saw little value in trying to teach operational skills to young children. "It would be completely useless," he said. "The child must discover the method for himself through his own creativity" (Hall 1970, 30).

Recent years have seen much criticism of Piaget's unflattering assessment of young children's thinking (Brainerd 1978, 1979, 1983; Flavell 1985; Gelman 1972, 1980, 1982; Gelman & Baillargeon 1983; Mandler 1983). The basis for criticism varies, but a recurring theme is that the mind of the preschooler is considerably more sophisticated than Piaget realized.

Most of the evidence used to challenge Piaget's description of the young child's thinking is found in the results of training studies, designed to induce operational skills in supposedly preop-

erational children. The point of such studies is to demonstrate that operational skills do not depend on a particular underlying cognitive organization, as Piaget believed, but upon the possession of specific information or a specific frame of reference needed to solve the problem. For example, Gelman (1982) suggested that nonconserving children may simply not be attending to the important features of the conservation problem and can be taught to do so. Their performance improves significantly once they understand what is being asked of them. Other advocates of training argue that children who fail to conserve may not understand the psychologist's instructions, or may not understand how to use equipment such as the scale in conservation of weight experiments.

Most training studies focus on conservation problems (Gelman & Baillargeon 1983). Typical of such research is the extensive work of Rochel Gelman on children's understanding of number. Whereas Piaget maintained that number conservation (the realization that the number of items in a display remains constant regardless of the arrangement of items) is not characteristic of preoperational thinkers, Gelman (1982) found that 3- and 4-year-olds can indeed conserve number. To induce conservation, she first showed children two rows of three and four objects and asked them to count aloud the objects in each row. After counting each row, the children had to tell her how many objects each row contained. Then she presented a standard conservation of number task (see page 180).

Gelman found that, contrary to predictions based on Piaget's theory, the preoperational children in her study could conserve number, presumably because they were influenced by the training phase of the experiment. Gelman did not suggest that the children actually learned to conserve during the training phase, but only that training may have given them a clearer understanding of what was being asked of them.

Positive effects of prior training have also been demonstrated in studies of classification. For example, Smiley and Brown (1979) found that, when given a group of objects to classify, preschoolers do indeed fail to use logical categories;

they group instead according to overall themes or patterns, exactly as Piaget suggested (see page 178 for a discussion of preoperational sorting strategies). However, the researchers then demonstrated logical categorization of the objects for the children and asked them to sort the objects exactly as they had been shown to do. The children proceeded to do so, leading Smiley and Brown to suggest that young children apparently prefer to use less mature perceptual sorting strategies but, if directed to do so, can classify logically at an earlier age than Piaget indicated (Inhelder & Piaget 1964).

Other critics of Piaget's assessment of preschool cognition argue that even *without* training, young children are better able to organize their perceived environments than Piaget realized. Rather than indicating a deficiency in the young child's ability to see the world as rational and orderly, failure on Piaget's operational tasks might indicate only that the task methodology is inappropriate for young children. In support of this argument is the finding of Ross (1980) that even in the second year of life children see the world in terms of categories rather than as a disorganized jumble of stimulation.

Ross did not follow Piaget's approach of asking children to sort objects into groups. Instead, she measured the attention paid by 12-, 18-, and 24-month-olds to a variety of objects. Seated on a parent's lap, the children were shown a number of objects in succession that belonged to the same category (e.g., men, animals, food, furniture). Then they were shown a pair of objects, each new to them but one belonging to a category they had become used to seeing and one belonging to a totally different category. The children displayed more interest in the different-category object than in the one belonging to the familiar category. On the basis of that finding, Ross concluded that very young children do perceive their worlds in terms of categories, even though they are obviously unable to actively sort objects into categories by themselves. In other words, by using what she considered a more appropriate methodology for preschoolers, Ross obtained results that directly contradicted those of Piaget (Inhelder & Piaget 1964).

Did Piaget underestimate the intellectual abilities of preschool children? It appears that he did.

Not only can preschoolers conserve and classify under certain conditions, but also they have a more sophisticated understanding of cause and effect than Piaget imagined (Bullock & Gelman 1979; Bullock, Gelman & Baillargeon 1982), and an easier time distinguishing between animate and inanimate objects (Gelman & Spelke 1981). The mind of the preschooler appears to be less confused and better organized than was initially believed (Flavell 1985).

Findings of elementary forms of categorization, classification, and causal reasoning in young preschoolers raise questions about Piaget's belief that cognitive structures gradually emerge as a result of environmental interaction. Modern cognitive psychologists suggest that Piaget erred in failing to realize that some structures that underlie human cognition may be innate (Gelman & Baillargeon 1983). Human beings may have built-in mechanisms for organizing and making sense of the world, and these basic mechanisms may differ little from childhood to adulthood. However, until the age of 5 or 6, children lack the ability to reflect upon and to talk about their approaches to problem solving (Flavell 1985). It is significant that Piaget (1964) insisted that before a child could be credited with adequately solving an operational problem, the child must provide a verbal explanation of how the problem was solved.

Preschoolers are also easily distracted, and often unable to attend to relevant aspects of a problem while ignoring the irrelevant. They are too easily influenced by appearances rather than substance, and they can indeed be very egocentric. Such characteristics could certainly be responsible for their failure to solve concrete operational problems, even though, as critics of Piaget suggest, the underlying cognitive structures that organize the world may actually be present in young children.

Few psychologists deny that significant cognitive development occurs during the preschool years. Few deny that Piaget was perhaps the greatest contributor thus far to current knowledge of the *facts* about children's cognitive development. His views that children are active rather than passive in the process of their own learning and that their cognitive structures influence their perceptions and their understanding of the world have gained

Preschool children are easily distracted, which may offer a partial explanation for their failure to solve concrete operational problems.

widespread acceptance among psychologists and educators (Gelman & Baillargeon 1983). However, while Piaget's descriptions of preschoolers' behavior were accurate, the prevailing view today is that his interpretations placed too strict a limit on the young child's cognitive capacities.

Beyond Formal Operations?

In recent years much speculation has taken place on the possibility that there is a level of intellectual functioning more advanced than the stage of formal operations. Arlin (1975, 1984) observed that formal operational thought is characterized by a convergent problem-solving process. That is, people use formal reasoning skills to discover correct solutions to problems. They discover, for instance, the correct way to combine flasks of colorless chemicals in order to produce the color yellow. In fact, many standard tests of formal reasoning do resemble scientific experiments—techniques of discovery or convergence upon truths about the world.

In contrast to the problem-solving approach, in which there is convergence upon correct answers, Arlin suggested a higher form of reasoning called the *problem-finding*, or divergent, approach, which includes "creative thoughts . . . the formulation of generic problems, the raising of general questions from ill-defined problems, and the slow cognitive growth represented in the development of significant scientific thought" (1975, 603).

To measure problem-finding ability, Arlin (1975) showed a group of unrelated objects (e.g., a scissors, a wooden cube, candles, thumbtacks) to a group of college seniors and asked them to make a list of questions about the objects. She then rated the questions in terms of their sophistication and determined the extent to which the students showed signs of problem finding.

When the same college students were also tested on Piaget's formal operational (problem-solving) tasks, Arlin found that a person has to be a problem solver in order to be a problem finder, but that being a problem solver is no guarantee that one will also be a problem finder. In other words, the creative problem-finding approach seemed to be a step beyond mere problem solving, leading Arlin to conclude that there is a fifth stage of cognitive development beyond Piaget's formal operations.

Arlin's work has been criticized on the grounds that problem finding may not be qualitatively different from problem solving (Fakouri 1976). That is, perhaps the two are related skills, and perhaps problem finding is merely a refinement of problem solving instead of a totally different way of thinking. Piaget never suggested that intellectual growth ends at adulthood, but only that continued growth occurs within the stage of formal operations. Perhaps the process of problem finding is still a feature of formal operational thought rather than a completely new stage of intellectual development.

Instead of trying to identify more sophisticated stages as Arlin (1975, 1984) did, some psychologists deal differently with the question of whether formal operations represents the high point of human thinking; they argue that in describing formal reasoning as the final stage, Piaget exposed a serious weakness in his whole theoretical model (Datan, Rodeheaver & Hughes 1987).

As an illustration of this type of criticism, Labouvie-Vief (1984, 1985, 1986a, 1986b) challenged Piaget's view that a pure state of logical reasoning is developmentally superior to, and therefore inherently better than, the subjective and intuitive thinking processes of the child. She suggested instead that in an adolescent or adult, pure, objective reasoning exists side by side with personal, subjective forms of thinking and that the two continuously balance and enrich one another. Young children are indeed limited because their thought processes cannot go beyond the egocentric, the perceptual, and the intuitive. Adolescents begin to use formal reasoning, but often neglect, or temporarily "forget," their powers of intuition. Adults are more successful at blending the two ways of knowing. Thus, there *is* a type of thinking that is beyond formal operations: it is a blend of rational/objective and intuitive/subjective elements of thought.

To understand the benefits of the rational-intuitive balance in thinking, consider the following question asked of adolescents and adults by Labouvie-Vief (1986b): A woman tells her husband that if he ever comes home drunk again she will leave him. Several days later he comes home drunk. What does the woman do?

Using the strictly logical hypothetico-deductive strategy characteristic of formal operations, the answer is very clear: the woman will leave her husband. Adolescents and young adults typically gave this undeniably logical answer. The older respondents in the study usually said, however, that logic alone will not provide an answer; the human dimension must also be considered. How much does the woman love her husband? Why was he drunk? How drunk was he? Is the wife usually a forgiving person? Is she prone to make idle threats? What are the consequences for her, and for him, if she leaves?

Many of the older adults spontaneously referred to their own life experiences, and their intuitive feelings about what would happen. In that sense they attempted to blend the rational and intuitive sides of thought and probably came up with more realistic answers to the question than did the younger respondents. Labouvie-Vief (1986b) suggested that complex social reasoning, requiring both propositional logic and intuition, is actually a step beyond formal reasoning, not because it is a qualitatively different stage but because social reasoning incorporates more aspects of the human thinking process.

Is there a stage of thinking beyond formal operations? The best that can be said at this point is that answers are elusive. Perhaps it is wise to remember, however, that Piaget's theory represents but one theoretical model of cognitive development. It may not reveal the complete truth about human cognition but as a theory it is successful in the sense that it generates questions that are likely to engage cognitive researchers for years to come.

Piaget's Theory and Education

Although Piaget himself had little to say about the educational process, it seems reasonable that a theory of children's cognitive development would have implications for classroom teaching. A person's educational philosophy would certainly be affected by acceptance of the view that cognitive structures underlie a child's thought processes, that thinking progresses through a series of qualitatively different stages, and that the motivation for intellectual growth is internal. Ginsburg and Opper (1979) summarized a number of classroom implications of Piaget's theory, including the following:

- *The language and thought processes of the child differ from those of the adult.* When teachers present material to children, they must realize that the children may be viewing the material from a perspective that differs from that of the adult. Many college professors are disappointed to learn that what they see as the exciting issues in their field are rather uninteresting to their students. In the case of the elementary school child, the misperception can be more serious since the child may be unable to appreciate the issues the teacher is trying to discuss.
- *Children learn best when they can manipulate their environments.* Activity should be an important aspect of learning. Verbal instruction may be effective for a college student, but a child learns best when the method of presentation is concrete. It is more effective to allow a child to carry out a physics experiment or to take a nature hike than it is to discuss principles of physics or ecology.

- *The material to be learned should be "moderately" new to the child.* The most interesting "food for thought" is that which is unfamiliar but not too alien to the cognitive structures of the child. Familiar material has already been adapted to and if repeated leads to boredom in the learner, but material which is far above the child's level cannot be adapted to and the learner will be confused. Since the appropriate level of presentation may vary from child to child, children should be allowed to work at their own pace.
- *Since the child's thinking progresses through stages, children should not be forced to learn material until they are ready for it.* If such forced learning occurs, the pupils become frustrated, the teachers become frustrated, and negative attitudes about schooling may be fostered in the child.
- *Children should be allowed to talk to one another, to argue, and to debate in the classroom.* Intellectual growth is stimulated by social interaction, as any college student knows who has experienced the benefit of an informed discussion of issues in the dorm or cafeteria. Much knowledge comes from student interaction both inside and outside the classroom.

Environmental Influences on Cognitive Development

Piaget's theory, like most organismic theories, is an interaction model. That is, development results when the organism and the environment interact in increasingly sophisticated ways. The environment is important, obviously, because it provides intellectual material for the cognitive structures to adapt to. Nevertheless, Piaget had little to say about the features of specific environments in which children are raised. For example, he never attempted to describe ideal environments for intellectual growth, nor did he write about environmental deficiences.

This section of the chapter deals with specific environmental factors that influence cognitive development. It looks first at cultural differences in the emergence of Piaget's stages and what the differences might mean. Then it looks at the influence of education, of child-rearing practices, and of diet on intellectual growth.

Cross-cultural Perspectives

Cultural anthropologists repeatedly maintain that what are considered "normal" human characteristics may be normal only within a specific cultural context. In the area of intellectual development, what is described as the normal developmental pattern may not be universally observed. For that reason, cross-cultural research is essential. Most cross-cultural research on cognition has been carried out within the framework of Piaget's theory, and there have been numerous attempts to determine whether Piaget's stages of development can be found beyond the mainstream European and American culture.

Turning now to the findings obtained in cross-cultural research on cognition, a fairly consistent pattern emerges: the stages of development appear to be universal but the rate of development varies from culture to culture.

Comparative research on the *sensorimotor* stage is rare, and what there is has been undertaken only recently. Some scholars suggest that the lack of standardized testing procedures is the reason for the scarcity of research (Dasen & Heron 1981). Whatever the reason, the few studies that have been done strongly support the view that the characteristics of sensorimotor development are universal. Whether the infants were American, French, Indian, English, or African, they performed in much the same way on sensorimotor tasks. Dasen and Heron commented on how the similarity is sometimes unbelievable, citing as an example the behavior of 1-year-old infants when given a plastic tube and a chain of paper clips. The infants typically tried to pass the chain through the tube. This was equally likely to occur in European countries, where the infants had seen the objects before, and in African countries, where the objects were completely unfamiliar.

Comparative research on the *concrete operational stage* of development has yielded similar findings. That is, there is evidence that children from a variety of different cultures all acquire the logical thought processes of concrete operations, although the ages at which these are acquired are quite variable. For example, children in the African nation of Kenya have been found to conserve mass, weight, and volume in precisely the same sequence as Piaget observed in European children (Kiminyo 1977). Thai children have been shown to perform in much the same way as Piaget's Swiss children on a variety of cognitive tasks, including seriation, class inclusion, and various forms of conservation (Opper 1977). Similar results have been found on studies of children in England, Australia, New Zealand, Holland, Poland, and Uganda (Goldschmid et al. 1973).

Finally, cross-cultural research on the *formal operational* stage of development has been somewhat disappointing. As Dasen and Heron (1981) pointed out, the few studies that have been done in this area found little or no evidence of formal operational reasoning. For example, Kelly (1977) noted that performance on a formal operational task in Papua and New Guinea was so poor that he decided not to administer the test to all of the children in his sample. Perhaps the failure on formal-reasoning tasks should not be terribly surprising, since a large percentage of American high school and college students fail on these tasks as well (Joyce 1977; Kolody 1977; Renner 1977; Sayre & Ball 1975).

Although the sequence of stages appears to be universal, the rate of progression through the stages is highly variable (Dasen & Heron 1981; Price-Williams 1981). Why are children in some cultures slower to progress through the stages of development than others? Explanations usually focus on variables such as urbanization, schooling, and task relevance (Dasen & Heron 1981). Perhaps the tests themselves measure skills necessary for survival in some cultures, but not in others. For example, Dasen (1975) observed more advanced spatial skills in Eskimo children who belonged to a wandering hunting-and-gathering society than in West African children who belonged to a sedentary, agricultural tribe. Presumably Eskimos need better spatial ability to survive. In contrast, the West African children outpaced the Eskimo children in the development of various forms of conservation—possibly because Africans need a sophisticated understanding of quantity to exchange their foodstuffs in the marketplace while the Eskimos do not.

Finally, it should be pointed out that there have been recent challenges to the "cultural differences" explanations of differences in the rate of Piagetian cognitive development. Cross-cultural psychologist Raphael Nyiti (1982) suggested that the quantitative differences among cultures occur because (1) the researchers are usually outsiders who have an insufficient knowledge of the children's language and culture, and (2) the researchers try to use standardized rather than "open" interviews. Nyiti noted that cultural differences in the rate of development disappear when an open-interview approach is used and when the questions are asked by an examiner from the child's own culture.

In summary, it appears that there are few qualitative differences in the developmental process among widely diverse cultures throughout the world. However, the rate of progression through the stages varies considerably, and the explanations of this variance focus on cultural opportunities for advancement, cultural necessities for advancement, and factors related to the data-gathering process itself.

The Influence of Education

An extensive amount of research on the effects of schooling on cognition has been conducted. The findings can be summarized as follows:

- Formally educated people are better than uneducated people at abstracting general rules and applying them to specific problems (Scribner & Cole 1973).
- Formally educated people are better able to verbalize their behavior than are uneducated people (Scribner & Cole 1973).
- Formally educated people are more likely to apply earlier-learned cognitive skills to totally new situations (Nerlove & Snipper 1981).
- Formally educated people do better on memory tasks than do uneducated people (Rogoff 1981).
- The findings based on performance on Piagetian tasks are inconsistent. Some studies indicate that schooling can improve a child's concrete operational skills, such as conservation, while others show no differences at all between the schooled and the unschooled (Rogoff 1981; Nerlove & Snipper 1981).

Actually, it is not surprising that formal schooling has little effect on operational skills. After all, Piaget believed that a child develops by interacting with the world, and the classroom is only one arena of that interaction. Everyday experiences can stimulate intellectual growth, and, as mentioned in an earlier section of this chapter, formal training is often of little help in the child's acquisition of operational skills.

It is important to remember that even though there may be a relationship between formal schooling and certain intellectual abilities, we are unable to conclude that schooling itself enhances cognitive growth. As Rogoff (1981) observed, in contrast to parents who do not send their children to school, parents who do send their children to school may be wealthier, may have more progressive attitudes, or may have a higher motivation to achieve and thus set higher goals for their children. In other words, a variety of factors may account for cognitive differences between schooled and unschooled children, when in fact these differences occur.

Family Factors

While the findings from studies of family factors in cognitive development are too numerous and diverse to summarize, there appears to be an overall pattern: children who are overly dominated—overly controlled by their parents—seem to be slower in their cognitive development. For example, Munroe and Munroe (1977) discovered that children of mothers who used harsh punishment performed less well on a conservation of mass study than children of more lenient parents. Children who were more self-directed were found in another study to score higher on a memory test than did more controlled children (Munroe & Munroe 1978).

In a study of Japanese children (Hatano, Mikaya & Tajima 1980), maternal directiveness was related to a child's ability to conserve number. Highly directive mothers were identified as those who, when playing with their children, selected tasks for the children to get involved in, paid very close attention to what the children were doing, pressured them to do well, and allowed them only a slight degree of freedom. The children were then given a basic conservation of number task, similar to the one described earlier in this chapter. They first agreed that two parallel rows contained equal numbers of marbles; then the marbles in one row were spread out and the children were asked if they were still the same. Children of directive mothers were less likely to conserve number than were children of nondirective mothers, and the authors concluded that this was because the directive parent actually inhibits a child's interaction with the world.

Since the cognitive structures develop because of a child's interaction with the world, it would stand to reason that a family's child-rearing patterns, and even the family structure itself (i.e., intact versus single-parent family), could influence that interaction. A small but interesting body of research suggests that cognitive development is, in fact, influenced by variables such as family size, father absence, or the child-care arrangements that have been provided (Nerlove & Snipper 1981).

Nutritional Factors

Much of what is known about the effects of nutrition on intellectual functioning is based on extensions of findings from animal research or on research with hospitalized children. In other words, little is known about the effects of chronic malnutrition on intellectual development in a "normal" human population (Townsend et al., 1982).

Another difficulty with nutrition studies is that a number of factors other than nutritional ones influence results. For instance, if it is found that children from malnourished segments of society are slow to develop intellectually, does their retardation result from the inadequacy of their diets, or from other factors often correlated with malnutrition: poverty, illness, lack of intellectual stimulation?

Keeping in mind the limitations described above, consider one of the most extensive studies of the effects of nutrition on preschool mental development. Townsend and his associates (1982) carried out a longitudinal study of nutrition and mental development. Four Guatemalan villages were selected for study; two small villages and two

large villages were matched on a number of characteristics. Children and nursing mothers in one member of each pair were then provided with a nutritional supplement. The children were later tested, using a battery of preschool tests. For example, the researchers tested the children's reasoning skills, verbal ability, perceptual skills, learning ability, and memory. With careful control for the possibility of confounding variables (e.g., intellectual stimulation at home, illness), the researchers found that the nutritional supplement significantly improved the children's mental performance for most tasks. Furthermore, they reported that follow-up research, suggested that the intellectual advantages attributed to an improved diet carry over into adolescence and perhaps into adulthood! Such findings were consistent with those of previous findings on the relationship of diet to intellectual functioning.

It may be discovered in future years that mental development is linked specifically to certain aspects of brain maturation, to hormonal factors, and even to physical growth. However, for now psychologists must be content with a certain amount of speculation, and with theoretical models of intellectual functioning, such as that suggested by Piaget, that appear to have predictive and explanatory value.

Summary

1. Organismic theories of cognitive development, such as Piaget's maintain that development is a process by which individuals progress through a series of qualitatively different stages of thought, each of which builds upon those which preceded it.
2. Piaget viewed intelligence as a form of biological adaptation, and he separated intelligence into its content, its structure, and its function.
3. Intellectual growth for Piaget involved the growth of the cognitive structures, and this occurred because of the constant interaction between structures and external experience.
4. Piaget considered the functioning of intelligence to consist of the two fold process of organization and adaptation, with the latter being further divided into assimilation and accommodation.

5. Piaget believed that children progress through four stages of thought: the sensorimotor stage (birth to 1½ years), the preoperational stage (1½ to 6 years), the concrete operational stage (6 years to 12 years), and the formal operations stage (12 years to adult).

6. Cross-cultural research on cognitive development indicates that the stages of development described by Piaget are universal, but that the rate of progression through the stages varies from culture to culture.

7. Amount of formal education is related to performance on tests of abstract reasoning and memory, and is also related to verbal ability. A link between education and success on Piagetian measures of cognitive development has been difficult to establish.

8. A child's cognitive development is related to parental disciplinary techniques and to degree of parental control.

9. Most of the research on biological influences on cognitive development has emphasized nutritional factors. An inadequate diet appears to have an adverse effect on children's reasoning ability, verbal ability, learning, and memory.

Key Terms

cognitive structures
assimilation
accommodation
disequilibrium
sensorimotor intelligence
schemes
preoperational
  intelligence
transductive reasoning
animism
artificialism

centration
concrete operations
classification
seriation
conservation
cognitive conceit
formal operations

Suggested Readings

Elkind, D. (1981). *Children and adolescents: Interpretive essays on Jean Piaget*. New York: Oxford University Press.

A collection of eleven well-written essays on various aspects of Piaget's theory. This book clearly illustrates the fact that cognitive developmental theory has numerous practical applications. Included are essays on children's questions, egocentrism, reading instruction, conceptions of time, educational applications of Piaget's theory, and a comparison of Piaget's educational views with those of Maria Montessori.

Flavell, J.H. (1985). *Cognitive development* (2nd ed.). Englewood Cliffs, NJ: Prentice-Hall.

An infancy-through-adolescence coverage of various aspects of cognitive development, written by one of the nation's foremost cognitive psychologists. Topics include intelligence, problem-solving, language, perception, memory, social cognition, and personality factors in cognition.

Furth, H.G. & Wachs, H. (1974). *Thinking goes to school: Piaget's theory in practice*. New York: Oxford University Press.

A clear and readable discussion of Piaget's theory followed by a well-defined educational curriculum based on the theory. This book is one of the most effective presentations of the educational implications of Piaget's work.

Ginsburg, H. & Opper, S. (1979). *Piaget's theory of intellectual development* (2nd ed.). Englewood Cliffs, NJ: Prentice-Hall.

One of the most thorough, accurate, and readable treatments of Piaget's theory. Many examples are used to illustrate major Piagetian concepts, and the practical implications of the theory are discussed.

Piaget, J. & Inhelder, B. (1969). *The psychology of the child*. New York: Basic Books.

A brief and very clear summary of Piaget and his associate Barbel Inhelder's work in the area of child development. Much of Piaget's work is spread out across a number of different volumes, many of which are difficult to read. But this book is highly readable and serves as an excellent introduction for the student interested in reading Piaget and Inhelder in the original.

Readings from the Literature

The following article deals with the seeming ability of toddlers to see the world in terms of consistent categories rather than as a disorganized mass of stimuli. It provides an interesting illustration of the ways in which research findings often depend on the methodology that is used. As you read the article, try to answer the following questions:

• What does the author mean by "habituation"? Explain what led the author to believe that young children see the world in categories.

• To what extent does the study disprove certain aspects of Piaget's theory? How might Piaget defend his theory in responding to the author's conclusions?

• Is there any way in which the findings of the study could be seen as offering support for general principles of Piaget's theory?

Categorization in 1- to 2-Year-Olds

Gail S. Ross
Harvard University

Children 12, 18, and 24 months old were shown successive members of one category followed by the simultaneous presentation of a new member of that category and a member of a novel category. Six categories—Ms, Os, men, animals, food and furniture—were presented in all. Children habituated to presentations of Ms, Os, and men. They also showed greater attention to the novel category stimulus during the choice trial for each category. There were no age differences. Findings suggest that 1- to 2-year-olds recognize some conventional categories.

Classic developmental studies indicate that young children's object groupings do not correspond to those of adults (Bruner, Olver, & Greenfield, 1966; Inhelder & Piaget, 1964; Vygotsky, 1962). When asked to sort objects into groups that are alike, adults form category groups based on concepts in which all members have a common attribute. Young children, on the other hand, form "complexes" or groups in which members do not share a single trait in common and may be entered for any of their attributes. Based on these findings, many cognitive psychologists have concluded that young, preschool children do not form conventional categories as do older children and adults.

This conclusion has been questioned on two grounds. First, it is argued that young children's groupings are not qualitatively different from adults', since most natural categories used by adults are similar to the "complexes" formed by children (Fodor, 1972; Lenneberg, 1967). For example, it is difficult to specify the common attribute of members of the category *furniture* that are as diverse as a table, beach chair, and dresser. Second, researchers have shown that children as young as 2 years appear to use adult categories such as animals, food, utensils, and body parts (Goldberg, Perlmutter, & Myers, 1974; Nelson, 1973, Rossi & Rossi, 1965).

Comparatively few studies have been made of the categorizing abilities of children below the age of 2. One possible reason is the difficulty in measuring cognitive capacities of children in this age group. Use of the free-recall and release from proactive inhibition methods for studying categorizing ability are limited to children who are already verbal, and the discrimination-learning procedure has not proven successful in demonstrating category knowledge in children below the age of 3 (Daehler & Butatko, 1974). Ricciuti (1965) used spontaneous grouping behavior to measure categorization in 12-, 18-, and 24-month-olds but found that many of the younger subjects either did not sort objects into groups or formed groups that were incomplete.

One promising method of tapping the category systems of preverbal children is the habituation–dishabituation paradigm. Since a category is a group of physically distinct objects to which one imputes equivalent meaning, one might expect children to habituate to successive members of the same category as they do to physically identical stimuli. Furthermore, as a novel stimulus causes recovery of attention, a member of a different category may elicit dishabituation.

Some recent studies (Cohen & Strauss, 1979; McGurk, 1972; Ruff, 1978) have used the habituation–dishabituation paradigm to demonstrate that infants recognize similar perceptual features within categories such as geometrical shapes and faces. In addition, Cohen and Caputo (Note 1) used a paired-choice trial following habituation trials to test category learning. They found that 12-month-olds who had habituated to slides of different dogs attended more to an antelope than to a new instance of a dog during the choice presentation.

Similarly, we assessed categorizing abilities by presenting habituation trials followed by a choice between a new member of the familiarized category and a member of a novel category. The research was designed to investigate whether 1- to 2-year-olds understand certain categories and whether there are any developmental changes in categorizing abilities from 1 to 2 years of age.

Method

Subjects

Subjects were 150 children—50 each at 12, 18, and 24 months of age. Half of the children each age were boys and half were girls. The majority were white and middle-class, and all were seen within 1 week of the targeted age.

Stimuli

Children in the experimental groups were presented with toy objects from each of six categories—Ms, Os, men, animals, food, and furniture. These categories were grouped into three sets. The first set consisted of the two categories in which members were designed to be most similar perceptually—Ms and Os of different sizes. The Ms were M-shaped red wooden blocks, ranging from 5.1 to 10.2 cm in length. The Os were O-shaped red wooden blocks, ranging from 5.1 to 10.2 cm in diameter.

The second set consisted of the two categories that were designed to be intermediate in perceptual variation—men and animals that differed in color and material as well as in size. The men consisted of male dolls that varied in height from 8.3 to 15.4 cm; were made of plastic, pipecleaners, or cloth; and wore clothing in a variety of colors. The animals were all four-legged and varied in length from 3.2 to 13.4 cm, ranged in material from soft, squeezable plastic to hard plastic, and came in a number of colors.

The third set consisted of the two categories designed to have the greatest perceptual variation; members of each category differed from each other in forms as well as in color, materials, and size. The food category was comprised of objects that ranged in height from 5.1 to 17.9 cm, in form from rectangular (bread) to oblong (hot dog) to round (slice of salami), in material from styrofoam to hard plastic, and in color from green to white to red. Furniture exemplars varied in height from 3.2 to 12.8 cm, in form from an oblong (couch) to a rectangle (bookcase) to a circle (round table); in material from wood to soft plastic; and in color.

194

Children in the control group were presented with three sets of toy objects in which every item belonged to a different category. Items in each set ranged in height from 3.2 to 15.4 cm and varied in color, form, and material.

There were, in addition, three pairs of comparison stimuli, each pair consisting of previously unexposed members of the two categories in a set. These were a red M and a red O of the same size; a black and white man (groom) and a black and white cow; and a round green apple and a round green chair.

Experimental Design

At each age, children were randomly assigned by sex to one of three treatment groups—two experimental groups of 20 children each and a control group of 10 children. The first experimental group was presented with one category from each of the three sets (Ms, men, and food); the other experimental group was presented with the other category from each set (Os, animals, and furniture). Control children were shown the three groups of objects from different categories. The three stimulus series for each condition were presented in six different orders to subjects of each age and sex; objects in every stimulus series were presented in random order.

Procedure

The child sat on a parent's lap facing a table with a curtain behind it, the experimenter sat at the side of the table, and an assistant and the stimuli were concealed behind the curtain. During habituation trials, the assistant placed each toy through a central aperture in the curtain. The experimenter positioned a cardboard screen in front of the curtain between presentations so the child could not view stimuli as they were exchanged through the aperture. Each toy was secured to the back of the table by a string, enabling the child to manipulate the object freely but not to throw it off the table.

Members of the appropriate stimulus category were presented singly and in succession to children in the experimental groups. Seven exemplars of the M and O categories were presented for 15 sec each, and 10 exemplars of the other four categories were presented for 30 sec each. Intervals between presentation were uniformly 15 sec. Fewer Ms and Os were presented and for shorter durations because children in a pilot study had paid less attention to objects of those two categories than the others.

Following presentations of objects forming the first category series, each child was shown a comparison pair consisting of a new member of the category previously presented and a member of the other category in that set (e.g., following food, the apple and the chair were shown). The comparison pair was simultaneously presented through apertures in the curtain that were equidistant from the child's midline. After presentation of the comparison pair, there was a short interval and the child then returned to view the second series and its comparison pair. This procedure continued in the same manner until all three series had been presented in the preassigned order.

Procedure for the control subjects was similar and designed for comparability with the experimental groups. Thus, control children were presented with items from a 7-member mixed-category series for 15 sec each and with items in two 10-member mixed-category series for 30 sec each, with 15-sec intervals between presentation. Children in the control group were also shown the same three comparison pairs as children in the experimental groups. Comparison pair presentations lasted 30 sec for all subjects.

The research assistant and experimenter, respectively, recorded the amount of time children looked at and touched each stimulus in ½-sec units on an Esterline-Angus event recorder. The experimenter also timed the duration of trials and intertrial intervals. Interrater reliability, based on the independent observations of the experimenter and assistant on six children, was .95 for looking and .93 for touching.

Results

Habituation

Habituation was measured by decreases in attention over familiarization trials. There were two separate measures of attention—number of ½ sec looking at and number of ½ sec touching each stimulus.

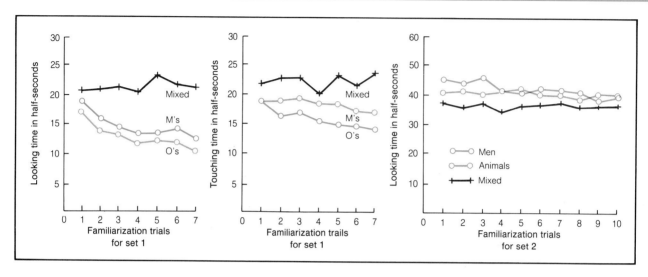

Figure 1 Average time attending to stimuli during familiarization

Major questions asked of the data were whether children habituated to categories and whether age or sex influenced habituation. The three category sets were analyzed separately, since categories in Set 1 were presented for fewer and shorter habituation trials than those in Sets 2 and 3. A Condition (3) × Age (3) × Sex (2) × Trials (7 or 10) analysis of variance (ANOVA) was performed separately on the looking and touching measures for each set, with trials as a repeated measure analyzed for linear and quadratic trends. F ratios were tested with the Geisser-Greenhouse conservative F test (Kirk, 1968).

There were no significant quadratic trends or interactions. There was a significant linear trend across trials in amount of looking, $F(1, 132) = 21.26$, and touching $F(1, 132) = 11.12$, for Category Set 1 (Ms, Os, mixed) and in amount of looking, $F(1, 132) = 10.01$, for Category Set 2 (men, animals, mixed)(all $ps < .001$). There was no significant linear trend in either measure of attention for Category Set 3 (food, furniture, mixed), indicating lack of habituation to any of the categories in that set.

A significant Condition × Linear Trend for Trials interaction was found for looking, $F(2, 120) = 7.16$, $p < .001$, and touching, $F(2, 120) = 4.79$,

$p < 01$, for Category Set 1, and for looking, $F(2, 119) = 3.73$, $p < .05$, but not touching, for Category Set 2. Post hoc linear trend analyses for each condition in Category Sets 1 and 2 indicated that children habituated in looking to Ms, Os, and men; and in touching to Ms and Os (all $ps < .01$). There was no habituation to all animal category or to either mixed category series in Sets 1 and 2. These results are shown in Figure 1. Neither age nor sex effects were significant nor were any other meaningful interactions.

Choice Test

The second measure of categorization was a comparison of the amount of time children attended to the novel and the familiar category stimulus during a choice trial. Attention measures were number of ½ sec looking at and number of ½ sec touching each stimulus.

Data were analyzed to determine whether children in the experimental groups preferred the novel category stimulus and whether age or sex influenced preference for the novel category. A 3 (condition) × 3 (age) × 2 (comparison stimulus) × 2 (sex) analysis of variance was performed for looking and touching, respectively, for each category set.

196

Table 1 Mean Time Looking at Comparison Stimuli by Stimulus Series (in ½ sec)

Comparison stimuli	Stimulus series presented		
	M	**O**	**7 mixed**
Ms	10.5	24.6	14.6
Os	28.3	10.9	19.1
	Men	**Animals**	**10 mixed**
Groom	15.5	22.5	29.3
Cow	30.6	14.0	22.1
	Food	**Furniture**	**10 mixed**
Apple	15.1	31.8	25.2
Chair	34.7	13.9	21.3

There was a significant Condition × Comparison Stimulus interaction in both looking and touching for each category set, $F(2, 132) = 14.78$, $p < .001$, and $F(2, 132) = 12.49$, $p < .001$, respectively, for Set 1; $F(2, 132) = 25.42$, $p < .001$, and $F(2, 132) = 20.23$, $p < .001$, respectively, for Set 2; and $F(2, 132) = 18.49$, $p < .001$, and $F(2, 132) = 34.94$, $p < .001$, respectively, for Set 3.

Tests of simple main effects showed that children in each experimental group significantly preferred the novel category stimulus for every category (all $ps < .01$ for looking and touching, respectively). Children in the control group showed no significant preference in looking or touching for either comparison stimulus in all choice tests but one, as they touched the apple significantly more than the chair, $F(1, 132) = 10.55$, $p < .01$. This is a minor result, as experimental children presented with furniture in familiarization trials preferred the apple to the chair significantly more than controls—touching the apple significantly more, $q'(2, 132) = 5.08$, $p < .01$, and the chair significantly less, $q'(2, 132) = 8.11$, $p < .01$ (Dunnett's test, cited in Kirk, 1968). No other relevant effects or interactions were significant. Table 1 shows the mean time children looked at each comparison stimulus following presentation of every familiarization series.

Thus, in comparison to the control subjects, children in the experimental groups attended significantly more to the novel than to the familiar category object in the choice test for every category. Furthermore, neither age nor sex influenced novel category preference.

Discussion

Results of this study showed that 12-, 18-, and 24-month-old children habituated to presentations of the two categories designed to be perceptually most similar, Ms and Os, but not to the categories designed to be perceptually most different, food and furniture. On the categories designed to be intermediate in perceptual variation, children habituated to men but not to animals. Post hoc examination of these two categories shows that men are physically more alike than animals. This difference may explain why children habituated to men as they did to Ms and Os and responded to animals as they did to food and furniture.

The finding that children did not habituate to animals, food or furniture does not necessarily mean that they were unable to recognize those categories. Modifications in methodology, such as using different stimuli or presenting more familiarization trials, might have elicited habituation to those categories as well. Although children did not show decreases in attention to all categories, they did show a preference for the novel rather than the familiar category comparison stimulus following every category series. This result suggests that with successive presentations of members of the same category, children develop an expectation for that group that is violated when a member of a different category is presented. Thus, use of a choice trial following a familiarization series may serve as an effective means of measuring categorizing ability in young children.

Children's significant preference for the novel category following presentation of all six categories indicates that 12- to 24-month-olds can not only extract the common physical features of categories whose members are perceptually alike but that they can also recognize superordinate categories such as food and furniture in which members vary considerably in perceptual characteristics and have a related function. However, whether similarity in perceptual features or similarity in function is the basis for categorization cannot be determined from this research.

The lack of age differences in either habituation or preference for novel category stimuli was unexpected. A likely explanation is that the categories selected for the study are equally familiar to 12-, 18-, and 24-month-olds. Another possibility is that changes in categorization abilities that occur during the 2nd year of life, such as better articulation of categories, may not be tapped by this methodology.

In sum, the results of this study suggest a conclusion different from that made by classical grouping studies (Bruner et al., 1966; Inhelder & Piaget, 1964; Vygotsky, 1962). By using a procedure that relied on productive activity (i.e., sorting) and that required both consistency and completeness in category groupings, they found that preschool children did not classify objects by category and concluded that young children do not form groupings as do adults. However, by using a procedure that relied on receptive behavior (i.e., attention) and that did not require that every category member be classified as such, this study provides evidence that 1- to 2-year-olds recognize conventional categories such as men, animals, food, and furniture. This finding suggests that sorting studies may have underestimated children's categorization abilities. Furthermore, it indicates that conclusions about children's categorization skills are dependent on the methodology employed, the response required, and the categories presented.

Reference Note

1. Cohen, L. B., & Caputo, N. F. *Instructing infants to respond to perceptual categories.* Paper presented at the meeting of the Midwestern Psychological Association, Chicago, May 1978.

References

Bruner, J. S., Olver, R., & Greenfield, P. M. *Studies in cognitive growth.* New York: Wiley, 1966.

Cohen. L. B., & Strauss, M. S. Concept acquisition in the human infant. *Child Development,* 1979, *50,* 419–423.

Daehler, M., & Butatko, D. Discrimination learning in 2-year-olds. *Child Development,* 1974, *45,* 378–382.

Fodor, J. Some reflections on L. S. Vygotsky's *Thought and language, Cognition,* 1972, *1,* 83–95.

Goldberg, S., Perlmutter, M., & Myers, N. Recall of related and unrelated lists by 2-year-olds. *Journal of Experimental Child Psychology,* 1974, *18,* 1–8.

Inhelder, B., & Piaget, J. *The early growth of logic in the child.* New York: Norton, 1964.

Kirk, R. F. *Experimental design: Procedures for the behavioral sciences.* Belmont, Calif.: Brooks/Cole, 1968.

Lenneberg, E. H. *Biological foundations of language.* New York: Wiley, 1967.

McGurk, H. Infant discrimination of orientation. *Journal of Experimental Psychology,* 1972, *14,* 151–164.

Nelson, K. Some evidence for the cognitive primacy of categorization and its functional basis. *Merrill-Palmer Quarterly,* 1973, *19,* 21–39.

Ricciuti, H. N. Object grouping and selective ordering behavior in infants 12 to 24 months old. *Merrill-Palmer Quarterly,* 1965, *11,* 129–148.

Rossi, E. L., & Rossi, S. I. Concept utilization, serial order and recall in nursery school children. *Child Development,* 1965, *49,* 293–306.

Ruff, H. A. Infant recognition of the invariant form of objects. *Child Development,* 1978, *49,* 293–306.

Vygotsky, L. S. *Thought and language.* New York: Wiley, 1962.

Received December 31, 1979. A version of this article was presented at the biennial meeting of the Society for Research in Child Development, New Orleans, March 1977.

Learning and Information Processing

7

If Larry receives an *A* on his algebra test, can his teacher be certain that he has learned her course material very well? Maybe not! Learning is a mental process; it is an aspect of an overall system of processing information—beginning with attention and ending when material is retrieved from memory storage.

Learning is said to occur when certain experiences bring about a change in behavior, but as a mental process, the learning itself is not directly observable. The experiences are observable: Larry attended his algebra class, did his homework, and studied for the test. The changed behavior is observable: Larry performed well on the test. But for learning to have taken place, the experiences would have to have caused the behavior. Larry's teacher assumes that they did, and it certainly appears that he learned his algebra. However, it is possible that the boy learned nothing, but cheated on the exam, or simply was a lucky guesser!

The point is that learning cannot be seen, but must always be assumed. A certain air of mystery surrounds the ways in which children process information in their minds. We see what is available to them as input, and we see the output in their behaviors; but what we cannot see are the processes by which information is registered, made sense of, stored, and retrieved at a later time. These internal processes of learning, attention, and memory will be the focus of this chapter.

The chapter begins by presenting basic principles of several varieties of human learning—especially conditioning and social learning—and by reviewing the literature on learning from infancy through adolescence. Included also will be a discussion of learning in the classroom—that most applied of all learning environments. Then the chapter discusses the information-processing approach to dealing with children's cognitive activity, involving attempts to trace the internal sequence of mental operations required when performing an intellectual task. The discussion will focus on attention—the cognitive activity that specifies which information the child will enter into the information processing system—and memory—the process by which information in the system is stored and later retrieved when needed.

Conditioning

The simplest form of learning is conditioning. In fact, conditioning studies made up much of the early research on processes of learning, and the "participants" in these studies were usually lower animals rather than human beings. Nevertheless, the conditioning literature, and particularly that on operant conditioning, offers useful information for understanding the developing child.

Principles of Conditioning

The technique of **classical conditioning** was first investigated by the Russian physiologist Ivan Pavlov (1849–1936). Pavlov placed dogs in a harness and trained them to salivate each time they heard a tone produced by a tuning fork. The training was accomplished by presenting the sound of the tuning fork at approximately the same time he inserted food powder into the dogs' mouths. Salivation in response to the food powder is an automatic response, whereas salivation to the sound of a tuning fork obviously is not. After the food powder and the tuning fork were presented simultaneously for a consecutive number of trials, the dogs came to associate the two stimuli, so the tuning fork alone produced salivation.

Pavlov referred to the food powder in his experiment as the *unconditioned stimulus* (UCS), and the salivation to the food powder as the *unconditioned response* (UCR). This is an unconditioned, or unlearned, stimulus-response connection because it occurs reflexively without the necessity of learning. The sound of the tuning fork in Pavlov's experiment was referred to as the *conditioned stimulus* (CS), and the salivation response to the sound was called the *conditioned response* (CR). The CS-CR connection obviously is learned, because it simply would not occur naturally. The actual learning in the classical-conditioning procedure involves the association of the UCS with the CS (the food powder and the tone in this case) so that both eventually elicit similar responses.

It is important to note that the conditioned behavior will not continue indefinitely. The conditioned dogs would not salivate every time they

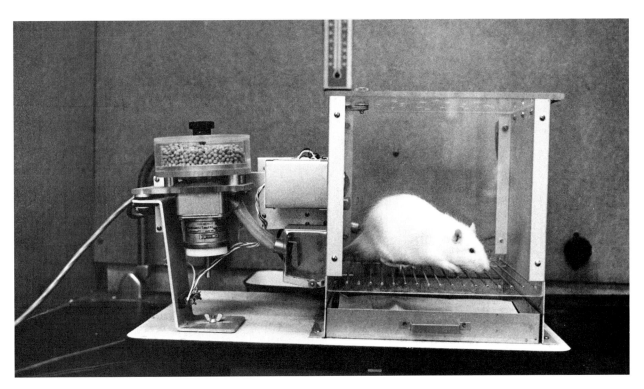

This rat is being conditioned to press a button in order to obtain food. When it leans on the button at right, a piece of food will come through the tube, thus reinforcing the button-pressing behavior and increasing the likelihood that it will occur again.

heard a certain tone on a tuning fork for the rest of their lives. In fact, if the CS is presented alone, without the reinforcement of the UCS, the CS soon will lose its effectiveness as an elicitor of a CR. This wearing away of the CS-UCS connection is referred to as **extinction.**

As will be seen in the discussion of learning in childhood, human beings are susceptible to classical conditioning. Consider for now the illustrative case of Albert in the classic experiment by Watson and Raynor (1920). Albert was a contented infant who showed very little fear. He exhibited no fear when a laboratory rat was introduced into the room in which he was playing. However, Albert soon was conditioned to respond with great distress to the rat. An extremely jarring and unpleasant sound (UCS) was produced each time the rat appeared. The sound elicited a distress response in Albert (UCR), and eventually the rat itself became a CS that produced a similar distress response in the child. The very sight of the rat, which was formerly

a neutral stimulus, was enough to make Albert cry with fright.

Although Albert has become a famous case in the annals of psychology, classical conditioning generally is thought to be of little significance to a study of human learning, because it involves a somewhat mechanical procedure that relies on involuntary responses. Of greater significance is the concept of operant conditioning.

Operant conditioning, also referred to as *instrumental conditioning,* developed from the research of Edward L. Thorndike (1874–1949), one of the pioneers of American psychology. In 1905 Thorndike produced a doctoral dissertation that dealt with the behavior of hungry cats as they attempted to free themselves from a puzzle box to reach a supply of food that was on the outside. The only way the cats could escape from the box was to press a latch that would open the door. The cats would make a number of responses, and eventually they all would manage to strike the latch. When they did so, the door would open, and the cats would receive their earned reward of food. They then were placed back in the box for another trial until they had fully learned the task.

Thorndike maintained that the cats learned to press the latch because a connection gradually was established between a stimulus, which might be the animals' hunger or the sight of the food, and the response of pressing the latch. Why was this particular stimulus-response bond established while other bonds (for example, between the stimulus of food and the response of scratching the floor) were not? Thorndike maintained that what bonded the stimulus with the correct response was the reinforcement of being rewarded. The bonding occurred because of what he described as the **law of effect**—the basic tenet of operant conditioning—which states that responses followed by reinforcement are increasingly likely to be repeated.

Positive and Negative Reinforcement

Reinforcement, then, follows an action and increases the likelihood that the action will be repeated. Reinforcement can be either positive or negative. *Positive reinforcement* is synonymous with reward—something of value (e.g., a piece of food, candy, or praise) is given to the learner. *Negative reinforcement* involves the removal of an unpleasant stimulus, as when a rat is exposed to an electric shock until it makes a desired response, after which the electricity is turned off. In a sense, positive and negative reinforcement are simply different ways of looking at the same behavioral outcome. Whether a pleasant stimulus is given or an unpleasant one is taken away, the net result is the same: the future likelihood of the behavior's being emitted has been increased.

Punishment

Another behavioral outcome that a learner may experience is **punishment,** which must not be confused with negative reinforcement. The intent of punishment is to decrease the likelihood of a future occurrence of a behavior, and not to increase it, as either type of reinforcement is intended to do.

There is little doubt that punishment can put a stop to unwanted behaviors. However, it generally is seen as less effective than reinforcement for a number of reasons. First, punishment may raise the learner's anxiety level to such a point that learning is actually inhibited. Second, punishment may teach the learner what not to do while failing to teach appropriate behavior. It is true that people can learn from their mistakes, but they can learn much more efficiently from their successes. Third, the threat of punishment often encourages the learner to make an avoidance response, a move designed to avoid the punishing authority. Parents may try to instill virtue in children merely by punishing instances of vice (e.g., lying, stealing). But instead they raise a child who, rather than being virtuous, is skilled at avoiding the parents' notice while engaged in practicing the vice.

Timing of Reinforcement or Punishment

To be effective, reinforcement must be given as soon as possible after the behavior is emitted; the longer the delay, the poorer will be the performance of the learned response (Logan 1976). If Thorndike's cats had been rewarded with food for pressing the latch even a few minutes after the action was taken, the stimulus-response connection would not have been made. A similar pattern applies to the use of punishment as a means of influencing behavior. Consider the case of a man who arrives home from work to discover that his dog chewed a hole in the sofa sometime during the day. He finds the dog in the kitchen innocently drinking from a pan of water, and he proceeds to slap the dog for his unacceptable sofa-chewing behavior. What has the dog learned from the punishment? Perhaps he has learned not to drink water when his master comes home.

Schedules of Reinforcement

A second consideration for those who use the operant-conditioning technique concerns the *reinforcement schedule.* Reinforcement may be given after every response (continuous reinforcement) or only occasionally (intermittent, or partial, reinforcement).

Schedules of reinforcement, and particularly the intermittent schedule, are of much interest to those engaged in animal research. However, there are some useful applications for human development as well. It has been found that learning occurs more rapidly if a continuous schedule of reinforcement is used, but that extinction occurs more slowly if an intermittent schedule is used—the latter phenomenon being known as the *partial-reinforcement effect* (Gleitman 1986). Therefore, to bring about the fastest and most durable learning, it might be wise to reinforce continuously at first but to gradually decrease the frequency of reinforcers once the task has been mastered. A child should not expect to be rewarded for desired behaviors every time those behaviors are emitted; such expectation may result in dependence on reward and the fairly rapid extinction of the behavior when the rewards are not forthcoming.

Defining Reward and Punishment

In addition to the timing and the schedules of reinforcement, many questions can be asked about the nature of reward and punishment themselves. In the case of reward, an experimental psychologist may be fairly certain that an animal deprived of food for a period of time will see food as an extremely satisfying reward. Human beings, however, are not so predictable. What is rewarding to one may not be rewarding to someone else; in fact, what is intended as punishment often may be seen as a reward, and vice versa. Many a child will never forget the painful embarrassment of being publicly singled out by an elementary school teacher as a positive example to the rest of the children in the class. Praise was the teacher's intended reward; but, in fact, the child may have been punished by the public recognition and by later teasing from classmates. The reverse may occur in the case of the child who views verbal or even physical punishment from a parent or teacher as rewarding because it provides much needed attention.

Classical Versus Operant Conditioning

Operant conditioning differs from classical conditioning in two major ways. Classical conditioning involves primarily reflexive behavior, whereas operant conditioning deals with voluntary

behavior. Second, as was noted, operant conditioning depends upon the law of effect; the learner must emit a response, the future occurrence of which is influenced by the consequences of that response. In other words, the learner must act in order to receive the reward or punishment. Classical conditioning relies primarily on the **law of contiguity** in that the learning occurs because of the simple association of the CS and UCS. In a sense, the reinforcer in classical conditioning is the UCS, but the learner's involuntary response does not lead to any reinforcement. (See Applying Our Knowledge "Conditioning as Therapy: Behavior Modification" for an example of the use of operant-conditioning principles.)

Classical and operant conditioning are neither easily comparable (because they involve essentially different forms of learning) nor easily separable. Very frequently, classical conditioning takes place during the course of operant conditioning (Ellis et al. 1979); an example of this confusion will follow in the discussion of conditioning during infancy.

Developmental Research on Conditioning

The vast majority of the studies of classical conditioning in humans have involved either infants or college students (Reese 1976). In fact, most of the infant-conditioning research has focused on the very young infant; in recent times, no studies have included infants over the age of 5 months (Hirschman, Melamed & Oliver 1982).

Classical conditioning appears to be possible with the newborn infant, but it has been difficult to demonstrate. As an example, Lipsitt, Kaye, and Bosack (1966) inserted a rubber tube into the mouths of infants ranging from 1½ to 4 days old and presented sweetened water through the tube, which caused the infants to begin sucking. The sweetened water was the UCS and the sucking was the UCR. Eventually, the tube itself elicited the sucking response, even though no water was fed through it. Thus, the tube became a CS producing a CR (sucking).

On the surface, it might readily be concluded that Lipsitt, Kaye, and Bosack were able to demonstrate classical conditioning in infants, but did

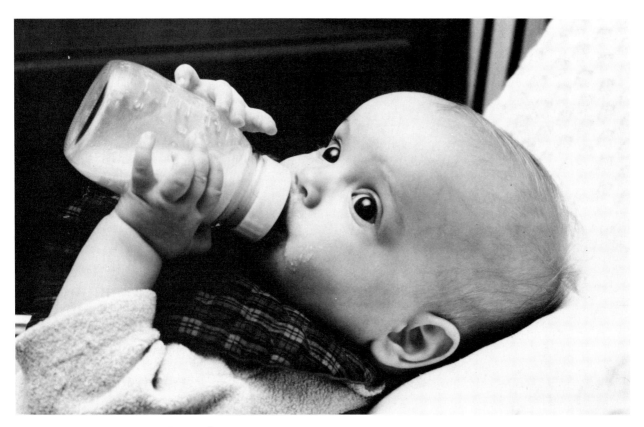

Would this young infant sucking reflexively (UCR) when presented with milk (UCS) also suck (CR) when presented with the nipple alone (CS)? If so, classical conditioning may have been demonstrated. On the other hand, no conditioning can be said to have occurred unless the nipple was a truly neutral stimulus.

they in fact do so? Sameroff (1971) later pointed out that the sucking response to the rubber tube would have occurred even without the association with sweetened water, and therefore the rubber tube is not a pure CS in the classical sense. In other words, the connection between the tube and the sweet liquid may have made the tube a more powerful inducer of the sucking response, but the tube was never a completely neutral stimulus, as the CS should have been to demonstrate that classical conditioning had taken place.

In a further comment on the Lipsitt, Kaye, and Bosack study, Reese (1976) noted that the findings are interesting from a technical standpoint, but that they have little practical value. They simply offer a scientific demonstration of what most parents already know: infants usually become con-

ditioned to the sight of a bottle or to the sounds made by the caretaker in preparing the bottle, evidenced by the fact that they engage in anticipatory sucking responses. In other words, particular sights or sounds become CSs when associated with food (a powerful UCS for a hungry infant).

Other studies of conditioning in the newborn have used heart rate (for example, Clifton 1974a, 1974b), reflexive head turning (Papousek 1967), and reflexive motor activity (Polikanina 1961) as the CRs. Results from such studies have been mixed, with greater conditioning success demonstrated in studies of 3- to 4-week-old infants than in studies of newborns (Sameroff 1971). However, classical conditioning of young infants has been successful often enough to indicate that it can be done if the circumstances are appropriate (Hirschman, Melamed & Oliver 1982).

Applying Our Knowledge

Conditioning as Therapy: Behavior Modification

Operant-conditioning principles have been used extensively with both normal and disturbed people of all ages to bring about desired behavioral changes. The application of these principles for "therapeutic" purposes has been referred to as *behavior modification*. As an example of this procedure, consider the case of Danny, a 6-year-old who had been brought by his parents to a child development clinic because he was bossy and manipulative. He ate when he wanted to, went to bed when he wanted to, and generally ran the household to his own liking. Whenever his parents confronted him, he would scream until they relented.

The psychologists at the child development clinic attempted to train Danny's mother in the effective use of behavior modification—the application of operant-conditioning procedures to the solution of behavioral problems. The mother was told to completely ignore every instance of Danny's commanding behavior ("You go over there, and I'll stay here!") and to respond only to Danny's cooperative behavior. In other words, she was taught to reward the behavior she wished to see continue and to ignore that which she wished to eliminate.

The results of the behavior therapy with Danny were precisely as would be predicted from a knowledge of operant-conditioning principles. Danny's cooperative behavior (the rewarded behavior) increased noticeably, and his commanding behavior decreased. What is more, Danny's mother reported that as the offensive behavior diminished, she felt increasingly comfortable in her interactions with her son.

Danny's case illustrates two important concepts. The first is that operant-conditioning principles can be effective in solving common behavioral problems. The second is that operant conditioning occurs even when we are unaware of using it. Danny's mother changed her reinforcement patterns after she was taught to do so. It is obvious that she had been reinforcing Danny all along, but for the wrong behaviors. She had been responding to him when he made manipulative demands and thus had rewarded unacceptable behavior. The training session forced her to realize that is was she who had been responding inappropriately to her son by rewarding him for his bossiness.

Source: R.G. Wahler, G.H. Winkel, R.L. Peterson & D.C. Morrison. (1968). Mothers as behavior therapists for their own children. In H.C. Quay (Ed.), *Children's behavior disorders*. New York: Van Nostrand Reinhold, 92–95.

Although classical conditioning appears to be possible with young infants, operant conditioning is considerably easier to demonstrate (Hirschman, Melamed & Oliver 1982; Sameroff & Cavanaugh 1979). For example, in the Lipsitt, Kaye, and Bosack (1966) study referred to earlier, the design included both operant and classical conditioning. Classical conditioning would have been demonstrated if the UCR of sucking elicited by the UCS of sweetened water later could have been elicited by a previously neutral stimulus because of its association with the sweetened water. Since there is a question as to whether the tube was a previously neutral stimulus, pure classical conditioning was difficult to demonstrate. Nevertheless, operant conditioning clearly occurred in this study: the infants increased their rate of sucking on the rubber tube after the sweetened water was introduced. In other words, because sucking was rewarded with sweetened water, the incidence of sucking increased.

Siqueland and DeLucia (1969) also conditioned young infants to increase their sucking rates by rewarding them not with food, but with the chance to look at an interesting visual display. They found that 4-month-old infants will suck more vigorously on a nipple if their sucking seems to produce an interesting visual display (e.g., cartoon figures, human faces) on a screen positioned directly in front of them. The Siqueland and DeLucia study seems to demonstrate not only that infants are susceptible to operant conditioning, but also that they seem to appreciate a little visual stimulation.

Other studies of infant operant conditioning have demonstrated successful conditioning of smiling (Brackbill 1958), vocalization (Rheingold, Gewirtz & Ross 1959; Weisberg 1963), and motor responses such as eye movements and head turning (Siqueland 1964).

Mediation Theory: Beyond Conditioning

Conditioning principles may indeed be age irrelevant; human beings of all ages may as readily form associations between UCSs and CSs, and work as diligently to earn rewards and avoid punishments. However, there appears to be a major developmental change in susceptibility to conditioning—a change first described by psychologists Howard and Tracey Kendler (1963) a quarter of a century ago. Understanding the significance of the Kendlers' work requires an understanding of the reversal learning experiments they carried out. Consider the figures in Figure 7.1. They differ from one another in the dimension of size and also in the dimension of color. Imagine that a child is presented with various pairs of these figures (e.g., large white, small black; large black, small white; large black, small black) over a series of trials and told that he or she must learn which member of the pair the experimenter has designated as the correct one. The experimenter will indicate each time a correct choice is made.

Suppose the experimenter has decided that the smaller figure always will be correct, regardless of color; the child soon will learn only to respond to the small ones, since such responses are the only ones that will be rewarded. However, to complicate the issue, after the child has learned to choose correctly, the experimenter changes the rules. Now only the large figures will be rewarded. This condition is what the Kendlers called a **reversal shift,** because the experimenter now is rewarding the

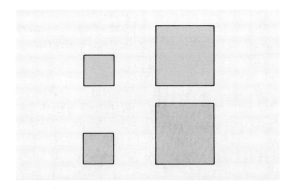

Figure 7.1   Stimuli Used in the Kendler Reversal Learning Task

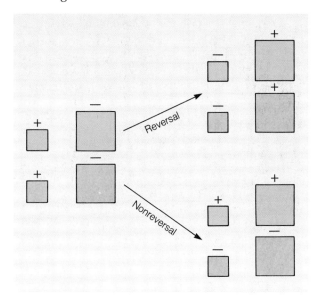

Figure 7.2   A Schematic Representation of the Reversal Shift and Nonreversal Shift Problems

opposite figure, but in the same dimension. (See Figure 7.2.) In contrast, if the new rule were to change from rewarding small figures to rewarding black figures, it would constitute a nonreversal shift in learning, because a new dimension (color) would be rewarded rather than simply the reverse figure in the previously rewarded dimension (size).

Which of the two—the reversal or the nonreversal shift—would be easier to learn? According to basic operant-conditioning principles, the nonreversal shift should be easier, because the learner already has been conditioned to respond positively to half of the new stimuli (the small black squares) designated as correct in the nonreversal condition. He or she needs only to unlearn the response to small white squares and learn to respond to large black squares instead.

In fact, rats and young children behave precisely as conditioning principles would predict. They find nonreversal shifts easier to learn than reversal shifts. However, human beings over the age of 5 or 6 typically find the reversal shift the easier to learn of the two. This is because the older child or adult, rather than blindly responding to the rewarded stimuli as a rat or a young child might do, first responds internally to the dimension of size; the internal response (size) must be changed in the case of a nonreversal shift, but not in the case of the simple reversal. This internal response is a mediating response, which comes between the presentation of the stimulus and the external response to it. Thus the Kendlers' theory became known as **mediation theory.**

The ability to use mediating responses radically alters the nature of the learning situation and sharply distinguishes between the human and animal response in a learning situation. The Kendlers' work highlighted the need to develop more sophisticated measures of human learning than are used with pigeons or rats because of the existence of whatever was occurring in the human thought process that rats are not capable of—whether this activity be referred to as internal responding, mediation, or concept formation. The Kendlers also emphasized the developmental aspect of human learning by discovering the age-related change in reversal learning. Finally, the Kendlers' work has generated a large amount of supporting data over the past twenty years—so much so that the classical stimulus-response explanations of human learning are no longer seen as totally adequate (Diamond 1982). Simply put, there are situations in which human beings do not continuously repeat previously rewarded behavior, but instead use mental strategies to determine which behavior will be appropriate in the future. If an adult told a joke at a party and was rewarded with laughter, it is unlikely that he or she would immediately repeat the joke. Young children might; in fact, they often do.

Social Learning

Parents often find it disconcerting to see their children engaging in behaviors that the parents definitely did not, or did not intend to, teach them. The fact is, of course, that much learning occurs not by direct reinforcement at all, but as a result of observing other people's behavior, as well as by observing the consequences of that behavior. Learning that occurs in this manner has been referred to as **observational learning;** the broader term used to describe any type of learning from a model, whether reinforcement is evident or not, is **cognitive social learning** (Bandura 1969, 1977).

Basic Principles

In its simplest sense, social learning, or modeling, involves the application of operant-conditioning procedures to the social arena. The early social-learning studies (e.g., Bandura 1965; Bandura, Ross & Ross 1963a, 1963b, 1963c), some of which will be discussed later in this chapter, focused on the effects on the learner of watching a model receive reinforcement for specific behaviors. As will be shown, observers are more likely to imitate the rewarded behaviors of models than the unrewarded ones. However, observational learning has been found to go far beyond learning based on vicarious reinforcement (i.e., the reinforcement received by the model). As Bandura (1986) noted, children often imitate a model's behaviors when no reinforcement of any kind is evident. They often fail to imitate a model immediately, but later they can be found at play engaged in a variety of imitative behaviors. To complicate the issue even further, imitation of a model does not guarantee that any learning has taken place. As the later discussion of the effects of television on children's behavior will show, imitation may not be indicative of learning, but rather a result of social facilitation. Previously learned behaviors are freely exhibited because the model has shown the observer that such behaviors are permissible.

Model Events	→	Attentional Process	→	Retention Process	→	Motor Reproduction Process	→	Motivational Process	→	Matching Performances
		Modeling Stimuli		Symbolic		Physical Capabilities		External Reinforcement		
		Distinctiveness		Cognitive Organization		Availability of Component Responses		Vicarious Reinforcement		
		Affective Valence		Symbolic Rehearsal				Self-reinforcement		
		Complexity		Motor Rehearsal		Self-observation of Reproductions				
		Functional Value				Accuracy Feedback				
		Observer Characteristics								
		Sensory Capacities								
		Arousal Level								
		Motivation								
		Perceptual Set								
		Past Reinforcement								

Figure 7.3   Subprocesses in the Social Learning View of Observational Learning

Source: From A. Bandura (Ed.) *Psychological Modeling: Conflicting Theories.* Reprinted by permission of the Publishers Lieber-Atherton Inc., Copyright 1971. All rights reserved.

Bandura (1971) outlined the social-learning view of observational learning by dividing the actual learning into four necessary subprocesses; attentional, retention, motor-reproduction, and motivational processes (see Figure 7.3). Attentional processes must be involved in observational learning; even though the learner is exposed to a variety of experiences, only some features of observed behavior are modeled. The features that tend to be modeled most often are those that are distinctive enough to be easily recognized, those that occur frequently, those that are exhibited by a highly valued model, those that have been reinforced in the past, and so forth. It would be inappropriate here to try to describe all of the characteristics of the model and of the observer that cause certain modeled behaviors to be singled out for imitation. However, an example of this attentional subprocess will be given in the following section on research on social learning, where a study on the effects of status and perceived power of an adult model on children's imitative behavior will be cited.

The second subprocess of observational learning is the process of retention. As noted earlier, learners often exhibit the behaviors of models not immediately after seeing them, but considerably later. Memory processes, therefore, are involved in observational learning. The learner must be able to encode the model's behavior and store it for later retrieval by some sort of rehearsal process.

The third type of subprocess involved in observational learning is the motor-reproduction process—the physical capability of the learner to reproduce a model's behavior and the self-monitoring of such processes. For example, a child might watch a talented gymnast perform a routine on the high bar, but even if the activity were particularly fascinating to the child and even if the child could mentally remember the details of the exercise, learning would not be said to have taken place if the child were physically unable to reproduce the routine.

Finally, the motivational process is involved in observational learning. Here Bandura meant reinforcement, whether direct, vicarious, or self-administered. Bandura noted that even after a modeled behavior has been carefully attended to, remembered, and reproduced, the learning may seldom be activated if it is not reinforced. A child or adult may learn a variety of behaviors from a model but may not dare to exhibit these behaviors for fear of social disapproval.

Developmental Research on Social Learning

Even an infant is capable of learning by observing the behavior of other people. Piaget, whose work was described in detail in Chapter 6, noted that his son Laurent engaged in imitative behavior at 2½ months. Piaget (1962) wrote that Laurent

> imitated me as soon as I uttered sounds identical with his own, or even when it was merely my intonation which recalled his. He again imitated me even when he had not been crooning himself immediately before. He began by smiling, then made an effort with his mouth open (remaining silent for a moment) and only then produced a sound. Such a behavior clearly indicates the existence of a definite attempt at imitation. (P. 9)

Even though Piaget described his son's behavior as imitative, he did not consider it to be a genuine example of social learning. Instead, he argued that it was a "preimitative" behavior—a forerunner of true imitation—because the child could imitate the adult only insofar as the adult first imitated the child's behavior. Piaget made sounds identical to those Laurent had made previously, and only then did Laurent "imitate" his father's sounds. In a sense, the child did not distinguish between his own sounds and those made by his father (Flavell 1963; Piaget 1962).

The question of when genuine imitations first occur in the human infant has become a controversial one in recent years. Piaget (1962) did not see genuine imitation as occurring before 7 or 8 months of age, but not all psychologists agree with Piaget's assessment. Meltzoff and Moore (1977, 1983) argued that even a newborn baby will spontaneously imitate such adult behaviors as sticking

out the tongue or opening and closing the mouth. To demonstrate this phenomenon, they placed newborn babies in a semi-reclining position in an infant seat in a darkened room. The babies were then presented with a spotlighted adult face about ten inches away from their own. The adult would slowly open and close his mouth four times during a twenty-second period, then remain passive, then slowly extend and withdraw his tongue four times, then remain passive, and so forth. The infants' facial gestures were recorded on videotape. When the tapes were analyzed, it was found that the babies opened their mouths most often during the experimenter's mouth-opening periods and stuck out their tongues most often during the tongue-protrusion periods. Meltzoff and Moore (1983) interpreted these findings as being indicative of true imitation at what is indeed a very early age.

While their actual findings are not in question, there continues to be controversy over whether or not genuine imitation occurred in the Meltzoff and Moore (1977, 1983) studies. Critics argue that what occurred was in reality a reflexive rather than an imitative act. For example, Jacobson (1979) found that the 6- to 14-week-old infants she tested did in fact stick out their tongues when an adult first demonstrated this behavior, but they also stuck out their tongues when presented with such objects as a moving pen or a dangling ring. She suggested that perhaps the mouth and tongue movements are not selective imitation at all but are adaptive feeding responses to any object that resembles a nipple.

In a later study Abranavel and Sigafoos (1984) found that some 4- to 6-week-old infants did stick out their tongues following identical behaviors by the experimenter, but most did not. Furthermore, the tendency to engage in imitative tongue movements did not improve with age, as might be expected if genuine selective imitation were really occurring. Tongue protrusion actually decreased with age from 4 to 21 weeks, leading the authors to echo Jacobson's (1979) belief that reflex mechanisms of a sort may have been in operation in the case of the younger infants.

Answers to the question of whether or not very young infants selectively and intentionally imitate the behaviors of adult models are still undetermined; perhaps, as Flavell (1985) suggested, there can never be a definitive answer. On the other hand, it seems quite clear that by 5 to 6 months of age genuine imitation of adult models does occur and that this imitation is intentional, selective, and nonreflexive (Kaye 1982; Kaye & Marcus 1978). It also seems clear that the mutual imitation which occurs throughout infancy, with parents and babies producing similar patterns of sounds and facial gestures (leaving aside the question of which one initiates the pattern), is of significant social value. Uzgiris (1984) described mutual imitation, which increases throughout the first year of life, as a meaningful shared experience that enhances the bonds of attachment between infant and parent. Furthermore, when parents imitate their infants' behaviors, there is an increased likelihood that the infants will attempt to imitate them in turn (Bandura 1986; Kauffman, Gordon & Baker 1978).

As children develop they are capable of increasingly sophisticated imitations. McCall, Parke, and Kavanaugh (1977) place infants aged 12, 15, 18, and 24 months in a playroom with a variety of toys (e.g., rattles, bells, a toy telephone, a stuffed animal, a toy car). The infants first were observed playing spontaneously and then as they watched an adult modeling certain prescribed behaviors with the toys. Imitation of adult behavior was found at all ages tested, although perfect imitaton was never seen earlier than 18 months of age. In general, imitative ability increased regularly from the youngest to the oldest group of children in the study.

Noting that even 1-year-olds are exposed to the influence of television, McCall, Parke, and Kavanaugh (1977) extended their investigation to examine the influence of televised models on the imitative behavior of young children. Children aged 18, 24, and 36 months either watched a videotape of an adult model playing with toys in a particular manner, or they watched a live model engaged in the identical activity. They then were observed playing with toys by themselves to determine whether social learning had occurred as indicated by the imitation that would take place. It was found that live models were more effective in "teaching" the younger children, but by the age of 3, the differences between the conditions had virtually disappeared. The authors suggested that by the time a child is between 3 and 4 years of age,

television models become potentially as effective as live models in inducing social learning.

In reality, of course, all models are not equally likely to be imitated by children. In an examination of the characteristics possessed by the most-imitated models, Bandura, Ross, and Ross (1963a) studied children ranging in age from 3 to 5 years who watched two adults in a playroom. One adult, designated as the controller, had the most attractive toys to play with, dispensed the snacks, and was clearly in charge of the situation. The other adult, the consumer, played a more passive role. The children later were asked to play a guessing game that consisted of determining in which of two boxes the experimenter—in some cases the controller and in some the consumer—had hidden a picture sticker. The real object of the game, however, was to see if the children were more likely to spontaneously imitate the activities of an adult perceived as powerful rather than those of an adult perceived as dependent. As they demonstrated the guessing game for the children, the controller and the consumer engaged in different activities, used different words to verbalize the instructions, and even wore "thinking caps" of different colors to help them guess which box contained the sticker.

Bandura, Ross, and Ross found that children were more likely to imitate the behaviors of the controller and that they obviously identified with the source of rewarding power. Apparently, some models have a greater influence on children than others do. Extending these findings from the laboratory to the world at large, it becomes obvious that parents—who are the ultimate dispensers of rewards to children, the ultimate sources of status and control—should have a greater influence than any other models available.

A positive relationship between dominance and the likelihood of being imitated has been found in other studies as well. For example, in studies of peer imitation in nursery school children at play, it appears that the children who most often attract the attention of other children are also the children most likely to be imitated (Abramovitch & Grusec 1978; Grusec & Abramovitch 1982; Hold 1976). Grusec and Abramovitch (1982) also noted that the amount of imitation in preschool groups declined from age 3 to age 5. Furthermore, they suggested

Like father like son. A parent is a highly significant model in a child's life—a source of affection and a symbol of power.

that peer imitation serves as more than just a means of learning new behavior; it is also a powerful means of facilitating social interaction with peers. Models generally responded positively to being imitated and by doing so rewarded their imitators. Apparently, even for preschool children, imitation is the sincerest form of flattery, and flattery may bring about friendly social interaction.

Television and Social Learning

A number of social-learning studies have dealt with the effects of televised models on children's behavior (e.g., Bandura 1965; Bandura, Ross & Ross 1963a, 1963b; Friedrich & Stein 1973; Hicks 1965). In some of these studies, children observed a televised model's behavior and then witnessed the consequences of that behavior to the model (e.g., punishment for aggression). In other studies, no behavior consequences were shown. The findings from the television studies were fairly consistent: children can learn by watching the televised behavior of others. Observing the consequence of a model's behavior has much the same effect as experiencing the consequences of one's own behavior (Stevenson 1970).

The question of the influence of television models becomes controversial when the modeled behavior is aggressive. Since the early days of television, when in 1952 a House of Representatives committee dealt with the issue, there have been questions about the possible effects on chidren of watching televised violence. Commercial television continues to have a high level of violence, and

Chapter 7. Learning and Information Processing

much of this violence can be found in Saturday morning cartoons (see Table 7.1).

The findings of studies investigating the effects of viewing televised violence have been fairly consistent: children display higher levels of aggression after watching adult models engaged in aggression—particularly if those models are rewarded for their behavior (Bandura 1965; Bandura, Ross & Ross 1963b; Hicks 1965). Children who watch much violence on television are the most likely to approve of it (Dominick & Greenberg 1972). Finally, children who watch a good deal of violent television programming are also likely to be quite aggressive in real life (Lefkowitz, Walder & Eron 1963), and their high level of aggression apparently stays with them into early adulthood (Lefkowitz et al. 1972).

At this time it cannot be concluded, based on the available research, that watching televised models of aggression actually causes children or adults to be aggressive. Children who witness acts of violence and then behave more aggressively may not have actually learned any new behaviors. They instead may have learned only that their previously learned aggressive behaviors are acceptable to display. When it is found that aggressive children are more likely than nonaggressive children to watch violence on television, might this not be an example of self-selection? Perhaps, instead of deciding that the television viewing brought about the aggression, we should ask whether the aggressive children simply sought out televised material that appealed to them.

Viewing televised aggression may facilitate real-life aggression rather than actually teach it. Friedrich and Stein (1973), for example, found that 3 to 5-year-old children exposed to nine weeks of violent segments of the television cartoon shows *Batman* and *Superman* showed a definite reduction in self-control; there was a loss in their tolerance for delay, as well as a decline in their willingness to obey rules. As might be expected, a loss of tolerance for frustration could increase the likelihood of aggressive episodes. Friedrich and Stein suggested that researchers should explore a variety of personality factors when they study the effects of aggressive models on children. They also reported

Table 7.1 Incidents of Violence Per Hour in Saturday Morning Cartoons for the Fall of 1986

High-Violence Cartoons:

Spiderman(NBC)	49
Mr. T(NBC)	46
Bugs Bunny Looney Tunes(ABC)	48
Droids(ABC)	36
Real Ghostbusters(ABC)	32
Super Powers(ABC)	31
Lazertag Academy(NBC)	27
Ewoks(ABC)	24

Above Average Violence:

Smurfs(NBC)	17
Foofur(NBC)	15
Bullwinkle(NBC)	15
Kidd Video(NBC)	14
Galaxy High(CBS)	14
Kissyfur(NBC)	12
The Littles(ABC)	12

Some Violence:

Snorks(NBC)	9
Muppet Babies(CBS)	8
Pound Puppies(ABC)	8
Wildfire(CBS)	7
Flintstone Kids(ABC)	7

Low Violence:

Laff Olympics(ABC)	5
Pee-Wee's Playhouse(CBS)	5
Get Along Gang(CBS)	4
Punky Brewster(NBC)	4
Berenstain Bears(CBS)	4
Alvin & the Chipmunks(NBC)	3
Pink Panther & Sons(NBC)	2
Teen Wolf(CBS)	1.5
Kids, Inc.(ABC)	0

Source: Reprinted by permission of Dr. Thomas Radecki, Chairperson, National Coalition on T.V. Violence, Champaign, Ill.

a finding from their research that calls into question any simple causal connection between aggression and television viewing: interpersonal aggression did not increase for all the children exposed to the violent programming, but only for those who were above average in aggression in the first place.

This section on the effects of television models on children's social learning will end on an optimistic note. Children also can learn much that is positive from watching television. In the Friedrich and Stein study just mentioned, one group of children watched not *Batman* but *Mr. Rogers' Neighborhood* for nine weeks. The latter program generally is recognized as one that promotes the values of friendship, sharing, cooperation, rule acceptance, understanding of others, and so forth. The children who watched *Mr. Rogers' Neighborhood* improved in such prosocial qualities as self-regulation, tolerance for delay, task persistence, and rule obedience—a pattern exactly opposite to what was found among the *Batman* group.

Studies of the influence of television on children's development have far-reaching social implications. Even though violent television programming has not been found to "teach" violence to children, it seems that such programming may create an atmosphere in which aggressive solutions to problems will dominate. Furthermore, television has a remarkable (and relatively unexplored) potential for bringing about positive change.

Learning in the Classroom

Most research on human learning is carried out in laboratories under carefully controlled conditions, but learning occurs constantly in all areas of everyday life. Many examples used in this chapter consist of illustrations of learning in realistic settings, such as the home and the classroom. This section of the chapter deals specifically with educational applications of learning research. This is not because learning is more likely to occur in the classroom than anywhere else, but because the classroom is a setting specifically designed to facilitate learning in children and adolescents. What is more, principles of conditioning and observational learning are used intentionally in the management of children's classroom behavior and in the teaching of academic material. Such principles may or may not be used in a child's home, and their application at home is often haphazard and inconsistent. The application of learning principles

in the classroom is often quite successful and sometimes less so. In either case, an examination of classroom applications of principles of learning offers an opportunity for testing the effectiveness of these principles in an applied setting. (Issues in Child Development "What Is a Learning Disorder?" discusses a problem that can complicate the application of learning principles.)

The Uses of Reinforcement

The second-grade teacher was increasingly irritated by the disruptive behaviors of two children in her otherwise well-behaved class. Despite the fact that classroom rules had been clearly established and that the two troublesome children had been reminded repeatedly of the rules, the teacher felt powerless in her efforts to get them to conform. They broke rules repeatedly; they spent about half their time in the classroom fighting, running around the room, disturbing other children, and damaging school property.

The teacher decided to apply principles of operant conditioning in her classroom. Realizing the potential effectiveness of reinforcement, she tried to reward specific instances of positive behavior, such as quiet cooperative play, with attention and praise; at the same time she reminded the children of the rules, but merely ignored them when the rules were violated. As reported in this often-cited study by Madsen, Becker, and Thomas (1968), the children's problem behavior began to decrease at last. Consistent with operant-conditioning principles, rewarding desired behaviors increased the likelihood of their occurrence in the future.

Despite the apparent effectiveness of the praise-and-ignore approach taken in that one particular second-grade classroom, it should not be concluded that such a technique is an instant cure-all for behavior problems. What would happen if the disruptive children did not perceive the teacher's praise and attention as rewarding? What if the disruptive behavior was in some way being rewarded by the children's classmates? In fact, an often-reported finding in studies of this type is that rewarding desirable behaviors alone, with no negative consequences for undesirable behaviors, does not eliminate behavior problems, but only lessens

Issues in Child Development

What Is A Learning Disorder?

Six-year-old Alan constantly is being reprimanded by his first-grade teacher for fighting with other children. Jennifer, age 9, has a 40 percent hearing loss in her right ear. Paula is a 7-year-old who regularly wakes up screaming in the middle of the night because of terrifying nightmares. Are any of these children obvious victims of a **learning disorder**? The answer is no, but learning specialists frequently are approached by worried parents of children similar to Alan, Jennifer, and Paula and asked if learning disorders are responsible for their children's conditions. One parent even wondered whether the fact that his college-aged son had a live-in girlfriend could be attributed to a learning disorder of some kind (Cruickshank 1972).

Confusion about the nature of learning disorders is not confined to anxious parents. Even educators and psychologists who work with

learning-disabled children consider a huge number of terms (for example, *brain injury, minimal brain dysfunction, educational handicap,* and *reading disability*) to be synonyms for *learning disorder* (Myers & Hammill 1976).

Is there any way to formulate a clear and precise working definition of *learning disorder*—a definition that will separate the truly learning-disabled child from the one who is not disabled but is having adjustment problems at home or at school? Myers and Hammill (1976) suggested that the following elements must be considered in a definition of the concept of learning disorder:

- *The principle of disparity must be present.* There must be a disparity between what the child is genuinely capable of accomplishing and what the child actually achieves in school. It is not poor performance alone that indicates the possibility of a learning disorder, but unexpectedly poor performance based on what is known about the child's basic mental abilities.

- *The locus of the disorder must be in one of the basic learning processes.* These learning processes—or channels through

which learning occurs—include the auditory, visual, tactile, motoric, vocal, and memory processes. For example, some people have difficulty interpreting certain types of sensory information, and others have difficulty remembering it. The specific disorder might be (1) the loss of a basic process (for example, a speech loss following a stroke), (2) a delay in the development of a basic process, or (3) an interference in the functioning of a basic process (for example, difficulties in proper word pronunciation).

Myers and Hammill pointed out that, by this definition, certain types of children are automatically excluded from the learning-disorder category. Excluded are those who are mentally retarded, those who are educationally or culturally deprived, those who suffer primarily from emotional problems, and those with specific sensory deficits. Thus, a person with a hearing loss might be learning disabled as well, but many hearing-impaired people experience no special learning difficulty. Finally, it seems safe to conclude that a couple's decision to live together without benefit of marriage cannot be attributed to any specific learning disorder.

them (Phiffner, Rosen & O'Leary 1985; Woolfolk 1987). The ideal situation consists of a blend of reward whenever possible and punishment if necessary to see that classroom rules are enforced.

A number of other considerations must be weighed when reinforcement such as praise is used for classroom management (Woolfolk 1987). The first is that praise must be given appropriately. It must depend upon the appearance of the desired

behavior, rather than being given casually or indiscriminately. Second, the teacher must tell the child quite specifically what he or she is being praised for. Surprisingly enough, in 95 percent of the cases the praise given by teachers is far too general. For example, a teacher will say, "You've done a good job on your homework" instead of "You spelled every word correctly" (Anderson, Evertson & Brophy 1979; Brophy 1981). A third consideration is that praise must be given in such

*A teacher might use reinforcement to encourage children to raise their hands to ask
or answer questions. Praising children for what they have to say should result
in an increase in hand-raising behavior.*

a way that children do not see it as the teacher's
insincere attempt at manipulating their behavior
(O'Leary & O'Leary 1977; Woolfolk 1987). Finally,
teachers must be aware that if praise is used too
freely, the children may come to expect it and depend upon it; thus, they may be motivated to do
well in class because they want the teacher's approval and not because learning is a valuable goal
in itself (Woolfolk 1987).

Intended reinforcement will not be effective,
of course, if it is not perceived by the child as being
rewarding, and what is rewarding for one child
may not be rewarding for another. For example,
words of praise from a teacher can be a highly
effective reinforcer for an average or above average
learner, but slow learners seem to prefer more concrete reinforcements: activities, special privileges,

or tangible rewards (Serralde de Scholz & Mc-
Dougall 1978).

Woolfolk (1987) recommended that teachers
try to determine what their pupils would find to
be desirable reinforcements. This may be done by
observing the children at play to see what activities
they particularly enjoy and later using these activities as rewards for appropriate classroom behaviors. Teachers might also talk to parents or other
teachers to learn what is reinforcing for a particular
child or they might ask the children themselves to
tell about their favorite activities.

The Role of Punishment

Punishment, as was pointed out earlier in this
chapter, is less effective as a learning technique
than reward because of a variety of unpleasant side

The most effective reprimand that a teacher can give a child is one that is a private affair between teacher and pupil. Loud public reprimands are less likely to eliminate undesirable behaviors.

effects. It raises anxiety levels, it allows for avoidance responses, and it teaches what is wrong without necessarily teaching what is right. Nevertheless, punishment works, whether in the laboratory or in the classroom, when the intended goal is to suppress unwanted behaviors in the learner.

The effectiveness of punishment will vary from child to child and from situation to situation, but three approaches to punishment appear to be most effective in classroom management: reprimands, response cost, and social isolation (O'Leary & O'Leary 1976; Woolfolk 1987).

A *reprimand*, or verbal criticism, from the teacher can be effective in reducing the incidence of unwanted behaviors in children. However, the effectiveness of reprimands depends upon the ways in which they are given. Many adults re-

member the humiliation of being soundly and publicly reprimanded for misbehavior at school, and such distant memories are often still painful ones. In fact, loud public reprimands are less effective in eliminating unwanted behaviors than are quiet private ones (O'Leary et al 1970). Perhaps the public humiliation is less effective because the child resents it so bitterly and loses a measure of respect for the teacher who administers it. On the other hand, the child might enjoy the public recognition as a means of showing the other children that he or she has the ability to upset the teacher so much (Woolfolk 1987). Some children may enjoy the image of toughness and resistance to authority that such public recognition brings to them, and what was intended by the teacher as punishment may actually be a reward. The most effective reprimand—as determined by its ability to reduce problem behaviors— is a quiet and private affair between the teacher and the offending student.

The *response-cost* approach is punishment by virtue of the removal of reinforcement (Woolfolk 1987). Nine-year-old Ellen eagerly awaits the arrival of the twenty-minute recess period every day, but lately Ellen has become disruptive in class, speaking out of turn and making silly comments to provoke laughter from her classmates. To eliminate the disruptive behavior, the teacher uses a response-cost approach. She tells Ellen that every time she speaks out of turn, three minutes will be deducted from her recess period. Thus, Ellen is held responsible for her own disruptive behaviors; in a sense, she determines the extent of her punishment, if any, on any particular day.

Social isolation is the "time-out" approach to punishment. A disruptive child is made to sit alone in an uninteresting empty room for five or ten minutes, and it is the pain of isolation from others that constitutes the punishment (O'Leary & O'Leary 1976). Effective as the punitive technique of social isolation can be, it is not without its problems. As Woolfolk (1987) noted, many schools have no time-out room and even if such a room is available, genuine social isolation requires total separation from others. If several children are being "isolated" in the same place, then no real isolation can be said to occur. Finally, there is no guarantee that children, and particularly older children and adolescents, will stay in an isolation area if not supervised by an adult. Many schools have no such supervision available.

Observational Learning at School

Little research has been done on the effects of observational learning in the classroom, but the few existing studies of this type indicate that children learn a good deal from teacher and peer models. As an illustration, consider the study conducted by Swanson and Henderson (1977), who wanted to encourage preschool children to ask questions of their teachers. They had the children watch a television program in which preschoolers asked frequent questions of adults. After the pro-

gram, the children were given practice at imitating what they had seen on the television set, and it was later found that the frequency of asking questions increased significantly. Perhaps it should not be surprising that learning from models can significantly affect children's classroom behaviors. As Bandura (1986) pointed out, modeling has long been recognized as "one of the most powerful means of transmitting values, attitudes, and patterns of thought and behavior" (pp. 47–48).

Psychologist Anita Woolfolk (1987) suggested a variety of ways that teachers can capitalize on the potential effectiveness of observational learning. First, teachers might model the behaviors and the attitudes they want the students to learn. Instead of teaching by merely telling others what to do, teachers might also want to demonstrate the physical and mental tasks required of the students. If teachers want to encourage pupils to develop enthusiasm for the subject matter, they should display enthusiasm in teaching it. Many college students report that a professor's enthusiasm in teaching even a fairly uninteresting subject was contagious, and that they developed an interest in the course primarily because the professor was so excited by the material.

A second suggestion offered by Woolfolk for using observational learning is to have peers serve as models. Teachers can have students demonstrate appropriate classroom behaviors to the class. They can require children to work together in pairs or groups so that good students model appropriate work habits for those who are less capable. Teachers can also ask one of the more popular students in the class to befriend and work with a student who is socially isolated, so that the popular student serves as a model of caring and helping behavior for others in the class.

The possibilities for applying principles of observational learning, or principles of operant conditioning, to the elementary or high school classroom are limitless. All that is needed is a thorough awareness of these principles, a sensitivity to the needs of individual students, and a degree of creativity in planning strategies for classroom management. A gifted teacher embodies the ideal combination of such attributes.

Attention and Memory in Information Processing

Ellen is a sixth grader who took a history examination and failed. Why did Ellen fail the test? Was it because she never learned the material adequately in the first place or because, although she learned the material quite well, she was simply unable to remember it? Or does learning always imply the ability to remember, so that her memory failure could only be interpreted as a failure to learn the material properly? As a matter of fact, it is unclear where the failing student experienced a breakdown in her system of processing information. The breakdown could have occurred at any point in the process from the minute the information first registered on the girl's senses to the minute when she tried, and failed, to retrieve the information from memory.

Psychologists who try to trace the sequence of mental operations involved when a person performs a particular intellectual task are said to be using an *information-processing* approach (Anderson 1985). Stages in the process are identified and efforts made to determine success or failure in dealing with information at each stage. If Ellen is unable to remember an answer to an exam question, it is apparent that the information was lost somewhere on its journey through her information-processing system. Perhaps she failed to hear the information when it was first presented in class. If she did hear the teacher presenting the material, did she attend to it or was she distracted by something else at the time? If she attended to it, did she use strategies to make it memorable while it was still fresh in her mind—in what psychologists refer to as her short-term, working memory? For example, did she mentally repeat it, a process known as rehearsal? Did she organize the material into meaningful "chunks" of information?

If Ellen was effective in her use of such strategies while the information was still in short-term memory, then the material was entered into "storage" in her long-term memory. If not, the material was probably lost. Finally, if the information was successfully stored in long-term memory but she was still unable to remember it on an exam, the failure in the system probably occurred in the process of retrieving the information from long-term storage.

An analysis of Ellen's problems on her history test makes clear the wisdom of looking at learning in the overall context of the information-processing system. Studies of human learning discussed in earlier sections of this chapter also involved attentional as well as memory skills. Attention, perception, learning, and memory are discussed separately for convenience, but they are all aspects of the cognitive processing of information.

The remainder of this chapter discusses attention—the cognitive activity that specifies which information will and which will not be entered into the system—and then memory—the process by which entered information is held and later retrieved.

The Development of Attention

"Pay attention!" is a comment frequently made to children by parents and teachers alike. If the child does not attend, it is unlikely that information being presented will get into the learning system to be processed. Attention, then, is the directed aspect of human perception. It is the screening mechanism by which certain features of the intellectual environment are selected to be processed and other features are ignored. In a very real sense, attention is the gateway to the information-processing system.

This section will deal with the development of attention. It will look first at the attentional limitations of the infant and young child. Then it will look at research detailing the increasing efficiency of attention as the child grows up.

The First Year
Chapter 5 discussed pattern perception and preferences in young infants. The fact that preferences exist indicates that infants are capable of selectively attending to features of their environments. That is, they are able to perceive as well as to sense the world around them. Attentional processes are limited during infancy, however, for several reasons. In the first place, the actual amount of time available for attending is initially somewhat restricted; a newborn infant sleeps a good deal, and

the average length of nonfeeding alert periods is only five minutes, with over 90 percent of the non-feeding alert periods lasting for ten minutes or less (Clifton & Nelson 1976). By 3 months of age, the average alert period lasts for about ninety minutes.

A second attentional restriction during infancy is that, even in the second half of the first year, infants have limited knowledge about the world; as Olson and Sherman (1983) pointed out, a person's knowledge base affects his or her ability to attend selectively. As an illustration of this point, compare the careful attention to detail displayed by a shopper who really knows the merchandise with the relative inattention to product features typical of less knowledgeable buyers. The fact that increasing familiarity with the world leads to increasingly selective attention can be demonstrated in the social behavior of infants; as other people become more familiar to them, selective smiling increases. Greater and greater attention is devoted to the mother, or primary caretaker, as the infant matures (Olson & Sherman 1983).

A third limit on an infant's ability to attend is related to the limits on human attention at any age. People can attend to only limited amounts of environmental information at any one time. A person cannot be an attentive driver and at the same time worry about an upcoming final exam! Infants seem to be even more limited than adults in their ability to share their attention with two or more environmental stimuli (Olson & Sherman 1983). Consider how quickly a first toy is "forgotten" by an infant who has just been offered a second one.

Before ending this discussion of attention during the first year of life, it should be noted that adults can directly influence the attentional processes of infants by providing them with certain experiences. Tamis-LeMonda and Bornstein (1986) observed that some mothers call attention to themselves when they interact with their babies, while others direct their children's attention to objects in the environment. Mothers who call attention to themselves are likely to have infants who attend more to them than to the environment. Mothers who direct their infants' attention toward the environment have infants who explore objects more and mother less, and these effects are found early in the first year—between 2 and 5 months of age.

Development During Childhood

As children mature, they attend with increasing efficiency to the world around them. They become more and more likely to attend to information that is useful, meaningful, and relevant and to ignore irrelevant information (Maccoby 1969; Walk 1981). One way to illustrate this increasing efficiency of attention is to photograph children's eye movements as they attempt to solve a perceptual problem. Typical of this research on what is known as "visual scanning" is a study by Vurpillot (1968). Vurpillot showed children aged 3 to 10 pairs of houses in silhouette (see Figure 7.4) and asked them to determine whether the members of each pair were identical or different. She photographed the children's eye movements to determine which features of the houses they attended to. Children aged 3 to 5 performed poorly on the task, perhaps because their eye movements were unsystematic; they often looked at irrelevant features of the displays while ignoring useful information. For example, these young children gave answers before they had even looked at all the windows. Older children compared pairs of windows one at a time and stopped as soon as they had found a pair that differed from one another. Thus, the visual scanning of older children was designed to produce the greatest amount of information in the shortest possible time.

Other studies of developmental changes in attention have involved a technique known as "dichotic listening." In studies of this type the child wears a headphone, and a different message is presented to each ear. For example, Maccoby and Konrad (1966) had children ranging from kindergarten age to fourth grade listen to a male voice saying words into one ear and a female voice saying different words into the other. The children were then asked to report as many words as they could remember. Kindergartners remembered significantly fewer words than did fourth graders. What is more, the younger children displayed the effects of attentional interference in another rather amusing way. They combined sounds from the two words played simultaneously to construct nonsense words. "Squirrel" and "turtle" were reported as "squirtle" (Walk 1981). Fourth graders rarely did this.

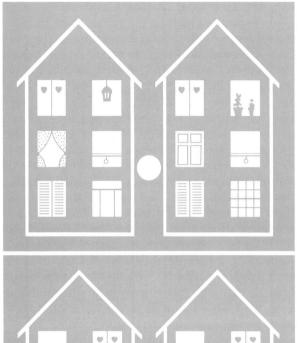

Figure 7.4 Sample Pairs of Silhouettes of Houses The top pair is a "different" pair, since three of the windows are not the same. The bottom pair is a "same" pair, with all windows identical.

Source: From Vurpillot, E. (1968) The development of scanning strategies and their relation to visual differentiation. *Journal of Experimental Child Psychology, 6,* p. 634. Orlando, Fla.: Academic Press. Reprinted by permission of the publisher and author.

The child's ability to direct his or her attention is by no means perfected by the age of 10; studies of visual scanning and dichotic listening indicate continued improvement through the years of childhood and adolescence, with maximum efficiency

of attention reached by early adulthood (Walk 1981). Frustrated parents and teachers would do well to remember that if a child, and especially a young child, fails to "Pay attention" when directed to do so, the problem may not be one of motivation. It may be related to the child's inability to tune out distractions and attend to the relevant information at hand—in this case the directives provided by the adult. (However, for a discussion of children whose attention does not improve developmentally, see Problems in Child Development "Attention Deficit Disorder.")

Television and Attention

Not all studies of children's attentional processes have used such exotic procedures as eye photography and dichotic listening. Some of the "equipment" for research on this topic is found much closer to home; many recent studies of attention have relied on the most often used entertainment and information source in American society—the television set (Comstock et al. 1978).

Studies of preschool children's visual attention to television programs have yielded a consistent pattern of findings: from the age of 1 to the age of 5, attention to television increases dramatically (Alwitt et al. 1980: Anderson & Levin 1976; Anderson et al. 1986). Typical of such research is a study by Anderson and Levin (1976) of children's attention to a *Sesame Street* program. The children were observed closely as they sat with one of their parents in a room containing a television set, as well as refreshments and interesting toys. The *Sesame Street* videotape was played, and the children were free to watch or not as they wished. It was found that spontaneous attention to the program increased with age; for example, the 1-year-olds spent only 15 to 20 percent of the time in the room looking at the television set, while the 4-year-olds watched the program for about 55 percent of the total time they spent in the room. The authors also found that this pattern closely matched the children's television-viewing patterns at home, as indicated on questionnaires completed by the parents. Children were most attentive, incidentally, when program segments were short rather than prolonged, when animation and lively music were

Problems in Child Development

Attention Deficit Disorder

As children grow up, improvement can be expected in their span of attention, resistance to distraction, and ability to attend selectively to the world around them. However, some children—between 3 and 5 percent of the population—do not show developmental improvement in these areas (Routh 1986). These children, about 90 percent of whom are boys, suffer from a syndrome formerly referred to as hyperactivity but now known as **attention deficit disorder** (American Psychiatric Association 1980).

Attention deficit disorder (ADD) is said to be present when a child gives signs of (1) developmentally immature forms of *inattention* (e.g., doesn't listen well, is easily distracted, is unable to concentrate on schoolwork, doesn't finish projects); (2) *impulsivity* (e.g., acts before thinking, is unable to wait for a turn in group games, needs much supervision, disrupts the class); and (3) *hyperactivity* (e.g., cannot sit still, runs about excessively, moves excessively during sleep). Furthermore, for a diagnosis of attention deficit disorder, these conditions must be present for at least six months, and must not be attributable to any specific known mental disorder or to mental retardation (American Psychiatric Association 1980).

Perhaps it is not surprising that the presence of such attentional problems has a significant impact on the social environment in which a child operates. ADD children often are rejected by their peers (Klein & Young 1979; Mainville & Friedman 1976). They are more likely than the average child to experience conflict with siblings (Mash & Johnston 1980), and to have stricter controls placed upon them by their parents (Cunningham & Barkley 1979). Finally, teachers are both more intense and more controlling when dealing with an ADD child, as well as with other children in a classroom in which an ADD child is present (Whalen, Henker & Dotemoto 1981).

The actual causes of attention deficit disorder are difficult to determine (Routh 1986). Some evidence indicates that genetic factors may be involved; for example, identical twins seem to resemble one another in level of distractibility (Torgersen & Kringlen 1978), and adopted children of hyperactive birth parents are often hyperactive even if their adoptive parents are not (Cunningham et al. 1975). Brain damage has been offered as a second possible explanation, but the relationship between ADD and specific brain damage is unclear; many brain-damaged children show no evidence of the condition (Routh 1986). Finally, in recent years there has been much interest in children's diets as possible influences on the kind of hyperactive behavior found in ADD children. For example, Feingold (1975) suggested that hyperactivity is the result of allergic reactions in some children to artificial flavors and colors in foods. Indeed, in one survey 70 percent of parents of children with behavior problems were convinced that diet was in some way responsible for the difficult behavior (Crook 1980). The actual evidence of dietary influences in attention deficit disorder is incomplete, but a number of studies point to links between food dyes and hyperactivity (Weiss et al. 1980) and between sugar and hyperactivity (Prinz, Roberts & Hartman 1980).

Whatever the causes of attention deficit disorder, the problem is a serious one, not only because of the previously mentioned negative social consequences, but also because the condition appears to carry over into adolescence and adulthood (Routh 1986). Among adolescents and adults, ADD has been associated with lowered self-esteem, difficulties in academic achievement, and even alcohol abuse (Routh 1986).

used, and when women rather than men were on the screen.

The developmental increase in preschooler's attention to television has usually been attributed to cognitive changes in the children themselves. That is, as children develop, they are better able to understand what they are watching, and because the material is increasingly comprehensible, it will be increasingly attended to (Anderson & Lorch 1983; Anderson et al. 1986). A person's knowledge base and degree of familiarity with what is perceived will certainly influence the efficiency of attentional processes (Olson & Sherman 1983).

Developmental changes in visual attention to television during the school years have rarely been examined, and when studies have been done, the results are inconsistent. In one of the most extensive studies of this type, Anderson and his associates (1986) observed television-viewing patterns in the homes of ninety-nine families, with an age range of family members from infancy to 62 years. The actual number of hours of television watching each week increased up to the age of 10 (an average of thirteen hours) and then declined gradually through adolescence and into adulthood. However, the percentage of visual attention—the amount of time a child actually attended to television out of the total time spent in a room with the television set on—increased only throughout the preschool years and then leveled off after the age of 6, indicating again the improvement in the efficiency of attention throughout the preschool years. What the authors observed is what so many parents are so regularly irritated by—the television set is often playing when nobody is actually attending to it. In fact, about 15 percent of the time when the set was on there was no one even present in the room (Anderson et al. 1986)!

Memory

All measures of learning, whether in the classroom or in the laboratory, invariably include a memory component, and many of the studies discussed in the previous sections tested memory as well as initial learning. In much the same way, many studies discussed in this section focus on the

process of encoding incoming material, as well as on retrieving it.

Thus, obtaining "pure" measures of memory is very difficult. After all, we cannot describe simple age changes in memory without referring to changes in other cognitive processes as well. For example, if young children cannot remember material as well as older children can, we must question whether the initial learning process was identical for the two groups. If young children have not learned as well as older ones, we could hardly expect them to remember as well either.

Types of Memory

Reference has already been made to different types, or stages, of human memory. It is appropriate to explain these stages in greater detail before discussing developmental changes during childhood. A frequently used distinction is between short-term and long-term memory. **Short-term memory**—also referred to as primary memory, active memory, or working memory—involves the retrieval of material still at the level of consciousness because it has recently been presented and is in the process of being rehearsed. Information in short-term memory will be held for only a very short time, one minute or less, and will be lost unless efforts are made to transfer it to long-term storage. Consider as an example of short-term memory the experience of locating a telephone number in the directory and keeping it in mind while closing the book, picking up the phone, and dialing. The caller may repeat the number several times to keep it in mind until the call is made—the process of rehearsal—but probably does not feel the need to "memorize" the number—that is, to transfer it to permanent storage. If the caller is interrupted before the call can be made, the number fades from short-term memory; and, if no efforts have been made to transfer the information to the more permanent long-term memory, the caller must go back to the telephone directory.

How much information can be held in short-term memory at one time? The answer is difficult to determine because the capacity of short-term memory seems to depend upon the meaningfulness of the material taken in (Anderson 1985).

This third-grader is struggling to remember the answer to the questions his teacher just asked him. If he is unable to remember the material, the failure may have occurred at any point in the intellectual process beginning with initial attention and ending with retrieval from storage.

Consider what happens when a list of words or syllables is presented and the listener is asked to repeat them immediately. A person can hold in short-term memory and repeat back four nonsense syllables (e.g., *GIB, BOF, DEX, WOB*) but not six; the short-term memory capacity for meaningful one-syllable words is six (e.g., *coat, dog, run, hand, cat, shoe*), but nine such words will not ordinarily be remembered. Finally, if a person is presented not with a list of words but with a meaningful sentence, the capacity of short-term memory goes up to nineteen words (Anderson 1985)! As the material increases in meaningfulness, the listener is better able to remember it immediately, and better able to process it into long-term memory storage.

Learned material that is not at a person's immediate level of consciousness is said to have been transferred from short-term memory to relatively permanent storage in **long-term memory**. Referring to the telephone-caller example discussed earlier, most people store in long-term memory several frequently called telephone numbers. A friend's telephone number may have been encoded but will not be brought to consciousness unless it is needed. If there is a need to call a particular friend, that person's number will be activated and brought from long-term to short-term memory—a process known as *retrieval*.

Factors Influencing Memory

A number of approaches can be used to help learners remember information better. Much opportunity for practice should be allowed so that the initial learning is firmly entrenched. The time between learning and retrieval should be minimized so that decay and interference are least likely to occur. The material should be presented in a form that is meaningful to the learner. Finally, mnemonic strategies involving rehearsal, organization, and elaboration can be taught to a learner who does not spontaneously use them—and this group is more likely to include children than adults—with the result that memory can be improved considerably.

The quality of the initial learning. Stated simply, the more completely a piece of information is learned in the first place, the easier it will be to remember. In a study by Anderson (1983), participants memorized sentences until they knew them by heart; they were later asked to select the memorized sentences from a list containing those sentences and others that had not been learned. It was found that the time required to identify a previously learned sentence was related to the number of days of practice. That is, the learners who had had more time to practice were better able to retrieve the information from memory. Such findings are consistent with those of numerous other studies indicating that practice increases the memorability of learned material.

Interval between learning and retrieval. As any student knows, the longer the delay between initial learning and the effort to remember what is learned, the more difficult it is to retrieve such information from storage. Two factors are involved in such memory loss. The first is *decay,* meaning that memory traces appear to fade with the passing of time (Anderson & Paulson 1977). Reasons for this decay of the memory trace are unclear, but there may be underlying physiological causes (Anderson 1985). The second factor in memory loss is *interference.* Earlier or later learnings can interfere with efforts to remember what is learned. As an illustration of this point, students who study French in their first year of high school and Spanish the following year may find that familiarity with one language interferes with their ability to remember the other. When asked to recall the French word for horse, which they learned as *cheval* in their

freshman year, some of them may remember only the Spanish word *caballo.* The greater the time interval between learning and retrieval, the greater is the likelihood of the interference that can result in forgetting.

The meaningfulness of the material. As discussed earlier, material that is meaningful is easier to remember than material that has little or no meaning for the learner. Perhaps this is because the learner can organize meaningful information into "chunks" and can relate new learnings to what has previously been learned, whereas there is no framework into which meaningless information can be placed.

The meaningfulness of material as an influence on memory has been demonstrated also in a number of studies of children's interests. Children are most likely to pay attention to what interests them, and more likely to remember things that are of interest than things that are not (Langsdorf et al. 1983; Renninger & Wozniak 1985; Wozniak 1986). As an illustration of this principle, Renninger and Wozniak (1985) had 3- and 4-year-olds look at nine toys, one at a time, which were then placed in a box. The children were asked, "What toys are in the box?" One of the toys had been identified previously as a toy the child had a particular fondness for, and it was this high-interest toy that was consistently the best remembered. The researchers concluded that interests and values definitely influence the cognitive performance of young children. Objects and experiences that have special meaning for a child are the easiest to remember later on.

The use of mnemonic strategies. As material is being learned, a number of strategies can be used to make that material more memorable. For example, learners may engage in spontaneous *rehearsal,* repeating the material over and over again to themselves, or if the material is presented visually, naming or labeling the items to be remembered. Another approach involves organizing the material into meaningful patterns. For example, the list of numbers *278147349* might be easier to remember if it were broken into segments *278 147 349.* Many grade school children remember the names of the Great Lakes only because the first letters of each name can be arranged to spell the word *HOMES*. A third mnemonic strategy is *elaboration*, in which the material to be learned is expanded upon in the mind of the learner. The larger the number of mental associations to the material, the easier it becomes to remember. Someone who has difficulty remembering people's names at a party might associate names with the colors of clothing worn by the guests: Jane-red, Mike-blue, and so forth. Elaboration is illustrated also by the strategy of making meaningful sentences out of lists of words (e.g., the list *child, hat, green, wall* becomes *The child threw his hat over the green wall*) or forming a visual image of the action described by such a sentence.

Memory Development

The findings from studies of children's memory development—an extensive and rapidly growing body of research within the past twenty years—have led to the conclusion that there are no age differences in short-term memory. In contrast, children's long-term memory improves significantly with age (Hagen 1971; Kail & Hagen 1982; Kunzinger 1985; Ornstein et al. 1985; Ornstein & Naus 1978, 1983). The results reported by Hagen (1971) illustrate this pattern of findings. Hagen found no age differences in the ability of children and adults to remember objects they had seen on a screen if they were asked to remember those objects immediately after they had seen them. However, if a delay were allowed to occur between the stimulus presentation and the recall trial, preschoolers seemed to forget more than older children and adults did. It appears that information enters the system with equal ease in young and older children, but once it has reached the short-term memory stage, young children are less able to process it into long-term memory storage.

Most explanations of developmental improvements in long-term memory emphasize improvements in the use of mnemonic strategies. That is, older children are thought to be more capable than younger ones of using sophisticated strategies to place learned material in storage so that it will be easily retrieved.

In a classic study of the strategies used by children to enhance the memorability of stimulus material, Flavell, Beach, and Chinsky (1966)

showed seven pictures to 5- , 7- , and 10-year-olds. The children were told that the pictures would later have to be remembered, and the researchers then observed the children's spontaneous verbalizations. Ten percent of the 5-year-olds, 60 percent of the 7-year-olds, and 85 percent of the 10-year-olds spontaneously spoke the names of the pictures to themselves as they studied them—presumably as a rehearsal strategy that would later aid their memory of the pictures. It appeared that the strategy worked, because the older children remembered the stimuli significantly better than the younger ones did.

In a later study, Flavell, Friedrichs, and Hoyt (1970) tested children ranging from nursery school to fourth grade on a simple memory task. The children were exposed to a series of objects in a horizontal row of windows, each of which could be lit up for viewing by pressing a button underneath the window. They were told to study the objects until they were ready to remember them in the order in which they were displayed. The researchers noticed that the older children used more efficient rehearsal strategies—testing themselves, rehearsing the names of the objects, and pointing at the objects in turn—than did the younger ones. Not surprisingly, the older children were better able to remember the objects than were the preschoolers.

Using a type of stimulus material familiar to every college student, Brown and Smiley (1978) examined the strategies used by children and adults as they studied textbooks with the intent of learning material to be remembered. In analyzing the study strategies of fifth graders, seventh and eighth graders, eleventh and twelfth graders, and college students, the researchers found striking differences in study patterns. The older children and the adults were more capable of ignoring irrelevant material and focusing on the most important material than were the younger ones. As a result of this increased organizational ability, the older learner does not waste time studying trivia, but uses instead a considerably more time-efficient study strategy. The older students were also much more likely to underline the textbook material and to take notes on it.

Effective studying involves the spontaneous use of mnemonic strategies to make material more memorable. It also involves a knowledge of the strengths and weaknesses of one's memory skills, or metamemory.

The finding that memorization strategies improve in efficiency as children mature does not mean, of course, that infants and young children cannot remember past experiences. Even by the age of 3 months, infants display evidence of fairly sophisticated long-term memory (Enright et al. 1983; Olson & Sherman 1983; Rovee-Collier 1984). An often-used procedure in studies of infant memory involves placing a ribbon on infants' ankles as they lie in their cribs. The ribbon is connected to a mobile hanging over their heads in such a way that a kick causes the mobile to move. The average number of kicks per minute is found to increase considerably when the kicks produce such stimulating results—an example of operant conditioning. More relevant to the discussion of memory, however, is the finding that when the babies are "reminded" of the experience two weeks later by being shown the mobile, the kick rate again increases. Clearly, there is a memory of past experience even at so young an age. Interestingly enough, such evidence of long-term memory does not appear when 2-month-old infants are tested in the same way (Vander Linde, Morrongiello & Rovee-Collier 1985).

Efficient strategies for transferring information from short- to long-term memory may indeed be lacking in the young child, but as any parent knows, preschoolers often display remarkable powers of memory. They will point out, for example, that when they visited the doctor's office six months ago, they were given a red lollipop by the nurse—a fact that had been completely forgotten by the accompanying parent. And yet the same child may fail to remember simple household rules that the parent has tried repeatedly to teach. Sometimes it appears that preschoolers remember the "wrong" things; they often forget what adults see as important and remember incidental events that apparently had special meaning for them. This pattern clearly indicates the inefficiency of their memory processes.

The fact that mnemonic strategies improve in efficiency with age does not mean that young children use no strategies at all. Even by the age of 18 months, primitive strategies have been observed (DeLoache, Cassidy & Brown 1985). Weissberg and Paris (1986) noticed spontaneous rehearsal in almost half of the 3- and 4-year-olds who were given lists of words and told they would have to remember them. The tendency in recent years is to see mnemonic strategies not as an all-or-nothing phenomenon but as being present in varying degrees from the years of early childhood and gradually improving with age (Ornstein & Naus 1978, 1983).

Summarizing the literature on the use of *efficient* rehearsal strategies as an aid to memorization, Kail and Hagen (1982) noted that such strategies are rarely used by children under 6 years of age. They are occasionally used by children 7 to 10 years old, depending on the nature of the learning situation. Mature strategies begin to appear consistently in children aged 10 or older. For these reasons the effectiveness of providing mnemonic strategies to children and training them to develop their own will depend on the age of the children in question. The results of such training will be more dramatic in young children than in older children or adolescents, who are probably already using efficient mnemonic strategies of their own.

Metamemory

One of the more interesting approaches to the subject of memory is the research on what is known as **metamemory,** the knowledge people have about their own memory processes (Flavell & Wellman 1977). Instead of viewing memory in isolation from other cognitive processes, advocates of the metamemory concept maintain that how well we remember is a function of how well we understand our own memory functions. People who remember best are those who best know the limits of their memory capacity, who best understand how to employ memory strategies, and who best realize how much effort will be needed to commit various materials to memory. Teachers routinely encounter students who believe they have prepared adequately for an examination but who fail it nevertheless because they underestimated the amount of study time needed to remember the material. Is memory failure responsible for their poor grades or a lack of understanding of their own memory processes?

In studies dealing with metamemory, older children are typically more knowledgeable about their own memory processes than are younger ones—a finding that may partially account for the long-term memory limitations of the younger child (Flavell 1985; Flavell, Friedrichs & Hoyt 1970; Yussen & Levy 1975). However, as is the case with other aspects of memory development, a person's ability to monitor his or her own memory is not an all-or-nothing phenomenon. Even preschool children display some signs of metamemory (Cultice, Somerville & Wellman 1983). Perhaps this should not be surprising since 3- and 4-year-olds, and particularly those who attend nursery schools, are often expected to please adults by memorizing songs, poems, stories, or parts in a school play. They are already capable of voluntary memory, and thus are conscious of their own memory processes and skills (Weissberg & Paris 1986).

Summary

1. Learning results in a relatively permanent change in behavior that is brought about by environmental experience. The process of learning itself is not directly observable.
2. Classical conditioning, first investigated by Pavlov, involves reflexive behavior and depends on an association between a neutral stimulus and an unconditioned stimulus. The association is formed by the law of contiguity.

3. Operant conditioning depends on the law of effect, which states that behaviors followed by reward are likely to be repeated, whereas those followed by punishment or by no consequences are likely to be discontinued. Operant conditioning deals with voluntary behavior.

4. Both classical and operant conditioning have been demonstrated successfully with human beings, even with young human infants.

5. Operant-conditioning principles have been less effective in explaining complex forms of human thinking than they have been in explaining simple behaviors. Mediation theory was developed to explain the developmental shift from the straighforward operant response of a young child in a problem-solving task to the more complex strategies employed by older children and adults.

6. Social learning is the application of conditioning principles to the socialization process. Observational learning, the basic mechanism described by social-learning theorists, is a complex form of learning that depends on attentional, retention, motor-reproduction, and motivational factors.

7. Observational learning includes the phenomenon of modeling, in which the learner imitates and identifies with a significant model, often in the absence of apparent reinforcement for doing so. Modeling is recognized as one of the most powerful means for transmitting values, attitudes, behavioral patterns, and patterns of thought.

8. Controversy surrounds the question of when children begin to use adults as models. There is general agreement that infants are capable of imitation by the middle of the first year of life, but some psychologists believe that it can occur even during the first month.

9. Operant conditioning and observational learning have been applied successfully in classroom management by teachers at all levels, but such application requires a thorough knowledge of basic learning principles.

10. There are developmental increases in the efficiency of attention. As children mature, they are better able to attend to meaningful information from the environment and to ignore what is irrelevant.

11. There is little or no developmental change in short-term memory during childhood, but long-term memory improves significantly. The probable reason for this improvement is that children's mnemonic strategies become more efficient with age.

12. Metamemory is the knowledge people have about their own memory process. Such knowledge increases throughout childhood and may contribute to the corresponding increased efficiency of long-term memory.

Key Terms

classical conditioning	mediation theory
extinction	observational learning
operant conditioning	cognitive social learning
law of effect	learning disorder
reinforcement	attention deficit disorder
punishment	short-term memory
law of contiguity	long-term memory
reversal shift	metamemory

Suggested Readings

Bandura, A. (1986). *Social foundations of thought and action: A social cognitive theory.* Englewood Cliffs, NJ: Prentice-Hall.

A work that goes far beyond other works on the subject of human learning. Written by the originator of the social-learning view of psychological modeling, the book deals with a wide range of issues involving human thinking, motivation, and behavior.

Lerner, J. W. (1981). *Children with learning disabilities.* Boston: Houghton Mifflin.

A book that discusses the variety of forms of learning disabilities in children. The reader will learn that the concept of learning disability is a highly complex one.

Reese, H.W. (1976). *Basic learning processes in childhood.* New York: Holt, Rinehart & Winston.

A book written for nonpsychology students and free from the technical jargon found in many books on learning. The author clearly describes children's learning in a variety of areas: conditioning, discrimination learning, verbal learning, and higher conceptual processing.

Woolfolk A.E. (1987). *Educational psychology* (3rd ed.). Englewood Cliffs, NJ: Prentice-Hall.

One of the most thorough and readable textbooks in the field of educational psychology. It contains up-to-date literature reviews on a variety of topics dealing with the psychology of the classroom, as well as numerous interesting and practical inserts.

Readings from the Literature

The following article is a developmental study of young children's attention to television, an area discussed in the preceding chapter. As you read the article, keep in mind the following questions, and then try to answer them when you have finished:

- How accurate are parents in estimating how much of their children's time in front of a television set is actually spent attending to the program?

- According to the findings of this study, what are some features of a television program that preschool children are most likely to attend to?

- What new information is provided by the results of this study? What did the authors of this study do that was not done in previous research on children's television watching?

Young Children's Attention to "Sesame Street"

Daniel R. Anderson and Stephen R. Levin
University of Massachusetts

This study analyzed 1–4 year-old children's attention to television as a function of age, sex, and the presence or absence of a number of relatively simple auditory and visual characteristics of a TV program. Children's attention and attributes of the "Sesame Street" program were rated and stored in a computer so that continuous information about the TV program could be related to continuous information about attention. There was an increase with age in attention to the TV, and attention was elevated in the presence of some attributes and depressed in the presence of others. Many of the attribute effects interacted with age, but very few interacted with the sex of the child.

While television viewing may have important beneficial as well as harmful effects on the behavior of preschool children (e.g., Ball & Bogatz 1970; Friedrich & Stein 1973), there has been little research on the development of attention to television and the factors that influence it (Stevenson 1972). From parental questionnaires, Schramm, Lyle, and Parker (1961) reported that by age 2.8 years 50% of children regularly "use" TV, and Lyle and Hoffman (1972) found that 76% of 3-year-olds were able to name their "favorite" program. By age 4, parents report that children spend about a third of their waking hours viewing TV (Friedrich & Stein 1973). With the exception of some informal and unpublished formative research done for the children's TV program "Sesame Street" (discussed by Lesser 1972), there have been no studies of the early development of television viewing based on actual observation of children, nor have there been any systematic attempts to analyze preferred TV programs to determine just what distinguishes these from other programs.

The present research contains the first formal descriptions of the development of visual attention to television based on direct observations of children. The study also provides a new methodology for examining the relationship of attention to variations in television content.

Method

Subjects

Seventy-two white, middle-class children from Amherst, Massachusetts, were observed. The research design called for 10 (five males, five females) children in each of seven age groups (12, 18, 24, 30, 36, 42, and 48 months ± 1 month). The 36- and 42-month age groups each contained an extra male.

The Television Program

The program employed was "Sesame Street" Test Show 4 and was shown in black and white. "Sesame Street" programs are constructed by sequencing short independent segments (bits) much like television commercials. This particular program was 57 min long and consisted of 41 bits. The bits ranged in length from 10 to 453 sec and averaged 87 sec. Although Test Show 4 has never been on the air, several of its bits have appeared in other "Sesame Street" programs, and it is fairly typical of early "Sesame Street" programs.

Viewing Room and Procedure

The viewing room measured 12 × 12 feet (3.66 m) and was comfortably furnished. Toys appropriate to preschool children were placed on open cabinet shelves and were readily available to the children. Coffee and tea for the parent and juice and crackers for the child were also provided.

Videotape equipment set up in an adjacent room was connected through the wall to a Sony 19-inch (48.26 cm) TV set. By switching back and forth between two TV cameras, the experimenter was able to constantly videotape the child as he/she moved about the room. After the parent and child were brought to the viewing room, the parent was given a home-viewing questionnaire to fill out during the viewing session. The door was closed, and the child was free to play with the toys and interact with the parent. After the parent and child were in the room for 5–10 min the experimenter started the "Sesame Street" program, and the child was videotaped for the duration of the program.

Subject Data Scoring Procedure

A computer was programmed to record the time (from the beginning of the TV program) that a key was depressed or released. An observer, viewing the videotape of a subject, pushed the key when the child appeared to be visually fixating on the television screen and released the key when the child looked away. Thus, a continuous record of the onset and offset of visual attention during the TV program was available for further analyses.

In order to estimate interobserver reliabilities, the onset and offset times were transformed to the number of seconds of attention for each of the 342 10-sec intervals (57 min) of the program. Independent rating of each of 10 pilot subject tapes by two observers produced an average interobserver reliability correlation of .98.

Attribute Rating Procedure

Test Show 4 was rated on the basis of the presence or absence of a number of visual and auditory attributes. The program was viewed by two observers, each with a four-channel keyboard which was connected to a computer. When the particular attribute an observer was rating appeared on the TV monitor, the appropriate key was depressed for the length of time the attribute occurred, thus providing a continuous record of the times of onset and offset of the attribute. The number of attributes an observer rated simultaneously depended in part on the observer's experience in rating and in part on the perceived difficulty of rating that attribute. In no case did an observer rate more than four attributes simultaneously, and typically an observer rated only one at a time. When visual attributes were being rated, the auditory portion of the program was turned off and vice versa. To reduce the possibility of interobserver bias, the two observers rated different attributes in a particular session. Over the course of the study, each attribute was rated at least two times by different observers.

For purposes of judging interobserver reliabilty, the amount of time an attribute was judged present was

230

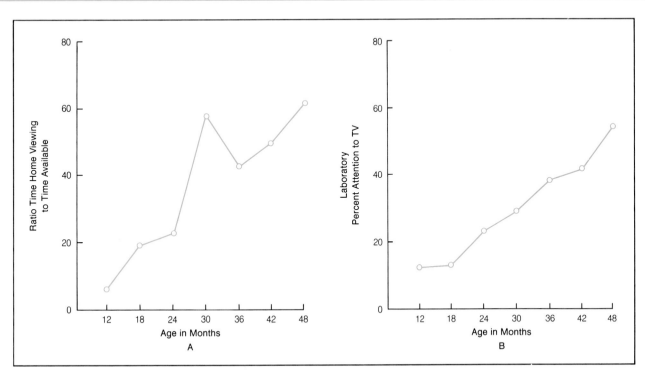

Figure 1 *a,* Home TV Viewing: Ratio of Viewing Time to Available TV Time as a Function of Age. *b,* Laboratory TV Viewing: Percentage of Viewing Time as a Function of Age.

calculated for each 10-sec interval of the program. For several attributes reflecting sudden transitions, such as cuts and auditory changes, the number of changes per 10-sec interval was calculated. An interobserver reliability coefficient was computed for each attribute using these 10-sec interval data. If the reliability was below .85, the attribute was discussed, redefined, and independently rated again by the two observers. This procedure was repeated until the ratings reached a reliability criterion of at least .85 (23 of the 44 attributes required more than one rating).

Results

Home Viewing

On the questionnaire, parents were asked to estimate the number of hours a TV was available to watch during the morning, afternoon, and evening of each day of the week. Each parent was also asked to estimate

the number of hours his child actually watched TV during each morning, afternoon, and evening. A 7 (age) × 2 (sex) analysis of variance of estimated hours per week of viewing time revealed a significant main effect of age, $F(6,56) = 9.12$, $p < .001$, such that older children watched more TV at home than did younger children (in this and subsequent analyses of variance one male subject in the 36- and 42-month groups was randomly excluded to produce equal cell sizes). There was, however, a tendency for TV availability to increase with age, $r(68) = .29$, $p < .05$. In order to gain a less confounded measure of TV viewing, the ratio of amount of home viewing to the amount of TV availability was calculated. An age × sex analysis of variance of the ratio data also revealed the significant age effect, $F(6,56) = 6.75$, $p < .001$, which is illustrated in figure 1a. Scheffe analyses (α set at .05) indicated that the 12–24-month-olds were not significantly different from each other, but had significantly smaller ratios than the 30–48-month-olds, who in turn were not different from each other. Thus, a sharp increase in

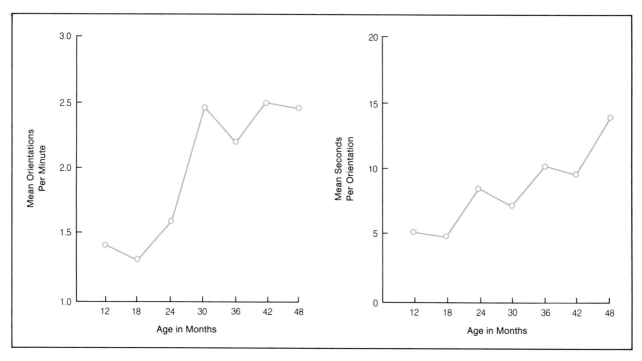

Figure 2 *a*, Mean number of visual orientations to the TV as a function of age. *b*, Mean duration of visual orientations to the TV as a function of age.

reported home TV viewing occurred at 2.5 years of age.

Attention to Television in the Laboratory

There was also an increase with age in percentage of attention to the TV in the laboratory ($F[6,56] = 8.37$, $p < .001$, as illustrated in fig. 1*b*). The increase in attention was due both to increasing frequency, $F(6,56) = 4.19$, $p < .01$, and duration of visual orientation, $F(6,56) = 5.28$, $p < .001$, as illustrated in figure 2. Scheffe analyses of frequency of visual orientation indicated a break between 24 and 30 months, quite analogous to the increase in home viewing at this age. There was no equivalent break in the average duration of visual orientation. Percentage of attention in the laboratory correlated positively with parents' estimates of home viewing, $r(70) = .485$, $p < .01$, and parents' education was significantly related to the average duration of a visual orientation, $r(70) = .338$, $p < .01$.

Bit Analyses

Attention decreased as bit length increased, $r(39) = -.55$, $p < .001$. Longer bits were initially low in attention. There was a negative correlation between attention in the first 10 sec of a bit and bit length, $r(39) = -.33$, $p < .05$, but the negative correlation of bit length and attention remained significant ($p < .001$) when the effect of initial attention was statistically removed.

"Sesame Street" producers often employ considerable repetition of concepts and bits. In Test Show 4, three bits were repeated. Attention was neither significantly enhanced nor diminished with repetition for any of these bits.

Attribute Analysis

Since the time of onset and offset of each attribute was known, and since the time of onset and offset of attention for each child was known, it was possible to

232

determine whether attention was elevated or depressed in the exact presence of a given attribute relative to the absence of that attribute. The percentage of attention in the presence and in the absence of each visual and auditory attribute was calculated for each subject. A 2 (presence vs. absence) × 7 (age) × 2 (sex) analysis of variance for the percentage of attention was performed for each attribute. Several attributes, rather than existing continuously in time, marked transitions of one sort or another (e.g. cut auditory change). The "presence" of these attributes was arbitrarily defined as existing for 3 sec following such a transition, unless another transition occurred within the 3-sec interval, in which case the end of the interval occurred 3 sec after the second transition, and so on. Since the age and sex main effects are redundant for each analysis, they are not reported.

There were 31 attribute main effects and 17 interactions with age. Three (black man, white man, inactive stationary central figures) showed progressively larger negative effects with age; and seven attributes (adult female voice, animation, motion through space, rhyming, repetition and alliteration, sound effects, auditory change, and change to an essentially familiar scene) showed progressively larger positive effects with age. The remainder of the attributes showed negative effects at some ages and positive effects at others. As an example of the latter type of interaction, attention to animals increased up to 24 months of age and declined precipitously thereafter. One attribute (white man on screen) interacted with sex of subject such that girls' attention was depressed more than boys'. Two attributes (puppets and peculiar voice) interacted complexly with both age and sex.

Multivariate analyses

In an attempt to determine how much of the variability of attention over time could be accounted for by the simple attributes, a number of correlational analyses were performed. Amount of attention and amount of each attribute (including elapsed time into the program) were calculated for each 1-min segment of Test Show 4.[1] In order to determine the degree to which children

[1] There was no significant trend at any age for attention to decrease with elapsed time into the program.

attended to the program *at the same time,* a random sample of 110 of the 2,556 possible pairwise intersubject correlations were calculated. The correlations averaged .10, indicating that by knowing a given child's minute-by-minute pattern of attention to a TV program, little of the variability of attention of another child may be predicted. This result stands in contrast to the apparent intersubject consistency for some of the attributes: *All* of the 72 children looked less at the screen in the visual presence of a white adult male, for example, than during other parts of the program. The children tended to be inconsistent with respect to each other, however, concerning just when a white adult male depressed attention. Given the intersubject inconsistency with respect to which minutes of the program are most attended, therefore, the attempt to account for the variability of attention over minutes was unsuccessful. The present data were subjected to stepwise multiple-regression analysis such that the number of seconds of attention for each subject in each of the 57 min of Test Show 4 was the dependent variable to be predicted by the number of seconds in each minute of each attribute. As expected, the regression analyses (a separate analysis was done for each age) accounted for relatively little of the minute-by-minute variability in attention (a maximum of 37.1% for the 48-month-olds).

Discussion

From 1 to 4 years of age, there was a dramatic increase in attention to television. Informal observation indicated that younger than 30 months, children did not systematically monitor the TV screen but rather had their attention "captured" for short periods of time. The younger children appeared to be far more interested in playing with toys and interacting with their mothers than watching television. Older children, on the other hand, appeared to more deliberately "watch" television: they sat oriented toward the TV, often playing with toys, but glancing up at the screen frequently. The older children looked at the TV for up to 7 min without glancing away, whereas the longest orientations of the younger children were about 60 sec.

Attention was increased in the presence of some visual and auditory attributes and decreased in the presence of others. Causal inferences, unfortunately, are not in order: elevated or depressed attention in the presence of a given attribute may be caused by that attribute, but also might be due to correlated factors. A clear example of this problem is the differential attention the children paid to men and women characters: attention was depressed in the presence of men and enhanced in the presence of women. While young children may find adult men inherently less interesting than women (a notion consistent with work on social reinforcement [Stevenson 1965]), it is the case that in Test Show 4 and in most TV programs men and women are in fact "programmed" differently (see Sternglanz & Servin 1974). Men tended to be absent when lively music was on the sound track and tended to be heard in the presence of still drawings and inactivity (based on minute-by-minute correlations of all attributes). Women, on the other hand, were seen and heard in the presence of child characters, singing, dancing, rhyming, repetition, and alliteration. At least on "Sesame Street" Test Show 4, men read books and are inactive whereas women dance, sing, recite poetry, and talk to children. Until experimental analyses can be performed, therefore, causal inferences about the role of men and women or any other attributes in determining attention must be entertained cautiously. Nevertheless, a problem for producers of educational television for children is to provide programs which can successfully compete with the violence-prone offerings of entertainment television (see Liebert, Neale, & Davidson 1973). To the degree to which Test Show 4 and the behavior of the present sample of young children are representative, one can cautiously suggest that children are more attentive in the presence of women, children, eye contact, puppets, peculiar voices, animation, movement, lively music, rhyming, repetition and alliteration, and auditory change. They tend to watch less in the presence of adult men, animals, inactivity, and still drawings. Camera work, however, appears to have relatively little effect. The rapid pacing which producers of TV programs feel is necessary to maintain children's attention (Cantor 1972) is probably most effective in the form of lively music, motion, and auditory change rather than a plethora of pans, zooms, and cuts. When a magazine format is employed, the present study indicates that attention to a bit decreases as bit length increases.

Both theoretical and empirical considerations (Bandura & Walters 1963; Yussen 1974) indicate a child learns that to which he or she attends, and yet there has been little work on what attracts and maintains a young child's attention to television. The present study provides preliminary data and a new methodology for investigating this. Further research is needed to assess the generality of the present findings for a variety of TV program materials and subject populations.

References

Ball, S., & Bogatz, G. A. *The first year of Sesame Street, an evaluation.* Princeton, N.J.: Educational Testing Service, 1970.

Bandura, A., & Walters, R. H. *Social learning and personality development.* New York: Holt, Rinehart & Winston, 1963.

Cantor, M. G. The role of the producer in choosing children's television content. In E. Rubenstein et al. (Eds.) *Television and social behavior: media control and content.* Washington, D.C.: Government Printing Office, 1972.

Friedrich, L., & Stein, A. Aggressive and prosocial television programs and the natural behavior of preschool children. *Monographs of the Society for Research in Child Development,* 1973, 38(4, Serial No. 151).

Lesser, G. G. Learning, teaching and television production for children: the experience of *Sesame Street. Harvard Education Review,* 1972, **42**, 232–272.

Liebert, R.: Neale, J., & Davidson. E. *The early window: the effects of television on children and youth,* New York: Pergamon, 1973.

Lyle, J., & Hoffman, H. R. Explorations of patterns of television viewing by preschool-age children. In E. Rubenstein et al. (Eds.), *Television and social behavior: television in day-to-day life: patterns of use.* Washington, D.C.: Government Printing Office, 1972.

Schramm, W., Lyle, J., & Parker, E. B. *Television in the lives of our children.* Stanford, Calif.: Stanford University Press, 1961.

Sternglanz, S. H., & Serbin, L. A. Sex role stereotyping in children's television programs. *Developmental Psychology.* 1974, **10**, 710–715.

Stevenson, H. W. Social reinforcement of children's behavior. In L. Lipsitt & C. Spiker (Eds.), *Advances in child development and behavior.* New York: Academic Press, 1965.

Stevenson, H. W. Television and the behavior of preschool children. In E. Rubenstein et al. (Eds.), *Television and social behavior: television and social learning.* Washington, D.C.: Government Printing Office, 1972.

Yussen, S. R. Determinants of visual attention and recall in observational learning by preschool and second graders. *Developmental Psychology,* 1974, **10**, 93–100.

235

Intelligence

8

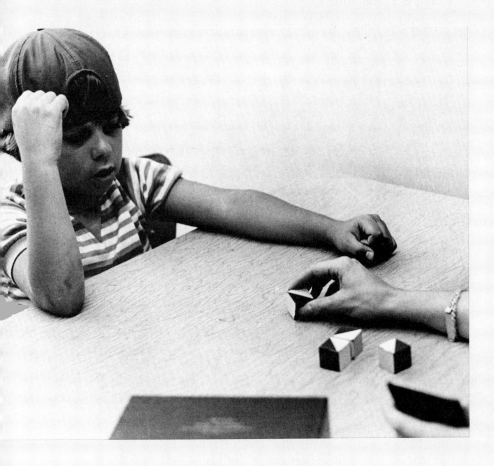

Randy was a high school junior whose entire scholastic career had been characterized by academic success. Then, for no apparent reason, his grades began to take a downward turn. His parents were surprised at first and eventually became alarmed. What would cause an excellent student to undergo such a radical transformation? All of the more obvious explanations—physical illness, emotional stress, and even difficulties with particular teachers—were ruled out. Then one day Randy mentioned to his parents that he had been in the office of the school guidance counselor several months before and had accidentally seen in his file that his IQ score was 90. Randy knew that a score of 90 is toward the lower end of the average range. He admitted that since that time he saw little point in pushing himself beyond what he now saw as his limited intellectual potential!

Randy's story had a happy ending: it turned out that the 90 he had seen was not his IQ score at all, but his percentile ranking in his class! It indicated high academic standing and not a low-average intelligence. Shortly after the mistake had been explained to him, he began to earn his customary As and Bs again—much to the relief of his worried parents.

Randy's story illustrates that intelligence, and particularly the IQ score, is too frequently misunderstood; even if Randy's information about his score had been accurate, the IQ is not a fixed entity that sets limits on academic achievement. The second and disturbing point of Randy's story is that IQ can have a frightening impact on a person's self-esteem—an impact so great that the belief a person has about his or her own intelligence can significantly affect intellectual performance. This is despite the fact that most people, including Randy, have only a vague notion of what intelligence really means, or how intelligence can be measured, or what intelligence test scores indicate.

This chapter deals with a variety of issues related to individual differences in human intelligence. It attempts to define intelligence in the quantitative sense in which the term is commonly used, in order to illustrate the difficulty psychologists have had in formulating adequate definitions. The chapter discusses the controversies surrounding the effectiveness of, and even the desirability of, attempts to measure intelligence, and

it describes some of the better-known intelligence tests currently in use.

The question of hereditary and environmental contributions to human intelligence is one of the most controversial issues in the study of child development. This chapter also examines the meaning of and the implications of current research suggesting inherited influences on intelligence. It discusses the swirl of controversy surrounding observed racial differences among American children in performance on IQ tests. The chapter then turns to an examination of specific environmental influences on the development of intelligence during childhood.

The last section of this chapter will address the question of what IQ scores really tell us about children and how such scores should be interpreted. Included will be a discussion of appropriate uses of IQ testing in clinical and educational settings, and some of the ways in which the IQ concept is frequently misused.

The Nature of Intelligence

The concept of intelligence is often misunderstood, perhaps because of a tendency to think of it as a "thing," an entity that a person possesses. A more accurate view is that intelligence is an abstract concept based on, or abstracted from, human behavior. In other words, we never see intelligence; we see examples of behavior that can be described as more or less intelligent. It is incorrect to say a person has a certain amount of intelligence, but it can be said a person behaved intelligently in a certain situation: he read a map correctly and found his destination, or she helped resolve a family crisis by acting calmly, or he answered questions properly on an intelligence test. In fact, within the same person there is the capacity for varying degrees of intelligent behavior, depending on the particular conditions under which the behavior occurs. The real danger in what anthropologist Stephen Jay Gould (1981) calls the "reification" of intelligence—the assumption that it is a thing rather than an abstraction—is that people often become needlessly concerned about "How much of it do I have?" or "Do I have as much intelligence as other people do?"

Definitions of Intelligence

Many different approaches have been taken to the definition of intelligence. Jean Piaget, for example, saw it as a form of biological adaptation to the environment—the mechanism that allows us to interact successfully with out surroundings (see Chapter 6). Lewis Terman, the developer of the Stanford-Binet Intelligence Scale, viewed intelligence as the ability to engage in abstract thinking. Alfred Binet, who constructed the first widely used intelligence test, believed that intelligence involves "judgment, practical sense, initiative, and the ability to adapt . . . to circumstances" (Sattler 1981). Perhaps the most comprehensive definition of intelligence came from David Wechsler, who developed two of the most widely used individual intelligence tests: intelligence is the ability to think rationally, act purposefully, and deal effectively with the environment.

One area of disagreement concerning the intelligence concept centers on the question of the number of cognitive components, or factors, that underlie a person's intelligence. For example, Spearman (1927) believed that intelligence involves two factors: a general reasoning factor (*g*), and a factor specific to the type of test taken. Therefore, each section of an intelligence test would call on the factor specific to that section (e.g., memory, spatial awareness) and would also call upon the *g* factor of general reasoning, which is required in every intellectual task. Thurstone (1938) rejected the concept of a single *g* factor and argued that there are seven basic abilities involved in intelligence. The "primary mental abilities" are: verbal meaning, inductive reasoning, perceptual speed, number facility, spatial relations, memory, and verbal fluency.

Perhaps the most complex analysis of factors involved in intelligence is that proposed by Guilford (1967), who developed a three-dimensional model of intellectual functioning (see Figure 8.1). Guilford believed that five types of mental operations can be performed (cognition, memory, divergent thinking, convergent thinking, and evaluation), that these can be performed on four types of content (figural, symbolic, semantic, and behavioral), and that six different products might result (units, classes, relations, systems, transfor-

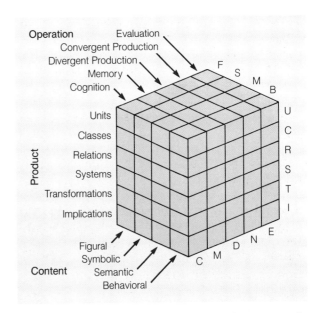

Figure 8.1 Guilford's Model of the Structure of Intelligence

Source: From Guilford, J.P. (1976) *The nature of human intelligence,* New York: McGraw-Hill. Reprinted by permission of the publisher.

mations, and implications). As an illustration, cognition (i.e., recognition or simple interpretation) of symbolic systems (i.e., dealing with letters, numbers, or other symbols) might be tested by a number series: what number is missing in the following series? 1 4 8 ___ 19. (The answer is 13.)

Guilford hoped to identify components of intelligence in each of the 120 cells produced by the 4 × 5 × 6 matrix, and to develop tests for each of the components. Unfortunately, he never reached his ambitious goal, and one critic remarked that such fragmenting of human intelligence gave the impression that people are "scatterbrained" (Cronbach 1984).

In an interesting recent approach to the issue of the various cognitive components of human intelligence, Sternberg (1985, 1986) suggested that three different aspects of intelligence must be examined. The *componential* aspect closely resembles the concepts of intelligence described by the theorists mentioned above. Found in people of all cultures, it deals with the internal mental processes that underlie intelligent behavior. A person high

Solving a practical problem, such as reading and understanding a map, requires intelligence. Intelligence includes the ability to deal effectively with one's environment.

in componential intelligence would perform well on tests requiring analytical reasoning, including most traditional intelligence tests and most school examinations. The *experiential* aspect of intelligence involves the ability to deal with new situations, and to display a degree of insight and creativity in deciding how to solve unfamiliar problems. A person high in experiential intelligence would approach a novel situation by easily deciding which information is relevant and which to ignore, establishing an overall picture of the situation, and relating new information to what he or she already has had experience with. Finally, the *contextual* aspect of intelligence involves adapting to a specific environment (e.g., adjusting to the routine of a new job), deciding when adaptation is no longer desirable (e.g., choosing to leave a job that no longer satisfied a person's needs), and attempting to change an

unsatisfactory environment (e.g., trying to improve conditions in a job a person cannot leave).

While the componential aspect of intelligence is universal, the experiential and contextual aspects differ from culture to culture. As an example, a person might be very insightful in problem solving (experiential) and very capable of adapting to the environment (contextual) of a small town, but might display considerably less intelligent behavior if relocated to a large metropolitan area. What is more, a person could be highly proficient in one or more aspects of intelligence but only average or even deficient in others, as in the case of someone who is adept at analytical reasoning but lacks insight when confronted with unfamiliar situations.

On first glance it appears that there is little agreement about what constitutes human intelligence, but in fact there is much similarity among the definitions. Most psychologists agree that intelligence requires a general ability to reason. Most agree that a number of more specific cognitive abilities (e.g., verbal skills, quantitative skills, spatial awareness, intuition, memory, and speed) are involved, and that these are correlated rather than isolated from one another. Finally, most theorists agree that intelligence involves the ability to deal effectively with, or adapt to, the particular environment in which a person lives. In other words, instead of viewing it only as an abstract mental ability, psychologists see intelligence as a problem-solving behavior, or class of behaviors, that occurs in a particular time and place, and depends upon the presence of certain mental abilities. The mental abilities in question, however, will vary to some extent depending on the nature of the problem to be solved. They are not easy to specify in every situation requiring intelligent behavior.

Intelligence Testing

Can intelligence be measured? Measuring human physical characteristics is a relatively simple task. Measuring psychological characteristics is considerably more difficult, particularly when, as in the case of intelligence, a clear and simple definition of the concept is not available.

Few psychologists deny that the concept of intelligence is a legitimate one, and few deny that human beings vary considerably in their effectiveness at problem solving. Disagreement arises, however, over the effectiveness of, and the desirability of, attempts to measure human intelligence and to quantify individual differences in intelligent behavior.

In this section of the chapter, a number of intelligence tests will be discussed. These were developed by advocates of the measurement, or *psychometric*, approach to intelligence. The tests mentioned are by no means the only ones of their kind, but they are among the best.

A good test of any kind has two essential characteristics. First, it must be *reliable*. This means that if the same person is tested on two different occasions, the test scores will be highly similar. **Reliability,** therefore, refers to the consistency of scores yielded by a test (Anastasi 1982). A good

test must also demonstrate **validity:** it must measure what it claims to measure, so that test results provide clear and meaningful information about a person's performance in a particular area. Validity is established with reference to some outside criterion, such as another well-established test or performance in a real-life situation (Anastasi 1982). Thus, a reliable intelligence test should provide consistent scores over time; a valid intelligence test should yield scores similar to those obtained on other valid tests, and the scores should bear some relationship to observed intelligent behavior in the outside world.

Critics of intelligence testing do not attack the reliability of the better-known tests such as those described in this section. Instead, they question the validity. They argue that the testing situation offers too artificial and too limited a sample of human behavior; a child who performs poorly on a test might still exhibit highly intelligent behaviors in his or her everyday world. To use Sternberg's (1986) terminology, critics argue that most intelligence tests measure the componential aspects but not the experiential or contextual aspects of intelligence. Testing advocates respond that the tests do in fact measure a number of factors related to human intellectual functioning in a variety of situations; they point to the relationship between intelligence-test performance and school success, occupational choice, and overall lifetime accomplishments as an indication that adaptive skills are indeed measured by the tests. Both perspectives should be kept in mind in the following discussion of the tests themselves.

The Binet Tests

In 1904, the minister of public instruction in Paris appointed a committee to determine the levels of mental ability of children in the school system and thereby to separate the normal from the subnormal. As members of the committee, Alfred Binet (1857–1911), a well-known psychologist, and Théodore Simon (1873—1961), a physician, developed the first widely used intelligence scale. The 1905 *Binet Scale* included thirty tests arranged according to difficulty level. It was expected that the number of tests passed would be determined by the age of the child. Among other abilities, the tests measured sensory and motor skills, vocabulary, spatial awareness, memory, and the ability to tell time. Critics argued that the scale relied too heavily on verbal ability and on memory, maintaining that children who had a facility with words would have a decided advantage over their less verbal peers. Nevertheless, the scale represented a breakthrough in intelligence testing and a number of American researchers introduced translations and variations of it into this country.

The *Stanford-Binet Intelligence Scale,* the most successful American version of the Binet test, was produced by Lewis M. Terman (1877–1956) at Stanford University in 1916. Terman used the Binet Scale for more than half of his test items, and to these he added forty items of his own. Test items were standardized; that is, they were tried out on about one thousand children and four hundred adults so that the questions could be placed at the appropriate age levels. (See Chapter 2 for a discussion of sampling procedures.)

The other major innovation of the 1916 scale was the use of the concept of the intelligence quotient, or IQ. A person's IQ was determined by dividing mental age by chronological age and multiplying the results by one hundred to eliminate the decimal—the **ratio IQ** formula.

The 1916 Stanford-Binet Scale was too heavily weighted with verbal as opposed to nonverbal items (a ratio of about two to one), and the instructions for administering and scoring it were not always adequate. In addition, although Terman attempted to standardize his test carefully, the standardization sample was relatively small, and contained too few cases at the upper and lower extremes of intelligence. As such, it was not representative of the general population.

The Stanford-Binet Intelligence Scale is still widely used today, although not in its original version. It was restandardized and updated in 1937, again in 1960, and most recently in 1985.

The Wechsler Tests

Many individual intelligence tests made their appearance in the 1930s and 1940s. The most noteworthy of these was developed by David Wechsler (1896–1981). Wechsler carefully analyzed the standardized intelligence tests available at the time and experimented with them for two years using various populations of known intelligence. Then, in 1939, he produced the *Wechsler-Bellevue Intelligence Scale,* which contained eleven of the most useful subtests taken from a variety of other tests. Included were tests of general information, arithmetical reasoning, memory, vocabulary, and spatial-reasoning skills.

The Wechsler-Bellevue Intelligence Scale has undergone much revision and restandardization since 1939. It was replaced by the *Wechsler Intelligence Scale for Children* (WISC) in 1949 and the *Wechsler Adult Intelligence Scale* (WAIS) in 1955. These were replaced by the WISC-R in 1974 and the WAIS-R in 1981, respectively. In 1963, Wechsler developed the *Wechsler Preschool and Primary Scale of Intelligence* (WPPSI), similar in basic form and content to the WISC but designed for use with children aged 4 through 6½ years. The WISC can be administered to children aged 5 through 15 and the WAIS to adults 16 years and older.

The eleven subtests of all three Wechsler tests are divided into verbal tests (1–6) and performance tests (7–11). Wechsler saw the verbal subtests as relying heavily on a factor called verbal comprehension, which is, roughly speaking, the ability to derive meaning from words. The performance tests seem to rely on a factor of nonverbal organization which Wechsler described as "the capacity to organize discrete spatially perceived units into larger wholes or configurations" (Wechsler 1958, 125). Other factors involved in intelligence, including a general reasoning factor and a memory factor, are found in both sections of the test.

Wechsler (1958) maintained that there are not different types of intelligence, but that intelligence shows itself in different ways. In fact, people who take a Wechsler test usually show a good deal of consistency across subtests. In other words, a person who scores well on the verbal subtests will probably score well on the performance subtests also—and vice versa.

Finally, Wechsler rejected as confusing the mental-age concept of the IQ, which Terman had used. He used instead the **deviation IQ,** which is determined by averaging the raw scores on the scales for each age group and arbitrarily equating average performance with an IQ score of 100. Virtually every IQ test in use today employs the same procedure, including the updated Stanford-Binet.

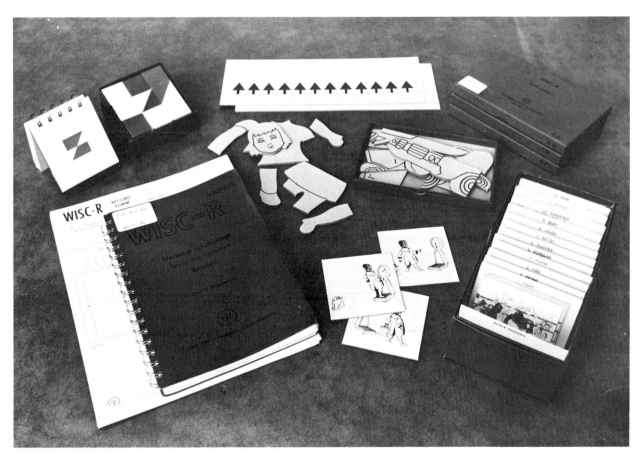

The Wechsler Intelligence Scale for Children-Revised.

When people take an IQ test, what they discover about themselves is not their mental age but the relationship of their performance to that of the "average" person who takes the test. (See Applying Our Knowledge "Interpreting an IQ Score" for more information on the meaning of IQ scores.)

Infant Intelligence Testing

Infant "intelligence" tests are more accurately called tests of infant development because they emphasize physical problem solving, basic motor skills, and indicators of social and emotional maturity. Needless to say, they do not contain the verbal emphasis so typical of IQ tests for older children and adults. Perhaps because the infant test examines different manifestations of human intelligence than does the standard IQ test, there is little relationship between scores earned on infant tests

and later IQ scores (Bloom 1964; Ebel & Frisbie 1986).

One of the more widely used infant intelligence tests is the *Bayley Scales of Infant Development* (1969). The Bayley Scales measure an infant's progress from birth to age 2½ in three different developmental areas. The mental scale is a measure of memory, learning, and problem-solving ability; of infant vocalizations, attempts at communication, and later understanding of speech; and of ability to generalize and to make simple classifications (which Bayley saw as the basis for later abstract thinking). The motor scale assesses motor coordination and manipulatory skills. For example, items deal with levels of proficiency in sitting, walking, and grasping objects of various sizes. Finally, the infant behavior record examines a child's emotions, activity level, energy, social tendencies, attitudes,

Applying Our Knowledge

Interpreting an IQ Score

You have been informed that your child's score on the Wechsler Intelligence Scale for Children (WISC-R) is 116. Do you know what this means? Even an awareness that modern IQ tests produce *deviation IQ* rather than *ratio IQ* scores and that a score of 100 indicates average performance does not equip you to understand the meaning of your child's score. You know, of course, that your child's performance is better than the mean, or average, attained by children taking the WISC-R, but how much better is it? To answer this question you need to know about the concept of the normal distribution and about the standard deviation of the test in question.

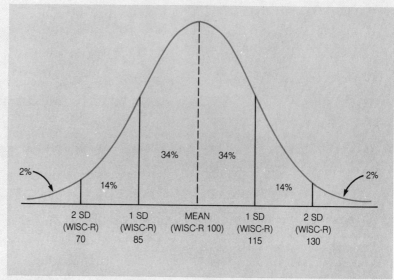

The **normal distribution** is a mathematical concept used to describe the way in which test scores distribute themselves around a mean. As the Figure shows, it is represented in the form of a graph known as a "bell curve."

The bell curve indicates that in a representative sample of a population, the closer a person comes

and interests. For example, the examiner looks at an infant's fearfulness, cooperativeness, goal directedness, and responsiveness to mother and to persons in general.

The mental and motor scales each produce a score referred to as the mental index and the psychomotor index, respectively. As is the case with other intelligence tests, results are expressed in standard scores with a mean value of 100, and each infant's score is expressed in terms of its relationship to the mean. The range is from 50 to 150 on each scale.

Performance on the Bayley Scales of Infant Development, or on any other test of its kind, does not predict later intelligence, but indicates how a particular infant is developing in comparison with the average infant of the same age. Bayley suggested that a value of the test is that developmental problems can be recognized early and corrective treatment begun. Poor performance on the Bayley Scales will not identify the cause of an infant's developmental problem (e.g., sensory deficits, neurological defects, emotional disturbances, or difficulties in the home environment), but will alert a physician or psychologist to the fact that a problem exists and that a search for its causes is warranted.

Group Intelligence Testing

The Stanford-Binet and the Wechsler tests are examples of an **individual intelligence test.** Administered by a professional psychologist to one

to the numerical average score on any particular test, the larger the number of scores that will be found there. Put another way, considerably more people are "average" on any measured characteristic than are exceptionally high or exceptionally low. In terminology more familiar to college students, if a class is distributed normally, more *C*s than *A*s or *F*s are earned on any examination.

The normal curve is segmented into percentages of the population defined by standard deviations above or below the mean. But what is a **standard deviation?** It is a numerical indication of the variance of the individual scores from the mean. To understand this concept, turn to a classroom example:

Sue discovers that her score on an exam was 79, while the average score in the class was 72. Her score is obviously better than the numerical average, but is a 79 a grade of *A* or is it still a *C*? The answer depends on how the other students' scores clustered around the mean. If the range of scores was limited, and most students earned scores between 67 and 75 (that is, the standard deviation was low), Sue's 79 is quite impressive and may correspond to a grade of *A*. If the majority of the class had scores between 62 and 82 and the range was considerably greater (that is, the standard deviation was high), Sue's 79 is less praiseworthy; it might now result in her getting a letter grade of *C*⁺ instead of *A*. It is obvious, therefore, that comparing Sue's score to the mean does not give her enough information; she also needs to know how the scores in the class were grouped around that mean.

A numerical standard deviation can be computed for any group of scores. If the distribution is normal, 34 percent of the population will fall within one standard deviation in either direction from the mean, 14 percent between one and two standard deviations from the mean, and so forth. Turn back now to the original question about the meaning of your child's score of 116 on the WISC-R. The standard deviation on the WISC-R is fifteen points (Wechsler 1974). Thus, 68 percent of children taking the test earn scores between 85 and 115, 14 percent fall between 70 and 84 and 14 percent between 116 and 130, and 2 percent fall above 130 and 2 percent below 70. You now know that your child's score of 116 is above the normal range; your child performed better than approximately 85 percent of the children who take the test and would be considered "high average (bright)" according to the intelligence classifications provided in the WISC-R manual.

person at a time, individual intelligence tests are costly and time-consuming to administer on a large-scale basis. Most people who take intelligence tests take a **group intelligence test.**

The earliest group intelligence test was developed by a committee of psychologists during World War I as a service to the United States Army. This was the *Army Alpha Test,* containing eight subtests—including measures of arithmetical skills, practical judgment, vocabulary, general information, and ability to follow directions. For those recruits who could not read or write, a nonverbal group test, the *Army Beta,* was also developed. More than a million men were tested during World War I, and when the war came to a close, group intelligence testing was fairly well established.

During the 1920s there was a surge of interest in intelligence testing. Psychologists were so pleased by the successful use of the army tests that they pushed for the development of group tests for civilian use; in fact, the Army Alpha Test itself was used in schools and in private industry as a predictor of future success (Haney 1981). Numerous other group intelligence tests made their appearance as the United States became increasingly IQ-conscious. Unfortunately, some of the early group tests were crude instruments and were administered indiscriminately to people of all ages and types, and for every conceivable reason (Anastasi 1982). The ease of administration and scoring (no psychology degree is required) and the possibility of mass testing for research purposes made group tests particularly attractive. These factors probably contributed to the growing IQ-consciousness, as well as to the eventual negative image of the intelligence-testing movement. Many group intelligence tests were and are well-standardized and sensitive instruments, but their indiscriminate use created a backlash in the early years; the result was suspicion and hostility directed toward all forms of psychological testing (Anastasi 1982). In fact, the controversy surrounding the appropriate uses of group intelligence tests still continues today, as will be pointed out in a later section of this chapter dealing with IQ testing in the schools.

The Development of Intelligence During Childhood

What are some of the changes in intelligence-test performance that occur as an individual moves through childhood? By looking at performance on two of the more widely used intelligence tests, the WISC-R and the WAIS-R, a typical pattern can be observed: performance on each of the subtests improves gradually and continually throughout childhood and adolescence until a peak is reached somewhere between the ages of 18 and 25.

There are two points to remember when thinking about age increases in the abilities involved in intelligence. The first is that while improvement occurs in the various abilities, this is not always reflected in improvement in the IQ score. The reason for this is that the test norms change as people get older so that expected improvements in performance are built into the tests themselves. As an example, it is expected that a 9-year-old will have a larger vocabulary than a 7-year-old and will outscore the younger child on the WISC vocabulary subtest. A 7-year-old who knows the meaning of nine words will be awarded four scale points, whereas a 9-year-old would have to define at least thirteen words correctly to get four scale points. However, when scale points are converted to IQ scores, the older child's IQ will not be higher than that of the younger child; the older child is expected to answer more questions than the younger one, and, if improvement does not occur, the IQ score will actually decrease.

A second point to remember about intelligence changes in childhood is that the group stability of the IQ does not rule out individual variation. It has generally been recognized that the IQ is stable throughout childhood, at least after the preschool years. Bayley (1949) found correlations ranging from .80 to .96 between childhood and young adulthood and adolescent and young adulthood scores, respectively. However, this stability is based on group data and does not mean that a particular child's IQ will not change with age. The high correlations between childhood and young adult IQs reveal only that scores change very little relative to one another *within* the group: the high scorers on the first test are the high scorers on the second test, and the low scorers on the first test are the low scorers on the second. However, the average scores for the group may have changed in either direction.

Much of the research literature (e.g., Honzik, MacFarlane & Allen 1948; Sontag, Baker & Nelson 1958; Bayley 1949; Moore 1967) suggests that there is improvement across the childhood and adolescent years in IQ scores, and that there are significant differences for individual children, with some improving markedly and some showing test-retest decline. What all of this means is that consistency *within* the group can exist despite changes in the group average, and even despite dramatic IQ changes for some individuals within the group.

Genetic Factors in Intelligence

Heredity and environment interact in such a manner in determining behavioral characteristics that it is virtually impossible to separate them. Attempts to do so typically focus on situations in which one of the two factors is held constant while the other is allowed to vary. In other words, researchers look for individuals whose genetic characteristics are similar or identical, but whose environments differ considerably, and for individuals whose genetic makeup is quite different, but whose environments are similar or identical. It is considerably easier, however, to find genetically similar individuals than to find those whose environments are identical because the concept of environment

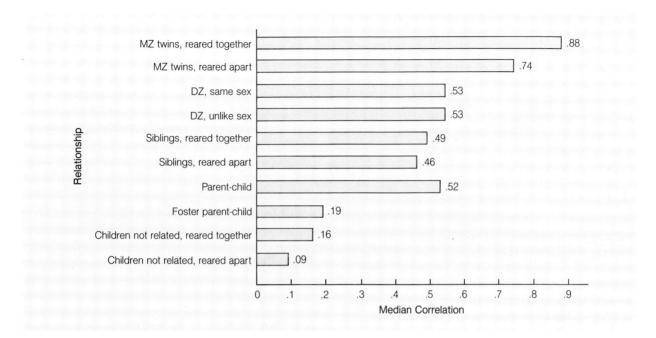

Figure 8.2   IQ Correlations for Various Degrees of Kinship

Source: From *The Psychology of Individual and Group Differences* by Lee Willerman. Copyright 1979 by W.H. Freeman and Company. Used by permission. Originally adapted from Erlenmeyer-Kimling and Jarvik, 1963.

is difficult to define. Are two children raised in the same family raised in the same environment? The physical environment is certainly the same, but the social and psychological environments might be markedly different.

To locate genetically similar people, researchers simply look at kinship patterns. Identical, or monozygotic (MZ), twins are genetically identical; siblings are genetically similar, as are parents and children. Kinship correlations in IQ are found by forming two groups—each containing one member of a kinship pair (e.g., a group made-up of parents and a group made-up of their children)—by determining the IQ scores of the entire sample, and by examining the degree of relationship between the two groups.

Figure 8.2 summarizes the findings of fifty-one kinship correlation studies containing over thirty thousand pairs. The closest family relationships are found at the top of the figure, and the most distant at the bottom. The numbers are cor-

relation coefficients; the higher the number, the higher was the degree of relationship in IQ. When a large number of cases are studied, a number below .40 is generally regarded as a low correlation, a number from .40 to .60 as moderate, and a number above .60 as high.

As can be seen from the figure, the most genetically similar group, monozygotic (MZ) twins, had the highest IQ correlations. That is, knowing the IQ score of one MZ twin would allow a person to predict fairly well the IQ score of the other. For children who were not related, however, there was little or no IQ relationship between the groups, and this was true even if these children were raised in the same environment. In the middle of the chart with moderate correlations in IQ were the fraternal—or dizygotic (DZ)—twins, the siblings, and the parent-child pairs, all of whom are genetically more similar than are unrelated children. What seems to be occurring, therefore, is that the correlations of the IQ scores increase as the individuals increase in genetic similarity, and this is precisely what would be expected if intelligence is genetically linked.

What does Figure 8.2 suggest about the influence of the environment on intelligence? It can be seen that the correlations for each group—MZ twins, siblings, and unrelated persons—differ very little from one another in the "reared together" and "reared apart" conditions. Furthermore, the IQs of MZ twins reared apart are more similar than the IQs of siblings reared in the same environment, and siblings reared apart resemble one another more than do persons reared together who are not related. If intelligence were influenced completely or even largely by the environment, why would unrelated children raised in the same family not be more similar in IQ than are identical twins reared in different families?

Environmentalists respond to the findings of kinship correlation studies by arguing that even when siblings are raised separately, they are usually raised in very similar environments. As Kamin (Eysenck & Kamin 1981) observed, in many studies of "separated twins," the children were hardly separated at all. For example, in one study (Shields 1962), three-quarters of the twins raised separately were raised by relatives, who in all likelihood provided the children with environments similar to what they would have experienced at home. Twins were considered to be separated if at any time during childhood they had lived apart for a period of five years or more. Many of them lived in the same houses during most of their childhood, went to school together, or at least saw each other frequently. Furthermore, Kamin (Eysenck & Kamin 1981) noted that when children are made available for adoption, there is usually an attempt by social-service agencies to place them in homes which closely resemble those of their natural parents (e.g., in race, in religion, and even in the IQs of the parents). Lastly, among identical twins raised separately, the pairs whose adoptive environments were most similar were also most similar in intelligence, while those from radically different adoptive environments differed most in adult intellectual ability (Cronbach 1984).

Kamin (Eysenck & Kamin 1981) also observed that identical twins are more similar in intelligence than are fraternal twins or siblings because identical twins have more similar environments. That is, they are often dressed alike, usually spend a good deal of time together, sleep in the same room, and so forth. On the surface, it does appear likely that identical twins have more similar home environments than other siblings do. However, the question of whether similarity of rearing patterns within a home affects the similarity of children's intelligence has never been answered satisfactorily, in part because sophisticated measures of child-rearing similarity have never been used. It is not enough to simply ask parents if they rear their twins in the same way, as has often been the methodological approach in studies of this type (Loehlin & Nichols 1976).

The Meaning of Heritability

Modern researchers in the area of human intelligence rarely view the hereditary-environment question as an either-or proposition. Instead, they focus on the extent to which genetic and environmental factors determine the IQ. Estimates of the percentage of the genetic contribution to intelligence have been set as low as 40 percent (Scarr 1981), in the middle of the range at 50 to 60 percent (Vernon 1979), and as high as 80 percent (Eysenck & Kamin 1981; Jensen 1981; Herrnstein 1971). These percentages are estimates of **heritability,** the degree to which certain characteristics vary in a given population because of genetic factors. To illustrate the concept of heritability, consider the following example:

Twenty-five children in a physical education class are learning how to play basketball. On the first day of class, each child attempts twelve foul shots. In keeping individual records of successes and failures, the teacher finds a good deal of variation among the children in their ability to throw a basket through a hoop from a specific distance. Assuming that the variation is probably an interaction of hereditary factors (e.g., body size, body proportion, motor coordination, rate of physical development) and environmental factors (e.g., previous experience, motivation, attitude toward sports), the teacher then attempts to determine the *relative* influence of hereditary and environment and to assign a rough percentage to each.

The teacher works with the children for a month—drills them, encourages them, motivates them. Then the original test is repeated. This time the average performance is better, but, more importantly, the variation is considerably reduced. The range of scores, which earlier had been 0 to 10, is now 8 to 11. The teacher concludes that the major reason for the initial variation among the children was that there was much variation in their experience at basketball (an environmental factor). On the other hand, if, despite practice and encouragement, the variation in the group had been reduced hardly at all by the practice sessions, the teacher might have concluded that ability to make foul shots is influenced more by innate characteristics than by experience.

Heritability means the variation within a group and the factors responsible for it. If most of the group variation in any human characteristic is due to hereditary factors, then most of the variation should be eliminated if genetic variation in the group is reduced (e.g., by studying family groupings), but very little variation would be eliminated if the environments of group members are equalized. On the other hand, if environmental factors account for most of the group variation, as in the case of our young basketball players, then reducing environmental variation (e.g., by training procedures) will significantly reduce the variation in the children's performance.

Heritability must always be thought of as a population characteristic rather than as an individual one. For example, the teacher might conclude that environmental factors account for perhaps 80 percent of the variation in basketball skills of the physical education class, but it does not follow that 80 percent of the skill of any particular child is determined by experience. It is possible to generalize from the population, of course, and say that environmental factors are *probably* more important than heredity in the athletic skills of any one child, but any generalization from group to individual characteristics contains the possibility of error.

Advocates of the so-called "hereditarian" approach to the IQ controversy—including Arthur Jensen, Hans Eysenck, and Richard J. Herrnstein—suggest that heredity is more important in determining intelligence variation within a population than are the effects of the environment—approximately twice as important, to be specific. They do not set percentages on the hereditary and environmental factors in the intelligence of an individual, nor do they argue that intelligence is fixed in an absolute sense. To quote from Eysenck:

> All that is said applies to conditions at a given time in a given place. Current environmental conditions in Western countries produce the results we have discussed. It is possible that new discoveries, either in physiology or in education, may alter conditions, and that in the new environment the population may achieve a different mean IQ, or a different distribution, or a different heritability. (Eysenck & Kamin 1981, 60)

In summary, the hereditary and environmental question is not an either-or issue. No one denies that a person's environment can influence his or her intelligence. Similarly, very few psychologists deny all genetic influence on intelligence. The question is one of the degree of influence of the two factors. Estimates of the heritability of intelligence range from 40 to 80 percent, but the heritability data apply to particular populations and not to individuals. Heredity may play a significant role in determining differences within a population, but no one can estimate the size of the genetic contribution to any one person's intelligence. Finally, the data on the heritability of intelligence apply only to the populations that have been studied in certain Western societies living in the world today. They cannot be applied to the past, nor should they be used to predict future intelligence patterns.

The Issue of Racial Differences

The question of differences in intelligence between groups of black and white American children may be the most controversial question raised by psychologists and educators today. Before examining the findings from studies of "racial" differences in intelligence, it should be pointed out that psychologists, anthropologists, and behavioral geneticists disagree as to whether race should be thought of as a biological concept, or even whether race is a legitimate concept at all. Races are subgroups of a particular species, identified as races because they exhibit different gene frequencies. However, although some genetic differences are found, human racial groups are not completely different. Gene exchange occurs continuously because the human "races" are not geographically isolated from one another and because we reproduce sexually. Therefore, the classification of the human species into races is somewhat arbitrary, depending on *which* genetic differences are attended to. There is no correct number of human racial groups. In fact, if detailed enough measurements are taken, any two breeding populations could be found to show some genetic differences (Loehlin, Lindzey & Spuhler 1975).

The Findings

Studies of black-white differences in performance on intelligence tests, in both American and European populations, yield a consistent pattern of results: whites score an average of fifteen points higher on IQ tests than do blacks, with average scores of 100 and 85 respectively, and these differences have been observed repeatedly for the past sixty years (Jensen 1969, 1981; Loehlin, Lindzey & Spuhler 1975; Vernon 1979). When Orientals have been included in the studies, the usual finding is of no IQ differences between Orientals and whites, or of minor variations in the pattern of their performances (Loehlin, Lindzey & Spuhler 1975; Vernon 1979). Occasionally, however, differences have been found in favor of Oriental populations. For example, Lynn (1977, 1982) administered the WISC-R to 1,100 Japanese children and reported an average score of 111, eleven points above the average for American and European whites.

The Attempts at Explanation

There are no widely accepted scientific explanations for racial and ethnic differences in IQ-test performance; there are only hypotheses. The genetic hypothesis, promoted by Arthur Jensen (1969, 1981), states that racial differences in IQ can be attributed to genetic differences among the races and, to a much lesser degree, to environmental

factors. Jensen's argument has two main thrusts: First, whenever there are differences between socially isolated breeding populations in a highly heritable characteristic, such as intelligence, the differences are probably genetically caused. Second, environmental explanations of IQ differences have failed to specify the factors which influence IQ or to explain why these factors appear to affect some racial groups more than others.

Opponents of the genetic hypothesis (e.g., Eysenck & Kamin 1981; Weiss & Mann 1981) argue that Jensen has misused the heritability concept. They point out that variation *within* a population may indeed have a genetic basis, but it does not follow that variations *between* populations are genetically caused.

To better understand the between-within distinction, consider the following example (Eysenck & Kamin 1981): A farmer fills a white sack and a black sack with equal mixtures of different genetic varieties of corn seed. He then plants the seed from the white sack in one field, and the seed from the black sack in another. The first of the two fields is more fertile than the second; when the crop comes in, the corn in the first field is taller and stronger. However, the amount of variance *within* each field is identical because the genetic variance in each sack was the same. Clearly, the variation *within* each field is genetically caused, but would the farmer also attribute the difference in yield *between* the two fields to genetic factors? In all likelihood, he would conclude that it was the difference in the soil (an environmental factor) which resulted in the different crops.

Kamin (1974; Eysenck & Kamin 1981) argued that racial differences in IQ result from differences in the social, intellectual, and physical environments in which blacks and whites are raised—differences in the "soil" in which they are grown. Such environmental hypotheses are difficult to prove, however. The farmer can easily test *his* environmental hypothesis by equating the environments in which the different types of seed are grown: he can plant both sacks of corn in the same field. Psychologists and educators have a much more difficult time of it. Can we ever really "equate" the environments of black and white children in this country in order to examine environmental influences? How can we even define all of the factors that make up any person's social and intellectual environment? Which of these factors do and which do not affect a person's intelligence?

Some equations of a sort can be effected by matching the populations studied on various sociocultural factors. For example, if psychologists examine not a random selection of the general population, but groups of black and white children matched according to parents' level of education, income, or occupation, they have "equated" the children on the factor of socioeconomic status. When this is done, the black-white IQ differences are reduced considerably; lower-class blacks and lower-class whites, for example, differ in IQ by an average of only three points (Loehlin, Lindzey & Spuhler 1975). Socioeconomic status may account for some of the racial differences in IQ that are observed when groups are not matched on this variable, since American blacks and whites as groups usually differ in social class as well as in ethnic origin. However, as Cronbach (1984) pointed out, even when racial groups are matched on such variables as years of parental education or job title, we still may not have truly equivalent groups; hidden differences may exist in the quality of education received or in the types of responsibilities and opportunities encompassed by a job title.

A second method used to "equate" the environments of black and white American children involves direct intervention: the implementation of educational programs designed to provide children with a richer variety of intellectual experiences than they would ordinarily receive at home or in the traditional school. A number of such programs were implemented during the 1960s and 1970s (Cronbach 1984). These have been referred to as intervention, enrichment, or **compensatory education** programs.

As an illustration of a successful enrichment program, consider the one designed by Heber and Garber (1970). Twenty black infants of low-IQ mothers living in a Milwaukee slum area were selected to participate in an intensive enrichment experience. This experience was not designed specifically to increase IQ but to prevent progressive retardation. Every day from the age of 3 months until they entered the first grade, the children were brought to an infant education center and were involved in an intensive program of sensory and language stimulation. The stimulated infants were tested periodically between the ages of 2 and 5½ and compared with a control group of children from similar backgrounds who did not participate in the program. The results were most encouraging—the children exposed to the enrichment program received average IQ scores of 125, approximately thirty points higher than the average for the control group.

Early critics of compensatory education (e.g., Jensen 1969) argued that children in such programs were being specifically trained in the skills required to perform well on IQ tests rather than experiencing any real gains in intelligence. In support of their argument, they pointed out that the IQ gains resulting from enrichment programs are often temporary; in fact, it was not an unusual occurrence, both in the United States and Europe, for such IQ gains to fade by the time follow-up studies were done (Tizard 1974).

Supporters of the compensatory education movement responded that IQ-test performance alone is not a meaningful indicator of program success because IQ tests measure too narrow a range of behavior (Bronfenbrenner 1979). They further pointed out the need for long-term follow-up studies of children who had *continuing* support for their intellectual growth. As Kagan (1969) observed:

> It would be nonsense to assume that feeding animal protein to a seriously malnourished child for three days would lead to a permanent increase in his height and weight, if after 72 hours of steak and eggs he was sent back to his malnourished environment. It *may be* that compensatory education is of little value, but this idea has not been tested in any adequate way up to now. (P. 128)

Finally, others noted that the success or failure of any particular program depends on the quality of the program itself, and that some types of programs appear to be more effective than others. As an illustration of this point, Sprigle and Schaefer

These children are in a Head Start class, designed to "equate" the intellectual environments of lower and middle class children by offering an enriched educational experience.

(1985) found that a structured program focused on teaching problem-solving strategies in small-group settings is more effective at the elementary school level than is a more general and less structured enrichment program.

As compensatory education programs flourished in the 1960s and 1970s, so, too, did the controversy surrounding their effectiveness. Now that it is possible to look back at this movement from the vantage point of the 1980s, what can we conclude? The view from the present is actually quite encouraging. Recent studies seem to provide evidence that gains made by children enrolled in a variety of preschool enrichment programs of the 1960s have lasted at least up to three or four years (Becker & Gersten 1982; Lazar et al. 1982). It is unlikely that such gains would be the result of nothing other than practice.

Lazar and his associates (1982) analyzed the long-term results of eleven intervention programs carried out during the years from 1963 to 1972. These programs involved black and poor preschool children from various cities and small towns in the Northeast, Midwest, and Southeast. Included were *home-based programs,* in which an educator brought toys and educational activities to the home and instructed the child's mother in their use; *center-based programs,* which used a standard nursery school format, small-group interaction, and parental observation but not direct involvement; and *combinations of home- and center-based programs.* At the time of the Lazar follow-up study, the children ranged in age from 8 to 18. A variety of measures were used to assess the impacts of the various programs in terms of children's intelligence, school success, and attitudes and values. Included also were interviews to determine what, if any, impact the intervention experiences had had on the children's families.

The findings of the Lazar follow-up study were quite encouraging. IQ gains, as measured by the WISC-R, persisted even four years after the terminations of the various programs. Children who had been enrolled in the intervention programs were higher in school competence than a control group of children who had had no such early education experience; they were less likely to be held back in school, and only half as likely to be assigned to special education classes. (School competence was defined as the ability of the child to meet the requirements of his or her school, without being required to retake classes or to enroll in special education programs.) In terms of their attitudes and values, graduates of the enrichment programs were significantly more likely than controls to have positive attitudes toward themselves that were linked to their school or their work achievements. Finally, one of the most promising findings reported in the study was that mothers of children who had been in enrichment programs were more satisfied with their children's current school performance and had higher aspirations for their children's futures than did mothers of children in the control group. Such parental support could be a significant factor in determining whether or not the intellectual gains from compensatory education programs are lasting ones.

The Controversy Today

Where do psychologists and educators now stand in their attempts to interpret black-white differences in IQ-test performance? Since the data on heritability of the IQ do not support a definitive conclusion that racial differences in IQ are genetically-linked, and since studies of environmental effects on human intelligence have barely begun to explore the issue in depth, there is no single satisfactory explanation for these differences. After completing what is perhaps the most exhaustive review to date of racial differences in IQ, Loehlin, Lindzey, and Spuhler (1975) could only conclude that the differences were due to (1) environmental conditions, (2) genetic differences, (3) inadequacies or biases in some of the tests themselves, and (4) interactions of any or all of the above factors. In

another survey of the research on racial-ethnic IQ differences, Vernon (1979) listed thirty conclusions that can be safely drawn. Thirteen of his conclusions supported the genetic interpretation of racial differences, eleven supported the environmental interpretation, four could be used to support either interpretation, and two supported neither. Such is the current state of knowledge in this area.

Environmental Influences on Intelligence

In an earlier section of this chapter, developmental changes in intelligence during childhood were discussed. It was pointed out that intelligence tends to increase throughout the elementary and high school years, but that the increase is expressed in terms of averages; some chidren have significant IQ gains, some have little or no gains, and some show IQ declines throughout childhood. What are the reasons for these individual differences? Answers to this question typically point in the direction of environmental influences on intelligence. This section examines some of the ways a child's cultural surroundings may influence intellectual growth.

Child-rearing Patterns

IQ gainers tend to come from families in which there is parental warmth, attentiveness, and a generally positive attitude toward the children (Skeels & Dye 1939; Bayley & Schaefer 1964). Overly strict or punitive parents tend to raise children whose IQs are less likely to increase (Bayley & Schaefer 1964). Furthermore, the parents of IQ gainers encourage academic achievement in their children and provide accelerated educational experiences (McCall, Appelbaum & Hogarty 1973), whereas children from intellectually impoverished home environments have actually shown IQ declines with age (Gordon 1923; Roberts et al 1965; Sherman & Key 1932).

When interpreting studies of child-rearing patterns in the homes of IQ gainers or decliners, a certain amount of caution should be used for two

Parents of children whose IQ's are likely to increase encourage academic achievement and provide accelerated educational experiences.

reasons. First, the evidence provided by such studies is correlational rather than causal. That is, parents who stress academic achievement may not actually be causing IQ gains in their children. Perhaps it is the case that some parents perceive in their children an advanced level of intellectual functioning and respond to this perception by stressing academic achievement. Thus, a child's intellectual level could influence parents' child-rearing patterns as easily as the reverse.

A second reason for caution in interpreting the results of such studies is that it may not be the child-rearing approach, but the IQs of the parents themselves that influences the intellectual growth of children. In other words, the parents who provide the most intellectually stimulating home environment might be the most intelligent parents to begin with; therefore, the intellectual gains of the children could be attributable to genetic rather than environmental factors. In fact, the mother's IQ alone predicts her child's intelligence very well, but only until the child is 2 years old; after that, maternal IQ alone is not a good predictor of a child's IQ—the intellectual stimulation of the home environment must also be considered (Yeates et al. 1983). In other words, the quality of the home environment becomes increasingly influential on the child's IQ as the child gets older.

Nutrition

It has long been recognized that nutritional factors and intellectual development in childhood are related. More specifically, severe malnutrition in the first few years of life is correlated with a lowered IQ in later childhood or adolescence (DeLicardie & Cravioto 1974; Galler, Ramsey & Solimano 1985; Richardson 1976; Ricciuti 1981; Puri et al. 1984; Winick, Meyer & Harris 1975). What has not been established is a direct causal link between malnutrition and intellectual impairment, or the degree to which diet alone affects the intellect. The difficulty faced by researchers in this area is that malnutrition among infants is related to a variety of negative factors in the home environment. Children who are malnourished often come from homes in which there is little social, emotional, or intellectual stimulation; as a result, nutritional factors are not easy to isolate as influences on intellectual growth.

Attempts have been made to separate the effects of malnutrition from adverse psychological effects in the home (e.g., Richardson 1976), but the relative contribution of nutritional factors varies from study to study (Ricciuti 1981). However, it appears that the possible negative effects on a child's intellect of even severe early malnutrition can be minimized or prevented by a positive home atmosphere; nutritional supplements for malnourished children have been found to reverse the negative effects on the intellect of an inadequate diet, but only if the overall home environment is supportive of emotional, social, and intellectual growth (Ricciuti 1981; Winick, Meyer & Harris 1975).

Birth Order and Family Size

The fact that a child's level of intelligence is influenced by parents' child-rearing patterns, as well as by within-family genetic similarity, would lead us to expect that siblings would be similar to one another in intelligence. Indeed, as noted earlier in the discussion of kinship correlations, siblings are more similar in IQ than are unrelated children, but within-family variations still exist. To explain these variations, the factors of birth order and family size have been cited. For example, Belmont and Marolla (1973) examined military records of nearly four hundred thousand men living in Holland, and found relationships between level of intelligence and both family size and birth order: firstborn children performed better on IQ tests than did second-

borns, and second-born children did better than third-borns, and so forth.

To explain this birth-order difference, which appeared in later studies as well, Zajonc and Markus (1975) developed what is known as the **confluence theory**: the intelligence of each family member is influenced by the average intellectual ability of the other family members. Thus, the firstborn child is influenced by the average intellectual ability of the parents, while later-born children are influenced by the average ability of the parents *and* the older siblings. The hypothetical average ability of the family decreases as family size increases, since children are intellectually less capable than their parents.

Intriguing as it may be, support for the confluence theory has not been impressive. A number of recent studies (e.g., Galbraith 1982; Price, Walsh & Vilberg 1984; Rodgers 1984; Rodgers & Rowe 1985) have questioned the notion that each additional child in a family is less intelligent than those who came before. In examining children's IQs within 1,173 families, Rodgers and Rowe (1985) found no evidence that family size or birth order had an influence on the intelligence of the individual child. As a further illustration that no simple birth-order model can explain IQ variation among siblings, and as a challenge to the notion that the firstborn is the most advantaged, McCall (1984) observed that IQ performance of an older child actually dropped ten points after a new sibling was born; fortunately, the drop was a temporary one.

Gender Roles

In examining IQ gains during childhood, researchers typically discover that males are more likely to experience gains than females (Bayley 1968; Moore 1967; Roberts et al 1965; Sontag et al. 1958), with the difference usually being attributed to cultural rather than to biological factors. It has even been suggested that girls who are the most accepting of the traditional feminine gender roles are least likely to experience IQ gains and most likely to show a pattern of actual decline during adolescence (Campbell 1976)! That the IQ difference between males and females becomes increasingly evident during early adolescence might be seen as further evidence that the difference is culturally determined; it is during early adolescence that gender roles become increasingly inflexible (Lamb & Urberg 1978), and the female gender role in our culture frequently involves a denial of intellectual potential (Datan & Hughes 1985; Troll 1984).

Uses and Interpretations of Intelligence Scores

Throughout this chapter, the difficulty of defining and measuring human intelligence has been emphasized, but the assumption has been made that there is some value in trying to do so. This final section deals with the practical value of IQ tests. It begins with a discussion of the tests and asks the question What is the relationship between IQ-test performance and success or failure in dealing with the worlds of school and work? Then follows a discussion of the controversial uses of IQ testing in the schools and a examination of some of the frequent misuses of IQ tests.

What IQ Scores Really Predict

There would be little value in a test of intellectual ability if the results were in no way related to performance in the real world. Since people presumably use their intelligence in their everyday functioning, we would expect a degree of relationship between IQ scores and success in meeting life's daily challenges. In fact, such relationships do exist.

Before discussing the predictive power of IQ tests, a few words about the meaning of prediction are in order. Prediction is being discussed here in the statistical sense; one variable is said to predict another if even a modest degree of relationship has been established between the two. Statistical prediction involves no guarantee of future performance and is based on group rather than on individual data. What this means is that a finding of a positive relationship between IQ and classroom performance may lead us to assert that IQ scores predict school grades. It does not mean, however,

that Jane will definitely be successful in school because she earns a high-IQ score or that John has little chance of succeeding in the classroom because his IQ score is low. In reality, a number of factors (e.g., gender, motivational level, self-image) other than the intellectual processes measured by IQ tests are related to school success. Parents concerned about a child's academic potential would receive more meaningful information from a sensitive teacher than from an IQ score.

IQ and School Performance

Throughout years of research a consistent pattern has emerged concerning the relationship between IQ and school performance. There are modest but significant correlations at various grade levels between IQ and school grades (Matarazzo 1972; Minton & Schneider 1980), between IQ and rank in class (Conry & Plant 1965; Willerman 1979), between IQ and tests of general academic achievement (Bossard & Galusha 1979), and between IQ and the ultimate educational attainment (years of schooling completed) of adults (Matarazzo 1972; McCall 1977). In addition, there are positive correlations between IQ and success in specific academic subject areas, such as mathematics, science, social studies, language arts, and reading (Bloom et al. 1981; Kavrell & Petersen 1986). Finally, there is a link between low-IQ scores and the tendency to drop out of high school (Brody & Brody 1976), although the decision to drop out of high school is related to many social, cultural, and personality factors as well as to intellectual ability.

In summary, a relationship exists between IQ-test performance and many aspects of school performance in children, adolescents, and adults. In fact, it would be surprising if intelligence were not related to academic achievement in some way, if only because classroom performance and IQ-test performance may require similar cognitive and verbal skills. Nevertheless, IQ scores themselves are thought to be of little predictive value for teachers because of the many variables involved in classroom performance; in fact, the best predictor of future academic achievement is not a standardized test score at all, but is the student's current level of academic achievement (Antonak, King & Lowy 1982; Ebel & Frisbie 1986).

IQ and the World of Work

An examination of the link between IQ and performance in the job world produces a mix of findings. There is definitely a relationship between IQ and occupational status (Matarazzo 1972; McCall 1977b; Willerman 1979). That is, people in high-status professional-level careers (e.g., accountants, engineers, teachers) tend on the average to have higher IQs than people in the lower-status nonprofessional careers (e.g., skilled laborers, truck drivers, miners).

There is another way of looking at the relationship between IQ and success in the work world, however. We might look *within* particular careers at the relationship of IQ and job success. That is, we might ask if teachers with higher IQs are more successful than teachers with lower IQs, rather than compare teachers as a group with a group of skilled laborers. Such within-career analyses do not yield significant findings; IQ scores may predict occupational status, but they are considerably less effective in predicting success on the job (Matarazzo 1972; Willerman 1979). The reasons are similar to the reasons discussed earlier for not using IQ scores to predict school achievement; many factors are involved in job success as in school success, and these include motivation, interest, and overall emotional well-being in the workplace.

IQ and Success in Life

To what extent is there a relationship between performance on an IQ test and life success as measured by conventional standards of wealth, fame, and educational attainment? To answer this question, Terman in 1921 identified a group of over fifteen hundred children and adolescents (aged 3 to 19) whose IQ scores placed them in the top 2 percent of the population. These children have been tested and interviewed repeatedly over the past sixty years, most recently in 1977; most of those who are still living are now retired. The goal of this massive longitudinal study has been to determine whether highly intelligent people live their lives any differently than does the general population.

According to psychologists Pauline and Robert Sears (Goleman 1980) the majority of Terman's highly intelligent people have done remarkably well for themselves. In terms of educational attainment, they were considerably ahead of the national average. Two-thirds of them were college graduates, and nearly 30 percent eventually earned advanced degrees (97 Ph.D.s, 92 law degrees, 57 medical degrees, 177 master's degrees). There was great diversity of career choice among the highly intelligent group—there were writers, lawyers, entrepreneurs, film directors, bankers, scientists, and mail carriers—and they seemed to be highly successful in whatever career they chose. Many were nationally known figures by the time they reached middle age. For example, one was an Academy Award-winning film director, another a highly popular writer of science fiction. As a whole the group had produced nearly three thousand books, monographs, and scientific articles. Perhaps it is not surprising that the income level of Terman's sample at middle age was remarkably high—four times the national average!

We cannot conclude, of course, that the lives of highly intelligent people are better in an absolute sense than those of people of lower intelligence, nor can we conclude that a high degree of intelligence is in itself a guarantee of accomplishment. However, by many standards of success (educational attainment, wealth, fame) the participants in Terman's study had certainly distinguished themselves. Performance on IQ tests clearly bears some relationship to performance in the "real world."

Intelligence Testing in the Schools

Throughout this chapter several references have been made to the potential for abuse of IQ scores. How should intelligence tests be properly used? This section attempts to answer that question by discussing the uses of IQ tests in the school system.

There are two primary purposes for using intelligence tests in the school system: clinical diagnosis and guidance (Ebel & Frisbie 1986). Clinical diagnosis involves identifying children who have specific intellectual deficiencies, for the purpose of placing such children in remedial programs or special education classes. Ordinarily, the intelligence tests used for this purpose are individual tests, administered and interpreted by a trained psychologist. Furthermore, the IQ test is only one of a

Problems in Child Development

Defining Mental Retardation

Approximately 6 million Americans, or 3 percent of the population, could be classified as mentally retarded, but what does this label mean? According to the American Association of Mental Deficiency (AAMD), mental retardation has three essential characteristics: (1) it is indicated by a score of 70 or lower on an intelligence test, (2) it involves an impairment in a child's ability to adapt to his or her environment, and (3) it first appears during the years of childhood or adolescence (Goldstein, Baker & Jamison 1986).

A low-IQ score *alone* is not an adequate indicator of mental retardation, primarily because a child may perform poorly on an IQ test for many reasons other than actual

mental impairment (e.g., visual or speech problems, motor-coordination problems, high anxiety, low motivation). Nevertheless, in a diagnosis of retardation based on a variety of relevant determining factors, IQ scores are used by the AAMD to define levels of impairment, as shown in the table.

For a diagnosis of mental retardation to be made, the criterion of a low-IQ score must be accompanied by the criterion of poor adaptive behavior. Adaptation problems are defined differently by the AAMD, depending on the age of the child in question, as indicated below (Grossman 1983):

Infancy and Early Childhood
- Problems in sensory and motor-skill development
- Problems in the development of communication skills

- Difficulty in taking care of self-needs (in the second year of life and beyond)
- Inability to interact socially with other children or adults

Later Childhood and Adolescence
- Problems in sensory and motor-skill development
- Inability to interact socially with other individuals or to participate in group activities
- Inability to apply basic academic skills to everyday life
- Inability to use appropriate judgment in everyday activities

The experience of mental retardation may be particularly trying for children, particularly if the people in their environments do not understand their problems. Mildly retarded children, who are aware of their limitations, do not perform as well in learning situations and, as a result, may be less motivated to

number of psychological tests administered to a child suspected of having a learning disability. No placement decision should be made on the basis of IQ-test results alone. (Problems in Child Development "Defining Mental Retardation" discusses the use of IQ scores as one indicator of mental retardation.)

The second purpose of intelligence testing in the schools—guidance—is to help teachers, counselors, parents, and administrators to make decisions about the effectiveness of current and future educational programs (Ebel & Frisbie 1986). Typically, group intelligence tests are used for this purpose, and, as in the case of clinical diagnosis, IQ

scores constitute only a part of the information obtained for program planning.

Even though the IQ score is only one part of the total picture of a child's intellectual functioning in the school, the use of intelligence testing has become controversial within the past twenty years. In reviewing the history of the controversy, Bersoff (1981) pointed out that in 1967 minority group members challenged the constitutionality of using group IQ-test scores to place school children according to ability level. The ruling in this case, known as *Hobson v. Hansen,* was that, in fact, such group measures were culturally biased instruments and were being used to discriminate against and deny educational opportunities to minority group

perform new tasks; they are often more anxious than the average child, more likely to feel frustrated by their limitations, and more likely to have lowered self-esteem (Goldstein, Baker & Jamison 1986). It seems clear that adults who work with children in any capacity need to have an understanding of the concept of mental retardation and how a diagnosis of retardation is reached; they need also to be sensitive to the dangers of applying negative labels to any child, since the psychological impact of intellectual limitations can vary depending upon a child's social circumstances.

Levels of Mental Retardation

IQ Score	Category	Description
50-55 to 70	Mild Mental Retardation	Children in this category, comprising three-fourths of all those diagnosed as retarded, are considered "educable." They are often placed in special classrooms that teach academic skills up to a sixth-grade level. Increasingly, such children are being "mainstreamed" into regular classrooms.
35-40 to 50-55	Moderate Mental Retardation	Between 10 and 20 percent of all retarded children fit into this category. They are usually said to be "trainable" and are taught basic skills (e.g., housekeeping, counting money) that will allow them to function independently as adults.
20-25 to 35-40	Severe Mental Retardation Profound Mental Retardation	Because their mental impairment is so great and because they often have physical handicaps as well, children in these categories are often institutionalized. However, in recent years there have been increasing attempts to train these children in basic skills, either in regular classrooms or in special centers.

members. (For an explanation of cultural bias, see Issues in Child Development "Is There a Cultural Bias in IQ Testing?") In 1979, in the *Larry P. v. Riles* case, similar charges of cultural bias were raised against two of the best-known individual intelligence tests—the Stanford-Binet Intelligence Scale and the Wechsler Intelligence Scale for Children (WISC-R). A California federal district court ruled in favor of the minority group plaintiffs; it said in effect that the Stanford-Binet and the WISC were culturally biased against minority group children, and their use in the placement of children in classes for the educationally mentally retarded was evidence of discrimination. To complicate the issue, however, a federal district court ruling in Illinois the following year directly contradicted the California ruling. In *PASE v. Hannon*, an Illinois federal judge ruled that the Stanford-Binet and the WISC were *not* culturally biased, and their use in clinical diagnosis was perfectly appropriate if they were used in conjunction with many other sources of information about children's academic potential.

The controversy about intelligence testing in the schools still remains, in part because the issue of cultural bias in testing has never been fully resolved and in part because not all social scientists and educators are convinced that the IQ score is viewed as only a small part of the total picture. Some would argue (e.g., Berk, Bridges & Shih 1981)

Issues in Child Development

Is There a Cultural Bias in IQ Testing?

One of the most frequently heard criticims of the IQ concept is that IQ tests themselves are biased in favor of people who grow up in the white middle-class culture. Members of minority groups, such as blacks, Puerto Ricans, and Mexican Americans, are at a distinct disadvantage when taking such tests for two reasons:

1. The questions themselves tap knowledge pertaining to the white middle-class culture (e.g., "Which word does not belong?" *cello, drum, viola, guitar, violin).* Such knowledge is less accessible to members of minority cultures.

2. The tests are presented in and responses must be given in the language of the white middle-class culture. Many minority group members speak a foreign language or a variation of "street English" that differs considerably from standard English; therefore, minority group test-takers are being tested in their second language.

In opposition to the cultural-bias argument, advocates of intelligence testing suggest that the most widely used intelligence tests have taken into account any cultural differences which may exist in our society. They have done this by including a broad cross-section of the American public in the standardization sample, and by carefully avoiding a sample that would give an advantage to any particular subculture. Furthermore, they argue that subcultural linguistic differences are greatly exaggerated; virtually all people in our society are exposed via the media to standard English, regardless of the dialect they choose to speak at home.

The cultural-bias argument appears to be one which nobody can win, because neither position can be proven conclusively. It seems fair to say, however, that a truly culture-free test would be extremely difficult, if not impossible, to develop; since we all function within a cultural framework, how can a test developer ever be completely separated from that framework? It also seems fair to conclude that no intelligence test is a perfect instrument, and test inadequacies contribute to some extent to observed racial/cultural IQ differences.

An interesting solution to the cultural-bias problem in IQ testing was offered by sociologist Jane Mercer of the University of California (Rice 1979). Mercer developed an instrument known as the *System of Multicultural Pluralistic Assessment* (SOMPA). The SOMPA consists of (1) a Wechsler IQ test, to measure the child's mental ability within the dominant culture; (2) a one-hour interview with the child's parent to obtain a health history of the child, a complete picture of the child's home life and family background, and a measure of the child's ability to function effectively in his or her everyday environment; and (3) a complete physical examination. After administering the SOMPA, Mercer combines all of the information she has gathered and adjusts the Wechsler IQ score accordingly. For example, a child who does poorly on the WISC, but who comes from an impoverished home environment and who handles everyday problems quite effectively, would have the WISC score adjusted upward.

The merits of the particular SOMPA battery have been hotly debated, but Mercer's approach illustrates an important point to be made about intelligence testing: the more information we have about a child's ability and performance, the better able we are to make meaningful decisions about that child's future. The IQ score should not be considered in isolation, but as only one piece of information in a complicated pattern of human intellectual functioning.

that schools use IQ scores for ability grouping far more extensively than they admit. This may be the case, despite the consistent warnings of testing experts that we should not rely too heavily on IQ scores, or on any one type of score, in deciding children's educational futures. Even if a test were a perfect instrument, it could be a highly destructive one if used irresponsibly.

Frequent Misuses of IQ Tests

Even advocates of IQ tests warn that, as may occur with any sensitive instrument, such tests can easily be misused. Misuse is particularly likely if persons who administer and/or interpret tests are inexperienced, careless, or simply insensitive. Among the common misuses of IQ tests, as discussed by Lutey and Copeland (1982), are the following:

- Overstatement of what the test is capable of assessing, as outlined in the accompanying test manual
- Failure to look at test results in the overall context of the subject's educational background, personal problems, and actual behavior during testing
- Failure of the examiner to provide a written report describing the meaning of the specific test results along with the score itself
- Examiner deviations from the standardized instructions for administering a test, such as offering rewards for good performance when no such practice is specified in the test manual
- Use of an IQ test to justify a decision about a person after that decision has already been made
- Careless errors in test administration and scoring.

It becomes clear from an examination of such abuses that the administration of IQ tests and the interpretation of results are highly demanding skills. Parents and teachers involved in making decisions about a child's future must recognize their limited ability to interpret intelligence-test results. They owe it to the child to acquire a full knowledge of the strengths and limitations of the test that was used, of the specific purposes for which it was developed, and of the circumstances under which it was administered. They must examine carefully the psychologist's written report that accompanies the score obtained from an individual test. They must recognize that any type of test is of little or no value unless administered and interpreted properly, and that the results from a single test should never form the basis of a judgment about a child's educational future. It is fair to say that much of the criticism of intelligence tests themselves should really be directed at the ways in which the results are often abused.

Summary

1. Intelligence should be considered as a concept which describes a person's problem-solving behavior in a particular setting rather than as an entity that people possess.
2. There is a large variety of definitions of intelligence, with some theorists arguing that a single general reasoning ability is involved in all intelligent behavior and others maintaining that many separate but related factors are involved.
3. Intelligence testing began in the early years of the twentieth century. The first widely used individual test was developed for the French Ministry of Education of Alfred Binet in 1905. Group tests were originally developed for the United States Army in 1917 and 1918.
4. A regular increase in intelligence occurs throughout childhood. Intellectual development reaches a peak in young adulthood.
5. There are wide individual differences in intellectual development, with some persons growing or declining faster than others.
6. Heredity plays a significant role in explaining IQ variation within a given population. However, no one has been able to determine the relative contributions of heredity and environment to the intelligence of an individual.
7. The heredity-environment question in intelligence should not be thought of an an either-or proposition. It is likely that both factors interact in determining intellectual ability.
8. The concept of race is not a purely biological one, but is psychological, cultural, political, and economic as well. The definition of races is somewhat arbitrary.
9. Racial differences are usually observed in performance on IQ tests, with whites and Orientals earning average scores approximately fifteen points higher than blacks. However, there is currently no adequate explanation for these findings.

10. Child-rearing patterns are related to IQ development in the sense that children's IQs are most likely to increase when parents are warm, attentive, and supportive of intellectual accomplishment.

11. The influence of birth order or family size on a child's intelligence is limited, and studies favoring such a relationship have come under increasingly heavy criticism in recent years.

12. Males are more likely to show IQ gains during childhood than are females, particularly when the girl assumes a more traditional gender role.

13. Childhood IQ scores are related to educational achievement in childhood and adolescence, to ultimate educational attainment in adulthood, and to adult occupational status.

14. Intelligence tests are used in the schools to identify children with intellectual difficulties and to engage in current and future program planning. Psychologists recommend that IQ scores never be used in isolation from other data about children's intellectual functioning.

Key Terms

reliability
validity
ratio IQ
deviation IQ
normal distribution
standard deviation

individual intelligence test
group intelligence test
heritability
compensatory education
confluence theory

Suggested Readings

Eysenck, H.J. & Kamin, L. (1981). *The intelligence controversy.* New York: Wiley.

The hereditarian and the environmentalist views of intelligence as presented by the leading advocate of each position. The format is that of a debate; the two "sides" of the issue were written separately, but each author was then asked to comment in writing about the other's argument. The result is a stimulating, and often heated, discussion of one of the major controversies in the field of human development.

Kamin, L. (1974). *The science and politics of IQ.* Potomac, MD: Erlbaum.

Sobering and important reading for human development or psychology students. Leon Kamin, an impassioned advocate of the environmentalist position on intelligence, argues that the IQ concept has been destructive since its inception. For example, he describes how intelligence testing was used to restrict immigration to the United States of racial and ethnic minorities perceived to be undesirable.

Loehlin, J.C., Lindzey, G. & Spuhler, J.N. (1975). *Race differences in intelligence.* San Francisco: Freeman.

A straightforward and comprehensive review of the literature dealing with racial/ethnic differences in IQ performance. The authors examine a number of complicated issues: the meaning of race, the concept of heritability, the difficulties in measuring intelligence, and the sociopolitical implications of research in this area. One-quarter of the book is devoted to a number of enlightening and useful appendices pertaining to the topic.

Sternberg, R.J. (1986). *Intelligence applied: Understanding and increasing your intellectual skills.* New York: Harcourt Brace Jovanovich.

An engaging presentation of Sternberg's theory of human intelligence, including numerous examples of tests of componential, experiential, and contextual intelligence. Included also are exercises for developing and three aspects of intelligence and a fascinating summary chapter devoted to the topic of why intelligent people often fail.

Readings from the Literature

Many research articles in the field of child development are based on data from major longitudinal studies. The article that follows contains information about participants in the Fels Longitudinal Study, begun in the 1930s and still in progress. The article deals in general with the impact of environmental factors on the IQ score, and specifically with the impact of the birth of a younger sibling on the IQ performance of children. As you read, keep in mind the following questions:

- *Could a researcher obtain information about long-term effects on IQ of the birth of a sibling by using any other type of research design? What are the unique advantages of a longitudinal design?*

- *Do the findings of the study give us any information about the ways in which parents treat siblings differently from one another?*

- *In what sense are the results consistent with Zajonc and Markus's confluence model of familial factors in intelligence? Why are the results not seen as conclusive proof of the confluence model?*

Developmental Changes in Mental Performance: The Effect of the Birth of a Sibling

Robert B. McCall
Boys Town Center

The IQ performance of children who experienced the birth of a younger sibling was found to drop 10 points during the next 2 years relative to singleton children and 5.8 points relative to last-born children from families of comparable size. These differences were no longer significant at 17 years of age. The method controlled for sex, family size, age at assessment, and IQ before the birth of the sibling. The results illustrate the possible contribution of 1 environmental factor to within-family developmental changes in mental performance.

The environmental factors thought to influence mental performance, specifically IQ, have typically included parental encouragement of intellectual activities, opportunities for enriching experiences, and so forth. Such factors characterize the "general intellectual climate of the home," and they are assumed to be present equally for all children within a family. As a result, while they contribute to differences between families, they should promote similarity in the IQs of siblings within families.

More recently, however, some scholars have argued that there has been too much emphasis on such general factors to the exclusion of other contributors (McCall, 1983; Rowe & Plomin, 1981). For example, while siblings are more similar than unrelated children in average IQ, they are not more similar in the pattern of IQ change over age (McCall, 1970), and such developmental changes can be substantial— approximately 30 IQ points on the average—even for normal, untreated, middle-class children (McCall, Appelbaum, & Hogarty, 1973). Indeed, by one estimate, half of all the environmental variation in IQ is within-family and not shared by siblings (Row & Plomin, 1981).

Such nonshared within-family factors might include differential treatment of siblings by parents, peers, and teachers; environmental events that match the abilities and interests of one but not another child within a family; age differences at the time of a divorce, relocation, death of a relative, and other events; and birth order.

Birth order is an obvious candidate for study in this regard because, by definition, the birth of a younger sibling is an event that the children of a family do not experience equally. Moreover, birth order has been studied for many years (e.g., Altus, 1966), perhaps because it is a convenient, unambiguous, independent variable. Unfortunately, the consequences of birth order have been anything but unambiguous, perhaps partly because the effects have rarely been studied longitudinally.

For example, a major theory of the effects of birth order and other family configuration variables, called the confluence model, suggests that the birth of a baby reduces the average intellectual climate of the home and should be associated with a temporary relative decline in intellectual growth rate among existing children in that family (Zajonc, 1976; Zajonc & Markus, 1975; Zajonc, Markus, & Markus, 1979).

The theory consists of other theoretical propositions plus an elaborate mathematical model. Specific predictions from the math model were first tested on very large samples of children of different birth orders (e.g., Belmont, Stein, & Susser, 1975; Page & Grandon, 1979; Velandia, Grandon, & Page, 1978; Zajonc, 1976; Zajonc & Bargh, 1980; Zajonc & Markus, 1975; Zajonc et al., 1979) and later cross-sectionally on siblings within families (Berbaum & Moreland, 1980; Brackbill & Nichols, 1982; Grotevant, Scarr, & Weinberg, 1977; Rodgers, 1984). These and other results have been heatedly debated (e.g., Berbaum, Markus, & Zajonc, 1982; Galbraith, 1982a, 1982b), and questions even have been raised about whether the mathematical model is a faithful incarnation of the theoretical propositions.

The research presented here is a test of the proposition that the birth of a younger sibling should be associated with a developmental decline, perhaps temporary, in

IQ relative to children with older rather than younger siblings, and especially relative to singleton children. An attempt was made to control a variety of other variables thought by some to influence IQ and IQ change—namely, family size, the age at which IQ tests were administered, and IQ prior to the birth of a sibling. Such control was favored over large sample size because, while large samples are common in the literature, controlled conditions and developmental data are not.

Although the theoretical propositions tested in this study derive from concepts proposed by confluence theory, this research is *not* a test of the confluence model. First, no attempt has been made to use the mathematical expression of that model to make predictions for these data. Second, because matching, control, and longitudinal data were emphasized, large samples were not available to estimate parameters with the precision required to use those parameters in multiplicative or exponential expressions that have the potential of magnifying error. Third, some critics (e.g., Galbraith) believe the mathematical model makes predictions that are at odds with the theoretical statements presumably underlying the model. In view of these circumstances, this paper focuses on the longitudinal examination of the single theoretical prediction stated above and ignores the other propositions and mathematical expression of the confluence model.

Method

Subjects

The subjects for this study were selected from the Fels Longitudinal Study to achieve maximum control over family size, sex, and completeness and comparability of IQ tests and the ages of assessments.

Eighty subjects were available from a previous study (McCall et al., 1973) who had been assessed with the same IQ test by the same examiner with minimum missing data. These subjects were born between 1930 and 1938, and were tested at 2½, 3, 3½, 4, 4½, 5, 5½, 6, 7, 8, 9, 10, 12, 14, 15, and 17 years of age with either the 1916 or 1937 (L and M) versions of the Stanford-Binet. (See McCall et al. [1973] for details of the sample, missing data procedures, and adjustments for test form.)

For the present study, subjects who were adopted in childhood (one) rather than infancy, who were twins (two sets) or triplets (one set), and who lacked complete family information (one) were omitted from consideration, leaving 70 usable subjects. A subject was defined to have no younger siblings (i.e., last-born) if there were no siblings born or adopted within 10 years following the subject's own birth. Because IQ tests were not used before 2½ years and at least one assessment prior to the birth of a sibling was required for the analyses, younger siblings had to be born when the subject was 3 years of age or older and had to live in the home with the subject during the age period of concern.

Comparison Groups. The focal group were subjects who had no older siblings and only one younger sibling born before their seventh birthday. This was the focal group because presumably the birth of a sibling will have maximum effect on such children. This group of four males and five females was called the "two-child family/one younger sibling" group. The age of the subject at the birth of the younger sibling ranged between 3½ and 7 years, with an average of 5.0 years.

To control for family size and sex, a two-child/no-younger group was selected from subjects who had no younger siblings but one older sibling. Nine subjects were available, four males and five females, who were matched perfectly for sex with the two-child/one-younger group.

Two three-child family groups were created to be as comparable as possible to the two-child family groups. A three-child/one-younger group consisted of nine subjects who had one younger and one older sibling and were matched as closely as possible to the sexes and ages at which a younger sibling was born in the two-child/one-younger group. The match for sex of subject was perfect. Six of the nine subjects were matched to subjects of the focal group within 6 months and eight of nine within 1 year of the age at which a sibling was born. Only one subject, who was least similar to a member of the focal group, was not used.

A matched three-child/no-younger group of nine subjects was also selected. Ten subjects were originally available in the subject pool for this group. Eight were matched for sex with the focal group. The unmatched additional subject, a male, was selected from the two available by coin flip.

Finally, eight subjects had no siblings. This singleton group was matched for sex with the focal group in seven of eight cases.

Target Age. A "target age" was determined for all subjects who had younger siblings. The target age was the age of the child when administered an IQ assessment closest in time to the birth date of the younger sibling, either before or after the actual date. The target age was within three months of the birth date for 16 subjects and within six months for all 18 subjets with younger siblings.

The two one-younger groups were matched as closely as possible for target age, and "dummy" target ages for the three groups without younger siblings were assigned to match subject for subject with those of the focal group. The target ages for the three-child/one-younger group were matched with the targeted ages for the two-child/one-younger group within 6 months for six of the nine subjects and within 1 year for eight of nine subjects. The target ages for the three groups not having younger siblings were the target ages of the subjects within the focal group with whom the control subjects were matched.

In summary, all groups were matched as closely as possible with the focal group (two-child/one-younger) for sex and the ages at which IQ assessments were made.

Results

The data for each subject consisted of Stanford-Binet IQ scores (adjusted to be equivalent across test forms; see McCall et al., 1973) assessed as closely as possible to the target age, 6 months prior to the target age (called the "target age − ½ year"), and yearly for 5 years following the target age (called the "target age + 1, + 2 . . . + 5"). The "target age − ½ year" assessments were made within 6 months of the actual date for 41 (91%) and within 1 year for all 45 subjects. Of the 225 annual follow-up scores, 155 (69%) were on the yearly anniversaries, and all were determined within 6 months of the actual dates.

Statistical Strategy. The longitudinal data for all subjects were aligned according to each subject's target age. Then the assessment for "target age − ½ year," which was known to occur before the birth of the sibling, was selected to be the covariate in the data analyses. This had the effect of equating the groups on IQ and its correlates (e.g., SES) prior to the birth of a sibling. It focused the analysis on change in IQ (Cronback & Furby, 1970) and reduced within-group variability associated with factors extraneous to the family configuration conditions. Other data using the Fels sample suggest that the stability and correlates of IQ approach asymptote at around 5 years of age, which is close to the average age when the covariate was measured in this study (McCall, 1977).

The assessment at the target age was not used in the analyses, because the sibling birth occurred before this age for some subjects and after this age for other subjects. The first two anniversary assessments following the target age were averaged and selected for analysis, because the birth effect should be maximum during this period. The other follow-up ages were not analyzed because the length and extent of the predicted "recovery" from the sibling birth might depend on the actual ages and spacing of siblings, factors that were not controlled in this sample. However, IQs at age 17 were analyzed. By this time, such differences might be expected to be minimal.

Preliminary Tests. Preliminary tests were conducted on the control variable of family size, which was not the primary focus of the study. A family size (two- vs. three-child families) + younger/no-younger siblings analysis of covariance was conducted using the IQ 6 months prior to the birth as a covariate and the average IQ at 1 and 2 years following the birth of the sibling as the dependent variable. The analysis revealed no differences for family size as a main effect or in interaction with younger/no-younger siblings, F's < 1.

Main Comparisons. As a result of this preliminary analysis, two- and three-child families were combined, thereby increasing group size for the main comparison. An analysis of covariance was then performed on the singletons ($N = 8$), combined no-younger ($N = 18$), and combined one-younger ($N = 18$) groups with pairwise comparisons tested a priori and directionally.

Assumptions for such an analysis were tested and found to be satisfactory. Specifically, there was no significant difference on the covariate, $F < 1$, which (contrary to widespread belief) is a preferred precondition for covariance (Appelbaum & McCall, 1983). Furthermore, a substantial pooled within-cells correlation (.82) occurred between covariate and dependent variable. This correlation approximates r's for IQs across 1½–2½ years for such ages and samples.

The covariance analysis produced a significant groups effect, $F(2,40) = 3.33$, $p < .05$. Simple effects tests showed that the one-younger group was significantly lower than both the singletons, $t(40) = 2.58$, $p < .01$, and the no-younger group, $t(40) = 1.85$, $p < .04$.

IQ at age 17 was then compared for these three groups after adjusting for presibling IQ by covariance. The groups did not differ in IQ at age 17, $F < 1$. However, it should be noted that the increased number of years between the assessment of the covariate and the dependent variable reduced the sensitivity of this test relative to the previous comparisons. Therefore, one cannot firmly say that the sibling effect diminished over age.

These results are presented in Figure 1. The adjusted mean follow-up IQ (years 1 and 2) was 125.7 for the singletons, 121.5 for the no-younger group, and 115.7 for the one-younger group. As can be seen, the effect seemed to derive both from a decline in performance associated with the birth of a younger sibling and from increases in relative performance by control subjects. Such increasing patterns are not unusual in longitudinal studies (McCall et al., 1973). Therefore, the sibling effect reported here is a relative one—relative to what might have been expected if the younger sibling had not been born.

266

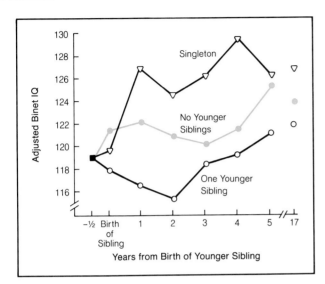

Figure 1 Adjusted Binet IQ over age for the singleton, no-younger, and one-younger sibling groups after equating the groups for IQ 6 months prior to the birth of a sibling and controlling for sex, age at testing, and family size where appropriate.

It appears in Figure 1 that the trends reported began even before the birth of the sibling, because the groups have begun to diverge at the target age (i.e., "birth of sibling"). Actually, however, this is probably the result of the procedural fact that the target age was a few months before or *after* the birth of a sibling, so some subjects already had a younger sibling by this time.

Discussion

The results of this study indicate that during the 2 years following the birth of a sibling, the IQ performance of an older child dropped 10 points relative to singletons and 5.8 points relative to last-born children with older siblings. These differences were not significant at age 17, although the statistical test at this age was not as sensitive as the other comparisons. This is the first confirmation of the hypothesized developmental effect of the birth of a sibling using longitudinal data and controlling for sex, family size, the age at which IQ tests were administered, and IQ prior to the birth of the sibling.

It is important to note that, although these data apparently support a major psychological premise of confluence theory, they do not provide evidence on other premises of the theory and certainly not on the specific mathematical model proposed by Zajonc and his colleagues. Indeed, another analysis of the Fels data conducted from that perspective does not support the formal mathematical predictions of the confluence model (Rodgers, 1984), although the conclusions are being debated.

No direct evidence exists that specifies the functional attributes that produce the change in IQ observed here. However, some research (Dunn & Kendrick, 1980, 1982) suggests that the birth of a younger sibling is associated with less maternal interest and sensitivity to the social initiatives of the older child, with fewer maternal initiations of conversations, verbal games, and activities, and with more negative mother-child confrontations over issues of behavioral control.

It is reasonable to speculate that the birth of an infant saps attention that otherwise might be paid to an older child, and the task demands of caring for an infant might increase stress in interpersonal relations. The net effect might be a dilution of the intellectual climate of the home for the older child. As the youngest child matures, the intellectual environment could be expected to return to more normal levels. Unfortunately, while it appears in these data that the sibling effect diminishes with age, the analyses do not permit a certain conclusion in this regard.

More generally, however, the results of this study make plausible the effect on IQ of the birth of a sibling, and they illustrate that at least one environmental event occurring within families and not shared equally by siblings can have an effect on mental performance.

References

Altus, W.D. Birth order and its sequelae. *Science,* 1966, **151,** 44–49.

Appelbaum, M.E., & McCall, R.B. Design and analysis in developmental psychology. In W. Kessen (Ed.), Vol. **1,** P. Mussen (Gen. Ed.), *Handbook of child psychology* (4th ed.), New York: Wiley, 1983.

Belmont, L., Stein, Z.A., & Susser, M.W. Comparison of associations of birth order with intelligence test score and height. *Nature,* 1975, **255,** 54–56.

Berbaum, M.L., Markus, G.B., & Zajonc, R.B. A closer look at Galbraith's "closer look." *Developmental Psychology,* 1982, **18,** 174–180.

Berbaum, M.L., & Moreland, R.L. Intellectual development within the family: A new application of the confluence model. *Developmental Psychology,* 1980, **16,** 506–515.

Brackbill, Y., & Nichols, P.L. A test of the confluence model of intellectual development. *Developmental Psychology,* 1982, **18,** 192–198.

Cronbach, L.J., & Furby, L. How should we measure "change"—or should we? *Psychological Bulletin,* 1970, **74,** 68–80.

Dunn, J., & Kendrick, C. The arrival of a sibling: Changes in patterns of interaction between mothers and first-born child. *Journal of Child Psychology and Psychiatry,* 1980, **21,** 119–132.

Dunn, J., & Kendrick, C. *Siblings: Love, envy and understanding,* Cambridge, Mass.: Harvard University Press, 1982.

Galbraith, R.C. Just one look was all it took: Reply to Berbaum, Markus, and Zajonc. *Developmental Psychology,* 1982, **18,** 181–191. (a)

Galbraith, R.C. Sibling spacing and intellectual development: A closer look at the confluence models. *Developmental Psychology,* 1982, **18,** 151–173. (b)

Grotevant, H.D., Scarr, S., & Weinberg, R.A. Intellectual development in family constellations with adopted and natural children: A test of the Zajonc and Markus model. *Child Development,* 1977, **48,** 1699–1703.

McCall, R.B. IQ pattern over age: Comparisons among siblings and parent-child pairs. *Science,* 1970, **170,** 644–648.

McCall, R.B. Childhood IQ's as predictors of adult educational and occupational status. *Science,* 1977, **197,** 482–483.

McCall, R.B. Environmental effects on intelligence: The forgotten realm of discontinuous nonshared within-family factors. *Child Development,* 1983, **54,** 408–415.

McCall, R.B., Appelbaum, M.I., & Hogarty, P.S. Developmental changes in mental performance. *Monographs of the Society for Research in Child Development,* 1973, **38** (3, Serial No. 150).

Page, E.B., & Grandon, G.M. Family configuration and mental ability: Two theories contrasted with U.S. data. *American Educational Research Journal,* 1979, **16,** 257–272.

Rodgers, J.L. Confluence effects: Not here, not now! *Developmental Psychology,* 1984, **20,** 321–331.

Rowe, D.C., & Plomin, R. The importance of nonshared (E_1) environmental influences in behavioral development. *Developmental Psychology,* 1981, **17,** 517–531.

Velandia, W., Grandon, G.M., & Page, E.B. Family size, birth order, and intelligence in a large South American sample. *American Educational Research Journal,* 1978, **15,** 399–416.

Zajonc, R.B. Family configuration and intelligence. *Science,* 1976, **192,** 227–236.

Zajonc, R.B., & Bargh, J. The confluence model: Parameter estimation of six divergent data sets on family factors and intelligence. *Intelligence,* 1980, **4,** 349–361.

Zajonc, R.B., & Markus, G.B. Birth order and intellectual development. *Psychological Review,* 1975, **82,** 74–88.

Zajonc, R.B., Markus, H., & Markus, G.B. The birth order puzzle. *Journal of Personality and Social Psychology,* 1979, **37,** 1325–1341.

Source: McCall, R.B. (1984) Developmental change in mental performance: the effect of the birth of a sibling. *Child Development, 55,* 1317–1321. Copyright by the Society for Research in Child Development, Inc.

Language

9

The Egyptians before the reign of Psammetichus used to think that of all races in the world they were the most ancient; Psammetichus, however, when he came to the throne, took it into his head to settle this question of priority, and ever since his time the Egyptians have believed that the Phrygians surpass them in antiquity and that they themselves come second. Psammetichus, finding that mere inquiry failed to reveal which was the original race of mankind, devised an ingenious method of determining the matter. He took at random, from an ordinary family, two newly born infants and gave them to a shepherd to be brought up among his flocks, under strict orders that no one should utter a word in their presence. They were to be kept by themselves in a lonely cottage, and the shepherd was to bring in goats from time to time, to see that the babies had enough milk to drink, and to look after them in any other way that was necessary. All these arrangements were made by Psammetichus because he wished to find out what word the children would first utter, once they had grown out of their meaningless baby-talk. The plan succeeded; two years later the shepherd, who during that time had done everything he had been told to do, happened one day to open the door of the cottage and go in, when both children running up to him with hands outstretched, pronounced the word "becos." The first time this occurred the shepherd made no mention of it; but later, when he found that every time he visited the children to attend to their needs the same word was constantly repeated by them, he informed the master. Psammetichus ordered the children to be brought to him, and when he himself heard them say "becos" he determined to find out to what language the word belonged. His inquiries revealed that it was the Phrygian word for "bread," and in consideration of this the Egyptians yielded their claims and admitted the superior antiquity of the Phrygians.

Source: From *The Histories* by Herodotus, translated by Aubrey de Sélincourt and revised by A.R. Burn (Penguin Classics, 1954, 1972). Copyright by The Estate of Aubrey de Sélincourt, 1954; copyright by A.R. Burn, 1972. Reproduced by permission of Penguin Books, Ltd.

As the preceding story from the historian Herodotus (500 B.C.) illustrates, language is surely one of our most intriguing mysteries. Despite re-

cent advances in describing linguistic growth, analyzing the various uses of language, and evaluating individual differences, the basic issue of how a child acquires this remarkable ability has not been satisfactorily resolved. On the one hand, thousands of different languages and dialect variations have been identified. On the other hand, essential similarities in the structure and functions of these languages, as well as in the process of their development, also have been observed.

As a complex system of sounds and symbols created to transmit meaning, language serves several crucial functions. First, language permits us to express our feelings, ideas, and demands. Second, we learn about and regulate our environment—including other people—through language. Finally, language allows us to clarify our thinking or to extend it imaginatively. Each of these functions may be applied to various cultures, to different ages, and across countless generations. Language, therefore, is a significant unifying characteristic of our species. Most of our knowledge about the history of the world and its different peoples—not to mention our accumulated wisdom or creative accomplishments—has been transmitted through oral, and ultimately written, language.

This chapter will explore both the universal sequences of language use and the influences that foster linguistic variations. Furthermore, it will discuss the major theories that attempt to explain the nature of language development. The first task, however, is to outline the formal aspects of language study.

Five Components of Language Study

To communicate effectively with each other, speakers and listeners must be aware of and use the rules of their language (Menyuk 1982). These interrelated sets of rules have been analyzed by linguists and developmentalists within the following five areas: phonology, morphology, syntax, sematics, and pragmatics (see Table 9.1). Defining each component will permit a clearer appreciation of the process of language acquisition. The five

Table 9.1   Five Types of Rules for Studying Language Development

Phonological	Rules related to the sound units used in a given language
Morphological	Rules for how to construct words and how to modify them
Syntactic	Rules for putting words into appropriate phrases or sentences
Semantic	Rules related to selecting words that express intended meaning
Pragmatic	Rules governing the behaviors for engaging in effective communication

Source: Paula Menyuk from C.B. Kopp and J.B. Krakow, *The Child* ©1982 by Addison-Wesley Publishing Company, Inc. Reading, Mass. Rules. Reprinted with permission.

types of rules, however, are distinguished only for the sake of reducing complexity. Engaging in everyday discourse does not imply a conscious application of these rules, nor do they develop independently from one another.

At a basic level, we must be able to recognize and articulate sound patterns. The knowledge of **phonology** consists of being able to pronounce, put together, and properly stress the sound system of a particular language. For example, a child familiar with the English language could say the word *solt,* even if it were not found in the dictionary. However, the same child also would realize that reversing those letters to form *tlos* does not yield a word that could exist in our language. Children are similarly attuned to small distinctions in sound that create wide variations in meaning, such as comparing *fig* with *fog.* Another illustration of phonological rules relates to how the speaker formulates a question. If English speakers proceed toward the end of a phrase or sentence with a steadily rising intonation, listeners will attempt to answer the question. This pattern of sound, however, would not be useful for communication in Finnish.

Two other rules of language concern the formation of words **(morphology)** and the arrangement of words within sentences **(syntax).** Just as children are taught something about phonology during a phonics lesson, their study of grammar

usually includes some analysis of language structure. Morphological rules relate to the basic word units for constructing a language and to the ways that modifying them transforms meaning. For instance, linking *with* and *drawn* creates a word that is not obviously related—*withdrawn.* Attaching an *-s* to *pot* indicates that we are referring to more than one. Adding an *un-* to *finished* suggests the opposite of the original word. A child who is very fluent in morphological rules (which vary considerably from one language to the next) is able to change the tense of a verb from present to past (*go* to *went*) or turn an adjective *(nude)* into a noun *(nudity).*

Syntactic rules govern the order in which words are placed in a phrase or a sentence. Arranging words in various sequences provides the opportunity for linguistic creativity and is equally important for accurate communication. Rephrasing *The hat is blue* into *Is the hat blue?* changes a statement into a question. A very simple juxtaposition may reverse the intended meaning—*Mary teased Jack* versus *Jack teased Mary.* The improper arrangement of words can make even routine conversation difficult *(horse put the before cart the).* Learning a second language is a challenge because mastery of vocabulary and pronunciation is only a preliminary accomplishment to understanding the syntax. For example, it is common for Spanish speakers and writers to place a noun before an adjective (*a table round*), but English speakers follow the reverse procedure. Every language has syntactical rules to help avoid ambiguous discourse.

Another aspect of language study is **semantics,** which concerns the meaning of words and sentences. Semantics is a controversial area because it is impossible to describe semantic development without simultaneously trying to understand how children think. It is also easy to see that the use of grammatical rules is intimately connected to the acquisition of semantic rules. Researchers interested in semantics study how a child comes to differentiate between an automobile and other moving objects on wheels (e.g., trains and buses), at what point a child achieves a knowledge of opposites (e.g., right and left or up and down), and in what ways the meanings of words change with development. Simply possessing a vocabulary cannot be equated with understanding, since a parrot can be trained to say many words without understanding a single one.

When children are conversing, their words and sentences do not provide the complete arena for communication. Pragmatic factors, such as gestures and facial expressions, allow language to be understood in context.

The last of the five components of language, **pragmatics,** has been seriously examined only since the 1970s. Pragmatic rules concern the social and contextual factors that govern conversation. For example, if a girl says to her mother, "These scrambled eggs are dry," she may mean that she dislikes the eggs *or* that she is pleased with the eggs. The pragmatic approach to language involves interpreting meaning according to a knowledge of the situation and the people within it (e.g., gesture, facial expression, personality, and life history). Pragmatics also refers to more general rules, such as knowing how to take turns in a conversation or being able to adjust speech for the benefit of younger children or foreigners. In other words, pragmatic rules imply the nonverbal accompaniments to expressing joy or anger, the appropriateness of

slang versus polite speech, and the interaction of linguistic, cognitive, and social factors in language development.

The next sections will relate some of the specific findings in the areas of phonology, morphology, syntax, semantics, and pragmatics to each of the following linguistic phases: infancy, early childhood, later childhood, and adolescence. Thus, the material will focus on developmental changes rather than on the validity of any one theory of language. This is for two reasons. First, there is little consensus that any one theory can explain the diverse aspects of language development much more effectively than another. Second, few of the researchers whose work will be cited here have indicated pure theoretical convictions. Tempering early environmental views of language development with the heredity perspective of the 1960s has appeared to result in a better balance within the past decade. Whitehurst (1982) has concluded:

> If the field of developmental psycholinguistics is now ready to shift toward a more social conception of language, we may be close to a point at which the interaction of biological preparation and social learning of language may be addressed productively. Paradoxically it is only a rigorous examination of the role of environmental variables that can clarify the contributions of biology to the acquisition of that most complex and intriguing of skills—human language. (P. 384)

Infant Antecedents of Language

In light of the derivation of the word *infancy* from the Latin *infantia* (an inability to speak), it may be puzzling why we should devote attention to this period of development. Although infants clearly are limited in their abilities to use an extensive vocabulary, to construct complex sentences, and to understand subtle abstractions, they are certainly not impossible to communicate with and are far more receptive to our speech than most people typically believe. Before examining the preliminary language of infants, especially in regard to the meaning and context of their words, we must see how infants respond to and manipulate basic sounds.

Early Sounds

The capacity of infants to perceive and attend to their environment from the first days of life was discussed in Chapter 5. This section will examine further the infant's response to the stimulus of human language. Condon and Sander's (1974) videotapes of neonatal movements have offered illuminating evidence in support of a biological readiness for language. They found that the apparently uncoordinated squirming and flexing of body parts are not merely random movements. When the videotapes were analyzed frame by frame, it was discovered that infant movements were highly syn-

chronized with the adult patterns of speech. Therefore, prior to the first spoken word, infants may be practicing the intonations of their native language with barely perceptible rhythms of their bodies. Using a variety of other procedures developed by researchers of infant perception (e.g., analyzing head turning, heart-rate changes, and sucking force), psycholinguists have demonstrated that "the infant early in life possesses many of the speech discrimination abilities that characterize an adult language user" (Molfese, Molfese & Carrell 1982, 307).

Just as infants learn to distinguish human from nonhuman sounds during the first weeks of life, and familiar from strange voices during the second or third month, they become increasingly adept at formulating sounds by the end of their first year (Kaplan & Kaplan 1971). All infants proceed through four stages of preverbal vocalizations. During the first six months of infancy, much to the chagrin of new parents, sound production largely takes the form of crying. Whether or not parents can determine if their infant's cries refer to pain, anger, or hunger on the basis of the pitch, pattern, and intonation of the cry alone (Schaffer 1971; Wolff 1971) or if knowledge of the context is also required (Muller, Hollien & Murry 1974), there is no doubt that crying provides a basis for communication and exercises the infant's vocal cords and breathing apparatus.

Sometime between the second and fourth months of life, infants begin to articulate sounds more clearly and to coo (produce squealing and gurgling noises). As in any sequence of developmental transitions, phonological changes are subject to much individual variability, and the stages certainly overlap. This second prelinguistic stage includes other sounds such as grunts, sighs, and noises that depend upon lip and tongue movements.

By around six months of age, the important third stage—babbling—dominates cooing and crying. Babbling consists of the repetition of actual speechlike sounds—simple combinations of vowels and consonants (such as "ga-ga-ga-ga") that may strike the unaware listener as a foreign language. In fact, adults tend to have much difficulty identifying the language background of babbling

Problems in Child Development

Language Acquisition in the Deaf

A primary concern of parents with deaf children is whether their child's language skills will be adequate for socioemotional and cognitive development to proceed successfully. Several methods have been used to help deaf children learn to communicate effectively: lipreading, fingerspelling, sign language, and many variations or combinations of these procedures. Evidence concerning the superiority of any one method is uncertain; however, multiple approaches, begun as early as possible, appear to be the best solution. In attempting the course of language remediation it is also necessary to consider factors such as the degree of deafness, the age of onset, the intelligence of the child, and the existence of other disabilities. The prognosis for normal development has improved in recent years, but for most deaf children, their deficient communication skills will hamper their progress (Dale 1976; Reich 1986).

Nonetheless, language acquisition in the deaf provides an amazing display of the apparently very powerful mechanisms through which children learn to communicate. Research by Susan Goldin-Meadow and Carolyn Mylander (1984) with deaf children who did not receive any form of language tutoring revealed the spontaneous creation of a system of gestures that parallel the typical course of early language development in hearing children. The researchers found no evidence that these deaf children were learning their gestural languages through either imitation or reinforcement. They concluded "that exposure to a conventional linguistic input is not a necessary precondition for a child to acquire at least certain of the properties of language" (p. 105).

In order for deaf children to refine their communication skills, however, a self-taught gestural system needs to be augmented by other procedures. Since fingerspelling is relatively slow and lipreading alone is not entirely effective, nearly all deaf children are now also taught a sign language. American Sign Language (known also as Ameslan or ASL) is the most widely used sign language in the United States. Based on a version originally developed by a French priest in the eighteenth century, ASL relies essentially on a set of hand movements for each morpheme, or meaningful word part, in the English language (see the Figure for several examples of ASL words). Although ASL is a manual language and regular English is an oral language, the similarities between the two outweigh the differences. ASL, for example, has more than one dialect, allows for puns and slips of the tongue (hand?), and follows the same developmental course as spoken languages (Bellugi & Klima 1982).

It is the last property mentioned that distinguishes ASL as a genuine language in which deaf children may develop at a rate similar to that of their hearing peers. In fact, some research has found accelerated initial language acquisition for users of ASL (Bonvillian et al. 1983). This finding can probably be explained by the visual and motoric activities that have been practiced during the months of infancy. The vocal apparatus and speech centers of the brain, in contrast, are maturing slowly; however, after 2 years of age, the advantages of ASL disappear.

infants at this stage (Thevenin et al. 1985). Most babies, even those who are born deaf, enjoy producing babbling sounds. The babbling of hearing infants continues to evolve after six months; however, deaf infants gradually cease their spontaneous vocalizations. Thus, the sounds of language provide essential stimulation for continued development of that language. (Note the accompanying Problems in Child Development "Language Acquisition in the Deaf.")

Between eight and ten months after birth, infant babbling usually becomes modified to such a degree that an adult sitting in the next room might

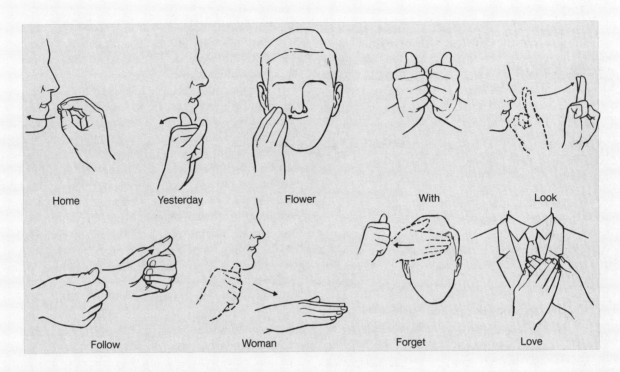

Examples of Signs from American Sign Language (ASL)

Source: From L.L. Riekehof (1978) *Talk to the deaf,* Springfield, Mo.: Gospel Publishing House.
Copyright 1978 by the Gospel Publishing House. Used by permission of the publisher.

Thus, ASL development may occur earlier and more rapidly than spoken English, but little else differentiates language acquisition in these two modes. As Dale (1976) contends:

The really important aspects of language and the really important abilities the child brings to the problem of language learning are independent of the modality in which the linguistic system operates. Language is a central process, not a peripheral one. The abilities that children have are so general, and so powerful, that they proceed through the same milestones of development as do hearing children. (P. 59)

mistake the sounds being produced for the native language itself. Kaplan and Kaplan (1971) have termed this fourth stage one of patterned speech. At this point babies babble in lengthy "strings" that accurately reproduce the sound combinations and intonation patterns of their own language. They no longer emit the sounds characteristic of other languages. Nevertheless, sounds common to several languages will be learned and properly articulated by all infants in the same approximate sequence (Jakobson 1968). For example, the vowel and consonant combinations required to produce *papa* (or *padre* in Spanish) is relatively easy for an infant.

Perhaps this is the reason some parents feel sure that their infant's babbling has meaning despite the fact that understanding lags months behind the apparent "word" production.

From Words to Sentences

One of the major events of infant development is the appearance of true language—the first word. The timing of this milestone varies from the age of 10 to 15 months; however, many infants achieve the first word around their first birthday. Dodd (1980) has cautioned:

> Identifying the first word is difficult because pronunciation is crude and the meaning may be different from the adult meaning; in fact, what seems to be a word may be only babbling. But, given an approximation to the correct sounds of some word, produced voluntarily, and paired with the appropriate referent, proud parents and language researchers will call it a first word. (P. 60)

On the basis of her detailed analysis of eighteen white, middle-class infants during their second year of life, Nelson (1973) concluded that the age when ten words have been acquired (about 15 months) offers a more stable index of this critical step in language development. Several dozen to several hundred additional words will become part of the infant's vocabulary by 2 years of age. Most observers have reported that the period between 18 and 24 months is one of significant vocabulary expansion.

Nelson's (1973) research was also concerned with the types of words first acquired. The most commonly spoken words at the fifty-word stage (approximately 20 months of age), for instance, were general nominals (categorical nouns, especially if they involve some type of action such as *ball*, *snow*, or *car*). General and specific nominals (such as a particular person, animal, or object) accounted for nearly two-thirds of the total vocabulary. The remaining types of words, in descending order of frequency, included action words (*bye-bye*, *look*, and *up*), modifiers (*cold*, *blue*, and *nice*), personal/social words (*no*, *please*, and *ouch*), and function words (*where*, *to*, and *for*).

Whereas much research has emphasized the speaking aspects of early language, Gruendel's (1977) study evaluated the listening processes. She noted that in a child's attempt to understand the world "a word may be attached to a concept as soon as the functional core relations have been articulated" (p. 1575). This notion suggests that children are not likely to use words with notable consistency until they are able to integrate them within a conceptual scheme.

Once children have mastered the core vocabulary of fifty words or more, they begin to use two-word utterances in an inventive and unique form of grammar. Children's language at this stage, which usually begins at the age of 21 months, is a constructed version of adult speech, but it is not imitation. However, these two-word sentences do not seem to violate the appropriate rules for word sequence in the adult version of the language.

Since all children, including those who learn sign language, use the two-word utterance in similar ways at approximately the same time, it appears likely that a universal tendency to create and attend to language arises from the development of cognitive abilities, an innate mechanism for language acquisition, or both. There is still much controversy over how to best describe the early grammatical rules children use to form the two-word utterance, as well as how to interpret the different meanings which may underlie these "sentences."

Bloom, Lightbown, and Hood (1975) reported that not all children construct identical combinations of two words, and that, in fact, relatively few consistent patterns are used. Slobin (1971), in contrast, suggested seven functional relationships which effectively characterize the two-word utterances of children from different cultures. For example, the demands of the child may be stated *mehr milch* (*more milk* in German), and *mai pepe* (*give doll* in Samoan). Negative expressions are equally common at this stage: *no wash* and *ei susi* (*not wolf* in Finnish). Children are also eager to indicate ownership or possession, as in *Mama dress* or *pop moya* (*my navel* in Russian). Other functions include questions (*where ball*), modifiers (*piypiy kech*, or *hot pepper*, in Luo), actions and objects (*hit ball* or *Bambi go*), and locations (*there book*).

Thus, infant grammar demonstrates a natural ability for abbreviating adult language. However,

Adults have no difficulty coordinating words with actions when they communicate, but this is a skill that must be gradually acquired by young children.

appreciating the meaning of a child's utterances requires an evaluation of the context within which they are spoken.

Understanding and Communicating

Communication during the months of infancy depends on strategies beyond the use of phonological and grammatical rules. Infants must attend to stress and intonation, to nonverbal signals such as hand gestures and facial expressions, and to cues associated with situations. The infant discovers such communication strategies even before producing recognizable words. Bates (1976) describes 1-year-old Carlotta's behavior:

> C. is sitting on her mother's lap, while mother shows her the telephone and pretends to talk. Mother tries to press the receiver against C.'s ear and have her *speak*, but C. passes the

receiver back and presses it against her mother's ear. This is repeated several times. When mother refuses to speak into the receiver, C. bats her hand against mother's knee, waits a moment longer, watches mother's face, and then, uttering a sharp, aspirated sound *ha*, touches her mother's mouth. (Pp. 54–55)

Similarly, infants learn how to share their visual perspective with others by pointing accurately at objects (Leung & Rheingold 1981). They are able to coordinate this activity with verbal labels by approximately 14 months (Murphy 1978). Other researchers have demonstrated that infants can even grasp the rules for taking turns in having a conversation (Ninio & Bruner 1978; Snow 1977).

The emergence of the first words does not imply that infants attribute the same meanings to these words as do adults. In fact, such words are known as **holophrases** because "they appear to be attempts to express complex ideas, ideas that would be expressed in sentences by an adult" (Dale 1976, 13). The infant pointing to the box of cookies on the table and saying "Cookie" may be labeling that object, expressing a desire to play with it, or indicating a state of hunger. Greenfield and Smith's (1976) analysis of the holophrastic speech of two infant boys suggested that these early words may serve different functions according to the context.

Sometimes a word is used in a very restrictive manner referred to as *underextended*. For example, the infant may label the family pet *dog* but not use that word for other dogs. The opposite phenomenon is more common and is found in all languages. According to one report, between 20 and 34 percent of all words produced were *overextended* (Nelson et al. 1978). Many a father has been disappointed to hear his infant call another man "Daddy." Infants also may refer to any round object (for example, a rock, marble, or cherry) as a *ball*.

Although the two-word utterance provides additional clues to the meaning of infant language, these primitive "sentences" are also challenging for adults to interpret. The infant who says "Momma book," for instance, could be trying to communicate that the book belongs to Mother or that it would be nice of Mother to read this book with him or her. Therefore, parents are forced to use similar strategies for understanding two-word expressions as they did in figuring out the meaning of holophrases.

Infants do offer some helpful hints in making themselves understood, however. In the expression *kitty food*, for example, stress on the first word could mean "This is the kitty's food," whereas stress on the latter word suggests "It is time to feed the kitty." These variations demonstrate that infant communication can be quite complex and necessitate careful attention to the subtleties of the language context.

Early Childhood and the Linguistic Explosion

Beyond the infancy stage, language acquisition proceeds very rapidly for the next three or four years. By the time a child is ready to begin receiving

a formal education, pronunciation is usually accurate, a basic vocabulary has been established, the rules of grammar are intuitively applied, the meanings of language are considerably extended, and the use of words is related appropriately to their context. Although language production continues to lag behind the comprehension of speech throughout early childhood, advances in cognitive development insure significantly easier communication than was possible for an infant. The following sections describe several of the ways in which the preschool period has been found to be exceptionally rich in language development.

Improving Speech

Young children react to the difficulties of acquiring the sounds of language in the same way they cope with grammar and meaning. That is, they reduce the complexity of what they hear from the speech environment. Dale (1976) has suggested that "the differences between the child's forms and those of the adult are not solely a matter of perceptual and articulation difficulties; rather, they reflect the workings of a rule-governed system that . . . appears to be quite similar in the early stages for children acquiring different languages" (p. 233). Most preschool children do not have persistent trouble in discriminating among the sounds of their native language. Eilers and Oller (1976) found that 2-year-olds could distinguish between *cow* and *pow*, had some problems with *rabbit* and *wabbit*, and were likely to confuse *monkey* with *mucky*. As children's short-term memory processes become more efficient, they pay greater attention to the finer distinctions in speech (including their own) and rely less on pragmatic clues to sound.

The ability of preschool children to produce sounds improves substantially between the ages of 2 and 6 years. Early attempts at pronunciation, such as "hefant" for *elephant* or "boon" for *spoon* (Ingram 1974), result in common childish simplifications. These are gradually overcome by comprehension of the differences and by coordination of the lips and tongue, which allows better articulation of sounds. Through a spectrographic analysis (sound wave patterns) of certain words, Macken and Barton (1980) found distinctions in children's production of speech that were undetectable to the untrained ear. Other researchers (for example, Hodson 1980; Ingram 1981) have been able to identify the processes of phonological acquisition. Children, for instance, characteristically say "Pay" before achieving the ability to say "Play." This cluster-reduction strategy involves simplifying the *pl* sound-blend to only one of its component sounds.

The Emergence of Grammar

When speech has progressed to the point whereby three or more words are combined into a single sentence, the child has grasped the essential elements of the language. For example, a preschooler who says "Daddy push truck" is expressing the relationships among a subject *(Daddy)*, a verb or action *(push)*, and an object *(truck)*. Similar statements, such as "I go bye-bye," communicate messages in a syntactic form that has been called **telegraphic speech.** Because the cost of sending a telegram is based on the number of words in the message, we try to eliminate any words that are not absolutely necessary for accurate communication. Young children's speech lacks the same type of words usually omitted from telegrams—articles, prepositions, conjunctions, and so forth. Nevertheless, a preschooler almost always produces sentences with a word order consistent with adult language.

Psycholinguists have been studying children's language by using (1) naturalistic methods of transcribing spontaneous speech and (2) experimental studies that probe for specific abilities. Intensive efforts to understand the telegraphic grammar of children have been under way for more than two decades. According to Slobin (1973), the task of these analyses is to chart the sequence of grammatical development and to explain the cognitive strategies children apply to learning a language. Based on data from over forty different cultures, Slobin tentatively arrived at his seven principles that appear to guide language development. Similarly, Brown's (1973) longitudinal investigation of three children led him to conclude that "the order of progression in knowledge of the first language . . . will prove to be approximately invariant

across children learning the same language and, at a higher level of abstraction, across children learning any language" (pp. 403–404).

One aspect of morphology that has received careful study is the suffix. Suffixes are added to the ends of words in order to change their meaning. These markers, such as plural forms *-es* or *-s* and the past tense *-ed*, are also known as *inflections*. It can be seen how two of Slobin's (1973) principles pertain to morphological development. Rather than learn language simply through imitation, children apparently try to abstract the rules of grammar by producing forms that do not exist, but that are sensible, syntactic arrangements. This process of "regularizing" the language, called *overregularization*, demonstrates Slobin's principles of (1) avoiding exceptions and (2) attending to the ends of words.

In a classic study of the early awareness of plural forms, Berko (1958) presented young children with an illustration of a cartoonlike character labeled a *wug*. After showing them another illustration with two of these unfamiliar creatures, she said to the children, "Now there are two _____." Giving children the opportunity to supply the plural form *wugs* almost always resulted in the correct response. Children often attempt to use the normal plural rule for irregular plurals such as *gooses* and *foots* or even as additions to the irregular forms themselves (*geeses* and *feets*). Clark and Clark (1977) pointed out that the overregularization of such rules can be found in a variety of languages.

The sequence of inflection development, however, is not what we might predict on the basis of a regularizing tendency. We might expect that regularizing would be the first stage, but Cazden (1968), for example, found it to be the third of the four stages in the acquisition of the past tense. At first, children do not use any past tense forms, such as *went* or *stopped*. Then they will use a few irregular forms (*went*) they have learned through imitation. In the third stage, children produce the regular form for both regular (*stopped*) and irregular verbs (*goed*). They even may extend the irregular forms to create novel words such as *wented* and *broked* (Kuczaj 1978). Finally, toward the end of the preschool years, children eliminate virtually all of the overregularized forms. These patterns of use reveal the active role of children in constructing language.

Although children often appear to be listening carefully to adult speech, they tend to pay more attention to the message than to the actual words or sentences. Thus, their own speech contains creative usage, such as "wented," that does not derive from imitation.

Besides acquiring greater flexibility with the structure of words themselves, children quickly elaborate on the construction of their formerly short and crude sentences. The process through which children create sentence order is still a very controversial area. However, most researchers acknowledge that certain regular transformations must occur. These rules are not consciously applied by either children or adults attempting to formulate sentences, yet indirect evidence suggests that they are used. For instance, if a person is asked to transform the statement "The lors bliged the grint" into a question, he or she could easily complete the task: "Did the lors blig the grint?" Since these words or sentences were never heard before, the only way to transform the syntax is by following an appropriate set of rules. Comparisons between children of different ages demonstrate that transformational rules develop during early childhood for many grammatical forms including questions, negatives, passives, conjunctions, and embedded clauses (Elliot 1981).

Semantics and Pragmatics

Although the growth of vocabulary itself during early childhood is an impressive feat—more than twenty words per day are added for a child of average intelligence (Miller 1978)—the meanings of language develop gradually. The most significant constraint on improvement in semantic knowledge is likely to be the level of understanding the child brings to the speech arena. Factors that influence a child's understanding include the labeling of the environment by parents, the value of certain objects for the child, the context of word and sentence use, and the perceptual features of the child's world. De Villiers and de Villiers (1978) illustrate the profound nature of semantic acquisition for the child with a quote from Elizabeth, who is 3½: "'You know what, Mommy? Yesterday today was tomorrow'" (p. 121).

One aspect of semantics that appears to give young children particular trouble is the use of relational and comparative terms (e.g., *big/little, now/later, right/left,* and *more/less*). The evidence concerning the proper use of such words depends on the particular linguistic comparison, as well as the child's language environment. For example, a study by Clark and Sengul (1978) of 2- to 5-year-old children's comprehension of *here/there* and *this/that* yielded an interesting developmental pattern. The children were asked to give to the experimenter one of two identical animals placed at different distances from them, yet within reach. The 2- and 3-year-olds could not differentiate the opposing terms and always chose the animal either close to themselves or close to the experimenter. Only the 5-year-old children could always make the correct selection.

Today, preschoolers are viewed as effective and sensitive communicators, whereas in the past their linguistic deficiencies were emphasized. For example, Shatz and Gelman (1973) demonstrated that 4-year-old children are capable of adjusting their descriptions of a toy to suit the various language levels of 2-year-olds, their peers, and adults. Even a child of 2½ years may be willing to engage in an active dialogue with an interested adult (Keenan 1975). Nevertheless, Bacharach and Luszcz (1979) have shown that communicative competence still needs to improve during the early childhood years. They compared the abilities of 3- and 5-year-old children to use **implicit information** during conversations. Implicit information means attention to material newly introduced in a conversation or to action versus content or to beginnings and endings of a topic. The younger children failed to make appropriate remarks in light of the experimenter's comments. In contrast, the older children's responses were governed by the context that the experimenter had structured.

Bacharach and Luszcz's (1979) results suggest that younger preschool children have not yet acquired the competence to engage in a completely meaningful conversation because they lack a sense of implicit information. The researchers, however, were not certain about how to explain the children's deficiency or why the 5-year-olds were more responsive to the experimenter's remarks. Is it a matter of learning to identify and use implicit linguistic cues? Are younger children unable to process that much information? Perhaps preschoolers do not pay attention to such information? Or are these children biased to respond to objects rather than actions? This last possibility is supported by the findings of Gentner (1978), who reported that preschoolers relied on perceptual features, not actions, to label an unfamiliar toy. In any event, the meanings of language during early childhood are intimately related to both grammatical skills and contextual cues.

Language Refinements of Later Childhood and Adolescence

Later childhood and adolescence are highlighted by the capacity not only to use the rules of language, but also to consciously create and interpret subtle distinctions. After the age of 5 or 6 years, children develop a fuller appreciation of the sounds making up language. They expand their knowledge of word meanings and relationships; they refine their use of grammatical irregularities and minor syntactic rules; they become more attuned to linguistic ambiguities; and they achieve greater ability in perceiving the needs of those with whom they wish to communicate. Although preschoolers have begun these processes, the skills have not yet emerged in a consistent fashion at the complex levels that characterize later development. For instance, we might ask a youngster above the age of 6, "Do you have the time?" He or she might reply, "Yes." Our immediate reaction may be that the child has a sense of humor, but, in fact, the simple reply shows how sensitive the child is to the distinction between interrogative sentences ("What time is it?") and declarative sentences ("Please tell me the time").

Words and Sentences Revisited

A study conducted by Shultz and Pilon (1973) demonstrates the grammatical confusion that obstructs the path of children's language development. They evaluated the skills of first, fourth, seventh, and tenth graders in detecting four types of linguistic ambiguities:

Phonological:
"The doctor is out of patience (patients)."
"He saw three pears (pairs)."
Lexical:
"No one liked the plant (factory)."
"He did not have enough dough (money)."
Surface-Structure:
"He sent her kids story books." (emphasis on her *or* kids)
"He saw a man eating fish." (emphasis on man *or* eating)
Deep-Structure:
"The duck is ready to eat." (duck could eat *or* be eaten)
"They are visiting sailors." (they could be going *or* here) (P. 730)

After the researchers explained and illustrated that sentences may have more than one meaning, the children were asked to listen to and interpret a random selection of sentences of the four ambiguous types or their unambiguous versions. For example, "The doctor has lost his temper" is the unambiguous version of "The doctor is out of patience." Similarly, "He saw a ferocious fish" is the unambiguous version of "He saw a man-eating fish."

Schultz and Pilon found that the particular type of ambiguity determined the children's detection ability. Improvement in explaining phonological types occurred earliest (between the ages of 6 and 9 years). The lexical ambiguities showed a gradual, steady improvement with age. Finally, deep- and surface-structure ambiguities were not detected until at least age 12. We can conclude that grammatical constructions of our language require various levels of transformation in order to be accurately interpreted.

Not only do children have to learn that the surface structure of their language may not always provide unambiguous clues to sentence meaning; they also have to grasp elaborations of previously acquired morphological and syntactic forms. Such sentences include complications, similar to this one, that embed secondary clauses within the main point (e.g., the research of Huang 1983). Word forms that are mastered during later childhood include stress shifts to distinguish a *greenhouse* from a *green house* and stem changes that alter *reproduce* to *reproduction*. Children continue to improve their articulation of language sounds, enlarge their vocabularies many times over, and further refine relational terms (e.g., *follow* versus *lead*). However, the most frustrating challenge for the later years of childhood is learning the exceptions to many of the rules that have so recently been acquired. For example, the irregular past tense form of many verbs (*bled*, *flew*, and *sent*) is but one aspect of this problem (de Villiers & de Villiers 1978).

Meanings and Conversations

Communication with school-aged children rapidly becomes easier as they develop the linguistic skills needed to convey intended meanings and to interpret speech subtleties. Semantic and pragmatic progress can be seen in the construction and comprehension of jokes, in the recognition that the form of address depends on the person to whom they are speaking (e.g., a parent as opposed to a playmate), and in their ability to tell an effective lie. By the time they are in the first grade, children have a fairly sophisticated understanding of commonly used words; in fact, such children are sensitive enough to subtleties in word usage that they can tell from the speaker's tone of voice and the context when someone is speaking sarcastically to them (Ackerman 1982). However, many of these same children make errors in speech when using words that are quite familiar to them, and they consistently fail to correct those errors.

Consider the words of 6-year-old Mindy, a child interviewed by Bowerman (1978): "You said what I was going to say . . .you *put* the words right out of my mouth" (p. 986). Why would Mindy make such a mistake? Certainly she had never heard an adult substitute *put* for *took* in the preceding expression. Bowerman explained the error by noting that a child who is trying to construct such a sentence must select from among semantically similar words, thus overloading mental limitations. In addition, children make rapid substitutions—either upon request or spontaneously—and never replace a correct word with an incorrect one. In sum, a child's semantic development proceeds as a consequence of information-processing advances in attending to his or her own speech, as well as to the linguistic environment.

Thus far, this section has reviewed language accomplishments with respect to sounds, words, and sentences. However, the area of pragmatics offers the most interesting changes in the child's linguistic development. The social context of communication—from the perspective of the speaker or the listener—demands new skills from the older child.

Research on the increasing sensitivity of children to the needs of both participants in a conversation commenced with Glucksberg, Krauss, and Higgins during the mid-1960s. Their investigations of school-aged children demonstrated an improving ability to provide accurate descriptions of objects and designs so that listeners who could not see the objects and designs were still able to draw them. Younger children typically produced brief, idiosyncratic communications that did not help the listener complete the task. Furthermore, they were relatively unresponsive to feedback from the listener who said "I don't understand." Whereas older children hearing this would try to explain the task in another way, 5- and 6-year-olds tended to repeat themselves or to remain silent.

Not only were kindergarten and first-grade children poor linguistic communicators; they were also poor listeners. Good listeners know when the information they are being given is unclear and can ask the speaker to clarify the message, as college students often do when they ask a professor to explain a point more fully. Glucksberg, Krauss, and Higgins (1975) noted that first graders do not even seem to realize when a speaker gives them confusing or contradictory information. A similar type of study by Sonnenschein (1986a) did reveal, however, that both first- and fourth-grade children had

an easier time communicating with friends than with strangers.

No one knows for certain why young children fail to accurately monitor their own comprehension, but Markman (1977) proposed that they seem to process spoken information very superficially. She based her conclusion on comparisons of the performances of first, second, and third graders in evaluating a totally inadequate set of instructions for playing a game and doing a magic trick. First graders seemed especially oblivious to the missing information and obvious misinformation recited by the experimenters. Although the tasks were simple and the children were specifically told to focus on faulty communication, the younger children appeared not to realize that they did not understand. More recently, Sonnenschein (1986b) found that young children evaluated ambiguous and inconsistent messages more accurately when the speakers were adults rather than if they were peers. Sonnenschein cautions teachers that their pupils "may be too ready to assume that the communications of adults are clear and that therefore failures in comprehension are due to errors by the children" (p. 168).

During adolescence language reflects both the powers of formal thought and the search for a secure identity. In the cognitive arena, linguistic abilities continue to improve so that the adolescent can appreciate poetic metaphors, complex analogies, ironic statements, and literary symbolism. These improved abilities, along with the normal expansion of vocabulary that occurs during adolescence, create a flexible speaking and listening language system. A cross-sectional study of 6-, 9-, and 13-year-olds and college students revealed that sarcastic remarks are not recognized until adolescence (Demorest et al. 1984). Researchers imply that like children with new toys, adolescents enjoy playing with and showing off their linguistic abilities.

Not only does language reveal the adolescent's development of biological and cognitive processes; it also exposes the need for strong social supports and identity formation. The slang expressions created by every generation of adolescents serve as an aid to effective communication, but

To express their emerging personalities, adolescents use several forms of language ranging from poetic to destructive. Graffiti may represent a bold attempt to state an identity to the rest of the world.

their more essential purpose may be to distinguish the adolescent culture from that of the adult world (Rice 1984). Teenagers have to make certain that their slang is current, however; users of last year's slang expressions may be viewed as hopelessly out of fashion. Expressions such as *far out* and *right on* were appropriate in the early 1970s, but an adolescent who uses them today may be regarded by peers as a refugee from the Stone Age. Finally, verbal dueling—whereby friends insult and challenge each other—is especially characteristic of adolescent boys. Adolescents use language to achieve status, claim dominance, vent anger, and avoid physical confrontation (Romaine 1984).

Theories of Language Development

Theories of language development can be most easily distinguished by noting the emphasis devoted to either innate (biological) or experiential (environmental) factors. Furthermore, each theory tends to focus on particular types of evidence that support the approach taken, while minimizing the findings that contradict the position. This section will introduce the three dominant theoretical views toward language acquisition. In brief, behavioral or learning theory stresses the acquisition of speech habits; nativistic or biological theory emphasizes the maturation of brain functions; and cognitive or

Table 9.2   Characteristics of Theories of Language Development

	Behavioral	Nativist	Interactionist
General Orientation	Environmental	Hereditary	Interactive
Basis for Development	Learning processes	Language acquisition device (LAD)	Cognitive Processes
Emphasis of Study	Surface structure	Deep structure	Deep and surface structure
Significance of Language Universals	Minimal	Maximal	Moderate
Role of Parents	Simplify speech for teaching rules	Exhibit speech during critical period	Use speech in the appropriate contexts
Special Features	Methods for remediation	Demonstrate creative qualities	Reciprocity of thought and language

interactionist theory focuses on the development of thought processes. Table 9.2 summarizes the major characteristics of the three theories of language development.

Behavioral Approach

According to learning theorists, language develops largely as a response to environmental stimulation. Aside from the vocal apparatus itself, and the capacity of the human species to learn, this perspective dismisses innate factors in language acquisition. Instead, behaviorists believe that children learn to speak because they are reinforced for producing sounds, for making associations between sounds and objects, and for imitating the sounds to which they are exposed. Behaviorists do not consider language to be different from other skills and therefore reject acquisition explanations that reflect unobservable processes or biological readiness. Although the behavioral approach was instrumental in stimulating a systematic analysis of language development, the influence of this view declined sharply after the late 1950s until the late 1970s (de Villiers & de Villiers 1978).

Since children learn to speak the language or dialect they hear during their early years, environmental variation would seem to be the crucial developmental variable. However, considerable research has indicated that such an explanation is quite incomplete. Certainly the influence of a child's native language cannot be ignored, but this does not verify the role of the environment as the principal cause for learning to produce and respond to speech. For instance, why would young children raised by well-educated parents ever say, "No go movie"? Such an expression is not found in the English language, is not likely to have been positively reinforced, and is not an imitation of a parental expression. The behavioral approach offers no convincing account for this phenomenon.

Even when parents make an effort to directly teach language to their children through modeling, the experience may be frustrating. The following dialogue reported by developmental linguist David McNeill (1966) illustrates this point:

> *Child:* Nobody don't like me.
> *Mother:* No, say "nobody likes me."
> *Child:* Nobody don't like me. (Eight repetitions of this correction and error)
> *Mother:* No, now listen carefully: say *"Nobody likes me."*
> *Child:* Oh! "Nobody don't likes me." (P. 69)

It would be less exasperating, if more time-consuming, for a parent to train appropriate speech patterns using a schedule of reinforcements. Aside from the fact that few parents are aware of the rules of grammar or the principles of operant condition-ing, there are not enough hours in the day to sys-tematically reward the complexities of human lan-guage that are acquired so quickly. Furthermore, it has been demonstrated that parents typically ex-press approval or disapproval of their children's speech on the basis of what the children are trying to say, not the grammatical accuracy of their ut-terances (Brown, Cazden & Bellugi 1969). The strategy of correcting infant speech, in fact, may backfire. Nelson (1973) found that language devel-opment proceeded more slowly for those 1- and 2-year-olds whose mothers imposed their own pronunciations and syntax on their children.

Nevertheless, it is clear that the environment is necessary for stimulating language development (Hoff-Ginsberg 1986). Parents will alter their sen-tence structure and simplify their vocabulary when speaking to infants and young children (Clark & Clark 1977). Snow (1972) suggested that the will-ingness of adults to modify their speech and to repeat themselves helps give children consistent information to create the rules of grammar. For ex-ample, one of the most frequently employed lan-guage-training techniques is known as **expansion.** If the child says, "Daddy drink," the parent may respond with an elaborated type of imitation: "Yes, Daddy is having a drink." There has been consid-erable controversy about the value of expansions for improving language development. Earlier re-search indicated that expansions were not highly useful (Cazden 1968; Feldman 1971); however, a more recent investigation (Newport, Gleitman & Gleitman 1977) found that certain linguistic struc-tures attained by children were significantly related to parental expansion.

The behavioral approach, then, concerns the ability of children to generalize from the speech of adults to their own use of the language. Contra-dictory findings in this area may be the result of such factors as the age of the children, the famil-iarity of the researchers with the children, the artificiality of a laboratory environment, and the differential effectiveness of parents in providing appropriate models or corrections. Therefore, be-havioral explanations of natural language devel-opment may not be able to account for the full richness and rate of acquisition but may provide

insights about the environmental features which build on biological foundations. Several special lan-guage situations undoubtedly are the products of specific learning processes. Teaching children to speak a foreign language, offering forms of therapy to language-disabled children, or finely tuning the grammatical abilities of adolescent speakers all de-pend on particular learning experiences.

Nativist Approach

From the perspective of nativist theory, the impetus for language acquisition can be attributed to innate features of the brain. Noam Chomsky (1957) and Eric Lenneberg (1967) have been the major proponents of the nativist approach. In con-trast to the behavioral view, these theorists focus on the biological aspects of language. Specifically, they are interested in universal patterns of lan-guage development, the basic similarities among all languages, and the relationship between ner-vous system maturation and linguistic ability. While few contemporary theorists totally dismiss the effects of the learning environment, many re-searchers have been persuaded that such factors are less relevant than innate determiners in guiding the process of language acquisition.

Perhaps the most impressive evidence which supports the nativist approach to language is the unfolding of developmental milestones. In spite of a wide range of differences in linguistic environ-ments for infants and young children, the sequence and timing of language achievements throughout the world are surprisingly invariant. A striking de-gree of "prewired" preparedness is suggested in all stages from babbling sounds to constructing sentences, in the errors in formulating questions or negatives, and in the synchronization of motoric and language skills. Even among deaf children—who spontaneously vocalize during the early months of life in a manner indistinguishable from that of hearing infants—the course of sign lan-guage development and rate of acquisition are vir-tually identical to those of normal speech. There-fore, whether a child is Polish or Portuguese, silent or vocal, or middle- or lower-class, the path toward language competence is remarkably alike.

Hearing-impaired children need not be isolated linguistically or unstimulated cognitively. Through the use of American Sign Language, communication can be as accurate and sensitive, and follow the same developmental course, as vocal language.

Another biologically based notion concerns the issue of whether children must acquire language during a critical period. Ethologists, for example, identify time intervals during which a species may be especially sensitive to certain types of change (see Chapters 1 and 11). (Issues in Child Development "Can Chimpanzees Use Language?" further discusses the notion of communication in a different species.) What support do we have for the applicability of critical-period constraints on language development? Since Lenneberg (1967) proposed that exposure to language is essential between infancy and puberty, it would be expected that language deprivation for much or all of this period would make it unlikely that complete command of a language would be acquired. Although the difficulties in either regaining linguistic functions following brain damage or learning a foreign

language beyond puberty are clearly recognized, a more stringent evaluation of the critical-period concept demands raising a child without the usual language environment until adolescence.

Naturally, no researcher would suggest that such an unethical experiment be deliberately conducted. There have been several examples, however, of infants abandoned in remote areas or of children reared under extremely deprived conditions. Attempts subsequently were made to teach the children to communicate using language rather than simply through gestures, grunts, and facial expressions. It is impossible to know exactly what physical and emotional traumas or possible mental retardation has influenced the development of these children; however, none have been successfully trained to demonstrate much language skill

(Brown 1958). The efforts to teach some language have been more rewarding in the case of children who were severely unstimulated due to parental insanity, sensory handicaps, or limited intelligence.

The discovery of a 14-year-old girl named Genie provided only some evidence for Lenneberg's position. Curtiss (1977) described Genie's life from the age of 20 months as one of physical neglect and abuse, darkened and roped confinement, and no linguistic stimulation. Despite years of language remediation, Genie's knowledge of phonological and syntactic rules is still impaired. However, her speech, especially the semantic aspect, has progressed well past the minimal level suggested by the critical-period hypothesis. The story of Isabelle, an equally deprived child, had a more encouraging ending (Brown 1958). After only a year of special training, her language skills were normal for her age. At the time of Isabelle's discovery, however, she was much younger than Genie (about 6 years old).

Chomsky's (1957) analysis of the process of language acquisition originates with the position that the mind is predisposed to construct and respond to language in specific ways. Children, therefore, have a tendency to attend to the language environment, formulate rules about how language functions, and modify the rules based on feedback. The reason for such similarity in language development, according to Chomsky, is that a language acquisition device (LAD) in the brain controls language learning as strongly as the child's biological endowment influences physical and perceptual development. No matter what language the child first hears, an identical set of basic structural rules is available for transformation to the rules of a particular language. Psycholinguists such as Slobin (1973) have been trying to establish the universal strategies used to relate these basic and specific language rules. Thus, the language children eventually learn consists of a subset of possible language rules—the ones which the child experiences.

Nativists also recognize the importance of the environment in achieving the specific rules of a language, just as the behavioral approach to language development admits to certain biological givens. However, nativists do not emphasize individual differences in language use. Instead, they have been fascinated by the child's capacity to generate an extraordinary variety of sentences to which they have never been exposed. Earlier, this chapter illustrated some of the common grammatical features often cited in support of the biological approach to language development. Although recognition of the universal acquisition elements and of the similarity in formal structure of different languages is noteworthy, the nativist approach has been criticized for "covering up" presently unexplainable developmental processes with a biological label. Nativists have left unanswered the question of just how children are able to create a language.

Interactionist Approach

The final theoretical perspective favors neither hereditary factors nor environmental input as the dominant contribution toward language acquisition. The interactionist approach can be characterized by a somewhat different question: how does the linguistically receptive mind interpret stimulation from the world? When language development is construed in this manner, controversial issues are addressed not through instincts or habits, but as an interactive process composed of many phenomena. Similarly, describing the phonological and grammatical aspects of language is minimized, with a shift toward semantic and pragmatic components. One of the major themes pervading the interactionist approach, for example, is the extent to which language is a product of thought or thought is rigidly constrained by language. In fact, it is still not resolved whether language and thought develop simultaneously or according to different mechanisms (de Villiers & de Villiers 1978).

Perhaps the most extreme view of the link between thought and language has evolved from the work of cultural anthropologists such as Benjamin Whorf (1956). They argue against the notion of universal sequences and biological determinants of language acquisition. Instead, they regard language as a tool of the culture for shaping the thinking process. A consequence of distinctly varied

Issues in Child Development

Can Chimpanzees Use Language?

There is little doubt that chimpanzees are intelligent and communicative creatures, yet they have not evolved a formal system of language. Researchers have been fascinated by the prospect of teaching apes to use language in order to demonstrate the relationship of human to ape intelligence and to learn more about the process of language acquisition. An early attempt to teach a chimp to talk ended in failure when Viki, raised as Catherine and Keith Hayes's own daughter, could produce only three poorly articulated words. Since the vocal apparatus of the chimpanzee is apparently not suited for making the sounds of human speech, another approach was necessary (Miller 1981).

Allen and Beatrice Gardner decided to capitalize on the ability of apes to use their hands. They reared an infant chimpanzee named Washoe using American Sign Language, the system of communication taught to deaf persons. Washoe's progress was quite impressive compared with the efforts of Viki. By the age of 4 years, Washoe used 132 signs alone and in combinations (Gardner & Gardner 1969). However, Edward Klima and Ursula Bellugi (1973) pointed out that Washoe's development did not match the level of a child of comparable age in terms of proper word order, size of vocabulary, or flexibility of language use.

The encouraging work of the Gardners nevertheless stimulated Ann and David Premack to train another chimpanzee, Sarah, to use a set of plastic tokens instead of hand gestures. The tokens were backed with magnets so that they would adhere to a large board, and they varied in size, color, and shape. Sarah was able to show more sensitivity to language flexibility and productivity than did Washoe (Premack 1976). In spite of Sarah's accomplishments, however, critics such as Herbert Terrace and associates (1979) remain convinced that chimpanzees have learned little more than to imitate their trainers and to pile up strings of signs or gestures.

A series of experiments conducted by Duane Rumbaugh (1977) involved a chimp who was taught to use a computer-based language. Lana learned to press keys on a keyboard representing various symbols; the symbols were then displayed on a video monitor. She made even more progress than Sarah, demonstrating an ability to ask questions, correct mistakes, and indicate the end of a sentence with a period. After further analysis, however, Rumbaugh and his colleagues contended that chimpanzees use symbols merely to replace their natural gestures so that they can obtain rewards (e.g., food, games, and reassurance) rather than to express ideas and opinions.

At present it is difficult to determine how effectively chimpanzees can learn to use human language. The process of language acquisition in chimpanzees appears to be both similar to, and different from, that of a child. The apes in the experiments certainly demonstrated a degree of novelty in using signs or symbols, an ability to comprehend some messages, and a limited knowledge of "word" order. Future research must answer important questions before we can be confident about apes' linguistic achievements, however. For instance, will they teach a sign language to their own offspring, will they be able to understand more complex forms of grammar, and will they modify their messages to match the needs of different listeners (de Villiers & de Villiers 1978)?

These Asian children develop in a culture that is quite different from the environment of most American youngsters. Do these differences lead to language variations that shape the children's thought processes or are they merely alternative ways of expressing similar ideas?

languages is, according to Whorf's **linguistic relativity hypothesis,** that children from different cultures perceive the world and communicate in dissimilar ways. Whorf himself believed that language actually causes thought to take a certain form. A more modest version of this approach suggests that "languages differ not so much as to what *can* be said in them, but rather as to what it is *relatively easy* to say in them" (Hockett 1954, 122). In other words, although Eskimo children have many different words to describe varieties of snow, English-speaking children could describe the same ideas using combinations of words.

Research on color naming, color memory, and color distinctions has yielded similar results that cast doubt on the extreme version of Whorf's hypothesis (Brown & Lenneberg 1954; Gleason 1961;

Lantz & Steffire 1964). The evidence on colors led Dale (1976) to conclude the opposite of linguistic relativity: "universal aspects of the human perceptual and cognitive apparatus lead to universal aspects of color naming" (p. 246). Slobin (1971) reminds us about the relationship between language and thought in summarizing the fate of Whorf's hypothesis:

> Cultural anthropologists are looking for ways in which the underlying structures of cultures are alike, and psychologists are moving out of Western culture to cross-cultural studies, in an attempt to understand general laws of human behavior and development. Perhaps in an age when our world has become so small, and the most diverse cultures so intimately interrelated in matters of war and peace, it is best

that we come to an understanding of what all men have in common. But at the same time it would be dangerous to forget that different languages and cultures may indeed have important effects on what men will believe and what they will do. (P. 133)

An opposing view to the linguistic relativity approach was proposed by Jean Piaget (1967). Piaget considered language to depend on, to reflect at times, and to help facilitate cognitive development. Language, however, is never more than a tool to aid in thinking or a vehicle to permit communication and the expression of ideas. Piaget believed that language serves to mentally represent the world as a means for liberating thought from the immediacy of perception. In other words, people can talk about events and objects in the world without simultaneously having to perceive them. Language is acquired, and increasingly becomes more complex, because it follows in the footsteps of intellectual development. Therefore, although language is a valuable medium to use for gaining knowledge, it cannot be regarded as a causative agent for thought.

Creative thinkers, such as Albert Einstein, frequently suggest that words—written or spoken—are not essential for the construction of new ideas (Ghiselin 1955). Images and symbols may provide equally significant methods for representing fantasy or reality, especially for younger children. Furth's well-known research on cognitive development in deaf children is particularly persuasive on this point. He found that many deaf children attained advanced levels of reasoning despite the lack of a verbal environment or a speech system (Furth & Youniss 1975). Investigators such as Beilin (1975) have attempted to explain how the difficulties children have in using complex grammatical structures are linked to their cognitive developmental status.

A third position, proposed by Lev Vygotsky (1962) in the Soviet Union, is less cognitively dominated than Piaget's theory. According to Vygotsky, language and thought develop separately during infancy; early speech is preintellectual and early intelligence is prelinguistic. These independent streams of development converge during early childhood so that language becomes rational and

thought becomes appropriately verbalized. Vygotsky suggested that the blending of cognitive and linguistic processes leads to **inner speech,** the unarticulated use of language to create meaning for the child. Therefore, speech arises from different roots than does thought—language is not controlled by cognition, nor is thinking exclusively verbal.

Reich (1986) cited a variety of supportive evidence for Vygotsky's general position (also see Berk 1986), which is less unidirectional than Piaget's approach to thought and language. Vygotsky's work does not contradict Piaget's ideas as much as it elaborates on how speech provides another source of stimulation for cognitive development. In sum, the interactionist perspective is made up of several shades of opinion that diverge on the extent to which language and cognition have mutual origins and reciprocal influences.

Variations in Language Development

Much of this chapter has discussed the common patterns of language use and development, regardless of the particular group or individual. Many linguistic variations could be described, in addition to the distinctions that generally accompany chronological age. This section will focus on two that are of special interest to those who study child development: the contrasts between middle and lower classes and the distinctions among language dialects. Both topics have generated controversy, yet they are intertwined with critical developmental issues. This section's consideration of linguistic variations is designed not simply to illustrate the nature of individual differences in language, but also to shed light on some sensitive issues in child and adolescent development.

Communication and Socioeconomic Status

The consistent observation that lower- and working-class children do not attain the same level of language skills as do middle- and upper-class children has challenged linguists to explore the reasons for this socioeconomic variation. However, the idea that socioeconomic status itself actually causes differences in speech or understanding is an oversimplification (and, as will be noted later, some theorists are not even persuaded that such differences should be considered deficits). Articulate speakers and creative writers have certainly emerged from less-than-ideal social circumstances. However, the bulk of evidence indicates that particular factors associated with poor language skills are more prevalent at the lower-socioeconomic levels.

The most unambiguous aspect of language variation between socioeconomic levels concerns the acquisition of vocabulary. A careful study by Stodolsky and Lesser (1967), which controlled for ethnic background and test bias, found significant differences on picture and word vocabulary between middle- and lower-class black, Hispanic, Jewish, and Oriental first graders. Ethnic variations were minor in terms of total vocabulary development, but all of the middle-class groups demonstrated clear verbal superiority. In his assessment of grammatical competence, however, Dale (1976) stated that equally convincing evidence for social-class differences has not been obtained.

A variety of research has examined the syntactic and morphological skills of the middle versus the lower classes. Although some investigations, such as the one by Dewart (1972) in Ireland, concluded that lower-class children have more difficulty with passive constructions and complex sentences than their middle-class peers, most research has yielded negligible differences. Furthermore, Dale (1976) argued that when socioeconomic-status variations are obtained, they may frequently be a function of dialect differences, a lack of familiarity with middle-class testers and environments typically used for testing, or test biases and researcher expectations. Confusion among these extraneous variables—along with the distinct vocabulary and grammatical structures of lower-socioeconomic speakers—probably has contributed to an image of the lower-class child as communicatively handicapped.

One study, however, is especially noteworthy because the researchers minimized vocabulary problems and did not introduce ethnic complications. Pozner and Saltz (1974) taught white, middle- and lower-class fifth graders (with approximately equal IQs) how to play a simple game involving the positioning of various shapes, colors, and coins. After half of the subjects had mastered the game, they were asked to teach the rules to the remaining children. No significant social-class differences were found in listening abilities, but lower-class children were less effective communicators (to both middle- and lower-class listeners). They tended to provide incomplete and inaccurate instructions while trying to use motoric demonstrations (the children could not see each other, since they were separated by a partition). Pozner and Saltz concluded that lower-class children have difficulty in verbal expression because of an "inability to take the perspective of their listeners in attempting to communicate information" (P. 770). However, this study does not help us with the task of specifying the origins of the presumed cognitive immaturity and linguistic egocentrism characteristic of some lower-class children.

Since social-class differences in either language or thought do not become evident until after 2 or 3 years of age, what are the components of a lower-class environment that ultimately may begin to take their toll? Bee (1978) suggested that malnutrition and generally poor health might retard brain development, resulting in inferior performance. Lower-class homes also may not provide adequate stimulation in terms of the amount or variety of exploratory experiences. These probably are important factors; however, the specific influences on language development are more controversial. At the heart of this debate is a sociopolitical dispute about the value of speaking a nonstandard version of a language. Linguists are convinced that one variation is not grammatically superior or more complex than another, but the utility of a nonstandard form for educational and vocational success is questionable. In sum, nonstandard language need not be viewed as a deficit unless it hinders the communicative effectiveness of the child.

Communication patterns within homes of lower-socioeconomic status differ in both style and substance from those of middle-class environments. Bernstein (1971) was the first theorist to describe social-class differences in language use.

He hypothesized that middle-class speakers engage in an elaborated style of speech, including lengthy sentences, detailed and complex explanations, fluent transitions from one thought to another, and an extensive vocabulary. In contrast, Bernstein suggested that lower-class speakers use a restricted form of language that is less explicit, is more concrete, involves a limited vocabulary, and is more private. Higgins (1976), Labov (1972), and others severely criticized the notion of elaborated versus restricted language codes. They challenged Bernstein's lack of evidence and pointed out research which does not support this distinction when the social context is controlled.

Bernstein (1971) also suggested that middle-class families tend to emphasize the individuality of each member, whereas lower-class families stress clearly defined and strictly observed roles. In her review of family interaction studies, Bee (1978) indicated that middle-class parents do talk to their children more often, provide frequent praise, and use rational explanations for controlling behavior. Lower-class parents tend to be more critical of their children and use authoritarian methods of discipline. Should we be surprised, then, that the speech of lower-class children is not highly sensitive to the communicative needs of their listeners, especially those who have middle-class expectations?

Dialect Differences

An alternative position to Bernstein's is the approach of Bryen, Hartman, and Tait (1978). They regard all language variations reflecting sociocultural factors to be equally effective dialects. From their perspective, language competence can be interpreted only within the framework of the dialect used by the child. Whether language variations are due to sex, age, race, social class, geography, or context, no dialect can be considered superior to another, nor does any particular dialect reflect linguistic immaturity or cognitive deficiency. Furthermore, Bryen, Hartman, and Tait reject the implication that impoverished environments produce language weaknesses. They believe that variant forms of a language are looked down upon because of negative attitudes toward people from other regions of a country, toward minority groups and

immigrants, or toward the poor. No single, standard form of any language really exists; rather, there are overlapping variations that share more similarities than differences.

Disentangling the various sociocultural influences on language development has proved to be difficult. Nevertheless, the pattern of all dialect acquisitions appears to be similar, and each dialect is a complete, complex language. Dale (1976) commented that moving away from the "deficiency approach" to a "differences model" may benefit society by promoting more extensive vocabularies, expanding the meanings of language, and offering new ways to communicate. The diversity of American culture can enrich our children's lives rather than foster snobbishness or dissension.

It is unfortunate that children with certain dialects are made to feel ashamed of their culture or their intelligence because they use a variant form of language. Sometimes such children feel compelled to imitate the dialect of more prestigious groups in order to compensate for their perceived deficiencies. This hypercorrect speech usually results in stilted pronunciations and awkward grammar. Bryen (1974) suggested that instead of trying to modify the language of variant-dialect children to insure that they achieve social mobility, "the responsibility for change [should] be placed on societal institutions, rather than the individual" (P. 596).

Researchers like Bryen and Labov have been somewhat instrumental in shifting attitudes toward increasing tolerance of variant dialects, but many children still must cope with the prejudices of teachers, peers, and institutional representatives. There is no reason why multiple dialects cannot coexist. Dale (1976) believes that knowing two dialects offers the child a choice of languages that may be appropriate in different settings without eradicating or demeaning cultural heritage. Simultaneously, an awareness that dialect differences are superficial variations that do not indicate intellectual ability should be promoted.

Black English, for example, one of many variant forms of our language, seems to function as a barrier to communication because it establishes negative expectations about the competence of the child. In fact, black English is actually several dialects that are spoken by many, but not all, black

The different dialects of these two girls should be viewed as equally acceptable versions of a language. Variant dialects rarely hinder communication, although they frequently are misjudged as indicators of cognitive ability.

children in the United States. These dialects also are used by many white southern children, especially those from rural, lower-class backgrounds. The confusion among ethnicity, social class, and dialect may be responsible for some of the performance variations observed on cognitive tasks. Research frequently has compared middle-class whites to lower-class blacks, leading to unfavorable racial connotations. Similar problems face Hispanic, American Indian, and French Canadian minorities today, as they did Jewish, Irish, and Italian immigrants earlier in this century.

This exploration of language has turned from a discussion of common developmental pathways to an evaluation of variations. Just as studying themes of universal language acquisition reveals our shared humanity, becoming aware of variations in use demonstrates the child's need to identify with a smaller group or tradition. However,

there is an additional level of analysis. Not only does each child speak a version of a specific language, but also each child creates a unique "idiolect." Since no two children speak or write in precisely the same fashion, language, like a fingerprint, also acts as a vehicle for expressing individuality (Bryen, Hartman & Tait 1978).

Although language is one of the primary mechanisms for bringing children closer together, it is also one of the most distinctive features about any child. Two children who speak the same dialect may be clearly distinguished by their tone of voice, rate of speech, vocabulary level, sentence style, volume and pitch, length of discourse, characteristic pauses, and numerous other factors. This adds to the complexity and variety of the communication process as it functions throughout language development.

Summary

1. Although language development is an elusive and intricate process, the expressive, regulative, and clarifying functions that language serves have been demonstrated to be invaluable.
2. Linguists and developmentalists have defined five types of rules that capture the interacting uses of language. These include phonological, morphological, syntactical, semantic, and pragmatic rules.
3. During the past fifteen years it has been demonstrated that infants have the capacity both to produce and attend to sound.
4. Throughout the world, the second year of life is characterized by the appearance of simple words and two-word utterances.
5. Infants use language in ways that are different from adult expectations. For the speaker or the listener, conversation with infants requires attention to the context in order to improve communication.
6. During early childhood, language development proceeds very rapidly. Phonological rules become highly refined and other aspects of language advance dramatically.
7. The struggle to acquire the rules of grammar follows a common, creative course for preschool children. The way to understand language acquisition is to analyze children's linguistic errors.
8. The young child's remarkable development of language is evident from the expanding vocabulary and sentence structure. No less significant is an increasing sensitivity to semantic and pragmatic rules.
9. A highlight of later childhood and adolesence is mastery of the subtleties of language in both the speaking and listening areas.
10. The major linguistic challenges in later childhood are the process of coordinating language skills with cognitive development and the need to share knowledge of the world within social settings.
11. Adolescents refine their linguistic skills and use language to help develop an identity as well as to demonstrate cognitive development.
12. Behaviorist, nativist, and interactionist theories have influenced the study of language development. The behaviorists emphasize environmental aspects of communication but neglect nonobservable language competence. Nativists are convinced that the principal determinants of language development are innate biological processes. Therefore, they examine universal aspects of language and minimize variations. Interactionist theories do not ignore either biological or environmental factors in language development. Research centers on the relationship between communication and cognition.
13. Exploring language variations provides insights about development that are as rewarding as those gained from examining universal patterns.
14. A controversial issue is whether the speech of lower-social-class children should be regarded as deficient or merely different. This dilemma is complicated by the lesser educational achievement of lower-class children.
15. Recent evaluations of language variation stress the legitimacy of all sociocultural dialects. Therefore, negative attitudes must be replaced by tolerance and appreciation of language diversity.

Key Terms

phonology
morphology
syntax
semantics
pragmatics
holophrases

telegraphic speech
implicit information
expansion
linguistic relativity
hypothesis
inner speech

Suggested Readings

Curtiss, S. (1977). *Genie: A psycholinguistic study of a modern-day "wild child."* New York: Academic Press.

The fascinating story of language remediation in a young child of unidentifiable origins. This book provides a rare example of research on the critical-period hypothesis of language acquisition in humans.

Dale, P.S. (1976). *Language development: Structure and function* (2nd ed.). New York: Holt, Rinehart & Winston.

The finest paperback in print on language acquisition. Dale's book is clear, interesting, and filled with useful examples and charts.

de Villiers, J.G. & de Villiers, P.A. (1978). *Language acquisition.* Cambridge, MA: Harvard University Press.

An excellent and thorough introduction to the processes and major issues related to the child's development of language.

Miller, G.A. (1981). *Language and speech.* San Francisco: Freeman.

A brief but extremely well-written overview of the nature of language and speech. The biological approach provides the foundation for this paperback volume.

Reich, P.A. (1986). *Language development.* Englewood Cliffs, NJ: Prentice-Hall.

A fine, new paperback that is filled with examples, charts, drawings, and so forth. This book also has good chapters on bilingualism and language problems.

Rumbaugh, D.M. (Ed.). (1977). *Language learning by a chimpanzee: The Lana project.* New York: Academic Press.

A firsthand evaluation of the work with primates on language acquisition. Several members of the project team present balanced perspectives.

Readings from the Literature

In the following study, Harriet Rheingold and Judith Adams (1980) demonstrate that even during the first days of life infants are exposed to a significant variety of grammatically correct speech. Whatever the merits of the nativist position, the linguistic environment of the newborn provides a rich and continuous foundation for language development. Rheingold and Adams suggest that early infant responsivity to speech is a powerful mechanism for stimulating social relationships. The following questions should help you understand the central themes of their research:

* What evidence do the authors cite for the potential value of conducting their study?

* How would you characterize the type of research or procedures followed by Rheingold and Adams?

* Do the results of this study lead you to conclude that talking to newborns is a very desirable or merely an optional parenting behavior?

The Significance of Speech to Newborns

Harriet L. Rheingold
University of North Carolina at Chapel Hill

Judith L. Adams[1]
University of North Carolina at Chapel Hill

Samples of speech to newborn infants in a nursery showed that most of the hospital staff, men as well as women, spoke to most of the infants even from the first day of the infants' lives. The adults' speech was extensive, grammatically well formed, and almost entirely limited to comments on the infants' behavior and characteristics and to verbalizations of the adults' own caretaking activities. Furthermore, their speech displayed a warm regard for the infants as well as efforts to instruct them on how they should behave for their own good. These findings led to the conclusions that newborns are already powerful evokers of speech, that the speech exposes them to a fair sample of the language of their culture, and, even more important, that speech provides experiences of consequence for the development of social behavior.

The answer to the simple question of whether people talk to infants from the day of birth could provide information on several issues of consequence for the development of social behavior. The issues relate in part to the behavior of the persons who speak to the infants and in part to the effect of their speech on the infants. As for the speakers, the specific issues include the effectiveness of newborns as a stimulus for speech and the characteristics of their speech as indications of how they view and hence may behave toward the infants. As for the newborns, the issues include the possible effect on them of early exposure to the language of their culture and of such auditory stimulation on the genesis of knowledge about the social world.

That parents, both mothers and fathers, speak to their newborn infants has been reported; Parke and O'Leary (1976) recorded that they "vocalized" during a considerable portion of a 10-minute sample. In the present study, the answer to the main question was sought in the speech of hospital personnel to infants in a newborn nursery, a choice dictated by the ease with which a considerable amount of speech could be obtained in a relatively short period of time. Furthermore, what these men and women, biologically unrelated to the infants and having different responsibilities for their care, said to the newborns provided a measure of generality beyond the speech of parents to their own infants.

The data include not only the speech recorded in the nursery but the identity of the speakers by sex and occupation, how often they spoke, and the duration of time they spent in the nursery. Of special interest here was determining whether men also spoke to the infants, given the cultural expectation that women are more disposed to speak and are more nurturing of infants. Similarly, the identity of the infants by age and sex was recorded, as well as how often they were spoken to.

The speech was analyzed for its grammatical form and content (i.e., the topics of discourse). The grammatical form has relevance for the nature of the infants' first experiences with language, and the content has relevance for what it can tell about adult behavior toward the immature. These two characteristics of the staff's utterances may be compared with those of mothers' speech to their infants and very young children. Maternal utterances have been shown to contain few words and subordinate clauses, a high incidence of questions, and a restriction to current events, in particular the children's feelings, wishes, and needs; to resemble conversations to the extent that the utterances are directed toward eliciting responses from the children; and to include the speakers' answers to their own words as they imagine the children might respond (for a review, see Snow, 1977).

After the speech was analyzed for its grammatical form and content, there remained yet another characteristic that seemed worthy of analysis—the sense of the message. This measure sought to capture the attitudes of the speakers toward the infants.

The finding that people speak to newborns conveys information about their own behavior but would have no relevance for infant behavior if the newborns could not hear. A considerable body of work, however, attests to the newborns' responsiveness to sound (Kessen, Haith, & Salapatek, 1970). Furthermore, newborns respond more readily to complex multidimensional sounds than to pure tones (Eisenberg, 1970; Turkewitz, Birch, & Cooper, 1972), and more frequently to patterned sounds with fundamental frequencies within the range of the human voice (Hutt, Hutt, Lenard, Bernuth, & Muntjewerff, 1968). The latter findings have been claimed to be of consequence for the learning of language (Eisenberg, 1970) and for the development of the affectional bond between parent and child (Hutt et al., 1968).

Overt behavioral measures show that sounds of low frequency inhibit the distress of newborns under states of high arousal (Birns, Blank, Bridger, & Escalona, 1965), and those of low intensity produce turning of the eyes (Hammer & Turkewitz, 1975) and the head (Muir & Field, 1979) toward the source; both low frequency and low intensity would likely characterize the speech of adults to newborns. Moreover, the human voice evokes eye opening (Alegria & Noirot, 1978) and visual scanning (Mendelson & Haith, 1976). Finally, it has been reported that newborns move in synchrony with adult speech (Condon & Sander, 1974), a finding held to support the contribution of the first speech heard not only to the later learning of language but also to the interaction between the newborn and other persons.

Method

The data comprise the speech addressed to newborns by the hospital staff in a newborn nursery during 10 2-hour samples. The samples were collected over a period of 2 months, 8 in the morning and 2 in the afternoon, separated by at least 2 days, with each weekday sampled at least once. The usual practices of a newborn nursery for infants without medical problems obtained. The infants, who usually stayed for 3 days, were taken to their mothers periodically and could remain with them as long as the mothers wished. Routine physical examinations and circumcisions were performed in the nursery.

298

The speech was recorded in longhand by an observer familiar with the nursery's procedures (the second author) seated in a corner of the nursery. The record also included the identity of the speaker and of the infant spoken to, as well as the time of each speaker's entry and departure. The duration of the infants' time in the nursery, however, was not recorded; infants were brought in after birth and taken to or returned from their mothers' rooms at different times within a 2-hour sample.

Before recording each sample, the observer spent 15–20 minutes in the nursery to facilitate identification of the personnel and the infants. Throughout the 2 hours the observer directed her attention to the infants, continuing to make notes even when no one was speaking to an infant. At the end of the study, the speakers were shown their utterances, and each granted permission for their use.

Analysis of the Speech

From transcriptions of the samples, the speech was divided into utterances. An utterance was defined as a word or group of words separated from others by a pause that usually appeared as a natural break.

Grammatical Characteristics. The syntax of the utterances was analyzed by the following categories:

Length of utterance. The number of words in an utterance, including single words, phrases, and fragments of speech. Sounds ("sh-sh") and compound words ("sweetie-pie") were counted as one word, contractions ("we'll" or "can't") and slurred words ("gonna") counted as two words.

Type of utterance. Sentence or not a sentence, a sentence being defined as a grammatically self-contained unit consisting of a word or a syntactically related group of words that expressed an assertion, question, command, or exclamation (*Webster's Third New International Dictionary*, 1961), including greetings, appellations, and conventional phrases ("Just a minute") but excluding incomplete utterances (". . . grinning up a storm"), single words ("there"), and sounds.

Complexity of sentence. Simple; compound, containing two or more main coordinate clauses; and complex, containing a main clause and one or more subordinate clauses.

Number of verbs. The number of verb phrases in an utterance.

Repetitions. Exact repetitions of the speaker's just previous utterance.

Colloquialisms. The use of informal and familiar words such as *ain't* and including the dropping of syllables or terminal *g*s ("'cause").

Related characteristics were *speaks for infant*—an utterance the speaker pretends the infant would say ("Say I haven't learned to eat yet") and *personal mode of address*—including the use of pet names ("Hey, Miss Porcupine"), terms of endearment ("Okay, sweetheart"), the infant's own name ("Come on, sweet Beth"), and sex ("Hi, little man").

Topics of Discourse. The contents of the utterances (excluding greetings, exclamations, names of things, sounds, and fragments of which the meaning was not clear) were analyzed by four mutually exclusive categories:

Comments on the infant. The speakers comment on the infants' behavior ("Is that my girl waking up?"); direct their behavior ("Now you can burp, please"); or comment on the infants' physical appearance or personality ("Oh dear, you got one of those nice soft curly heads"), feelings ("Yes, say I'm mad about that, now stop messin' with me"), or wants and preferences ("Would you like me to hold you"). This category also includes the speakers' verbalizing what the infant might say or think.

Verbalizes own behavior. The speakers talk about what they are doing for the infant ("I gave you 30 cc, now I'm just quitting"), express their feelings ("I like you 'cause you make such nice baby noises") or wishes for the infants ("I hope by tomorrow your head will shape up some—a whole lot"), or express their thoughts about the infants ("I wonder if you're goin' to be this easy when you get home").

Talks about other persons. ("Your mama's a little under the weather").

Talks about other things. ("That's 30 cc").

Sense of the Utterance. The utterances were next divided into two main categories, one expressing warm regard, the other conveying instructions.

Warm regard. Included utterances expressing solicitude ("What's your problem, love"), sympathy ("Something's ailing you, poor baby"), appreciation ("You're looking like a little angel, dreaming up things to do"), soothing words and sounds ("Okay, little tot"), and expressions of affection ("We really love ya").

Instruction. Included admonishment ("If you don't eat more, I'm going to send you back"), encouragement and guidance ("You can do better than that"), explanations ("No, it's not poison; we give it [water] to all the children; they survive it"), and general information ("Your mama will be down to get you").

Coder Agreement

Two observers independently counted the number of utterances and the number of words in an utterance, categorized 250 randomly selected utterances by their grammatical characteristics, and analyzed all utterances for the topics of discourse and the sense of the message; the median percentages of agreement for each measure by samples ranged from 93 to 100.

Results

During the 20 hours of observation, 40 persons and 74 infants were in the nursery at some time. A few persons and most of the infants were present during only one sample, whereas many persons and a few infants were present during more than one sample.

Over the 10 samples, the mean number of persons in the nursery at some time during the 2-hour period was 7.1 (range, 3–12); of this number, 79% (M = 5.6; range, 3–8) directed one or more comprehensible utterances to the infants. Correspondingly, the mean number of infants in the nursery during a sample was 8.9 (range, 5–13); of these, 88% (M = 7.8; range, 5–11) were the recipients of one or more utterances. Thus, the greater part of the staff spoke to the infants, and by far the greater number of the infants were spoken to.

The 10 samples provided a total of 1,124 comprehensible utterances (range, 27–179). The mean number of utterances per speaker within samples was 24.3 (range, 4.5–55.7), and the mean number of utterances addressed to an infant by all who spoke, again within samples, was 15.0 (range, 4.5–25.6). Furthermore, more than half (59%) of the infants were spoken to by two or more different persons. Thus, not only did the staff speak to the newborns, but they spoke a great deal, and the infants were the recipients of a considerable amount of speech.

Characteristics of the Speakers. The 40 persons in the nursery comprised doctors and medical students; registered, practical, and student nurses; and laboratory technicians, secretaries, and a housekeeper. Of these, comprehensible utterances were recorded for all but 5 of the 12 doctors, 3 of the 5 medical students, and 1 of the 2 secretaries.

The different occupations, of course, entailed different responsibilities for the care of the infants and required different amounts of time in the nursery. For example, the 6 practical nurses present for 64% of the 1,200 minutes of observation gave 53% of the 1,124 utterances. In contrast, the 4 laboratory technicians, present for only 7% of the time, gave 2% of the utterances. Occupation was also related to sex; all the nurses, the secretaries, and the housekeeper were female, and the majority of the other persons were male. Ten of the 18 males who spoke to the infants gave a mean of 10.2 utterances, and 21 of the 22 females who spoke gave a mean of 48.7 utterances. However, when duration of time in the nursery was taken into account, no difference was found between males and females (χ^2 = 1.35, by the median test) in the number of utterances per minute they were present.

In summary, men and women, regardless of the operations they were responsible for, spoke to the infants. How much they said, as one might expect, was related to how much time they spent in the nursery, a variable related to occupation, which in turn was related to the sex of the speakers.

Characteristics of the Infants. Over the 20 hours of observation, 74 different infants were present, 63 of whom were spoken to; of those spoken to, 14 were present in two samples and 1 in three. Thus, a total of 78 infants were spoken to when each infant's appearance in a sample was counted. Here we considered the relationship between the number of utterances addressed to them by their age and by their sex, but this was viewed with caution because these characteristics may have interacted with duration of time in the nursery within a sample.

The infants ranged in age from the day of birth to 11 days, 85% being less than 5 days old. Of the 16 newly born infants, a mean of 10.5 utterances were addressed to 15 of them. Of the 29 2-day-old infants, 27 received a mean of 12.9 utterances; of the 19 3-day-olds, 14 received a mean of 13.4 utterances; and of the 12 4-day-olds, 11 received a mean of 21.2 utterances. Although these findings would suggest that as the infants grew older they were spoken to more often, the means for the few older infants did not show a similar increase. The most noteworthy finding is the considerable amount of speech addressed to the newborn.

Of the 47 male infants, 41 (87%) were spoken to; of the 42 females, 37 (88%) were spoken to. The males were the recipients of a mean of 12.5 utterances (range, 1–97), the females of 16.5 (range, 1–109), but the difference was not reliable ($\chi^2 = .24$ by the median test). In general, then, males were spoken to as well as females and in similar amounts.

Characteristics of the Utterances. *Grammatical form.* The mean length of the 1,124 utterances was 4.85 words (range, 1–21); of the 965 utterances of 2 or more words, the mean length was 5.49 words; and of the 10 longest utterances, the mean length was 17.4 words. Within speakers, the mean length of utterances was 4.33 words, and the mean length of the 10 longest

utterances was 10.2 words. Of all utterances, 87% were classified as sentences; the other 13% included incomplete utterances, single words, and sounds. Declarative statements accounted for 40% of the sentences; questions, 23%; commands, 14%; exclamations, 2%; and greetings, appellations, and conventional phrases, the remaining 8%. Although the majority of the sentences were characterized as simple, 15% qualified as compound or complex, and 25% contained two or more verb phrases. Repetitions characterized only 6% of the utterances, and only 14% were judged as colloquial speech. In 7% the speakers spoke as though they were the infants, prefacing most of these utterances with the verb *say,* and in 15% of the utterances the speakers used a personal mode of address, calling the infants by their own names, pet terms, or addressing them as Mr. or Miss, boy or girl. For the most part, then, the persons spoke grammatically correct sentences, some of which were relatively complex in structure.

Topics of discourse. Of the 1,124 utterances, 900 could be coded by topics of discourse. Of these 900, in 616 (68%) the speakers spoke directly about the infants. In 28% of these 616 utterances, the speakers commented on what the infants were doing, in 21% on what they should do, in 19% on their appearance or personality, in 7% on the infants' feelings, and in 21% on their wants or preferences. In the 215 utterances (24%) in which the speakers verbalized their own behavior in relation to the infants, they spoke about what they were doing for the infants (59%) or their feelings and wishes for, and thoughts about, the infants (41%). Only 5% of the 900 utterances concerned other persons besides the speakers and the infants, primarily the infants' mothers, and 3%, other things. Thus, all but a small fraction of what the speakers talked about were the infants or themselves in relation to the infants.

The sense of the utterances. In contrast to the analysis of the topics of discourse, only 65 utterances could not be assigned to the categories labeled as *warm regard* or *instruction.* Of the other 1,059 utterances, 60% fell into the category of warm regard. Within this category, a third (221 utterances) expressed solicitude, a third (208 utterances) were soothing words and sounds and expressions of affection, and the last third (211 utterances) were about evenly divided between statements of sympathy and of appreciation.

The other 40% of the utterances were judged to fit the category of instruction. Of these, 168 utterances provided general information; 161 offered the infants encouragement or guidance; 59 gave explanations about what the persons were doing or what the infants should do; and only 31 fell into the category of admonishments.

Speakers' Intentions. In obtaining the speakers' permission to use their utterances, some were asked why they spoke to newborns. Several persons (nurses, an intern, and a student nurse) reported that their talking evoked a response; for example, "I get a response. Sometimes infants stop crying. . . . They also turn in the direction of the sound and they focus on my face," and "Sometimes I really do believe that the babies understand what I say to them." A more general reason is revealed in a nurse's statement that "it just seems the natural thing to do. You are interacting with them, and talking gives more meaning to what you are doing." The most general response came from a medical student: "It is a matter of personal philosophy . . . it is never too early to start relating to infants as people."

Discussion

Newborn infants were indeed spoken to from the day of birth. That as many of the hospital staff, men as well as women, of different professions, spoke as much as they did attests to the effectiveness of the newborn as a stimulus for evoking the verbal behavior of adults.

The analysis showed that the speakers did not engage in baby talk or utter just soothing sounds but in the main spoke in properly formed speech. The mean length of the utterances compared favorably with those reported for mothers speaking to older infants (Snow, 1977). Also, in the large proportion of questions, and in limiting the content of the speech to the infants themselves and to what the speakers were doing for them, what the staff said closely resembled the speech of mothers to their very young children (Snow,

1977). Clearly, they spoke as though the newborns understood what they said. Furthermore, on many occasions the speakers created the illusion of engaging the infants in a dialogue. Asking questions may be viewed as an example. More striking still was the number of times the speakers answered the questions by playing the role of the infant or spoke as they imagined the infant might in response to the activity the speaker was then carrying out. In these ways the speakers were not only talking to the infants but engaging in conversations.

What the staff said revealed their kindly attitudes toward the newborns. Young as the infants were, the staff already saw them as individuals, often calling them by name, referring to their sex, and commenting on their attractive features. They saw the infants as needing help in adjusting to a new environment and sympathized with their distress. Not a laboratory technician drew blood from the heel of an infant without cajoling, encouraging, and pitying them. Yet the speakers also saw the infants as capable of learning. Thus, they explained to the infants why, for their own good, they should behave in certain ways, as though the infants could understand. Their words showed that they saw the infants as persons with feelings, wants, wishes, and preferences about which they often consulted them. The special nature of the staff's responsibility for the welfare of the newborns may be thought to account for the warm regard their speech revealed. To some extent the staff may well have been selected for the work by virtue of their kindliness, or may themselves have chosen their occupation out of such kindliness. Yet against these possibilities should be considered the alternative: that the daily routine of care for countless infants whose stay was so short and who were biologically unrelated to them might just as well have dulled their sensibilities.

Considerable in amount and rich in variety as the utterances of the samples proved to be, they must represent only a small part of all speech addressed to the newborns. In the first place, only comprehensible utterances were recorded; the observer's records often contained notes of people's speech that was unclear to her. Then, the infants would also be spoken to by their parents, visitors, and other observers. Not only would they be the recipients of a variety of types of utterances of varying content from a variety of speakers, all with their own characteristic intonations, but they would also hear people speak to other infants in the nursery as well as to each other.

Now we consider the potential effects on the infants of the speech reported here. When people speak, the findings show that they produce a fair sample of the language of their culture, of the language the infants will hear all the days of their lives. Thus, from the day of birth infants are provided auditory experiences that, continued day by day, acquaint them with the sounds and intonations that lay the foundation for learning language, as proposed by Eisenberg (1970) and Condon and Sander (1974). It may not be too farfetched to say that language is learned from the first utterance heard.

Of similar consequence for the development of social behavior is the association an infant can begin to form between people and their speech (Condon & Sander, 1974). To consider that the infant's sensitivity to the human voice contributes to the development of an affectional bond between child and parent (Hutt et al., 1968) places too narrow a construction on that sensitivity. The experience has far wider implications for its role in the genesis of social behavior, of which the relation to parental figures is only a part.

In the first place, the pairing of speech with persons, and not with things, lays the foundation for the basic distinction between people and things; the association provides the infant the means to distinguish between social and nonsocial objects. In the second place, as each speaker presents a unique combination of auditory stimuli, the foundation for distinguishing among different persons is laid. Repeated pairings of different voices and varying types of utterances with different persons builds on that foundation to effect distinctions between persons of different ages and sexes, degrees of familiarity, and kinds of responsibility for the infant's care. Each pairing, then, may be viewed as providing a template against which different associations can be formed.

Heretofore, vision has been ascribed a major role in the responsiveness of infants to people and in their increasing ability to distinguish among persons. In an attempt to account for the infant's special responsivity to people, contrasts drawn between social and nonsocial objects have usually favored the visual attributes of the human face and body, along with the nigh infinite changes produced by movement (Rheingold, 1961). Because the human voice evokes visual scanning (Mendelson & Haith, 1976), the preeminence of audition in the genesis of social behavior cannot be claimed. Yet sounds, in this study the human voice, possess the special characteristic that they do not demand the focusing required of vision and, furthermore, the full range of an infant's responses to sound cannot be detected. Responses such as opening the eyes or turning the head to a source of sound and even scanning are indeed but minor behavioral indexes of hearing compared to the amount of information speech conveys. Even though for the infant, and for the newborn especially, the grammatical form, content, and "sense" of speech are not yet comprehensible messages, timbre, inflection, intonation, duration, and rhythm, at the least, may well be. Just as the visual aspects of people differ, so do their voices. And the variations of sound in even a simple utterance must be at least equal to the visual changes wrought by movement.

Attention to the role of audition in the genesis of social behavior, then, in no way detracts from the role of vision but adds another and, it is proposed, as important an element. Given the newborns' advanced auditory apparatus and the evidence that speech is addressed to them from the moment of birth, the contribution of the auditory sense to the development of social behavior must now be recognized.

References

Alegria, J., & Noirot, E. Neonate orientation behaviour towards human voice. *International Journal of Behavioral Development,* 1978, *1,* 291–312.

Birns, B., Blank, M., Bridger, W. H., & Escalona, S. K. Behavioral inhibition in neonates produced by auditory stimuli. *Child Development,* 1965, *36,* 639–645.

Condon, W. S., & Sander, L. W. Neonate movement is synchronized with adult speech: Interactional participation and language acquisition. *Science,* 1974, *183,* 99–101.

Eisenberg, R. B. The organization of auditory behavior. *Journal of Speech and Hearing Research,* 1970, *13,* 453–471.

Hammer, M., & Turkewitz, G. Relationship between effective intensity of auditory stimulation and directional eye turns in the human newborn. *Animal Behaviour,* 1975, *23,* 287–290.

Hutt, S. J., Hutt, C., Lenard, H. G., Bernuth, H. V., & Muntjewerff, W. J. Auditory responsivity in the human neonate. *Nature,* 1968, *218,* 888–890.

Kessen, W., Haith, M. M., & Salapatek, P. H. Human infancy: A bibliography and guide. In P. H. Mussen (Ed.), *Carmichael's manual of child psychology* (Vol. 1, 3rd ed.). New York: Wiley, 1970.

Mendelson, M. J., & Haith, M. M. The relation between audition and vision in the human newborn. *Monographs of the Society for Research in Child Development,* 1976, *41* (4, Serial No. 167).

Muir, D., & Field, J. Newborn infants orient to sounds. *Child Development,* 1979, *50,* 431–436.

Parke, R. D., & O'Leary, S. E. Family interaction in the newborn period: Some findings, some observations, and some unresolved issues. In K. F. Riegel & J. A. Meacham (Eds.), *The developing individual in a changing world* (Vol. 2): *Social and environmental issues.* The Hague, The Netherlands: Mouton, 1976.

Rheingold, H. L. The effect of environmental stimulation upon social and exploratory behaviour in the human infant. In B. M. Foss (Ed.), *Determinants of infant behaviour.* London: Methuen, 1961.

Snow, C. E. The development of conversation between mothers and babies. *Journal of Child Language,* 1977, *4,* 1–22.

Turkewitz, G., Birch, H. G., & Cooper, K. K. Responsiveness to simple and complex auditory stimuli in the human newborn. *Developmental Psychobiology,* 1972, *5,* 7–19.

Webster's third new international dictionary of the English language, unabridged (14th ed.). Springfield, Mass.: Merriam, 1961.

Received January 2, 1980.

304

Personality and the Self

305

Before exploring theories of personality and the development of the self, it would be worthwhile to simulate the way in which much of the research in this area is conducted—that is, through the analysis of personality inventories. The following inventory by Lee Willerman (1975) provides a brief example of this method for assessing personality.

Item	How true is this of you?				
	Hardly at all				A lot
1. I make friends easily.	1	2	3	4	5
2. I tend to be shy.	1	2	3	4	5
3. I like to be with others.	1	2	3	4	5
4. I like to be independent of people.	1	2	3	4	5
5. I usually prefer to do things alone.	1	2	3	4	5
6. I am always on the go.	1	2	3	4	5
7. I like to be off and running as soon as I wake up in the morning.	1	2	3	4	5
8. I like to keep busy all of the time.	1	2	3	4	5
9. I am very energetic.	1	2	3	4	5
10. I prefer quiet, inactive pastimes to more active ones.	1	2	3	4	5
11. I tend to cry easily.	1	2	3	4	5
12. I am easily frightened.	1	2	3	4	5
13. I tend to be somewhat emotional.	1	2	3	4	5
14. I get upset easily.	1	2	3	4	5
15. I tend to be easily irritated.	1	2	3	4	5

To score this inventory, reverse the numbers of items 2, 4, 5, and 10; that is, for those items only, change any selection of 1 to 5, 2 to 4, 4 to 2, and 5 to 1 (there is no need to alter selections of 3 for these items). Next, add your responses to the statements for items 1 through 5, then for 6 through 10, and finally for 11 through 15. You should now have three total scores; these pertain to the basic personality dimensions of sociability, activity level, and emotionality, respectively.

By examining the chart on p. 307, the inventory, you can compare your standing on each of the three personality categories with a college-age sample tested by Willerman. It may be interesting to think about how your perceptions of yourself match these results. According to Willerman, "If your score falls below or above these ranges, you may regard yourself as exceptionally high or low [in that disposition]" (p. 35). Also note the different ranges for males versus females.

A recurring dilemma in attempting to grasp the nature of child development, and one that is particularly important for the study of personality and the self, is the issue of stability versus change. This book has shown that the concept of development implies certain changes beyond mere physical or quantitative growth. On the one hand, most definitions of personality include the notion of an enduring, characteristic pattern of behavior. Maddi (1980), for instance, conceptualized personality as a set of tendencies that determine thoughts, feelings, and actions over time. On the other hand, theory and research in personality development also have indicated that patterns of behavior do not remain unaltered from birth through adolescence.

There is considerable disagreement about the extent to which change is possible and what sources may promote personality development. For example, how critical are the early years of life in establishing the foundation for later characteristics? Does an inherited disposition persist throughout development despite environmental influences? What kinds of experiences, and with what regularity, are necessary to effect personality change? Are developmental changes in personality relatively predictable, or do random events foster a gradual evolution of individual styles of adaptation?

Answers to these questions, which are only beginning to emerge, illustrate the complexities of personality. Interactions between biological and environmental factors produce both continuity and

The biological roots illustrated by the obvious physical similarity of this mother-daughter pair suggest the strong role of heredity in child development. Is this equally significant for personality characteristics?

Personality Disposition	Statement Numbers	Typical Range for Males	Typical Range for Females
Sociability	1 to 5	13 to 19	15 to 20
Activity Level	6 to 10	13 to 19	13 to 20
Emotionality	11 to 15	9 to 16	11 to 18

Source: From Willerman, L. (1975). *Individual and group differences*, Austin, Tex.: Hogg Foundation. Reprinted by permission of Dr. Wayne H. Holtzman, President, Hogg Foundation, Austin, Tex.

transformations of personality. Furthermore, whereas fairly regular changes might be anticipated, dramatic events or unusual circumstances may modify more predictable patterns. Although there are several dozen widely recognized theories of personality, categorized in many different ways, this chapter will attempt a detailed analysis of only

two theorists. Sigmund Freud (1856–1939) and Erik Erikson (b. 1902) have provided numerous insights concerning the dynamic stages and interpersonal relationships within child development. Their work, characterized by the term *psychodynamics*, emphasizes the flow of personality changes across time. In contrast, behavioral and trait theories of personality tend to be more situational or static and will not, therefore, be addressed in this discussion of development. Humanistic (i.e., biological) theories are similarly nondevelopmental, but they will be mentioned later in the chapter because of their impact on personality research.

Following the presentation of Freud's and Erikson's theories, this chapter will explore the nature of the self-concept and self-esteem; that is, children's own awareness of their personalities. Finally, it will raise issues that pervade the analysis of personality development and introduce some examples of appropriate research.

Psychoanalytic Revolution of Freud

Sigmund Freud set himself the task of analyzing the dynamic workings of the human mind. His medical training and his background in literature and philosophy helped him to formulate an insightful theory that linked the physical, social, and psychological aspects of development.

Basic Principles

Freud postulated several interrelated themes that contribute to the development of personality. The first is the principle of **psychic determinism,** which states that every mental activity or event is caused by the activities or events that preceded it. Telling a joke, having a dream, saying something "by mistake," or even singing a certain song for no apparent reason always are caused by influences from the past. Although we may not be able to identify the sources of our thoughts or feelings, there are no mental accidents. If we find ourselves wondering why a friend's comment angered us so much or why we are so fearful about attending a forthcoming party, Freud would suggest that the answers may be found in previous events; past events determine our reactions to the present. Although this notion is restrictive—allowing little room for either random behavior or creative change—it is not altogether incompatible with most assumptions about how child development operates.

A second principle of personality is the significance of **unconscious motivation.** Not only is our mental activity determined by the past, but also we are often completely unaware of the processes that guide our daily lives. Because we are not conscious of the motivating factors for all that we think and feel, we tend to perceive a gap between our superficial mental activities and the reasons for their occurrence. If we could become aware of the entire psychic pattern, both conscious and unconscious, a consistency would be revealed. For example, the friend's remark that angered us so easily may be a reminder of the criticism and tone of voice that we heard so frequently from one of our parents. It is, therefore, the unconscious aspects of our personalities that add an element of mystery to our mental functioning. According to Freud, the unconscious also is the source of our psychological problems, since it is the repository of forgotten early experiences and memories that may be unpleasant.

In addition, Freudian theory is based on two instinctual energy forces that are responsible for stimulating the course of personality development. The most important of these instincts is termed *Eros,* or the life force. The life force includes such physiological drives as hunger, thirst, and sex. The energy of the life force, known as **libido,** generates a sense of mental excitement or tension concerning sexuality; this energy was the object of Freud's intense analysis. He maintained that the human being attempts to reduce the demands of libido and seek gratification through sexual pleasure. Freud did not mean to suggest that sexual intercourse is the only way to reduce erotic drives. For instance, even the pleasure which an infant may derive from sucking would be considered an appropriate means for satisfying erotic tensions. Other pleasurable activities that might be associated with libidinal energy include touching, kissing, defecating, and displaying the body to others.

Later in his career Freud introduced an opposing instinctual force, known as *Thanatos,* which functions as a kind of perpetual, yet unconscious, death wish. This instinct becomes more powerful as the individual ages, but it is present from birth and is responsible for our hostile or self-destructive behaviors. In the case of suicide, for example, the aggressive energy that is usually expressed out-

Emotions and the behaviors which emanate from them are often complex and ambiguous. An adolescent Halloween costume may contain elements of diverse feelings (such as fear, anger, sensuality, or joy) that reflect the developing personality.

wardly is turned inward as Thanatos overwhelms Eros to reach the ultimate state of reduced anxiety.

Just as Eros means more than the desire for intercourse and food, Thanatos does not always refer to death itself, but to hostility and aggression in general. Moreover, the aggressive drive operates in a fascinating and simultaneous interplay with the life force. The infant, for example, may use the mouth to gratify opposite instincts by both sucking and biting. A toddler can deliberately urinate on the rug to anger a parent, as well as to satisfy a physical urge. The genitals, which we usually associate with sexual pleasure, also can be thought of as weapons. It is now recognized that rapists are performing an act of hostility, not merely reducing sexual tensions.

Freud's concept of the death instinct was not as clearly elaborated as were his ideas about sexuality. Consequently, it has been treated less favorably by critics of psychoanalysis and often relegated to a minor role in development. As each of the previous examples demonstrates, however, it is often quite difficult to separate the erotic from the hostile components of our behavior. Since Freud believed that the two instincts are usually fused (although one may dominate at a particular time), it is possible to understand how we can have contradictory feelings (of love and hate, for instance) toward another person. Each of us, has, at least occasionally, felt confused about our motives for certain behaviors or thoughts. Freud would suggest that we need to disentangle our early sources of instinctual satisfaction to see how the intricate pieces of the personality became assembled.

Personality Structures

The instinctual forces in children—one pushing them toward self-centered gratification of physical needs and the other, toward aggressive behaviors—will certainly bring them into conflict with society. This conflict is at the heart of Freud's theory. In attempting to resolve the clash, certain structures of the personality—the id, the ego, and the superego—must be understood.

Id

Present from birth, the **id** is the irrational, unconscious, greedy, and selfish component of our personalities that seeks gratification at any cost. Being pushed toward immediate tension reduction by the id, we are led to engage in what Freud called **primary process thinking,** an example of which is provided by infant behavior. In a sense, the infant personality is pure id. Infants are not interested in logical consistency, societal restrictions, or the problems of other people. When they want to be fed, changed, or held, they cry impatiently. Around-the-clock feedings are not considered to be unreasonable demands, because infants have yet to develop moderating personality structures.

Ego

During the second year of life, infants become increasingly aware that things do not always work in the way they demand. Sometimes a toddler will have to wait for what is wanted or may even be denied the pleasure sought. To handle the restrictions imposed by reality, a new structure emerges. Freud labeled this component of personality the **ego.** By siphoning off some of the energy that the id possesses, the ego functions primarily at the conscious level to help the individual deal sensibly with other people and the rest of the world. Freud felt that the ego promotes the use of **secondary process thinking,** which is characterized by an ability to postpone instinctual gratification. In contrast

to the id, which seeks fulfillment through any means available, the ego develops as a patient and rational means for alleviating demands. Ego development is not a sudden change in the child's outlook, but a gradual and sometimes painful adjustment to the restrictions on immediate gratification. As the mechanism for placating the demands of both id and eventually society, the ego's purpose is to serve as the great mediator of personality.

Superego

The last structure to emerge, beginning by the age of 3 or 4 and developing over the next few years, is known as the **superego.** Like the ego, this component of the personality arises by using energy from the id in a largely conscious or preconscious (readily brought to awareness) way so as to establish acceptable, internal standards of behavior. Through identification with parents, children learn to view themselves as members of a culture and to incorporate the society's values as their own. Thus, the id represents the needs of the self, the superego represents society's point of view, and the ego serves to moderate the demands of the id to accommodate civilization.

Freud believed that the superego is composed of two highly interconnected parts: the conscience and the ego ideal. On the one hand, the little voice inside us that warns about doing something wrong is our conscience (be certain to distinguish this from *conscious*). The infant may refrain from a particular activity because adults will physically prohibit it, not because of the pangs of conscience. Older children who are developing a superego, however, may behave to avoid violating standards which they have adopted, not because they were literally prevented from carrying out the activity.

Our ego ideal, on the other hand, is the embodiment of what we should be doing—the perfection of parental and cultural values that create a personal, internal hero for us to imitate. Once established, this image and the rules for conduct derived from it are as rigid and demanding in their own moralistic fashion as are the instinctual drives of the id. Therefore, the ego takes on a more difficult and critical role than ever before. It must check the "I want" of the id, as well as placate the "I should" or "I should not" of the superego.

Table 10.1 Freud's Psychosexual Stages of Development

Stage of Development	Emerging Structure	Approximate Age Range	Erogenous Zone and Gratification	Characteristic Area of Tension
Oral	Id	Birth to 18 months	Mouth/Breast	Weaning
Anal	Ego	1½ to 3 years	Anus/Feces	Toilet training
Phallic	Superego	3 to 6 years	Genitals/Opposite-sex parent	Oedipal conflict
Latent	Balance of personality	6 to 12 years	None	None
Genital	Re-integration of personality	Puberty to death	Genitals/Opposite sex	Instincts versus society

Somewhere in the conflict between the other two structures, the ego attempts to maintain a functional system. If the id gains the upper hand, our selfish behaviors will lead to condemnation and rejection by society. If our superego is permitted too much control, however, we will experience so much anxiety or guilt that we will become incapable of effective and creative functioning. Freud felt that civilization could not survive unless the demands of the id are sufficiently curbed, but that the individual could not maintain psychological health (relatively free of anxiety) unless tensions also are released.

Stages of Development

Child development, from a psychoanalytic perspective, is the process of learning to cope with the various manifestations of instinctual energy. Libido is focused on certain areas of the body at different times in life. Thus, psychological gratification depends upon a biological source of tension and excitement that defines a particular stage of development.

Freud identified five stages of development. The terms used to identify each of the stages—oral, anal, phallic, latent, and genital—clearly indicate Freud's greater concern with erotic, or psychosexual, drives than with other life or death instincts (see Table 10.1). Freud's theory is especially interesting because his stages represent the first comprehensive attempt to synthesize physical and mental functioning. All stages are generally related to chronological age, but they also overlap with preceding and subsequent stages. The following sections describe the sequence of psychosexual development and its consequences for the personality.

Oral Stage

Libidinal energy, according to Freud, is concentrated in the mouth during the first year or so of life. Infants derive much pleasure from sucking and mouthing objects in their world throughout this oral stage. It appears that oral activities, especially the experience of being fed, constitute the mechanism for incorporating and knowing reality. Compared with other activities, infants spend considerable time sucking, biting, chewing, teething, spitting up, vocalizing, crying, and breathing. Some of these behaviors satisfy the instinctual demands of aggression as well as infantile eroticism. Freud believed that the pattern of frustration and indulgence of oral needs, which parents help the infant to establish, determines the foundation for adult personality characteristics. However, it is important to recognize that the oral stage represents the initial arena for human gratification and conflict.

Anal Stage

A second source for psychosexual energy becomes dominant sometime during the second year and remains especially crucial for a year or two thereafter. Libidinal energy now is centered at the

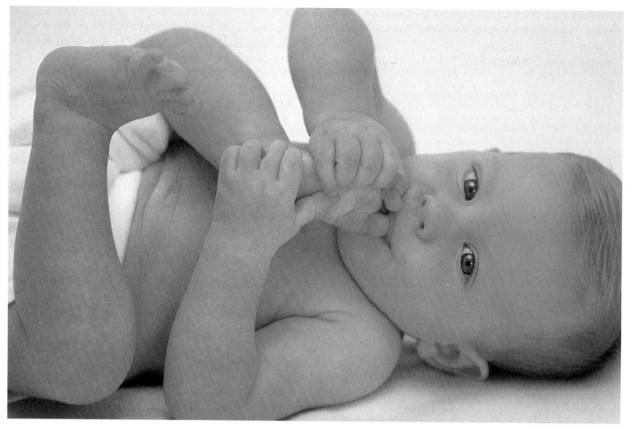

According to Sigmund Freud, personality is formulated early in life through the resolution of tensions relating to oral activities. Infants engage in many forms of oral tension reduction, such as sucking toes.

anal region. Therefore, the sensations accompanying retention and evacuation of feces are very satisfying for the toddler. (To a lesser extent, similar gratification is associated with urination.)

At the same time that feelings of pleasure surround anal activities, there is also greater opportunity for the child to express aggressive drives. Whereas infants, who are catered to and protected, are not expected to delay impulses or to control their behavior, toddlers begin to be faced with explicit social demands. Freud speculated that as the child moves slightly closer toward death, the aggressive drive begins to exert a bit more influence over the life force. The ego must develop to help the young child confront the competing pressures of libido and society. No longer can the world be readily incorporated or rejected; the child must reduce anal tension in light of restrictions imposed by parents. Although the problems involved in weaning an infant from extensive dependence on oral activities should not be minimized, the conflicts regarding toilet training tend to be more difficult to resolve. In psychoanalytic theory, parental-toddler interactions concerning toilet training, which may range from punitive to permissive, can encourage personality characteristics that last a lifetime.

Phallic Stage

By the end of the second year or the beginning of the third year of life, the child has entered the most important stage of psychosexual development: the phallic stage. Libidinal energy now is concentrated in the genital region, which becomes the focal point of physical pleasure. Although children do not understand the reproductive nature of the genitalia, Freud believed they have an unconscious tendency to associate their phallus (erect penis) or clitoris (small penis) with some kind of activity with the parent of the opposite sex. Genital tensions lessen at approximately 5 or 6 years of age, bringing the phallic stage to a close. However, the events that occur during this period have major consequences for sexual and gender-role identity, for the formation of the superego (and, therefore, the preservation of society), and for the fusion of personality structures. It is necessary to discuss the course of phallic stage development separately for boys and girls, since Freud proposed different patterns for each.

At some deep level of knowing, rooted in the history of the human species, a boy relates his feelings of genital tension to his mother. Freud labeled the circumstances surrounding these feelings the *Oedipal complex,* based on the Greek myth of Oedipus, who unknowingly killed his father and married his mother. While the boy wishes to displace his father and physically possess his mother, he recognizes his father as a powerful rival for his mother's affections, and he knows he cannot compete with a person who is so strong and who has so much control over his world. He even fears that his father will emasculate him.

The antagonism generated between the boy and his imagined rival, therefore, is termed *castration anxiety.* This anxiety is particularly heightened when a boy notices that the sexual anatomy of a girl seems to be lacking his valued organ. Since anxiety is not a pleasurable state, the boy seeks to reduce his jealousy of his father by becoming as much like him as possible. Freud called the process through which a boy imitates his father and adopts his values an *identification.* Because the boy becomes socialized by identifying with his father (simultaneously reducing his interest in mother and his castration anxiety), Freud felt that the Oedipal complex is responsible for superego development.

A girl also undergoes experiences analogous to the Oedipal complex, but they are not as clear or dramatic as those occurring in a boy. There are two reasons for this difference. First, very young girls are less attached to their fathers than little boys

are to their mothers, so girls have a head start on feminine identification. Second, and of greater significance, girls do not have obvious, external genitals to arouse castration anxiety. Although a girl may have an unconscious desire to possess her father, she does not have to actually fear her mother.

Instead, having observed the male anatomy, the girl may believe she has already been castrated and blame her mother for allowing this to happen. This resentment and insecurity Freud labeled *penis envy.* The girl's attraction to her father may reflect a longing to substitute his penis for the one she has "lost." The girl must work out her feminine identification as libidinal energy lessens by imitating her mother and delaying her maturity until she can obtain a husband and a baby of her own to replace her father. Since hostility toward and competitiveness with mother are not entirely reduced during early childhood, Freud believed that female resolution of the Oedipal complex is not complete, resulting in a weaker superego than for males.

Latent Stage

Freud believed that from the ages of 6 or 8 until puberty, libidinal energy is diffuse; that is, it is not concentrated intensely at any one part of the body. As a result, and in conjunction with the resolution of Oedipal strivings, the child moves into the latency stage. During this period, sexual interests usually diminish (*latent* means "hidden"). The attraction to the opposite-sex parent, which was not permitted to be completely fulfilled, turns to an affectionate attachment. Social roles and sexual identification become increasingly solidified as the child is encouraged to emulate the same-sex parent. In other words, the increasing demands of society force the ego to reorient libidinal energy away from the id and toward a less selfish compromise with reality.

Freud never maintained that sexual feelings and experimentation do not occur during the latency stage. In fact, they can occur and are especially likely to do so in a sexually permissive environment. In cultures in which sexual play is common among children, there may be no latency stage at all. In more restrictive societies such as our own, sexual interests are usually discouraged, leading to a curious interruption in psychosexual development.

Genital Stage

As adolescence emerges, libidinal energy returns to the genital organs, which now have a reproductive function. Psychosexual development, therefore, culminates in a genital stage that continues throughout adulthood. The young adolescent experiences a reawakening of oral, anal, and phallic conflicts. In particular, Oedipal strivings may stimulate the adolescent to fall in love with, or have a crush on, older persons of the opposite sex. Movie stars, sports figures, or teachers, for example, are often the targets of the renewed Oedipal complex. As knowledge about sexuality increases, expressions of libidinal energy may take more direct forms. In contrast, adolescents who are embarrassed or confused about their sexual feelings may seek outlets other than masturbation, necking, or intercourse itself. Instead, they channel libidinal energy into "safe" areas such as political activism, athletics, or volunteer work.

Psychoanalytic Controversy

Even among Freud's followers, serious disagreements surfaced within a decade of the founding of the psychoanalytic movement. Controversy centered on his overemphasis of sexual and unconscious motivation, his fatalistic stress on early personality formation, and his pessimistic view that all behavior is essentially defensive. Freud's followers also questioned his view that even scientific inventions and works of art are examples of *sublimation* (the release of libidinal tensions in socially desirable ways). The rejection or modification of Freud's ideas by his followers led to the establishment of interpretations of personality development that differed from his, but still maintained important elements of the original position.

Erikson's Psychosocial Modifications

Discontent with the limitations of Freudian theory stimulated others to reassess psychoanalytic

principles from new perspectives. One of the most notable attempts to preserve the spirit of psychoanalysis, while infusing it with new life, has been fostered by Erik Erikson. In contrast to the relatively narrow range of opportunities experienced by Freud, Erikson has brought a wealth of cultural diversity to his theory of child development.

Basic Principles

Erikson has been responsible for extending and transforming the psychoanalytic account of personality development. Despite his belief in basic Freudian structural and functional characteristics, Erikson shifted emphasis from the unconscious and irrational id to the aware and rational ego. Not only does he feel that the ego is present at birth rather than emerging from the id, but also he assigns to the ego its own energy and a goal beyond that of helping to satisfy the id. For Freud, the ego was an arbitrator between instincts and civilization. The Eriksonian ego is a creative force for change that accounts for both the biological needs of individuals and the cultural and historical contexts of their lives.

In comparing the conceptions of Freud and Erikson, it is clear that the latter takes a more optimistic view of human nature. The crises of development originate in the accommodation of personal goals to social expectations, not simply in the inhibition of sexual demands. Thus, Erikson stresses psychosocial—rather than psychosexual—drives. Erikson is interested in how individuals are able to develop healthy egos that can be accepted and confirmed by those around them. Development is a continuous growth process in which the ego thrives on the challenge of resolving the potential conflicts between the self and society. Crises are not seen as pitfalls to be avoided or escaped from, but as opportunities for successful maturation. Although Freud recognized the significance of social conflict—particularly parent-child relationships—he tended to stress their negative outcomes and early foundations.

Stages of Development

Another major change that Erikson brought to psychoanalytic theory is the addition of adult stages of personality development. He replaced

Table 10.2   Erikson's Psychosocial Stages of Development

Phase of Life	Psychosocial Crisis	Favorable Outcome	Significant Relations	Social Modality
Infancy	Basic trust versus mistrust	Hope	Mother	To get—to give in return
Toddlerhood	Autonomy versus shame or doubt	Willpower	Parents	To hold (on)—to let (go)
Early Childhood	Initiative versus guilt	Purpose	Family	To make (going after)—to "make like" (playing)
School Age	Industry versus inferiority	Competence	Neighborhood and school	To make things—to do together
Adolescence	Ego identity versus role confusion	Devotion	Peer groups	To be oneself—to share oneself
Young Adulthood	Intimacy versus isolation	Love	Partnerships and friends	To lose and find oneself in another
Middle Adulthood	Generativity versus stagnation	Care	Divided labor and shared household	To make "be" (create)—to take care of
Maturity and Old Age	Ego integrity versus despair	Wisdom	"Mankind"	To be through having been—to face not being

Source: Adapted from *Childhood and Society*, 2nd Edition, by Erik H. Erikson, Copyright 1950 (1963) by W.W. Norton & Company, Inc. Copyright renewed 1978 by Erik H. Erikson; and from *Identity and the Life Cycle* by Erik H. Erikson. Copyright 1980 by W.W. Norton & Company, Inc. Copyright 1959 by International University Press, Inc. Used by permission of W.W. Norton & Company and of Chatto & Windus, Ltd. For British Empire rights.

Freud's genital stage with four phases of life ranging from adolescence to old age. Therefore, instead of five developmental stages as Freud had suggested, Erikson postulates an eight-stage sequence that parallels Freud's theory only in the childhood aspects (see Table 10.2).

Each of Erikson's stages is defined by a universally determined **psychosocial crisis** that builds upon and incorporates previous development, as well as cultural influences and biological change. Erikson's theory is not strictly tied to chronological age, nor are the stages always easy to separate. However, Erikson feels that each stage throughout the lifespan offers an important contribution to the total personality. The **epigenetic principle,** Erikson's (1968) summation of development, states that "anything that grows has a ground plan, and that out of this ground plan the parts arise, each part having its time of special ascendancy, until all parts have arisen to form a functioning whole" (p. 92).

Failure to deal adequately with early crises jeopardizes, but does not render impossible, the successful resolution of later crises. In contrast to Freud's pregenital-stage determinism, Erikson does not dismiss the capacity of the individual to again confront and reintegrate previous conflicts.

Infancy

According to Erikson, the young infant's first major crisis is whether a sense of basic trust or mistrust of the world will be established. To allow healthy ego functioning to develop, infants must learn to sleep deeply and to feed easily; they must gain a feeling of confidence that their needs will be met regularly. Since this is the most helpless period of life, it is essential that infants obtain consistent and loving care so that they will feel secure. However, Erikson (1968) states that

the amount of trust derived from earliest infantile experience does not seem to depend on absolute quantities of food or demonstrations of love, but rather on the quality of the maternal relationship. Mothers create a sense of trust in their children by that kind of administration which in its quality combines sensitive care of the baby's individual needs and a firm sense of personal trustworthiness within the trusted framework of their culture's lifestyle. (P. 249)

Ultimately, the infant should tolerate parental absence without undue anxiety, gain a sense of certainty about social relations, and have hope for a positive future. Of course, an infant should also develop a certain measure of mistrust. To survive in this world, it is unwise to trust blindly everyone and everything. However, an infant's failure to achieve a favorable balance in the direction of trust sets the stage for later anxiety about satisfying essential needs, creates suspicion of other people's motives, and leads to feelings of depression.

Toddlerhood

Instead of centering the source of conflict in the second stage exclusively on issues of toilet training, Erikson describes this stage as a crisis of autonomy and self-control versus shame or doubt. Toddlers must learn to accept the privileges and the limitations that growing up entails. The task of parents is to help children become independent— literally "stand on their own feet." At the same time, the infant must learn to control muscular activity that is socially unacceptable. Obviously, the anal and urethral muscles can become a battleground for this conflict. Erikson (1963) explains how the delicate balance of this stage

> becomes decisive for the ratio of love and hate, cooperation and willfulness, freedom of self-expression and its suppression. From a sense of self-control without loss of self-esteem comes a lasting sense of good will and pride; from a sense of loss of self-control and of foreign over-control comes a lasting propensity for doubt and shame. (P. 254)

Parents should protect their toddlers from experiences leading to failure and destructiveness without curbing their desires to do things for themselves. If Mary insists on pouring a glass of milk

by herself, for example, perhaps she should be allowed to do so, even though she is apt to make a mess of it. In contrast, no parent would or should allow a toddler to play with matches. As in all of Erikson's stages, a delicate balance is required. Parental control is both realistic and necessary. Yet, if toddlers are habitually punished for their strivings toward independence, they may begin to doubt their decision-making abilities, feel ashamed of their "incompetence," and become inflexible and secretive adults.

Early Childhood

The third stage of psychosocial development builds on earlier trust and autonomy to overcome the crisis of initiative versus guilt. Children who successfully resolve this conflict learn to plan their own activities and organize the directions for channeling their energy. As a consequence, they have a feeling of purpose that is expressed by their imagination, curiosity, and experimentation. If parents resent the questions their child frequently asks (including those about sexuality and sex differences), if they are not models of responsible behavior, if they belittle the child's fantasies or ideas, and if they discourage interaction with the peer group, the child will develop a sense of resignation and guilt about initiating new tasks or pondering the mysteries of life.

For the individual who does not establish a favorable ratio of initiative to guilt during early childhood, particular personality characteristics may hinder subsequent development. Adults who are passive, impotent, or irresponsible might still be fearing the punishment and ridicule they received from their parents many years ago. Erikson (1967) suggests that such people lack a sense of purpose or "the courage to envisage and pursue valued goals uninhibited by the defeat of infantile fantasies, by guilt and by the foiling fear of punishment" (P. 122).

School Age

With the advent of later childhood comes a shift from family and fantasy toward a more formal introduction to the culture. Now that children are physically and intellectually stronger, in addition

Parents have to tolerate the exploratory and sometimes risky activities of their preschool children. Children may later become passive and excessively guilty if their parents severely restrict their exploratory behavior.

to more emotionally stable, they are expected to demonstrate relevant forms of competence:

> Thus the inner stage seems all set for "entrance into life," except that life must first be school life, whether school is field or jungle or classroom. The child must forget past hopes and wishes, while his exuberant imagination is tamed and harnessed to the laws of impersonal things— even the three R's . . . he now learns to win recognition by producing things. (Erikson 1963, 258–259)

Virtually ignored by Freud, the latency period is a crucial conflict between industry and inferiority, according to Erikson. Children must learn to use the tools of their society, whether the tools

include spears or computers, rain dances or written language, pottery or mathematics. Although children are rarely expected to contribute much to the traditions or direct survival of the culture, they must prepare for entrance into adulthood by showing perseverance and diligence in the completion of assigned tasks. Productive activities and the mastery of complex skills are demanded of children in diverse ways—for example, doing chores around the house, participating in religious ceremonies, earning good grades in school, and playing constructively with friends.

The danger of this crisis is the sense of inferiority that might result from failure to compete effectively with peers or from constant criticism from significant adults (mostly parents and teachers). Failure may lead not only to humiliation, but also to the possibility of becoming a conformist slave to achievement while neglecting socioemotional growth. Again, a delicate balance is required here, too. Children must learn that failure is a normal part of life; experience with, as well as learning to cope with, occasional failure can actually strengthen children.

Adolescence

Adolescence, the period of the lifespan in which Erikson has shown the greatest interest, is designated by the crisis of ego identity versus role confusion. Although the biological changes of puberty may trigger the onset of this crisis, Erikson does not view a conflict between society and sexuality to be the chief source of adolescent anxiety. Instead, the ego's task is to integrate previous childhood experiences in order to create a commitment to a set of values, a sense of personal identity, and a direction for the future. Searching for a sense of who they are and where they are going is particularly difficult for adolescents raised in contemporary, technological civilizations. In addition to coping with the dramatic physical changes of puberty that cause them great concern about their appearance to others, adolescents must negotiate a complex array of choices on the road to adulthood.

Erikson regards the interval between the role confusion of early adolescence and the achievement of a secure identity by adulthood as a psychosocial moratorium. He feels that this is a time of delaying adult commitments. It is

> characterized by a selective permissiveness on the part of society and of provocative playfulness on the part of youth, and yet it also often leads to deep, if often transitory, commitment on the part of youth, and ends in a more or less ceremonial confirmation of commitment on the part of society. (Erikson 1968, 157)

Through such free experimentation, the adolescent may find a unique and appropriate sociocultural niche. However, the turmoil and dilemmas of the period may result in perpetual role confu-

sion, premature and unexplored identities (possibly adopted from parents), temporary over-identification with popular heroes or ideologies (e.g., rock musicians or revolutionary movements), and socially deviant identities (e.g., the attitude that it is better to be a delinquent gang member than a nobody). If self-consciousness and the protection of cliques and slogans can be overcome, fidelity—"the ability to sustain loyalties freely-pledged in spite of the inevitable contradictions of value systems" (Erikson 1964, 125)—can emerge.

Young Adulthood

Having constructed the basis for an adult identity, the individual is ready to face the crisis of intimacy versus isolation. Only when people are comfortable with themselves are they capable of sharing their intimate feelings and ideas with another person in a mature, nonselfish way. Neither the dependent attachment of infants nor the blind infatuation of adolescents qualifies as genuine love. However, the young adult, "emerging from the search for and the insistence on identity, is eager and willing to fuse his identity with that of others" (Erikson 1963, 263).

Middle Adulthood

If people learn how to love and how to share in early adulthood, they will be able to care for and guide the next generation effectively. Erikson considers the crisis of this long seventh stage of personality development, which may extend until the fifth or sixth decade of life, to be one of generativity versus stagnation. The adult who does not make a contribution to children's development or to humanity is left with a sense of impoverishment and stagnation. These feelings may be reflected by excessive self-indulgence and other manifestations of a middle-age crisis.

Maturity and Old Age

Erikson believes that the final conflict of development focuses on how people look back over their lives and how they approach impending death. Thus, the elderly must negotiate between integrity and despair. On the one hand, individuals who have achieved favorable ratios with regard to the earlier conflicts may attain wisdom. In reviewing their past, they have a sense of satisfaction, rather than regret. On the other hand, some people are filled with despair and fear of death. Instead of fulfillment, these people long for another chance to imbue their lives with meaning.

Psychosocial Evaluation

Erikson's theory is the culmination of the psychodynamic approach to personality development. In his emphasis on flexibility, optimism, and environmental factors, he has created a contemporary variation of Freudian theory. Although Erikson credits his own contributions to Freud's foundation and maintains much of the flavor of psychoanalytic theory in his writing, there are definite anthropological and behavioral elements in his work that might have made Freud quite uncomfortable. Chapter 7 described how the processes of learning theory represent an important component of child development. The mechanisms of reinforcement and observational learning play a role in the formation of personality, just as they do in affecting cognitive activities. Erikson, by no means a behavioral theorist, supports a position that regards the nurture aspects of development in a more equal balance than the dominant nature position that Freud never relinquished.

Nevertheless, there are certainly legitimate criticisms of Erikson's theory; often these parallel weaknesses in Freud's approach. For instance, both psychodynamic theories fail to make adequate distinctions between the personality development of boys and girls. Although Erikson's ideas have been somewhat less offensive than Freud's views, the section on the self in this chapter and the discussion of gender roles in Chapter 14 will elaborate on these weaknesses. A different limitation of both theories is the lack of systematic data that would either support or refute Freud's and Erikson's positions. Their theories were created on the basis of clinical sessions with patients rather than from the collection of empirical evidence. As vague and difficult to demonstrate as some of these ideas are, more and more research on the details of Erikson's theory, at least, are proving to be not only testable, but also valid. The crisis of identity versus confusion, in particular, has attracted the attention of many personality development researchers in recent years.

Development of the Self

A number of personality theorists, such as Gordon Allport (1961), Carl Rogers (1961), and George Kelly (1955), view the study of the self as the central issue in personality and its development. Their humanistic views emphasize that almost everything we do influences the self and the self-concept; conversely, the self and self-concept influence almost everything we do.

What Is the Self?

A simple task, used in a number of studies on the self, can demonstrate several points about the nature of the self: Label the top of a blank sheet of paper with the question "Who am I?" Now proceed to respond to this question, taking about fifteen minutes to do so; be sure to answer with the first things that come to mind. Try to list twenty answers to the question. Now try to answer again as if you were an 8-year-old, then a 12-year-old, and then a 16-year-old.

Answering the Twenty Statements Test (Kuhn & McPartland 1954), as the foregoing task is called, requires *objectification* on the self. For some adults, this may not be as easy as it looks; adults may run out of answers after the fourth item. This task of objectification is especially hard for young children. As you look over the responses generated, you may find that they typically fall into a number of categories that reflect physical aspects of the self (e.g., tall, thin), social roles (e.g., student, daughter), and personality qualities (e.g., moody, conservative). Thus, people tend to think of themselves along a variety of dimensions. These dimensions may change with age, as may be seen by comparing your hypothetical children's responses with your adult responses. Thus, the self is a developmental phenomenon, which undergoes significant change and modification.

Some of these insights are a part of psychology's heritage. William James, a professor of the early 1900s who is considered to be the father of American psychology, devoted a large portion of his textbook *Principles of Psychology* (1890) to the self. James divided the self into the subject, or knower (the "I"), and the object, or the known (the "me"). The study of the self as "I" (the active and engaged self) has only recently received attention in the developmental literature (Damon & Hart 1982; Harter 1983; Logan 1986), but the self as "me" (the reflective and descriptive self) has been the focus of numerous theoretical and empirical studies since James's original work. James further divided the self as known into the *material me* (physical self and possessions), the *social me* (roles and interpersonal relations), and the *spiritual me* (consciousness and thoughts).

The term **self-concept** refers to the aspect of the self that is objectively known. The self-concept includes all the ideas, concepts and attributes linked to the awareness of the self. **Self-esteem** is the evaluative, or subjective, aspect of the self-concept. When labels and emotions such as "good" or "bad" are related to the social, physical, and personality/spiritual aspects of the self, the level of self-esteem can be raised or lowered. Often, as James (1968) noted, comparisons are made between an "ideal" self and the current status of the self (the "real" self). When an individual rates a large discrepancy between the ideal and the real self, low levels of self-esteem may result. In contrast, a close resemblance to an indivdual's ideal self serves to raise self-esteem.

Finally, for purposes of reducing the complexity of the self, it is helpful to view the self-concept as influenced by three major developmental components. The first component involved cognitive development. Because the self-concept is a result of thinking, qualitative changes in thinking will significantly affect ideas about the self. Contemporary self-concept theorists have discovered a number of parallels between self-concept development and the stages of preoperational, concrete operational, and formal operational development as presented by Piaget (Harter 1983; Noppe 1983).

The second component involves interpersonal development. The notion that the concept of the self arises out of social interaction has a long history (Baldwin 1897; Cooley 1902; Mead 1934). According to this view, as children develop they construct a "looking-glass self"; that is, the reflection of the self in the eyes of others is what forms the basis of the self-concept. People who are highly valued *(significant others)* are especially likely to

have their appraisals and ideas incorporated into an individual's sense of self. The cast of significant others changes with development. Thus, parents and teachers are significant others during the early childhood years; their influence gradually defers to the influence of peers and best friends during adolescence (Harter 1983).

Personality development, particularly in the Eriksonian sense of achieving a sense of unity and self-consistency, is the final major component to influence the self-concept. According to Erikson (1968), certain developmental tasks are necessary for the achievement of an integrated personality. These tasks—leading to a sense of self-trust, self-autonomy, self-initiative, and self-competence—have important implications for the concepts of self, self-esteem, and the "I" as the self that organizes and interprets experience.

Development of the Self-Concept

Using the previous analysis of the self as a conceptual framework, this section analyzes the developmental course of the self-concept from infancy through adolescence.

Infancy

Infants need to establish a subjective and objective sense of self. They must first learn that they can cause things to happen, such as mother's approach, the shake of a rattle, and the scratching sound on their sheets. Such a sense of self emerges from the feedback babies receive in their everyday interactions with people and objects (Lewis & Brooks-Gunn 1979). In particular, parental imitation of the baby's actions seems to be a significant source of feedback (Harter 1983). These experiences are important for the emergence of the "I," as well as the "me."

Theoretically, the objective sense of self may be linked to the development of object permanence (the knowledge that objects continue to exist even when they are out of view). The development of the self as object has been studied by presenting a mirror to infants and noting how they respond. One of the earliest studies to use this technique was published by Dixon (1957). He longitudinally

Does this infant recognize himself in the mirror? A primitive conception of the self, according to several developmental researchers, begins to evolve during the second year of life.

observed five infants, from the ages of 4 months to the age of 12. He found a four-stage developmental sequence of visual self-recognition:

Stage 1. The baby has no interest in the reflection in the mirror.
Stage 2. The baby responds to the image in the mirror as if it were an interesting playmate.
Stage 3. The baby is able to differentiate between his or her own reflection and the mirror image of another child.
Stage 4. The baby shows definite signs of self-recognition.

Later studies on visual self-recognition have supported Dixon's developmental sequence, al-though the age at which true self-awareness becomes evident varies between 12 and 20 months.

Observing self-recognition through mirror play is difficult, because the researcher has to determine whether infants perceive their own facial features or those of "another child" in the mirror. Several studies have attempted to separate these factors. Amsterdam (1972) and Lewis and Brooks (1975) placed rouge on the noses of infants, as a point of reference for evaluating self-recognition. Infants showed obvious signs of self-recognition if they looked in the mirror, saw rouge on the nose of the image, and then touched their own noses. This occurred sometime during the latter half of the second year. Finally, Lewis and Brooks-Gunn

(1979) found that infants, beginning at about 15 months of age, were able to distinguish between live television images of themselves, television images of themselves taken one week earlier, and television images of another infant.

Research on the self-concept during infancy has been limited, of course, by the infant's lack of language. Yet, the evidence seems to strongly point out—at least on a visual basis—that older infants have constructed a sense of "I" and "me," are able to tell themselves apart from others of the same age, and can distinguish between their knowledge of themselves and their knowledge of their mothers (Pipp, Fischer & Jennings 1987).

Childhood

During the childhood years, changes in the self-concept are related to a number of important developmental processes. First, the child can now use words to label himself or herself and can verbalize what aspects are of the self and what are "not-self" (Markus 1977). Second, ways of conceiving the self become more diverse with increasing age (Mullener & Laird 1971). There is a differentiation of the self during childhood that leads older children to think of themselves using more ideas and categories than do younger children. Third, children's self-concept development appears to parallel the general cognitive developmental sequence of preoperational to concrete operational to formal operational thought. That is, children's self-descriptions begin by focusing upon physical, external aspects of the self; then, as they grow older, they refer to themselves more often in psychological terms. For further details on this observation, see the Research Close-up "Who Am I?"

Many of these points were studied by Guardo and Bohan (1971). They examined the sense of self exhibited by 6- to 9-year-olds. To do this, the researchers asked the children if they could become a pet (testing for the sense of humanity), an opposite-sex peer (testing for the sense of sexuality), or a same-sex peer (testing for the sense of individuality), and whether they were the same person in the past and future (testing for the sense of continuity). All of the children expressed a sense of their humanity, individuality, sexuality, and continuity. But, Guardo and Bohan found that the 6- and 7-year-olds emphasized their physical characteristics (e.g., not being able to assume the identity of a friend because their traits are different).

Adolescence

Many people consider adolescence to be the crucible of self-concept development. As previously discussed, Erikson (1968) views adolescence as a time of the establishment of a sense of identity. Identity involves a sense of unity across different components of the self; a sense of continuity between past, present, and future selves; and a sense of mutuality between the individual's self-concept and the views that significant others have of the self. Adolescents strive for self-consistency, which is a fundamental aspect of a mature self-concept (Lecky 1945), at a time when the self as others view it takes on a heightened importance. They are very self-conscious about the view others may have of them (Elkind & Bowen 1979) and anchor much of their self-concepts in social roles (Noppe 1983). Additionally, the emergence of formal-operational reasoning opens the way for an increase in self-reflection—thinking about the self in a hypothetical plane, and generally using more psychological and abstract concepts to describe the self.

Adolescence is the time for the construction of a "self-theory." A self-theory is much like a scientific theory; it has principles, serves to generate hypotheses, attempts to be internally consistent, and can be verified by experiments (Epstein 1973). The major difference between a self-theory and a scientific theory is that it is constructed by an individual about himself or herself. Much of the self-reflection during adolescence, therefore, functions to develop a self-theory that can be used as an aid to interpret experience. Abstract thoughts, broadened and more intimate social relationships, and a newly acquired future orientation act as catalysts for the emergence of the self-theory, which maintains its importance throughout adolescence and in the years beyond.

Self-esteem

Self-esteem becomes increasingly important as children learn to evaluate themselves. Research using pictorial self-esteem scales has indicated that young children (aged 4 to 7) do not have a general

Research Close-up

Who Am I?

Measuring the self-concept is not an easy task. Despite the problems associated with scoring an open-ended type of questionnaire, self-concept researchers prefer this method because responses are not as influenced by the questions asked, as they are in more structured questionnaires. The Twenty Statements Test (TST) is an open-ended, self-concept instrument that requests subjects to respond to the question "Who Am I?" Answers are then placed into one of a number of categories, such as social roles, physical characteristics, personality attributes, and a sense of unity. The TST has traditionally been used with adults. Montemayor and Eisen (1977) charted the development of the self-concept by giving the TST to children aged 10 to 18 years. When the researchers classified the children's answers, they found that younger children described themselves in concrete ways: their sex, name, age, likes, dislikes. For example, here are the responses of a 9-year-old fourth grader:

> My name is Bruce C. I have brown eyes. I have brown hair. I have

brown eyebrows. I'm nine years old. I LOVE! Sports. I have seven people in my family. I have great! eye site. I have lots! of friends. I live on 1923 Pinecrest Dr. I'm going on 10 in September. I'm a boy. I have a uncle that is almost 7 feet tall. My school is Pinecrest. My teacher is Mrs. V. I play Hockey! I'am almost the smartest boy in the class. I LOVE! food. I love fresh air. I LOVE School.

Older children and young adolescents described themselves more in terms of their interpersonal relationships and personality characteristics. Here are the statements made by an 11½-year-old girl in the sixth grade:

> My name is A. I'm a human being. I'm a girl. I'm a truthful person. I'm not pretty. I do so-so in my studies. I'm a very good cellist. I'm a very good pianist. I'm a little bit tall for my age. I like several boys. I like several girls. I'm old-fashioned. I play tennis. I am a *very* good swimmer. I try to be helpful. I'm always ready to be friends with anybody. Mostly I'm good, but I lose my temper. I'm not well-liked by some girls and boys. I don't know if I'm liked by boys or not.

The older adolescent in this study was much more focused on psychological aspects of the self. Relative to the younger children, more was said about moods,

beliefs, feelings, and interpersonal relations. A 17-year-old twelfth grader wrote:

> I am a human being. I am a girl. I am an individual. I don't know who I am. I am a Pisces. I am a moody person. I am an indecisive person. I am an ambitious person. I am a very curious person. I am not an individual. I am a loner. I am an American (God help me). I am a Democrat. I am a liberal person. I am a radical. I am a conservative. I am a pseudoliberal. I am an atheist. I am not a classifiable person (i.e., I don't want to be).

Self-conception, according to Montemayor and Eisen, becomes less concrete and increasingly more abstract with development. Older children's self-concepts also seem to be more differentiated, because they use a greater number of categories to describe themselves. Overall, these trends parallel the trends of cognitive development proposed by Piaget.

Source: Montemayor, R. & Eisen, M. (1977). The development of self-perceptions from childhood to adolescence. *Developmental Psychology, 13,* 314–319.

sense of self-esteem; rather, they evaluate themselves on specific behaviors (Harter 1981).

During the child and adolescent years, feedback from parents, peers, and teachers becomes an important source of self-esteem. Older elementary school children are fairly stable in their levels of self-esteem. Puberty—and the accompanying shift

from elementary to junior high school—seems to bring with it lowered levels of self-esteem, particularly for girls (Noppe 1983). As the adolescent matures, a rise in self-esteem is observed. Interestingly, researchers have also found that young elementary school children are just beginning to formulate an idea of what their ideal selves may

This child's self-esteem is bolstered by success at a spelling bee contest. However, it is very difficult to determine whether achievement causes self-esteem to rise or whether high self-esteem leads to high achievement.

be, and, as they age, the distance between ideal and real selves increases. This discrepancy, which is a part of developmental maturation, may also tie into the lower levels of self-esteem found during the young adolescent years.

What promotes or lowers a child's self-esteem? A classic work by Coopersmith (1967) with 10- to 12-year-old boys provides important clues to this question. Coopersmith found that parents of boys with high self-esteem were more affectionate and child-centered, but that they also enforced rules carefully and consistently. Furthermore, these parents always tried to explain the reasons underlying their disciplinary actions. Harter (1983) cited evidence that the same parenting style has a positive effect on girls' self-esteem, too. Such par-

enting communicates to children that they are of value, loved for who they are, and capable of measuring up to their parents' expectations.

Another important factor related to self-esteem in children is their school performance. Whether low self-esteem leads to poor academic achievement or whether poor academic achievement lowers self-esteem, it is clear that the two are interrelated. In all probability low self-esteem and poor school performance form a vicious cycle that is difficult to break. Several experimental programs have worked at maximizing school success, and they have yielded promising results in terms of raising self-esteem in children (Harter 1983); teachers who communicate positive attitudes and high expectations for their low-self-esteem students may also see a corresponding rise in their pupil's schoolwork. Such research findings emphasize how significant the self-concept and self-esteem are to developing children, in both their personal and academic lives.

Issues in Personality Development

The study of personality and the self raises many questions concerning the influence of biology, cultural variations, and the stability of individual differences in child development. This section will discuss these issues, as well as the difficult question of distinguishing between normal and deviant patterns of personality. Caution is essential to avoid the mislabeling of children's behavior that may be temporary or does not extend beyond the typical range of healthy personality variations.

Does Personality Have Biological Origins?

Parents of difficult babies often wonder why their infant is so irritable. Why does the baby next door sit quietly in the mother's arms while their own child wiggles, squirms, and fusses when held? Such troubled parents may assume that it is they who made the child so fussy. Putting it another way, some people believe that an infant's personality is acquired completely from the environment. On the other hand, the parents of a difficult baby may assume that this is just the way the baby is. Their infant would act the same way no matter what they did. But is this really the case? Are certain aspects of personality "wired into" a child at birth?

Reliance on genetic influences as the major impetus for personality development is a concept that has waxed and waned in popularity for decades. Several theories of recent vintage—most notably those of Buss and Plomin (1975) and Thomas and Chess (1977)—lend some empirical support to the idea of **temperament** (inborn behavioral characteristics) as the forerunner of personality.

The temperament theory of Buss and Plomin contains three basic assumptions:

(1) individuals begin life with a small number of broad, *inherited* dispositions to act in certain ways; (2) the environment reacts to and modifies these dispositions (within limits); and (3) temperaments are more concerned with stylistic than content aspects of personality. (P. 227)

Buss and Plomin's theory is related to Willerman's personality inventory presented at the beginning of this chapter. The temperament dimension that sets the tone for future interactions with other people is sociability, an adaptive quality manifested in friendliness and cooperation. Individual differences between infant cuddlers versus noncuddlers (Schaffer & Emerson 1964), genetic evidence from twin research (Buss, Plomin & Willerman 1973), correlations between infancy and adolescence (Schaefer & Bayley 1963), and correlations between early adolescence and adulthood (Kagan & Moss 1962) support the notion of a sociability temperament.

Activity level, a second dimension of temperament, refers to the energy for initiating plans and contacts. Willerman and Plomin (1973) found strong relationships between the activity level of children and their parents' own activity level when they were children. Although the evidence of stability for activity level is less impressive then for sociability, Willerman (1979) remains convinced that it should be retained as a temperament dimension.

Finally, the emotionality component of temperament reflects the likelihood of arousal. Expressions of fear, joy, or anger may indicate varying degrees of the emotionally reactive dimension. A study by Rose and Ditto (1983) on the heritability and stability of fears from adolescence to adulthood illustrates that such research is continuing and has extended beyond the early years of development. Remember though, all three biological dispositions are subject to parental and sociocultural modification.

For more than twenty years, Thomas, Chess, and their colleagues have studied the identification and development of temperament in infants and

Table 10.3 Characteristics of Categories of Temperament

	Activity Level	Rhythmicity	Distractibility	Approach/Withdrawal
	The proportion of active periods to inactive ones	Regularity of hunger, excretion, sleep, and wakefulness	The degree to which extraneous stimuli alter behavior	The response to a new object or person
Type of Child				
Easy	Varies	Very regular	Varies	Positive approach
Slow to Warm Up	Low to moderate	Varies	Varies	Initial withdrawal
Difficult	Varies	Varies	Varies	Withdrawal

	Adaptability	Attention Span and Persistence	Intensity of Reaction	Threshold of Responsiveness	Quality of Mood
	The ease with which a child adapts to changes in the environment	The amount of time devoted to an activity, and the effect of distraction on the activity	The energy of response, regardless of its quality or direction	The intensity of stimulation required to evoke a discernible response	The amount of friendly, pleasant, joyful behavior as contrasted with unpleasant, unfriendly behavior
Type of Child					
Easy	Very adaptable	High or low	Low or mild	High or low	Positive
Slow to Warm Up	Slowly adaptable	High or low	Mild	High or low	Slightly negative
Difficult	Slowly adaptable	High or low	Intense	High or low	Negative

Source: From Thomas, A., Chess, S., and Birch, H.G. (1970) The origin of personality. Copyright 1970 by *Scientific American, Inc.* All rights reserved.

children. In their theory, nine factors make up the individual differences in infant temperament. Babies are grouped into three categories of behavioral style (easy, slow to warm up, and difficult).

In actual testing, however, nearly one-third of all babies examined did not fit neatly into any of these classifications. Table 10.3 outlines the temperamental factors and behavioral categories. Note that there is some overlap between these temperaments and those of Buss and Plomin.

Thomas, Chess, and Birch (1970) found temperamental stability across ten years for many of the characteristics listed. The "difficult baby" category, for example, was overly represented among

"problem children" years later. Infants at the age of 2 months who resisted diapering and cried when their carriages were rocked did not adjust well to new schools and cried when they could not solve a homework problem in the fourth grade. Although it was assumed that biological dispositions were very important in determining the children's subsequent personalities, Thomas and his associates were careful to point out that "there can be no universally valid set of rules that will work equally well for all children everywhere" (1963, 85). Therefore, not only does each infant have a particular set of temperaments, but also the reactions of parents to those qualities help to shape future personality.

Obviously, research and theory on temperament suffer from some of the same confusion that pervades the nature-nurture debate on intelligence. We cannot separate the inherited factors from the environmental factors that make up human personality. Few contemporary developmentalists doubt that genetic influences offer at least a moderately significant perspective on personality. Studies comparing identical with fraternal twins provide powerful support for this approach. Loehlin and Nichols (1976), for example, tested 850 pairs of twins on a wide variety of personality measures. They found greater similarities between identical than fraternal twins on virtually every dimension.

Of course, as Loehlin and Nichols acknowledged, most parents of identical twins tend to treat them more similarly than they do fraternal twins. In fact, environmental influences cannot be ruled out even for the few reliable studies of separated twins because of the possible influences of prenatal and perinatal (labor and delivery) experiences. An extensive review of the literature on genetic effects on personality development did not lead Goldsmith (1983) to any firm conclusions. Nevertheless, he tentatively offered the idea that the stability of personality dispositions over time may itself be a heritable characteristic. In other words, some children may be more inclined than others to maintain consistent personality attributes.

How Does Culture Affect Personality?

It would be surprising if personality were totally unaffected by the surrounding culture (which here is defined broadly to include parental influences and expectations, gender roles, and friendship roles). Obviously, no child lives in a vacuum; leaving questions of temperament aside, we can readily observe that all children are influenced in one way or another by the environment.

The early work on culture and personality, pioneered by Margaret Mead and others more than half a century ago, focused largely on intensive investigations of a single culture. More recent stud-

ies have employed a comparative approach in which at least two distinctly different cultures are researched on selected characteristics. Whiting and Whiting (1975), for example, compared six cultures that were organized according to either nuclear family groupings or extended family groupings. In the nuclear family—where parents and their children form small, intimate units—interactions tended to be sociable and relatively democratic. In contrast, extended families consisting of several generations (often segregated by sex) tended to encourage aggressive and authoritarian behaviors.

Other research has identified more similarity than variability among cultures. Heath (1977), for example, evaluated the criteria for student maturity in Italy, Turkey, and the United States. Mature students in all cultures were labeled as realistic, purposeful, rational, and fulfilling their potential, among other descriptions. However, U.S. judges also selected energetic, enthusiastic, and aggressive as characteristics of mature students. Thus, the values to which a culture aspires will inevitably be reflected by the personalities that are, in part, molded by that society.

Of course, culture and personality operate in an interactive fashion, and the differences among cultures are frequently not very dramatic. There is probably more variation within most cultures than would be found, on the average, from one culture to the next. Nonetheless, in the extensive work of Holtzman, Diaz-Guerrero, and Swartz (1975), over 80 percent of the more than one hundred variables studied yielded significant differences between Mexican and U.S. groups. The samples were carefully matched according to age, sex, and socioeconomic status in a sequential design. The study was initiated with first, fourth, and seventh graders who were followed for six years. A major distinction between the two cultures emerged from the data analysis. Holtzman (1982) offers the following personality portraits:

> An active style of coping, with all of its cognitive and behavioral implications, involves perceiving problems as existing in the physical and social environment. A passive style of coping assumes that, while problems may be posed by the environment, the best way to cope with them is

The responsibilities of the adolescent Nigerian girls—sex segregated and ritualized for centuries—suggest the powerful influences of culture on the lives and personalities of developing children.

to change oneself to adapt to circumstances . . . American children tend to be more actively independent and to struggle for a mastery of problems and challenges in their environment, whereas Mexican children are more passively obedient and adapt to stresses in the environment rather than try to change them. (Pp. 245–246).

It seems clear, therefore, that whatever individual differences are always present within a society, fundamental values may subtly affect the roles, perceptions, and behaviors of its members.

Although anthropologists have long been interested in studying the personality characteristics of other cultures, the controlled comparisons

needed are, with certain exceptions, frequently absent. A number of attempts have been made to translate personality tests into other languages, but often this research is fragmented, not carefully controlled, and rarely concerned with developmental issues. There are, of course, inherent difficulties in equating the meaning and understanding of personality in other cultures to our own. Furthermore, the notion of personality assessment itself may appear unusual or incomprehensible from another cultural perspective. Although it is undoubtedly easier to conduct cross-cultural research with children, particularly using nonverbal methods, the full impact of social variations may be felt most acutely during adulthood. We can expect to find increased interest in studying the comparative patterns of child development as concomitant advances are made both in cross-cultural research designs and in techniques for evaluating the personality.

Does Personality Change from Infancy to Adolescence?

The two preceding sections have noted the biological and cultural components of personality development. Based on the evidence available, the conclusion might be drawn that personality remains relatively unchanged from infancy to adolescence. Despite strong biological foundations and the possibility of a consistent cultural background, the notion of personality *development* suggests that change can and does occur. Developmental change is a consequence of hereditary and environmental factors interacting to create unique patterns of individual growth. Therefore, the particular experiences that children have as they grow up do influence the nature of personality development.

Research on the stability of personality is not as convincing between infancy and adolescence as it is during the adulthood years; difficulties in using the same assessment methods across this earlier time interval may be largely responsible. In other words, the temperament of an infant or a toddler cannot be measured with the same tools used to evaluate the personality of an older child or an adolescent. Block (1971), MacFarlane (1963), and others have, nevertheless, demonstrated a number of aspects of consistency in child personality. Kagan and Moss (1962) provided similar data, while pointing out the need to look for gender differences and to note how stable aspects of personality may appear in a somewhat different form at various stages of development.

One of the most detailed studies of personality development was conducted by Murphy and her associates (Murphy & Moriarty 1976). She began her longitudinal work when the subjects were infants and examined their development at the preschool level and again at early adolescence. The focus of the research was continuity or change in coping abilities. Murphy used a variety of observational and quantitative methods for assessing her

subjects—home visits, parent and child interviews, psychological tests, pediatric examinations, and parent diaries. Much careful thought was devoted to analyzing the children's developmental status at each juncture of the study.

Many findings can be derived from Murphy's work. For example, the stability of physiological responses during infancy—such as heart rate or perspiration—was correlated with preschool personality characteristics. Greater physiological stability was associated with more independence from parents. On the other hand, physiological instability was related to higher levels of anxiety. More surprising, due to the longer time interval between measurements, were relations that linked infant and adolescent behaviors. For instance, the sensory reactivity of babies was associated with social perceptiveness, pleasure in tactile stimulation, and a curiosity about new experiences in adolescence. The researchers suggested an openness to the environment at infancy continues to elicit positive social and physical feedback throughout childhood, encouraging a pattern of highly aware and perceptive interactions.

At the same time as they noted consistency from infancy to adolescence, Murphy and Moriarty also suggested patterns of change. Some aspects of personality development (e.g., greater degrees of impulse control) seem to be a predictable function of maturity. However, the ability to adapt to change itself showed variations in style. The coping patterns of 57 percent of the sample remained consistent over the years, while the remainder of the sample showed a wide range of styles and effectiveness. Moriarty and Toussieng (1976), in completing the analysis of Murphy's subjects during adolescence, emphasized the significance of parenting style in contributing to the coping strategies developed. For example, extremely obedient and traditional adolescents probably had parents who were overly controlling and inflexible, whereas imaginative and risk-taking teenagers were likely to have had parents with unusual, less conservative values.

Chapter 11 will describe in further detail family contributions to personality development. For now, the point to stress is that variations in the child's environment build on the temperament foundations established at infancy. By the time a child reaches adolescence, he or she has been exposed to a variety of influences. These influences may have been fairly stable or quite irregular or some mixture of these two extremes. At this time, we are not able to specify the exact effects of the countless environmental factors impacting on personality development. Only when we look at the more negative deviations from typical developmental patterns, as discussed in the next section, do we have a fairly confident sense that the consequences of certain environmental factors will be unfortunate.

How Does Personality Development Deviate from "Normality"?

Since Freud's pioneering work at the turn of the century, a great deal of interest has been shown in abnormal variations of personality development. However, only since the 1970s has a genuine effort been made to create a specialty that blends the expertise of child clinicians with that of child developmentalists (Cicchetti 1984). Before then, most child psychologists were either practitioners who tried to alleviate the child's personality problems or academicans who researched the normative development of the "typical" child. The focus on pathology has now been joined with the perspective of "normal" development to create a specialty known as *developmental psychopathology*. Sroufe and Rutter (1984) proposed that developmental psychopathology be defined "as the study of the origins and course of individual patterns of behavioral maladaptation" (p. 18).

Sroufe and Rutter pointed out the difficulties of tracing the path of psychopathology across child development, as well as the promise such research presents to our understanding of personality changes in the child. Studies of developmental psychopathology will need to be expensive, demanding, and time-consuming. Longitudinal designs should be framed within the context of relevant developmental theory, although uncovering the links between earlier behavior and later pathology will not always be easy. The connections may be paradoxical and initially ambiguous. However, this

exploration of abnormal development will help to clarify the issue of stability versus change in personality. A more significant effect of progress in this field is the potential to prevent serious child pathology and to remediate any problems before they become rigid patterns.

Perhaps the central issue in the study of developmental psychopathology is where to draw the line between normal and abnormal behavior in children. In cases of extreme deviation from typical development—such as a 4-year-old child who does not use any language, a 10-year-old boy who still sucks his thumb, or a 16-year-old girl who has no friends—there is little disagreement that the child has a problem. We need to recognize, however, that as behaviors, particularly social and emotional ones, become less deviant from typical patterns of development, the classifications of a child as abnormal is increasingly colored by personally and culturally defined judgments. Labeling a child according to a statistical departure from the "average child" or from the "ideal child" is, nevertheless, the common yardstick for determining psychopathology.

Whereas the values of the culture, and the typical behaviors found within it, provide a standard for judging deviance, caution in designating a child as abnormal is still warranted. For example, how far from the average does a child need to be—in the ability to throw a ball, to understand words, or to get along with peers—in order to be considered deviant? On what basis do we determine whether a child's behavior is sufficiently divergent from the ideal so that he or she requires therapeutic intervention—the guidelines of a particular theory, the context of the family or classroom or neighborhood, or the child's own previous actions? The answer, of course, is that all of these factors need to be taken into account. In addition, the longevity of a problem, its age of onset, and its impact on other children or adults must be incorporated by a professional evaluating the child.

Beyond knowing whether or not to label a child as deviant, we may also have doubts as to how the psychopathology itself should be classified. For instance, how do we distinguish mental retardation from autism or hyperactivity from learning disabilities or anxiety from depression?

Smoking marijuana may be an illegal activity, but it remains unclear whether this male adolescent is simply engaging in curious experimentation and social behavior or has crossed the line and entered the realm of developmental psychopathology.

There are often overlapping symptoms, multiple abnormalities, and similar causes. This confusion is compounded by the differences between child and adult pathology and the communication difficulties therapists have with younger children or infants.

While the reliability and validity of current diagnostic criteria are debatable (Garber 1984), three broad categories of abnormality simplify the situation. First, the most widely reported category of deviance is undercontrolled behavior disorders, such as hyperactivity and aggression. Substance abuse or delinquency may also reflect a similar lack of control. Overcontrolled behavior disorders represent the second, and in many ways opposite, category of psychopathology. This category includes fears, anxiety, and depression that can have physical manifestations such as eating disorders, tics, stuttering, or sleepwalking. Finally, the rarest and most extreme disturbances are termed pervasive developmental disorders. Such children are highly incapacitated and may be out of touch with reality. Examples of this category range from infantile autism to mental retardation to adolescent schizophrenia.

The debate about classification of developmental psychopathology is too extensive to be treated further here. Similarly, another textbook could be written to describe possible treatment approaches. For example, do we use medication or family counseling to help the hyperactive child? Is depression best treated in play therapy or through behavior modification? Most research on intervention in developmental psychopathology is relatively recent, and the likelihood is that serious deviations will require multifaceted treatment programs. Throughout this book, abnormal patterns of development have been discussed at appropriate topical points. Integrating aspects of pathology in this manner contributes to the attitude that such developmental deviations be viewed as continuous with normative patterns of change.

Summary

1. Personality is a complex phenomenon involving both stability and change. Two theorists—Freud and Erikson—have focused on how the interactions of biology and the environment lead to the development of personality.

2. Two fundamental principles of Freud's theory are psychic determinism and unconscious motivation. Two opposing energy forces, Eros and Thanatos, stimulate personality development.

3. Freud believed that personality is made up of three major structures: the id, the ego, and the superego. Conflict among these structures is related to mental health.

4. Early development, according to Freud, can be analyzed by the main biological feature of each stage. The oral stage of infancy and the anal stage of toddlerhood are followed by the phallic stage (and Oedipal complex) of early childhood. Middle childhood, called latency, lacks a strong psychosexual component.

5. The adolescent and adult years are labeled the genital stage, during which sexuality, aggression, and the experiences from previous development need to be reconciled.

6. Erikson offers a contemporary interpretation of psychoanalytic theory. His theory is more social, optimistic, ego-oriented, and lifespan-oriented than was Freud's perspective. Erikson views development as a series of eight psychosocial crises within a cultural context: basic trust versus mistrust, autonomy versus shame or doubt, initiative versus guilt, industry versus inferiority, identity versus confusion, intimacy versus isolation, generativity versus stagnation, and ego integrity versus despair.

7. Investigations of self-concept and self-esteem represent a valuable, integrative way to explore personality development. The self is influenced by cognitive and social components of development, as well as a tendency toward a sense of unity.

8. The concept of self is quite varied among children of different ages. Research clearly suggests that infants, children, and adolescents focus on very different qualities in themselves and do not construct their worlds from similar perspectives.

9. Temperamental origins may provide the basis for future personality. The theories of Buss and Plomin and of Thomas, Chess, and their associates have offered extensive evidence to support this position.

10. The environmental constraints of cultural background play a crucial part in personality development. Cross-cultural research, despite limitations, has revealed both similarities and differences among various groups.

11. Disentangling the research on stability versus change has been difficult. The evidence for personality consistency in the child is incomplete; however, patterns of change can be attributed to both normative development and to environmental variation.

12. Developmental psychopathology is a relatively new and important speciality. It combines interest in normative patterns of change with an understanding of deviant children. Neither classification nor treatment of such children is easy because defining pathology is colored by cultural and personal values.

Key Terms

psychic determination	superego
unconscious motivation	psychosocial crisis
libido	epigenetic principle
id	self-concept
primary process thinking	self-esteem
ego	temperament
secondary process thinking	

Suggested Readings

Erikson, E.H. (1963). *Childhood and society* (2nd ed.). New York: Norton.

An illuminating group of essays by our foremost contemporary psychoanalyst on infantile sexuality, cross-cultural patterns, play, developmental stages, and psychohistory.

Hamachek, D.E. (1978). *Encounters with the self* (2nd ed.). New York: Holt, Rinehart & Winston.

A thorough, interesting, and practical paperback that describes research and theory about the self in a very understandable fashion.

Offer, D. & Offer, J.B. (1976). *From teenage to young manhood.* New York: Basic Books.

A detailed and interesting account of a longitudinal study of adolescent boys developing over ten years.

Rychlak, J.F. (1981). *Introduction to personality and psychotherapy: A theory-construction approach* (2nd ed.). Boston: Houghton Mifflin.

A lengthy and detailed textbook that analyzes major theories of personality in a philosophical, comprehensive way. Rychlak is extremely authoritative, but this is not easy reading for students.

White, R.W. (1975). *Lives in progress: A study of the natural growth of personality* (3rd ed.). New York: Holt, Rinehart & Winston.

An enjoyable account of how patterns of childhood lead to adult personality. This paperback, a delightfully written classic, incorporates theory in personality development with several excellent case histories.

Readings from the Literature

The adolescent identity crisis has become a familiar concept to most people. While the identity concept was derived from Erik Erikson's clinical work with adolescents, it was James Marcia who pioneered the efforts to empirically define and elaborate Erikson's model. The following article by Sally Archer and Alan Waterman (1983) provides an excellent summary of the research on adolescent identity built on Marcia's interesting interview technique. Archer and Waterman themselves have been intrigued by the study of adolescence within the framework suggested by Erikson. Bearing in mind the questions below, you should learn how a theory gets translated into empirical studies:

- *What are the four categories of identity that Marcia believes are related to Erikson's theory? Describe each category.*

- *What are some examples of developmental sequences an adolescent could experience in the quest to establish a sense of identity?*

- *Although Archer and Waterman do not discuss this, research has found differences between males and females in identity development. What variations can you predict in the identity status achievement of adolescent boys and girls?*

Identity in Early Adolescence: A Developmental Perspective

Sally L. Archer
Trenton State College

Alan S. Waterman
Trenton State College

Ego identity status definitions with examples are elaborated upon with particular reference to early adolescents. Patterns of potential identity status change for this age group are discussed within the context of Waterman's developmental model. From the findings of seven separate studies employing the Ego Identity Status Interview with samples ranging from the 6th grade to college entrance, it appears that a substantial majority of early and mid-adolescents are either identity diffuse or foreclosed. However, some instances of the moratorium and identity achievement statuses were found to occur even at the 6th grade level. In line with Erikson's developmental theory, with increasing grade level, the frequency of identity achievers and moratoriums increased while the frequency of foreclosures and diffusions decreased. The use of age appropriate scoring criteria for studying identity formation is discussed.

Erikson (1968) theorizes that the establishment of one's ego identity is a major life task. It involves the development of a clear self-definition through consideration of alternatives pertaining to vocation, family and personal ideologies. Through his epigenetic principle, Erikson suggests that activity directed toward this goal commences early in life, reaches its ascendency during adolescence, and continues to be refined during the adult years. Individuals who crystallize their identity are thought to be more likely to engage in productive adult work and relationships.

To understand the place of early adolescence within a life-span perspective on identity formation, information is needed with respect to a series of interrelated questions. How far along is the process of identity formation at the start of the stage? What is the nature of changes in identity during early adolescence? What background and personality characteristics contribute to the process of identity development? At present answers to these questions can be offered from theory and from an emerging body of empirical research.

The Ego Identity Statuses

Marcia (1966) developed an interview technique that measures the process of identity formation along two dimensions: exploration (crisis) and commitment. Exploration (crisis) refers to the examination of alternatives with an intention to establish a firm commitment. Commitment refers to a stable investment in one's goals, values, and beliefs evidenced in supportive activity. Four modes of decision making are derived from various placements on these two dimensions. These four models are referred to as ego identity statuses. Extensive definitions and examples of these identity statuses for early adolescence are presented here.

The least developmentally sophisticated status is *identity diffusion*. Individuals in this status have made no commitment, nor are they attempting to arrive at a commitment in a given content area of the interview. They may or may not have experienced active questioning of alternatives in the past, but the end result is an absence of commitment. Early adolescents, when questioned about a particular topic, e.g., vocational plans, might respond that they have no idea about what they'll do, nor have they given much thought to it. Other things are more important in their lives. Sometimes an early adolescent will display knowledge or activity regarding a given content area but there will be no personal investment demonstrated. For example, there may be an ability to discuss political ideologies as these have been learned in school, but there will be no evidence that this knowledge is incorporated into a personal political philosophy. Similarly there may be instances of political action such as letter writing to government officials, but these are instigated by teachers or parents and do not reflect a personal investment in the views expressed.

Some adolescents may appear verbally committed to a viewpoint expressed in the interview without having thought about the meaning of that commitment in their lives. An identity diffusion might express a plan to parent someday because everybody does; it's the expected thing to do. Yet when asked to project into the future about the rewards and costs of parenting or the place of this commitment relative to others, the adolescent may have no information to provide.

Individuals in the *foreclosure* status have not actively questioned alternatives but they have made a commitment that they will strongly defend. This commitment is typically an extension of the values and expectations of significant others, particularly the parents, and is accepted without the consideration of other possibilities. For example, an early adolescent whose mother is a medical doctor may express plans to pursue the same career. The desire to be a doctor may have arisen in early childhood when the parents provided a play doctor's kit as a gift. In view of the attractiveness of this goal, no other career has been of sufficient interest to be seriously considered. By adolescence, exposure to relevant books and television programs, along with fantasy play and verbal assertions of this career plan may result in its incorporation into the self-definition.

One consequence of forming a commitment based on early identifications is that the opportunities for exposure to experiences that could generate consideration of alternatives will be curtailed. Alternatives that might be more rewarding or expressive may thus never be explored. For this reason, foreclosed commitments may be labeled premature and deemed developmentally unsophisticated.

Individuals in the *moratorium* status are in the process of actively seeking information in order to select from among alternatives. They are looking to make a decision in the near future. They are in crisis. For example, an early adolescent may be studying evolution in a science course and find that the information conflicts with religious teachings. If religion is important to this person's identity, a crisis to choose between science and religion may arise. The moratorium initiates activity to resolve this question, perhaps by reading, talking to friends, teachers, clergy, or reflecting on which feels more personally expressive. By contrast, some adolescents in the identity diffusion status might note the

335

existence of such a conflict and indicate an interest in trying to work out the issue some day. The diffusion lacks the moratorium's current investment in the question.

Identity achievers have experienced moratorium and have made a commitment that they are currently implementing or anticipate implementing in the near future. They have explored alternatives and have selected the one that they believe fits their individuality best at the present time and in the context of their anticipated future. For example, a tomboy might become fascinated with "adult" feminine clothes and feel torn between her rough and tumble friendship with males and the desire to become ladylike in her activities and appearance. As a consequence of the felt need to resolve this dilemma and choose a sex-role she can live with comfortably, a sense of identity may be achieved by deciding to become feminine in her behavior and appearance. Similarly, the forming of a commitment to maintain her tomboyish ways would be evidence of entrance into the identity achievement status. Consideration of alternatives reflects efforts to clarify one's self-definition; hence, moratorium and achiever decision-making modes are deemed sophisticated.

The Developmental Model

Since the four identity statuses represent strategies individuals use to handle the task of identity formation, it is useful to view them from a developmental perspective. Although Erikson (1968) postulates movement from diffusion toward an increasing sense of identity during the period from adolescence to adulthood, the use of the four statuses allows for the possibility of a complex set of developmental patterns to emerge (Waterman, 1982). A schematic presentation of the potential patterns of identity status change is given in Figure 1. In the present paper, the focus will be on the patterns of change more likely to be shown by persons in the early adolescent age group.

On the basis of Erikson's theory, one would expect to find early adolescents primarily using the less sophisticated decision-making modes of identity diffusion

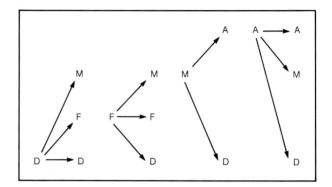

Figure 1 A model of the sequential pattern of ego identity development
D = Identity Diffusion; F = Foreclosure; M = Moratorium
A = Identity Achievement.
Source: Waterman (1982)

and foreclosure. The normative biological, cognitive, and social structures of this age group provide support for this expectation.

Early Adolescent Diffusion

It could be assumed that initially everyone is diffuse, lacking an identity. The continuance of diffusion into adolescence may be facilitated by pubertal changes. Early and mid-adolescents are often immersed in the physical aspects of their development, spending time agonizing over their body image, comparing themselves with others, and speculating about their ultimate body appearance (Blyth, Simmons, Bulcroft, Felt, Van Cleave & Bush, 1980; Petersen, 1979). The everyday reminders of their physical changes are highly tangible, identity concerns about their future are nebulous by comparison.

Most early adolescents do not have the cognitive capacity for formal operational thought (Martorano, 1977; Moshman, 1979); therefore, generating and comparing alternatives as required for the moratorium and achievement statuses would be a difficult task. Although these adolescents may have knowledge relevant to various alternatives, they may be unable to contrast the information in order to make choices. Other formal operational skills that might be lacking include the ability to generate possibilities and ideals, and the capacity to project them into the future. Early adolescents may be most comfortable with concrete observables and hence, likely to be diffuse (or foreclosed).

The most important social influence on the early adolescent will probably be the parents. Parents may help to maintain a diffuse state by refusing to relinquish the dependency the child has on the adult and discouraging attempts at independence. They may encourage diffuse behavior by being diffuse themselves. Further, they may convey a message that commitments are irrevocable; decisions, even if unsatisfactory, cannot be discarded. The result may be the development of a fear of making commitments. Also, for many parents who grew up during the depression or the war years, options may have been minimal. These parents could have difficulty recognizing that the present historical context is different from that of their own development and thus fail to help their adolescents to make the adjustments needed.

Early adolescents may make a deliberate choice to be diffuse in an area of considerable concern to their parents (e.g., religious ideology) as an expression of rebellion. Similar resistance to making identity choices may be directed against pressures arising from teachers or other adults.

Not only the parents but also the broader community, including the schools and the media, can contribute to diffusion through the failure to provide models worthy of emulation and by limiting access to knowledge and to opportunities for exploration among alternatives. Dictating the "age of appropriateness" of certain behaviors may deny some adolescents the timing most suitable to their individual need to explore and/or commit themselves to their first tentative choices.

Early Adolescent Foreclosure

Pubertal changes could facilitate self-appraisal culminating in the desire to discard childlike behaviors and don the adultlike values and beliefs of identification figures (Peterson & Taylor, 1980). In parallel, adults might generate expectations for increasingly responsible behavior to correlate with increasing physical maturity.

The first adolescents to engage in identity activity may be the early maturers. They in turn may function as models for their peers.

Given the limitations of the cognitive capacities of early adolescents, they may grasp the first available alternative recommended by significant people in their lives. Exposure to parents, peers, teachers, and media could provide ample information for a genuine commitment to evolve. A payoff derived from making premature commitments may be an increased sense of security. For some, it will be a false sense of security. Adult roles would be designated, models to emulate identified, and life goals clarified on a simplistic and often unrealistic level. "When I grow up, I'm going to get married and be taken care of for the rest of my life" is an all too frequent example of thinking from an early adolescent foreclosure. Lacking the cognitive skills to find the weakness of this assumption and settling into this "secure" expectation could set the stage for a severe emotional and/or identity crisis later in life.

Parents of early adolescents have been known to pressure their offspring into conforming to expectations expressive of parental preferences. Parental unfulfilled goals have a second chance if played out through their adolescents' lives. Such parents might try to maintain sufficient control over their early adolescents' access to information and range of activities to thwart the development of values and goals counter to parental wishes.

Many young adolescents are very happy in their family relationships (Hamid & Wyllie, 1980) in which case they may wish to emulate their parents. They internalize the family's values and have no desire to be different. The commitment to the family's way of life at an early age may preclude exposure to other life styles. Alternatively, early adolescent foreclosure may represent a first attempt at separateness, of individuality, of movement away from the family. The content of such commitments may derive from identification with teachers, neighbors, television characters or others.

In line with Waterman's (1982) model of the sequential patterns of ego identity development, these diffusions and foreclosures can remain in their respective statuses or move into others. Movement into the moratorium or achiever statuses represents the initiation of reflective consideration of identity alternatives or the development of personally meaningful commitments.

Early Adolescent Moratorium and Identity Achievement

The self appraisal caused by pubertal changes could trigger identity questions, such as "who am I," "what do I value," "which behaviors do I want to engage in." Some early adolescents are attempting to use formal operational skills. Identity tasks for them might be experienced as pleasurable opportunities for exercising these new skills. Some parents (perhaps themselves achievers) may encourage access to a variety of models and information. They may structure experiences which allow for exploration. They may recognize that "age appropriate" behaviors are relative to the individual adolescent. Further, parents may encourage commitments while conveying the message that decisions can be tentative. Should a choice prove unsatisfactory, it is advisable to reexamine alternatives and try again.

Moratorium behavior should be facilitated in a social milieu which provides opportunities for exploration and encourages such activity. Since it is also uncomfortable to continue indefinitely without a clear sense of direction, one might expect adolescents to spend as little time in this moratorium status as is necessary. Movement into the achiever status is likely to occur if realistic alternatives are weighed, a self expressive choice is identified and the individual is ready to make a commitment.

However, the models, knowledge and activity to which adolescents are exposed can increase dramatically as they become more independent from the parental environment. Consequently, some achievers may return to the moratorium status. Exploration may be reintroduced because more appealing options arise or because a lack of abilities in a chosen area is realized. Changes may be precipitated by continued disapproval of a choice by significant others, such as parents, teachers or peers, et cetera.

Early Adolescent Regression into Less Sophisticated Identity Statuses

A change into the diffusion status from any of the other statuses can be viewed as developmentally regressive, since it involves putting aside of identity concerns, at least temporarily, without having established a satisfactory resolution. Achievers may regress to the diffusion status. Disenchanted with a chosen life goal, early adolescents may find no other personally expressive options at that point in time. Pressures for unacceptable alternatives from signficant people in their lives may force some adolescents into apathy. Others simply need time out from the exploration and/or commitment process.

Moratoriums can also become diffusions. The decision-making process may become overwhelming due to cognitive inabilities or limited options. The timing may be inappriate for identity activity. Other life events, such as the dissolution of a romantic relationship, may suddenly overshadow the process.

Foreclosures may regress to the diffusion status. Premature foreclosures in particular may find it difficult to cope when a childhood commitment proves inappropriate. Rather than entering moratorium, they become diffuse due to having had little or no experience considering alternatives. They thus retreat to avoid decision making, at least temporarily. Adolescents may also be torn between several foreclosure routes, concomitantly or sequentially. Rather than disappoint either identification figure, the early adolescent may choose noncommitment as a diffusion.

Neither achievers nor moratoriums can become foreclosures. By definition, foreclosures have made a commitment without consideration of alternatives. Some achievers may sound like foreclosures since after having made a choice to which they are genuinely committed, they no longer invest their energies in thought about other possibilities.

Given the above scenarios, where are most adolescents to be found with regard to these identity statuses?

338

Summary and Conclusions

Early and mid-adolescents are primarily diffuse, lacking in identity concerns, or foreclosed, committed without the benefit of the examination of alternatives. This finding is in line with Erikson's developmental theory and congruent with the normative biological, cognitive, and social structures characteristic of this age group which might limit identity activity. It would appear that the greatest movement during early and mid-adolescence is taking place between the 10th and 12th grades. Consistent with Waterman's developmental model, there are increases in instances of moratorium and achiever behavior and decreases in diffusion and, to a lesser degree, foreclosure decision making. However, some sophisticated identity activity is taking place even among the youngest adolescents studied to date.

Several background and personality characteristics contributing to the process of identity formation have been identified, such as SES (socioeconomic status), poetry writing, and family disruption. However, given that the vast majority of early and mid-adolescents are diffuse or foreclosed, it will be difficult to generate a sufficient number of moratoriums and achievers to allow for meaningful comparisons among all four statuses on background and personality characteristics for this age group.

It is evident from this review of the literature that there is an emerging body of research on the ego identity functioning of early adolescents. This research is important for gaining an understanding of the psychological situation of early adolescents and for the development of teaching and counseling techniques responsive to their identity-related needs. The authors hope, however, that the findings will not be used for the purpose of constructing interventions designed to induce identity crises in those early adolescents not so predisposed or to otherwise attempt to accelerate the process of identity formation.

Certainly during early adolescence, and perhaps at all ages, there are advantages and disadvantages to each form of identity decision making. To be identity diffuse during early adolescence can be viewed as stage appropriate. Until the developmental concerns that provide the foundation for identity decision making have been successfully resolved, attempts to induce the making of identity choices will likely prove confusing and counterproductive. With respect to the foreclosure status, there is a function to be served by identification and the holding of a stable set of goals, values and beliefs while others are being worked through. To undermine these early commitments before the skills needed to experience a productive moratorium have developed is to invite disorientation and insecurity. Even pressure to seek an early resolution of identity crises may be misplaced if the result is a less than thorough consideration of alternatives that might be personally expressive. Any gains in commitment are likely to be short-lived since the probability of an identity achiever in high school remaining with the same commitments through four years of college is modest.

Professionals working with early adolescents might best proceed by responding directly to the questions and concerns coming from the adolescents themselves, rather than endeavoring to speed development toward some presumably desirable end state. There is much to recommend respecting the internal time-table of developing individuals.

References

Blyth, D.A., Simmons, R.G., Bulcroft, R., Felt, D., VanCleave, E.F., & Bush, D.M. The effects of physical development on self-image and satisfaction with body image for early adolescent males. In R.G. Simmons (Ed.), *Handbook of community and mental health* (Vol. 2), Greenwich, Conn.: JAI Press, 1980.

Erikson, E.H. *Identity: Youth and crisis.* New York: Norton, 1968.

Hamid, P.N., & Wyllie, A.J. What generation gap? *Adolescence,* 1980, *15,* 385–391.

Marcia, J.E. Development and validation of ego identity status. *Journal of Personality and Social Psychology,* 1966, *3,* 551–558.

Martorano, S.C. A developmental analysis of performance on Piaget's formal operational tasks. *Developmental Psychology,* 1977, *13,* 666–672.

Moshman, D. Development of formal hypothesis-testing ability. *Developmental Psychology,* 1979, *15,* 104–112.

Petersen, A.C. The psychological significance of pubertal changes to adolescent girls. Paper presented at the meeting of the Society for Research in Child Development, San Francisco, 1979.

Petersen, A.C., & Taylor, B. The biological approach to adolescence: Biological change and psychological adaptation. In J. Adelson (Ed.), *Handbook of adolescent psychology,* New York: Wiley, 1980.

Waterman, A.S. Identity development from adolescence to adulthood: An extension of theory and a review of research. *Developmental Psychology,* 1982, *18,* 341–358.

Source: Archer, S.L. and Waterman, A. Identity in early adolescence: a developmental perspective. Reprinted from the *Journal of Early Adolescence,* 1983, *3,* p. 203–214. By permission of the Publisher, H.E.L.P. Books, Inc., Tucson, Ariz.

Family Relationships

Two-year-old Steven surprised his parents one day by asking them to take his baby sister back to the hospital and leave her there. "I don't like her much," he said. Steven's parents were amused, but they also realized the impact of his sister's arrival on Steven's life. His world, and the path of his development, had been changed forever by the birth of his little sister. Indeed, how could this not be the case? A child's development may be an individual process, and yet every child develops within the social context of a family, however the term is defined. While we are all individual and unique human beings, we are also fathers, mothers, sisters, brothers, sons, or daughters. All of us are grandchildren, and many are grandparents. We influence and are influenced by every other person with whom we interact, and, perhaps most particularly, we influence and are influenced by our families.

This chapter focuses on family relationships. The formation of the bond between parents and their new offspring will be examined. Theoretical perspectives on attachment and parent and infant characteristics that promote or work against a close and secure attachment pattern will be presented. Also considered will be some consequences of inadequate attachment on the later development of the child.

The chapter will also deal with issues related to parenting styles and parenting roles. The classic distinction in parenting research is between the dimensions of affect (love versus hostility) and control (freedom versus restrictiveness). Research suggesting the necessity of parental warmth for optimal child development will be presented, as will questions surrounding the need for structure in the child's life. Particular issues to be addressed include the traditional neglect of the father's role and the likelihood of conflict between parents and their teenagers.

The relationship between siblings has received little attention until recently. The chapter will examine the quality of that relationship in the average family, the effect of birth order on the sibling relationship, and the advantages and disadvantages of growing up as an only child.

Finally, the chapter will discuss variations in the American family. A large number of families today do not fit the mold made popular by television situation comedies of the 1950s and 1960s—one happy mother, one happy father, and two or three happy children. Four in ten marriages today end in divorce and half of the children born in the 1970s will spend at least some of their childhood or adolescence in households headed by single parents. The characteristics of the single-parent household will be examined. Finally, the chapter will look at children's adjustment to divorce and to the remarriage of their parents.

Parent-Child Attachment

The bond between parents and children is perhaps the closest and most enduring of all human relationships. When psychologist Lillian Troll (1972) asked people ranging in age from 10 to 91 to describe any person they knew, most respondents of all ages described a parent.

Attachment is the process by which the parent-child bond is formed. This section deals first with the major theoretical perspectives on how attachment takes place. It then discusses variations in the degree of attachment, the reasons for those variations, and the importance of secure attachment for other areas of a child's development.

Theoretical Perspectives

There are two major theoretical perspectives on human attachment. The first, derived from the behaviorist tradition in psychology, is social-learning theory. The second, which emerged from the study of the bonding process in lower animals, is ethological theory.

Social-Learning Theory
Social-learning attachment theory proposes that attachment is a learned behavior, or a set of learned behaviors. Mothers dispense reinforcements that condition dependency responses in their infants. For example, infants experiencing hunger will seek in any way possible to have the basic physiological need for food met. They soon learn that the only way to satisfy this need is to demand the attention of, to seek contact with, their

An infant rhesus monkey demonstrates its need for contact comfort by clinging to a warm and cuddly terry cloth "mother."

mothers. By feeding her child, the mother rewards the infant's attention-seeking dependent behaviors. In other words, the dependent behaviors that underlie attachment pay off handsomely. And because they pay off, the infant, and later the child and adult, will continue to depend on others. Although not a primary physiological drive, dependency becomes a *secondary drive;* that is, dependency/attachment behaviors are learned rather than innate.

Suggesting that infants attach themselves to their mothers only to satisfy physiological drives is hardly a romantic view of the parent-child relationship. In fact, the secondary-drive hypothesis

was eventually rejected even by social-learning theorists themselves because (1) infants form attachments to people, such as peers, who have never satisfied their physiological needs, (2) infants attach themselves even to caretakers who mistreat them badly, (3) infants respond socially even in situations in which physiological needs are not involved, and (4) infants apparently require much more from a caretaker than simply the reduction of bodily needs (Joffe & Vaughn 1982).

Harlow (1963) carried out a series of studies to test the secondary-drive hypothesis of attachment. He removed infant rhesus monkeys from their real mothers and provided them with two surrogates. One surrogate mother was a dummy made of wire; she was a cold and forbidding figure, but equipped with a nursing bottle. The other mother was made of terry cloth; she was warm and cuddly, but offered no food to the infants. Harlow found that the infant monkeys went to the wire mother to satisfy their physiological need for food, but they went to the cloth mother for contact comfort, particularly when they were stressed. If the secondary-drive hypothesis had proven correct, the monkeys would have become more closely attached to the figure who satisfied their physiological needs. This was not the case, and it is apparent that infant rhesus monkeys, and also human infants, need more than food to bring about an attachment with a caretaker.

The secondary-drive hypothesis of attachment was the earliest but certainly not the only position set forth by social-learning theorists. Many others followed, but all had in common a desire to explain infant-mother bonding as a learning process. Typically, the two-directional nature of attachment was ignored (Joffe & Vaughn 1982). That is, social-learning theory emphasized the way infants attach themselves to their mothers and not the reverse. The mother's role was usually that of a reinforcer or facilitator of the process, rather than an equal partner in it.

Ethological Theory

Ethology is the naturalistic study of animal behavior and its underlying mechanisms. Ethologists maintain that much of animal behavior is genetically "wired in" as a result of a long evolutionary process (Gould 1982). The **ethological**

attachment theory, then, stresses that behaviors involved in the attachment process are innate rather than learned.

An example of the ethologist's view of human mother-infant attachment is the theory of John Bowlby (1969, 1982). Rejecting the secondary-drive hypothesis as one that "arises from an assumption and not from observation or experiment" (1969, 211), Bowlby argued that attachment is not learned, but is an instinctive system that evolved as a survival mechanism in human as well as nonhuman species. When infants experience the threat or fear of separation from their mothers, the attachment system is activated. The infants begin to exhibit certain behaviors designed to bring them closer to their mothers. These behaviors have either a *signal* function (e.g., calling, crying, babbling, smiling) or an *executive* function (e.g., reaching, grabbing, clinging, following). Consider the irresistible charm of an infant's smile! The infant's behaviors then serve as *elicitors* to the mother, producing in her certain reactions (e.g., smiling, approaching, entering the room, touching), and these maternal behaviors in turn terminate the infant's attachment-seeking behaviors. This is the dynamic character of a two-directional interaction, an element lacking in early secondary-drive theories of attachment.

One of the more interesting, and controversial, issues emerging in recent years from ethological conceptions of attachment concerns the question of bonding. In the literal sense of the word, bonding is the process by which the parent-offspring attachment is initially formed. Recently, however, the term **bonding** has been used in a more restrictive sense to refer to a biologically determined attachment mechanism that must be activated within a critical period after the infant's birth. Ethologists point out that the newborn offspring of lower-animal species that constantly move about in their environment (e.g., cattle, sheep, chickens) must quickly recognize and learn to follow their parents if they are to survive infancy. In such animals, a type of preprogrammed learning occurs called *imprinting*: the infant and mother automatically form an attachment if exposed to one another within a critical period of one or two days after birth. The infant automatically follows the parent (or other imprinted object) if such exposure occurs, and emits a species-specific call as the imprinted object moves away from it.

Might human infants also possess such a built-in attachment to their mothers? Ethologically oriented researchers, such as pediatricians Marshall Klaus and John Kennell, suggest that they do. Noting that some animal parents reject their newborns if separated from them immediately after birth, but form an irreversible bond if mother-infant contact is not interfered with, Klaus and Kennell (1976, 1982; Kennell & Klaus, 1984) suggested that there may be a critical bonding period for human beings as well as for lower animals. They produced evidence that mothers who had their infants with them immediately after delivery were more affectionate in interacting with them; they fondled their babies more, attempted to soothe them more frequently, and maintained eye contact with them more often and for longer periods of time.

Intriguing as the ethological theory of human attachment is, it has been challenged repeatedly for a lack of supporting evidence (Goldberg 1983; Myers 1984a, 1984b; Reed & Leiderman 1983). For example, Goldberg (1983) reviewed a large number of studies and concluded that there is no specific evidence to support a critical period for human parent-infant attachment. She pointed out that contact between mother and newborn varies considerably in quality. It is difficult to conclude that early contact itself promotes attachment when the attitudes of new mothers engaged in such contact range from euphoria to near indifference. What is more, in most bonding studies no efforts were made to separate timing of contact from actual amount of contact. Mothers who were given their infants immediately after birth had more overall time with them than did mothers who did not have this early experience. Therefore, if a closer level of attachment was observed in the former group, it could have been that these mothers simply had more time to spend with their babies and not that they were exposed to them during a critical period after birth.

Goldberg (1983) did not suggest that early parent-infant contact has no value. Indeed such contact may be highly desirable. She pointed out, however, that strong and lasting attachments can

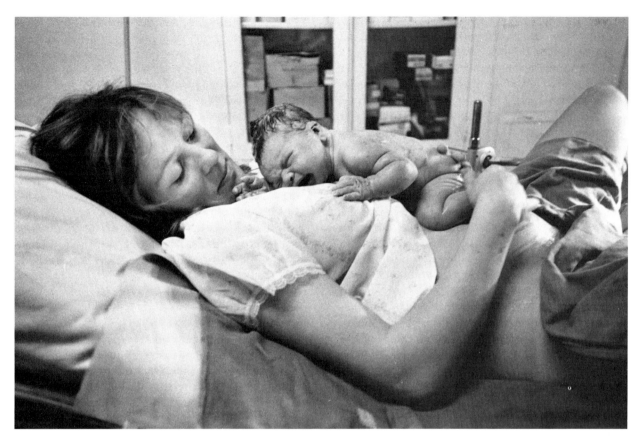

Holding her newborn baby only minutes after delivery is a very satisfying experience for many mothers. However, if such contact is not possible, a strong bond of attachment between parent and child can still be formed.

be formed between parent and child even if contact does not occur shortly after birth. Parents who for any reason may not hold their infants immediately after delivery need not fear that the parent-child relationship will be deficient in any way.

In support of Goldberg's reassuring conclusion, research on human attachment indicates that a strong infant-caregiver bond can be formed even under the most adverse conditions. For example, no differences exist in degree or quality of parent-infant attachment when preterm and full-term babies are compared (Frodi & Thompson 1985; Goldberg et al. 1986). Not only are preterm babies unavailable for handling immediately after delivery, but also they are often less alert than full-term infants, less responsive to stimulation, and less coordinated; they smile less often in the early months

and are more irritable in general (Bakeman & Brown 1980). We might expect that under such conditions the attachment process would be disrupted, since a parent would find a preterm infant difficult to relate to. In fact, parents seem to adapt their caregiving behaviors to meet the needs of the individual child; a full-term infant may be easier to warm up to, but parents of preterm infants try harder to form a bond of love by accommodating themselves to their child's limitations (Frodi & Thompson 1985).

Research on the security of attachment between parents and adopted children also indicates that no simple bonding mechanism can fully account for the closeness of the parent-child relationship. Singer and associates (1985) compared the security of parental attachment of a group of twenty-seven nonadopted children with a group of forty-six children adopted during the first year of life. No group differences were found. Adopted children were just as securely attached as the natural children of a family.

The study of children whose early life circumstances could easily lead to attachment difficulties but who are, in fact, closely attached to their parents leads psychologists to the following conclusion: there might indeed be some genetic predisposition toward attachment between human parent and child, as ethologists suggest, but the learning process seems to be at work as well. Perhaps the Goldberg (1983) review makes clear the necessity of blending social-learning and ethological perspectives in order to understand the attachment process in an organism as complex as a human being. Such a blending allows for the possibility that nature and nurture are interacting in the attachment process, and also makes clear the necessity of seeing attachment in two-directional terms.

Individual Differences in Attachment

By whatever mechanisms it occurs, the process of attachment is of great significance to the establishment of the parent-child relationship. It is fairly evident, however, that not all parent-child relationships are alike in quality. Some children are particularly close to their parents while others are more distant. This section emphasizes individual differences in attachment. The varying degrees of attachment will be discussed as well as the techniques for measuring them. The section also examines the characteristics of parents who are easiest to attach to, and the relationship between secure attachment and the young child's social and emotional development.

Degrees of Attachment

The attachment between a parent and child has been discussed thus far with little reference to individual differences. In fact, attachment should not be thought of as an all-or-nothing phenomenon. Instead, there are degrees of attachment, with some infants and young children very securely

attached to their parents and others decidedly less so.

To identify individual differences in degree of attachment, Ainsworth (1977; Ainsworth et al. 1978) developed a testing procedure known as the Strange Situation. In this procedure, an infant and his or her parents are brought into a playroom containing a variety of toys and a strange adult. After a brief introductory period, the parents leave the room and then return on two occasions. The infant's reaction to their departure and return is observed. When their parents return, secure, closely attached infants at first seek closeness and contact with them, but then easily return to their independent play. A less-secure group of infants, referred to as "insecure-avoidant," react to their parents' return with hostility and resistance. A third group, described as "insecure-ambivalent," appear angry and resist contact with the returned parents while at the same time expressing a need for such contact.

Attachment and Parenting Style

Why are some infants more securely attached than others to their parents, as indicated by responses in the Strange Situation? Ainsworth, Bell, and Stayton (1971) carried out extensive observations of mothers and their babies at home. They noticed that mothers of securely attached infants aged 9 to 11 months were particularly sensitive to their babies' attempts to signal their needs. Not only were they better able to determine what their children needed, but also they were quicker to respond to those needs than were mothers of less closely attached children. As but one illustration of this point, mothers of securely attached children responded faster and more consistently to their infants' crying than did mothers of children less closely attached.

A more general personality and behavioral profile of mothering styles related to the security of attachment was provided in a study by Egeland and Farber (1984): Mothers of securely attached children feel good about themselves and are confident about their parenting skills. They handle their infants affectionately and seem to be both interested in and skilled at feeding and playing with them. In contrast, mothers of insecure children are anxious and irritable; they lack self-confidence and react negatively to motherhood.

One 20-year-old mother reported that she would prefer to be traveling than at home taking care of her child. Mothers of insecure children appear to have little interest in their infants; they feed and handle them mechanically and only as necessary. The general impression is that insecure babies have limited access to their mothers; mother is simply not very available to them (Main 1981).

Not only is the security of attachment in infants related to the quality of the mother-infant relationship at the time, but also there seems to be considerable stability in the parenting approaches that contribute to attachment. Bates, Maslin, and Frankel (1985) found that secure attachment at 13 months predicted secure attachment at 24 months. In fact, most studies of attachment indicate a high degree of stability both in degree of attachment and in the parenting characteristics that appear to promote it (Jacobson & Wille 1984; Main, Kaplan & Cassidy 1985; Thompson, Lamb & Estes 1982).

Correlates of Secure Attachment

A number of studies indicate a link between mother-infant attachment and later cognitive and social behaviors. Secure, closely attached preschool children have been found to be more capable of relating to their peers than are less secure children (Lieberman 1977; Waters, Wippman & Sroufe 1979) and more comfortable in interacting with a strange adult (Lutkenhaus, Grossman & Grossman 1985). Their make-believe play is both more sustained and more complex than that of anxious children (Slade 1987). Closely attached 6-year-olds are likely to be verbal and at ease in exploring their thoughts and feelings (Main, Kaplan & Cassidy 1985). Secure children display a greater interest and ability in exploring their environments (Cassidy 1986; Joffe & Vaughn 1982) and are more environmentally oriented in free play (Belsky, Garduque & Hrncir 1984). Perhaps as a consequence, they have been found to score higher on tests of spatial ability (Hazen & Durett 1982). The most secure, closely attached children also appear to have advantages in solving simple problems, such as removing a desired object from a tube (Matas, Arend & Sroufe 1978). In short, the most securely attached infants frequently become the most competent toddlers. They are close enough to adults to depend on them

when necessary, but independent enough to act on their own and even to defy their caretakers. Frustrated parents of defiant toddlers may take some consolation from the conclusions drawn by Matas, Arend, and Sroufe (1978) about the competent 2-year-old problem solver:

> The competent two-year-old . . . is not the child who automatically complies with whatever the mother tells him/her. Rather, it is the child who shows a certain amount of noncompliance when requested to stop playing and clean up the toys. When, however, cooperation has clear adaptive advantage, as in the tool-using situation, these children become readily involved in the task . . . they work hard, independently at first, then request help from the mother when they get stuck. (P. 554)

Parenting: Styles, Roles, Issues

Raising a child is one of life's most significant responsibilities, and yet most people enter parenthood with little or no preparation for the role. This section focuses on variations in the qualities of parents, or, more accurately, in the qualities of the parent-child relationship in the United States. The section deals, first of all, with the degrees of affection and control displayed by parents and the importance of love and of structure in a child's life. It examines the particular significance of fathers in the child-development process. Finally, it discusses the relationship between parent and adolescent—a relationship that is often misunderstood and is usually more positive than people are led to expect.

Dimensions of Affect and Control

Research on the impact of parenting styles on children's development has focused primarily on two parental dimensions: the affective dimension, referring to the degree of parental affection and approval perceived by the child, and the restrictive dimension, referring to the degree of parental control (Maccoby & Martin 1983).

Little disagreement exists on the point that loving, accepting parents are more likely to enhance the psychological well-being of their child

Table 11.1   A Two-Dimensional Classification of Parenting Patterns

	Accepting, Responsive, Child-Centered	Rejecting, Unresponsive, Parent-Centered
Demanding, Controlling	Authoritative	Authoritarian
Undemanding	Permissive	Indifferent, uninvolved

than are hostile parents. However, the dimension of restrictiveness is far more complicated than was once imagined. To illustrate this point, a home may be characterized as restrictive because children are expected to obey many rules, but parents might be either firm or casual in implementing these rules. Furthermore, control can be psychological as well as physical; the presence or absence of rules may reveal little about the actual degree of autonomy or control in a home. Some parents impose few concrete restrictions; instead, they control their children by instilling in them a strong sense of anxiety or guilt for misbehavior (Maccoby & Martin 1983). Finally, other parenting dimensions, such as the degree of responsiveness to or interest in the children, can affect the way autonomy or control is interpreted by the child. The involved and interested parent who grants autonomy may communicate an attitude of trust; the uninvolved and unresponsive parent who allows children a high degree of autonomy may seem indifferent or even negligent!

A helpful framework for understanding the current information on the effects of parents on their children, and one that recognizes the complexity of the autonomy-control dimension, was provided by Maccoby and Martin (1983) and is illustrated in Table 11.1.

Authoritarian, Authoritative, and Permissive Parents

Three of the four parenting categories in the chart—the authoritarian, the authoritative, and the permissive—have been investigated extensively by psychologist Diana Baumrind (1975). Her characterization of each style and their impacts on children are as follows:

- **Authoritarian parents** attempt to shape their children's behavior according to precise and absolute standards of conduct. They attempt to instill in their children such values as respect for authority, for work, and for tradition, and they leave little room for discussion of their standards. The child's role is simply to obey the parents without question.
- **Authoritative parents** are also quite willing to exercise control over their children, but they attempt to be rational in doing so. That is, they are willing to reason with their children, to explain rules, and to allow appropriate degrees of independence. These parents value obedience and conformity in their children, but they also value independence and self-direction.
- **Permissive parents** are unwilling to exert power or control over their children. They see themselves as accepting and nonevaluative resources to which children can turn if they need help, but not as shapers of their children's behavior. They impose few regulations on their children and place a low priority on household responsibility and order.

On the basis of a number of studies (Baumrind 1967, 1968, 1971, 1975; Baumrind & Black 1967), Baumrind concluded that authoritative parenting is the most effective of the three approaches. Children of authoritative parents were the most independent, the most socially responsible, and the most achievement-oriented. They were the most likely to be self-controlled, self-reliant, assertive, explorative, and friendly.

In contrast, children of permissive or authoritarian parents were equally likely to be anxious, dependent, lacking in self-confidence, and inca-

Authoritative parents discuss family rules with their children. They exercise control but in a rational way.

pable of making decisions for themselves. Children of authoritarian parents displayed a lesser degree of internal moral control, or conscience, than did children exposed to the other child-rearing patterns (Hoffman 1970). Children of permissive parents tended to be more impulsive and more aggressive (Maccoby & Martin 1983).

Baumrind suggested that the authoritative parenting style is the most beneficial of the three because it shows children that the world is orderly and rational, while leaving room for challenges to the established order, and because it teaches them to be responsible for their own actions. Children need rational structure in order to learn independence. To stand up for themselves, they need something to stand up against. Unreasonable structure, as might be found in the authoritarian home, suppresses dissent and teaches children that

they are incapable of exerting any control over their own lives. Total lack of structure—the characteristic of the permissive home—not only encourages demanding, inconsiderate behavior on the part of the child, but also fails to teach self-control. Permissively reared children often feel anxious and guilty about their own unstructured behavior.

Indifferent and Uninvolved Parents

Indifferent and uninvolved parents communicate a desire to keep their children at a distance. They have little interest in their children's activities and are often unaware of their children's whereabouts. Their primary concern is for their own immediate comfort and convenience. This emphasis is reflected in their approach to discipline: they may ignore a child's bad behaviors rather than make efforts to correct them, or fail to teach positive attitudes because of the time and trouble involved in doing so.

Children of uninvolved, indifferent parents lack self-confidence; have lowered self-esteem (Loeb, Horst & Horton 1980) and lowered achievement motivation; and are impulsive, moody, and disobedient (Block 1971). They seem to lack a clear sense of direction in life and are the most likely to engage in antisocial behaviors, such as drug abuse, truancy, and criminal activities (Pulkkinen 1982; Maccoby & Martin 1983).

Considering the range and seriousness of the consequences of parental indifference, children exposed to this last pattern are probably the least fortunate of the four groups. As Maccoby and Martin (1983) concluded on the basis of a review of the various child-rearing patterns, active parental involvement in a child's life and decisions—even into the years of adolescence—serves to promote optimal child development.

The Neglected Role of the Male Parent

Within the past ten years interest in the role fathers play in their children's development has surged (Lamb 1981). Until the end of the 1960s, the father's role in the family was unappreciated, even by social scientists; father was then "rediscovered" for the following reasons (Lamb 1981):

- Research on parental influence was so weighted in favor of the mother-child relationship that social scientists began to wonder if fathers were totally irrelevant.
- Rapid social changes (e.g., the rising divorce rate) caused social scientists to speculate on the future of the family—and the factor most often associated with family disruption was father absence. In a sense, fathers became visible by their absence.
- In recent years, fathers themselves have become increasingly interested in their part in child rearing, while mothers have begun to explore new options outside the home.

The recent research on fatherhood is making it increasingly clear that fathers not only play a role in children's development, but also that a man's role in child rearing may be qualitatively different in certain aspects from that of a woman. As of today, we can only speculate on the full impact of fathers as parents, since research on fatherhood is still very limited (Lamb 1981). As men take a greater interest in child rearing and as women discover options for themselves outside the home, we should continue to learn about the unique and important role of the human male parent.

Fathers and Sons

The father's special influence on the development of his son has been investigated in three areas: gender role development, cognitive development, and socioemotional development. In terms of gender role, it has been found that the presence in the home of a father who is affectionate, who is seen as a competent decision-maker, and who is involved in family functions has a positive impact on the masculine development of male children. The sons of such fathers are likely to feel positive about their own masculinity and to possess the competencies associated with their gender. The result is a feeling of security and self-confidence (Biller 1981, 1982). In the cognitive area, sons of nurturant, competent fathers have been found to earn higher scores on achievement and intelligence tests as well as higher grades in school than do sons of "inadequate" fathers or boys from father-absent homes (Biller 1981; Blanchard & Biller 1971; Radin 1972). Finally, the presence of a nurturant and competent father has been associated with high self-esteem in elementary school boys (Coopersmith 1967), personal adjustment in college-age males (Reuter & Biller 1973), and successful heterosexual adjustment in early adulthood (Biller 1974, 1982).

Fathers and Daughters

Girls raised in families that include a loving and respected father are most likely to become healthy well-adjusted young women who feel pride in their femininity; this effect is observed particularly if their mothers and fathers had a warm and satisfying relationship with one another (Fish & Biller 1973). Evidence also suggests that a warm and close father-daughter relationship is positively correlated with the daughter's later marital satisfaction (Biller 1974). Finally, the absence of a father

A father who is actively involved in family functions is likely to raise children who are self-confident and well-adjusted.

during his daughter's childhood has been linked to her later negative attitudes toward masculinity (Biller 1982), as well as to insecurity in dealing with boys and men during the girl's adolescence (Hetherington 1972).

The Parent-Adolescent Relationship

The teenage years are often thought of as a phase of life that can gray a parent's hair. The popular media have given much attention to the con-

flict of generations and to the conflicting influences of parents and adolescent peer groups. Such stereotypes often contain a grain of truth, but—like all human relationships—the parent-adolescent relationship is a highly complex one that defies simple explanation.

This section addresses the issue of conflict between parent and teenager. Is it inevitable? When is it most likely and least likely to occur? Parent-peer cross-pressures and the influences of parent versus peer advice on the behavior of the adolescent will also be examined.

Is Conflict Inevitable?

American parents often dread the adolescent years, assuming that even the most pleasant children will turn overnight into rebellious, disrespectful, and hostile teenagers. Is there any real reason for such concern? Is conflict between parent and adolescent an unavoidable and unpleasant phase in child development?

Research, theory, and popular wisdom about adolescent-parent relationships often produce contradictory images of the degree of conflict in the American home. To illustrate this point, there was much discussion in the late 1960s and the early 1970s of the "generation gap" between parent and adolescent. Margaret Mead (1970) described the gap as the inevitable result of a cultural clash between those who were raised before World War II and those who had grown up after it. And yet, in 1969, at the height of the American domestic conflict over the morality of the Vietnam War and at the time Mead was writing her book, a national survey (Yankelovich 1969) indicated that two-thirds of adolescents and two-thirds of their parents felt that generational conflict was not serious. In the same survey, three out of four adolescents said their values were similar to those of their parents and any existing differences were minor. Such findings agree with those of a number of studies conducted during the 1960s and 1970s. For example, after studying five thousand adolescents, Douvan and Adelson (1966) discovered few serious disagreements between teenagers and their parents. Similarly, Meissner (1965) observed in his study of over twelve hundred high school boys that 90 percent of them were happy in their homes, and three out of four said they were proud of their parents and would like them to meet their friends. In another study, Larson (1975) questioned fifteen hundred seventh, ninth, and twelfth graders in a small Oregon city. He found that nearly half of the students had a highly satisfying relationship with their parents and three-fourths had at least a satisfying relationship.

It would appear that the adolescent-parent relationship in American society is often a very

healthy one, and yet there are some difficult contradictions to explain. On the one hand, adolescents seem to share the values of their parents and to be happy in their homes; there seem to be few serious disagreements between the generations. On the other hand, real-life experience indicates that our society is not without parent-child conflicts (e.g., concerning music, clothing styles, drug use, sexual behavior) during adolescence. These conflicts may not illustrate the deep and serious generation gap Mead described, and yet they cannot be ignored, even if, as Rice (1984) contended, they are exaggerated by the media.

Perhaps the best approach to reconciling the conflict-ridden and conflict-free descriptions of the parent-adolescent relationship is to conclude that intergenerational conflict is highly variable (Ellis 1986), occurring frequently in some families, but rarely in others.

Factors Related to Conflict

The recognition that intergenerational conflict during adolescence is highly variable, and therefore avoidable, leads to a logical question: can we identify factors that promote conflict between parents and teenagers? Ellis (1986) identified three factors contributing to parent-adolescent conflict. The first is the *speed of social change*. Rapid social change is likely to induce intergenerational conflict. For example, in upwardly mobile families, the children may be better educated and better off economically than their parents were during adolescence. The children may have access to drugs their parents have never even heard of. They may be challenged to deal with a permissive set of sexual standards unheard of in the previous generation. In a sense, the children grow up in a world far different from the one their parents grew up in, leading to the cultural conflict Mead (1970) was referring to in her discussion of the generation gap.

A second contributor to parent-adolescent conflict according to Ellis is *delay of adult status*. Societies that deny adult status to older adolescents and even young adults are the most likely to experience rebelliousness among disenfranchised young people. Delay of adult status is characterized by withholding adult privileges and responsibilities (e.g., driving, holding a job, marrying, voting, drinking) and by extending the years of education.

Finally, a highly significant predictor of conflict is the *amount of control exercised by parents*. The relationship between conflict and control is not a linear one, however. That is, conflict does not increase directly as the amount of control increases. Instead there is a curvilinear relationship, with the greatest intergenerational conflict at the extremes of too much or too little control and the least amount of conflict in the middle range. This pattern is illustrated in Figure 11.1. The authoritative approach to control, with discipline tempered by rational discussion, is associated with a lower level of conflict than is found in authoritarian or permissive families.

Ellis noted that the strength of the conflict-control relationship is influenced by several other variables. One variable is the degree to which adolescents adopt their parents' values. When the child shares the parent's values, control is internal rather than imposed from the outside, and the likelihood of conflict is reduced. A second variable influencing the conflict-control relationship is the timing of parental control: if control is imposed early in childhood, the child is likely to have internalized parental values by adolescence and conflict is minimized. On the other hand, if parents are permissive with young children and attempt to impose greater control when these children reach adolescence, the result will be resentment and conflict. Ellis suggested that "early permissiveness" and "later constraint" is a pattern often found in families in the United States; thus, the stage for intergenerational conflict is set. By way of contrast, parents in Denmark follow a reverse pattern of "early control" and "later independence" in raising their children, and parent-adolescent conflict in that country is practically nonexistent (Ellis 1986; Kandel & Lesser 1969).

Finally, the conflict-control relationship is influenced by the degree to which the adolescent sees parental control as legitimate (Ellis 1986). If the control is perceived as fair, rational, and legitimate, conflict is unlikely; if the control is seen as arbitrary or unreasonable, conflict is often the result. Again, authoritative parenting is linked to conflict reduction, since authoritative parents attempt to be rational in imposing constraints on their children and indicate respect for their children by being willing

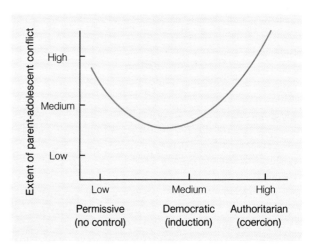

Figure 11.1 The Curvilinear Relationship of Parent-Adolescent Conflict and Parental Control

Source: Reprinted from *Adolescents in Families*, Copyright 1986, by Geoffrey K. Leigh and Gary W. Peterson. Used by permission of South-Western Publishing Co.

to explain their rules. Oftentimes, adolescents are not rebelling against the rules but against the ways in which the rules are imposed.

Parental Versus Peer Influence During Adolescence

An analysis of the parent-child relationship during adolescence invariably leads to the question of the relative influence of parents and peers on adolescent decision making. Parents often blame the influence of peers for their children's insubordinate behavior; a parent's common lament is "they never seem to listen to me anymore, but everything their friends say is right."

Does parental authority really give way to peer influence when a child enters adolescence? Two conceptual frameworks have been applied to the study of parent-peer cross-pressure in an attempt to answer that question. These are the situation hypothesis and the individual differences hypothesis (Berzonsky 1981).

According to the *situation hypothesis,* adolescents sometimes look to parents for guidance and sometimes to peers, depending on the situation. They look to their peers and reject parental suggestions in areas in which social values are changing rapidly and no long-range effects are involved.

For example, an adolescent might ask peers for advice on how to dress or on which class to take in school, but would ask parents for advice on which part-time job to take or on basic moral decisions (Brittain 1963, 1967/1968; Kelley 1972). Most adults probably remember feeling that their parents were old-fashioned in their choice of music, hairstyles, and clothing and that the "kids" knew what was really happening. However, in making major decisions affecting their future lives, those same adults probably sought advice and encouragement from their parents rather than from their peers.

Instead of focusing on specific decision-making situations, the *individual differences hypothesis* focuses on the characteristics of individual decision makers, particularly on their styles of thinking and on the degree to which they have established a sense of personal identity (Berzonsky 1981). Some adolescents are **information-oriented decision makers.** That is, they gather relevant information from every possible source before making decisions. These are self-reliant, psychologically mature people with well-formed identities. Other adolescents are **source-oriented decision makers:** they rely heavily on the opinions of others when making a decision—some primarily on the opinions of parents and some on the opinion of peers. They lack the self-reliance connected with the establishment of a clear identity of their own.

The normal developmental progression in decision making involves a shift from parental source-orientation to information-orientation, accompanying a shift from a poorly formed to a well-formed identity. In fact, young adolescents have been found to be more parent-oriented than are older ones (Floyd & South 1972; Larson 1975).

Many adolescents remain parent-oriented in decision making, even as they move into adulthood. Others seek to break away from parents but are not yet ready to make independent decisions; therefore, they rely heavily on peers as sources of information and advice. Finally, some adolescents are encouraged by their parents to become independent information-oriented decision makers.

Berzonsky (1981) argued that personality characteristics of decision makers are at least as significant as characteristics of the situation. From

No human relationship is characterized by such extremes of love and hatred as is the sibling relationship.

a developmental standpoint, when the adolescent begins to shift from reliance on parental advice to a greater reliance on other information sources—teachers, employers, reading materials—adolescent-parent conflict can result, particularly if parents are reluctant to relinquish authority. (See Problems in Child Development "Children Who Run Away" for comments on the relation of conflicts with parents and peers to the nation's runaway problem.)

The Sibling Relationship

Parents are often asked how well their children get along with one another. The answer is difficult because the quality of the relationship can vary from day to day or even from hour to hour. A child may love a sibling intensely and may leap to his or her defense if there is a threat of harm from a playmate. The same child can hate the same

Problems in Child Development

Children Who Run Away

In 1975, nearly a quarter of a million American children between the ages of 10 and 17 ran away from home. Boys and girls ran away in fairly equal numbers. The typical runaway was 16 years old and from a low-income broken home (although all social classes were well represented in the runaway population). The runaway did not go very far from home and was gone for less than three days; however, one in six runaways was gone for a month or more (Nye & Edelbrock 1980).

Why do children run away from home? To answer the question, we must differentiate among several types of runaway children; Nye

(1982) suggested three basic types:

1. The *adventurers* run away to meet new people, visit exciting places, and have experiences not available at home. This is the "positive" runaway, who is not unhappy at home but who is looking for greater challenges in life. Only one in five runaways belongs in this category.

2. *Dissatisfied runaways* are unhappy about certain aspects of their lives. They hope to run to a happy place, where their problems cannot follow them. These runaways have problems at home, in school, or with peers; some may have problems with the police. This category makes up the majority of runaways—roughly 75 percent.

3. The *pushouts* are unwanted adolescents who are told, either in words or by the actions of their parents, that they must leave home. Many are abused, physically or sexually, and they run to escape intolerable home situations. Approximately 5 percent of all runaways are pushouts.

The reasons for running away from home—and the solutions to runaway problems—are varied. Positive runaways might be encouraged to postpone their adventures until they reach adulthood. Dissatisfied runaways need counseling to deal with their problems. The pushouts, unfortunately, will require special attention because their families generally do not want them to come home.

brother or sister with a passion rarely found in other relationships.

This section examines the sibling relationship from the time the new baby arrives until the end of adolescence. It also looks at the experiences of children without siblings and at the ways in which a child's place in the family is related to his or her psychological development.

Coping with a New Sibling

The entry of a baby brother or sister into a family has a dramatic effect on the life of an older child. Four in ten children express mixed feelings about their mother's pregnancy, one in four is ambivalent about the postbirth reunion with mother,

and the majority of firstborns—a striking 64 percent—display negative changes in behavior within a few weeks after a sibling's birth (Nadelman & Begun 1982).

To provide an in-depth analysis of the psychological impact of new siblings, Dunn and Kendrick (1982) observed the family situations of forty firstborn English children coping with baby brothers and sisters. They noticed that mother-child confrontations, both verbal and nonverbal, increased considerably over prebirth levels. Naughty behaviors, involving deliberate disobedience or a direct attack on the mother, were three times more likely to occur after than before the sibling birth. Since these outbursts generally occurred while the mother was handling the newborn, the naughtiness can be related to the presence of the new baby.

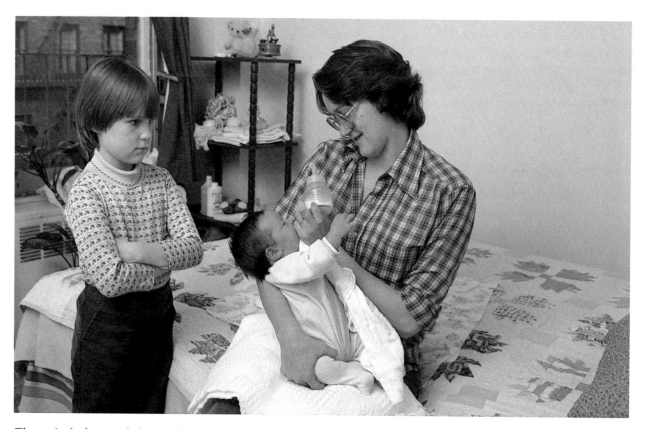

The arrival of a new baby in a family has a profound effect on an older sibling, nearly two-thirds of whom display negative changes in behavior after the baby's birth.

What is more, even when parents made substantial efforts to prepare the first child for the baby's arrival, the presence of the "intruder" still caused considerable adjustment difficulties.

Why are firstborn children so affected by the arrival of a baby brother or sister? A possible answer to this question was suggested by Dunn and Kendrick (1982) when they looked at pre- to postbirth changes in the quality of the mother-child interaction. Mothers of newborns spent less time playing with their older children, showing things to them, giving them things, helping them, and initiating conversations with them. Thus, a major consequence for an older child of the arrival of a new sibling is a significant decline in mother's attention.

A number of characteristics related to the ease of postbirth adjustment have been identified in children. *Sex of child* is a significant factor; boys are typically more upset by a new sibling than girls are and more likely to withdraw. *Temperament* of the older child is also related; children described as being negative in their mood are most likely to show withdrawal and/or sleeping difficulties after the baby arrives. *Age of child* is a factor as well, with younger children more likely to be disturbed by the loss of mother's attention. Younger children are the most likely to become clingy and overly dependent and to display regressive behavior, such as toileting accidents (Dunn & Kendrick 1982; Nadelman & Begun 1982; Stewart et al. 1987). *Mood of mother* is also a predictor of the firstborn's adjustment; if the mother is overly tired or depressed after the birth of the second child, the older child is more likely to engage in negative behavior, such as withdrawal. Finally, children who adjust most easily to the arrival of a new brother or sister have had close, intense involvements with their fathers (Dunn & Kendrick 1982). While the mother's attention to the firstborn declines after the birth of a sibling, the father's attention does not; in fact, whether or not they realize they are doing so, fathers of newborns actually increase the amount of time they spend with the firstborn child (Stewart et al. 1987).

Sibling Interactions in the Preschool Years

Since young children spend a great deal of their time at home, it is likely that in families of two or more children an extensive amount of sibling interaction will occur. To examine the quality of that interaction, Abramovitch, Pepler, and Corter (1982) carried out home observations of nearly 120 families with two preschool children. They described a level of sibling interaction that was striking both in its quantity and in its diversity.

Parents often pity the younger sibling, who seems to be the object of aggression from an older brother or sister. In fact, in the Abramovitch study, older siblings initiated aggressive activity about 80 percent of the time. On the other hand, older children also introduced two-thirds of the prosocial activity. It appears that older children usually initiate social activity of any sort, probably as a result of their greater social maturity. In the Abramovitch study, younger siblings initiated one-third of the prosocial activities but only 20 percent of the aggressive ones. Perhaps they are simply less aggressive than older brothers or sisters or perhaps they are just realistic: they recognize they are not likely to win if a conflict occurs. Not surprisingly, the younger siblings did display more imitation; thus, an older child can serve as a role model and teacher for the younger one. In fact, older siblings have been found to be good models for facilitating cognitive development in infants (Wishart 1986).

Abramovitch and her associates observed that girls were more prosocial than boys; boys were involved in sibling conflict more often and were more likely to display physical aggression. On the other hand, girls were just as verbally aggressive as boys and just as likely to take things from a younger sibling. Finally, older sisters seemed to be

kinder to younger siblings, particularly in same-sex pairs.

As a final note on the Abramovitch study, no differences in any aspect of the sibling relationship were attributable to the age differences between sibling pairs. This finding runs contrary to the popular belief that parents can use some ideal spacing formula to promote harmonious sibling relationships. In fact, experts on sibling interaction observe that the ideal-age-difference concept is a myth; as Dunn (1985) pointed out, whether the age gap is eleven months or four years, play, companionship, and affection appear just as frequently in siblings—and so do aggression, hostility, and teasing.

Considering the extent and variety of sibling relationships during the preschool years, we might expect that patterns acquired in socializing with siblings would be transferred to peer relationships. To investigate the degree to which social interaction patterns in the home are carried into the school, Berndt and Bulleit (1985) examined the behaviors of thirty-four preschoolers in both settings. A link between peer play and sibling play was found in two areas: the incidence of aggression and the incidence of onlooker play. Children who tended to be aggressive with siblings also tended to be aggressive with peers; children who were often passive watchers rather than active participants in school play often assumed the same role at home. The most passive children were girls without brothers, leading Berndt and Bulleit to suggest that a male sibling may draw a sister into stereotypically masculine active play.

An Ambivalent Relationship

The sibling relationship beyond the preschool years is characterized by a high degree of love and hate. The intensity of the sibling relationship is not surprising when we consider the advances in social and self-awareness that characterize the years from middle childhood through adolescence and the closeness of the physical environment that siblings share; not only do they live in the same house, but also one in three American siblings shares a bedroom and virtually every child shares household chores with a brother or sister (Bryant 1982).

The sibling relationship during childhood and adolescence is one of the most stressful of all human relationships because of its ambivalence; stress might result from any relationship that combines such high degrees of love and hate (Pfouts 1976). As Bryant (1982) observed, even the same relationship can range from a positive extreme of psychological closeness and support to a negative extreme of frustration, anger, and competition, which is often referred to as sibling rivalry. The closer in age the siblings are, the greater is the degree of ambivalence. That is, closely spaced siblings tend to say more positive *and* more negative things about one another than do siblings who differ greatly in age (Bigner 1974).

When sibling rivalry occurs during childhood and adolescence, it seems to arise from two sources: competition for parental approval and competition for status according to ground rules established by the siblings themselves (Pfouts 1976). In other words, even if children feel thoroughly approved of by their parents, sibling rivalry can still exist as children compare themselves with their brothers and sisters.

Why would children who feel equally approved of by their parents still need to see themselves as better in some way than their siblings? The answer may be that parents unintentionally treat siblings differently and thus set up a basis for social comparison. For example, mother may dispense equal amounts of affection to her two children (Dunn, Plomin & Daniels 1986), but she may provide a greater degree of attention and emotional support to the younger one (Bryant 1982; Bryant & Crockenberg 1980). Of the nearly four hundred adolescents and young adults studied by Daniels and Plomin (1985), 40 percent reported that their parents treated them differently from their siblings. And differential parental treatment is only one aspect of environmental differences that may lead to social comparisons and sibling rivalry! Daniels and Plomin also discovered that nearly two-thirds of the participants in their study believed they and their siblings lived in very different environments in terms of sibling interaction, peer characteristics, and specific life events. The researchers concluded that two children raised in the same family may be living in radically different environments.

Environmental differences in sibling experiences are reflected in research findings on the effects of birth order on characteristics of sibling relationships. Firstborns are more negative toward siblings than later-borns are; they are bossier, more dominant, and more likely to use power-assertive techniques (e.g., hitting, bribing, referring to their status) to get what they want. In contrast, later-borns more often resort to pleading, crying, and sulking; they are also more likely to appeal to parents for help (Dunn 1985).

Children Without Siblings

Ask one hundred people to describe the child without siblings, and the response will be overwhelmingly negative. In one public opinion poll, 80 percent of the respondents believed that an only child is disadvantaged (Blake 1974). The only child has been described as maladjusted, self-centered, temperamental, anxious, unhappy, and unlikeable—among other negative traits (Thompson 1974). In keeping with their negative stereotype, only children have been found to be more egocentric and less cooperative than children with siblings (Jiao, Ji & Ching 1986). On the other hand, when only children themselves and their parents are asked to describe their life experiences, they present a considerably more positive view (Falbo 1978a, 1978b, 1982).

What is the truth about the life of the only child in the American family? In the first place, being an only child seems to be a much more positive experience than most people believe. Secondly, the life of the only child is not unique; only children and firstborn children share a considerable number of characteristics.

Only children and firstborns have higher educational aspirations than do later-borns, and they are more likely to achieve success in life as measured by conventional standards. Only children and firstborns experience greater pressure from parents for mature behavior; perhaps as a result, they are more responsible and self-controlled. Only children and firstborns have fewer friends and typically have a less intense social life than do later-borns, perhaps because the first or only child receives more parental affection and therefore requires less affection from peers. On the other hand, only children and firstborns have just as many *close* friends as do later-borns and report being just as satisfied with their lives. No consistent differences between children with and without siblings have been found in the areas of overall popularity or in self-esteem (Falbo 1982).

Observed differences between the only child and the child with siblings may occur for many reasons. Falbo (1982) suggested that the social and personality development of the only child is influenced more by the characteristics of the parent-child relationship in the one-child home than by the absence of siblings in itself.

The Impact of Divorce

The so-called nuclear, or "intact," family unit—mother, father, and children residing under the same roof—is but one of several variations in family composition. The single-parent family, for example, is not an uncommon situation in the United States. Consider the following statistic: between 40 and 50 percent of all American children born in the 1970s will probably live, for at least a short time, in a single-parent household (Hetherington 1979). Furthermore, the single-parent household is not, as is commonly believed, a phenomenon peculiar only to the 1970s and 1980s. Data on familial patterns since 1900 indicate that one-quarter to one-third of American children have always had some exposure to "disrupted" families (Bane 1979).

In the past, parental death was a major factor contributing to marital disruption. One in five children born in 1900 could expect to see a parent die before the child's eighteenth birthday; only one in twelve born in 1960 could expect a similar occurrence (Bane 1979). Today, however, divorce is the largest single cause of marital disruption and the major reason why single-parent households are created. Between 1966 and 1976 the divorce rate per thousand population actually doubled, possibly because divorce is gaining widespread acceptance as a solution to marital problems (Norton & Glick 1979). It has been estimated that 40 percent of all marriages contracted today will eventually

end in divorce (Fine, Moreland & Schwebel 1983).

Divorce is rarely a civilized and friendly business between a husband and wife; it is often accompanied by anger, depression, a lowering of self-esteem, and a degree of temporary mental confusion (Kelley 1982; Wallerstein & Kelly 1980). The divorce statistics convey an even greater sense of pain, however, when we realize that many divorcing husbands and wives are fathers and mothers as well, and a family breakup is keenly felt by the children involved. About fourteen percent of all American children born in 1955 experienced a divorce in the family before they reached the age of 18. Estimates suggest that of children born in 1970, 23 percent already have or will live through a divorce; while of those born in the 1980s, fully one-third will see their parents' marriages dissolve (Bane 1979). Clearly, divorce can no longer be regarded as an isolated phenomenon, and American parenting cannot be discussed without reference to the single-parent household that typically results from divorce. (See Issues in Child Development "What Happens When Mother Goes to Work?" for information on another major influence on the contemporary American family.)

The Single-Parent Household

According to the 1980 census, there are approximately 60 million families in the United States today; 10 million of these are headed by a single parent, and, in five cases out of six, the parent with custody of the children is a woman (U.S. Census Bureau 1980).

To understand the impact of divorce on children, we must first recognize the significant changes that occur in a household as a result of marital disruption. The changes are in three areas: (1) economic factors, (2) emotional reactions of the custodial parent, and (3) the "loss" of the noncustodial parent.

Economic Factors
In 1980, 54 percent of the children living in single-parent families headed by white women and 70 percent in families headed by black women were living below the established U.S. poverty level; only 8 percent of the children living in male-headed

One of every six American families is headed by a single parent, and in the vast majority of such homes, the single parent is the mother.

(predominantly two-parent) families in the late 1970s found themselves in such dire economic circumstances (Bane 1979).

The particular economic disadvantage of the female-headed family has been attributed to a number of factors. First, the levels of alimony and child support received by single mothers are quite low, and payments tend to be irregular. Second, single mothers may be unable to find adequate child-care facilities, which would free them to work outside the home. Third, our society provides fewer employment opportunities for women (many of whom lack marketable job skills) than for men. Finally, when women do find work, it is mostly in areas in which low wages are paid (e.g., clerical work, service work, private household work); and, even when they have equivalent skills and experience, women workers in the United States earn lower wages than men (Bane 1979).

The first effect of divorce on children, therefore, is that their standard of living may be lowered.

Issues in Child Development

What Happens When Mother Goes to Work?

More than half of the mothers of school-aged children, and slightly less than half of the mothers of preschoolers, are employed outside the home (Hoffman 1979). What is more, maternal employment cannot be thought of as a temporary reaction to difficult economic times, since three out of four working women say they would continue to work even if they did not need the money (Dubnoff, Veroff & Kulka 1978). Hetherington (1979) attributed the increase of mothers in the American work force to (1) the reduction in the size of the family, (2) a decrease in the amount of time needed to complete regular household chores, and (3) an increase in women's level of education.

Not surprisingly, child psychologists have been particularly interested in the effects of maternal employment on children. To date, however, the research has been somewhat limited, particularly that involving infants and young children. Furthermore, the findings are mixed: maternal employment appears to affect children both positively and negatively. Thus far, however, the positive has been found to outweigh the negative. Comparisons between children of working and nonworking mothers for the different age groups follow.

Infancy and Early Childhood

Positive

In the event of divorce, mothers who had worked while married are better able to cope, both psychologically and economically. Thus, some negative effects of divorce on preschoolers are diminished. (Hetherington 1979). Four-year-old children of working mothers experience better social adjustment than do 4-year-olds whose mothers do not work (Gold & Andres 1978c).

Negative

In the second year of life, children of nonworking mothers are more vocal, experience more positive social interactions, and score higher on tests of normal development (Cohen 1978).

School Years

Positive

School-aged children with working mothers are more likely to be given greater household responsibilities and are more likely to behave independently than their age-mates with nonworking mothers (Hoffman 1974). They are more likely to have democratic gender role concepts and less likely to hold rigid gender role stereotypes (Gold & Andres 1978b). They also are more likely to have a positive view of femininity (Hoffman 1974). Finally, daughters of working mothers are higher in achievement motivation, set higher career goals for themselves, and are more likely to see their mothers as successful models to be emulated (Huston-Stein & Higgins-Trenk 1978).

Negative

Sons in lower-class families experience strained relationships with their fathers, perhaps because maternal employment is seen as a sign of the father's failure (Hoffman 1979). Sons of all social classes score lower on mathematics and language achievement tests when their mothers work (Gold & Andres 1978a).

Adolescence

Positive

Adolescent daughters of working mothers are more socially outgoing, independent, achievement-oriented, and personally and socially well adjusted than those of non-working mothers.

Adolescent sons of working mothers are higher in self-esteem, social adjustment at school, and personal adjustment (Gold & Andres 1978a).

Issues in Child Development (continued)

personality characteristics of the mother. Consider the findings from a study by Benn (1986), who examined the quality of attachment between working mothers and their 18-month-old sons and found much variety in the relationships. Working mothers whose children were the most secure and the most closely attached were warm and loving parents and were relaxed and happy in their parenting roles. They were sensitive to their children's needs and conscientious in their choice of substitute caregivers, whom they regarded not as replacements but as extensions of themselves. They were secure, self-confident people who saw their jobs as opportunities to expand themselves rather than as means of establishing their self-worth. In contrast, working mothers of the least secure children were angry and frustrated; they took little pleasure from motherhood, and they saw their jobs as means of keeping them from being depressed and of filling a void in their lives. They were careless in their choice of day-care arrangements and communicated very little with their children's caregivers.

In conclusion, it would seem that employment outside the home is not the only variable to be considered in research on working mothers. In an analysis of a relationship as complicated as that between mother and child, numerous other variables must also be kept in mind.

Emotional Reactions of the Single Parent

The quality of a child's home atmosphere may be affected adversely by the custodial parent's reactions to the divorce. In fact, divorced and separated mothers (the typical custodial parent) have been found to suffer greater anxiety and to experience deeper depression than do married mothers (Hetherington 1972; Pearlin & Johnson 1977; Longfellow 1979). Divorced single mothers have also reported feelings of anger and feelings of incompetence in their roles (Hetherington, Cox & Cox 1976). Finally, the divorced mother may experience a substantial loss in her social contacts and, as a consequence, may lose much-needed emotional support and advice from family and friends. Such losses may adversely influence her relationship with her children (Longfellow 1979).

If their mother is stressed, the children of divorce will feel the stress as well. Divorced mothers report having less time and emotional energy to devote to their children than they did while married (Brown, Bhrolchain & Harris 1975; Longfellow 1979). Parent-child conflict is more frequent as the children become at least slightly disillusioned about the personal qualities of their parents (Tessman 1978; Hetherington 1979). In two of every three cases studied, the mother-child relationship seems to deteriorate within the first year after the divorce (Wallerstein & Kelly 1975).

The "Loss" of the Noncustodial Parent

Research on parent-child separation after a divorce has focused almost exclusively on the "loss" of the father as a continuing source of influence. Hetherington (1979) described several effects on children of the loss of the father, a loss that can best be understood by referring to the father's functions in the intact nuclear family. Fathers participate in child rearing directly by disciplining children, by teaching them, and by serving as adult models. Mothers serve as models, of course; but, as Hetherington observed, two adult models expose the child to a wider range of interests, attitudes, and behaviors than does only one. A second adult in the family can also serve as a buffer of emotional support if the other adult rejects a child on a continuing basis or on an occasional basis (perhaps because of a difficult day at work). In the single-parent family, such an adult refuge is rarely available.

Fathers participate in parenting indirectly by providing economic aid to the family, by sharing household chores, and by providing emotional support for their wives. Such activities promote the harmonious functioning of the family unit and, as a consequence, improve the overall quality of the child rearing. The loss of a father may have a reverse effect.

Single-Parent Family Versus Other Family Patterns

In combinations or separately, economic hardship, a stressed parent, or the absence of a second adult can adversely affect a child's development. To assess the impact on children of a variety of family patterns, Dornbusch and his associates (1985) looked at a representative group of 7,500 adolescents whose family structures fit into one of three categories: (1) the household headed by a single mother and containing no other adult, (2) the household headed by both biological parents, and (3) the household headed by a single mother but containing an additional adult (e.g., boyfriend, uncle, grandparent).

The adolescents were rated on a number of conventional measures of deviancy, including contacts with the law, arrests, truancy, disciplinary problems at school, and attempts to run away from home. Children from two-parent families displayed significantly fewer deviant behaviors than did children from single-mother households. What is more, children from single-mother households in which a second adult was living were less deviant than those from households in which the mother was the only adult.

Dornbusch and his associates were also interested in the relationship between family structure and decision-making patterns in the family. That is, to what extent are decisions affecting the adolescent's life shared and to what extent are they the sole responsibility of the parent or the adolescent? The researchers found that in households headed by a single mother as the only adult decisions were most often made by the adolescent alone. Parental decision making and joint decision making were more typical of two-parent households. A relationship was found between degree of deviant behavior exhibited by an adolescent and

the amount of parental influence in decision making, with the more involved parents having the less deviant adolescent children.

The authors of the study did not conclude that single mothering in itself is a cause of deviant behavior among adolescents. Certainly a number of other factors (e.g., economic conditions, outside sources of emotional support) must also be considered in explaining the relationship. However, they did suggest that raising an adolescent is an extremely difficult task for a mother alone, and that an additional adult in the household seems to provide a degree of adult involvement that adolescents need and helps to reduce adolescent deviant behavior.

Children's Reactions to Divorce

Thus far, this section has described the structural changes in the child's home life that occur as a result of marital disruption. However, developmental changes in children's characteristic reactions to divorce can also be noted (see Table 11.2). As the child grows older, he or she is more likely to express freely a variety of complex feelings, understand those feelings, and realize that the divorce cannot be attributed to any one simple cause. Self-blame virtually disappears after the age of 6, fear of abandonment diminishes after the age of 8, and the confusion and fear of the young child are replaced in the older child by shame, anger, and self-reflection.

Children not only react differently to divorce according to their age but also according to their sex. The impact of divorce is initially greater on boys than it is on girls and considerably longer-lasting as well (Hetherington, Cox & Cox 1978; Hetherington 1979). Compared with daughters, the sons of divorced parents tend to be more aggressive, to be less compliant, to have greater difficulties in interpersonal relationships, and to exhibit problem behaviors both at home and at school. Furthermore, the adjustment problems of boys are still quite noticeable even two years after the divorce, whereas any adjustment problems for girls have disappeared by that time.

Hetherington suggested a number of possible explanations for the relatively greater impact of divorce on boys than on girls. The boys' aggression

Table 11.2   Developmental Changes in Children's Reactions to Divorce

Age	Reaction
2½ to 6 Years	Children had difficulty expressing their feelings, lacked an understanding of what the concept of divorce meant or implied in terms of parental separation or change in living arrangements, and tended to blame themselves for the situation, regardless of how carefully the parents explained that the children were not responsible (Wallerstein & Kelly 1975).
7 to 8 Years	Children did not blame themselves for the divorce. They were aware of their feelings and easily verbalized their sadness, but not their anger. Feelings of rejection were common. There was no understanding that the divorce was a mutual arrangement between the two parents; instead, the children believed that one parent simply got angry and left, or told the other one to leave. Fear that they, the children, could as easily be abandoned or thrown out were common (Kelly & Wallerstein 1976).
9 to 10 Years	Children did not blame themselves for the breakup, and freely expressed their feelings, including anger toward either or both parents. However, the anger was often combined with loyalty—a sense of loving and hating the parent at the same time. Unlike younger children, there was a tendency among nines and tens to hide their sadness, to present a "tough" exterior. Feelings of loneliness and fear of being unloved were common (Wallerstein & Kelly 1976).
Adolescence	Strong feelings of anger, shame, sadness, and embarrassment were found in this age group. Adolescents also displayed an ability to analyze the nature of their parents' marriage relationship, and to understand the needs and feelings of both parents. Adolescents experiencing a parental divorce related to their parents as real and complex human beings much better than they did earlier. Also, there was a tendency to give careful consideration to the nature of and requirements of marriage itself (Wallerstein & Kelly 1974).

and noncompliance may reflect the fact that such behaviors are tolerated and even encouraged in males in our culture more than they are in females; even in the two-parent family males exceed females in the prevalence of aggressive, noncompliant behaviors (Hetherington 1979). Furthermore, boys may have a particular need for a strong male model of self-control, as well as for a strong disciplinarian parent. Divorce frequently removes this control. Boys are more likely to be exposed to their parents' fights than girls are and thus have a model for hostility. After the breakup, boys are less likely

than girls to receive sympathy and support from mothers, teachers, or peers; their anti-social behavior may be an attempt to gain attention (Hetherington 1979).

Children's Adjustment to Divorce

The most extensive information available on children's long-term adjustment to divorce is contained in the California Divorce Study (Wallerstein & Kelly 1980). The children of sixty California families were interviewed five years after the divorce;

however, no single pattern emerged from the interview data.

The study found that some children were quite happy and well adjusted. The authors defined *well adjusted* as the absence of depression, adequate or high self-esteem, and a positive and realistic view of life. They identified a number of factors related to a child's successful long-term adjustment. These factors were

- a continuing stable relationship with both parents
- a warm, nurturant relationship with the custodial parent
- a close relationship with the noncustodial parent
- the presence of good friendships outside of the home
- the presence of other sources of emotional support, including grandparents, teachers, neighbors, and clergymen
- the psychological stability of the parents.

Unfortunately, just as some children adjusted quite successfully to the trauma of divorce, others were not as successful. Many children continued to be angry, lonely, and depressed. A number of factors were related to poor adjustment, including

- the failure of the divorce to resolve the conflict between the parents
- the presence of stress in the custodial parent
- inadequate parenting, which had been inadequate even prior to the divorce
- inability of the children to understand the divorce in the first place.

Only one recent study has attempted to investigate effects of divorce beyond the five-year point. Fine, Moreland, and Schwebel (1983) interviewed a group of college students (average age: 19.6) whose parents had been divorced for an average of ten years, and a group of similar students from intact families. Young adult children of divorced parents, in contrast to young adults from intact families, were likely to characterize their homes as colder, less affectionate, more distant, and poorer in communication. Students from divorced families typically rated their current relationships with their parents as average in quality, while those from intact families rated their relationships with parents as above average. Lastly,

the authors noted that the parent-child relationship that suffers the least after a divorce is that between a mother and her daughter. They suggested in explanation that the daily experience of living with mother as a role model strengthened the mother-daughter relationship, or that daughters sympathized with their mothers and became sensitive to the stresses they were experiencing (Fine, Moreland, & Schwebel 1983).

What do these follow-up studies of children of divorce reveal? Divorce *can* have significant long-term effects on a child's self-concept, as well as on the relationship with either or both parents. However, such negative effects can be counteracted by maintaining high-quality relationships with both the custodial and the noncustodial parent. Divorce can be a painful and emotionally trying experience for children, but psychological recovery is possible—and even very likely—if parents are sensitive to their child's feelings and needs.

Stepparents and Stepchildren

Approximately 85 percent of the men who become divorced and 75 percent of the women decide to marry again—usually within five years after their divorces are final (Duvall 1977; Glick 1984). Children in our society will be affected by parental remarriage just as they are affected by divorce: six in ten of the divorced people who marry again are the parents of at least one child under the age of 18 (Bigner 1985), and one in three children born in the United States in the early 1980s will spend at least some time in a stepfamily (Glick 1984). Thus develops what is known as a reconstituted family, members of which take on the unfamiliar roles of stepparents and stepchildren.

In general, the effects of remarriage on the family are positive. Children in reconstituted families differ little in their psychological profiles from children living in unbroken homes (Wilson et al. 1975). One exception is the case of adolescent boys living with stepfathers. Perhaps because of the particular qualities of the stepfather-stepson relationship, adolescent boys in this category more closely resemble boys in single-parent households in the frequency of their deviant behaviors than they do boys who live with both natural parents (Dornbusch et al. 1985).

The "reconstituted" family resulting from the marriages of couples who already have children is an increasingly familiar phenomenon in the United States today.

The general observation that a parent's remarriage can relieve the stresses experienced by children in single-parent households does not imply that problems never arise when families are reconstituted. In fact, the establishment of the stepparent and stepchild relationship is often a difficult process for several reasons. New stepparents take on an unfamiliar and sometimes frightening role as they attempt to incorporate themselves into the "culture" of an existing family; they may be perceived as and may perceive themselves as outsiders (Bigner 1985). Stepparents may face particular difficulties in their role as disciplinarians; their style of discipline may deviate from what the stepchildren are used to, and there may not be adequate time to coordinate the disciplinary approaches to stepparent and natural parent. Compromise is often required, and children may take advantage of the initial inconsistencies by playing one parent against the other. Children may also take merciless advantage of a new stepparent who has never been a parent before (Bohannan & Erickson 1978).

Another complication in the relationship between stepparent and stepchild is that children may hold a strong allegiance to the natural parent and may resent the stepparent as a poor substitute for the absent parent (Kompara 1982). They may hope, consciously or not, that their natural parents will reunite; obviously, they see the stepparent as an obstacle to that reunion (Bigner 1985).

Stepmothers in particular may find themselves struggling against a negative stereotype: the "wicked stepmother" is a stock character in many children's fairy tales. As a result, the stepmother may try too hard to be accepted by her stepchildren, and may find herself in the stressful situation of trying to make everyone in the family happy (Nelson & Nelson 1982). Stepfathers, on the other hand, may have their own special problems. They often face the difficult prospect of trying to provide financial support for two families at once, and they may feel guilt for "abandoning" their natural children as they move into the new family.

Summary

1. Theoretical perspectives on parent-infant attachment focus on social learning or on instinctive bonding; human attachment seems to involve learning to a greater extent than does the bonding process in lower animals.
2. The security of attachment varies from one parent-child relationship to another and is related to sociability, sense of competence, and amount of exploratory behavior in young children.
3. The major variables in research on parenting style are the degree of child- or parent-centeredness and the degree of parental permissiveness or control.
4. Authoritative parenting, combining acceptance and understanding of children with a high degree of parental control, is most effective in promoting independence and positive self-esteem in children.
5. In recent years, there has been much interest in the relatively neglected role of fathers in the parenting process; it appears that the roles of male and female parents are not interchangeable but instead complement and enhance one another.
6. Despite stereotypes concerning intergenerational conflict, the parent-adolescent relationship is generally a close one in American society. Conflict that does occur is related to several sociological variables, to parenting approaches, and to the personality of the adolescent involved.
7. Studies of sibling relationships indicate that children within the same family are often treated differently by parents, and that the quality of the sibling relationship is influenced by the children's developmental level, gender, and position within the family.
8. The divorce rate has risen rapidly in recent years, and single-parent households are increasingly common in the United States.
9. Children are invariably stressed by the divorce of their parents, but the severity of the impact depends on the children's level of development at the time, on their gender, on the possibility of maintaining close relationships with both parents, and on the availability of outside sources of emotional support. Some children adjust poorly to divorce, but others adjust remarkably well.

Key Terms

social-learning attachment theory
ethological attachment theory
bonding
authoritarian parents
authoritative parents
permissive parents
indifferent and uninvolved parents
information-oriented decision makers
source-oriented decision makers

Suggested Readings

Dunn, J. & Kendrick, C. (1982). *Siblings: Love, envy, and understanding*. Cambridge, MA: Harvard University Press.

A discussion of the variety of topics surrounding the sibling relationship. The book is based on an extensive study of forty English children. Included are discussions of the reactions of young children to the arrival of baby brothers and sisters, the nature of communication and understanding among siblings, developmental changes in the sibling relationship, and implications for parents.

Leigh, G.K. & Peterson, G.W. (1986). *Adolescents in families*. Cincinnati: South-Western.

A book containing useful articles on the experiences of adolescents within the family. Among the issues covered are intergenerational conflict, independence training, and familial influences on the self-image, vocational aspirations, and mental health of adolescent children. Included also are papers dealing with specific adolescent problems, such as delinquency and drug abuse, and with the experiences of adolescents in minority subcultures.

Parke, R.D. (1981). *Fathers.* Cambridge, MA: Harvard University Press.

A short and highly readable treatment of various aspects of fatherhood as illustrated by current research in the field. Included are discussions of expectant fathers, the father-infant interaction, and the influence of fathers on children's social and intellectual development.

Wallerstein, J.S. & Kelly, J.B. (1980). *Surviving the break-up: How children and parents cope with divorce.* New York: Basic Books.

A discussion of the findings of the California Divorce Study, one of the most extensive studies to date of the effects of divorce on both children and adults.

Readings from the Literature

The following article deals with the behavior of infants and toddlers in the Strange Situation, as discussed on page 346 of the chapter you have just read. As you read the article, keep in mind the following questions:

- In terms of research strategy, does this study represent an experimental or a nonexperimental design?

- What does the study add to our knowledge of the importance of secure attachment in a child's normal development?

- Does the study prove that secure attachment in infancy actually produces a high degree of self-confidence in later childhood?

Infant-Mother Attachment at Twelve Months and Style of Interaction with a Stranger at the Age of Three Years

Paul Lütkenhaus
Max-Planck Institut für Psychologische Forschung

Klaus E. Grossmann
University of Regensburg

Karin Grossmann
University of Regensburg

This study explores the relation between the quality of infant-mother attachment at 12 months and the child's style of interaction with an unfamiliar visitor at age 3 years. Quality of infant-mother attachment was assessed in Ainsworth's Strange Situation. At age 3 years, the children were visited in their homes and a competitive game interaction between child and visitor was videotaped. Children classified as securely attached at 12 months interacted faster and more smoothly with the visitor than children who had been avoidantly attached. Microanalyses of the competitive game also revealed different styles of interaction. Failure feedback led to increased effort in the secure-attachment group and to decreased effort in the insecure-attachment group. After failing, securely attached children tended to display sadness more openly than insecurely attached children.

A substantial body of researchers have linked qualities of the early infant-mother attachment bond to differences in the quality of the child's responses to other people at later ages (Arend, Gove, & Sroufe, 1979; Escher-Gräub & Grossmann, 1983; Lieberman, 1977; Main & Weston, 1981; Pastor, 1981; Sroufe, Fox, & Pancake, 1983; Thompson & Lamb, 1983; Waters, Wippman, & Sroufe, 1979). The aim of the present study was to investigate these later reactions in more detail. We assessed how 3-year-old children with different attachment histories reacted to a visiting stranger, and how they responded to success and failure in a competitive social game with an adult. According to both theory and empirical findings, children with a secure attachment will have had a history of smooth, reciprocally regulated, and joyful interactions with the mother, whereas those with an insecure attachment will have experienced inappropriate and/or delayed maternal responses to their signals (Ainsworth, Blehar, Waters, & Wall, 1978; Egeland & Farber, 1984; Grossmann, Grossmann, Spangler, Süss, & Unzner, in press). We consequently hypothesized that due to this difference in interpersonal experiences, children who had been securely attached in infancy should be more ready to interact with a visiting stranger than children who had been insecurely attached.

Maternal responsiveness and sensitivity toward her infant have been viewed as providing conditions under which an infant can exert control over what happens by influencing the mother's behavior. An infant "is competent to the extent that he can, through his own activity, control the effect that his environment will have on him" (Ainsworth & Bell, 1974, p. 98). Such early experiences of control are considered important in fostering the development of a general sense of confidence and competence on the part of the child (Ainsworth & Bell, 1974). Following this line of thinking, different early attachment histories may lead to different reactions in a context that challenges the child's sense of competence. Specifically, we predicted that the possibility of failure in a competitive game would induce children who had been securely attached to exert more effort (in an attempt to control the environment), whereas insecurely attached children would not do this.

Finally, there is evidence that mothers of securely attached infants tend to respond both promptly and appropriately to their infants' emotional expression, whereas the less sensitive mothers of insecurely attached infants tend to react inappropriately and/or rejectingly (Ainsworth et al., 1978; Egeland & Farber, 1984; Escher-Gräub & Grossmann, 1983; Grossmann et al., in press). Assuming that one of the consequences of such insensitive reactions may be to teach the child not to show distress or sadness in interpersonal situations, we predicted that securely attached children would feel more free to display their disappointment in failing at competition than children who had had an insecure attachment relationship.

Method

Sample

Forty-nine children (23 girls and 26 boys) participated in the study at age 12 months, and 44 of them (20 girls and 24 boys) were observed again at age 3 years. The sample, which is part of the North German Longitudinal Study, was composed of Caucasian, predominantly middle-class families that were heterogeneous with regard to education, profession, and age. For further details see Grossmann et al. (in press).

Assessment of Infant-Mother Attachment

At age 12 months (± 1 month) each infant-mother pair was observed in Ainsworth's Strange Situation (see Ainsworth et al., 1978). The procedure consists of eight episodes involving the infant, the mother, and a stranger. The degree to which the infant seeks contact and interaction with the mother following two brief, mildly stressful separations determines classification of the child's quality of attachment as secure, insecure-avoidant, or insecure-ambivalent. Sixteen (33%) of the 49 infants were classified as secure and 30 (61%) were classified as insecure (24 avoidant and six ambivalent); three infants could not be classified. This distribution of classifications differs from what has been typically reported; in our sample the number of infants classified as avoidant is double that usually reported. This is discussed in greater detail in Grossmann, Grossmann, Huber, and Wartner (1981).

Assessment of Behavior with Visitor

At about age 3 years (range 35-37 months), 44 of the children were observed again in their homes during a 3- to 4-hour visit. The visitor was in all cases the first author, who was unfamiliar to the child and had no knowledge of the child's 12-month attachment status. The child's social reactions were assessed by examining narrative records made during the first part of the visit when the visitor greeted the mother and child, and during a subsequent 30-min interview with the mother. The child's first reactions to the visitor (at greeting and during the interview with the mother) were rated on a 7-point "Readiness to Interact" scale ranging from (1) "Child hides from visitor, clings to mother, cries or whines; during all of the maternal interview he/she avoids eye-contact with the visitor and answers no questions," to (7) "Child approaches visitor without hesitation and talks to him without being asked to do so."[1] Agreement between two independent raters, established on half of the sample, was 100%.

Following the interview, the mother and child played together for about 10 min, then the child played alone for about 10 min. Subsequent to this, the visitor requested that the child play a game with him. All children consented. The child and the visitor sat opposite each other and were provided with a 12-cm peg. The goal of the game was to build a tower of 10 wooden rings by stacking them on the peg. The rings were each 1 cm thick and 6 cm in diameter, and constructed so that only one ring could be placed on the peg at a time. The "winner" of this game was the person who first completed a tower. By varying his own building speed, the visitor could inconspicuously manipulate the outcome. All children won on the first trial, and success and failure were alternated on subsequent trials. The game ended when the child did not want to play longer. Because about 30% of the children stopped wanting to play after the third trial, only behavior in the second (i.e., first failure) and the third (success) trials were used in the analysis.

Two measures were derived from the videotaped records of the competitive game. For each measure, reliability was assessed by independent codings of a different sample of five randomly selected records. The first measure was the child's response to potential failure or success, measured as a change in building speed. To derive this measure, we analyzed behavior in the middle of each trial, between the child's placement of the fourth and eighth rings on the peg. We recorded the child's glances at the visitor's tower during this time (interobserver agreement on glancing was 82%), and noted whether the child received potential

failure feedback (the visitor's tower was taller) or potential success feedback (the visitor's tower was shorter).[2] We then measured the child's building speed (the mean time required to place a single ring on the peg) prior to looking at the visitor's tower, and immediately after looking. Thus we measured the reaction to potential success or failure by comparing building speed before and after feedback about the visitor's tower. Interobserver agreement on building speed was $r = .99$. The second measure was the child's display of sadness at actual, not potential, failure. We coded the child's facial expression in the second (failure) trial for "sad face" displays during each of the 7 sec preceding and the 7 sec following completion of his or her tower. A sad face was defined by Izard's (1979) Max-Code 56 (corners of mouth drawn outward; chin may push up center of lower lip); intercoder agreement was 73%. In addition to total frequency of such displays, frequency of sad face concurrent with eye contact with the visitor was also established (intercoder agreement on eye contact was 84%).

Results

Of the 44 children tested at 3 years, 12-month attachment classifications were possible only for 41. These included 15 securely attached, 21 avoidantly attached, and five ambivalently attached infants. In the results to be reported here, the avoidant and ambivalent groups are combined into a single, insecurely attached group. Differences within the insecure group are noted where appropriate.

On the Readiness to Interact scale, the mean score of the securely attached group of children ($N = 15$) was 5.40 and that of the insecurely attached group ($N = 26$) was 4.58; as assessed by U test, this difference is significant at $p < .02$ (one-tailed; $U = 272.5$). Within the insecure group, the mean score of the ambivalent children ($N = 5$) was 5.90 and that of the avoidant children ($N = 21$) was 4.29; only the latter subgroup differed significantly from the securely attached group ($U = 236$, $p = <.02$, two-tailed).

[1] Scale definitions are available from the first author.

[2] Prior to the fourth ring, a slight difference in performance level can rarely convey potential success or potential feedback. After the eighth ring, outcome is rather certain and can hardly be changed by increased effort output.

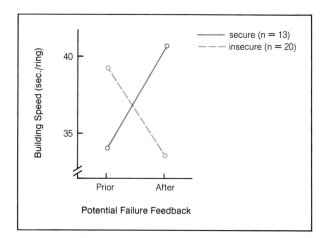

Figure 1 Mean Building Speed (sec/ring) Prior to and after Potential Failure Feedback for Each Attachment Group.

The children's responses to potential failure were analyzed by a 2 (secure/insecure) × 2 (prior to/following first glance at visitor's taller tower) repeated-measures ANOVA to the index of building speed. There was a significant interaction between these two factors, $F(1,31) = 4.85$, $p < .05$: securely attached children increased, whereas insecurely attached children decreased, their building speed after obtaining the "potential failure" information. These results are displayed in Figure 1. A similar analysis of effects of "potential success" feedback on building speed showed no significant results.

Among the 33 children who displayed a sad face at the end of the failure trial, the mean total number of such displays did not distinguish between the securely ($N = 12$, $X = 3.08$) and insecurely ($N = 21$, $X = 3.43$) attached groups. Our prediction, though, was that the groups would differ in communicating their reactions to another. A more sensitive test of this is whether children made a sad face while seeking eye contact with the visitor. Thus, we computed the proportion of sad faces "with eye contact" out of all sad faces the child showed. On this measure the mean proportion of the securely attached group of children ($N = 12$) was .35, and that of the insecurely attached group ($N = 21$)

was .14; as assessed by U test, this difference approaches significance at $p < .07$ (one-tailed; $U = 160$).

Discussion

This study's finding, that children with a secure-attachment relationship with their mother show a greater sociability in subsequent interactions with unfamiliar persons than children with an insecure-attachment relationship, fits in with findings reported by others (Main & Weston, 1981; Pastor, 1981; Thompson & Lamb, 1983). In addition, we found that children also reacted differently in a different type of social interaction—a competitive game. These differences appeared both in the amount of effort expended and in the communication of emotional reactions to failure, although the hypothesis that securely attached children would be more free in displaying their sadness at losing a game received questionable support. Whether this is due to our simple index of an "open expression of sadness," or whether the kind of situation/emotion we used is insensitive for the test of the hypothesis, awaits further research.

In line with our predictions, potential failure feedback during the interaction had opposite effects on the two attachment groups. Children from the secure-attachment group increased their performance speed, while children from the insecure-attachment group slowed down. Potential success feedback had no differential effects. These results lend support to the claim of Ainsworth and Bell (1974) that early experiences of being effective in influencing the behavior of a responsive, sensitive mother are predictive of later self-confidence, here defined as having control over an interactional outcome. The securely attached children's increase of effort when faced with the possibility of failure may indicate their confidence in their capacity to change the potential outcome failure. For us, this is the most important finding of the present study.

Another way of viewing the behavior in the competitive game we used focuses more on the social interactional aspect of the situation. The outcome of the competition establishes a dominance relation between winner

372

and loser. Viewed in this way, an increase of effort in the face of failure could stand in the service of a social motive, to be the winner or to resist against being the loser. In future studies it would be interesting to see whether the quality of the infant-mother attachment relationship is generally predictive for later individual differences in social motives. A recent result from Sroufe (1983) points in that direction, in that it shows a positive relationship between the security of the infant-mother attachment and the popularity of the child in the preschool.

Behavior in the competitive game we used can be viewed in two ways: At first, the game resembles an achievement situation in which one has to compete with a standard of excellence, that is, to built faster than the other. In the patterns of effort the children expend in the face of failure, we find that securely attached children increased their effort, in order to win, and insecurely attached children slowed down—gave up. These patterns of effort are similar to those found by Halisch and Heckhausen (1977) in older children in the same situation: success-motivated subjects increased their effort in the face of failure and failure-motivated subjects slowed down. For future studies it would be interesting to see whether the quality of the infant-mother attachment relationship is predictive for later individual differences in achievement motivation.

References

Ainsworth, M. D. S., & Bell, S. M. (1974). Mother-infant interaction and the development of competence. In K. Connolly & J. Bruner (Eds.), *The growth of competence* (pp. 97-118). New York: Academic Press.

Ainsworth, M. D. S., Blehar, M., Waters, E., & Wall, S. (1978) *Patterns of attachment*. Hillsdale, NJ: Erlbaum.

Arend, R., Gove, F. L., & Sroufe, L. A. (1979) Continuity of individual adaptation from infancy to kindergarten: A predictive study of ego-resiliency and curiosity in preschoolers. *Child Development, 50,* 950-959.

Egeland, B., & Farber, E. A. (1984). Infant-mother attachment: Factors related to its development and changes over time. *Child Development, 55,* 753-771.

Escher-Gräub, C. D., & Grossmann, K. E. (1983). *Bindungsunsicherheit im zweiten Lebensjahr-Die Regensburger Querschnittuntersuchung.* Research Report, University of Regensburg.

Grossmann, K. E., Grossmann, K., Huber, F., & Wartner, U. (1981). German children's behavior towards their mothers at 12 months and their fathers at 18 months in Ainsworth's Strange Situation. *International Journal of Behavioral Development, 4,* 157-181.

Grossmann, K., Grossmann, K. E., Spangler, G., Süss, G., & Unzner, L. (in press). Maternal sensitivity and newborn's orientation responses as related to quality of attachment in northern Germany. In I. Bretherton & E. Waters (Eds.), Growing points in attachment theory and research. *Monographs of the Society for Research in Child Development.*

Halisch, F., & Heckhausen, H. (1977). Search for feedback information and effort regulation during task performance. *Journal of Personality and Social Psychology, 35,* 724-733.

Izard, C. E. (1979). *The maximally discriminative facial movement coding system (Max).* Newark: University of Delaware.

Lieberman, A. F. (1977). Preschooler's competence with a peer: Relations with attachment and peer experience. *Child Development, 48,* 1277-1287.

Main, M., & Weston, D. (1981). The quality of the toddler's relationship to mother and to father: Related to conflict behavior and the readiness to establish new relationships. *Child Development, 52,* 932-940.

Pastor, D. L. (1981). The quality of mother-infant attachment and its relationship to toddlers' initial sociability with peers. *Developmental Psychology, 17,* 326-335.

Sroufe, L. A. (1983). Infant-caregiver attachment and patterns of adaptation in preschool: The roots of maladaptation and competence. In M. Perlmutter (Ed.), *Minnesota Symposium on Child Psychology* (Vol. **16,** pp. 47-83). Hillsdale, NJ: Erlbaum.

Sroufe, L. A., Fox, N.E., & Pancake, V. R. (1983). Attachment and dependency in developmental perspective. *Child Development, 54,* 1615-1627.

Thompson, R. A., & Lamb, M. E. (1983). Security of attachment and stranger sociability in infancy. *Developmental Psychology, 19,* 184-191.

Waters, E., Wippman, J., & Sroufe, L. A. (1979).
Attachment, positive affect and competence in the
peer group: Two studies in construct validation. *Child
Development,* **50,** 821-829.

Social Interaction

Chapter Outline

Jack was a second grader whose social interactions with his classmates were very unsuccessful. An aggressive child with little ability to empathize with others, Jack quarreled constantly, picked on children weaker than himself, and often made cruel and insensitive comments to his classmates. His sense of morality and his self-control were so poorly developed that he saw nothing wrong in bullying smaller children into giving him their lunch treats and even their pocket money. Needless to say, Jack was openly rejected by his peers, and at the age of 7 he had already become a social isolate.

Fortunately, Jack's problem finally came to the attention of a sensitive guidance counselor, who arranged to meet with him twice every week. At these meetings she drew him into discussions of how an imaginary child named Bill should deal with a variety of moral issues that arose in his interactions with classmates. She also encouraged Jack to imagine himself in the role of the victim who is attacked by a stronger child, and to talk about how it might feel to be victimized. She coached him intensively in skills involved in cooperation, sharing, making positive statements to others, and making constructive suggestions when in a group; she also observed his subsequent social interactions and gave him feedback on his progress. Within a few months, Jack's bullying behavior had stopped, and he had gained considerably in social status. While not exactly a group leader, he was no longer openly rejected either, and he was happier than he had ever been in his school experience.

Jack's story illustrates the importance of successful social interaction in a child's development and the pain of social isolation. It also illustrates that children with little social or moral awareness who are unable to relate well to peers can be helped, if adults are sensitive enough to realize that their love and approval of a child are not enough; children need to be accepted and approved by peers as well. The special significance of a child's interaction with other children is that the peer relationship is a "mutual" one, whereas the adult-child relationship is often "unilateral" (Piaget 1965). In other words, adults typically make the rules in adult-child interactions, while peers establish their own mutually agreed-on rules and, in the

process develop an understanding of concepts such as cooperation and mutual respect—concepts essential for successful social relationships and for the development of moral reasoning (Smollar & Youniss 1982).

This chapter discusses the nature of social interaction from infancy through adolescence. It first analyzes the development of children's awareness of their peers, from the earliest attempts at communication in infancy to the sophisticated role-taking ability of adolescents. It then discusses the development of morality, emphasizing that morality involves an awareness of the perspectives of others and a sensitivity to their needs. The final section of this chapter will deal with the structure and functions of groups throughout childhood and adolescence. In a sense, the chapter moves from the psychological awareness of other people to a sociological analysis of social relationships—the outward concrete manifestation of social awareness. Included also will be a discussion of characteristics required for group acceptance and methods for helping rejected or neglected children to become more popular with their peers.

Social Awareness

How does a child develop an awareness of other children? That is the central question in this section of the chapter. Children display developmental changes in interest in peers and in efforts to interact with them. This section describes how, related to their increasing intellectual maturity, children display increases in knowledge about friends and in knowledge about the concept of friendship itself. There is an increasing ability to understand the thoughts and feelings of others and an increasing concern for the welfare of others. Such developments are necessary if successful social interaction is ever to take place.

The First Three Years of Life

The infant and young child have often been described as selfish and self-centered and therefore incapable of understanding or caring about peers. As can be seen in this section, even an infant is

Infants and toddlers have a much greater interest in peer interaction than was once believed, and cooperative peer play begins to merge in the second year of life.

considerably more peer-oriented than many people believe. Infants are definitely interested in communicating with peers, and, by the second year of life, there are even glimmers of cooperative play.

Attempts to Communicate

Even during the early months of the first year of life, infants are definitely interested in one another. Fogel (1979) observed infants 5 to 14 weeks old in three different social settings: while alone, while looking at their mothers, and while seated on their mothers' laps facing another infant. When the babies were alone, they usually appeared relaxed and content. When mother approached, they smiled at her, made gestures with their arms and legs, and often stuck out their tongues. When they saw another infant, however, there seemed to be a qualitatively different reaction—a sense of uncontrolled excitement; they stared at the other baby, leaned forward as if straining to have a closer look, and made abrupt head and arm movements.

Although even young infants are capable of making social gestures to peers, these gestures are still somewhat limited during the first year of life. First of all, they are of very short duration; as the child develops through the first year and into the second, the time spent on individual social gestures increases (Hay, Pederson & Nash 1982). A second limitation of the young infant's social gestures is that they are relatively simple, consisting only of one or two specific behaviors at a time (e.g., smiling and vocalizing, smiling and waving the arms). The second year of life brings an increasing complexity of social overtures. Individual social behaviors are combined into more complex patterns; social interactions are increasingly controlled and predictable (Brownell 1982, 1986).

Ross, Lollis, and Elliott (1982) observed a variety of communicative gestures in the play of children ranging in age from 20 to 22 months: showing toys to their partner, offering a toy, giving a toy, requesting something, inviting a partner to play, making declarative statements, protesting a partner's action, and so forth. Not only were communicative overtures common among the children, but also they were often quite effective. In other words, even these very young children could understand and comply with the needs of peers fairly well; in the few instances when children failed to do so, the researchers believed that the issue was one of unwillingness to communicate rather than inability.

Cooperative Play

Cooperative play involves two or more participants in a shared activity with a common goal. Such play between child and adult occurs even in the first six months of life, as any parent knows who has played peekaboo with a child. However, true cooperative play has been observed only rarely in peer relationships in the first two years of life (Eckerman & Stein 1982). Nevertheless, such play has been observed with increasing frequency in recent years. As an example, Brenner and Mueller (1982) described what they called **shared meanings** in the play of toddlers—themes which organize their social interactions. Such themes include "motor-copy," in which children copy one another's motor behavior; "peekaboo," in which one child hides and then reappears suddenly, to the delight of the other child; or "run-chase," in which the children run after each other.

These shared meanings, which increase in frequency and variety throughout the second year of life, are definitely social behaviors and often quite sophisticated ones at that. The stereotype of the 1- and 2-year-old as an antisocial, totally egocentric little being with an interest only in toys and not in other children is being challenged by much of the recent research (e.g., Mueller & Lucas 1975; Goldman & Ross 1978; Brenner & Mueller 1982; Hodapp & Mueller 1982; Ross 1982; Howes 1983). Not all toddlers participate in social games, but some of them certainly do. Perhaps, as Ross (1982) suggested, those children who do not play cooperatively might do so if the social setting were conducive to cooperative play.

Effects of Early Peer Interaction

Does the experience of being with other babies have an effect on an infant's social skills or social interests? The answer appears to be no for social skills and yes for social interests. Social skills (e.g., ability to take leadership roles, to interact

without conflict, to display confidence in social settings) do not seem to be affected by experience during the first two years of life. Age alone, and not the amount of experience with other infants, is the best predictor of an infant's social maturity. In other words, there seem to be developmental limits on the quality of a child's social interactions from birth until the age of 2 (Brownell 1986).

When the infant's social interests are examined, however, a different pattern emerges. Ricciuti (1974), for example, compared 12- to 19-month-olds exposed to day care with those who were not. He noticed that children in the former group were more likely to move away from their mothers when mother and child were observed together in a playroom. The day-care "veterans" were also more likely to play at a greater distance from mother during the observation period, more likely to look at their peers rather than at mother, and less likely to seek physical contact with her. These findings are typical in studies of the effects of day care on the young child's social development: children exposed to the day-care setting tend to be somewhat more peer-oriented than those who have not been in day care (Belsky & Steinberg 1978). The intense peer interaction provided in a day-care setting may even be related to a child's social development for many years after the actual experience. Moore (1975) reported that adolescent boys who had been placed in day-care settings before the age of 5 were more interested in social activities than were home-reared boys, and were more often rated as likable by their peers.

However, actual day-care experience is not the only predictor of later social interests. An even better predictor may be the closeness of attachment between parent and child. In a number of recent studies of children 3 years or older, social interest and social skills were most often found among those who had secure, close attachments to a parent or parents (Jacobson & Wille 1986; La Freniere 1983; Lieberman 1977). It appears that exposure to other children at an early age is not in itself a guarantee of a child's later social success.

From Preschool to Adolescence

As children develop throughout the years of elementary and high school, they mature considerably in their understanding of friendship and in their ability to relate to friends. They become increasingly skilled at role taking and thus get beyond their self-centeredness to appreciate the world from other people's points of view. They develop increasing concern for others. Finally, there emerge gender differences in peer relationships that reveal much about the processes of gender-role socialization in our society today.

Social Cognition

In recent years, interest in children's developing awareness of interpersonal relationships has grown rapidly. Psychologists are studying children's conceptions of, expectations of, and definitions of friendship (Smollar & Youniss 1982). There has also been considerable interest in the development of children's understanding of the needs, thoughts, feelings, and intentions of others (Shantz 1975; Damon 1977), the development of a sense of fairness (Berndt 1982a), and the development of a sense of compassion (Mussen & Eisenberg-Berg 1977). Taken as a whole, the study of the child's developing awareness of others and his or her changing conception of friendship is known as **social cognition**—the application of cognitive skills in social interactions.

The Beginnings of Friendship Selection. Even by the time children are 3 or 4 years of age, they are able to provide consistent reasons for liking and disliking nursery school peers. Hayes (1978) interviewed forty children ranging in age from 3 to 5 years. He asked them questions such as "Who do you like/dislike more than anyone else?" and "Why do you like/dislike _____?" The most typical reasons for liking another child were

- common activities
- general play (e.g., "Because she plays with me")
- propinquity (e.g., "We live near each other")
- evaluation (e.g., "He is a nice boy")
- physical possessions.

The most typical reasons for disliking a preschool peer were

- violation of rules
- aggression
- deviant behavior.

In investigating developmental changes in social awareness at the preschool level, Furman and Bierman (1983) used a variety of measures to assess young children's conceptions of friendship. A group of 4- and 5-year-olds was found to differ significantly from a group of 6- and 7-year-olds in reasons for describing children as friends. Responses in the categories of "affection" (liking, loving, emotional attachment) and "support" (sharing, helping, comforting) increased significantly with age; responses in the categories of "common activities," "physical characteristics," and "propinquity" did not.

The same trend was illustrated in a study by Boggiano, Klinger, and Main (1986). They looked at the types of directions that would encourage children to play with a classmate they did not know. Children aged 5, 7, and 9 years saw "Robby" on a television monitor; some of the children were asked if they wanted to play with Robby "because he's real nice," while others were asked if they wanted to play with him "because he has a new Lego® game." The suggestion that Robby was a nice person increased the interest of 9-year-olds in playing with him but had no impact on the 5-year-olds. On the other hand, Robby's new Lego® building set significantly increased interest among 5-year-olds but not among 9-year-olds.

The research on childhood friendship suggests that thoughts, feelings, motives, and personality characteristics become increasingly important as criteria for selecting friends. Perhaps, as a result, there is also a developmental increase in the stability of friendship; the friendships of grade school children are highly stable, particularly when contrasted with the friendships of preschoolers (Berndt, Hawkins & Hoyle 1986).

Knowledge About Friends. As children progress through the elementary school years, knowledge about their friends' psychological characteristics increases (Berndt 1982b). As an illustration of this trend, Diaz and Berndt (1982) asked a group of fourth graders and a group of eighth graders a variety of questions about their best friends. These questions dealt with external characteristics (e.g., "What clubs or teams does your friend belong to?"), with preferences (e.g., "What is your friend's favorite subject at school?"), and with personality characteristics (e.g., "What does your friend worry about most?"). The friends were asked to answer the same questions about themselves, and the two sets of answers were then compared.

No age differences were observed in external knowledge about friends—birth date, telephone number, names of siblings, and so forth. However, there was a significant age difference in knowledge of a friend's personality and preferences: adolescents apparently were more knowledgeable than children were about their friend's internal characteristics. Diaz and Berndt concluded that adolescent friendships are more "intimate" than are those of children, presumably because adolescents are more likely to share intimate information with their friends.

Similar results were found by Volpe (1976) in an investigation of age differences in selecting friends. Younger children (aged 6 to 10) expressed the view that the way to make friends is to do things together. Their answers focused on actions rather than on personality characteristics. As one 10-year-old boy remarked, "'Friends are easy to make. All you have to do is go up to a guy, say hello, and ask him if he wants to play ball; then he's a friend. If he don't want to play ball, then he's not a friend, unless you decide to play something else'" (Smollar & Youniss 1982, 283). By contrast, 12- and 13-year-olds in the Volpe study stressed the importance of a friend's personal qualities and the need to get to know one another, especially what the other person likes and dislikes. As in the Diaz and Berndt study, we see the shift from external, surface characteristics to in-depth knowledge of a friend.

Obligations and Expectations of Friendship. Evidence suggests a developmental change in a child's understanding of the obligations of friendship. Of the 10-and 11-year-olds Ryan and Smollar (1978) interviewed, 80 percent saw the major obligation of friendship as acting "nice" to one another: doing things with or doing things for one another, and avoiding fights. Only 24 percent of the 13- and 14-year-olds mentioned "niceness" obligations, and, by the age of 16 or 17, such action-oriented obligations were mentioned by only one in ten. Emphasis shifted from actions to the per-

sonal qualities of a friend and concern for the friend's feelings and emotional needs.

Not only is there a developmental change in what a child feels is owed to a friend, but also there is a change in what is expected from a friend as well. Studies of children ranging from grade 1 to grade 8 have found an increasing tendency to expect common interests, similarity of attitudes and values, and the potential for intimacy from a friendship and a decreasing tendency to expect a friend to give one things, to share common activities, or to enjoy the same games (Bigelow & La Gaipa 1975; Bigelow 1977). Again, the age-trend is away from external characteristics and towards the internal qualities of friends.

Role-Taking Ability. A child's development in the area of peer relationships involves more than an increase in knowledge of the psychological characteristics of others and an understanding of the concept of friendship. To interact successfully with peers, children must also go beyond their own self-centered perceptions and try to see the world from other people's points of view. Such role-taking ability may be a prerequisite for close interpersonal communication (Harter 1983), and is related to altruistic, or helping, behavior among older children (Cialdini, Baumann & Kendrick 1981; Froming, Allen & Jensen 1985). The most popular children in the grade school classroom are the most sophisticated role takers (Kurdek & Krile 1982), and role-taking skill is related to the ease of establishing intimate peer relationships in childhood (McGuire & Weisz 1982).

The ability to take the point of view of others does not appear suddenly at some point during childhood; it develops gradually, reflecting the child's growing awareness of the world, as well as the gradual transition from concrete to more abstract forms of reasoning. Psychologist Robert Selman and his associates (Selman 1980; Selman & Byrne 1974; Selman & Jacquette 1978) have identified the following developmental stages in the progression from total self-centeredness to sophisticated role-taking ability:

• *Stage 0: Egocentrism.* Children are able to see only their own perspectives. They assume that what they see, feel, and want is what everybody sees, feels, and wants. This stage is typical of children from the age of 3 to the age of 5 or 6.

- *Stage 1: Subjective Role Taking.* Children now realize that others have different perspectives, but they think that the differences occur only because of differences in available information. ("If you knew what I know, you would see things the correct way—my way!") They judge the actions of others only from their own perspectives, and they cannot see themselves as others see them. The age range for subjective role taking is from 6 to 8 years.
- *Stage 2: Self-reflective Role Taking.* Individual differences in perspectives are no longer attributed to simple information differences but to basic differences in values and purposes. Knowing what another person's values are, the child can then predict that person's reaction to a future situation. Children can now examine their own behavior as it must appear to another person. The age range from self-reflective role taking is from 8 to 10 years.
- *Stage 3: Mutual Role Taking.* Adolescents and adults can distinguish their own perspectives from those of the "average" person in society. They can *simultaneously* evaluate their own point of view and that of a second person; they can even imagine how an objective third party would simultaneously evaluate their perspective and a different perspective held by the second person. For example, a skilled role taker involved in a debate could understand the philosophical basis of an opponent's argument, could predict an opponent's position on related issues, and could imagine how an objective observer would evaluate arguments on both sides and understand them in the context of the differing philosophical views of the debaters.

In Selman's model, individual differences in role-taking ability appear to be related to differences in level of intellectual development. However, additional reasons for individual variations may exist. For example, role-taking ability is somewhat related to performance on standard intelligence tests (Shantz 1983). It is also related to such environmental factors as child-rearing practices and direct exposure to role-taking experiences. In regard to child rearing, children who are the most skillful role takers have parents who use a disciplinary approach known as **induction** (Hoffman 1970; Maccoby & Martin 1983). Induction emphasizes the impact of the child's behavior on other

people (e.g., "It makes me happy to see you sharing your toys" or "Your sister is very sad because you don't want to play with her"). By contrast, less effective role taking is found among children whose parents discipline by referring to general rules that must be followed, to status differences, or to their own positions of power (e.g., "Children should share their toys" or "You'll play with your sister because I *told* you to do so!") (Bearison & Cassel 1975).

Since a child's experience can influence the degree to which he or she is able to take the perspective of others, we might expect that role-taking skills could be taught to children who lack them. In fact, role-taking training can be quite effective (Feshbach 1979; Iannotti 1978). For example, Iannotti (1978) trained kindergarten boys and third-grade boys in role taking by reading stories to them and having them act out the parts of the story characters. During training, he asked the children questions about how their characters feel, why they behave as they do, what they plan to do next, and how the other characters might feel about them. Role-taking skills were assessed both before and after the training by having children answer questions about hypothetical social or moral dilemmas. Children who received role-taking training improved significantly in role-taking skills, while a group who did not receive the training showed no such improvement.

To summarize the research on social cognition, it would seem that the nature of friendship changes from the years of early childhood to the years of early adolescence. Intimate knowledge of friends increases, conceptions of friendship shift from an emphasis on shared activities to an emphasis on shared psychological characteristics, the sense of responsibility and commitment to friends becomes deeper, and expectations of friends increase.

Understanding the needs, feelings, values, and unique perspectives of other people improves as children gradually rid themselves of their egocentric world views. Intimate communication, as opposed to surface level social interaction, becomes the basis for mature peer relationships.

Acts of kindness, such as sharing one's possessions, are fairly common among preschoolers in the age range of three to six.

Social Concern: The Development of Altruism

The developing social awareness discussed in the previous section might be thought of as the cognitive aspect of peer relationships. This section emphasizes the affective, or feeling, dimension— the constellation of *prosocial* qualities that include generosity, kindness, caring, and helping. The term used to describe a variety of such prosocial behaviors is **altruism,** literally meaning "concern for other people," and here referring to the presence in the child of thoughts or actions concerned with the welfare of another person or persons. (The Research Close-up "Concern for the Victim" describes a study that dealt with the development of altruistic behavior.)

Concern for other people is found very early in life, and certainly comes before a child has acquired mature social awareness. Even newborn babies cry reflexively when they hear the cries of other newborns (Simner 1971; Sagi & Hoffman 1976), and such reactions to the distress of peers have been found throughout the first and second years of life (Radke-Yarrow, Zahn-Waxler & Chapman 1983). Actual helping behaviors can also be found quite early in life: Rheingold (1979) observed that nine out of ten 2-year-olds in a laboratory setting will spontaneously help their mothers with routine household chores. As mentioned earlier in this chapter, evidence of cooperative play with peers can be found even during the second year of life (Brenner & Mueller 1982). Finally, by the age

Research Close-up

Concern for the Victim: The Development of Altruistic Behavior

As children develop, they might be expected to become increasingly capable of displaying concern for other people. One form of that concern is caregiving behavior toward victims in distress. Carolyn Zahn-Waxler, Sarah Friedman, and E. Mark Cummings (1983), of the National Institute of Mental Health, carried out a developmental study of children's responses to a baby's cry. The subjects in the study were five boys and five girls at each of the following age or grade levels: 4 years old, kindergarten, first grade, second grade, fifth grade, and sixth grade. These children were placed individually in a room and

exposed to the sound of an infant crying in the next room. Then the infant was carried by the mother into the room in which the child was sitting, and the mother said, "I'm looking for the baby's bottle."

The experimenters were interested in finding out what types of altruistic, or prosocial, responses the children would make and whether or not older children would be more concerned about the baby's well-being than younger children were. Prosocial responses were expected to occur in the form of verbal help (e.g., telling the mother where to find the bottle, saying "poor baby"), gestural help (e.g., pointing to the bottle), or physical help (e.g., getting the bottle for the mother, feeding the baby).

While the findings concerning gestural and physical help were somewhat mixed, grade school children expressed significantly more verbal concern and offered more ver-

bal help than did preschoolers and kindergartners. Furthermore, an analysis of composite overall ratings of prosocial behaviors indicated that in general school-aged children were more altruistic than 4- and 5-year-olds. Interestingly enough, although girls are often thought of as being more prosocial than boys, no sex differences in helping were found in this study; in fact, most studies of this type do not find sex differences in altruistic behavior (Radke-Yarrow, Zahn-Waxler & Chapman 1983).

The findings of this and other studies of helping behavior in children are consistent with the pattern of findings in social cognition research in general: as a child develops, an awareness of, understanding of, and concern for other persons increase. Prosocial attitudes and behaviors are increasingly sophisticated, and egocentrism declines.

of 2, children will indicate in a variety of ways that they feel sorry for another person in distress: they will verbalize sympathy, give things to a suffering person, make helpful suggestions, and make efforts to protect a victim from harm (Radke-Yarrow, Zahn-Waxler & Chapman 1983).

Studies of preschool children, ranging in age from 3 to 6, typically indicate that altruistic behavior is quite common in this age group (Zahn-Waxler & Radke-Yarrow 1982; Radke-Yarrow, Zahn-Waxler & Chapman 1983). Cooperative play continues to increase, but beyond that it cannot be said that preschoolers are any more or less altruistic

than they were in the first three years of life. Furthermore, the motivation for altruistic behaviors in this age group is unclear: many kindly behaviors among preschoolers may actually be motivated by fear, by a desire to control others, or by attempts to gain approval from adults (Radke-Yarrow, Zahn-Waxler & Chapman 1983).

An examination of developmental changes in altruistic behavior during the elementary and high school years produces a complex pattern. In the first place, it might be expected that as social awareness improves, acts of altruism will increase. In fact, the frequency of overall prosocial behavior does not seem to change at all; increases are seen in some behaviors, decreases in others, and no change in the rest. There is no basis for a simple conclusion that children become kinder to one another as they advance through the years of childhood and adolescence (Radke-Yarrow, Zahn-Waxler & Chapman 1983). On the other hand, if we look not at the number of altruistic behaviors but at their quality, developmental changes can be seen in reasons for prosocial behavior; the sense of caring, which was reflexive in infancy and primarily emotional in the young child, becomes increasingly linked to reasoning ability. This transition, corresponding to the development of role-taking ability and decreasing egocentrism, has been described by Eisenberg, Lennon, and Roth (1983) as a series of levels of prosocial reasoning, and these are contained in Table 12.1.

Gender Differences in Friendship Patterns

When gender differences are examined in friendship research on children and adolescents, a pattern seems to emerge. If we look at the development of a child's understanding of what friendship means, we do not find gender differences (Bigelow & La Gaipa 1975; Furman & Bierman 1983). Similarly, no gender differences appear in children's and adolescents' intimate knowledge of their friends (Diaz & Berndt 1982), and boys do not claim to have more friends than girls do and vice versa (Berndt 1982).

On the other hand, gender differences have been discovered in friendship expectations. Even among preschoolers the expectations of friendship seem to be different for girls than for boys; in one study 3- to 5-year-old girls were more willing to share a favorite food with a friend than with a mere acquaintance, but boys of the same age made no such distinction (Birch & Billman 1986).

During the grade school years, girls are more likely than boys to mention the potential for intimacy and sharing of feelings (Bigelow, 1977). Girls are also more likely than boys to list emotional assistance as an obligation of friendship; and, when asked why emotional assistance is an obligation, girls more often give reasons related to benefiting the other person (Ryan & Smollar 1978). Girls also

seek closer attachments and greater degrees of trust and loyalty than boys do (Sharabany, Gershoni & Hofman 1981), and female friendships appear to be more exclusive. For example, girls are less willing to include a nonfriend in an ongoing conversation than boys are (Eder & Hallinan 1978). Gender differences in friendship expectations apparently continue into adolescence. As an illustration of this trend, Douvan and Adelson (1966) conducted a nationwide survey of adolescents aged 14 to 16—one of the most extensive studies of adolescent friendship ever undertaken. They found that boys and girls clearly wanted different things from their friends. Boys wanted friends to help them establish their independence and to join with them in resisting adult control. They wanted friends who could give them concrete help when they needed it **(instrumental needs)**. Girls wanted friends who could help them understand themselves, who could share their private thoughts and feelings, and who could offer emotional support **(expressive needs)**.

There is no single explanation of gender differences in expressed friendship needs; such differences might be interpreted in more than one way. For instance, it is possible that males, for whatever combination of cultural or biological reasons, simply do not need the closeness and emotional support that females do. It is also possible that males do have emotional needs similar to those of females, but feel less free to express them. An adolescent boy might be unwilling to admit that he seeks friends who are warm and sensitive to his needs, because such an admission might imply that he is soft, weak, or unmasculine. However we choose to interpret these data, it seems wise to follow Berndt's (1982) suggestion to avoid such broad generalizations and value judgments as "female friendships are closer (better?) than male friendships" and "males are too emotionally inhibited to form close friendships." Instead, we might speak of gender-related *patterns* of friendship seeking—patterns which require greater exploration than they have thus far received, and which offer a potentially rich source of information about gender-role socialization in our culture.

Table 12.1 Levels of Prosocial Reasoning

Level	Orientation	Description	Group
1	*Hedonistic, Self-focused*	The individual is concerned with self-oriented consequences rather than moral considerations. Reasons for assisting or not assisting another include consideration of direct gain to self, future reciprocity, and concern for others whom the individual needs and/or likes (due to the affectional tie).	Preschoolers and younger elementary school children
2	*Needs of Others*	The individual expresses concern for the physical, material, and psychological needs of others even though the other's needs conflict with one's own needs. This concern is expressed in the simplest terms, without clear evidence of self-reflective role taking, verbal expressions of sympathy, or reference to internalized affect such as guilt.	Preschoolers and elementary school children
3	*Approval and Interpersonal and/or Stereotyped*	Stereotyped images of good and bad persons and behaviors and/or considerations of others' approval and acceptance are used in justifying prosocial or nonhelping behaviors.	Elementary and high school students
4	*a Empathic*	The individual's judgments include evidence of sympathetic responding, self-reflective role taking, concern with the other's humanness, and/or guilt or positive affect related to the consequences of one's actions.	Older elementary school and high school students
	b Transitional (Empathic and Internalized)	Justifications for helping or not helping involve internalized values, norms, duties, or responsibilities, or refer to the necessity of protecting the rights and dignity of other persons; these ideas, however, are not clearly stated.	Minority of people high school age
5	*Strongly Internalized*	Justifications for helping or not helping are based on internalized values, norms, or responsibilities, the desire to maintain individual and societal contractual obligations, and the belief in the dignity, rights, and equality of all individuals. Positive or negative affect related to the maintenance of self-respect for living up to one's own values and accepted norms also characterizes this stage.	Only a small minority of high school students and virtually no elementary school children

Source: From Eisenberg, N., Lennon, R., and Roth, K. (1983) Prosocial development: longitudinal study. *Developmental Psychology, 19,* 846-855. Copyright 1983 by the American Psychological Association. Reprinted by permission of the publisher and author.

Morality

In its simplest terms, morality is the ability to distinguish what is right from what is wrong. In actuality, the concept of morality is considerably more complex, involving cognitive skills (e.g., role taking, reasoning, decision making), feelings (e.g., empathy, altruism, care), and behaviors (e.g., helping others, resisting temptation). In theory, the cognitive, affective, and behavioral dimensions can each be examined separately, but in practice they can never be completely separated (Rest 1983). A person described as having high-moral standards is aware of the needs and feelings of others (cognitive), concerned about others (affective), and likely to display that awareness and concern in dealing with other people (behavioral). Deficiencies in any of the three dimensions would indicate a less than perfect moral character. Thus, the ability to understand the perspectives of others will not guarantee moral behavior if a sense of care is lacking. Social awareness and social concern do not indicate a high degree of morality if they are not translated into courses of action; a vast difference often exists between what people believe is right and what they actually do when confronted with moral dilemmas! Finally, level of morality cannot be determined from an analysis of behaviors alone, but must also include reference to underlying motives. What a person does is often a less meaningful indicator of moral sophistication than is the reason why the person does it.

There are a number of different theoretical perspectives on moral development, each with its own emphasis. Social-learning theory emphasizes the behavioral dimension, psychoanalytic theory the affective dimension, and cognitive developmental theory the cognitive dimension. Disagreements among these theories do not focus on what is right or what is wrong behavior, but on the dimensions the theorists choose to emphasize and on the mechanisms by which they see morality as being acquired.

Social-Learning Theory

The social-learning approach to moral development stresses the role of experience in the acquisition of a set of morally appropriate behaviors.

Right and wrong behaviors are learned in a variety of ways. In some situations reinforcement or punishment is experienced directly: children learn that what is right is what they have been rewarded for doing and what is wrong is what they have been punished for. Behaviors not acquired by a direct experiential learning process are often acquired through the process of *observational learning*. For example, a child sees another child being rewarded or punished for a certain behavior and therefore learns that this behavior is acceptable or unacceptable. In a sense, the observer also shares in the reward, but the reinforcement is *vicarious:* the observer receives it by imagining himself or herself in the place of the child who was rewarded directly.

Examples of observational learning of moral behavior can be found most notably in the area of learned aggression (Bandura, Ross & Ross 1963a, 1963c; Bandura 1965; Hicks 1965). The typical procedure in these studies is to have young children observe aggressive behaviors, expose them to a frustrating situation—such as having toys they are playing with taken away—and then record subsequent instances of aggression in their play. Children become more aggressive if they have recently seen aggressive models, especially if the models are rewarded for their aggressive behaviors. (See Applying Our Knowledge "Coping with an Aggressive Child.")

Finally, much of a child's moral education takes place through the process of "generalized imitation" (Gewirtz 1969) or **identification** (Aronfreed 1969): the child uses a significant adult, often a parent, as a model for his or her behavior, and from that model the child acquires a set of behaviors that are not intentionally taught. As an illustration of the impact of models as teachers, Baer and Sherman (1964) had children observe a puppet who taught them a variety of simple behaviors using direct reinforcement techniques. Later, the puppet began pressing a bar, and the children imitated the behavior even though they were not specifically rewarded for doing so. Apparently, the imitation of anything the puppet did became a rewarding experience.

When children use parents as models, they learn not only the things that parents deliberately try to teach, but also their parents' attitudes toward life, and their religious and moral behaviors and

Applying Our Knowledge

Coping with an Aggressive Child

Parents often complain that the most irritating antisocial behavior displayed by their children is aggression, and, based on the high incidence of aggression observed in children of all ages, the complaint is easy to understand. One study found that approximately 80 percent of children between the ages of 3 and 17 occasionally use physical aggression against their brothers or sisters (Straus, Geller & Steinmetz 1980)!

Aggressive acts occur more often among younger than among older children (Hartup 1974; Straus, Geller & Steinmetz 1980; Feshbach & Weiner 1986), a fact that may provide hope to parents who feel like referees at a boxing match. However, evidence indicates that aggression may be a stable trait across childhood; highly aggressive children at age 2 seem to grow into highly aggressive adolescents (Huesmann et al. 1984; Olweus 1979; Parke & Slaby 1983). Boys have typically been found to be more aggressive than girls, particularly when the aggressive act is specifically intended to harm another child (hostile aggression), rather than simply to achieve a goal such as getting the toy another child is playing with (instrumental aggression) (Hartup 1974).

We do not know the extent to which biological factors may contribute to human aggression, but we do know that some parental characteristics are closely related to aggression in children. Parents of very aggressive children tend to be permissive in dealing with their children's aggression. They make few demands for positive prosocial behavior. They are often lax in their supervision and inconsistent in their discipline. Finally, they tend to be cold or rejecting in their dealings with their children (Feshbach 1970; Feshbach & Weiner 1986; Parke & Slaby 1983).

What can a parent or teacher do to help reduce aggression in children? A number of approaches have been tried, some successful and others not. Among the least successful approaches has been harsh punishment, which may inhibit aggressive behavior but may actually increase the child's underlying anger and resentment. Milder forms of punishment are more effective, particularly if the punishment is given a prosocial slant (e.g., requiring that the aggressor do something nice for the victim). Also successful have been attempts to train children in social awareness and empathy—to encourage them to imagine how their victim feels ("How would you like it if someone punched you?"). A third successful approach involves changing the meaning of the stimulus that produces the aggressive response. For example, Johnny is told that when Billy takes his toys,

it is not because Billy is naughty but that he is too young to know better, and for this reason Johnny should not "punish" Billy by striking him. An approach that has often been successful in the classroom is for the teacher to ignore the aggressor, but comfort the victim. The teacher offers the victim something interesting to do and suggests ways for him or her to be assertive and still avoid confrontations with aggressive children. In this way, the teacher models tolerance and assertiveness, and, more importantly, the teacher does not reward the aggressive child with attention (Feshbach & Weiner 1986).

Children's aggression may not be easy for parents and teachers to tolerate, but perhaps they can ease their anxiety if they realize that some aggression is normal, that adults themselves may—without knowing it—encourage aggression in children, and that levels of children's aggression can be reduced.

Acts of physical aggression, particularly among boys, are extremely common throughout childhood, but, fortunately, aggressive behaviors decrease with age.

beliefs. Since parents are the most readily available models for their children, they must do more than just teach moral principles directly; they must also practice them. It makes little sense for parents to punish a child for lying or stealing and then to engage in these behaviors themselves. The child who lies may point out with embarrassing accuracy that Mommy lies, too, when she tells a boring caller that she is too ill to talk on the telephone.

Psychoanalytic Theory

While social-learning theory stresses learning in the acquisition of moral behaviors, the psychoanalytic approach emphasizes the resolution of conflict between the individual's needs and society's expectations. Conflict produces anxiety, and the establishment of a moral code helps the child

to reduce anxiety; thus, psychoanalytic theory focuses on internalized feelings rather than external behaviors. (Refer to Chapter 10 for a discussion of psychoanalytic theories of personality development.)

Young infants experience little conflict with society, and little of the resulting anxiety, because they are indifferent to societal restrictions. Adults typically accommodate to infants' needs rather than the reverse. By the end of the first year, however, these same infants are beginning to learn that they cannot always have what they want when they want it. The conflict between what they want and what the world will allow becomes increasingly apparent.

The toddler acquires what is referred to as **instinctual anxiety** (Freud 1966)—a fear of those basic instincts (e.g., aggression, sexual curiosity) that society considers to be unacceptable. Toddlers submit to societal restrictions because they know they will be rejected if they allow their instinctual needs free expression; therefore, their very instincts cause them to suffer anxiety. For example, children may feel anxious about wanting to steal from the cookie jar because they fear the disapproval of authorities who have control over them. However, in circumstances when authorities are not in a position to supervise, they may slip and give way to temptation.

At approximately 5 years of age, children begin to assume the values and restrictions of society as their own, by the process of identification with an adult—usually the same-sex parent. In a sense, the values of society are internalized, and the control over the child's behavior comes not just from authority figures but from within the self. The child develops a conscience. Freud (1930) felt that conscience development is civilization's way of achieving control over the often dangerous and aggressive impulses of individuals; but, unlike the external control felt by the toddler, the conscience of an older child or adolescent is internal. The child who has internalized the values of society will still experience conflict, but the conflict will arise from opposing forces within the self. Now if the child wishes to steal a cookie before dinner, the impulse will be held in check, not by fear of authority, but by the internal discomfort usually referred to as guilt.

Cognitive Developmental Theories

The cognitive developmental approach to morality emphasizes the cognitive rather than the affective dimension in the socialization process. Moral development involves a growing awareness of the needs and viewpoints of others, and, with this, a growing sensitivity. As people develop, they become increasingly capable of role taking, of imagining the consequences of their actions on other people's lives, and of recognizing the need for an impartial system of morality that can be applied to society as a whole.

Jean Piaget's Theory
Jean Piaget's work focused on stages of cognitive development, and his theory of morality was not as completely articulated. Nevertheless, Piaget

did make significant contributions to the understanding of the child's moral development. More than fifty years ago Piaget rejected the view of morality as a system of controls imposed on children by adults. He argued that a mature concept of morality is based on underlying cognitive structures; the child is actively involved in the construction of his or her moral values, which are based on an awareness of the perspectives of others.

Piaget distinguished between two types, or levels, of morality. The **morality of constraint** is acquired directly from adults during early childhood. Young children simply accept the definitions of right and wrong provided by their parents, who are seen as wiser and more powerful than they. Conformity to parental rules results from a combination of fear, admiration, and affection. Preschool morality is concrete in the sense that the rightness of wrongness of an act resides in the act itself, and not in the intention behind it. Breaking a dish by accident is just as wrong for the young child as is breaking it on purpose.

The second level or type of morality begins to appear at the age of 6 or 7 and does not reach mature status until the age of 10 or 11. This is the **morality of cooperation,** which children construct on the basis of their interaction with peers. Thus, for Piaget, peer relationships are extremely important in the child's moral development. When children interact with peers, a certain amount of give-and-take is required; they learn to abide by rules, and they are required to share, to cooperate, and to delay gratification of their own needs. Out of such interactions will emerge a sense of justice, the cornerstone of a mature set of moral values.

Moral development, according to Piaget, involves a move from egocentrism to an awareness of the perspectives of other people. It involves a move from a moral code imposed by parents to a moral code mutually agreed on as a result of peer interactions. It involves a move from a belief that moral rules are fixed and absolute to a belief that such rules are arbitrary—that morality resides not in the rules themselves but in the reasons for their establishment. Finally, in moral development the child is increasingly involved in constructing a set of personal values that facilitate harmonious peer relationships.

Table 12.2   Classification of Moral Judgment into Levels and Stages of Development

Level	Stage of Development	Example
I *Preconventional*	*Stage 1* Moral decisions are based on the desire to avoid punishment. Social norms will not be violated because such action will result in unpleasant consequences.	A child decides not to steal candy from a store because the risk of detection and punishment is great.
	Stage 2 Moral decisions are based on a desire to obtain rewards. In this form of what Kohlberg called "marketplace morality" the question is "what's in it for me?"	An adolescent does not report a classmate for vandalism because the classmate may return the favor by lending a homework assignment.
II *Conventional*	*Stage 3* Moral decisions are based on a desire for social approval. This is the "good boy" or "good girl" orientation.	A person contributes to charity only because it is expected by members of the community, and failure to make a donation would be seen by peers as selfishness.
	Stage 4 Morality is determined by those in legitimate authority. What is legal is moral. The social order must be maintained as an end in itself.	If the leaders of a nation declare war, citizens must go to war because it would be immoral to challenge those in command.
III *Postconventional*	*Stage 5* Morality is based on the assumption of a contract among members of a society to behave in an acceptable manner. The individual submits to a moral code designed to benefit the community as a whole.	People do not commit acts of violence because they realize that if all citizens were free to commit such acts, society could not maintain itself.
	Stage 6 Moral decisions are based on self-chosen ethical principles directed toward promoting what is good for humanity as a whole.	People may believe that no human being may take the life of another; if forced to do so, they would be morally bound to refuse. Kohlberg described Jesus Christ, Mahatma Gandhi, and Martin Luther King, Jr., as stage 6 thinkers.

Lawrence Kohlberg's Theory

The most completely formulated cognitive developmental theory of moral development is undoubtedly that of Lawrence Kohlberg (1927–1987), who extended and refined many of the concepts discussed by Piaget. Kohlberg (1969, 1984) described moral development as a gradual progression through six increasingly sophisticated stages, as outlined in Table 12.2. As can be seen in the table, moral judgments at the lower stages (1 and 2) are based on an egocentric satisfaction of personal needs, at the middle stages (3 and 4) on an effort to follow social convention and obtain social approval, and on the upper stages (5 and 6) on adherence to a set of personal moral standards that promote the general welfare of society. The move is from concrete self-centeredness to abstract conceptions of social responsibility. (See Issues in

Issues in Child Development

Are There Sex Differences in Moral Reasoning?

All of our major theories of moral development were formulated by men. In the case of Kohlberg's theory, some of the early research used only male subjects. In a recent book entitled *In a Different Voice,* Harvard psychologist Carol Gilligan (1982) argued that current theories of morality, most notably that of Kohlberg, typically describe only male behavior. To support her argument, she cited research (Haan, Smith & Block 1968; Holstein 1976; Gilligan 1982) to indicate that females regularly score lower than males according to Kohlberg's classification; males are usually at stage 4, females at stage 3.

Gilligan maintained that the reported gender difference can be attributed to the failure of "male" theories to recognize that moral decision making may differ along gender lines: boys are taught from infancy to separate themselves from others as they form their identities. As a result, males seek out a moral code that emphasizes the rights of the individual. Girls are taught from infancy to value their relatedness to others, to identify by relating to rather than by separating from others. Hence, females prefer a moral code based on caring for and empathizing with others ("I would not steal from you because I don't want to hurt you" as opposed to "I would not steal from you because I respect your property rights").

Gilligan's thesis reminds us of the value of keeping an open mind about all developmental theory; none is so sacred that it should not be regularly questioned. She has also called attention to the importance of representative sampling in the formulation of theory. Nevertheless, the overwhelming body of research evidence does not indicate any gender differences in children's moral functioning, and, in the few studies in which differences are found, females display a greater degree of moral maturity than do males (Keasey 1972; Blatt & Kohlberg 1975; Rest 1976, 1979, 1983; Walker 1984, 1986; Walker & deVries 1985).

Child Development "Are There Sex Differences in Moral Reasoning?" for another perspective on Kohlberg's theory.)

In the normal course of events, a person will progress upward through the stages in sequence; skipping stages does not occur. Evidence for such a progression was obtained in a twenty-year longitudinal study of adolescent boys (Colby et al. 1983). The same study found a degree of consistency between childhood and adulthood patterns of moral judgment. The most morally mature children seemed to become the most morally mature adults.

The stimulus for moral development in Kohlberg's model is internal disequilibrium: individuals who encounter examples of moral reasoning more sophisticated than their own will be driven to incorporate that form of reasoning into their own moral system, provided of course, that the more sophisticated reasoning is understandable to them. The goal of a moral educator, therefore, is to stimulate and to challenge rather than to preach. Blatt and Kohlberg (1975) and Colby and his associates (1977) engaged junior high and high school children in regular discussions of moral issues and found that approximately one-third of the students moved from a lower- to a higher-moral stage; no noticeable change occurred in matched control groups. Kohlberg (1977) achieved similar results with college undergraduates. He concluded that exposure to more sophisticated forms of moral reasoning rather than pressure from parents or educators helps children to become true moral philosophers.

Moral Judgment and Behavior

While Kohlberg's model describes the developmental progression in moral reasoning and judgment, it was not based on observations of children's behavior in real-life settings. Instead, it was based on analysis of children's statements about how they would resolve imaginary moral dilemmas.

To what extent are a person's moral-reasoning skills related to behavior in everyday settings? A considerable amount of evidence suggests a high degree of relationship (Blasi 1980, 1983; Gibbs et al. 1986; Kohlberg & Candee 1984). Consider as an example the findings of a study by Schwartz and his associates (1969) who examined cheating among college students. Thirty-five undergraduates were given a Kohlberg moral interview and a very difficult vocabulary test specifically designed to allow for the possibility of cheating. The students were carefully watched and indications of cheating recorded. Evidence of cheating was found to be related to a student's level of moral judgment; more than half of the stage 3 and stage 4 thinkers cheated, while only one in five of those at stage 5 and stage 6 did so! Such findings parallel those of a number of studies of cheating in the classroom, involving participants ranging from elementary school to college age; it certainly appears that one factor determining a student's willingness to cheat is level of moral reasoning.

Using a slightly different approach to the question, Gibbs and his associates (1986) compared moral-reasoning level with teachers' ratings of the "moral courage" of high school students. Teachers were asked questions such as: "Would this student consistently stand by his or her principles . . . support an unpopular cause if he or she believed it was right . . . defend someone who is being attacked by the group . . . support a cause only if the cause is popular with his or her friends?" Degree of moral courage was significantly related to moral maturity as indicated by responses on the standard Kohlberg interview.

The findings of studies of cheating, moral courage, and a variety of other morally challenging situations (e.g., helping friends in need, sharing, keeping a promise) seem to indicate a fairly consistent pattern. In general, a relationship exists between a person's moral judgment and his or her actual behavior in a social setting.

Factors Related to Moral Development

It would be surprising if a person's level of moral development were not related to other aspects of development or to that person's particular set of life experiences. In fact, moral development is closely related to a child's or adolescent's level of intellectual growth. Furthermore, moral reasoning can apparently be influenced by environmental conditions. The experience of education or of being forced to deal with moral dilemmas in everyday life can affect the course of moral growth.

Cognitive Factors.   Sophistication of moral judgment in the cognitive developmental framework is related closely to measures of intellectual functioning (Rest 1979; Carroll & Rest 1982). For example, the progression through Kohlberg's moral stages is related to the progression through Piaget's cognitive stages, in the sense that cognitive development is a necessary, although not a sufficient, condition for moral development (Kohlberg 1976). Thus, a preoperational or concrete operational child cannot reach Kohlberg's stage 5 or stage 6, since these stages require formal operational thinking; however, an adolescent can be at Piaget's stage of formal operations and still not be functioning at Kohlberg's highest moral stages (Walker & Richards 1979). The cognitive aspects of moral development have also been suggested by the consistency of the significant correlations between tests of moral judgment and tests of IQ, aptitude, and achievement (Colby et al. 1983; Rest 1979, 1983).

Relevant Life Experiences.   The experience of coping with difficult moral issues seems to influence the rate of progression through Kohlberg's stages of moral development. This pattern is certainly suggested by results of moral education programs discussed earlier (Blatt & Kohlberg 1975; Colby et al. 1977). It is also suggested by patterns of moral development observed in adolescents and adults in real-life settings. Adults who advance most rapidly through the stages attribute their gains to the experience of dealing with challenging responsibilities, such as those involved in mar-

What cognitive or personality variables would lead one child to steal nail polish from a drug store while a classmate might refuse to do so under any circumstances? Different answers to this question would be provided by social learning, psychoanalytic, and cognitive-developmental theorists.

riage, career choice, or financial planning (Rest 1975).

Level of moral reasoning is also linked to level of education, with rapid progress through the stages occurring more often among those who attend college than among those who do not. Since intellectually capable individuals are also more likely to attend college, it is not possible to conclude that the college experience itself brings about ad-

vances in moral reasoning. It is interesting, however, that moral progress is greatest among those who enter fields of study such as philosophy and theology, where moral decision making is discussed or even required. Apparently, a society in which there is a free exchange of ideas and a willingness to discuss moral issues is a society conducive to moral development, at least according to the cognitive developmental model (Colby et al. 1983; Rest 1975; Rest, Davison & Robbins 1978).

Cross-cultural Differences. Most of the studies of Kohlberg's stages have been done in the United States, but a growing body of research is also examining cultural variations in moral development. Both cross-sectional and longitudinal studies have been carried out comparing the moral reasoning of children, adolescents, and adults in numerous countries, including the United States, England, Canada, India, Kenya, Israel, New Zealand, Nigeria, Mexico, and Turkey (Kohlberg 1969; Turiel, Edwards & Kohlberg 1978; White, Bushnell & Regnemer 1978). Summarizing the findings of these studies, Edwards (1981) concluded that there is preliminary support for the universality of both the stages and sequence of stages. She goes on to say, however, that while the first three stages are found in most cultures, stages 4, 5, and 6 are found only in more complex societies. Edwards suggested that the complexity of the stages reflects the complexity of the society in general. A complex sociopolitical order may require more complex moral judgments than would be required in a simpler, more "primitive" society. This interpretation agrees with Rest's (1975) findings discussed earlier: American adults who showed the greatest moral advances attributed these advances to the demands placed on them to be responsible members of our complex society.

Social Structures

The chapter thus far has emphasized what might be considered the psychological aspects of social interaction—the individual development of social awareness, social concern, and moral reasoning. The chapter now turns to an analysis not of the individual but of the group. This section examines the emergence of and the functions of the childhood peer group, the changes in group constitution during adolescence, and individual characteristics that lead to acceptance, rejection, or neglect by the other members of the group.

The Emergence of the Peer Group

From the age of 6 to the age of 10, peers become more and more important in a child's life. Family orientation decreases, while organization into peer groups increases (Minuchin 1977). While its composition may change from week to week, the group is, nevertheless, a very close-knit society, with definite rules for membership. Occasionally such groups even have special languages, handshakes, secret passwords, and secret clubhouses.

Not all children attach themselves to organized groups. Some prefer one-to-one relationships, while others associate with neighborhood "gangs"—loose and frequently changing confederations having no group names, secrets, or specific membership requirements (Williams & Stith 1980). Rules will exist in the gang, although perhaps not as clearly specified as in the more organized groups. Children who do not like the games their peers play, or who do not own bicycles, or who are not allowed out after dark may be excluded. Indeed, children may be excluded if they are different in any way, even if the difference is regarded as a positive one by adults. In some groups, children may be ostracized if they will not cooperate in stealing or in vandalism, or if they like going to school while their peers do not.

Peer Group Functions

The peer group in middle childhood functions as a major socializing agent. In the group the children learn about the peer culture. They learn to obey rules and to follow a certain moral order. They learn to compromise. They develop a variety of physical skills, as well as acquire a large supply of riddles, jokes, stories, and knowledge about games. They learn what their peers consider to be masculine and feminine behavior, and they will firm up sexual identity accordingly. In essence, they learn how to function in society (Williams & Stith 1980). The peer group in middle childhood is also a source of playmates. It provides the child with a number of other children to do things with, and is the pool from which friends are chosen.

Gender Differences

The middle childhood peer group, at least in our culture, may be primarily a male phenomenon.

Dating, which typically begins about the age of fourteen provides adolescents with pleasant recreational activity, companionship, and an opportunity to gain status within the peer groups.

Waldrop and Halverson (1975) obtained careful records of children's weekly social interactions and found that highly sociable boys were more likely to have **extensive peer relations** (i.e., group activities), but highly sociable girls more often had **intensive peer relations** (i.e., one-to-one activities). The authors concluded that the sex difference may occur because (1) girls are more likely than boys to be kept close to home and therefore group activities are limited; (2) girls are discouraged more often than boys from being noisy, and groups tend to be noisy; or (3) girls are more likely than boys to experience close one-to-one relationships at home, with mothers and daughters often being particularly close.

Adolescent Groups and Dating

Peer groupings in the early years of adolescence usually consist of same-sex children only. In middle and late adolescence, however, the tendency toward heterosexual interaction increases. Unisex groups gradually become heterosexual groups, and heterosexual groups eventually break down into couples.

The process of pairing off into heterosexual couples—the phenomenon of dating—may begin as early as 12 years of age, but today's adolescent typically begins dating at age 14 or 15 (Hansen 1977). Girls begin dating earlier than boys do, perhaps because girls are more physically and emotionally mature and because girls typically date partners older than themselves. By the age of 17, virtually all adolescents have dated at least once.

A rather obvious function of dating is mate selection; but, in fact, the majority of American adolescents do not see the dating process as preparation for marriage. Rice (1984) lists a variety of reasons why adolescents date, and these are:

- *Recreation.* Dating is simply an enjoyable social experience that often becomes an end in itself rather than a means of selecting a spouse.
- *Companionship without marriage.* The need for emotional closeness expressed by adolescents is frequently met in a dating situation. In dating, adolescents may learn to share their intimate thoughts and feelings.
- *Status and achievement.* Successful dating experiences may indicate to the peer group that a boy or girl is emotionally and socially mature and is sexually desirable. Nondaters may look up to the adolescent who dates and admire and envy the dater's "grown-up" heterosexual behavior.
- *Sexual experimentation.* Throughout the past fifty years sexuality has played an increasingly greater role in adolescent interpersonal relations. Dating is an avenue for sexual experimentation and sexual satisfaction.
- *Mate selection.* Whether or not an adolescent consciously seeks a lifelong mate when dating, the process usually leads to mate selection, especially among older adolescents.

Characteristics of Popularity

In recent years, a number of psychologists (e.g., Masters & Furman 1981; McGuire & Weisz 1982) have emphasized the need to distinguish between friendship and popularity. Friendship refers to the degree of liking in a one-to-one relationship, whereas popularity refers to the degree to which a person is valued by the peer group as a whole. A distinction between the two concepts may be necessary because it appears that certain characteristics (e.g., altruism, understanding, sensitivity) are related to friendship development, but not to popularity (McGuire & Weisz 1982). Other characteristics (e.g., sociability, ability to give praise and affection, social status) seem to be related to popularity, but not to individual friendship selection (Masters & Furman 1981).

Childhood

The most popular children in elementary school are friendly, intelligent, high in academic achievement, athletically skilled, and physically attractive. They engage in much cooperative play and successful social conversation; they are seen as good leaders and as children who know how to share with others (Dodge 1983).

Children are likely to be rejected if they are antisocial, hostile, physically unattractive, or low in achievement. Rejected children are seen as poor leaders. They have difficulty sharing, and they often exclude other children from their play (Dodge 1983; Dodge, Coie & Brakke 1982; Hartup, Glazer & Charlesworth 1967).

A third group of children are neither liked nor actively rejected. Instead, they are virtually ignored by the peer group. This category of neglected, or socially isolated, children has received much attention in recent years (Gottman 1977; Dodge, Coie & Brakke 1982; Asher, Hymel & Renshaw 1984). Neglected children are not seen as hostile or aggressive and, in fact, are often thought of as shy. (See Problems in Child Development "The Origins of Shyness.") They are usually more physically attractive than clearly rejected children. What they share in common with rejected children is that they lack social skills or social experiences. Summarizing the differences between rejected and neglected groups, Dodge (1983) noted that the former group lacks social skills *and* is antisocial, while the latter group lacks social skills but is not antisocial. What is more, actual peer rejection seems to be quite consistent throughout elementary and high school, while peer neglect is variable and seems to depend on the particular social setting the child is in (Coie & Krehbiel 1984). A neglected child might become more popular if moved to a different classroom or a different school; a rejected child seems to be rejected everywhere.

Adolescence

Certain characteristics make adolescents popular with their peers. Table 12.3 lists the qualities Snyder (1972) found important for being a "big wheel" in one midwestern high school. As you can see, personal qualities (e.g., personality, good looks) were most frequently mentioned, followed in order by material possessions (e.g., cars, money,

Problems in Child Development

The Origins of Shyness

Not long ago, a television program on the topic of shyness was broadcast nationwide. Over six hundred people who saw themselves as being shy wrote letters in response, and their overriding message was that shyness is a real problem for many people, but one that is not taken seriously enough in our society (Harris 1984). Just how serious an obstacle to a child's normal social development is the characteristic of shyness? In the first place, the number of self-defined shy children may be greater than many of us realize. Lazarus (1982a) found that 38 percent of the approximately four hundred fifth graders he surveyed labeled themselves as shy. Nearly half of those shy children felt that being shy was a personal problem, and nearly half expressed a desire to participate in a counseling group to overcome their shyness. Shyness is related to peer rejection and social isolation in childhood (Asher, Hymel & Renshaw 1984; Richmond 1985), as well as to low self-esteem (Lazarus 1982b). Among adolescents, extreme shyness has been associated with eating disorders (Segal & Figley 1985), with anxiety, and with depression (Traub 1983).

Where does shyness originate? Is it learned, or does it have a genetic basis? In fact, a growing body of evidence suggests that shyness is a stable characteristic of temperament that may have biological origins (e.g., Buss & Plomin 1984; Jacklin, Maccoby & Doering 1983; Plomin & Rowe 1979). As an illustration of research in this direction, Daniels and Plomin (1985b) examined 152 adopted infants at 12 and 24 months of age and 120 nonadopted infants at the same ages. The researchers obtained parental reports on degrees of shyness (i.e., fearfulness in strange situations) observed in the infants, including reports from the biological mothers of the adopted children. The amount of shyness exhibited by the parents was also measured, by means of standard personality tests. Results of the study indicated a high degree of similarity between children and biological parents in their tendency to be socially outgoing or socially withdrawn—and this relationship existed even when the child was being raised by someone other than his or her biological parent!

Before we rush to the conclusion, however, that shyness is a genetic and not an environmentally influenced personality characteristic, we should look at another finding of the Daniels and Plomin study: there was also a degree of similarity in sociability between adoptive parents and their infants, who were obviously genetically dissimilar groups. Both genetic and environmental factors apparently have to be considered in explaining the origins of shyness. The researchers suggested that a tendency toward shyness may be inherited, but that shy mothers—by failing to expose their children to novel situations—may also set up environments that encourage shyness in their children. Exposure to novelty could be a key element in promoting a socially outgoing attitude in children. The encouraging results of programs designed to help children overcome their shyness further suggest that the environment can influence the sociability of children. Exercises in relaxation, activities to foster greater self-awareness, training in social skills, forced participation in group games and activities, and involvement in drama therapy all have been found useful in bringing shy children out of themselves (Biemer 1983; Lowenstein 1983).

nice clothes), activities-athletics, academic achievement, and the "right" friends.

Certainly we might expect that personal qualities would be most closely related to popularity. After all, the possession of nice clothes or a sports car or success on the football field will be of little help to an adolescent who is inconsiderate, dishonest, bad-tempered, or extremely withdrawn. The fact that material possessions rated second in Snyder's list of criteria suggests a degree of superficiality in at least some adolescent relationships. It is likely that many adolescents are so involved

Table 12.3 Criteria Necessary for Being a "Big Wheel" on Campus, as Listed by High School Students

Criteria	Boys (N = 142)	Girls (N = 178)
Personal Qualities	60.6	89.3
Material Possessions	49.3	55.1
Activities—Athletics	35.9	23.6
Academic Achievement	21.8	25.8
"Right Friends"	17.6	10.1

Source: From Snyder, E.E. (1972) High school perceptions of prestige criteria. *Adolescence, 6*, p. 132. ©1972 Libra Publishers. Reprinted by permission.

in developing their own identities that they are not yet ready to look beneath the surface of others and to establish intimate relationships.

An interesting and frequently observed finding was Snyder's discovery that, for boys at least, athletic success takes precedence over academic achievement. In 1961, Coleman asked adolescent boys how they would like to be remembered after graduation from high school and discovered that 44 percent of them wanted to be remembered as outstanding athletes, 31 percent as brilliant scholars, and 25 percent as the most popular students. Twenty-five years later, Eitzen (1975) found that the figure for athletics was 47 percent, for scholarship 23 percent, and for popularity 30 percent. Apparently little had changed from the 1950s to the 1970s. If anything, the value of scholarship seems to have slipped.

Helping the Unpopular Child

When a child is either rejected or neglected by peers, a number of unfortunate consequences may result. Childhood peer rejection in particular has been associated with emotional difficulties during adolescence, with dropping out of school, and with juvenile delinquency (Asher, Oden & Gottman 1977; Hartup 1983). Neglect by peers is a cause of childhood loneliness. Considering the possible

negative impacts of social isolation, we might wonder how a caring adult might help a child who is disliked or ignored by his or her peers. The traditional adult response has been to pressure the peer group into becoming more accepting, and this approach has usually been ineffective. Within the past ten years, however, a new and more promising approach to dealing with children's social isolation has emerged. This involves working not with the group as a whole, but directly with the socially isolated child, and coaching that child in specific social or academic skills necessary for peer acceptance.

In one of the earliest studies illustrating this new approach, psychologists Sherri Oden and Steven Asher (1977) selected third- and fourth-grade children judged by their classmates to be socially undesirable, and coached them individually for four weeks in strategies for participation, cooperation, and communication. Oden and Asher reported that the coaching seemed to have the desired effect. Approximately one week after the coaching sessions ended, the formerly unpopular children experienced a significantly greater degree of acceptance from their peers. Indeed, half of the coached children were now ranked in the top half of the class in popularity. Even more encouraging was the finding that the effects of coaching were long lasting: the researchers returned one year later and found that the children they had worked with were accepted by their peers to an even greater degree than they had been one week after coaching.

Within the past ten years, a number of other studies (e.g., Bierman 1986; Bierman & Furman 1984; Coie & Krehbiel 1984; Gresham & Nagel 1980; Ladd 1981; La Greca & Santogrossi 1980) have supported the view that coaching children in a variety of social skills (e.g., sharing, cooperating, initiating friendships, making conversation, playing games) can lead to a greater degree of peer acceptance. Typically, these studies included refinements and extensions of the Oden and Asher technique. For example, Ladd (1981) was concerned that some of the social success achieved by unpopular children in the earlier study could have been the result of the special attention provided by the psychologists, and not of the skill training itself. In his study, he provided a group of unpopular third graders with

Neglected children often experience a childhood filled with loneliness.

training in asking questions of, making suggestions to, and offering supportive statements to peers, as well as giving them opportunities to practice these skills and evaluate their own successes. A second group of children received the same amount of attention from the psychologist and the same "practice" exposure to peers, but no skills training. It was found that children trained in social skills showed significant improvement in their tendency to be accepted by peers, but those given adult attention without skills training did not. Special attention from caring adults is not enough to help a socially isolated child become more accepted by other children; skill training is needed as well.

As noted earlier, factors other than personality characteristics are related to social status in childhood. One of these factors is academic achievement. Rejected children tend to have problems in academic performance and are more likely to need help in the classroom (McMichael 1980; Coie & Krehbiel 1984; Dodge 1983; Coie, Dodge & Coppotelli 1982). Why do social rejection and academic difficulties often go hand in hand? Coie and Krehbiel (1984) suggested three reasons:

1. Children with academic problems may begin to engage in antisocial activities because they are bored or anxious in the classroom.
2. Children might be looked down on by other children specifically because they are not successful academically.
3. The same immaturity that causes social problems may cause academic problems in the classroom; thus, the two sets of problems are related.

If academic failure is related to social failure, might a child's social status be improved as a result of special efforts to remedy academic problems?

Coie and Krehbiel (1984) investigated this question. They worked with third graders identified as having both social and academic problems. Some of the children were provided with two sessions a week of individual tutoring in academic subjects. Others received social-skills training similar to what was provided in the Ladd (1981) study mentioned earlier. A third group received training in both academic and social skills. The result was that children who were tutored in academic subjects actually showed greater improvement in social status than did those receiving only the social-skills training. This does not mean, of course, that social-skills training is ineffective, or that academic tutoring can help the social image of all rejected children. It does reinforce the idea, however, that adult intervention can benefit a child's standing in the peer group, and it further suggests that the intervention can be accomplished in more than one way, depending on the reasons for a particular child's unpopularity. This should provide much encouragement for parents and educators, and much hope for children who for any reason experience the pain of isolation from their peer groups.

Summary

1. Infants and toddlers have a definite interest in peer relationships, as can be seen by their communicative gestures and by their attempts at cooperative play.
2. Extensive peer interaction during the first two years of life is related to later social interests but not to later social skills.
3. Even by the age of 4, children have definite preferences in friends. As children develop throughout the elementary school years, their knowledge about psychological characteristics of friends increases, and they have a deepening understanding of the nature of friendship itself.
4. Role-taking skills improve from the preschool years to the years of adolescence. Decreases in egocentrism are accompanied by an increase in ability to see the world from the point of view of another person.
5. Altruism, or concern for others, is found even during infancy. While the number of altruistic behaviors do not increase with age, the quality of those behaviors is enriched, as the sense of caring is enhanced by a growing social awareness.

6. There appear to be sex differences in friendship needs in American society, with males seeking friends who can provide concrete, practical support and females more often seeking emotional closeness in a friendship.
7. Moral development has been described from the perspectives of the behaviorist, psychoanalytic, and cognitive developmental theorists. The three viewpoints differ considerably in their analyses of the reasons why human beings usually engage in morally "right" behaviors and tend to avoid those that are morally "wrong."
8. There is some evidence in support of the universality of stages of moral development, but it appears that the degree of complexity of the stages is related to the complexity of life in a particular society.
9. The peer group is a major socializing agent in childhood, particularly for males who seem to be more group-oriented in their friendships than are females.
10. Adolescents typically begin to date at age 14 or 15. Dating serves many functions for American adolescents, including recreation, companionship, status, and the opportunity for sexual experimentation.
11. In both childhood and adolescence, popularity is related to the possession of a pleasant personality, sociability, academic achievement, and physical attractiveness. Unpopular children can be thought of as fitting into either of two categories: the rejected and the neglected.
12. Adults can have an influence on the social status of children by coaching the unpopular child in social skills or in skills indirectly related to peer acceptance.

Key Terms

shared meanings	identification
social cognition	instinctual anxiety
induction	morality of constraint
altruism	morality of cooperation
instrumental needs	extensive peer relations
expressive needs	intensive peer relations

Suggested Readings

Bronfenbrenner, U. (1972). *Two worlds of childhood: U.S. and U.S.S.R.* New York: Simon & Schuster.

An often-fascinating discussion of child rearing, family life, and peer relationships in the United States and the Soviet Union. A number of interesting comparisons and contrasts are drawn, and the reader clearly sees that a person's social development is influenced by the values of his or her culture.

Damon, W. (1977). *The social world of the child*. San Francisco: Jossey-Bass.

A discussion of social development throughout childhood. The author focuses on issues of morality and justice, and presents his stages of distributive justice through which all children are assumed to pass.

Livesley, W.J. & Bromley, D.B. (1973). *Person perception in childhood and adolescence*. London: Wiley.

A treatment of the development of children's understanding of other people—the transition from reliance on superficial characteristics to an appreciation of subtleties and contradictions in human personality.

Rest, J.R. (1979). *Development in judging moral issues*. Minneapolis: University of Minnesota Press.

A review of research on moral development using the Defining Issues Test, an objective measure based on Kohlberg's principles. The author reviews developmental differences in moral reasoning and discusses factors that affect moral development.

Rubin, K.H. & Ross, H.S. (1982). *Peer relationships and social skills in childhood*. New York: Springer-Verlag.

A collection of sixteen articles dealing with current theory and research on social interaction in childhood. This book well represents the state of the art in the rapidly expanding field of social development. Included are articles on fairness and friendship, social-problem solving, social interaction in infancy, and the positive effects of early socialization.

Readings from the Literature

The topic of the following study is self-reports of loneliness in children. Rather than attempting to identify the actual causes of loneliness or to suggest remedies, the authors are validating the usefulness of a loneliness questionnaire. As you read the study, try to answer the following questions:

- What need were the researchers responding to in developing their questionnaire?

- What did the researchers demonstrate about the relationship between a child's self-report of loneliness and the way the child is actually treated by his or her peers?

- In this study, the responses of actively rejected children were not separated from those of neglected children. The authors suggest that this may be one reason why the overall correlation between sociometric status and reported loneliness was not as high as expected. Why might the correlation be higher if the two categories of children were separated?

Loneliness in Children

Steven R. Asher
University of Illinois at Urbana-Champaign

Shelley Hymel
University of Waterloo

Peter D. Renshaw
Murdoch University

Children experiencing difficulties in their peer relations have typically been identified using external sources of information, such as teacher referrals or ratings, sociometric measures, and/or behavioral observations. There is a need to supplement these assessment procedures with self-report measures that assess the degree to which the children themselves feel satisfaction with their peer relationships. In this study, a 16-item self-report measure of loneliness and social dissatisfaction was developed. In surveying 506 third-through sixth-grade children, the measure was found to be internally reliable. More than 10% of children reported feelings of loneliness and social dissatisfaction, and children's feelings of loneliness were significantly related to their sociometric status. The relationship of loneliness and sociometric status to school achievement was also examined.

Research focused on children who lack friends in school is growing rapidly. Given evidence that poor peer relations are predictive of serious adjustment problems in later life (see Hartup, 1983; Putallaz & Gottman, 1983), and given repeated documentation of the social skill deficits of children who lack friends (for a review, see Asher & Renshaw, 1981), investigators have sought to improve the peer relations of unpopular children through direct instruction in social skills (e.g., Gottman, Gonso, & Schuler, 1976; Gresham & Nagle, 1980; Ladd, 1981; LaGreca & Santogrossi, 1980; Oden & Asher, 1977). Children in this research typically are selected for participation based on external sources of information, most notably, teachers, peers, or unfamiliar adult observers (for a review, see Asher & Hymel, 1981). For example, many intervention studies with unpopular children use sociometric measures to select children who are least liked in their classrooms. In some studies, sociometric data are supplemented by direct observations of children's social interaction style.

One limitation of the intervention literature has been the absence of information concerning unpopular children's perspective about their own situation. To date, no attempt has been made to learn whether the children who are chosen for intervention feel lonely or are themselves dissatisfied with their social relationships. This contrasts with research with adults in which self-report measures, especially measures of loneliness, have been widely used to identify people having problems in social relationships (for an excellent review, see Peplau & Perlman, 1982).

The goals of the present research were to develop a reliable measure of children's feelings of loneliness and social dissatisfaction and to learn whether the children who are least accepted by their classmates are indeed more lonely. There are several reasons for learning whether low-status children are dissatisfied with their peer relationships. The argument could be made that some children by virtue of normative selection criteria, have to be at the bottom of their class in terms of peer acceptance and are not necessarily unhappy with their social situation. Therefore, assessment of children's own feelings about their peer relations might be useful in identifying children for participation in intervention programs. Data on the child's perspective would also be useful in evaluating whether social-skill training decreases children's feelings of loneliness or social dissatisfaction and in determining whether intervention efforts are differentially successful as a function of children's feelings prior to training. There is also the possibility that children's feelings of loneliness will predict to later adjustment beyond the prediction that can now be made based on measures of children's participation in a social network. Finally, the phenomenon of loneliness in children merits investigation in its own right, since relatively little is known about the concerns and emotional lives of children. This study, therefore, was designed to provide a first step in this heretofore neglected area.

Method

Subjects

Five hundred twenty-two children from third through sixth grade initially participated in the study. Of the 522 children in the original sample, 16 children had incomplete loneliness data, leaving a total of 506 children (243 females, 263 males) in the final sample. The children came from 20 classrooms in two schools in a moderate-size midwestern city in the United States.

Procedure

A 24-item questionnaire was developed to assess children's feelings of loneliness and social dissatisfaction (see Table 1). The 16 primary items focused on children's feelings of loneliness (e.g., "I'm lonely"), feelings of social adequacy versus inadequacy (e.g., "I'm good at working with other children"), or subjective estimations of peer status (e.g., "I have lots of friends"). The other eight items focused on children's hobbies or preferred activities (e.g., "I like to paint and draw"; "I watch TV a lot"). These eight "filler" items were included to help children feel more open and relaxed about indicating their attitudes about various topics.

Children responded to each of the 24 items by indicating on a five-point scale how much each statement was a true description of themselves (i.e., always true, true most of the time, true sometimes, hardly ever true, not true at all). The scale was administered in a group testing session in each classroom by a male experimenter (the third author). Children were first trained in use of the rating scale by responding to several activity preference statements (e.g., "I like roller skating"). After children understood the task, the experimenter read aloud each of the 24 items, waiting for children to record their ratings for each item before going on to the next item.

Two weeks later, sociometric measures were administered in each classroom by a female experimenter (the second author). Two different sociometric measures were used: (1) a positive-nomination measure in which children were asked to name their three best friends in the classroom; and (2) a rating-scale measure on which children rated each classmate on a 1-5 scale according to how much they liked to play with

Table 1 Questionnaire Items

1. It's easy for me to make new friends at school.
2. I like to read.
3. I have nobody to talk to.*
4. I'm good at working with other children.
5. I watch TV a lot.
6. It's hard for me to make friends.*
7. I like school.
8. I have lots of friends.
9. I feel alone.*
10. I can find a friend when I need one.
11. I play sports a lot.
12. It's hard to get other kids to like me.*
13. I like science.
14. I don't have anyone to play with.*
15. I like music.
16. I get along with other kids.
17. I feel left out of things.*
18. There's nobody I can go to when I need help.*
19. I like to paint and draw.
20. I don't get along with other children.*
21. I'm lonely.*
22. I am well-liked by the kids in my class.
23. I like playing board games a lot.
24. I don't have any friends.*

Note: Items 2, 5, 7, 11, 13, 15, 19, and 23 were classified as hobby or interest items.
*Items for which response order was reversed in scoring.

that person at school (Singleton & Asher, 1977). As in past research (e.g., Oden & Asher, 1977), sociometric scores were computed and analyzed on the basis of nominations and ratings received from same-sex classmates.[1] For the nomination measure, a child's

score first was computed as the number of nominations received from same-sex peers. Next, to permit comparison of nomination scores across classrooms that varied in size, a proportion score was also computed for each child, operationally defined as the number of same-sex nominations received divided by the number of same-sex classmates. For the rating-scale measure, a child's score first was computed as the average rating received from same-sex peers, with a higher score indicative of greater peer acceptance. Then, to permit comparison of scores across classrooms, these average-rating scores were converted to standard scores ($Z = X_1 - \overline{X}/SD$), using means and standard deviations for each sex group in each classroom in the computations.

Results

Descriptive Findings

Table 2 presents descriptive information concerning the distribution of children's responses to each of the 16 primary items. It can be seen that on nearly all items over 10% of the sample reported feelings of considerable social dissatisfaction. For example, on the item "I'm lonely," 5.8% of the children indicated "that's always true about me," and another 5.6% said "that's true about me most of the time." On the item "I feel left out of things," 8.5% said "that's always true about me," and 9.8% said "that's true about me most of the time." Thus, a sizable number of children reported feelings of loneliness and social dissatisfaction.

Factor Analysis and Internal Reliability

Children's responses to all 24 questionnaire items were subjected to factor analysis (quartimax rotation). The results indicated a primary factor that included all 16 of the loneliness and social dissatisfaction items. None of the hobby or interest items loaded significantly on this factor. Factor loadings for each scale item are given in Table 3 along with the item-to-total-score correlations.

The resulting 16-item scale was found to be internally consistent (Cronbach's $\alpha = .90$) and internally reliable (split-half correlation between forms = .83; Spearman-Brown reliability coefficient = .91; Guttman split-half reliability coefficient = .91).

[1]Data reported here are based on sociometric ratings and nominations received from same-sex peers since this scoring procedure is typical in the intervention literature addressed. However, data based on sociometric scores received from all classmates were also analyzed, and the results were highly similar to those reported here for same-sex sociometric scores.

Table 2 Percentage Distribution of Children's Responses to Loneliness Items

	Always True	True Most of the Time	Sometimes True	Hardly Ever True	Not True at All
It's easy for me to make new friends at school.	29.2	29.8	29.0	6.2	5.8
I have nobody to talk to.	5.6	6.2	14.1	18.5	55.6
I'm good at working with other children.	29.2	34.2	25.3	5.8	5.4
It's hard for me to make friends.	9.6	8.1	19.8	20.2	42.3
I have lots of friends.	56.0	20.8	13.5	5.6	4.2
I feel alone.	5.0	8.7	20.2	21.7	44.4
I can find a friend when I need one.	39.1	23.6	23.4	6.4	7.5
It's hard to get other kids to like me.	8.1	11.2	19.5	22.6	38.6
I don't have anyone to play with.	5.4	5.4	17.7	19.4	52.1
I get along with other kids.	37.5	37.3	20.2	2.1	2.9
I feel left out of things.	8.5	9.8	22.5	27.1	32.1
There's nobody I can go to when I need help.	6.7	5.4	11.7	18.3	57.9
I don't get along with other children.	5.0	6.7	15.8	24.9	47.6
I'm lonely.	5.8	5.6	15.6	20.4	52.6
I am well-liked by kids in my class.	32.6	32.6	23.7	6.8	4.2
I don't have any friends.	3.3	2.1	5.4	11.0	78.1

Note: Figures do not always total 100% because of rounding.

Loneliness and Sociometric Status

Next we examined the relationship between self-reported loneliness and sociometric status. On the basis of the factor analysis, all 16 loneliness items were used to compute a total loneliness score for each child. Responses to each of the loneliness items were scored from 1 to 5, with order reversed for particular items (see Table 1) such that a score of 5 was always indicative of greater loneliness or social dissatisfaction. Responses for each of the 16 items were then summed to create a total loneliness score for each child that could range from 16 (low loneliness) to 80 (high loneliness). In our sample, loneliness scores ranged from 16 to 79, with a mean score of 32.51 and a standard deviation of 11.82.

Correlational analyses were performed to examine the relationship between loneliness and sociometric status. As noted earlier, to permit comparisons across classrooms, the proportion of same-sex nominations received and standardized average rating scores from same-sex peers were used as sociometric indices in these analyses. The results are presented in Table 4 for the entire sample and separately for males and females and for children in each of the four grade levels. Three children within the sample had moved prior to administration of sociometric measures; thus the sample size for these analyses was reduced to 503. As can be seen in Table 4, for both sexes and at each grade level, a significant negative relationship was found between loneliness and both friendship nominations and play ratings received from same-sex peers.

405

Table 3 Factor Loading for Each Item and the Correlations of Each Item with the Total Score

Item Number	Factor Loading	Item-to-Total-Score Correlation
1	.54	.62
3	.57	.58
4	.43	.50
6	.63	.66
8	.58	.65
9	.69	.70
10	.51	.59
12	.67	.70
14	.66	.66
16	.59	.65
17	.64	.66
18	.57	.56
20	.60	.62
21	.73	.72
22	.55	.62
24	.67	.67

Note: Items 3, 6, 9, 12, 14, 17, 18, 20, 21, and 24 had their response order reversed in scoring.

To examine loneliness further as a function of sociometric status, we considered whether children who might be targeted for intervention on the basis of sociometric measures reported greater loneliness and social dissatisfaction than their higher-status peers. A typical procedure in intervention studies has been to target as candidates for intervention the three lowest-rated children on a rating-scale sociometric measure. Accordingly, we selected the three children in each class who received the lowest ratings from same-sex peers ($N = 59$, 26 females and 33 males, with one targeted child omitted because of incomplete loneliness data). These least-accepted children were compared with the rest of their classmates ($N = 444$) in terms of loneliness in a three-way (sociometric status × grade × sex) analysis of variance. Results indicated a significant main effect for sociometric status, $F(1,487) = 31.28$, $p < .001$. Lowest-rated children reported significantly greater feelings of loneliness and social dissatisfaction ($M = 40.61$, $SD = 12.46$) than did their more accepted peers ($M = 31.36$, $SD = 11.13$). All other main effects and interactions were nonsignificant. Thus, the children typically selected for intervention on the basis of rating-scale sociometric data do report more loneliness than the rest of their classmates.

A second analysis was conducted to examine whether children with few or no best-friendship nominations within their classroom would experience greater loneliness. For this analysis, the number of best-friend nominations received from same-sex peers was used to identify six groups of children: those who received no friendship nominations, and those who received one, two, three, four, or five or more friendship nominations. These groups were compared in terms of self-reported loneliness in a three-way (number of friends × grade × sex) analysis of variance. Results indicated a significant main effect for number of friends, $F(5,455) = 7.30$, $p < .001$, with all other main effects and interactions nonsignificant. Means and standard deviations of loneliness scores for each of the six levels of friendship are presented in Table 5; as can be seen, loneliness scores increased as the number of friends decreased. Post-hoc Scheffé comparisons of the means for these groups indicated that children receiving zero, one, or two best-friend nominations reported significantly more loneliness than children receiving five or more best-friend nominations.

It appears, then, that lower-status children do experience and report considerably more loneliness and social dissatisfaction than their more accepted peers, regardless of the type of sociometric measure used to identify such children. Still, the magnitude of the relationship (see Table 4) suggests that there must be considerable variability within particular levels of status. To examine this issue further, we used both rating-scale and nomination measures to identify three groups of children: unpopular, average, and popular. Unpopular children ($N = 69$) were defined as those who received average play-rating scores that were 1 SD below the mean for their same-sex classroom peers and who were nominated as a best friend by only one or

406

Table 4   Correlations of Loneliness with Sociometric Status

Group	Sociometric Measures	
	Standardized Same-Sex Ratings	Proportion of Best Friend Nominations
Males (N = 261)	−.37***	−.27***
Females (N = 242)	−.25***	−.23***
Third-grade Students (N = 118)	−.28**	−.31***
Fourth-grade Students (N = 128)	−.32***	−.21*
Fifth-grade Students (N = 125)	−.35***	−.32***
Sixth-grade Students (N = 132)	−.30***	−.19*
All Students (N = 503)	−.31***	−.25***

*$p < .05$.
**$p < .01$.
***$p < .001$.

Table 5   Number of Best Friends and Average Loneliness Scores

Groups	Loneliness Scores	
	M	SD
No friends ($N = 70$)	36.27	12.89
One friend ($N = 102$)	35.66	12.79
Two friends ($N = 91$)	33.85	10.91
Three friends ($N = 89$)	30.37	10.56
Four friends ($N = 58$)	30.64	9.78
Five or more friends ($N = 93$)	27.79	10.18

no same-sex classmates. Popular children ($N = 60$) were defined as those who received average play rating scores that were 1 SD or more above the mean for their same-sex classroom peers and who were nominated as a best friend by four or more same-sex classmates. The remaining children ($N = 374$) were considered to be average in popularity. Of the 69 children classified as unpopular, 29% had loneliness scores that were at least 1 SD above the mean for the entire sample. However, 6% actually had loneliness scores that were 1 SD below the mean, and the remaining 65% were average in self-reported loneliness (i.e., within 1 SD of the mean). Loneliness scores varied among popular children as follows: 33% reported low loneliness, 62% reported average loneliness, and, interestingly, 5% reported high loneliness.

Variability is also evident when children's responses to individual items are examined. Many of the items did show considerable differences between popular and unpopular children. For example, on the item "I feel left out of things," 23% of the unpopular children indicated the statement to be "always true" of them as compared with none of the popular children and 6% of the average children. Still, it is also clear from the individual items that a few popular children experience difficulty in their relations with peers and that many unpopular children do not experience, or at least do not report, serious dissatisfaction. For example, 8% of the popular children indicated that they felt left out of things most of the time, and 41% of unpopular children said it was not at all true that they felt lonely.

Achievement, Sociometric Status, and Loneliness.

There are several studies indicating a relationship between children's sociometric status and their school achievement (e.g., Glick, 1972; Green, Forehand, Beck & Vosk, 1980). For move of the children in the present study, achievement test data were available from the schools, and we were interested in assessing the reliability of the relationship of status to achievement, as well as in examining the relationship of achievement to loneliness.

Two different achievement tests, the Comprehensive Test of Basic Skills (CTBS) and the Stanford Diagnostic Reading Test (SDRT), had been administered by the schools approximately 1-2 months prior to our study. CTBS scores were available for 364 of the 506 children in our sample; SDRT scores were available for 293 of the 506 children. To compare students across the various grade levels, percentile rank scores were obtained on these measures and used in the correlational analyses described below. These analyses examined the relationship among achievement, sociometric status, and loneliness for a large subsample of the children included in the study. As in past research, modest but significant correlations were obtained between achievement scores and sociometric status: $r(362) = .27$, $p < .001$, between CTBS scores and standardized play ratings; $r(291) = .19$, $p < .001$, between SDRT scores and standardized play ratings; $r(362) = .20$, $p < .001$, between CTBS scores and the proportion of friendship nominations received; and $r(291) = .14$, $p < .05$, between SDRT scores and the proportion of friendship nominations received. Loneliness was unrelated to SDRT achievement scores, $r(287) = .02$, and only slightly related to CTBS achievement scores, $r(348) = .10$, $p < .05$.

Discussion

Results of this study indicated that children's feelings of loneliness and social dissatisfaction can be reliably measured and that children's feelings about their social relationships do relate to their sociometric status in the classroom. Indeed, the children whose status was lowest reported more loneliness and social dissatisfaction. This suggests that the children who have been

selected in previous intervention research were likely to have been more lonely than their classroom peers.

Still, the overall relation between loneliness and sociometric status was modest. Several explanations can be suggested. As in other areas that rely on self-report measures with children (e.g., Sarason, Davidson, Lighthau, Waite, & Ruebush, 1960), there is the possibility of social desirability or defensiveness on the part of respondents. Many low-status children may have been uneasy about admitting feelings of loneliness or social inadequacy and, instead, responded in a socially desirable fashion. Recent research by Kagan, Hans, Markowitz, Lopez, and Sigal (1982) provide data relevant to this issue. These investigators examined the validity of third graders' self-reports in a number of domains, including popularity among classmates. Kagan et al. found that when children acknowledge negative or undesirable personal attributes these tend to be confirmed by external assessments from peers and teachers. However, using peer and teacher ratings as standards, positive self-evaluations were suspect for about one-third of the sample. These results suggest that, when children do admit to undesirable personal characteristics such as loneliness, the reports are probably valid. However, there may be children who report positive feelings who are in fact experiencing dissatisfaction.

A moderate relation between status and loneliness also may result from sociometric assessment being done only in the child's classroom. Some children identified as unpopular may have friends in other classes or schools (e.g., neighborhood friends), and thus are not particularly lonely or discontent. Similarly, children's parents and siblings may serve as emotional buffers, and satisfactory home relationships may help when school peer relationships are not going as well as they might. We have some anecdotal evidence to support these speculations. In a later sample, individual responses to the loneliness items were discussed with the children in an attempt to understand how children interpreted the statements and how they decided on their responses. It was clear in several cases that children responded to particular items with consideration of their neighborhood and/or family social relations. For example, some children indicated that they did not feel alone because they had brothers or sisters at home or had neighborhood friends with whom they could play. Further research on the relative contributions of parents, siblings, and classroom versus neighborhood peers would be welcome. Also it may be useful to assess children's feelings of loneliness in various relationship and situational contexts (for a recent example of research with adults, see Schmidt & Sermat, 1983). Only two items (1 and 22) in our questionnaire explicitly referred to a school context; others referred to peers but without context, and still others make no mention of peers at all.

It would also be advisable in future research to subclassify unpopular children into those who are rejected and those who are neglected. This long-recognized distinction (e.g., Gronlund & Anderson, 1959) has been difficult to implement because of hesitancy about administering negative nomination measures (e.g., "name three children you don't especially like"). However, recent research by Cole, Dodge, and their colleagues indicates that the distinction is essential. Rejected children are more likely to remain rejected when placed in a new group or new class, whereas neglected children are more likely to become average or even popular (Coie & Dodge, 1983; Coie & Kupersmidt, 1983). Furthermore, the two groups exhibit quite different behavioral styles (e.g., Coie, Dodge, & Coppotelli, 1982; Dodge, 1983; Dodge, Coie, & Brakke, 1982). Overall, it appears that rejected children may be the group particularly at risk for later adjustment problems. Given the findings emerging from this research, it would not be surprising if rejected children report stronger feelings of loneliness than neglected children. This pattern, too, would explain why the overall correlation between status and loneliness, although significant, was not higher.

Finally, it seems important to consider the influence of certain social-cognitive processes that may mediate the relationship between actual peer status and loneliness. Children's awareness of their acceptance by peers may be one important mediating variable. Some unpopular children simply may be unaware of their poor acceptance by peers and, therefore, may not report social dissatisfaction. Another potentially important factor is children's perceptions of the reasons or causes of their difficulties with peers. Research on children's attributions for social success and failure (e.g., Ames, Ames, & Garrison, 1977; Sobol, Scott, & Earn, Note 1) suggests considerable variation in children's causal attributions. Children who attribute social rejection or failure to external causes rather than more internal, personal causes may be less dissatisfied with their personal relationships.

In our discussion of the moderate relationship of sociometric status to loneliness, it should be kept in mind that loneliness is in fact a subjective experience (Peplau, Russell, & Heim, 1979) and cannot be equated with the objective condition of number of friends. From this perspective, the correlation between loneliness and sociometric status will always be far from perfect. Although unpopular children would be expected to feel more dissatisfaction than popular children, all children may feel the need for more social support and intimacy. It is also important not to lose sight of the fact that many children in our study reported being very lonely. Indeed, the number of children reporting extremes of loneliness and social dissatisfaction typically exceeded 10% on each item. This percentage is similar to that obtained with a single question in a recent national survey of 7–11-year-olds in the United States (Zill & Peterson, in press). Our hope is that the present research will serve to stimulate further inquiry into the causes and ramifications of loneliness during childhood.

Reference Note

1. Sobol, M., Scott, C., & Earn, B. *Children's sociometric status and explanations of social experience.* Paper presented at the annual meeting of the American Psychological Association, Los Angeles, August 1981.

References

Ames, R., Ames, C., & Garrison, W. Children's causal ascriptions for positive and negative interpersonal outcomes. *Psychological Reports,* 1977, **41,**595-602.
Asher, S. R., & Hymel, S. Children's social competence in peer relations: Sociometric and behavioral assessment. In J. D. Wine & M. D. Smye (Eds.), *Social competence.* New York: Guilford, 1981.

Asher, S. R., & Renshaw, P. D. Children without friends: Social knowledge and social skill training. In S. R. Asher & J. M. Gottman (Eds.), *The development of children's friendships.* New York: Cambridge University Press, 1981.

Ausubel, D., Schiff, H. M., & Gasser, E. B. A preliminary study of developmental trends in sociempathy: Accuracy of perception of own and others' sociometric status. *Child Development,* 1952, **23,** 111–128.

Coie, J. D., & Dodge, K. A. Continuities and changes in children's social status: A five-year longitudinal study. *Merrill-Palmer Quarterly,* 1983, **29,** 261–282.

Coie, J. D., Dodge, K. A., & Coppotelli, H. Dimensions and types of status: A cross-age perspective. *Developmental Psychology,* 1982, **18,** 557–570.

Coie, J. D., & Kupersmidt, J. B. A behavioral analysis of emerging social status in boys' groups. *Child Development,* 1983, **54,** 1400–1416.

Dodge, K. A. Behavioral antecedents of peer social status. *Child Development,* 1983, **54,** 1386–1399.

Dodge, K. A., Coie, J. D., & Brakke, N. P. Behavioral patterns of socially rejected and neglected preadolescents: The roles of social approach and aggression. *Journal of Abnormal Child Psychology,* 1982, **10,** 389–410.

Glick, O. Some social-emotional consequences of early inadequate acquisition of reading skills. *Journal of Educational Psychology,* 1972, **63,** 253–257.

Gottman, J. M., Gonso, J., & Schuler, P. Teaching social skills to isolated children. *Journal of Abnormal Child Psychology,* 1976, **4,** 179–197.

Green, K. D., Forehand, R., Beck, S. J., & Vosk, B. An assessment of the relationship among measures of children's social competence and children's academic achievement. *Child Development,* 1980, **51,** 1149–1156.

Gresham, F. M., & Nagle, R. J. Social skills training with children: Responsiveness to modeling and coaching as a function of peer orientation. *Journal of Consulting and Clinical Psychology,* 1980, **18,** 718–729.

Gronlund, N. E., & Anderson, L. Personality characteristics of socially accepted, socially neglected, and socially rejected junior high school pupils. *Educational Administration and Supervision,* 1959, **43,** 329–338.

Hartup, W. The peer system. In E. M. Hetherington (Ed.), P. H. Mussen (Series Ed.), *Handbook of child psychology.* (Vol. **4**): *Socialization, personality, and social development.* New York: Wiley, 1983.

Kagan, J., Hans, S., Markowitz, A., Lopez, D., & Sigal, H. Validity of children's self-reports of psychological qualities. In B. Maher (Ed.), *Progress in experimental personality research* (Vol. **2**). New York: Academic Press, 1982.

Ladd, G. W. Effectiveness of a social learning method for enhancing children's social interaction and peer acceptance. *Child Development,* 1981, **52,** 171–178.

LaGreca, A. M., & Santogrossi, D. A. Social skills training with elementary school students: A behavioral group approach. *Journal of Consulting and Clinical Psychology,* 1980, **48,** 220–227.

Oden, S., & Asher, S. R. Coaching children in social skills for friendship making. *Child Development,* 1977, **48,** 495–506.

Peplau, L. A., & Perlman, D. *Loneliness: A sourcebook of current theory, research and therapy.* New York: Wiley, 1982.

Peplau, L. A., Russell, D., & Heim, M. The experience of loneliness. In I. H. Frieze, D. Bar-Tal. & J. S. Carroll (Eds.), *New approaches to social problems: Applications of attribution theory.* San Francisco: Jossey-Bass, 1979.

Putallaz, M., & Gottman, J. M. Conceptualizing social competence in children. In P. Karoly & J. J. Steffen (Eds.) *Improving children's competence: Advances in child behavioral analysis and therapy.* Lexington, Mass.: Heath, 1982.

Sarason, S. B., Davidson, K. S., Lighthau, F. F., Waite, R. R., & Ruebush, B. K. *Anxiety in elementary school children.* New York: Wiley, 1960.

Schmidt, N., & Sermat, V. Measuring loneliness in different relationships. *Journal of Personality and Social Psychology,* 1983, **44,** 1038–1047.

Singleton, L. C., & Asher, S. R. Peer preferences and social interaction among third-grade children in an integrated school district. *Journal of Educational Psychology,* 1977, **69,** 330–336.

Zill, N. *Happy, healthy, and insecure: A portrait of middle childhood in the United States.* New York: Doubleday/Anchor, in press.

Source: Asher, S.R., Hymel, S. and Renshaw, P.D. (1984) Loneliness in children. *Child Development,* 55, 1456-1464. ©1984 by the Society for Research in Child Development, Inc.

Playful and Creative Activities

13

For several weeks after the death of their family dog, the Smith children and their friends gathered occasionally in their basement to play "funeral." Watching one of these play episodes, Mrs. Smith was struck by the degree of imagination involved in the game. None of the children, aged 4 through 8, had been to a funeral, and yet their game was both elaborate and precise. The children had cleverly used common household items to represent the trappings of a funeral ceremony, and their "eulogies" were original, humorous, and very creative.

It was not only the creative aspects of the play, however, that impressed Mrs. Smith. She realized that she was seeing her children use play as a means of understanding and coming to terms with the death of their beloved pet. Apparently they could express in play—their natural language—the confusion and the grief they could not express in other ways. When the funeral games finally stopped a few weeks later, Mr. and Mrs. Smith knew that the children's grief was close to being resolved. Thus, the playful and creative activities of these young children had become for them a way of coping, a way of solving problems.

This chapter deals with children's play and creativity. Play is often thought of as a frivolous activity—a way for children to keep busy when adults are occupied with more urgent matters. As the funeral game in the Smith family's basement indicates, this is far from being the case. Play has significant implications for a child's social, emotional, and intellectual development. Creativity, on the other hand, is widely recognized as the foundation of civilization's highest accomplishments, and the creative process must be understood if we are to foster the development of children capable of original and useful achievements.

The goal of this chapter, therefore, is to describe both the potential value of play for children's development, and the antecedents of adult creativity as expressed in children's playful activities. First the chapter discusses play and creativity separately; then it examines the ways in which the two may be connected. The play-creativity relationship is an aspect of child development that received little attention from psychologists prior to the 1970s. Today, however, it is widely believed that the two are linked. The child's ability to be playful is thought to form the basis of adult creativity and adult problem-solving skills (Hofer 1981; Pepler & Ross 1981; Vandenberg 1980).

What Is Play?

A natural activity for children, play is so interwoven into the fabric of their daily lives that it is often difficult to know where play begins and other activities end. Adults may be able to segment their lives into work and playtime, but the boundaries are less clear for children. Children can easily transform cleaning their room, washing the dishes, or taking out the garbage from work into play; indeed, children sometimes maintain a playful attitude toward everything they do. For these reasons, a clear and consistent definition of play must be established.

For an activity to be thought of as play, it must have a number of characteristics. First, the activity must be *intrinsically motivated.* That is, there are no external reasons for engaging in the activity; it is done only for the sake of doing it. If the only reason a child plays soccer is to win a trophy or to please his or her parents, then the activity is not play; it is work. Second, for an activity to be thought of as play it must be *freely chosen* by the child or children involved. Kindergarteners have been found to regard an activity assigned by their teacher as work, even though they would consider the same activity as play if they had initiated it themselves (Johnson, Christie & Yawkey 1987; King 1979).

A third essential ingredient of play is that it must be *pleasurable* (Garvey 1977). The child, or adult, must enjoy the activity. If a child riding a bicycle is in constant terror of falling off and being hurt, then the activity can hardly be described as playful. A fourth characteristic of play is that it is *nonliteral.* That is, it involves some degree of pretense. Children in a playground may wrestle with each other; the activity is play because it is "pretend" fighting. The children do not intend to hurt each other, at least in the beginning. Finally, play is *actively engaged in.* The player must be physically and/or psychologically involved in the activity, as

*Melissa certainly enjoys looking through the contents of her mother's purse, but
such exploration of relatively unfamiliar objects is not considered play. Once the
objects become familiar she will probably discover imaginative ways of playing with them.*

opposed to being passive or indifferent while the activity is going on (Rubin, Fein & Vandenberg 1983).

When the essential components of play are examined, it becomes obvious that many supposedly playful activities are not play at all. As an example, can we automatically conclude that a child involved in sports is playing? Many sports activities do not meet the definition of play: they may be motivated by external goals, they may not have been freely chosen, and quite often they are not even pleasurable activities for the participants. For some children, involvement in sports is a very serious, stressful, and externally motivated undertaking. In such a case, an activity originally intended as play can often end up being closer in appearance to work.

In defining play, it is also important to distinguish play from exploration. In general, play appears to be a more relaxed, more flexible, less intense, and less stereotypic activity than exploration (Hughes & Hutt 1979; Hughes 1978; Hutt 1979). When children are engaged in exploration, they are more cautious and more resistant to interruption; they have a less variable heart rate and behave in a more stereotypic manner.

A key issue in distinguishing exploration from play is familiarity. Play occurs when the child controls the object or environment and finds novel ways to extend what is already familiar about a toy or an activity or a place. Exploration is a process of transforming new materials and new situations into more familiar ones. The child who is exploring something novel is externally dominated until complexity or unfamiliarity is reduced. At this point, when the materials or situations are safe and familiar, they can be incorporated within established repertoires of play behavior (Rubin, Fein & Vandenberg 1983). The second half of this chapter describes more fully the value of both play and exploration for the creativity of the child.

Developmental Patterns in Play

Play is a major activity in the life of the child, and the characteristics of play reflect the child's level of biological, social, emotional, and intellectual development. Children's play changes from early infancy through the adolescent years. The following discussion incorporates several observations from the work of Jean Piaget.

The First Two Years of Life

Play is observed even in the first weeks of life among infants who are given toys and and allowed to engage in interaction. Much early play is purely physical. Sensorimotor play, or **practice play,** consists of banging rattles, feeling stuffed animals, and mouthing almost anything. Social play, however, can also be found in infant-adult interactions: reciprocal smiling, peekaboo, and vocal expressiveness are games usually initiated by the infant's caretakers. As infants develop, their play becomes more complex, less exploratory, more repetitive, and increasingly self-initiated. After 6 months of age, infants begin to play with more than one object at a time and start to use objects for their appropriate functions (Rosenblatt 1977).

While the first year of life is characterized by sensory and motor play—the simple repetition of actions for the sheer pleasure of doing so—a new element appears in the second year—the element of make-believe. Just as words come to represent objects, empty plates begin to represent steak dinners, mud pies represent food, or an empty box represents a boat.

Pretend play does not emerge all at once, however. Its appearance is a gradual process characterized by several stages (Piaget 1962; Watson &

Jackowitz 1984). The earliest pretend behavior, occurring even at 12 months of age, is usually a solitary activity and involves the performance of actions familiar to the child, such as sleeping, eating, or talking on the telephone. The element of pretense is present because the pretend activities are in no way related to the child's real needs; that is, children may pretend to sleep even when they do not feel at all tired.

A second stage of make-believe occurs when a child begins to substitute one object for another. A block becomes a boat, or an empty cereal bowl serves as a hat. And, finally, the child begins to combine make-believe objects with make-believe action sequences, as when the child pretends that a toy teddy bear is eating pretend food from an empty dish (Johnson, Christie & Yawkey 1987).

While the earliest forms of symbolic play usually occur when the child is alone, the more sophisticated pretend play is often a social activity. Toward the end of the second year, children become interested in watching the play of their peers (*onlooker play*) or in playing independently beside them (*parallel play*), but they do not yet engage in genuine interactive behaviors (Rubin, Maoni & Hornung 1976). Solitary play gradually gives way to mature social play with peers, but this will not occur until the child is between 3 and 4 years of age.

What value does the play of infants have for their later development? Sensorimotor play may contribute to the advancement of perceptual awareness and muscular coordination (both fine-motor and gross-motor skills). Playful vocalization, or "sound play," can stimulate the acquisition of the phonemic, morphemic, syntactic, semantic, and pragmatic rules described in Chapter 9. Social play with parents may enhance bonding and the desire for human relationships. And, finally, all repetitive play serves to consolidate infants' understanding of newly developed concepts in their social and physical environment.

Early Childhood

The preschool years have typically been considered the golden age of play. **Symbolic, or fantasy, play** is particularly characteristic of early childhood, but mastery of physical skills and an increasing interest in social play compete with the time spent at pretense. On a physical level, the improving dexterity of preschool children makes possible large-muscle play activities such as throwing a ball, climbing a ladder, or jumping on the furniture, as well as small-muscle activities such as cutting with a scissors, painting with a brush, or stringing beads.

Preschool children's social play also matures considerably. Play involving other children occurs more often and becomes more complex. The size of children's play groups increases, and preschoolers become increasingly selective in choosing their playmates. Five-year-olds prefer playmates of their own age, sex, and developmental level; the undiscriminating 2-year-old will play with anybody who is willing (Parten 1933).

The solitary, onlooker, and parallel play of the 1- and 2-year-old is enhanced by the addition of associative and cooperative play (Parten 1933). *Associative play* involves sharing and taking turns ("I'll lend you my red paint if I can borrow your green") and *cooperative play* involves working together with other children on a common activity and with common goals. Dramatic play (playing "house" or "supermarket") requires cooperation because, unless everyone agrees to play his or her assigned role, the game cannot proceed.

The make-believe world of early childhood can be classified according to three different types of roles: (1) functional, (2) relational, and (3) character (Garvey, 1977). Functional roles are defined by particular plans of action (e.g., fighting a fire). Relational roles are family roles (e.g., mommy, daddy, baby). Finally, character roles are those defined by occupation, habitual behaviors, or personality features, and include real (e.g., bride, doctor) and fictional (e.g., Cookie Monster) characters. Relational roles, according to Garvey and Berndt (1977), are the roles most frequently enacted by preschoolers.

Unlike the often solitary pattern of activity found in the younger child, the make-believe play of the preschooler typically involves friends. Johnson and Ershler (1981), for example, reported that between 70 and 80 percent of the pretend play of 3- to 4-year-olds occurs in groups. This pattern continues to evolve throughout early childhood and does not reverse until the early elementary school years (Rubin, Watson & Jambor 1978).

Another progression in the pretend play of preschoolers, regardless of solitary or group setting, is the movement away from a literal form of object substitution. Older preschoolers are increasingly able to use their imaginations and to symbolize absent objects or places rather flexibly (Elder & Pederson 1978; Overton & Jackson 1973). In fact, as playmates become more familiar with each other, their fantasy behavior is significantly less realistic (Matthews 1977). There is a movement away from a preoccupation with familiar themes—such as playing out the roles of doctors, teachers, or mommies and daddies—to an interest in themes far removed from the child's everyday experiences. For example, children graduate to playing roles of storybook characters or characters from their own imaginations (Johnson, Christie & Yawkey 1987).

A similar development toward greater flexibility in play has been observed by Mueller and Lucas (1975). They described how the social-fantasy play of preschoolers is extremely ritualized at the start of early childhood, but becomes much less so as the children develop. As an illustration, young preschoolers imitate the dialogue and actions of their friends quite literally:

> Rachel: My bunny is going down the slide.
> Jennifer: My teddy is going down the slide.

Older preschoolers more easily vary the structure of their conversations and the different behaviors their words are narrating:

> Johnny: My truck is climbing over the mountain.
> Bobby: My boat is going across the river.

Both the freedom from ritual and the abstraction from object reality illustrate the preschool child's gradually maturing cognitive abilities.

What is the value of make-believe play for the preschool child? In attempting to answer the question, Singer (1973) emphasized the development of self-confidence and self-regulation. He suggested that lengthy involvement in pretense leads to improvements in concentration and reflective thought. Further implications of pretend play for the development of creativity will be explored later in this chapter. For now, it can be said that the functions of early childhood play, and especially that involving make-believe, may be more significant for individual development than is the earlier play of the infant and the toddler.

Middle Childhood and Adolescence

Two issues dominate the study of play during the middle-childhood and adolescent years. First, it becomes difficult to observe such behavior as the times and locations of these children at play are increasingly remote from adult supervision. Children beyond the preschool age tend to be more private about their activities, often deliberately retreating as far as possible from parental interference. Second, genuine play behaviors begin to be subordinated to and absorbed within more structured and worklike tasks. The amount of time available for play is reduced by the time needed for chores around the home, part-time jobs, school-related activities and homework, organized sports, music or dance lessons, and so forth.

A major change occurs in play as children develop from preschool age to the early elementary school years. Symbolic, or make-believe, play gradually declines and games-with-rules begin to appear. **Games-with-rules** have two essential characteristics. First, they involve at least two players who compete with each other for the purpose of winning the game. Second, the behavior of the players is regulated by a strict set of rules that either are made up for the occasion or are handed down from one generation of children to another (Rubin, Fein & Vandenberg 1983). Games-with-rules include formal games such as baseball or basketball, informal games such as tag or tug-of-war, or even superstitious rituals shared by children (e.g., "Step on a crack; break your mother's back").

Games-with-rules appear, not surprisingly, at the same time as the emergence of logical thinking—the beginning of Piaget's stage of concrete operations (see Chapter 6 for a discussion of this concept). They are increasingly in evidence from kindergarten until the end of fifth grade, after which they begin to decline in frequency (Eifermann 1971; Hetherington, Cox & Cox, 1979; Rubin, Fein & Vandenberg 1983; Rubin & Krasnor 1980).

What is their function? Ellis (1973) suggested that being required to play by the established rules of the group helps children to overcome the self-centeredness of the preschool years. It also encourages them to become more socially mature.

Many psychologists, however, question whether these games should be considered play at all. For example, Garvey (1977) maintained that games-with-rules do not qualify as genuine play because they are relatively inflexible, tradition-dominated, goal-directed, competitive, formalized, and explicit. They lack the characteristic of spontaneity, and the goal of winning goes beyond the sheer enjoyment of the activity in itself.

While games-with-rules dominate their activities, school-aged children also participate in activities that more easily fit the definition of play offered at the beginning of this chapter. For example, children still engage in a great deal of goal-free functional play (e.g., shooting baskets, throwing a ball around, riding a bicycle). Constructive play with materials such as blocks, plastic bricks, models, and clay continues throughout this period. In addition, children engage in much wandering about the neighborhood, which is not specifically exploratory or goal-directed. Even fantasy play continues throughout the middle-childhood period. An 8-year-old boy might dress up like Superman and fly around the neighborhood faster than a speeding bullet.

Middle-childhood play should be encouraged because it provides expressive freedom and opportunities for both solitary behavior and comfortable social experiences for children. This is particularly necessary when we consider the competitive and more structured academic environment children encounter in school, the daily hours of passive television viewing, and the highly organized rules of formal games.

Many of the characteristics of middle-childhood play also apply to the adolescent. Functional and fantasy play are further absorbed by more organized activities. Games-with-rules remain important in increasingly complex forms—athletic teams, school clubs (e.g., debating, theater, and community services), video arcades, and board games (e.g., chess, Scrabble, and Dungeons and

Much of adolescent play behavior consists of "hanging out" with friends, talking, teasing, and simply relaxing.

Dragons). Nevertheless, playful behavior does exist in spontaneous and unstructured ways. In a physical sense, there are wrestling matches among the boys. Then, there are teasing games between girls and boys, and much same- or mixed-sex language play for all teenagers (see Chapter 9). The largest proportion of adolescent play seems to occur in the arena of verbal behavior. This may have social, cognitive, and linguistic functions, but primarily adolescents have fun relating verbally with, showing off to, and teasing their peers. Thus, the play of adolescents is not always visible to developmental researchers, but it contributes to a balance of relaxation and enjoyment with the more serious and stressful aspects of maturation.

Why Children Play: An Examination of Theories

There is no one simple answer as to why children play. However, a number of theoretical views, in combination, emphasize the value of play for a child's social, emotional, physical, and intellectual development. No one theory should be considered complete or totally correct. Instead, each should be thought of as contributing pieces to a puzzle yet to be solved. Table 13.1 summarizes the play theories discussed in this section.

Early Theories

In the late 1800s and early 1900s, a number of theories of play were expressed. They all had in

Table 13.1 Theories of Play

Theory	Reasons for Play	Area of Greatest Benefits
Surplus Energy H. Spencer	To discharge natural energy of the body	Physical
Renewal of Energy G.T.W. Patrick	To avoid boredom while the natural motor functions of the body are restored	Physical
Recapitulation G.S. Hall	To relive periods in the evolutionary history of the human species	
Practice for Adult Living K. Groos	To develop skills and knowledge necessary for functioning as an adult	Physical, intellectual
Psychoanalytic S. Freud A. Freud E. Erikson	To reduce objective and instinctual anxiety by giving a child a sense of control over the world and an acceptable way to express forbidden instincts	Emotional, social
Cognitive J. Bruner J. Piaget B. Sutton-Smith	To facilitate general cognitive development To "consolidate" learning that has already taken place while allowing for the possibility of new learnings in a relaxed atmosphere	Intellectual, social
Arousal Modulation D.E. Berlyne	To keep the body at an optimal state of arousal To relieve boredom and to reduce uncertainty	Emotional, physical
Bateson's Theory G. Bateson	To help a child to distinguish between reality and imagination To facilitate social interaction	Social, intellectual

common a belief that play was natural to the human organism and that it fulfilled some biological function in a child's development. For example, British philosopher Herbert Spencer (1873) suggested the *surplus energy theory*: every human being is supplied by nature with a certain amount of energy to be used in efforts at survival. Any energy not used up must be discharged somehow, and children do this by playing.

An opposite interpretation of play was offered by G.T.W. Patrick (1916), who thought that play would occur only when the child is relaxed and fatigued. Thus, play allows for the *renewal of energy,* avoiding idle boredom while waiting for the natural motor functions to be restored. G. Stanley

Hall's *recapitulation theory* was discussed in Chapter 1. He believed that the child's individual development parallels the evolutionary development of the human species, and so a child's play reflects our species development. For example, the hunting and chasing games of grade schoolers mirror an age in human history when people lived in caves and hunted and gathered in order to survive.

The German philosopher Karl Groos (1901) saw children's play as *practice for adult living*. In play, the child rehearses skills that will be needed later on, just as the play fighting of young animals prepares them for hunting as adults.

Early theories of play were limited because each seemed to explain only a small aspect of the range of children's playful activities. What is more, they were all based on unscientific views of human instincts and human evolution, and numerous exceptions could be found to challenge each of them (Johnson, Christie & Yawkey 1987). For example, parents often notice that their children will play to the point of total exhaustion (therefore discharging their "surplus energy") and then get up and begin to play again!

These older theories did stimulate an interest in children's play and in its adaptive significance, and in some cases they contain elements of accuracy. For example, while no one today would accept the view that the *only* function of play is to prepare children for adulthood, some play does have this function: for example, a child playing house could learn something about family roles that might be useful later on.

Contemporary Theories

Modern theories emphasize the psychological rather than the physical significance of play. The psychoanalytic theory, with its view of play as anxiety reduction, stresses the emotional and social benefits. Cognitive theories, on the other hand, emphasize the intellectual value. Perhaps the best approach to keep in mind while examining contemporary theories is that each looks at play in relation to a particular aspect of children's development. As stated earlier, no one theory is completely correct; but, if taken as a whole, the combination of theories provides much information about the value of play.

Psychoanalytic Theory

According to Sigmund Freud's psychoanalytic view, play is an activity used by the child to help reduce anxiety (Freud 1974). Infants and children experience two types of anxiety. *Objective anxiety* occurs because children realize they are helpless in dealing with the huge, adult-controlled world. Play can alleviate this anxiety by giving children added strength, by providing them with at least the illusion of power and control. For the infant, a rattle might become an extension of the self, allowing the child to manipulate and control the environment more effectively. Preschoolers extend themselves through play not just physically, but psychologically as well. For example, they can reduce the large and powerful world to a size they can handle by building with blocks or by playing with dolls or miniature toys. Fantasy play allows them to transform the world into a less threatening environment. The child who is frightened of monsters becomes one, and frightens other children. Children who feel that their parents are unfair become parents to their toys—symbolically reversing an anxiety-producing situation. The child who is disturbed by conflicts at home role-plays domestic scenes with happier endings.

The second major anxiety of early childhood is *instinctual anxiety* (Freud 1974). Children fear expressing instincts forbidden by society. These include anger, unreasonable fears, sexual curiosities, and the need to be messy or destructive. Play allows children to confront and explore antisocial instincts in socially acceptable ways. For example, breaking a dish or throwing a rock through a window are unacceptable behaviors, and the feeling of destructiveness that motivated them is equally condemned. However, when a child builds towers of blocks or sand castles and then proceeds to destroy them with great enthusiasm, this destructiveness is acceptable to most adults.

The psychoanalytic view is also represented by Erik Erikson (1963). Taking a more developmental approach than Freud did, Erikson stated that children play in order to master bodily and social skills rather than to relieve anxiety. During the first year of life, the child's behavior is referred to as **autocosmic play** because it involves exploration of the bodily self. Talking, walking, looking, listening, and playing with one's hands or feet illustrate such play. In **microsphere play,** during the second year of life, the child's world is expanded to include an examination of toys and other objects. Such play enables the child to acquire actual mastery over the world, not simply mastery through the power of fantasy. Finally, the preschool child engages in **macrosphere play,** building on the physical manipulations of body and objects to learn about social interaction. The sharing of reality and fantasy with other children represents an important step in the child's capacity to understand the culture.

Cognitive Theories

Cognitive theorists typically regard play as a tool that facilitates general cognitive development. For example, both Jerome Bruner (1972) and Brian Sutton-Smith (1967) believe that play allows a child to solve problems in a relatively stress-free and relaxed atmosphere and that these experiences may be useful later on when the child is faced with more complex real-life problems.

According to Jean Piaget (1962), play is the dominance of assimilation, (the incorporation of reality into the child's cognitive structures) over accommodation (the changing of the child's cognitive structures in response to environmental input). To understand assimilation-without-accommodation, consider the following example: in the mind of a child at play, an empty box becomes a boat sailing on the ocean. An accommodation to reality would involve the recognition that the box is really just a box, but the child does not conform to reality. Instead, reality is made to conform to the child's view of it, and this is "pure" assimilation.

Since intellectual development requires adaptation, and since adaptation requires both assimilation and accommodation, it follows that for Piaget, play is not the equivalent of intellectual development. In fact, Piaget wrote about the difference between play and "serious adaptation," with play involving the repetition of an activity which has *already* been learned, for the sake of itself. As an example, he cited the case of the 3-month-old boy who threw his head back to look at the world from an unusual position. Initially, this behavior involved serious learning, but soon the child lost interest in the result and threw his head back time and again, laughing loudly, for the sheer enjoyment of the activity. The activity had become play.

Play in Piaget's theory has been thought of as a form of "consolidation": an activity is first learned (adaptation) and is then repeated over and over again (play) as a means of incorporating the new activity into the child's previously learned activity patterns (Rubin, Fein & Vandenberg 1983; Sutton-Smith 1985). As an illustration of the concept of consolidation, consider the case of the little girl who learns how to "pump" on a swing so that

she can keep herself in motion without needing to be continually pushed. After the learning has taken place, the child consolidates the activity, repeating it over and over again in the same way, and also introducing variations (e.g., swinging while standing up, swinging on her stomach).

While play is not the same as learning in Piaget's theory, play can lead to learning. This can be illustrated by an examination of Piaget's three types of play, corresponding roughly to his stages of cognitive development. Sensorimotor, or practice, play is characteristic of the first twelve months of life. As mentioned earlier, *practice play* is the intrinsically satisfying repetition of simple, motoric skills. Infants learn to master their own bodies and to manipulate the objects in their environment. Playing with balls, rattles, spoons, and cups is not only an enjoyable pastime; these activities also may enable the infant to grasp the nature of physical reality.

By the second and third years of life, sensorimotor play is merged with an increasing proportion of make-believe, or symbolic, play. *Symbolic play* differs from real learning, but Piaget believed that the second often follows from the first. For example, in the process of symbolic play, a child might imagine that a stone or a piece of wood is a house, but the same child might then develop an interest in making the house as realistic as possible. He or she might make a serious attempt to reproduce the house faithfully with blocks or clay. Therefore, what had begun as symbolic play gradually became a serious learning project, a constructive game, which Piaget saw as falling on a continuum somewhere between symbolic play and adaptation.

The third type of play, *games-with-rules,* emerges as the child attains the level of concrete operational thought. With firmer notions about reality and decreasing egocentrism, the child's play can become both more social and more logical. At this point, fantasy play diminishes and becomes subordinated to games-with-rules. The play of older children and adolescents begins to resemble the interactions of adults, in which shared communication, organized cooperation and competition, and more sophisticated strategies prevail. Or-

The simple repetition of motor activities, such as the shaking of a rattle by this four-month-old girl, is an example of what Piaget called sensorimotor, or practice, play.

ganized sports now become very popular—as do board games requiring mental skill, such as Monopoly® and checkers, and games requiring physical dexterity, such as hopscotch and Pacman®. The games of concrete operational children require skill, intelligence, and, above all, knowledge of the rules. Children who cheat or who simply do not know the rules of the game may find themselves quickly excluded from the organized games of their peers.

Arousal Modulation Theory

According to the arousal modulation theory of play developed by D.E. Berlyne (1969), a drive in the human central nervous system keeps our bodies at an optimal level of arousal. Extremely high or extremely low levels of stimulation create feelings of uncertainty or boredom. Exploratory play can relieve boredom while repetitive play can reduce uncertainty. This position is related to the psychoanalytic approach to play as tension reduction. Berlyne, however, emphasizes the optimum state of arousal within the central nervous system rather than the presence of intrapsychic conflict. Other researchers (e.g., Ellis 1973; Fein 1981) have proposed variations of Berlyne's model. They focus more on increasing arousal, as well as the conscious control a child may have over the arousal mechanism.

Bateson's Theory

A very different interpretation of play, although not inconsistent with arousal theory, has been promoted by Gregory Bateson (1972). He believes that the make-believe play of children enables them to communicate about the symbols of their culture. The opportunity to distinguish between reality and imagination is more important for the child than is the actual content of playful behaviors. Children who are *pretending* to fight or to go to the doctor are communicating with each other and understanding their world in a different way than they would by actually engaging in these activities. Thus it is the element of make-believe as well as the messages and negotiations during play that create a framework for understanding interpersonal relationships.

The Context of Play

There may be many reasons why children play, but one fact is certain. A child's play always occurs within a social and cultural context. By looking at cross-cultural differences in play, we can realize the influence of a culture's needs and values on the play of its children. This section also evaluates differences within a culture and the impact of parents, peers, and physical surroundings on children's play activities.

Cross-cultural Differences

Children's play is found in virtually every culture in the world, but the amount of play, the type of play, and the complexity of the games vary widely. The study of play in any particular culture provides much information about the nature of the culture itself. The following sections discuss cultural differences in the amount of competitive play and in the types of games children play.

Competition Versus Cooperation

A general finding of the cross-cultural research on play is that the most primitive cultures, where survival is a day-to-day affair, have the lowest overall amount of play, whereas technologically advanced societies have the most. In addition, simpler cultures seem to emphasize cooperation in play, whereas more complex Westernized societies, such as that of the United States, put greater emphasis on competition (Kagan & Madsen 1972; Knight & Kagan 1977; Shapera 1976; Sutton-Smith 1980). Perhaps the differences in cooperative versus competitive play reflect the larger cultural val-

ues of the societies in question. In more primitive cultures, people need to cooperate within their family units simply to survive. In a subsistence economy, the child who competes for more than his or her share of food is criticized, and competitive, aggressive behavior serves no adaptive purpose. In more advanced cultures, however, the "breadwinner" often must compete outside the home to ensure the economic survival of the family (Madsen 1971). Thus, competition is more highly valued in such cultures, and this value seems to be reflected in children's play.

In addition to economic conditions, the amount of cooperation versus competition in children's play reflects the society's political philosophy. For example, Bronfenbrenner (1972) observed that competitive play is rarely found in the Soviet Union, where the government emphasizes the submission of individual needs to those of the state. Soviet caregivers stress cooperation, group loyalty, and group dependence. Soviet children are urged to play group games and are often provided with complex toys that work only if two or three children play with them at once. But, in the United States, where the government encourages free enterprise, competitive play is extensively seen. Child rearing emphasizes individual development and individual achievement. However, even within the United States certain child-rearing values increase the likelihood of cooperative play behavior; children raised in a commune, with an emphasis on communal property and communal achievements, have been found to engage in little competitive play (Plattner & Minturn 1975).

Types of Organized Games

When the organized competitive games of a culture are analyzed, differences in cultural values and environmental experiences become clear. As noted in the previous section, competitive games are emphasized more heavily in some cultures than in others, but most cultures have at least some element of competition. Sutton-Smith (1981) identified three types of competitive games and described the cultures in which these games are found:

1. *Games of physical skill.* The outcome—win, lose, or draw—is determined only by the players' motor skills. A foot race is an example of such a game.

Hockey is a game of physical skill, of chance, and of strategy. As such, it reflects the values of American society. However, if the game becomes too serious and stressful for a child, it may resemble work more than play.

2. *Games of chance.* The outcome is determined by a guess or a chance occurrence such as a lucky roll of the dice or spin of the wheel.
3. *Games of strategy.* The outcome is determined by the players' intellectual skills and by rational choices made during the course of the game.

Cultures that are highly complex, technologically advanced, and characterized by clearly defined social-class groupings typically have all three types of games, and typically emphasize games of strategy. In such cultures—and the United States is included—children have much to learn as they grow up, and Sutton-Smith (1980) believes that games of strategy are adaptive in societies in which people must use their wits to get ahead in life.

Games of physical skill are the only competitive games found in primitive cultures with subsistence economies, while games of chance are most often found in wandering cultures whose survival depends on uncontrollable factors, such as the weather. Thus, the risks of life are reflected in the children's games as well.

Games and Cultural Values

Cross-cultural research on children's play reveals much about the cultures in which the children live. The type of play a culture emphasizes is related, perhaps not surprisingly, to cultural values. American parents who discourage aggressive, competitive sports for their children might be interested in an analysis by Montague and Morais (1976) of the relationship between football and the adult world of work in the United States. Football is a game requiring physical skill, chance, and a great deal of strategy. As in the business world, football emphasizes hard work, dedication, teamwork, and competition. In both areas there is a strict hierarchical organization; players must know their places, their status, and how to play their roles. Both activities require team efforts, but both reward individuals for exceptional performance or blame them for their failings. On the negative side, both football and business involve a degree of manipulation and dishonesty as players attempt to trick their opponents. Whether or not we accept the details of the football-work relationship, the point is similar to that made in much of the cross-cultural research: the games of a society did not develop accidentally; the play of children reflects the values of adults.

Family and Peer Influences

Just as playful activities vary from culture to culture, they may also vary within a culture. Family values and peer-group interaction influence the type and amount of play.

In the United States, one area of variation is fantasy play. Fantasy play may be especially encouraged by certain parents, whereas other parents tend not to promote this imaginative play. The support for fantasy play, however, must be fairly subtle because parents typically do not initiate, join in, or extend these behaviors (Dunn & Wooding 1977). Instead, children are more likely to express their imaginations if they have been provided with a safe and responsive social environment (Arend, Gove & Sroufe 1979; Freyberg 1973; Matas, Arend & Sroufe 1978; Rubin, Fein & Vandenberg 1983; Singer 1973). Children do not need their parents to teach them how to engage in fantasy play but rather to establish secure attachments that will naturally lead them to exploration and imaginative expression. Nevertheless, Garvey (1977) suggested that adults can increase the extent to which children use fantasy in their play "by providing role-playing models, suggesting relations between roles and plans, proposing imaginative solutions, and using evocative toys over a period of time" (p. 98). (See the Research Close-up "The Effects of Divorce on Children's Play" for additional comments on the influence of families.)

The relatively sparse yet consistent research on peer influences has suggested that the degree of familiarity a child has with his or her peers is the primary variable in determining play behavior (Rubin, Fein & Vandenberg 1983). Toddlers seem to play at a more sophisticated cognitive level with friends than by themselves (Rubenstein & Howes 1976). Preschool children interact more frequently and in a more complex manner when playing with familiar—as compared with unfamiliar—peers (Doyle, Connolly & Rivest 1980). Since the research on peer influences on play has largely investigated fantasy play, similarity between peer and parent effects on the child's play can be noted. A child who is secure with a parent or a friend senses an atmosphere of acceptance and freedom in which make-believe play can flourish.

The Physical Setting

Not only is children's play influenced by diverse cultural, socioeconomic, family, and peer contexts but also the physical context is significant. One simple example is the effect of spatial density on playful activity. McGrew (1972) noted less running and less physical contact as the amount of play space was reduced. Smith and Connolly (1976) also found less rough-and-tumble play with decreasing play space. In contrast, reducing spatial density leads to an increase in imaginative play (Peck & Goldman 1978).

The type of materials or objects in the play environment will determine, in part, how children play. For instance, nonsocial play in preschoolers is associated with clay, crayons, paints, and scissors; whereas cars, blocks, and dress-up materials

Research Close-up

The Effects of Divorce on Children's Play

In view of the current high-divorce rate, approximately 50 percent of our children are likely to spend at least some of their growing years dealing with a relatively stressful home environment (see Chapter 11). As part of a two-year longitudinal study on family reactions to divorce, Hetherington, Cox, and Cox (1979) examined the impact of divorce on children's play.

The researchers followed the development of twenty-four boys and twenty-four girls from white, middle-class backgrounds who

were in the custody of their mothers. These children were matched with a control group consisting of an equal number of boys and girls who were attending the same preschool programs but whose parents were not divorced. At the beginning of the study, the children were approximately 4 years of age. By the end of the period, the average age of the children was nearly 6 years.

Each child was observed for six half-hour sessions at two months, one year, and two years after the parents were divorced. Observers saw the children in both classroom and playground free-play situations. They rated the play behaviors according to social and cognitive categories, as well as for emotional state, imaginative processes, fantasy themes, and other related factors.

Hetherington, Cox, and Cox reported that the play patterns of children from divorced homes were more fragmented and less socially or intellectually mature than those of the control group. The imaginative play of children from divorced homes was more restricted, and boys in particular had trouble assuming roles in dramatic play. The play of boys also showed considerably more aggression.

From this study, it becomes clear that the influences of a family on the play of children are considerable. It is also clear that an analysis of play can help psychologists understand the stresses that a particular child is going through at any given time.

encourage more social and fantasy play. Rubin & Seibel (1981) observed objects used in different ways, depending on whether or not the child was alone. Blocks, for example, were used more frequently for construction when children were alone but became the materials for fantasy play in group interactions. Campbell and Frost (1978) observed that at a playground with traditional equipment (i.e., conventional swings and seesaws), 7-year-olds played in a typical way. In contrast, at a creative playground (i.e., with mobile and unusual equipment), the children engaged in significantly more imaginative play.

Of course, whether children play indoors or outdoors influences play activities. Sanders and Harper (1976) found that older preschoolers preferred to spend more time playing outdoors than did younger preschoolers. Furthermore, the out-

door play of the older preschoolers took on a greater fantasy quality than did the outdoor play of the younger preschoolers. Smith and Connolly (1972) have observed more rough-and-tumble play outdoors than indoors, and boys were especially vigorous in their outdoor activity. The girls tended to play in smaller groups, somewhat more quietly, and in closer proximity to playground equipment or supervising adults.

The Construct of Creativity

Defining, evaluating, and predicting creativity are tasks that generate much interest among psychologists, but little agreement. There is agreement, however, that the study of creativity somehow deals with the essence of development. As

The quality of play is greatly influenced by the physical setting. Children play more imaginatively in creative playgrounds than in those that contain more traditional equipment.

Kogan (1983) pointed out, creativity is a major value in practically every literate society ever known.

Creativity is difficult to define because it is a complex construct, or concept, containing three related elements. It is a *personality characteristic*, and an *intellectual process*, and it results in a type of *product*. In the first sense, creativity is a way of being, an attitude toward the world and the self that reflects the personality characteristics of flexibility, spontaneity, curiosity, and persistence. In the second sense, it is a way of thinking, an intellectual approach to solving problems. Finally, a creative product can be defined as any original contribution to the appreciation, understanding, or improvement of the human condition. (In this last sense of creativity as a product, it is generally more accurate to describe children and adolescents

as having the potential for being creative rather than as actually producing creative works.)

The Creative Personality

A common belief about the personalities of creative children is that they are highly neurotic, at least bizarre, and possibly even frightening. Actually, this is not the case at all. Although some well-known creative individuals, such as Vincent van Gogh and Edgar Allan Poe, seem to have developed little emotional control, most children or adults designated as creative are psychologically quite healthy (Gough 1979; Kubie 1958; Maslow 1964). Creative individuals who are emotionally disturbed are creative despite their personality handicaps, and not as a result of them.

A number of personality characteristics differentiate the creative from the less creative child during the elementary and high school years. These include persistence, high-energy levels, self-confidence, independence of judgment, flexibility and openness to new experiences, tolerance of ambiguity, and a good sense of humor. Also, creative children seem to be aware and accepting of their feelings, playfully curious about their world, and less attached to conventional sex-role stereotypes (Barron & Harrington 1981; Janos & Robinson 1985). Such characteristics may not describe the typical child, but they can hardly be labeled as unhealthy. This creative outlook on life seems to be fostered by parents who are not overly strict, who encourage the child's independence, and who are not excessively concerned with neatness, obedience, or emotional control (Nichols 1964; Schaefer 1961).

The Creative Process

Besides knowing the personality characteristics of creative children, it is also essential to identify the mental processes that bring about the production of new ideas and material creations. A popular belief is that a creative person waits around for a brilliant solution to instantly occur. For example, Sir Isaac Newton supposedly discovered the principle of gravity while he was sitting under an apple tree. Blind luck, however, can play only a small role in creativity. Austin (1978) proposed that both chance and creativity depend on an exploratory style, a highly prepared mind, and persistent activity. To illustrate this point, Mozart's brilliant musical compositions were not due to a flash of insight, but instead were the result of a long process of developing an incredible grasp of symphonic structure, an accurate memory for melodic themes, and a great flexibility in perceiving tonal relationships (Gardner 1982a).

Thus, the processes of creativity sound like a variation of the definition of intelligence. In fact, much of the research on creative thinking has attempted to distinguish the concept of intelligence from that of creativity. How are creativity and intelligence related? There appears to be no more than a modest correlation between intelligence and

creativity. Put simply, high levels of intelligence do not guarantee creativity, but at least average intelligence is necessary to be creative. Creativity is unlikely in a person of low intelligence (Barron & Harrington 1981).

A major task for researchers interested in the creative process is to determine which cognitive skills are necessary for creativity. Guilford (1967), whose theory of intellectual functioning was discussed in Chapter 8, suggested that creativity involves **divergent thinking,** the ability to branch out from a starting point to reach a variety of possibilities. The opposite is **convergent thinking,** the ability to bring bits of information together to come up with a single correct solution. To illustrate these concepts, asking in what year George Washington crossed the Delaware River requires a child to use convergent thinking, because only one answer is correct. Creativity is not involved in coming up with an answer. Asking how Washington might have felt as he crossed the river requires the child to use divergent thinking; there is no correct answer, and the child can be quite creative in considering a variety of possibilities.

The convergent-divergent distinction in defining the creative process is appealing, but research on this model has produced mixed results (Kogan 1983; Wallach 1985). Because divergent thinking is itself composed of several subprocesses—quantity of free-flowing ideas, flexibility of alternative solutions, elaboration of the ideas generated, and novelty of the proposed solutions—it is not surprising that inconclusive results have been reported. Moreover, the tasks used to assess divergent thinking (e.g., "In addition to holding pieces of paper together, what other ways can you think of to use a paper clip?") frequently are not very motivating to a child. An evaluation of a divergent-thinking assessment is presented in Issues in Child Development "How Do We Test Creativity?"

Convergent thinking, which is frequently related to traditional intelligence-test results, has been incorrectly viewed as having little significance for creativity. Hudson (1966) claimed that divergent thinking may be characteristic of creativity in the arts but convergent thinking is essential to creativity in the sciences. Actually, both divergent and convergent thinking seem to be required for all

Issues in Child Development

How Do We Test Creativity?

Tests of creativity are at a very early stage of development, perhaps because of the difficulty of defining the construct. However, one creativity test is frequently administered to children: the *Torrance Tests of Creative Thinking* (TTCT). The TTCT were developed more than two decades ago by psychologist E. Paul Torrance (1962; 1966). He conducted his work within the context of stimulating divergent thinking through educational experiences. Keep in mind that Torrance's approach does not emphasize personality factors or the actual production of creative works.

The TTCT include versions of a picture form and a verbal form, each containing several subtests. Picture subtests ask the test taker to complete or construct drawings and to label them. Verbal subtests require, for example, guessing consequences, improving products, and suggesting unusual uses for ordinary objects. ("How many uses can you think of for a brick?"). Each subtest may be scored for at least two of the fol-

lowing four categories: fluency (the number of responses), flexibility (the variety of responses), originality (the novelty of responses), and elaboration (the amount of detail provided). According to Torrance, these tests may be used for children from kindergarten age through the high school years and beyond. The verbal subtests may be administered orally for children prior to the fourth grade. The entire test battery can be completed in approximately seventy-five minutes; most children enjoy the challenge.

Technically, the TTCT receive mixed reviews from specialists in psychological assessment. Weaknesses of these tests include

- the inappropriateness of timed-tests for creative thinking
- the problems of the scoring-system criteria
- the inconsistent relationships between test scores and real-world creativity
- the limitations of predicting adult creativity from childhood test scores.

However, favorable reactions to the TTCT include

- the clear instructions and interesting format
- the satisfactory consistency over extended times of measurement
- the adequate relationship with other means of assessing creativity
- the low relationship with standard measures of intelligence in order to distinguish between the two constructs.

Balancing the positive and negative evaluations of the TTCT, users should probably be cautious in their interpretations of the results (Anastasi 1982; Chase 1985; Gronlund 1985; Treffinger 1985).

How can creativity tests like the TTCT be used? The individual test results should not be used to make decisions for a child in the absence of other information concerning creativity. They may be used, according to the author and test publisher (Scholastic Testing Service, 1985-1986), for assessing programs, for creating an awareness of potential, for individualizing instruction, and, ultimately, for understanding the processes of creative thinking.

---

forms of creativity, although this may not always be apparent to the casual observer.

Beyond divergent thinking, other mental processes thought to be involved in creativity include the tendency to form unusual associations, to relax conscious thought in order to gain access to more primitive modes of cognition, to use analogical and metaphorical reasoning, to formulate visual im-

ages, and to ask original questions (Barron & Harrington 1981).

The Creative Product

As mentioned earlier, a child can have a creative personality and can engage in creative mental processes, but it is doubtful that children really

This young boy's drawings are imaginative and colorful, but are not usually defined as creative products. They are not seen as "original contributions to the appreciation, understanding, or improvement of the human condition."

produce creative products. Their products may be skillful, cute, unusual, and imaginative, but they are never creative in the real-world sense of Michelangelo's sculpture, Dostoyevski's novels, or Einstein's theories. Even the musical compositions Mozart wrote prior to the age of 20 are regarded more for their historical interest than as examples of extraordinary creativity.

Kogan (1973) stated that "there is reason to doubt that a creativity criterion can be found at the elementary school level that is more 'real' than the performance on divergent-thinking tasks" (p. 155). Thus, the issue of creative potential versus creative production, which is also of relevance to adolescents who have not yet expressed their potential, remains a problem. Gowan (1977) suggested that the potential to be creative as an adult may be found in the gifted child. However, not every gifted child will become a creative adult, and likewise, all creative adults were not gifted children (Gruber 1982). We can review the creative work of historical figures and judge the timeless quality of a painting or a poem; we can also judge the value of a biological or a sociological theory. However, what products can we use to predict which childhood "creators" will be viewed as creative in the future? Perhaps our best hope at this point is to adopt the evolving-systems approach of Wallace (1985), who recommended a rich case-study analysis of creative persons to determine the developmental path of creativity. Therefore, the next section turns to a discussion of the changing flavor of creativity from infancy through adolescence.

The Development of Creativity

The elusive nature of human creativity becomes all the more obvious when psychologists try to explain how creativity develops. This section first examines two stage theories of creativity development, each of which attempts to distinguish between genuine adult creative endeavors and the spontaneous, flexible, and playful activities of childhood, which may or may not represent true creativity. Then it examines the research on creativity at various points during childhood and adolescence in an attempt to determine what changes and what remains the same as the child grows up.

Theories of Creative Development

Only a few theorists have presented a continuous sequence that attempts to describe the changes in creativity from childhood to adulthood. I.A. Taylor (1974), for example, proposed a model of creative development that outlines the qualitative changes appearing at different points in the life cycle. After its initial appearance, each change can be found at any time in the life cycle. First there is *spontaneity* in early childhood, as seen in the language, play, and drawings of children and in the work of adult creative artists. From late childhood through adolescence *technical proficiency* appears, as children take advantage of specific forms of training and refine their skills. *Inventive ingenuity*, appearing during adolescence or early adulthood, involves working with gadgets and tinkering with materials. The inventor Thomas Edison exemplified this type of creativity in his ability to combine many elements to solve old problems in new ways. *Innovative flexibility*, appearing in early to middle adulthood, involves changing ideas and systems for new purposes, as Erikson did when he modified Freud's theory. Finally, in middle- and old-age, there is *emergentive originality*—the development of totally new ideas such as those of Freud.

A similar developmental approach to the study of creativity was suggested by David H. Feldman (1974). In his system, creativity is potentially developed over four stages:

1. the universal achievements of all human beings

2. the cultural advances common to members of particular social groups
3. the idiosyncratic accomplishments of specific persons within a given culture
4. the unique creative developments which "may alter for all time a mode of expression or a domain of knowledge" (p. 68).

Universal creativity refers to the normal discoveries of infancy and childhood. **Cultural creativity** reflects the knowledge acquired from being raised in a specific society. **Idiosyncratic creativity** means the special achievements that accompany changes within a limited area of expertise. Finally, **unique creativity** implies the invention of something totally new and extraordinary. Certainly creativity, at stages 1 and 2 at least, is within the capabilities of children or adolescents.

A problem with theories of creative development such as Taylor's and Feldman's is that they fail to explain why some children reach the original and unique levels associated with genuine creativity while others do not. Furthermore, it is probably not a good idea to rely too heavily on age-related or developmental factors in creativity, because in doing so we might neglect important historical, generational, and cultural factors (Romaniuk & Romaniuk 1981).

Developmental Patterns

This section discusses questions concerning the developmental changes in creativity throughout childhood and adolescence. When can a child be thought of as creative? Are infants creative? How may creativity be influenced by the various social pressures children deal with as they develop?

Infancy and Early Childhood

The notion of infant creativity may seem ridiculous to some people and very obvious to others. The discussion might even begin at an earlier point; Anderson (1959) asserted that creativity is "characteristic of development [and] a quality of protoplasm" (p. 124). Biologist Edmund Sinnott (1959) similarly concluded that life itself is a creative process in which organization and regulatory properties are inherent in living organisms. It was Piaget (1981), however, who alerted us to the infant's creativity by regarding the sensorimotor pe-

Inventive ingenuity, a form of creativity that emerges during adolescence or young adulthood, is illustrated by students in a chemistry class looking for new solutions to old problems.

riod as "incredible in its amount of invention and discovery" (p. 229). The infant's creativity does not introduce new products or ideas to the world, but it does lead to original constructions of time, space, and language for the infant (see Chapter 6). More significantly, the process of solving sensorimotor problems suggests an inclination toward originality (Noppe & Noppe 1976). Also, some infants, by virtue of their basic temperaments, could be more curious and more inclined to seek novelty than others are (Thomas, Chess & Birch 1970).

Early childhood elaborates on the creative development that began in infancy. The young child is extremely playful and open to new experiences. The preschool years are a golden age of fantasy and imagination as indicated by the rich, imaginative quality of children's symbolic play. It is not

easy to tell, however, which of these young children will maintain their creative imaginations into the years of adolescence and adulthood, although a longitudinal study by Harrington, Block, and Block (1983) provides some encouraging evidence for the predictability of preadolescent creativity from preschool tests of divergent thinking. The researchers administered creativity and intelligence tests to seventy-five children between the ages of 4 and 5 years. When the children were 11 years old, their sixth-grade teachers were asked to evaluate these students' levels of creativity. Results indicated significant correlations between the various tests of creativity at different ages. It is particularly interesting that there was no meaningful relationship between preschool intelligence and later teacher-rated creativity. Apparently, some common element of creative thinking was maintained over a six- to seven-year span despite the controversy concerning the value of divergent-thinking tests as valid measures of creativity.

Middle Childhood and Adolescence

During the middle-childhood and adolescent years, creative potential appears to reach a critical point. Because of advances in logical thought, elementary and high school students have a tremendous opportunity to expand the range of their imaginations. However, conformity to parental and cultural expectations, the imitative rather than imaginative techniques of much of our educational process, and the capacity to be harshly self-judgmental may place severe limits on the freedom and playfulness essential for creativity to flourish. Children of this age need a firm foundation of knowledge and a clear sense of reality, but they should not be permitted to give up the spontaneity and imagination of their earlier childhood. Older children must learn to combine the discipline and purpose of working with the flexibility and joy of play.

Although the orientation to concrete reality limits the potential for truly creative thought during middle childhood, teachers can strive to follow the five principles suggested by Klausmeier (1985) for promoting creativity:

1. Provide for variety in instructional materials and forms of student expression.
2. Develop favorable attitudes toward creative achievement.
3. Encourage continuing creative expression.
4. Foster productivity.
5. Provide assistance and feedback.

Teachers and parents must do more than simply hope that creative activity will occur spontaneously. They need to pose challenging questions, accept a variety of solutions to problems, and suggest tasks that will allow children to develop new ways of perceiving their world.

If Piaget (1981) could describe childhood as the most creative time in the life of a human being, why is much of this creativity apparently lost by adolescence? Wolf and Larson (1981) proposed that younger children are not nearly as creative as we often suppose, because their creations are accidental and often the result of their own ignorance of

the world around them. Furthermore, the apparent loss of creativity in some adolescents may reflect peer pressure to conform, because conformity is the enemy of creative expression. Noppe and Noppe (1976) pointed out, though, that the formal operations that may emerge during adolescence contain the seeds of true creativity—the flexible system of combinatorial reasoning, the reversal of reality and possibility, and the tolerance of incomplete solutions and contradictions. Finally, adolescent creativity apparently can be stimulated through the use of imaginative methods and materials, active involvement in trying new ideas, and the provision of a receptive, encouraging atmosphere (Davis, 1975).

Play, and Creative Problem Solving

Thus far, the nature and developmental progression of children's play and creativity have been discussed separately. This section attempts to integrate the two by looking at research relating play to childhood problem solving. (Applying Our Knowledge "Education of the Gifted and Talented" discusses creativity as a criterion for assessing giftedness.)

Since the 1970s, a variety of research has been conducted, mostly with preschool children, that examines the relationship between play and convergent- or divergent-problem solving. Over two decades ago, Wallach and Kogan (1965) suggested the value of play for improving children's thinking. More recently, Rubin, Fein, and Vandenberg (1983) concluded that a playful attitude may allow children to come up with unique and unusual solutions to problems. Playful activity may bring about the flexible and relaxed attitudes necessary for the occurrence of creative thought.

Play with Objects

There seems to be a relationship between children's levels of creative problem-solving and the types of objects they are given to play with (Pepler & Ross, 1981; Smith & Dutton, 1979; Sylva, Bruner & Genova, 1976). Illustrating this point are the find-

Applying our Knowledge

Education of the Gifted and Talented

Americans seem to have a curious attitude about the necessity of special education for their gifted and talented children. While innovative programs and additional resources have been directed toward a number of exceptional groups—for instance, learning-disabled, mentally retarded, and sensorily handicapped students—virtually no attention has been paid to offering the gifted and talented child or adolescent much beyond a standard curriculum. Why is it less tragic for gifted and talented students to fail to live up to their potential than for learning-disabled students not to have their needs addressed? Why do we doubt whether the return on the investment of appropriate resources for teaching the gifted and talented would equal the benefits of educating the mentally retarded (DeLeon & VandenBos 1985)?

Much effort has occurred in recent years to coordinate information about gifted and talented children; to promote public awareness of their needs; and to develop national, state, and local agencies for their support. An obvious starting point would be to agree on how to define and identify the gifted or talented student. According to the Gifted and Talented Children's Act of 1978, the term "gifted" applies to:

. . . children, and, whenever applicable, youth, who are identified at the preschool, elementary, or secondary level as possessing demonstrated or potential abilities that give evidence of high performance responsibility in areas such as intellectual, creative, scientific, academic, or leadership ability, or in the visual and performing arts, and who by reason thereof, require services and activities not ordinarily provided by the school. (*Congressional Record*, 1978)

A somewhat different definition has been suggested by Renzulli (1978) emphasizing three criteria for a gifted child: (1) greater than average intellectual ability, (2) high levels of task commitment, and (3) creativity.

Since any single assessment procedure selected for distinguishing gifted children is controversial, most school districts will use a variety of methods for identifying the students on whom they wish to focus special education. These approaches may include any of the following: individual or group intelligence tests, achievement tests, personality or maturity tests, personal interviews, parent and teacher observations or ratings, creativity tests, and expert judgments of written, artistic, or musical productions. Another basic unresolved issue concerns the specificity of the child's strengths as a criterion for giftedness. For example, do we wish to consider a third grader with outstanding artistic potential, but no special talents or abilities in other areas, to

be a gifted child? This would appear to be an easier way to identify the gifted or talented student as well as a more effective means of incorporating a larger proportion of children into special programs (Passow 1981).

Once children have been identified for participation in a program for the gifted and talented, the task is to determine how to best meet their educational needs. The two most typically adopted models of education for gifted and talented students are the enrichment strategy and the acceleration strategy, or some combination of the two. Renzulli (1978) pioneered the enrichment strategy that consists of special activities, independent study, after-school or weekend programs, learning centers, mentor programs, and so forth. In contrast, the acceleration strategy, supported by a Johns Hopkins University group (Fox & Washington 1985), emphasizes grade skipping, early admission to college, credit by examination, fast-paced instruction, telescoping four years of high school into three years or three years of junior high school into two years, and correspondence or telecommunication courses.

The early recognition of gifted and talented children in the classroom and the implementation of appropriate educational programs will enable them to maximize their school experiences and to achieve their intellectual/creative potentials.

ings of Pepler and Ross (1981), who provided sixty-four preschool children with the opportunity to play with convergent (e.g., puzzles) or divergent (e.g., blocks) materials on several occasions. They later administered several problem-solving tasks to the children and found that those who had engaged in divergent object play were more flexible and original in their problem-solving responses. For example, they were quicker than those in the convergent play group to adandon ineffective solutions to problems and to come up with new approaches. Working with puzzles may teach that there are right answers and may encourage children to seek them out; working with blocks may tell a child that the possibilities for creative imagination are as diverse as the variety of structures into which the blocks can be formed.

Fantasy Play

In addition to research on object play and creativity, several investigations have related make-believe play to divergent thinking (Dansky 1980; Hutt & Bhavnani 1976; Johnson 1976). In Dansky's study, ninety-six preschoolers were observed in a free-play situation in order to categorize them as either high- or low-make-believe players. After permitting interactions with a set of materials in a free-play, imitative, or problem-solving condition, the children were given a divergent-thinking task. The highest scores were attained by those children who were in a free-play situation, but only if they were spontaneously high in make-believe play. Dansky (1980) emphasized that individual differences among children, and not simply the type of environment created for them, account for variations in divergent thought.

While such research should not discourage parents or teachers from establishing a climate of freedom and providing interesting materials for young children to play with, it does suggest that some children may have an innate capacity for make-believe play and others may not. Furthermore, a child's basic capacity for fantasy seems to influence the degree to which he or she can engage in divergent problem-solving. Why? It is the cognitive concept of decentration (see Chapter 5) that links fantasy play and divergent thought. Rubin, Fein, and Vandenberg (1983) explained that pretend play lets children transform objects and sit-

uations while at the same time understanding their original identities and states. Therefore, they come to see the world from a variety of perspectives at once, and this perception enhances their intellectual flexibility.

The spontaneity and imagination of children's play may indeed enhance creativity, but such characteristics are also healthy qualities for living. If play offers nothing more to the child than the chance to create and experiment with multiple versions of reality, then it is certainly an activity worth pursuing. It is a child's language. To a certain extent, it is a child's life.

Summary

1. Play is an activity that is intrinsically motivated, freely chosen, pleasurable, nonliteral, and actively engaged in by the child.
2. Infant play rapidly becomes complex through social interactions, sensorimotor behaviors, and vocalizations. By the end of infancy, play becomes more structured and may exhibit simple fantasy episodes.
3. During early childhood, fantasy play becomes very extensive. The value of preschooler pretense can be linked to increasing social cooperation, fine- and gross-motoric advances, and maturing cognitive abilities.
4. From middle childhood to adolescence, playful behaviors occur less frequently, especially in the presence of adults. Play may be transformed to games and to work, but it is also seen through language, teasing, and rough-and-tumble.
5. Classic theories of play emphasized only limited purposes for this activity, such as releasing surplus energy, renewing an exhausted body, or practicing skills necessary for being an adult.
6. Psychoanalytic accounts of play focus on the release of objective and instinctual anxiety. Erikson incorporated the physical and social aspects of development in his theory.
7. Piaget constructed an influential cognitive view of play that corresponds to the changes in a child's level of thought. He labeled three stages of play as practice play; symbolic, or fantasy, play; and games-with-rules.
8. More contemporary theories of play have blended physical, cognitive, and socioemotional themes of development, as well as the concepts of arousal, communication, and flexibility.

9. Play occurs in almost every culture. However, economic conditions and cultural values influence the amount of play and the characteristics of games.
10. Creativity can be thought of as a personality characteristic, an intellectual process, and an activity resulting in an original and interesting product.
11. Infants display a very personal form of creativity that has no cultural ramifications. Similarly, the fantasy of preschool children is an individual, not a societal, expression of imagination.
12. Individual differences in creativity during middle childhood and adolescence may be blunted by pressures to conform and the educational system's structure. Nonetheless, creative expression is demonstrated and can be encouraged.
13. The link between play and problem solving is sound theoretically but empirically limited. Flexible and relaxed attitudes necessary for creative thinking parallel playful activity.
14. Fantasy play, in particular, seems to be related to divergent-thinking ability in preschoolers. The concept of decentration may offer the crucial connection between these two activities.
15. While the long-term consequences of play may not yet be easily traced, children must be given the freedom and opportunities to pursue spontaneous, voluntary, and imaginative behavior for its own sake.

Key Terms

practice play	divergent thinking
symbolic, or fantasy, play	convergent thinking
games-with-rules	universal creativity
autocosmic play	cultural creativity
microsphere play	idiosyncratic creativity
macrosphere play	unique creativity

Suggested Readings

Elkind, D. (1981). *The hurried child: Growing up too fast too soon.* Reading, MA: Addison-Wesley.

A controversial attempt to understand stress in our children. In the conclusion, play and creativity are nicely integrated.

Feldman, D.H. (Ed.). (1982). *Developmental approaches to giftedness and creativity.* San Francisco: Jossey-Bass.

A collection of five interesting and authoritative essays from several perspectives. Each one is worth reading—all are creatively written.

Garvey, C. (1977). *Play.* Cambridge, MA: Harvard University Press.

The best available treatment of children's play in one short volume. It includes many examples and discusses play from several different angles.

Rubin, K.H. (Ed.). (1980). *Children's play.* San Francisco: Jossey-Bass.

Another group of valuable essays that focus on a variety of issues in the study of play. The topics range from games to fantasy to language to creativity.

Wallach, M.A. & Kogan, N. (1965). *Modes of thinking in young children: A study of the creativity-intelligence distinction.* New York: Holt, Rinehart & Winston.

A classic account of the interrelationships of intelligence, creativity, thinking processes, and education for the middle-childhood years.

Readings from the Literature

The relationship between problem solving and play was discussed in the last section of Chapter 13. The following study by J. Allan Cheyne and Kenneth H. Rubin follows up on the work of Dansky (1980) and Pepler and Ross (1981). While none of these authors claim to have resolved the issues, their results do suggest that particular types of play may affect certain kinds of problem solving. Cheyne and Rubin (1983) have also helped to clarify why sex differences exist in problem-solving behavior. Use the following questions as a guide for understanding the major aspects of this research:

- What characteristics of play do the authors feel may be especially significant for leading to effective problem solving?

- After examining the methodology of this study, what are the principal limitations of the measures used?

- How can various types of play affect the ability of a preschool child to solve either convergent or divergent problems?

Playful Precursors of Problem Solving in Preschoolers

J. Allan Cheyne
University of Waterloo, Waterloo, Ontario, Canada

Kenneth H. Rubin
University of Waterloo, Waterloo, Ontario, Canada

The results of a number of recent studies suggest that play serves to create specific skills as well as a special, flexible set for innovative thinking and problem solving. In this study, an analysis was made of object play components to determine whether the specific skills evidenced in the combinatorial activity of play and/ or the flexible set suggested by the use of fantasy were related to performance on a problem-solving task. Seventy-six female and 64 male preschoolers were permitted to play for 8 minutes with a number of sticks of varying length as well as with a number of blocks. A subset of these materials was subsequently made available in a problem-solving session in which solution could be achieved by joining sticks to create a tool to retrieve a lure. Significant correlations were found between (a) the discovery of the solution principle and (b) the quality of combinatorial activity during play and problem-solving solution time. Nonsignificant correlations were found between all other play measures, including nonliteral object use and solution time. The results are discussed in relation to recent research relating play and convergent and divergent problem-solving skills. Some resolutions to a number of apparent inconsistencies in the literature are suggested.

It has frequently been documented that a variety of mammals and birds appear to take great interest and enjoyment in object manipulation (Candland, French & Johnson, 1978; Groos, 1898; Van Lawick-Goodall, 1968; Vandenberg, 1980). Given the ubiquity of object play, it is not surprising that there is a long history of speculation concerning the possible adaptive functions of such activity (Bruner, 1972; Groos, 1898). Recently, a number of researchers have begun to investigate experimentally the potential functions of object play.

One potentially significant function of object play that has received experimental support is the facilitation of logicospatial problem-solving skills in children (e.g., Smith & Dutton, 1979; Sylva, Bruner, & Genova, 1976; Vandenberg, 1981). The studies cited have all used a paradigm that was developed over the years in research with nonhuman primates (Birch, 1945; Kohler, 1925; Schiller, 1957). Briefly, children are allowed a period of relatively unconstrained free play with sticks and some means for joining them. Following the free-play period, the subjects are presented with one or more problems, the solution of which involves the creation of a long extending tool by connecting two or more of the longest sticks available to them. Taken together, the results of these studies (Smith & Dutton, 1979; Sylva et al., 1976; Vandenberg, 1981) suggest that free play with the objects is often as effective (or more so in some cases) as direct or indirect (observational) tuition in promoting problem solving.

Thus far, however, the major thrust of this research has been to demonstrate a general, or global, relation between object play and problem solving. Only incidentally have the researchers attempted to relate specific components of such play to success in problem solving (Rubin, Fein, & Vandenberg, 1983). One possible method of identifying those specific play components that may be operative in improved problem solving would be to conduct a series of parametric studies using manipulations that preclude certain activities and/or experiences as explanatory variables. However, this approach would necessarily entail a large number of manipulations and might change the phenomenon (play) under investigation. An alternative procedure is to relate specific behaviors and strategies that occur during play with outcome measures of problem-solving proficiency. Sylva (1974), for example, found that the complexity of play constructions (or configurational richness) was positively related to problem-solving skill. Unfortunately, Sylva's play sample was small and varied widely with regard to age. Because the lure-retrieval problem appears to be age sensitive (Sylva, 1977; Vandenberg, 1981), and because Sylva did not control for this latter variable, her finding must be regarded as highly tentative. Moreover, Vandenberg

(1981) failed to find significant relations between configurational richness and problem solving. However, Vandenberg used a different and more quantitative measure of richness than did Sylva.

Schiller (1957) reported that chimpanzees discovering and utilizing the principle of joining two sticks during object manipulation were able to solve lure-retrieval problems, whereas animals not discovering the principle were unable to solve this problem. Again, both discovery and problem solving were correlated with age. More recently, Sylva (1974) examined the relation between the appearance of the principle of extension in children's play and problem solving but did not have sufficient observational data to compute an adequate statistical test. Vandenberg (1981) also examined the performance of certain components of problem solution during play, which he labeled "task specifics." He obtained partial support for the hypothesis that performance of task specifics in play would aid problem solving. Given this background, we attempted to test a number of theory-based hypotheses regarding the potential role of object play in the development of problem-solving skills.

The first set of hypotheses is based primarily on the observations and speculations of Schiller (1957), who emphasized that the role of play is to provide a context within which specific possibilities of, and strategies with, objects may be discovered and practiced in play. Such possibilities and strategies lead to the use of the objects as tools for solving problems. That is, the player discovers specific object uses or principles that may later be effective for problem solution. First, at one level the player may practice very elementary task specifics (Vandenberg, 1980), leading to the assimilation of the principle that sticks may be joined to blocks. This leads to the prediction that the frequency of joining sticks to blocks during play would be correlated with problem-solving proficiency. Second, and at a higher level, the player may discover somewhat more sophisticated principles such as that of extension through joining (i.e., stick/block/stick connections). Because the latter construction more closely approximates the principle that is the solution to the problem, it would seem even more likely than simple joining to predict problem solving. We further predicted that the discovery, in play, of the particular double-stick extension principle (long stick/block/long stick) specifically required for problem solving would better predict problem-solving proficiency than would the discovery of other double-stick constructions.

The fourth hypothesis followed from Piaget's (1962) theory and Schiller's (1957) theory that play is essentially assimilative and thereby promotes the consolidation of newly learned principles and actions through repetition. Thus, given that a child discovers the long stick/block/long stick principle of extension in play, it was hypothesized that the assimilation of this principle, as measured by frequency of use, would predict problem-solving proficiency.

Although the foregoing hypotheses all make predictions from the assumed acquisition of relatively specific skills or knowledge in play, the subsequent hypotheses are based on a view of play as occurring within a relaxed, tension-free field. This playful context has been thought to promote a *combinatorial* style of interaction with the environment (e.g., Bruner, 1972). One hypothesis deriving from such a view is that playful interchange with materials promotes more elaborate and complex combinations of materials than would be the case in nonplayful contexts. Such elaboration may render the possibilities of the materials more evident. This, in turn, may facilitate the discovery of solutions, which involve the materials, for problematic situations when they arise (Birch, 1945). Thus, we predicted that the greater the combinatorial complexity of play, as indexed by the elaboration or complexity of play constructions, the more effective problem solving will be.

Given the lack of external constraints on the player, he or she is purportedly free to use the given set of materials in any way he or she chooses. This lack of constraint on behavior has been postulated to create a "flexible cognitive set" whereby the player comes to realize that given materials can be used in multiple fashions (Bruner, 1972; Dansky & Silverman, 1973, 1975; Pepler & Ross, 1981). The flexible set engendered in play has been suggested as conducive to the development of problem solving and creativity. As Vandenberg (1980) has recently noted, object play

experiences lead the child to develop generalized models or schemes of applicability. Thus, when confronted with a problem to solve with materials earlier used in play, the child may access the self-produced schemes of multiple object use to aid in problem solution.

The flexible set engendered by object play may also lead the player to "go beyond the information given" (Bruner, 1957) and to discover nonliteral or fantasy object usages. Such representational schemes have also been found to aid in the development of problem-solving skills (Dansky, 1980; Pepler & Ross, 1981). Thus, in this study we predicted that the more evidence a child gave of flexibility in play and/or in nonliteral object use, the better would be his or her problem solving. Finally, because the lure-retrieval problem has proven to be extremely age sensitive, both chronological and mental age were included as dependent variables.

Method

Subjects

Seventy-six girls and 64 boys who attended nine different preschool/daycare settings served as subjects in the study. The mean age of the children was 56 months ($SD = 4$ months).

Procedure

Each child was brought individually to a testing room by one of three female experimenters. The child was seated at a low table and was given a set of three 24-cm, three 15-cm, and three 6-cm wood dowels and five wood cubes, each of which had four holes drilled into it. The experimenter pointed out that the sticks were of different lengths and then demonstrated the insertion of a stick into one of the holes in a block. Each child was then permitted to play with these materials for 8 minutes. Following this period, all children were presented with six sticks (two of each length), a block, and the problem of retrieving a piece of chalk or a marble, which they had previously chosen, enclosed in a transparent box placed out of arm's reach. The child was told that he or she could use

438

any of the materials to help in the solution of the problem but that he or she must remain seated. The ultimate solution to the problem involved the joining of the two longest sticks by means of a block, releasing the latch on the box, and raking in the lure. The specific measures of problem-solving proficiency are described below.

Hints, as used by Sylva et al. (1976) and Smith and Dutton (1979) were given to the child at 1-minute intervals. The hints were (a) "Have you used everything you can think of that might help you?"; (b) "Can you think of a way you can use the block to help you?"; (c) "Can you think of a way that you can use both the block and the sticks to help you?"; (d) "You could join the two long sticks together with the block and make a longer stick"; and (e) "I will hold this stick (a 24-cm stick). Can you put the block into the end of it? Now pick up the other long stick and joint that to the end of the other one."

Measures

During the child's play with the sticks and blocks, the experimenters, who had no knowledge of the specific hypotheses or of the specific measures to be derived from their recordings, recorded the child's verbalizations and dramatic play activities (e.g., "flying," "driving," or "eating" their constructions), as well as recording, diagramatically, the constructions made with the sticks and blocks. From these diagrams a number of measures were derived by two coders who were not the experimenters. First, a measure of the most basic task specific was taken, namely, the number of *joins* (i.e., number of insertions of sticks into blocks) made by the child during play. Second, it was noted whether or not the child gave evidence of discovering the long stick/block/long stick principle during play. The frequency of symmetrical double-stick constructions was recorded, for long sticks (the "correct" principle of extension with regards to the problem), and as control measures, for short and intermediate length sticks. These scoring procedures allowed the testing of the hypotheses concerning the discovery of the extension principle and the assimilation of the principle with these materials.

To test the combinatorial complexity hypothesis, two measures were used. First, a measure comparable to Sylva's configurational richness was used in which constructions were classified as *simple* (one stick and one block, one stick, and two blocks, two blocks and two sticks) or *complex* (multiple stick-block constructions). Frequencies of each type of construction were calculated and the number of simple constructions was subtracted from the number of complex constructions for each child, yielding a measure of construction complexity. In addition, a measure of complexity analogous to that used by Vandenberg (1981) was computed by recording the average number of elements (blocks and sticks) used for construction by each child.

Two measures were used to examine the flexibility hypothesis. First the average number of different operations or procedures engaged in by each child was tabulated. The operations recorded were (a) stacking blocks, (b) inserting sticks into blocks, (c) seriating sticks, (d) grouping sticks by size, and (e) making two- or three-dimensional configurations with the materials. Second, dimensional flexibility was determined by computing the number of joins per block. Because the blocks had holes on four surfaces, such a measure was taken to reveal the child's tendency to elaborate his or her constructions in several spatial dimensions. Finally, the number of fantasy constructions was recorded when the child's actions or utterances indicated some representational activity with regard to the object (e.g., flying an airplane-like structure or saying "I made a lollipop!").

These measures of play were related to a measure of problem-solving proficiency. Proficiency was defined as *solution time,* or the time elapsed between the end of the experimenter's instructions and the point at which the child had made the appropriate double-stick construction and had extended the tool toward the box. All children were successful following this maneuver, but because of coordination and dexterity differences, some children took longer than others to release the latch and roll the lure. Thus, this latter period of time was not included in the computation of solution time.

Table 1 Means and Standard Deviations for Major Dependent Variables for Girls and Boys

Dependent Variable	Girls		Boys	
	M	SD	M	SD
Solution Time	223.61	119.54	188.14	132.23
Joins	14.74	6.06	13.35	5.52
Short Constructions	1.37	1.34	1.46	1.23
Medium Constructions	.88	.98	.78	.91
Long (Principle) Constructions	1.18	1.46	1.00	1.11
Configural Richness	6.76	4.71	10.43	2.72
Elements/Construction	8.09	3.03	8.65	3.07
Operations	2.53	1.19	1.82	1.02
Joins/Block	2.67	1.23	3.13	1.17
Fantasy Constructions	1.71	2.25	2.50	2.32
*MA**	68.23	15.15	68.98	14.80
Age (Months)	57.04	4.49	56.02	4.25

Note: MA = mental age.
*Measured by the Peabody Picture Vocabulary Test.

Results

Two independent raters, blind to the outcome performance of the children, each recorded the object play scores for 30 subjects. Percentages of agreement for each play category ranged from 87% to 100%.

The means and standard deviations, for girls and boys, for each of the major dependent variables of the study are presented in Table 1. A series of t tests revealed sex differences for the number of operations, $t(136) = 2.68$, $p < .05$; and for configurational richness, $t(136) = 5.40$, $p < .001$. Girls tended to use the "correct" double-stick principle more often in play and scored lower on the measure of configurational richness than did boys.

Correlations between the problem-solving and the object play variables are presented separately for girls and boys in Table 2. The same correlation matrix for the entire sample is presented in Table 3. Separate correlations were computed for girls and boys and for the total sample. Because we were interested in discovering general principles relating play to problem solving, and because we were testing several hypotheses, we took the rather conservative approach of accepting as significant only those consistent relationships that were obtained for girls and boys separately as well as for the entire sample.

As shown in Tables 2 and 3, the use of the "correct" problem-solving extension principle in play (long stick/block/long stick) and the index of configurational richness were both consistently, negatively, and significantly correlated with time to solution. Both girls and boys who used the double-stick principle and who had higher configurational richness scores in their play tended to solve the problems relatively quickly. The average number of elements per construction, the num-

440

Table 2 Correlations Between Solution Time and Object Play Variables

Variable	1	2	3	4	5	6	7	8	9	10
1. Solution time		−.33*	−.09	−.01	−.32*	−.27*	−.27*	−.31*	.15	.00
2. Joins	−.01		.23*	.24*	.09	.68*	.09	−.01	.00	−.24*
3. Short constructions	−.27*	.14		.15	.27*	.08	.09	−.16	.16	−.11
4. Medium constructions	.04	.36*	.14		−.08	.14	.06	.00	.07	−.13
5. Long constructions	−.30*	.27*	.28*	.15		.23*	.20	.16	−.13	.03
6. Richness	−.24*	.53*	.38*	.25*	.27*		.58*	−.09	.24*	−.30*
7. Elements/construction	−.01	.06	.26*	.27*	.20*	.57*		.05	.10	−.30*
8. Operations	.25*	−.45*	−.23*	−.16	−.20*	−.40*	−.31*		−.45*	.10
9. Joins/block	−.10	.27*	.20*	.22*	.22*	.19	.20*	−.53*		.05
10. Fantasy	.00	.00	.05	.02	.13	−.09	−.25*	.04	−.05	

Note: Correlations for boys are above the diagonal; correlations for girls are below the diagonal.
*p < .05.

Table 3 Correlations Between Solution Time and Object Play Variables: Total Sample

Variable	1	2	3	4	5	6	7	8
1. Solution time	1.00							
2. Joins	−.11	1.00						
3. Use of principle	−.27*	.28*	1.00					
4. Configural richness	−.29*	.05	.24*	1.00				
5. Elements	−.15	.06	.18*	.57*	1.00			
6. Operations	−.02	−.10	−.12	−.17	−.18*	1.00		
7. Joins/block	−.06	.14	.28*	.28*	.20*	−.03	1.00	
8. Fantasy	−.01	.15	−.10	−.10	−.17	.03	.13	1.00

*p < .05.

ber of joins, and the number of operations in play were inconsistently correlated with the measure of problem-solving proficiency. The average number of elements and the number of joins were negatively correlated with solution time for boys but not for girls. Moreover, the number of operations used in play was significantly and negatively correlated with solution time for boys and was significantly but positively correlated with solution time for girls. Neither the number of joins per block (dimensional flexibility) nor the number of fantasy-dramatic constructions were significantly correlated with solution time for either sex.

Both mental age (MA; as measured by the Peabody Picture Vocabulary Test) and chronological age (CA) were significantly correlated with solution time for both sexes separately and for the total group. The total group correlations for MA and CA were $r(115) = -.33$, $p < .001$ and $r(139) = -.45$, $p < .001$, respectively. Although there were no consistently significant correlations between these developmental variables and the object play measures, second-order partial correlations were computed controlling for MA and CA. The only substantial difference between the original and the partial correlational analyses was that the correlation between configurational richness and time to solution was no longer significant for girls.

Given that the most consistent findings emerging from the analyses were the significant correlations between the use of the double-stick principle (long stick) in play and solution time, further analyses with respect to these relations were examined. First, the frequencies of symmetrical constructions using short or midlength sticks were not consistently significantly correlated with solution time. Second, analyses were conducted to specifically test the discovery and assimilation of the principle hypotheses because computations of Pearson product-moment correlation coefficients do not allow distinctions to be made between these two separate hypotheses. To determine whether the significant correlations noted above resulted from a difference between children who used the principle in play and those who did not (discovery hypothesis), or whether the correlations resulted from an approximately linear relation between the frequency of *use of principle* and solution time, a two-way analysis of covariance (ANCOVA) with CA as the covariate was performed. The ANCOVA was computed because CA was highly correlated with solution time. The independent variables were sex and use of principle. Solution time was the dependent variable. Because only 20 children repeated the use of principle two or more times in play, only three levels of the use-of-principle variable were analyzed, namely, zero, one, or two or more repetitions. The ANCOVA revealed significant effects for sex, $F(1, 129) = 4.70$, $p < .05$, and use of principle, $F(2, 129) = 4.91$, $p < .01$, respectively. With CA covaried, males solved the lure-retrieval problem more rapidly than did females. The main effect for use of principle was further explored by means of a series of pairwise t tests. Experiment-wise error was controlled by adjusting the alpha level to $p < .02$. The only significant differences were between children

who never made use of the principle and those who used the principle once, $t(88) = 2.46$, $p < .02$, and those who used the principle more than once, $t(45) = 7.68$, $p < .001$. There was no difference between children who used the principle once and those who used the principle more often during play. In short, children who had never made use of the double-stick construction in play took significantly longer to solve the problem than those who used the principle during play.

Discussion

The clearest and most consistent finding in the present study was that children who appeared to discover the long-stick extension principle during play were better able to solve a lure-retrieval problem that required the use of this principle than were their counterparts who did not discover the principle. Moreover, discovery and use of the long-stick extension in play was a better predictor of problem-solving proficiency than other forms of extension.

In recent research, Vandenberg (1981) had examined the relation between the use of task specifics in play and subsequent problem-solving skills. Task specifics have been defined as behaviors that are necessary for problem solution (e.g., stick/block/stick extensions; joins). Drawing from the work of Schiller (1957) and Birch (1945), Vandenberg predicted that the use of task specifics in play would become more helpful as the difficulty of the problem to be presented increases. Yet Vandenberg himself reported the opposite effect (i.e., the use of task specifics in play predicted the solution of a simple problem better than a difficult problem). Interestingly, the particular task specific that Vandenberg observed to predict performance on his simple problem was directly analogous to our "use of the principle" construction. It involved the exact construction (in play) necessary for subsequent problem solution. Alternately, the task specific that Vandenberg observed in the play session prior to the presentation of the difficult problem was analagous to our measure of "number of joins." Given our own and Vandenberg's data, we suggest that the potency of the task specific discovered in play becomes greater with increasing resemblance to the central principle required for problem solution, regardless of task difficulty.

Our results are, of course, correlational in nature and do not necessarily imply that the children discovered the extension principle for the first time in the play session or that the use of the principle was instrumental in the problem-solving process. However, in a recent experiment, Darvill (1981) found that children who were permitted to play with sticks and blocks that precluded stick/block joins performed more poorly on the lure-retrieval problem than did children who played with materials identical to our own. Thus, it would appear that the discovery or performance of the principle in play does have an impact on problem-solving skill.

It was originally hypothesized that the complexity of the object play constructions would predict problem-solving proficiency. Our data indicated that configurational richness was significantly, consistently, and negatively correlated with the lure-retrieval time. The finding is supportive of Sylva (1974), who also discovered a significant relation between configurational richness and problem-solving skill. However, our data conflict with Vandenberg's (1981) report of a nonsignificant relation between configurational richness and problem solving. Perhaps these differences can be reconciled by a simple comparison between Sylva's and Vandenberg's definitions of configurational richness. Sylva's measure closely approximated ours, whereas Vandenberg's measure was similar to our computation of the average number of elements per construction. Although these measures were consistently and significantly correlated with one another, only the former index of configurational richness was consistently and significantly related with lure-retrieval time. These results suggest that the relevant feature of play for problem solving may be the organizing or patterning features of ongoing object play. An examination of this suggestion will require sequential analyses of the constructive processes during object play rather than the analysis of static products.

The nature of the sex differences found were also consonant with the findings relative to play and problem solving. Boys received higher scores for configurational richness, and as one would predict given the relation between configurational richness and problem solving, they solved the problem in less time than did girls. Sex differences have not been notable in studies using the present paradigm. However, studies generally suggest a modest superiority of boys in the lure-retrieval problem (Sylva, 1977). Given that boys are more likely to play with constructive materials (Rubin et al., 1983) and given the inference that there is a causal relation between features of constructive play and problem solving, the obtained sex differences are readily interpretable.

Our hypotheses concerning the measures of flexibility and fantasy were not consistently supported. The failure to find consistent significant relations between flexibility of play construction, fantasy play constructions, and problem-solving skill may be attributed, in part, to the type of problem presented to the children. Pepler (1979; Pepler & Ross, 1981), for example, found measures of flexibility and fantasy to predict skill at solving divergent but not convergent tasks. In the former case, there were multiple problem solutions, whereas in the latter, convergent case, as in our problem, there was but a single task solution. Researchers would do well to examine further the different forms of play and construction that may predict and indeed aid in the solution of different types of problems.

An issue may be raised as to whether the object manipulation engaged in by children participating in this paradigm can be said to constitute play (Cheyne, 1982). Several considerations bear on this issue. First, many of the measures taken in this study are, by definition, play activities involving elaboration of materials into varied forms that had no functional goal except, in some cases, for fantasy or nonliteral manipulation. Children smiled, laughed at, and talked about their constructions in a manner suggesting an interest in the nature of the transformations they were effecting on the materials. There was little exploration of the materials as indicated by simple palpation or visual inspection. This was probably attributable to the simple nature of the materials as well as to the fact that the experimenter initially familiarized the child with the materials and their essential function. Nonetheless, future researchers would do well to further document the validity of the designation of play to the children's behavior by (a) evaluating the affective component, (b) attempting to separate exploration from play (Hutt, 1979), and (c) further separating both of these from desultory functional manipulation.

443

In summary, it seems apparent that there are several potential determinants of success in the oft-used lure-retrieval paradigm. For one, chronological age is important (Schiller, 1957; Vandenberg, 1980). Even within our restricted age range of 18 months, age was the strongest correlate of problem solving. Second, the availability of the correct extension principle seems to be important. Given the data of Schiller (1957) with chimpanzees and those of the present study, it seems unlikely that the act of insight in problem solving (Kohler, 1925) consists of the discovery of a previously unknown principle. Rather, insight may be better conceptualized as the discovery that a previously known principle will serve as a solution to a problem. We are not, incidentally, suggesting that the preschoolers in the present study were discovering for the first time the general principle of extension. Instead, we are suggesting that they were learning the principle with specific reference to the available materials.

The third significant predictor of problem solving was the construction of complex structures within the playful context. Again, knowledge of the structural possibilities of the objects may have had some impact on the insightful discovery of the problem solution. Future research in this area may shed light not only on the functional nature of play but also on the prerequisites for insightful problem solving.

References

Birch, H.G. The relation of previous experience to insightful problem-solving. *Journal of Comparative Psychology,* 1945, *38,* 267-283.

Bruner, J. Going beyond the information given. In H. Gruber (Ed.), *Contemporary approaches to cognition.* Cambridge, Mass.: Harvard University Press, 1957.

Bruner, J. The nature and uses of immaturity. *American Psychologist,* 1972, *27,* 687-708.

Candland, D.K., French, J.A., & Johnson, C.N. Object play: Test of a categorized model by the genesis of object play in *Macacca fuscata.* In E.O. Smith (Ed.),*Social play in primates.* New York: Academic Press, 1978.

Cheyne, J.A. Object play and problem-solving: Methodological problems and conceptual promise. In D.J. Pepler & K.H. Rubin (Eds.), *The play of children: Current theory and research.* Basel, Switzerland: S. Karger AG, 1982.

Dansky, J.L. Make-believe: A mediator of the relationship between play and associative fluency. *Child Development,* 1980, *51,* 576-579.

Dansky, J.L., & Silverman, I.W. Effects of play on associative fluency in preschool-aged children. *Developmental Psychology,* 1973, *9,* 38-43.

Dansky, J.L., & Silverman, I.W. Play: A general facilitator of associative fluency. *Developmental Psychology,* 1975, *11,* 104.

Darvill, D. *Effects of play with relevant and non-relevant materials on problem-solving.* Unpublished master's thesis, University of Waterloo, 1981.

Groos, K. *The play of animals.* New York: Appleton, 1898.

Hutt, C. Exploration and play. In B. Sutton-Smith (Ed.), *Play and learning.* New York: Gardner Press, 1979.

Kohler, W. *The mentality of apes.* New York: Harcourt, Brace, 1925.

Pepler, D.J. *The effects of play on convergent and divergent problem-solving.* Unpublished doctoral dissertation, University of Waterloo, 1979. *Dissertation Abstracts International,* 1979, *40,* 5039B-5040B.

Pepler, D.J., & Ross, H.S.: The effects of play on convergent and divergent problem-solving. *Child Development,* 1981, *52,* 1202-1210.

Piaget, J. *Play, dreams, and imitation in childhood.* New York: Norton, 1962.

Rubin, K.H., Fein, G.G., & Vandenberg, B. Play. In E.M. Hetherington (Ed.), *Handbook of child psychology: Social development.* New York: Wiley, 1983.

Schiller, P.H. Innate motor action as a basis of learning. In P.H. Schiller (Ed.), *Instinctive behavior.* New York: International Universities Press, 1957.

Smith, P.K., & Dutton, S. Play and training on direct and innovative problem solving. *Child Development,* 1979, *50,* 830-836.

Sylva, K. *The relationship between play and problem-solving in children 3-5 years old.* Unpublished doctoral dissertation, Harvard University, 1974.

Sylva, K. Play and learning. In B. Tizard & D. Harvey (Eds.), *Biology of play.* Philadelphia: Lippincott, 1977.

Sylva, K., Bruner, J., & Genova, P. The role of play in the problem-solving of children 3-5 years old. In J. Bruner, A. Jolly, & K. Sylva (Eds.), *Play.* New York: Basic Books, 1976.

Van Lawick-Goodall, J. The behavior of free living chimpanzees in the Gombe Stream Reserve. *Animal Behavior Monographs,* 1968, *1,* 161-311.

Vandenberg, B. Play, problem-solving, and creativity. In K.H. Rubin (Ed.), *New directions for child development: Children's play.* San Francisco: Jossey-Bass, 1980.

Vandenberg, B. The role of play in the development of insightful tool-using strategies. *Merrill-Palmer Quarterly,* 1981, *27,* 97-110.

Received February 17, 1982. Revision received March 23, 1982.

Gender Development

14

The following problem has stumped many college students (and their professors):

> A father and his son were in a car accident. The father was killed, and the son was seriously injured. The father was pronounced dead at the scene of the accident, and his body was taken to a local mortuary. The son was taken by ambulance to a hospital and was immediately wheeled into an operating room. A surgeon was called. On seeing the patient, the attending surgeon exclaimed, "Oh, my God, it's my son!" How can this be? (After Hyde 1985)

If you had a difficult time recognizing that the surgeon was the boy's mother, you may have fallen prey to a brainteaser designed to demonstrate how easily male and female roles are stereotyped. To compound the issue, gender is a very prominent characteristic of self and others for most people.

When people are asked to describe themselves, often one of the first terms that comes to mind is *man, woman, boy,* or *girl*. And, associated with those terms may be a whole grab bag of attributes and stereotypes that emphasize the differences, and not the similarities, between the sexes. Notions of what the two sexes are like seem to cut across sex, socioeconomic class, religion, age, educational level, profession, and marital status (Broverman et al. 1972). Typically, traits denoting activity and competence (e.g., aggressive, dominant, self-confident) are linked to maleness, whereas traits of warmth and expressiveness (e.g., gentle, tender, talkative) are linked to femaleness.

Such a consensus on the differences between males and females seems to suggest simple and direct links between biological sex and behavior. However, the study of the nature of sex differences and their origins has revealed that the links between biology and behavior are quite complex. Researchers now recognize many dimensions of sex typing. It is not sufficient to refer to a child as a "boy" or an adult as a "woman" as a way of explaining possible differences in behaviors, attitudes, and self-perceptions. Rather, within the context of biological sex, researchers recommend that activities and interests, concepts or beliefs about sex typing, values, social relationships, and personality characteristics, as well as sociocultural ex-

pectations and prohibitions also be taken into consideration (Huston 1983).

Along these same lines, researchers use the term *gender* as opposed to *sex* because sex may refer to both biological (e.g., chromosomal or reproductive) characteristics and psychological characteristics and behaviors that differentiate male from female (Deaux 1985). A distinction between gender and sex makes it less likely to attribute the psychological characteristics to biological factors or the other way around. Thus, the term **sex** is reserved for references to biological characteristics, and **gender** is used to describe the nonphysiological aspects of sex that social convention teaches are appropriate for either males or females (Deaux 1985; Unger 1979). Biology and psychology are intertwined, but more and more contemporary researchers are finding the distinction between the two is helpful. Therefore, the terminology in this chapter will adhere to the distinction between sex and gender as much as possible.

The term **gender identity** can take on a number of meanings. Gender identity may simply refer to the recognition that a person is a boy or girl from noting the physical differences between males and females. Another definition of gender identity emphasizes a personal awareness of being either male or female. Gender identity may or may not parallel a person's **gender role, gender-role stereotype,** or **gender-typed behavior** (e.g., "I like to play with trucks, *not* dolls"). These refer to the overt behaviors (as opposed to an internalized identification) that society recognizes as appropriate for men and women. **Gender-role preference** refers to the desire to adopt the behaviors and attitudes of one sex over the other (e.g., "I prefer feminine clothes"). In early childhood, such preferences may be seen in the choice of toys (trucks versus dolls) and play activities (baseball versus playing house). Later on in development, gender-role preferences may manifest themselves in career and life-style choices. Finally, we can talk about sex differences when we are making comparisons between males and females on particular traits and characteristics.

Attitudes and behaviors regarding gender may not be congruent within the same individual. For example, many women can recall their childhood as a time of climbing trees, pushing trucks across the kitchen floor, and hating frilly dresses.

Gender-related behavior and attitude may not always correspond. A child may identify herself as female (her gender identity), yet prefer to engage in gender-typed behavior of the opposite sex.

For these tomboys, behaviors and preferences for play and toys were inconsistent with social expectations of feminine behavior. Yet, playing as boys would not necessarily mean that such women thought of themselves as anything but females. Men who take paternity leaves to care for their newborn infants may not manifest gender-role stereotypic behavior but may have strong gender identities. Conversely, people who are insecure about their gender identities may exhibit macho or ultrafeminine behaviors—gender-role behaviors in all of their stereotyped glory.

As this discussion of terminology suggests, the study of gender development is a complex affair. This chapter addresses the developmental path that gender roles take from infancy to adolescence (or what develops). It examines a number of theoretical explanations of how gender develops and considers issues such as gender typing in the schools and androgyny.

The Development of Gender Roles: The Contributions of Biology and the Environment

Gender is an aspect of the self that undergoes a great deal of change and rethinking as children progress from infancy to adolescence. As children develop, both biological and environmental forces shape their emerging masculine or feminine identities, as well as behaviors that may or may not conform to socially defined gender roles. In considering the complex changes in gender during childhood, try not to view the biological and environmental as either-or contributors to the developmental process, but rather as factors that enter together into the gender formula.

Prenatal Development

Each egg cell in a woman's body contains an X chromosome, whereas the man's sperm cells contain either an X or a Y chromosome. If an X-bearing sperm fertilizes an egg, the resulting sex chromosome combination will be XX, and a genetically female child will be produced. If the fertilizing sperm bears a Y chromosome, a genetically male child will be produced with the XY sex chromosome pattern. Therefore, the father determines the gender of the child.

The process of sex differentiation does not end with the meeting of the two sex chromosomes. Throughout prenatal development, several significant turning points, or "gates," influence the future maleness or femaleness of the organism (Money & Ehrhardt 1972). Once a particular genetic or hormonal event has occurred, the choice cannot be redirected—the gate has closed. Gate 1 occurs at conception when the genetic sex of the organism is determined.

Regardless of genetic sex, during the first six weeks after conception the unborn child has the potential to develop into either a male or a female, because the organs of reproduction, or gonads, are undifferentiated. After six to eight weeks of gestation, the Y chromosome will direct the formation of testes, which, in turn, begin secreting two male

hormones (androgens). Testosterone stimulates tissues to differentiate into male internal organs, and *Müllerian-inhibiting substance* inhibits the development of female internal organs. If androgens are not produced, the gonadal organs will differentiate into ovaries by the sixth month of gestation. Thus, gate 2 has closed (Money & Ehrhardt 1972).

Gate 3 closes at around three to four months after conception, when the external genitals of the fetus are differentiated. The hormone testosterone influences the formation of male external genitalia (i.e., the formation of a penis). If the male's tissues are not responsive to testosterone at this point, female external genitalia will develop. Likewise, a female exposed to the male hormone at this point may develop male external genitalia.

Gate 4 leads from the genitals to the brain. At this point testosterone affects the midportions of the brain (the hypothalamus), rendering the brain sensitive to male hormones and insensitive to female hormones (estrogens). The hypothalamus controls the pituitary gland, which stimulates the production of testosterone in the testes and suppresses the female hormonal cycle in male adults. For female adults, the pituitary gland stimulates estrogen production in the ovaries and controls the menstrual cycle.

Gate 5 occurs during birth, when parents and medical staff look at the external genitalia of the newborn; exclaim triumphantly, "It's a boy!" or "It's a girl!"; and initiate the complex socialization process that usually results in a correspondence between sex and gender.

Several important conclusions should be drawn from this "relay race." First, at each of the turning points, the fetus will develop into a female unless a Y chromosome or androgen is introduced. Estrogen, however, is not necessary for the feminization of gonadal tissue. Second, there must be a correspondence among genes, hormonal secretion, and tissue receptivity in order for the proclamation of sex at gate 5 to match the preceding in utereo events. Third, the prenatal process of sex differentiation has an impact on the entire lifespan of the individual, not only in terms of the match (or mismatch) between sex and gender, but also in the programming of the portion of the brain that controls the cyclical production of hormones during adult life.

Infancy

There are few observable behavioral differences between girl babies and boy babies. Some evidence suggests that infant females are more sensitive to touch and that infant males are more active (Block 1976). In terms of biological differences, boys, on the average, tend to be slightly longer and heavier at birth, but they are more neurologically immature and irritable than females. Girls mature between 2 to 2½ years faster than males, and their skeletal development is more advanced.

Such differences may encourage the differential treatment shown by parents toward their young sons or daughters. For example, because females mature faster physically, parents may expect greater maturity of social skills from their daughters than from their sons (Parsons 1980). This partly may be due to parental expectations, but also by the differences in the ways male and female babies react to adults. Adults also tend to handle male babies more roughly (Maccoby & Jacklin 1974), and, when mothers think that a baby is male, they will more likely offer the child a train to play with than a doll; conversely, a baby assumed to be female will be offered a doll more frequently than a train (Will, Self & Datan 1976).

In addition to studying the behavioral differences between male and female infants, researchers have also examined the possible effects of prenatal hormones on behavior. For example, one condition for study is **hermaphroditism.** Genetic male hermaphroditism (the external genitalia are female but the internal reproductive system is male) may be caused by a failure to manufacture androgens during the prenatal period or by a lack of receptivity to androgen by target tissues. This androgen-insensitivity syndrome cannot be alleviated by administration of androgen after birth, but there are cases of children who were able to metabolize androgens at puberty. Both forms of male hermaphroditism are genetic in origin; and, in most cases, the child looks like and is raised as a female.

Hermaphroditism in genetic females can be caused by an overproduction of androgen by the adrenocortical glands during fetal development, which does not affect the gonads but does cause the external genitalia to assume a masculine appearance. This problem, known as **adrenogenital syndrome** (AGS), differs from progestin-induced hermaphroditism, which occurs when the fetus is exposed to synthetic steroid hormones taken by the mother.

John Money and Anke Ehrhardt have concentrated their research efforts on assessing the psychological consequences of hermaphroditism. The logic behind the research program is as follows: if AGS females who were raised as females after corrective surgery manifest a relatively greater number of masculine-type behaviors than the normal (unaffected) controls, such findings would provide a powerful argument for the dominance of prenatal hormones on later behavior.

In one study, Money and Ehrhardt (1972) selected twenty-five fetally androgenized genetic females, aged 4 to 16 years, who had received cortisone, surgical treatment, or both and were raised as females. The researchers compared these girls with a control group of normal girls matched on age, IQ, socioeconomic background, and race. Ehrhardt and Baker (1974) compared seventeen AGS females and ten AGS males (who were exposed to higher levels of androgen than normal prenatally) to their normal male and female siblings. In yet another study, Ehrhardt and Money (1967) presented data from ten girls whose mothers had received progesterone while pregnant. All three investigations focused on the results from IQ tests, structured doll play, and interviews with the children and their mothers.

The most persistent finding from this research is that girls identified themselves as female, but they were more tomboyish than their controls. For example, they liked to play outdoor sports and games; had a tendency to fight more often; preferred pants to dresses; were not interested in babysitting or dolls; and liked to play with cars, trucks, and blocks. Although most wanted to get married and have children of their own, they were more interested in pursuing careers than were the controls. In addition, the AGS girls exhibited a higher-activity level than is typical of normal girls, which was also true of AGS males relative to unaffected boys (Ehrhardt & Baker 1974). No differences in IQ were found between AGS females and normal females. There is some evidence that males with androgen-insensitivity syndrome manifest the typical female cognitive pattern of better verbal and poorer visual-spatial skills (Shepherd-Look 1982).

This research appears to provide a convincing argument in favor of prenatal hormonal influences on later gender-typed behavior. However, a number of methodological problems in the design of the research make it difficult to pinpoint exactly what caused the behavioral differences between AGS females and their controls. For example, parental perceptions of their AGS daughters may have been influenced by the fact that they knew their daughters had a unique prenatal history. After all, any parent may be quick to call a daughter's activities tomboyish knowing that she looked like a little boy in the delivery room. From such research, the difficulties of separating nature from nurture become clearer. Indeed, Money (1987) concluded from his work on hermaphroditism that prenatal hormones may predispose the human brain toward either masculinity or femininity, with postnatal experiential factors either facilitating or diminishing the prenatal hormonal effects.

Childhood

During the preschool years, a child's gender identity takes on a clearer focus. Children have learned to label themselves boy or girl and are very aware of many of the gender-role stereotypes in our culture. Most theories of gender-role development—including psychoanalytic, cognitive, and learning theories—also agree that the preschool years are significant for the acquisition of a gender identity. By the time children are 3 years old, definite differences in behaviors and activities may be found between the sexes. For example, when they are given a choice, either in free-play or laboratory situations, preschool boys and girls choose to play with same-sex toys.

During middle childhood, the preference for gender-typed toys and activities continues for boys. However, girls become increasingly interested in masculine activities (Huston 1983). The divergence in the male-female preferences for toys and activities could be due to the greater latitude

given to girls for cross-gender play (Langlois & Downs 1980). It is also possible that boys' toys and activities are more fun and challenging and override the attractiveness of the dollhouse. During middle childhood, boys also become more noticeably active, particularly when other boys are around (Shepherd-Look 1982), and both boys and girls begin to exhibit preferences for their own sex as evidenced in their doll play (Katz 1979).

As the elementary school years go by, the preference for same-sex friends becomes increasingly pronounced. The term *sex cleavage* refers to the division by sex in children's friendships and group activities. "No boys allowed," or "Do not enter if you are a girl" are familiar signs on the clubhouse doors of grade school children. Such adherence to same-sex friends almost takes on moral overtones, for children often claim that to engage in cross-sex behavior is not only deviant, but also wrong (Damon 1977). Again, this is particularly true of boys. As children become more sophisticated about concepts of gender and confident of their own gender identities, some flexibility enters during the latter part of middle childhood (Russo 1985).

Sources of Stereotyping

As mentioned, even young children are aware of gender-role stereotyping. Another indicator may be found in the kinds of toys children acquire. Rheingold and Cook (1975) analyzed the contents of children's rooms and discovered that girls had more dolls and domestic toys; boys more vehicles, sports equipment, and military toys. Robinson and Morris (1986) obtained a list of over five hundred toys that eighty-six preschool children received for Christmas. The parents of these children were asked to indicate which of these toys the children themselves had requested. Approximately 75 percent by age 5 of the toys requested were gender-stereotyped. Parents tended to provide more gender-neutral toys suggesting that children are the major contributors to the stereotyped toy box.

What are some of the sources from which children learn stereotypes? The media—especially television—influence gender-role development. Children under 5 years of age have been estimated to view an average of 25½ hours of television per week; by the time they reach high school, they will have viewed more than fifteen thousand hours of television. Analyses of the content of gender roles portrayed on television have been remarkably consistent across all sorts of programming, including cartoons and advertisements. There are more male than female roles on television, and often these roles conform to gender stereotypes. Males engage in more activities and are more aggressive and constructive than females; the activities of females tend to be ignored (Sternglanz & Serbin 1974). Males also are portrayed in professional roles, but most television females portray a nonprofessional romantic, married, or family figure. Similar trends have been observed for commercials: 75 percent of all television commercials using women have them selling bathroom or kitchen products. Even *Sesame Street* has been criticized as presenting gender stereotypes. There are more male actors than female actors on this prize-winning educational program, and the loudmouthed female puppets are hardly worthy of emulating (Action for Children's Television 1978).

Recent concern about television and gender stereotyping has addressed the more subtle features of televised messages that convey stereotypes. Even when the content of advertisements was sex-neutral, Huston and her associates (1984) found that children from 6 to 12 years of age recognized that fast-paced commercials with loud music, sound effects, and numerous scene changes were designed for boys. Children were also aware that soft music and many fades and dissolves were representative of commercials for girls' products. If television's portrayal of men and women has any impact on the development of gender concepts, then attention must be paid to the technical format, as well as to the intended content.

Proving that televiewing has a definite impact on the gender-role development of children has been difficult. However, the evidence, though mostly correlational, is beginning to mount up. McGhee and Frueh (1980), for example, found a relationship between gender-role stereotyping and the amount of time children spend watching television. The researchers classified first, third, fifth,

and seventh graders as either heavy viewers (twenty-five or more hours of televiewing per week) or light viewers (ten or less hours of televiewing per week) and then administered a children's gender-stereotype questionnaire. The heavy televiewers made more stereotyped responses than light televiewers. Furthermore, there was a progressive increase in such stereotyping from grades 1 through 5 and a leveling off from grades 5 through 7. The researchers felt that although television may not be responsible for teaching stereotypes, it may strengthen such notions acquired elsewhere and make it more difficult to modify stereotypes in the face of contrary evidence. Research studying the long-term impact of television on children's concepts of gender is needed.

Television probably has been the most visible source of gender stereotyping in the media, but others also have been identified. Children's storybooks and shool readers have typically placed more male characters in the central role; they are the doers as females passively look on. Men and women in traditional roles and occupations also are heavily represented in children's books. Although recent efforts have attempted to overcome stereotypes in children's literature, female appearances still are relatively meager, and their behaviors tend to follow the traditional lines (Huston 1983). Furthermore, many Sunday comics also provide examples of gender stereotyping (Chavez 1985; Brabant & Mooney 1986). An analysis of popular comics that appear nationally (e.g., "Blondie," "Dennis the Menace," and "Peanuts") finds the traditional gender roles still in fashion. Men are shown in outdoor activities and at their occupations, and women are more often found in the home, taking care of children and rarely reading. The ultimate symbol of the female role, the apron, still abounds in comics.

Gender and Aggression

A noteworthy distinction between boys and girls has been in aggressive behavior. Maccoby and Jacklin (1974), in a classic review of research on sex differences in children, found that one of the few dimensions on which boys and girls differ is aggression. The difference begins to appear at 2 to

One of the few well-documented sex differences is that males are more aggressive than females. This difference probably is due to biological factors that interplay with cultural expectations for male aggressiveness and female docility.

3 years of age and continues throughout adulthood. These differences appear across many different types of aggression that have been examined, such as physical aggression, verbal aggression, and fantasy aggression. Maccoby and Jacklin concluded, on the basis of such pervasive evidence, that the sex differences in aggression are biological in origin.

While such male-female differences in aggression are found in other cultures, the renowned anthropologist Margaret Mead (1935) reported gender-role variation in three "primitive" tribes in New Guinea. In the Arapesh tribe, both men and women were nurturant and nonaggressive—they both manifested expressive roles. The males and females of the Mundugumor tribe, in contrast, were equally competitive and aggressive. Finally, in the Tchambuli tribe, women were independent

and aggressive, while men were dependent, nurturant, and interested in arts and crafts. While Mead's work has been subjected to misinterpretation and criticism, her conclusions are important: how the parameters of culture help to define and shape the behaviors of males and females cannot be ignored.

Additionally, Tieger (1980) claimed that males are more aggressive because of their socialization. For example, parents encourage more gross-motor activity in their young sons than in their daughters and supervise their sons' play to a lesser degree than their daughters' play. Boys, therefore, may inadvertently be given more opportunity to engage in spontaneous aggressive behavior. Furthermore, Tieger pointed out, there are numerous models of male aggression within our culture. For example, television glorifies male aggression and often conveys the message that aggression pays off. Maccoby and Jacklin (1980) countered that male aggression has been observed in primates, cross-culturally in humans, and in very young children who have not yet had much opportunity to learn about such differences. Thus, they believe that sex differences in aggression are biologically based, although modified by social interaction.

Adolescence

During adolescence, becoming a man or a woman is no longer the fantasy of childhood; it is the reality of the not-so-distant future. Contemplation of that future and its concomitant roles and activities is enhanced by the hypothetical and abstract nature of newly emerging formal operational skills (see Chapter 6).

Gender and Personality

Erikson (1968) believes a reformulation of gender identity is a crucial dimension of the normative crisis of identity versus diffusion (see Chapter 10). According to Erikson, figuring out the answer to the question *Who am I?* includes the "part crisis" of **sexual polarization versus bisexual confusion.** This part crisis involves the adolescent's anticipation of an intimate relationship with a person of the opposite sex and the coming to grips with himself or herself as a mature male or female. Thus, says Erikson, gender identity develops early in life but becomes crystallized into identity during adolescence.

These social and psychological changes are significant, but it is the biological changes that make confrontation with gender identity and gender role unavoidable. Puberty brings about dramatic changes, such as a growth spurt, the onset of menstruation or seminal ejaculation, the development of secondary sex characteristics, and a surge of sexual arousal and interest. As a result of these changes, gender identity assumes a sexual orientation that was not quite as significant during the childhood years. Furthermore, both adolescent boys and girls become concerned with their appearance and how they present themselves to

others. Problems in Child Development "The Riddle of Anorexia and Bulimia" discusses how body image concerns have led to an increase in eating disorders among adolescent girls.

According to Lamb and Urberg (1978), young adolescents become rather inflexible and rigid in playing out their gender roles. The flexibility gained in late middle childhood is lost because of the uncertainty of the young adolescent's new sexual status. There is a parallel here between young children and young adolescents in their adherence to gender-role stereotypes: both conform to tradition in their quest for a strong foothold on their gender identities. However, young children view such transgressions as altering the physical identity of the individual, whereas young adolescents see such transgressions as socially deviant behavior (Stoddart & Turiel 1985). Ullian (1976) supported this observation in her analysis of interviews with children aged 6 to 18 years. She found, for example, that while 14-year-olds recognize that the differences between males and females are largely socially defined, they also claim that members of each sex must conform to gender-role stereotypes. Here are the comments of a 14-year-old "self-confessed feminist" when asked what she would think of a man who dressed in a feminine style coat and shoes with high heels:

> "I wouldn't go near him, ugh!" (Why not?)
> "They have some psychological problem." (Why?)
> "They must have something wrong with them, maybe they were brought up that way, because they shouldn't act feminine, that is our identity, that is our position, not theirs. They should be masculine." (Why?) "Because that is the way it is always—men are masculine and women are feminine. If they were feminine, it would really be strange." (P. 41)

By the time most adolescents are 17 years old, a greater flexibility towards gender roles and gender identity develops. No longer uncomfortable with the physical changes of pubescence and more practiced in behaving as a mature male or female, the adolescent no longer bends quite so far to the pressures of gender-role stereotypes. Thus, Ullian (1976) found that 18-year-olds no longer believe

The consequences of the self-starvation characteristics of anorexia nervosa *is evident in this young woman.*

that the differences between males and females are basic to their personal identities. Tolerance of cross-sex behavior (e.g., females calling males for dates and sharing expenses) is observed, and males feel freer to disclose their thoughts and feelings to both male and female peers. Failing to recognize the adaptive value of the temporary rigidity of their early teens, many college youths look back on the gender-role conformity of their younger adolescent years with distaste and amusement.

Sex Differences in Cognition

Although differences between males and females on several characteristics (such as aggression and activity level) appear early in childhood, sex differences on certain measures of intellectual ability do not consistently appear until adolescence. The source of much of this information is a review

by Eleanor Maccoby and Carol Jacklin in 1974 of over two thousand studies on sex differences that were published from 1966 to 1973.

Girls may be more developmentally advanced than boys in verbal ability at around ages 2 and 3, but during childhood the gender differences are not significant. Maccoby and Jacklin found that the sex difference appears during early adolescence and continues to increase throughout adolescence and early adulthood: girls score higher on both simple verbal measures and high-level verbal tasks such as reading comprehension, verbal creativity, and understanding complex logical relationships.

Another sex difference that emerges during adolescence is in the area of visual-spatial ability. Beginning in adolescence and continuing throughout the high school years, males have been found

Problems in Child Development

The Riddle of Anorexia and Bulimia: To Be Female Is to Be Slender

They are the children of privilege. They come from upper-middle-class families headed by parents who are older, better-educated, and financially better-off than the average person in the United States. Nine out of ten are girls, and they face a world which offers them greater career and social opportunities than their parents had. Indeed, in some ways they might be seen as belonging to the first generation of adolescent girls to reap the full benefits of the women's liberation movement. And yet, they suffer from puzzling disorders that cause them either to starve themselves to the point of emaciation (anorexia nervosa) or to binge on high-caloric food and then purge themselves by vomiting or other means (bulimia). Some girls will manifest symptoms of both disorders.

Dr. Hilde Bruch is a psychiatrist who has worked extensively with victims of anorexia and who has authored many articles and books on the subject, most recently *The Golden Cage* (1978). In attempting to explain the recent prevalence of anorexia, Dr. Bruch mentions the fascination with slimness that typifies our culture. Fashion models, actresses, and characters in one-calorie diet-soda television commercials are usually excruciatingly slim. The message is that the slender woman is loved and desired but the fat woman is not. There is also a link between femininity and thinness. Even women who have abandoned many of the traditional behaviors associated with womanhood may be reluctant to give up their feminine (i.e., thin) look (Striegel-Moore, Silberstein & Rodin 1986).

Another possible factor in the increased incidence of anorexia is the relative freedom of choice available to young women today. No longer does the high school girl face a future in which her most likely roles will be those of homemaker and mother. If she chooses a career outside the home, she no longer feels restricted to nursing or teaching. Freedom of choice is a highly desirable goal, but the greater the number of choices available, the greater the stress generated by choosing. The choice also involves compromising the dependence for which girls traditionally are valued, for the image of the independent successful woman.

Finally, the adolescent girl of today may feel greater stress because of her greater sexual freedom. Girls today are dating earlier and more often than in the past and are more likely to be sexually active at an early age. Pressure to conform to expectations of an active social life may encourage young girls to seek refuge in the thinner prepubescent body attained through starvation or purging (Striegel-Moore, Silberstein & Rodin 1986).

Whatever the specific reasons for the increased prevalence of anorexia and bulimia in the 1970s and 1980s, one fact appears certain: the disease is not merely a physical ailment; it is a psychological one as well. As one of Bruch's patients remarked, "The real illness has to do with the way you feel about yourself . . . You are afraid of not living up to what you think you are expected to do" (Bruch 1978, 135).

to be superior to females on nonanalytic spatial tasks that involve manipulating objects in space either mentally or physically. Such tasks usually involve finding a path through a maze, fitting shapes into their appropriate-sized holes, performing mental rotations of two-dimensional objects in three-dimensional space, and estimating the number of blocks in a two-dimensional array.

Maccoby and Jacklin found that males, again beginning at adolescence, were also superior on analytic-spatial tasks, particularly those that involve the process of "decontextualization," or the ability to separate a figure from its surrounding context. This ability, also known as **field independence,** has been linked to thinking styles, and has led to the belief that females think in a more global manner while males think in a more analytic manner. This conclusion has been questioned by a number of investigators (Caplan, MacPherson & Tobin 1985; Sherman 1967) who claim that tests of cognitive styles may demonstrate that males perform better in tasks of spatial ability, but such results do not necessarily mean males are more analytic in their thinking than females.

As in the cognitive abilities already discussed, the research suggests that sex differentiation in mathematical ability does not begin until early adolescence. Prior to this age, the two sexes are similar in their acquisition of quantitative concepts and arithmetic skills. After puberty, males tend to perform better than females on tasks assessing quantitative skills. Maccoby and Jacklin (1974) did find evidence that males' quantitative superiority shows up in comparisons of males and females who have taken the same number of mathematics courses. In general, however, the male adolescent does receive greater encouragement for active participation in mathematics-type activities than does the adolescent female and is more likely to anticipate a career that involves the use of mathematics (Meece et al. 1982). Thus, interest in mathematics during the adolescent years is generally more true of boys than girls.

At present, it is unclear as to why such sex differences in cognitive abilities appear during adolescence. Along with puberty may come a reorganization of brain functions related to a growth spurt of the central nervous system (Waber 1979). It also has been proposed that the cognitive differences between male and female adolescents are manifestations of social pressure to conform according to gender-stereotyped lines. In yet another hypothesis, Dweck (1986) suggested that girls (especially bright girls) experience different motivational patterns than boys; these patterns cause girls to avoid courses that initially may be confusing or involve new conceptional frameworks (as is found in secondary school mathematics courses). Each of these explanations has its value, but it also is important to recognize that such differences in cognitive abilities do not necessarily mean large dif-

ferences. Hyde (1981) reanalyzed the studies on verbal, spatial, and quantitative abilities reviewed by Maccoby and Jacklin. When results of the research were combined for each of the cognitive abilities, the differences between the sexes were extremely small. For example, the amount of variability in scores on verbal and quantitative tests due to gender was 1 percent; for nonanalytic visual-spatial ability, 4 percent; and for analytic visual-spatial ability, 2.5 percent!

Theories of Gender-Role Development

The preceding discussion of gender-role acquisition described "what" develops. The following discussion presents a number of theories that attempt to explain "how" gender roles develop. As you read, try not to view any one theory as the only "right" position, but rather as one contribution to our understanding of gender development. Thus, the psychoanalytic perspective contributes to our understanding of the emotional component of gender-role development; learning theories contribute to our knowledge of how social interactions influence gender-role development; and cognitive theories contribute to our knowledge of how gender-role concepts are acquired.

Psychoanalytic Theory

As you will recall from Chapter 10, Freud (1950) believed that gender roles and gender identity result from the resolution of the Oedipal complex encountered during the phallic stage. Boys perceive their fathers as competitors for their mothers' affections and, as a result, fear castration. To resolve the conflict, they become more like their fathers. Girls' desires for their fathers and rivalry with their mothers is properly resolved through the female aspiration of growing up to be a mother and symbolically attaining the penis (believed lost by "castration") through the birth of a child, especially a male child.

Erikson (1968) has taken a more positive view of female gender development than his theoretical ancestor, although his view also emphasizes the anatomical differences between males and females. His emphasis shifts from the notion of a lack of a penis to the presence of a woman's child-bearing and child-rearing potential. Erikson's observations of the play construction of 10-, 11-, and 12-year-old boys and girls led him to propose that boys' identities center on active, erect, and projectile models (i.e., boys built towers and tall buildings, knocking them down when complete), whereas girls' identities center on enclosed, protected, and receptive models (i.e., girls built interior, peaceful scenes). Thus, the core of the female identity is an "inner space" that leads to a more humanitarian, compassionate, and nurturant approach toward self and society.

Many criticisms have been levied against the psychoanalytic interpretation of gender-role development. The research community has found fault with the lack of empirical support for the notion of the Oedipal complex. Feminist scholars have taken exception to Freud's support of the traditional female-expressive role. In Freud's theory, healthy psychosexual development for women involves no aspirations for work and achievement. However, such low-achievement motivation may be more a reflection of living within a patriarchical society than limitations of a female's biology (Horney 1973). Freud's notion of penis envy has also upset many theorists and researchers. Clara Thompson (1974), a neo-Freudian, contended that women envy the penis because it symbolizes man's greater status and power, not because it is a coveted sexual organ. As a matter of fact, men consciously or unconsciously may envy the reproductive capabilities of women. For example, in some cultures, men go through a ritual pregnancy, childbirth, and recovery period—a practice known as *couvade.*

Erikson has not escaped criticism either. Whereas he takes a more favorable view of women, he also reaffirms the central significance of a woman's reproductive capability and her role as mother as the major dimension of her identity. For Erikson, healthy female ego development seems to require bearing children.

Despite these criticisms, the psychoanalytic approach has made several positive contributions to the understanding of gender-role acquisition. It underscores that gender identity is an early acqui-

sition and that the process of identification is central to its development. This perspective also points out that long-term father absence can seriously hamper a young boy's socioemotional development, and it calls attention to the harsher socialization practices directed towards males. Certainly, the early policies of the Boy Scouts of America support this claim (see Applying Our Knowledge "The Boy Scouts of America").

Learning Theories

Two types of learning theory are significant to the study of gender development. The first to be discussed, operant-conditioning theory, applies the principles of learning-contingent-on-reinforcement to the acquisition of gender-typed behavior. The second, social-learning theory, introduces the role of imitation in the development of gender roles and behavior.

Operant Conditioning

The appeal of conditioning theory (see Chapter 7) is that it explains many different behaviors by the same set of fundamental principles. Gender-role acquisition, according to behaviorists, involves the shaping of children's behaviors so that eventually they approximate masculine or feminine forms. Parents, peers, and teachers reward of praise gender-appropriate behavior and punish, ignore, or criticize gender-inappropriate behavior. The acquisition of a gender role and a gender identity, therefore, is based on socialization pressures applied to children; their gender roles are defined by the consequences of their actions.

In contrast to the psychoanalytic perspective—which uses clinical, or case-study, evidence for support—the conditioning perspective garners most of its support from research that uncovers differential treatment of boys and girls with respect to gender-typed behavior. Do the findings show that parents interact differently with their male and female children? The answer must be a qualified yes, for it really seems to depend on the sorts of behaviors and activities being observed. It does not appear that parents treat their boys or girls differently when it comes to discouraging aggression and dependence (Lamb & Urberg 1978). Parents

Applying Our Knowledge

The Boy Scouts of America: An Example of Male Gender-Role Socialization

Psychologists have speculated that it is harder for a boy to identify with masculinity than for a girl to identify with femininity. This is due to the father's absence for most of the day and the boy's initial attachment to his mother. Little boys are rarely told what they should do. Rather, their behavior is defined negatively in terms of what they should not do (i.e., anything that smacks of femininity or "sissy" stuff) (Hartley 1959).

Hantover (1978) speculated that such avoidance of feminine behav-

ior may have been one of the prime motivators behind the formation of the Boy Scouts of America in 1910. According to Hantover, the Boy Scouts was rapidly accepted among the middle class because of perceived threats to American masculinity. People feared that men could no longer flex their muscles because of the closing of the American frontier and the absence of war. More and more men entered white-collar jobs, and adolescent boys stayed at home longer to complete their educations. Scouting was portrayed as the means by which masculinity could be restored:

> The wilderness is gone, the Buckskin Man is gone, the painted Indian has hit the trail over the Great Divide, the hardships and privations of pioneer life, which did so much to develop sterling manhood are now but a legend in history, and we must depend upon the Boy Scout Movement to produce the MEN of the future. (Beard 1914, as cited by Hantover 1978, 189).

Furthermore:

> The REAL Boy Scout is not a "sissy." He is not a household plant, like little Lord Fauntleroy. There is nothing "milk and water" about him; he is not afraid of the dark. . . . He is not hitched to his mother's apronstrings. While he adores his mother, and would do anything to save her from suffering or discomfort, he is self-reliant, sturdy and full of vim. (West 1912, as cited by Hantover 1978, 191).

In the contemporary United States, such goals of achievement and competition for the male gender role may be producing many sources of conflict. As Pleck (1976) pointed out, little boys are socialized according to the traditional male role, but adult men are expected to exhibit expressive skills in business collaboration and in their relationships with women. They are expected to show tenderness and emotional intimacy, but also to remain levelheaded and cool.

also expect their sons and daughters to behave according to similar values such as being helpful around the house (Lambert, Yackley & Hein 1971). Yet, when parents work with their sons and daughters on a task, they communicate higher expectations and a desire for more independent behavior from their sons (Block 1978). Additionally, parents do seem to treat their sons and daughters differently when it comes to play activities and toy preferences. Such differential treatment occurs as early as 6 months and continues to be observed with older children.

A unique study by Langlois and Downs (1980) directly assessed and compared the rewards and punishments that mothers, fathers, and peers ad-

ministered to 3- and 5-year-olds on the basis of their gender-appropriate and gender-inappropriate play behavior. The researchers escorted a child to a room, where he or she was given either "girl" toys to play with (a dollhouse with furniture, a stove with pots and dishes, and women's clothing), or "boy" toys (an army set, a gas station with cars, and cowboy outfits with guns and holsters). The child was instructed to play with the toys in a gender-appropriate fashion. While the child was playing, his or her mother, father, or friend was escorted into the room. Thus, in the event of a cross-sex situation, a parent or peer could encounter a boy playing with a dollhouse or a girl setting up

Research findings suggest that gender-typed behavior in children are encouraged more by fathers than by mothers. Fathers are particularly attentive to bringing out masculine behavior in their sons.

soldiers from the army set. Fathers, mothers, and friends did not know that their behaviors toward the child's playing with the toys were the main focus of the researchers' observations.

Langlois and Downs found that the treatment the children received for playing along gender-appropriate or -inappropriate lines depended both on the sex of the child and on the person observing the child's play. For example, the researchers found that when boys engaged in cross-sex play they received punishment in the form of ridicule, interference with play, or a suggested alternative from both peers and fathers. Mothers, however tended to reward such behavior. When boys played with the masculine toys, they were ignored by their peers, received mild approval from their mothers,

and were clearly rewarded by their fathers. Mothers, fathers, and peers all approved of and rewarded same-sex play from girls, and disapproved of their cross-sex play.

Several important conclusions can be drawn from these findings. First, it appears that girls are treated more consistently than are boys by several different agents of socialization. Second, both peers' and fathers' responses were stronger than mothers' responses, and fathers exerted the greatest amount of pressure. These findings suggest that fathers are very significant teachers of gender-appropriate behavior. Indeed, Johnson's (1975) sociological analysis of the father role concludes that it is the father who brings out masculinity in his sons and femininity in his daughters. Finally, the difference in the amount of reward the fathers gave their sons for same-sex, as opposed to cross-sex, behaviors was greater than for daughters.

Langlois and Downs's study also emphasizes that gender-role behavior is not learned solely from parents. That peers reinforce gender-appropriate play and discourage cross-sex play has been observed in natural preschool settings (Lamb & Roopnarine 1979), as well as in laboratory settings. Siblings also have their impact. Although more cross-gender toys are available in homes with mixed-sex siblings, boys and girls are more likely to engage in cross-sex play activities if they come from homes where all of the children are of the same sex. Perhaps greater diversification of gender-role behavior is permitted and necessary in all-sister or all-brother families. After all, when there are no brothers to mow the lawn, a girl may find herself behind the mower.

Why is play so vulnerable to the lessons of gender typing? Perhaps play is an important, but fairly safe, arena for figuring out how to act in a boy-like or girl-like manner. In play, a boy or girl may be particularly responsive to the feedback that others provide. Thus, within certain areas of a child's life, the conditioning perspective offers valuable clues as to how gender roles are acquired. Although the development of gender roles and gender identity cannot be explained totally in terms of rewards and punishments, it is clear that when people important to the child reward either masculine or feminine behavior, their reactions have a significant impact on the child's development.

Social-Learning Theory

The social-learning, or observational, perspective (Bandura & Walters 1963) places more responsibility for the acquisition of gender-typed behaviors on the child than does conditioning theory (behavior and reinforcement/punishment). As you will recall from the discussion of social-learning theory in Chapter 7, new behaviors are acquired by observing and imitating the behaviors of others (models), particularly when rewards for imitation are anticipated. As applied to the development of gender roles, boys learn gender-appropriate behavior from observing and imitating the masculine behaviors of their fathers; girls learn gender-appropriate behavior from observing and imitating

the feminine behaviors of their mothers. The social-learning perspective acknowledges that anyone (teachers, siblings, grandparents, and so forth) may be a model for gender typing, particularly if that person is perceived by the child as warm, nurturant, or powerful. However, parents are particularly important models because of the amount of time they spend with their children and the intensity of their relationships with their children. Such factors seem to be particularly significant for males: the degree of masculinity in sons has been found to be related to how warm and competent they perceive their fathers to be (Lamb & Urberg 1978).

A major criticism levied against the social-learning perspective concerns research methodology used by its advocates. The typical study involves a child viewing either a male or female (usually an adult) engaged in an originally gender-neutral activity. For example, a female or male model may fashion an object out of clay or claim to prefer a balloon over a plastic horse. The child is then led to a room where a variety of objects (including those used by the model) are available and told to play with whatever he or she wishes. Observations usually are made through a one-way mirror or concealed camera to determine whether or not the child plays with the object used by the same-sex model or avoids the object seen with the opposite-sex model. In their review of this type of research, Maccoby and Jacklin (1974) found little evidence supporting the view that a child will imitate a model on the basis of sex, and they discounted imitation as a significant determinant of gender-typed behavior.

Because the relationship between gender-typed behavior and imitation makes such intuitive sense, Maccoby and Jacklin's conclusions did not put an end to social-learning theory. Instead, it was recognized that concepts and research drew too simple a line between the behavior of a model and imitation by the child. Huston (1983), for example, claimed that children learn facets of both masculine and feminine gender typing but will behave in a gender-appropriate way when the situation and situational cues demand it. And Perry and Bussey (1979) proposed that children do not just imitate any one model. Instead, children observe the behavior of many males and females and form abstractions as to what is gender appropriate. These

Social learning theory proposes that children learn gender roles through imitating a number of individuals of their own sex, particularly those with whom they have a warm and nurturant relationship.

abstractions are based on the child's memory of the relative frequencies of behaviors performed by one sex over the other. Thus, children form a composite picture of a gender role from the many models encountered over the course of their short lifetimes. In their research, Perry and Bussey also found that imitation will increase when the number of same-sexed models displaying a particular behavior increase. Finally, because boys and girls often seek out different types of activities, they may be exposed to different sources of gender-role socialization. There is evidence, for example, that girls, more often than boys, seek out experiences that place them in adult-led situations (Huston et al. 1986). In terms of the modeling framework,

this means that girls receive more feedback and modeling from adults, and boys receive more feedback and modeling from peers.

Can modeling also encourage cross-sex behavior in children? Research on the effects of maternal employment on children's behaviors suggests that this is the case. In the United States, children of working mothers tend to be less gender-stereotyped (Cordua, McGraw & Drabman 1979). Girls of working mothers generally are more achievement-oriented and have higher educational and career goals than daughters of nonworking mothers (Hoffman 1979). Furthermore, Baruch and Barnett (1986) found evidence of reduced gender stereotyping in children whose fathers performed more traditionally feminine chores at home. A second major criticism contends that the social-learning perspective fails to acknowledge that a child must have an initial awareness of being a boy or a girl in order to imitate. To complete the picture begun by the learning perspective, then, the cognitive component of gender identity must be addressed. Cognitive theories offer additional insight as to why children actively attend to models of their sex.

Cognitive Developmental Theory

In addition to his theory of moral development, Lawrence Kohlberg (1966) discussed the role of cognition in the acquisition of gender identity and gender role. Children go through three stages in the development of a complete understanding of gender:

1. Basic **gender identity,** in which children recognize that they are boys or girls on the basis of physical differences between males and females.
2. **Gender stability,** in which children realize that their gender will always remain the same and that they will grow up to be men or women.
3. **Gender constancy (conservation),** in which children understand that people's gender remains the same despite such superficial changes as hairstyles, dress, or activities.

Once children use the label *boy* or *girl*—first to themselves and then to others—they begin to organize ideas and experiences actively according to the categories of maleness and femaleness. Such labeling does not depend on any one model or person but rather comes from abstractions derived from a variety of sources, such as parents, siblings, and the media. Engaging in gender-typed behavior becomes pleasurable, because it confirms the child's self-categorization system: "I am a boy, therefore, I want to do boy things; therefore, the opportunity to do boy things (and to gain approval for doing them) is rewarding" (Kohlberg 1966, 89).

When an understanding of the stability of gender is acquired, there is an associated preference for the child's own sex (Smetana & Letourneau 1984). Just as children's knowledge of rules and obligations is rigid and inflexible when first acquired, so is their understanding of gender roles. Thus, 6- and 7-year-olds view acting in a gender-appropriate manner as a moral imperative—a boy

Figure 14.1 The Gender-Constancy Test

Source: From Emmerich, W., Goldman, K.S., Kirsch, B., and Sharabany, R. (1977) Evidence for a transitional phase in the development of gender constancy. *Child Development, 48,* 930-936. ©1977 by the Society for Research in Child Development, Inc.

who puts on a dress, for example, is naughty (Damon 1977).

Gender constancy is reportedly acquired at around age 6 or 7 and may be based on the concepts of conservation (see Chapter 6). This is exactly what Marcus and Overton (1978) found when they tested kindergarteners, first graders, and second graders on conservation and gender constancy: the former concepts were acquired prior to the latter. This sequence in the development of gender understanding has been observed cross-culturally in children from Belize, Kenya, Nepal, and American Samoa (Munroe, Shimmin & Munroe 1984).

Researchers use gender-constancy tests to see if children have acquired this concept. The test in Figure 14.1 is adapted from Emmerich and his associates (1976). In this test, drawings of a boy and a girl are placed into a ring binder. the drawings are cut at the neck so that the "heads page" can be turned over. On the following page, the positions, of the boy and girl heads are reversed. In this way, the boy's head can be presented with feminine clothing and vice versa. Starting with an all-girl picture, the researcher would say, "This is Janie." Then the researcher turns the page and asks the following questions (Emmerich et al. 1977):

- If Janie wants to be a boy, can she be?
- If Janie played with trucks and did boy things, what would she be? Would she be a boy or a girl?
- If Janie puts on boys' clothes (like this), what would she be? Would she be a girl or would she be a boy?
- If Janie has her hair cut short (like this), what would she be? Would she be a girl or would she be a boy?
- If Janie has her hair cut short (like this), and wears boys' clothes, (like this), what would she be? Would she be a girl or would she be a boy?

The same questions are then asked with the boy's picture and a boy's name.

In contrast to Kohlberg's claims, some evidence suggests that gender constancy can be acquired as early as 2 years of age. Kuhn, Nash, and Brucken (1978) gave 2- and 3-year-olds a gender-constancy test, as well as a test for gender typing and gender preference. The children were presented with two dolls, Michael and Lisa, and were asked to associate a picture of an activity with one of the dolls. Not surprisingly, children at this very early age have already learned the basic fundamentals of gender stereotyping: Lisa liked to play with dolls, cook dinner, and clean house, whereas Michael liked to play with cars, build things, and help his father. More importantly, Kuhn, Nash, and Brucken found a very high correlation between gender constancy and stereotyping. Children who understood the permanence of their gender were more likely to stereotype than those who did not. These same children also preferred their own gender to a significantly greater degree.

Why does stereotyping occur at such a very early age? Perhaps these researchers have found that when children are first learning about the permanence of their genders, their ability to process the subtleties and nuances of gender roles is limited to a few fundamental dimensions and concepts. As

you shall see in the next section of this chapter, flexibility in gender roles and gender identity may only come after a child is sure of what it means to be a male or a female.

Social-learning theory considers gender identity to follow or parallel the imitation of gender-typed behaviors. Children imitate models of their sex because they perceive a similarity between themselves and the models, and because they are rewarded for such imitation. Gender identity is then derived from such imitations. Cognitive developmental theory, in contrast, claims that imitation follows the acquisition of concepts of gender. There is some evidence supporting this cognitive developmental position. For example, Slaby and Frey (1975) gave 4-year-olds a gender-constancy task and then showed them a film. Each half of the screen had either a man or woman simultaneously building a fire, popping corn, playing instruments, and drinking juice. The children were able to look at only half of the screen at a time. Unknown to the children, Slaby and Frey observed their movie viewing through a one-way window beneath the screen, recording the amount of time spent looking at one half of the screen over the other. Boys and girls who had high-gender constancy scores spent a considerably longer period of time looking at the models than those children with low-gender constancy scores. Thus, something about gender constancy cues children into paying particular attention to the behavior of others. Furthermore, boys high in gender constancy spent a significantly greater amount of time attending to the male actor. A similar, but nonsignificant trend was noted for the girls. These findings have subsequently been replicated by Ruble (as cited by Maccoby 1980) for boys and girls 4 to 6 years old.

A More Contemporary Cognitive View: Information-Processing Theory

Both information-processing and cognitive developmental theories of gender typing and gender-role development claim that thinking serves to regulate gender-typed behavior. According to the information-processing perspective, the **schema** is the main determinant of gender typing. A schema is a set of ideas (naive theories) that guide

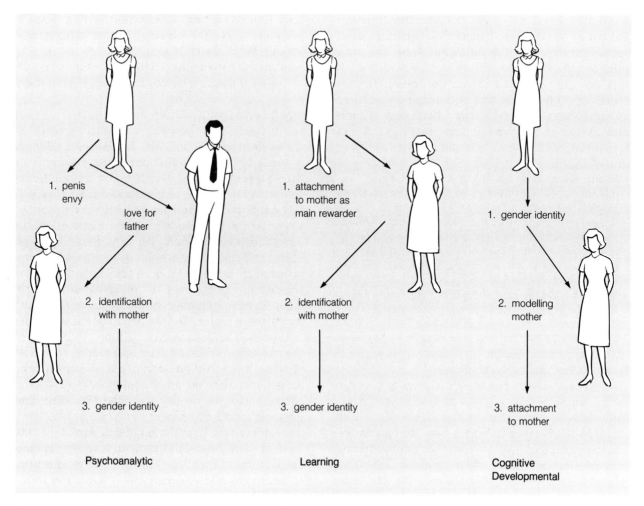

Figure 14.2   Theoretical Sequences in the Girl's Gender Identification

Source: Reprinted from *The Development of Sex Differences,* edited by Eleanor E.
Maccoby, with the permission of the publisher, Stanford University Press. ©1966 by
the Board of Trustees of the Leland Stanford Junior University.

decisions and behavior (Martin & Halverson 1981).
People form schemas about many aspects of their
world. We have schemas of our daily routines, our
school, and our selves. Schemas serve as a cognitive framework that helps us to organize information.

Schemas based on gender typing and gender
roles help children categorize information in terms
of what is appropriate and characteristic of males
and females. Children form schemas of both masculine and feminine stereotypes. When children

encounter something they judge as appropriate for
their own sex, they explore it, ask questions about
it, and generally show more interest in it. In this
way, an additional "own-sex" schema is formed
that helps children form concepts and plans of action necessary for behaving in ways considered appropriate to their own sex. For example, a boy
would learn that trucks are for boys and dolls are
for girls; he also would know considerably more
about trucks than about dolls. The opposite would
be true for girls. In general, children would be able

to recall more—and more in-depth information—about same-sex objects than about objects thought to be appropriate for the opposite or both sexes (Bradbard et al. 1986).

Whereas gender-based schemas function much like other stereotypes, children are likely to form gender schemas earlier than other schemas for characterizing people. The precedence of gender-based schemas may be due to the significance of gender and sex to the self, as well as to the prominence of gender in our society. Martin and Halverson (1981) emphasized that gender stereotyping may be necessary for children to help them simplify information from the environment. Such stereotypes help children to sort actions, attributes, and preferences into the categories "things for me" and "things not for me," although evidence suggests that preschoolers will more readily stereotype others than the self (Cowan & Hoffman 1986). Research has found relationships between gender schemas and behavior. For example, Fagot, Leinbach, and Hagan (1986) found that preschoolers who classified pictures of men and women by gender (as opposed to other classification schemas) spent more time playing with members of their own sex.

Simple gender schemas may have their value during childhood, but with the more complex forms of thinking that accompany cognitive development, gender stereotypes and concepts of gender roles become more differentiated and flexible. Conversely, an older adolescent or adult who remains gender-typed may have retained the narrowly defined gender schemas of early childhood.

The three major perspectives of gender acquisition are psychoanalytic, learning, and cognitive. Each differs in the order of attachment to parental figures, modeling, and gender identification. Figure 14.2 presents the sequences of gender identification for each of the theoretical perspectives.

Current Issues in Gender Development

The topic of gender development easily lends itself to a number of controversial issues and debates. The final section of this chapter considers two issues that have recently come under the scrutiny of those interested in gender-role development. Both issues to be discussed—androgyny, and gender roles and schooling—examine further how stereotypes affect gender-role development.

Androgyny

Prior to the late 1970s, the research and theory on gender typing emphasized the acquisition of sex-appropriate behavior. The literature of the past ten years has shifted its focus to an analysis of the significance of **androgyny,** a term which combines the Greek words for "male" and "female." Androgyny implies the incorporation of masculine and feminine characteristics in one person. According to the major proponents of androgyny theory, an androgynous person is more flexible and adaptable, because he or she is not constrained to act in accordance with gender-typed expectations (Bem 1974; Spence & Helmreich 1978). An androgynous person can act in a feminine manner (nurturant and expressive) in one instance, and in a masculine manner (assertive and independent) in another. Thus, behavior conforms to the situation rather than to expectations based on stereotypes.

Bem (1974) criticized personality tests that sought to measure masculine or feminine traits because they put such traits on the same continuum. In other words, a person rated "high" on masculinity would have to be rated "low" on femininity. Bem constructed her own test of gender roles, the Bem Sex Role Inventory (BSRI). The BSRI treats masculinity and femininity as two separate scales, each composed of twenty traits. The BSRI also has twenty neutral traits that serve as filler items. Subjects rate the masculine traits (e.g., "competitive" and "forceful"), feminine traits (e.g., "loves children" and "tender"), and neutral traits (e.g., "happy") on a scale of 1–7 indicating the degree to which these traits are true for themselves.

Four types of people can be scored by this scale: the androgynous person scores high on both masculine and feminine scales; the masculine or feminine person only scores high on either the masculinity scale or the femininity scale respectively; and the undifferentiated person scores low on both scales. A similar type of test is the Personal

Attributes Questionnaire (PAQ) of Spence and Helmreich (1978). It measures instrumental and expressive characteristics and yields a categorization scheme similar to that of the BSRI.

Do androgynous people behave differently (and more flexibly) than gender-typed people? This question has guided Bem's research since the construction of the BSRI. In one study, Bem (1975) observed male and female college students in social conformity and nurturant situations. In the social conformity condition, the students—along with a group of their peers—were asked to judge the funniness of cartoons. The task involved exercising independence (a masculine trait), because the situation was rigged so that the peer ratings did not match the funniness of the cartoons. In the nurturant condition, the students were given the opportunity to play with and handle a small kitten. Bem found that androgynous individuals were both independent in rating the cartoons and nurturant toward the kitten. Masculine students were independent, but ignored the kitten. Interestingly, the feminine students were neither independent nor nurturant. Bem speculated that these subjects were influenced by group pressure and were too inhibited to play with the kitten. Subsequent research has found that androgyny correlates with a variety of positive attributes, such as high self-esteem, low anxiety, high creativity, and effective parenting skills (Bem 1976; Spence & Helmreich 1978).

Hall and Halberstadt (1980) extended the work on androgyny to younger children. These researchers developed a children's version of the Personal Attributes Questionnaire and administered it to third- to sixth-grade boys and girls. Hall and Halberstadt also measured the children's self-esteem and obtained teacher and maternal ratings of the children's behavior. In addition to finding that masculinity, femininity, and androgyny can be assessed in children, the researchers also learned that for girls, higher-masculine scores were related to higher-IQ scores; high-feminine scores were negatively related to math achievement. For both girls and boys, higher-masculinity scores were related to more positive self-concepts. Interestingly, Hall and Halberstadt found that the androgynous children had the most positive self-concept, but

teachers reported that the gender-typed children were the most socially mature.

Recently, a number of psychologists have begun to critically examine the research of androgyny. Lenney (1979) and others (Baumrind 1982; Lamb & Urberg 1978; Shepherd-Look 1982) are concerned that androgyny may become the new standard of mental health, just as being appropriately gender-typed was the hallmark of competence until about ten years ago. This issue and the findings of Hall and Halberstadt raise several important questions. Is androgyny always superior to gender typing? Should we encourage children to be androgynous? Do androgynous adults always make the best parents? The Research Close-up "Androgyny and Parenting" describes a study designed to answer these questions.

Gender Roles and Schooling

School—a most powerful agent of socialization—has been examined with respect to its differential influences upon boys and girls. Sex often is used as the basis for dividing up a class in seat assignments, gym classes, classroom chores, and spelling bees. In addition, boys often have difficulty in elementary school because the norms reward "feminine" behaviors such as sitting quietly, following instructions, and turning in neat work. In countries where there are more male teachers, such as Germany and Japan, boys have fewer reading problems than do girls (the reverse is true for the United States). Similar results on reading tests have been obtained for U.S. and English boys who have been taught by male teachers (Shepherd-Look 1982).

Girls like elementary school more than boys do, demonstrate high levels of achievement, and receive much less attention for disruptive behavior. However, despite all of their positive experiences, girls' achievement in school declines as they progress up the educational ladder, as does their motivation for achievement. Conversely, boys become more serious and studious as they enter high school. If schools are unsupportive of males, why do they as a group excel? If schools provide a com-

Research Close-up

Androgyny and Parenting

Diana Baumrind (1982) recently published the results of an excellent study that tried to determine the consequences of androgyny. Baumrind has been involved with the Family Socialization and Developmental Competence Project at the University of California at Berkeley for several years. This project has attempted to relate parental child-rearing styles—primarily involving the dimensions of discipline and warmth (or receptivity)—to the cognitive and social competence of children.

The project involves collecting interview, questionnaire, and observational data on parents, their children, and the ways in which they interact. As one part of this project, Baumrind had the parents of 9-year-old children fill out the Bem Sex Role Inventory (BSRI) to see whether androgynous adults were more personally competent than gender-typed adults, whether androgynous parents were more effective in terms of the cognitive and social competence of their children, and whether BSRI scores could predict parental child-rearing styles.

The results underscore the necessity of critically examining androgyny theory. Baumrind found that androgynous adults were generally more *personally competent* than gender-typed adults. For example, androgynous adults were more internally directed and had higher self-esteem scores; androgynous men were more unconventional and autonomous than other men. However, in terms of parenting skills and the concomitant competence of their children, the androgynous parents did not score higher than the gender-typed. Androgynous parents were child-centered, but not authoritative; they were responsive to their children, but less demanding. There was a greater likelihood of finding both responsivity and demandingness (i.e., authoritative parenting) among gender-typed parents. Furthermore, Baumrind found that the children of androgynous mothers and fathers were less competent in several areas than those of gender-typed parents. For example, sons of androgynous mothers were less socially responsible than those of gender-typed mothers, and daughters of androgynous fathers were less cognitively competent than those of gender-typed fathers.

Baumrind's study is important because it indicates that both androgynous and gender-typed behaviors have positive and negative aspects. Androgyny may be beneficial to adulthood competence in some areas, whereas gender typing (which Baumrind did not find to be a sign of maladjustment) fosters competency in children. How do we reconcile the discrepancy in these findings? Perhaps one of the consequences of the traditional differentiation of gender roles when adults become parents is the demonstration of traditional gender-typed behavior to children. Perhaps androgynous parents would foster greater competence in their children if they recognized that it may be necessary for their children to firmly understand the gender component of their identity, and for their adolescents to understand the significance of gender to their sexual maturity. Thus, Baumrind asks, "Logically, how could an individual who had never internalized gender polarity transcend it?" (p. 70).

fortable environment for girls, why do they fail to achieve? Answers to this paradox may be found in the literature on differences between teacher-female and teacher-male interactions, as well as the literature on parent and teacher expectations for school achievement.

Gender and Teacher-Student Interaction

Boys and girls are treated differently by their teachers as early as nursery school. Analysis of teacher-student interactions indicates that boys receive more scoldings and discipline from their teachers than girls (Serbin et al. 1973). When boys behave in an approved fashion, they receive their teacher's attention no matter where they are in the classroom. Serbin and her associates found that girls must remain close to their teacher's side in order to get their teacher's attention. Thus, boys are viewed as the troublemakers, but their independence and on-task behavior are also attention getting. Girls, in contrast, are encouraged to maintain close proximity to their teachers, even to the point of seeking the physical contact associated with dependence.

In elementary school, girls manifest a phenomenon that Dweck (1977) called *learned helplessness in school*. In her analysis of teacher feedback to fourth and fifth graders, Dweck found that teachers are more likely to respond to their male pupils in regard to conduct problems or to nonintellectual aspects of their work, such as lack of neatness and motivation. Thus, boys learn that teachers are generally negative towards them because they are boys and that criticism is directed towards rather superficial features of their schoolwork. Girls, in contrast, are reprimanded far less often than boys, but when they do receive negative feedback, about 90 percent of it pertains to the accuracy and intellectual quality of their work. Thus, girls attribute their school failure to lack of ability rather than to lack of effort. The implications of these findings are far-reaching. Boys learn to try harder or to discount criticism in the face of failure, whereas girls are quick to doubt themselves and to give up trying. Perhaps this is one of the reasons why boys begin to outshine girls as they progress further up the educational ladder. The finding that boys and girls receive different types and amounts of attention from their teachers has been replicated at both the preschool and elementary school level. However, it should be noted that teachers usually do not *actively* seek to treat boys and girls differently. Rather, teachers' behavior may reflect the fact that boys misbehave more frequently, call out answers, and demand teacher attention whereas girls seek to comply with the teacher-determined constraints of the classroom. Thus, teachers sustain or reinforce whatever sex differences already exist (Brophy 1985).

Gender and Expectations for Academic Achievement

In the 1970s, educational psychologists focused on how self-fulfilling prophecies influenced academic achievement. Research beginning with the work of Rosenthal and Jacobson (1968) suggested that children often perform up to the level of their teacher's expectations. Later work in this area suggested that this "Pygmalion effect" is more potent and consistent when teachers' expectations, formed on the basis of group and individual attributes of their students, affect the self-perceptions of students (Brophy & Good 1974; Proctor 1984). Characteristics such as race, socioeconomic status, and gender are particularly prone to expectancy effects. In general, teachers attend less to their low-expectation students, place fewer demands on them, question such students less often, and do not give as much feedback as they do to high-expectation students.

The implications for gender and academic achievement are evident: in those classrooms where teachers have differential expectations of performance for males and females, the interaction between the predispositions of the students and teacher expectations may lead to gender-related differences in academic achievement (Lindow, Marrett & Wilkinson 1985). Such expectations may be particularly troublesome when the students' own expectations for achievement are segregated according to gender. The differential appeal of computers to boys and girls is one such example (see Issues in Child Development "Boys, Girls, and Computers").

Studies of self-perceptions of mathematics achievement provide another example of differential treatment. Parsons, Kaczala, and Meece (1982) compared fifth- through ninth-grade classrooms in which boys and girls had equally high expectations for success in mathematics with classrooms in which boys had higher expectations than girls. Boys and girls were given equal amounts of praise and criticism in the same-expectation classrooms. However, in the sex-differentiated classes, teachers were found to rely more on public responding, to have fewer private interactions, and to make more use of student volunteers for answers. In such classrooms, boys interacted more

Educators are concerned that their female students are avoiding computer studies. It is unclear why many girls avoid working with computers and boys are so drawn to them. Girls may avoid computer studies because such activities are often linked to mathematics and science courses, traditionally masculine domain.

with teachers and received more of their praise. In a related study, Parsons, Adler, and Kaczala (1982) demonstrated that parental attitudes reinforced teacher and student expectations of differential mathematics achievement for boys and girls. Even when boys and girls performed similarly, parents believed that daughters had to work harder at math than sons, and that sons needed upper-level math courses but daughters did not. Furthermore, Parsons, Adler, and Kaczala found that parental expectations had a powerful influence on their children's own expectations for math performance.

The discussion of gender and education is a suitable conclusion to a survey of the development of gender roles and gender differences. This is a topic of pragmatic, theoretical, and empirical significance. To be educated in the developmental implications of gender is to support programs to reduce teacher-expectancy effects and differential treatment of children because of their gender. To be educated about the development of gender roles is also to be more understanding of children's and adolescents' own stereotyping as they forge their way toward mature concepts of masculinity and femininity.

Issues in Child Development

Boys, Girls, and Computers

A computer attracts boys like moths to a flame. In the classroom, at after-school projects, in video arcades, and in computer summer camps, the ratio of boys to girls is weighted heavily in the boys' favor. The research indicates that boys and men spend more time with computers and like them more than females do (Lockheed 1985). Such sex differences are most notable in the areas of computer programming and recreation. Sex differences are smaller for word-processing activities, projects involving cooperative efforts, and activities that are personally relevant. Because computers are considered to be on the crest of the technological wave, girls may increasingly be left behind in a technological society (Lockheed 1985).

Many girls and women, therefore, may not develop the cognitive skills that will further their economic and career status in the future.

There may be several reasons why boys are more drawn to computers than girls are. Hawkins (1985) argued that schools often incorporate computer instruction within science and mathematics, two areas that have a long history of male domination. In addition, girls may steer away from computers because programming is a competitive, rule-based activity, and they fail to perceive the relevance of computers for their personal lives. Girls also do not receive as much support for computer activities as do boys; their parents purchase fewer computer games and tend not to send their daughters to computer camps. Computer games generally are gender-stereotyped, and the competition,

violence, and loud noises of these games are more appealing to boys than to girls.

Interestingly, these gender differences in computer use tend to be quite strong. Hawkins (1985) reported that even in elementary school classrooms where teachers were sensitive to the need of making computers relevant and available to girls, boys demonstrated greater interest and skill. School administrators and teachers must consider how computers are differentially perceived by their male and female students. Placement of computer curricula in an area designated as "Computer Literacy," as opposed to incorporation into math and science programs, may be an important step in the reduction of a gender-based caste system in technology.

Summary

1. The study of gender differences requires that a distinction be made between a personal awareness of being either male or female (gender identity), and stereotypes of suitable male and female behavior (gender-role stereotypes).
2. Both biological factors, such as prenatal hormones, and experiential factors, such as whether or not mothers work, have important consequences for gender-role development.
3. Although children learn a great deal about gender roles from their parents, toys, television, and books have been found to be powerful socialization agents of gender roles.
4. The crystallization of a sexual identity into an overall identity becomes a central issue for the adolescent.
5. Male-female differences on measures of verbal, quantitative, and visual-spatial abilities emerge most consistently in the literature on adolescence.
6. According to the psychoanalytic perspective of Freud, gender identity is accomplished through resolution of the Oedipal complex, whereby the child incorporates the feminine or masculine behaviors of his or her same-sex parent.
7. Conditioning theory claims that gender roles are acquired through the shaping of children's behavior. Gender-appropriate behavior is praised or rewarded, and gender-inappropriate behavior is punished, ignored, or criticized.

8. According to the social-learning perspective, boys learn gender-appropriate behavior from observing and imitating the masculine behavior of men; girls, from observing and imitating the feminine behavior of women.

9. According to the cognitive developmental theory of Lawrence Kohlberg, children first label themselves either as male or female, next learn that their gender remains the same despite superficial changes in appearance and behavior, and then seek out gender-appropriate models to observe.

10. The acquisition of gender schemas may help young children to sort the behaviors and characteristics of people into appropriate-for-male and appropriate-for-female categories.

11. Androgyny implies the incorporation of masculine and feminine characteristics in one person. Major proponents of androgyny theory claim that an androgynous person is more flexible and adaptable.

12. Schools provide different socialization experiences for boys and girls. The evidence suggests that teacher-student interactions and teacher expectations may reinforce gender differences and the self-perceptions of their students.

Key Terms

sex	adrenogenital syndrome
gender	sexual polarization versus
gender identity	bisexual confusion
gender role	field independence
gender-role stereotype	gender stability
gender-typed behavior	gender constancy
gender-role preference	schema
hermaphroditism	androgyny

Suggested Readings

Huston, A.C. (1983). Sex-typing. In P.H. Mussen (Ed.), *Handbook of child psychology.* (4th ed., vol. 4). New York: Wiley.

A thorough survey of the literature since 1970 on sex-typing in children. Included are topics such as definitions of sex typing, the development of sex typing, and socialization of sex typing in the family and clinical interventions.

Maccoby, E.E. & Jacklin, C.N. (1974). *The psychology of sex differences.* Stanford, CA: Stanford University Press.

Probably the most widely cited survey of the empirical literature on gender roles. This is an important book for those interested in examining the myths and realities of gender and sex differences.

Money, J. & Ehrhardt, A.A. (1972). *Man and woman, boy and girl: The differentiation and dimorphism of gender identity from conception to maturity.* Baltimore: Johns Hopkins University Press.

A fine discussion of prenatal sex differentiation and the significant findings of John Money's work on hermaphroditism. This book is for those interested in the psychobiology of sex and gender.

Tavris, C. & Wade, C. (1984). *The longest war: Sex differences in perspective* (2nd ed.). New York: Harcourt Brace Jovanovich.

A delightful overview of the field of gender roles. The authors provide a thorough and entertaining multidisciplinary discussion of gender and sex differences.

Wilkinson, L.C. & Marrett, C.B. (Eds.). (1985). *Gender influences in classroom interaction.* Orlando: Academic Press.

Discussions of the relationships between gender and school at the preschool, elementary, and high school levels. Students who wish an in-depth treatment of the relationship between educational practice and gender stereotyping will find current research and critical evaluation of the literature in this book.

Readings from the Literature

The following study by Miller, Danaher, and Forbes (1986) indicates that boys and girls have different ways of handling conflicts with their peers.

As you read, consider these questions:

- What method did the researchers use to observe conflict resolution among peers? Did their procedures effectively capture and measure the flavor of the children's interpersonal conflicts? Why or why not?

- How do boys and girls differ in their methods of conflict resolution? How are they alike?

- How do the findings of this research relate to what you have learned about gender-role development? For example, is there a link between the findings on sex differences in aggression and peer interactions?

Sex-Related Strategies for Coping with Interpersonal Conflict in Children Aged Five and Seven

Patrice M. Miller
Harvard University

Dorothy L. Danaher
Harvard University

David Forbes
Harvard University

Conflict situations present children with two very different challenges. One challenge is to resolve a conflict through active persuasion and negotiation. The second challenge is to mitigate a conflict or the resulting negative interpersonal affect, without disrupting social harmony between the interactors. This article explores differences between boys and girls in their use of these two kinds of strategies. Two groups of 6 five-year-olds and two groups of 6 seven-year-olds were videotaped in twelve 1-hr long playgroups. Both direct persuasion attempts and conflict mitigation attempts were coded from the videotapes. Boys were involved in conflict more often than girls. Once within a conflict situation, boys tended to use threat and physical force significantly more often, whereas girls tended to attempt to mitigate the conflict significantly more often, especially when interacting with other girls. These results are discussed in terms of boys and girls having different perspectives with respect to coping with conflict: Boys are more concerned with and more forceful in pursuing their own agendae, and girls are more concerned with maintaining interpersonal harmony.

The ability to cope effectively with interpersonal conflict situations has been recognized as an important component of social skills (Boulding, 1971; Converse, 1968; Main & Roark, 1975; Nye, 1973). Most studies that have investigated children's behavior in conflict situations have focused on the use of strategies for persuading or negotiating with the other (Blumenfield & Klinghorn, 1977; Clark & Delia, 1976; Delia, Kline, & Burleson, 1979; Findley & Humphreys, 1974; Flavell, Botkin, Fry, Wright, & Jarvis, 1968; Forbes, 1981; Forbes & Lubin, 1984; Piche, Rubin, & Michlin, 1978). The strategies examined in those studies are direct negotiating strategies, aimed at advancing a child's own point of view and getting others to adopt this view.

Conflict situations can be viewed in at least two distinct ways. In the perspective taken by the majority of past research, conflict is seen as a competition of viewpoints. Studies that adopt this perspective naturally focus on how conflict is met by efforts at direct persuasion. From a second view, conflict may also be seen as an occasion that threatens to produce negative affect in either one's interactive partners or oneself. Studies examining conflict from this viewpoint should focus more on the strategies that children employ to maintain interpersonal harmony. This study combines these two perspectives in examining sex-linked differences in responses to conflict.

Studies from several different traditions within psychology support the notion that sex plays a role in determining styles of response to interpersonal conflict. Lever (1976) collected diaries from children on their daily activities and observed children's play in playgrounds. Although the focus of her study was not on conflict, she found a difference between boys and girls in the amount of conflict in which they engaged. She speculated that boys were involved mainly in games with variable or debatable rules that provided many opportunities for negotiation and conflict resolution. Girls engaged more often in turn-taking games and other activities in which conflict was unlikely or indirect. When conflict did arise, girls tended to leave the situations rather than deal with the conflict. Because Lever did not code particular behaviors that lead to conflicts, she could not examine the possibility that it was the use of particular styles of conflict resolution that related to the different frequency of conflict between boys and girls. In a study of three-year-old dyads that may partially address this issue, Jennings and Suwalsky (1982) found that girls were more likely to join in the activity of their playmate, whereas boys were more likely to pursue their own ideas for play. Another set of findings that supports the notion that boys and girls may approach conflict differently is that boys have been found to be involved in aggressive interactions more frequently than girls (Barrett, 1979; Frodi, Maccaulay, & Thome, 1977; cf. also Maccoby & Jacklin, 1974).

Piaget (1965) and then Gilligan (1982) reported that males' and females' orientations to moral conflict take two forms. Females' solutions to hypothetical situations of conflict between moral principles were less likely than males' to stress legal elaborations and more likely to stress tolerance (Piaget, 1965), and to stress the primacy of maintaining relationships within intimate social groups (Gilligan, 1982). Males, by contrast, displayed a moral orientation that was more attuned to principles of justice, and they were more prone to espouse the primacy of considering the interests of society at large (Gilligan, 1982; Piaget, 1965).

We suggest how males and females behave in interpersonal interaction by generalizing from these findings about differences in the intrapersonal realm. Females should be more likely than males to use tactics that diffuse conflict or otherwise try and maintain interpersonal harmony in the face of conflict. Males should be more likely than females to resolve conflicting claims to further the group enterprise and be less concerned with the maintenance of interpersonal harmony as a primary goal. This may result in their being in conflict situations more often.

Method

Subjects

Twenty-four children were recruited from each of two classrooms in six different Cambridge, Massachusetts schools. The parents of each child in a class were sent a letter explaining that the study was designed to "better understand how children make friends with each other and play together." An average of three parents from each classroom both consented to their children's participation in the study, and indicated that their children would be able to attend at the appointed times. Of these children, one from each classroom was included in the final sample.

After the parents had consented to having their child participate in the study, four experimental playgroups were created. Each group consisted of three boys and three girls. Two playgroups were made up of five-year-olds, ranging in age from 4.9 to 5.3 years, and two were made up of seven-year-olds, ranging in age from 6.9 to 7.3 years. Although the groups were racially integrated and included children from varying socioeconomic backgrounds, with parent occupations ranging from blue- and white-collar to professional, no effort was made to control for race or socioeconomic status, either within or across groups.

Procedure

Behavior observations. A research assistant picked the children up after school and transported them to a 20′ by 25′ laboratory playroom at the Harvard Graduate School of Education. Children met for 1 hr a day, four times a week, for 3 weeks, giving a total of 12 hr of meeting time for each group. The playroom was supplied with age-appropriate toys and games selected by a teacher-consultant, who also was present in an adjacent room during data collection. The teacher did not intervene in or supervise the play except to put out new materials and to prevent physical injury or property damage. The play was constant and free flowing. Sessions were videotaped. If a child were absent, the playgroup was held as usual. The individual scores were adjusted accordingly as described below.

Coding Procedures. There were three steps in the coding procedure: (a) A subset of sessions were selected to be coded, (b) Conflict episodes were located within these sessions (c) Specific behaviors within conflict episodes were coded as to whether they represented persuasion or conflict mitigation.

The magnitude of the coding task was reduced by selecting 7 of the 12 playgroup sessions to be coded. A representative sample of sessions was included by choosing three sessions from the first week, two sessions from the second week, and two sessions from the last week.

To determine which episodes contained conflict, all episodes with two children interacting were examined using the "focal-child" observation method (Altmann, 1974). In focal-child coding, each of the six children's interactions with one other was focused upon and observed continuously in turn. Therefore, for each session, six separate passes were made through the data. Because a particular child could serve as both the initiator of a conflict in an episode (the persuader) and, at some later point, the recipient of a different conflict episode (the persuadee), only episodes in which the child was the persuader were transcribed when that child was focal. The first child within an episode to aggress was defined as the persuader.

One of the two following criteria had to be met for an interaction to be labeled a conflict episode: (a) There was overt disagreement between the children. That is, the persuader gave at least *one* negative command (a simple persuasion tactic such as "No . . ." "You can't . . ."), along with one persuasion tactic containing a reason or justification. (b) There was covert disagreement between the children. That is there was *no* negative command but the persuader used *two* or more persuasion tactics, with or without justifications.

Once some part of an episode had been detected using these criteria, the coder would look earlier on the tape to find the comment that introduced the topic of conflict. For an utterance to be considered a part of the same episode, two things had to remain constant. An utterance had to involve the same persuader and persuadee, and the topic mentioned in the utterance had to be the same. Conversely, episodes were seen as ending if either the persuader or the persuadee changed, if the topic changed, or if there was a temporal break of more than 60 s.

In order for a conflict episode to be included in the data base two coders, working together, had to agree that this was a conflict episode. Once episodes had been located, the audio portion of the tape of the session was transcribed, starting from the comment that started the episode. The identity and the sex of both the focal child and the other participant in the interaction, as well as key actions and context were noted. Both same-sex and cross-sex dyads were included.

476

During the third step, the episodes chosen in the second step were coded as containing either persuasion or conflict mitigation behaviors or both. A social behavior used by a child during a conflict episode was coded as exemplifying one of 18 persuasion tactics whenever it seemed to be aimed at directly changing the behavior of a second child, either by convincing the other child to cease a behavior that was already being engaged in, or by convincing the other child to engage in a different behavior.

A persuasion tactic was usually just one utterance, but could consist of more than one utterance if the coder judged that the additional utterances were simply re-phrasings of the original. The individual persuasion tactics have been collapsed into more global persuasion strategies for purposes of the analyses to be presented here. These persuasion strategies could be either heavy-handed or moderate. A heavy-handed persuasion strategy was one in which physical force or threat was used to persuade the other. A moderate persuasion strategy was one in which any of the following tactics were used: simple proposition, check desire, check ability, give directions, entreaty, appeal to situational constraints, appeal to social norms, effusion of affect, appeal to past compliance, co-opting, justification by appropriateness, justification by desired outcome, offers exchange, de-escalation of request, clarification of social intent, clarification of reference. The coding scheme, with definitions for each of these tactics, is available from the authors (Forbes, Katz, and Miller, 1984).

A behavior used by a child during an episode of conflict was coded as exemplifying one of the six conflict mitigation tactics whenever it seemed to avoid ad-dressing the issue in conflict directly. Table 1 defines these tactics and illustrates a few typical episodes.

All episodes had persuasion tactics. Some had, in addition, conflict mitigation tactics. Using the corpus of 1,146 conflict episodes, a total of 2,812 persuasion strategies and 202 conflict mitigation tactics were coded. Episodes that had only conflict mitigation tactics were not possible because at least one oppositional— and hence persuasive—exchange had to occur for a conflict episode to have been detected. While an overt disagreement could signal the presence of a persuasion episode, simple one-line disagreements with

Table 1 Description of Conflict Mitigation Strategies

Name of Strategy	Description
Clarification of other's Feelings	Clarifying and acknowledging the other's feelings, intent, or desires in order to facilitate co-operation. Example: #1. I'll be the mother. #3. (no response). #1. You want to be the mother?
Changing the Topic	Ignoring an issue of disagree-ment, and making an unrelated comment. Example: #1. You be the sister. #3. Hold it, this is the beans.
Peaceful Acquiescence	Doing what the other person wants with only a brief protest or no protest at all.
Proposal of Compromise	Child suggests an activity that in effect provides some satisfac-tion for both children. Example: #6. I found it. #5. I found it too. #6. I found it *first*. (grabs) #5. We both . . . hey, we both found it, O.K.? O.K.?
Indirect Display of Anger	Communication of anger to an-other in a displaced or indirect fashion. Example: #4. Can't I have daddy (doll) for a second? #6. I need daddy and mommy. #4. I'll trade you the boy for that . . . for a second be-cause I want to buy some-thing. #6. I buy something, you give *me* the money. #4. (Stages doll fight, no verbal response to #6).
Avoidance	Physically leaving the situation.

simple responses ("Will you do this?" "No.") were also not included.

To assess reliability for coding persuasion, each of the seven coders coded the same six episodes from six

477

different tapes. A Cohen's Kappa (1968) was then calculated for each of 21 combinations of coders, and these kappas were averaged. The average coding reliability for the 18 persuasion tactics was 68%, and the average Cohen's Kappa was .65. Once the 18 tactics were collapsed into heavy-handed persuasion versus moderate persuasion the average percentage agreement was .98, with an average Cohen's Kappa of .95. For the two coders who coded all the conflict mitigation data, the percentage agreement was .89, and the Cohen's Kappa was .86.

Results

The results focus on sex differences. An examination of differences between five- and seven-year olds' use of different persuasive and conflict mitigation behaviors showed no significant age differences. Therefore data from both age groups were combined.

Frequency of Conflict Episodes

First, the boys and girls initiated conflict episodes at different rates. Boys started an average of 55.9 episodes ($SD = 19.05$) over the seven sessions, whereas girls started an average of 39.9 episodes ($SD = 26.37$). However this measure is biased because the girls spent more time in dyads than did boys (Forbes & Lubin, 1981). Hence, the overall frequency of initiating conflict for each child was weighted by dividing it by that child's amount of dyadic interaction time. Dyadic interaction time was coded for each child using a "scan sampling" technique (Altmann, 1974) in which videotapes were paused each minute on the minute, and a record was made of who was playing with whom. The intercoder agreement for these judgments was 79%. The boys' average number of conflict episodes per dyad interaction hour was 30.0 ($SD = 17$), whereas the girls' was 18.6 ($SD = 12$). Eight boys were above the median number of conflict episodes, whereas only 4 girls were. A Wilcoxon Mann-Whitney U-test (Wonacott & Wonacott, 1977) indicated that these differences between the boys and girls were significant ($W = 181$, $z = 1.78$, $p < .04$).

Behavior in Conflict Episodes

In the stream of behavior during conflict episodes, each behavior exemplified one of the three types of tactics possible—heavy-handed persuasion, moderate

Table 2 Mean Proportion of Episodes Containing (a) Heavy-Handed Tactics, (b) Moderate Persuasion, and (c) Conflict Mitigation for Girls and Boys

	Girls		Boys			
Tactic	M	SD	M	SD	W	z
Heavy-handed Persuasion	.18	.10	.26	.10	183	1.90*
Moderate Persuasion	.59	.10	.64	.11	171	1.21
Conflict Mitigation	.22	.07	.10	.05	89	3.52**

*$p < .03$.
**$p < .001$.

persuasion, and conflict mitigation. Furthermore, the three types of tactics could occur in one of three different patterns within an episode: (a) the child who verbally initiated the conflict (called the persuader) engaged in one or more instances of heavy-handed persuasion and no conflict mitigation, (b) the persuader engaged only in moderate persuasion, but no conflict mitigation, and (c) the persuader engaged in both some persuasion (of either type) and some conflict mitigation.

The analyses to be presented were done on a child-by-child basis. Because individual children initiated a different number of conflicts, proportion scores rather than number of strategies and tactics were calculated for each child. This enabled the analysis to control for the child's overall rate of conflict and for other factors such as absenteeism.

The proportion of each type of episode was calculated for each child. The means of these proportions are shown in Table 2 with their corresponding Wilcoxon Mann-Whitney tests of gender differences for each type of episode.

Table 2 shows that boys were significantly more likely than girls to be in conflict situations in which heavy-

478

Table 3 Number of Children Above Group Median in Using Conflict Mitigation Strategies

Strategy	No. of Girls (Total = 12)	No. of Boys (Total = 12)	Fisher Exact Test
Clarification of other's feelings	8	0	**
Changing the topic	9	1	**
Peaceful acquiescence	6	3	
Proposal of compromise	6	4	
Indirect display of anger	7	2	*
Avoidance	4	2	

*$p < .04$.
**$p < .005$.

handed persuasion tactics (and no conflict mitigation) were used. They were significantly less likely than girls to be in conflict situations in which conflict mitigation tactics were used. While boys' and girls' conflict episodes were almost equally likely to consist of moderate persuasion ($W = 171$, $z = 1.21$, $p < .11$), an average of .26 of the boys' conflict episodes had heavy-handed tactics (8 boys were above the median) whereas an average of .18 of the girls' conflict episodes had heavy-handed tactics (4 girls were above the median), a significant difference ($W = 183$, $z = 1.90$, $p < .03$). On the other hand, on the average .22 of the girls' conflict episodes had conflict mitigation (9 girls were above the median), whereas only .10 of the boys' episodes did (3 boys were above the median, $W = 89$, $z = 3.52$, $p < .001$).

Girls were significantly more likely than boys to use three of the six individual conflict mitigation tactics shown in Table 3. Using medians tests, significantly more girls than boys used Tactic 1, acknowledgement of the feelings of the other ($p < .005$), Tactic 2, changing the topic ($p < .005$), and Tactic 5, indirect display of anger ($p < .04$).

Structure of Conflict Episodes

Third, to see if boys used more heavy-handed persuasion tactics early in a conflict episode than did girls and whether girls used conflict mitigation earlier than boys, the rate at and latency with which heavy-handed tactics and the latency with which conflict mitigation tactics were used was examined. An average proportion of .17 of boys' conflict episodes began with heavy-handed tactics, whereas only .11 of girls' episodes began in this fashion, a significant difference ($W = 185.5$, $z = 2.05$, $p < .02$). Latency was defined as the number of turns a child waited, on average, before using either a heavy-handed or a conflict mitigation tactic. Once past the first tactic, boys and girls did not differ significantly in their latencies to use heavy-handed tactics: the boys' mean latency was 2.74 ($SD = .64$), while girls' was 3.03 ($SD = .86$). Because conflict mitigation rarely occurred first in an episode, by definition, only latencies can be examined for this kind of tactic. In episodes with conflict mitigation, girls' mean latency to use conflict mitigation was 4.4 ($SD = .9$) while boys' was 4.6 ($SD = .9$), a nonsignificant difference.

Same-Sex and Cross-Sex Dyads

The last analysis examines whether the use of heavy-handed persuasion, moderate persuasion, and conflict mitigation differs between same-sex and cross-sex dyads. The proportion and number of episodes (the latter shown in parentheses) containing heavy-handed persuasion, moderate persuasion, and conflict mitigation were examined for girl-girl, boy-boy, girl-boy, and boy-girl dyads. The results are presented in Table 4.

Boys behave in a similar fashion, whether their behavior is directed towards another boy or towards a girl; if anything they are slightly more aggressive towards girls than they are towards boys. Girls, on the other hand, change their behavior according to whether they are interacting with another girl or with a boy. Very little of their behavior towards other girls is heavy-handed, whereas when they are interacting with boys their behavior resembles that of the boys more, except that they continue to use a greater proportion of conflict mitigation than do boys at any time.

Table 4 Proportion and Number (N) of Episodes Containing a Given Persuasion Strategy for Different Dyads

	Moderate Persuasion	Heavy-handed Persuasion	Conflict Mitigation
Girl-girl	.66 (173)	.09 (23)	.26 (68)
Girl-boy	.57 (140)	.24 (58)	.19 (47)
Boy-boy	.70 (310)	.22 (100)	.08 (36)
Boy-girl	.62 (112)	.30 (55)	.08 (15)

Note: $x^2(6, N = 1137) = 76.07, p < .001$.

Discussion

The results support the notion that there is a significant sex-linked difference in how children behave in interpersonal conflict situations. When conflict occurred, girls were more likely than boys to engage in behavior that defused or mitigated the conflictual quality of the interaction. By contrast, boys were more apt than girls to engage in heavy-handed behavior. Third, boys were more likely than girls to start a conflict episode with a heavy-handed tactic before less confrontative means of resolving differences had been tried. Boys tended to behave in the same fashion in their use of conflict behavior, whether they were interacting with other boys or with girls. Girls, on the other hand, changed their behavior, rarely using heavy-handed behavior with other girls, only with boys. It could be that these differences in how boys and girls interacted once within a conflict situation are related to the observed frequency with which they end up in those situations. These findings for sex can be contrasted with a lack of age differences in the same kinds of behaviors. Work published elsewhere (e.g., Lubin & Forbes, 1984) has described age differences in other aspects of persuasive behavior, therefore it is the sex differences that will be focused on here.

There is evidence that two sex differences affect the way that boys and girls behave in conflict situations. Boys' tendency to dominate others and aggress against them more often (as summarized in Maccoby & Jacklin, 1974) may result in higher rates of conflict, and greater use of direct confrontative behavior when in conflict. This openness to engaging in and pursuing conflict in the five- and seven-year old boys may lead to a greater concern with justice in older male subjects (Gilligan, 1982; Piaget, 1965).

Girls' tendency to be more nurturant than boys (e.g., Whiting & Edwards, 1973) and to behave more cooperatively (e.g., Kagan & Madsen, 1972; Szal, 1972) may result in girls' lower overall rates of conflict relative to the boys and their tendency to mitigate conflict more often, especially when they interact with other girls. Nurturance is taken here in the broad sense as consisting of offering help and emotional support (Whiting & Edwards, 1973) and avoiding the loss of each. A greater nurturant tendency would produce more interpersonal cooperation as a way of accomplishing tasks rather than confrontation and competition for control over the tasks. More interpersonal cooperation and less confrontation is consistent with maintaining social harmony and social relationships (Gilligan, 1982; Piaget, 1965).

The results of this study provide two distinct additions to the literature on sex differences in social reasoning and behavior. First, they document differences in behavior in real-life situations rather than just the reasoning differences about hypothetical conflicts that Piaget (1965) and later Gilligan (1982) studied.

Second, this study shows that although there are differences in the behavior of males and females, there is also considerable overlap. While noting the sex-linked differences in relatively extreme responses to conflict—the mitigation efforts by girls and the more confrontative heavy-handed persuasion by boys—the bulk of all children's responses to conflict are what we have termed *moderate persuasion*. This type of response makes up 64% of boys' responses and 59% of girls' responses. In addition, girls' patterns of using the different persuasion and conflict mitigation techniques do resemble boys' when they are interacting with boys.

This overlap in boys' and girls' observed patterns of behavior during conflict situations suggests that gender differences of this type may involve a difference in emphasis rather than a qualitative discontinuity. Rather than conceiving of sex differences in social development as reflecting two distinct paths, which is what Gilligan (1982) proposes—one concerned with "justice" and the other concerned with "relationships"—the results of this study suggest that there may be a continuum of responses to conflict. This continuum ranges from avoidance of conflict to aggressive or heavy-handed responses. Males and females are represented by overlapping distributions on this continuum that are centered more towards direct persuasion and negotiation for males, and more towards maintaining interpersonal harmony for females. Although males do engage in conflict mitigation, their predominant mode of dealing with conflict is initially more direct. Similarly, females do engage in heavy-handed persuasion, but their predominant mode of dealing with conflict is more indirect. In addition, there is no indication that boys and girls are not equally manipulative, they merely use different means to attain their respective ends.

Such differences between individual behavior during social interaction have implications for the design of research into the social behavior of children, especially when such research seeks to describe developmental progress. It suggests that many instances in which one sex or group is found to be highly developed on a particular scale, and another sex or group is found to be less developed, may be instances in which there is another (implicit) scale that more appropriately describes the behavior of the "lower" rated group. Unless there is a priori basis for assuming differences in developmental level of the groups studied, it will most likely be the case that either a different perspective or a simple set of biases to behave in a given way will account for group differences in terms of social styles or social priorities, rather than levels of development. A strategy that makes both scales explicit and so explores in a positive manner the social goals of both sexes is one that could provide much richer information about both sex differences and the variety of social behavior.

References

Altmann, J. (1974). Observational study of behavior: Sampling methods. *Behavior, 49*, 227-267.

Barrett, D.E. (1979). Relations between aggressive and prosocial behaviors in children. *Journal of Genetic Psychology, 134*(2), 317-318.

Blumenfield, P.C., & Klinghorn, S.N. (1977). Influence of role perception on persuasion. Paper presented at the bienniel meeting of the Society for Research in Child Development.

Boulding, K.E. (1971). *Collected papers (Vol. 2).* Boulder: Colorado Associated University Press.

Clark, R.A., & Delia, J.G. (1976). The development of functional persuasive skills in childhood and early adolescence. *Child Development, 47,* 1008-1014.

Cohen, J. (1968). Weighted Kappa: Nominal scale agreement with provision for scaled disagreement or partial credit. *Psychological Bulletin, 70,* 213-220.

Converse, E. (1968). The war of all against all: A review of the Journal of Conflict Resolution, 1957-1968. *Journal of Conflict Resolution, 12(4),* 391-550.

Delia, J.G., Kline, S.L., & Burleson, B.R. (1979). The development of persuasive communication strategies in kindergarteners through twelfth-graders. *Communication Monographs, 46,* 241-256.

Findley, G.E., & Humphreys, C.A. (1974). Naive psychology and the development of persuasion appeals in girls. *Canadian Journal of Behavioral Science, 6,* 75-80.

Flavell, J.H., Botkin, P.T., Fry, C.L. Wright, J.W., & Jarvis, P.E. (1968). *The development of role-taking and communication skills in children.* New York: Wiley.

Forbes, D. (1981). Verbal social reasoning and observed persuasion strategies in children's peer interactions. Unpublished doctoral dissertation, Clark University, Worcester, MA.

Forbes, D.L., Katz, M.M., & Miller, P.M. (1984). Coding manual for children's persuasion. Unpublished coding manual.

Forbes, D.L., & Lubin, D. (1981). Overview of results from the first three years of the Peer Interaction Project. Section II: The cognitive component. Unpublished manuscript, Harvard University.

Forbes, D.L., & Lubin, D. (1984). Verbal social reasoning and observed persuasion strategies in children's peer interactions. In H.E. Sypher and J. Applegate

(Eds.), *Understanding interpersonal communication: Social cognitive and strategic processes in children and adults*. Beverly Hills, CA: Sage Publications.

Frodi, A.M., Maccaulay, J., & Thome, P.R. (1977). Are women less aggressive than men? A review of experimental literature. *Psychological Bulletin, 84,* 634-60.

Gilligan, C. (1982). *In a different voice*. Cambridge, MA: Harvard University Press.

Jennings, K.D., & Suwalsky, J.T. (1982). Reciprocity in the dyadic play of three-year-old children. In J.W. Loy (Ed.), *The paradoxes of play* (pp. 130-140). West Point, NY: Leisure Press.

Kagan, S., & Madsen, M.C. (1972). Rivalry in Anglo-American and Mexican children of two ages. *Journal of Personality and Social Psychology, 24,* 214-20.

Lever, J. (1976). Sex differences in the games children play. *Social Problems, 23,* 478-487.

Maccoby, E.E., & Jacklin, C.N. (1974). *The psychology of sex differences*. Stanford, California: Stanford University Press.

Main, A., & Roark, A. (1975). A consensus method to reduce conflict. *Personnel and Guidance Journal, 53*(10), 754-759.

Nye, R.D. (1973). *Conflict among humans*. New York: Springer.

Piaget, J. (1965). *The moral judgment of the child*. New York: The Free Press.

Piche, G.L., Rubin, D., & Michlin, M. (1978). Age and social class in children's use of persuasive appeals. *Child Development, 49,* 773-780.

Szal, J.A. (1972). Sex differences in the cooperative and competitive behaviors of nursery school children. Unpublished master's thesis, Stanford University.

Whiting, B.B., & Edwards, C. (1973). A cross-cultural analysis of sex differences in the behavior of children aged three through eleven. *Journal of Social Psychology, 91,* 171-188.

Wonacott, T.H., & Wonacott, R.J. (1977). *Introductory statistics for business and economics*. New York: Wiley.

Glossary

Accommodation The adjusting of cognitive structures to adapt to new information from the environment.

Adrenogenital syndrome A form of hermaphroditism in genetic females caused by an overproduction of androgen during fetal development and resulting in masculinized external genitalia.

Affordances In differentiation theory, those things that the environment offers, or provides, to the perceiver. Affordances yield possibilities for action.

Afterbirth The third and last phase of the birth process, during which the amniotic sac and placenta are expelled from the uterus by uterine contractions.

Altruism Concern for the welfare of another person or persons.

Amniotic sac The fluid-filled sac in which the embryo and fetus will develop throughout the pregnancy.

Androgens Male sex hormones.

Androgyny The incorporation of masculine and feminine characteristics in one person.

Animism The belief of preoperational children that because they themselves have life, all things are alive. Thus, rocks are piled together in a rock garden because "they like each other."

Anoxia A lack of oxygen at birth which may lead to cerebral palsy or neonatal death.

Artificialism The belief that there must be a psychological reason for everything that exists, even natural phenomena.

Assimilation Part of the adaptive function of human intelligence that involves the fitting of new intellectual material into already existing cognitive structures.

Attention deficit disorder Formerly referred to as hyperactivity, a syndrome characterized by inattention, impulsivity, and hyperactivity lasting for at least six months and not attributable to any specific mental disorder or to mental retardation.

Authoritarian parents Parents who tend to shape their child's behavior according to precise and absolute standards of conduct. The children are expected to be respectful and to value tradition. Little room for discussion of parental standards is allowed.

Authoritative parents Parents who exercise control over their child's behavior but who also allow and encourage the child to be independent. Such parents value obedience but are willing to discuss their expectations with their children.

Autocosmic play The infant's activities during the first year of life that involve the exploration and manipulation of the body.

Axon A long projection that extends from the cell body of a nerve cell. Axons and dendrites are referred to as *nerve fibers*.

Baby biography The informal and personal diary that certain educated and middle-class parents keep concerning the development of their infants.

Behaviorism The theoretical view that stresses that environmental factors are largely responsible for influencing the observable changes of development.

Binocular disparity The tendency of each eye to view a visual display from a slightly different vantage point.

Blastocyst A cluster of about five hundred cells that the fertilized egg has become by the time it has moved from the oviduct to the uterus.

Body image The view a person has of his or her body. Body image may or may not correspond to objective reality, as when physically attractive people with poor self-concepts see themselves as being physically unattractive.

Bonding Literally, the process by which the parent-offspring attachment is initially formed. In the more restrictive sense, bonding refers to a biologically determined attachment mechanism that must be activated within a critical period after the infant's birth.

Canalized Behaviors that follow a prescribed genetic course. Canalized behaviors are relatively unmodifiable by the environment.

Case-study method An individual research strategy, derived from the methods of psychoanalysis, in which the details of a child's life are carefully documented and discussed within a flexible format.

Centration A characteristic of preoperational thought whereby a child centers on the most noticeable features of the environment and ignores other important features.

Cephalocaudal growth Physical growth that proceeds from the head to the trunk, as can be seen in the gradual progress made by infants in raising their heads when placed on their stomachs.

Cerebral cortex The outer surface of the human brain, which is responsible for the sophisticated psychological functioning that differentiates human beings from lower animals.

Chromosomes Microscopic, threadlike structures found in the nucleus of every cell in the human body. Chromosomes contain hereditary materials in the form of genes.

Classical conditioning A basic form of learning involving primarily reflexive behavior, in which two stimuli are associated by virtue of being presented at relatively similar points in time.

Classification The ability to perceive logical similarity among a group of objects and to sort them according to their common features.

Clinical method An individual research strategy popularized by Jean Piaget, in which the child is provided with certain materials and problems to solve within a flexible format and then observed closely, one on one. This strategy has more recently been termed the method of critical exploration.

Cognitive conceit A phenomenon described by David Elkind whereby children who recently have attained the level of concrete operations develop too much faith in their reasoning ability and cleverness. A cocky, know-it-all attitude may be the result.

Cognitive social learning A type of learning characterized by imitation of, or identification with, observed models.

Cognitive structures The ways in which people organize their knowledge—that which determines their intellectual view of the world. Structures are formed as a result of interaction with the intellectual environment.

Compensatory education Educational programs designed to provide children with a richer variety of intellectual experiences than they would ordinarily receive at home or in a traditional school.

Concrete operations The stage of thinking in Jean Piaget's theory that extends from approximately the age of 6 to at least the years of early adolescence. The child now has a logical system within which to organize representational acts but is limited in the use of logic to reasoning about concrete situations or events.

Confluence theory A theory developed by Zajonc and Markus (1975) suggesting that the intelligence of any particular family member is influenced by the average intellectual ability of other members of the family.

Conservation A Piagetian task designed to measure a child's logical understanding of the concept of amount. To succeed at such a task, the child must recognize that variations in the physical appearance of a substance do not alter the amount of the substance present.

Contrast sensitivity The sensitivity of the perceiver to contrast between object and background in a visual display.

Convergent thinking An aspect of intelligence that brings together various bits of information to formulate a single solution (*see also* Divergent thinking).

Correlational statistics (positive and negative correlations) Mathematical procedures that organize data in a manner that shows the strength and direction of relationship between two or more variables. Positive correlations indicate that as scores on one variable increase, scores on a second variable also increase. Negative correlations indicate that as scores on one variable increase, scores on a second variable decrease.

Cross-sectional design A developmental research method that compares the data from different chronological age groups simultaneously.

Cultural creativity A type of creativity reflecting knowledge acquired by being raised in a specific society.

Demand characteristics The cues about the nature of a research project to which the children unknowingly may react, thereby biasing the results.

Dendrites Branchlike projections that extend from the body of a nerve cell and that increase in number as people mature.

Descriptive statistics Mathematical procedures that simplify and succinctly summarize data (e.g., averages and percentages).

Developmental stage A period within the life cycle that is characterized by a cohesive cluster of physical, emotional, intellectual, or social characteristics.

Deviation IQ The IQ computation employed in virtually every intelligence test today. It indicates the relationship between the performance of a given test taker and the "average" person who takes the test.

Differentiation theory The theory of human perception expressed by Eleanor J. Gibson and James J. Gibson, which states that perceptual development allows people to attend more and more closely to the distinctive features differentiating one stimulus from another.

Disequilibrium The imbalance that occurs when there is a discrepancy between perceived reality and a person's way of thinking about the world. Disequilibrium is the motivation for intellectual growth in Jean Piaget's theory.

Divergent thinking An aspect of intelligence that requires the ability to branch out from a single starting point to reach a variety of possibilities (*see also* Convergent thinking).

Down's syndrome A chromosomal disorder in which there is an extra chromosome 21. The disorder results in mental retardation and physical abnormalities.

Ectoderm The outer layer of the embryo which gives rise to such structures as the skin, sensory organs, brain, and spinal cord.

Ego In psychoanalytic theory, a personality structure that develops during the second year of life to consciously and rationally deal with the restrictions that reality imposes on the infant.

Embryo The organism in utero between the ages of 2 and 8 weeks after conception (from the time of implantation to the time when bones can be seen in X rays).

Empiricism The philosophical position that maintains that knowledge is derived only from the senses and that the human organism is "empty" at birth.

Endoderm The inner layer of the embryo which gives rise to such structures as the digestive system, respiratory system, and the lining of the internal organs.

Enrichment theory A type of perceptual theory emphasizing the view that as people develop, their perception is increasingly influenced by what they bring of themselves to the act of perceiving.

Environmentalism The theoretical point of view that describes children as developing according to influences in their environments.

Epigenetic principle According to Erik Erikson, the notion that development proceeds from a universal plan that continually builds upon itself at the appropriate times.

Estrogen The major female sex hormone, which is secreted from a woman's ovaries and is responsible for the "feminizing" of a woman's body.

Ethological attachment theory The view that attachment behaviors are not learned but are "wired into" the organism by nature as a means of ensuring its survival.

Ethology The naturalistic study of animal behavior and its underlying mechanisms.

Expansion An informal language-training technique frequently employed by parents in which the child's simple sentences are reiterated in a more elaborate form.

Experimental strategy A type of research in which one or more variables are manipulated and isolated to determine cause-and-effect relationships. The part of the sample that is given a treatment is known as the *experimental group.* The part of the sample that is not given the treatment, for comparative purposes, is known as the *control group.*

Expressive needs Needs for emotional closeness and support in a relationship.

Extensive peer relations Social interactions characterized as group activities.

Extinction The process by which learned responses are unlearned because the stimulus-response connections cease to be made.

Fetal alcohol syndrome A set of congenital problems that may result from maternal ingestion of alcohol during pregnancy. Typical of the syndrome are mental retardation, facial anomalies, and poor growth in height and weight.

Fetus The newly developing organism in utero from 8 weeks after conception—when bone cells appear in X rays—to the moment of birth.

Field experiment A type of experimental strategy in which the research is conducted relatively unobtrusively in a natural setting rather than in a laboratory.

Field independence An analytic-spatial ability to separate an embedded figure from its surrounding context.

Formal operations The highest of Jean Piaget's stages of logical reasoning, reached only by the adolescent or adult. Formal reasoners are aware of their own thought processes and can deal with abstract, hypothetical, and contrary-to-fact propositions.

Frequency A characteristic of sound waves that is perceived by human beings as variations in the pitch of sound. Frequency is measured in a unit known as a hertz.

Games-with-rules The logical, rule-dominated games of elementary school children.

Gender The nonphysiological aspects of sex that social convention designates as appropriate for either males or females.

Gender constancy The child's understanding that his or her gender will remain the same despite such superficial changes as hairstyle, dress, or activity.

Gender identity The personal awareness of being either male or female. It is an internalization of the characteristics, attitudes, and feelings of one sex over the other.

Gender role The behaviors that society recognizes as appropriate for males and females.

Gender-role preference The desire to adopt the behaviors and attitudes of one sex over the other.

Gender-role stereotype Well-defined cultural prescriptions for appropriate male and female behavior. This is also referred to as *gender-typed behavior.*

Gender stability The child's realization that his or her gender will always remain the same and that he or she will grow up to be a man or a woman.

Gender-typed behavior Behavior that is stereotyped according to conventional prescriptions of "appropriate" male or female behavior.

Genes Hereditary material found in the chromosomes. Genes are composed of the chemical substance deoxyribonucleic acid (DNA) and carry coded information that influences physical characteristics.

Genotype The total genetic inheritance of a living organism.

Group differences statistics Mathematical procedures that organize data in a manner to permit comparisons between two or more groups within a sample.

Group intelligence test An intelligence test that can be administered on a large-scale basis. Because of the ease of administration and scoring, group intelligence tests have been widely used. However, their results must be interpreted very carefully and used cautiously.

Gyri The ridges of the cerebral cortex.

Habituation The process by which a stimulus becomes familiar and gradually ceases to bring about an orienting reflex.

Heritability The degree to which a certain characteristic or characteristics vary within a population as a result of genetic factors.

Hermaphroditism A condition in which the internal reproductive system matches one genetic sex, but the external genitalia do not.

Heterozygous Having two different genes for a trait. Each gene is at the same location on its corresponding chromosome in a pair of chromosomes.

Holophrases The first words infants use, which tend to convey more meaning (that is, the meaning of whole phrases) than the typical adult usage would imply.

Homozygous Having two of the same genes for a trait. Each gene is at the same location on its corresponding chromosome in a pair of chromosomes.

Humanism The philosophical and theoretical perspective that maintains that the freedom, subjectivity, and creativity of the person are essential for understanding the process of development.

Hypothalamus The area in the lower-central portion of the brain that regulates body temperature, blood pressure, and blood flow to the brain and controls the endocrine system.

Hypothesis The formal statement of a researcher's educated guess about how two or more variables are related.

Id In psychoanalytic theory, a personality structure that is present from birth and contains the irrational, unconscious, and selfish aspects of human beings.

Idealism The philosophical position that maintains that reality cannot be known independently from the mind that perceives it.

Identification The process by which one person perceives himself or herself as being similar to another and, in a sense, shares in the identity of the other person. For example, a child may identify with a parent, or a person may identify with a religious or ethnic group.

Idiosyncratic creativity Creative accomplishments of specific individuals within the context of a particular culture.

Implicit information The skills that competent users of a language possess and take for granted in the process of having a conversation. For example, competent speakers are aware when the topic of conversation changes.

Indifferent and uninvolved parents Parents whose primary concern is for their own comfort and convenience and who have little interest or involvement in the day-to-day aspects of their children's lives.

Individual intelligence test An intelligence test administered by a professional psychologist to one person at a time. The Stanford-Binet Intelligence Scale and the Wechsler tests are among the better-known individual intelligence tests.

Induction A disciplinary approach that emphasizes the impact of the child's wrong behaviors on other people in the environment.

Infant states A continuum of levels of sleep and wakefulness that has been observed in neonates and young infants.

Inferential statistics Mathematical procedures that estimate the probability of obtaining similar data with a different sample from the same population.

Information-oriented decision makers Self-reliant, mature adolescents who gather relevant information from every possible source before making a decision.

Inner speech According to Lev Vygotsky, the process by which spoken language becomes a silent, private form of thinking.

Instinctual anxiety In psychoanalytic theory, the fear children have of their own instincts whose expression is forbidden by society.

Instrumental needs Friendship needs that are concrete and practical as opposed to emotional. An example is the need for a friend who will offer financial assistance in times of economic hardship.

Intensity A characteristic of sound waves that is perceived by human beings as variations in the loudness of sound. Intensity is calculated in decibels.

Intensive peer relations One-to-one social interactions.

Interaction A dynamic two-directional process in which the behaviors of each party continuously influence the behaviors of the other.

Karyotype A picture of the chromosomes of a cell, which have been stained and arranged in an ordered series of pairs.

Kwashiorkor A disease that results from a diet lacking in protein. In third-world countries, children are at risk for this disease when they are weaned.

Labor The first and longest phase of the birth process, during which uterine contractions push the fetus downward into the cervix, eventually causing the cervix to open to a diameter of ten centimeters.

Law of contiguity The basic principle upon which classical conditioning relies: learning occurs because two stimuli (the unconditioned stimulus and the conditioned stimulus) are presented at roughly the same time and therefore become associated.

Law of effect The basic tenet of operant conditioning, which states that responses followed by reinforcement are increasingly likely to be repeated.

Learning disorder A condition that results from a dysfunction in one of the basic learning processes (for example, visual, auditory, tactile, motoric, or memory), causing a disparity between a child's basic ability and actual intellectual performance.

Libido According to Sigmund Freud, the instinctual psychosexual energy force that provides the motivation for thought and behavior.

Linguistic relativity hypothesis The position held by cultural anthropologist Benjamin Whorf that a language actually determines the nature of thought for the speaker of that language.

Longitudinal design A developmental research method that compares the data from one sample at different chronological age intervals.

Long-term memory Memory for information that is no longer being held at the level of consciousness and must be retrieved from permanent storage.

Macrosphere play Preschool children's activities, in conjunction with peers, which enable them to understand their culture and learn about social interaction.

Maternal sensitization A condition that occurs during pregnancy when an Rh-negative mother creates antibodies to attack the red blood cells of the Rh-positive fetus she is carrying.

Maturationism The theoretical view that stresses that hereditary mechanisms are largely responsible for influencing the path of development.

Mediation theory A theory that attempts to explain developmental differences in human learning by suggesting that internal "mediated" responses come between an external stimulus and an external response. These mediated responses are generally not produced by children until the age of 6 or 7.

Meiosis A process of cell division by which a body cell divides into two new cells, each containing only half the number of chromosomes found in the parent cell. This is the process by which sex cells are produced.

Menarche The first episode of menstrual bleeding, which can occur at any time from age 10 to age 16 in the developing adolescent girl.

Mesoderm The middle layer of the embryo which forms such structures as the circulatory system, muscles, and blood.

Metamemory The area of study that deals with people's understanding of their own memory functions.

Microsphere play The toddler's activities, especially the examination of toys and other objects, that enable the child to acquire mastery of the world.

Mitosis A process of cell division by which two new cells are formed from a parent cell. Each new cell is genetically identical to the parent cell.

Morality of constraint A morality characterized by the child's simple acceptance of definitions of right and wrong supplied by the parents.

Morality of cooperation A morality constructed by children themselves on the basis of their interactions with their peers.

Morphology The study of the basic word units of a language, including how they are constructed and how they are modified.

Motherese A pattern of speech used by adults when speaking to infants. Motherese is characterized by a raising of the voice's pitch and exaggerated intonations.

Multivariate statistics Mathematical procedures that are used to analyze the data of multiple dependent variables simultaneously (*see also* Univariate statistics).

Myelination The developmental process by which the nerve fibers are surrounded by a fatty layer (myelin sheath). The myelin sheath serves as an insulator and increases the efficiency with which a nerve fiber conducts a nerve impulse.

Natural experiment A type of nonexperimental strategy in which the researcher is able to take advantage of a naturally occurring manipulation instead of deliberately intervening.

Naturalism The philosophical view that nature provides the child with a plan for development and no harm will result if the child is allowed to grow without much supervision.

Neuron A nerve cell.

Normal distribution A mathematical concept that describes the way test scores distribute themselves around a mean, or average, score.

Normative The research approach, based on maturational theory, that attempts to establish the natural timing and sequence of typical developmental change.

Nutritional marasmus A severe form of malnutrition resulting from an insufficient amount of protein and calories in the diet. The name for this condition literally means "wasting away."

Observational learning Learning that results from observing the behavior of other people and, most particularly, from observing the consequences of that behavior.

Observational research Data collection procedures that use checklists, rating scales, narrative methods, or behavioral samples to obtain results. Researchers or their appointees usually try to obtain the data relatively unobtrusively in natural settings.

Operant conditioning A type of learning in which the consequences of the learner's behavior (e.g., reward or punishment) influence the future occurrence of that behavior.

Operational definition The specific meaning, in quantitative or categorical terms, assigned to the use of a variable.

Organismic theory A type of developmental theory that stresses the importance in development of factors within the organism itself.

Orthogenetic principle According to Heinz Werner, the observation that development involves movement from relative globality to ever-increasing levels of differentiation and integration.

Permissive parents Parents who are unwilling to exert authority or control over their children. Few regulations are imposed, and there is little emphasis on responsibility and order in the home.

Phenotype The actual manifestations of genetic information as evidenced by the appearance of an organism. Thus, a person may inherit genes for both brown and blue eyes (the genotype) but may have brown eyes (the phenotype).

Phonology The study of the patterns of sound in a language, including intonation, stress, pronunciation, and blending.

Pituitary gland The body's master gland. Located at the base of the brain, the pituitary gland—on receiving signals from the hypothalamus—stimulates and controls all of the other glands in the endocrine system.

Placenta The disklike membrane, rich in blood vessels, that is formed at the juncture of the newly developing fetus and the uterine wall and that serves as an exchange filter between the maternal and fetal bloodstreams.

Polygenic A trait or characteristic that is determined by a multiple number of gene pairs.

Practice play The intrinsically satisfying repetition of simple motor skills that occurs during the first eighteen months of life. Practice play is also called sensorimotor play.

Pragmatics The study of the social and contextual factors that govern conversation, as well as the nonverbal aspects of language.

Preoperational intelligence A form of mental activity found in preschool children who are capable of mental representation but as yet have no system to organize their thinking.

Primary process thinking According to Sigmund Freud, the tendency of the id to strive for immediate gratification of needs or reduction of tensions by any available means.

Proximodistal growth Growth that proceeds from the center of the body to the extremities, as when infants can move an arm as an entire unit before they can control the movement of their individual fingers.

Psychic determinism The psychoanalytic principle that all mental activity is caused by previous events that continue to influence the present.

Psychoanalysis The theoretical view and therapeutic practice stressing that unconscious mechanisms are largely responsible for influencing the course of development.

Psychoanalytic theory The theoretical view that stresses the importance of unconscious mechanisms in development and sees the human organism as a creature of appetite rather than reason.

Psychosocial crisis A predominant conflict that is associated with each of Erik Erikson's eight stages of development. The crisis results from both biological and cultural demands and may be favorably or unfavorably resolved.

Punishment An outcome that follows a behavior and decreases the likelihood that the behavior will occur in the future.

Ratio IQ The original formulation of the intelligence quotient, which was obtained by dividing a person's mental age by chronological age and multiplying the result by 100.

Reaction range The extent of possible variations in the expression of a particular genotype as a result of different life experiences.

Realism The philosophical position that maintains that reality has an existence independent of the perceiver's consciousness of it.

Reflexes Automatic behavioral reactions found in the newborn infant. Some reflexes have obvious survival value, whereas others do not. Reflexes are thought to form the basis for more complex learned behaviors.

Reinforcement An outcome that follows a behavior and increases the likelihood that the behavior will occur in the future. Positive reinforcement is accomplished by presenting the learner with a reward. Negative reinforcement involves the removal of an unpleasant stimulus.

Reliability The consistency of scores yielded by a particular psychological test.

Response set The tendency of either subjects or researchers to react in a constantly similar manner despite variations in stimulation, thereby biasing the results of an experiment.

Reversal shift A condition in a discrimination learning task in which the learner initially is rewarded for responding to one example (white, for example) of a particular dimension (in this case, color) and later rewarded for responding to an opposite example (black, for example) of the same dimension.

Sample The persons, or subjects, who participate in a research project. They are generally chosen to reflect the characteristics of the larger similar group, or population, that the sample represents.

Schema According to information-processing theorists of gender development, a set of ideas that help children categorize information in terms of what is appropriate and characteristic of males and females.

Schemes Consistent action sequences made up of classes of acts that have regular common features. Schemes are the sensorimotor equivalent of concepts.

Scoop model A model of gene-environment interaction that illustrates the relative significance of genetic factors early in development and of environmental factors later in development.

Secondary process thinking According to Sigmund Freud, the tendency of the ego to postpone instinctual gratification through the use of logic and the testing of reality.

Secular trend The tendency for each generation since the early 1800s to be taller and heavier than the generation that preceded it, as well as to reach puberty earlier.

Self-concept All the components of a child's personality of which he or she is aware.

Self-esteem The evaluative component of the self-concept whereby "good" or "bad" labels are attached to aspects of the self.

Semantics The study of the meaning of the words and sentences of a language.

Sensorimotor intelligence The action-oriented type of intelligence and problem solving engaged in by infants up to the age of 1½ years.

Sequential design A developmental research method that blends elements of cross-sectional, longitudinal, and time-lag designs to maximize the advantages and minimize the disadvantages of these simpler methods.

Seriation A Piagetian task designed to measure a child's understanding of ordinal relations.

Sex The term used by researchers of gender development to refer to biological characteristics and differences between males and females.

Sexual polarization versus bisexual confusion As proposed by Erik Erikson, a part of the adolescent identity crisis. It involves accepting oneself as a physically and psychologically mature male or female.

Shape constancy The realization that the actual shape of an object remains the same even though the shape seems to change when the object is viewed from different angles.

Shared meanings Themes that organize a social interaction between young children. An example might be a peekaboo game.

Short-term memory Memory for material still at a person's level of consciousness because it has recently been presented and is in the process of being rehearsed.

Size constancy The realization that the actual size of an object remains the same even though the size of the object's visual image changes in relation to its distance from the viewer.

Social cognition Children's developing awareness of other people and their changing conceptions of friendship. Cognitive skills are applied in social interactions.

Social-learning attachment theory The belief that attachment consists of a set of learned behaviors resulting from the child's associating his or her caretaker with the satisfaction of physiological needs.

Source-oriented decision makers Adolescents who lack self-assurance and rely heavily on the opinions of others when making a decision.

Standard deviation A numerical indication of the variance of all reported scores from the mean, or average, score.

Standardized tests or tasks Systematic methods for obtaining samples of categorical or numerical information that are inferred to represent a child's characteristics.

Stereopsis Depth perception resulting from binocular disparity and involving the convergence of the eyes on a single target and the fusion of the different visual images perceived by each eye.

Sudden infant death syndrome The unexplained death of an apparently healthy infant.

Sulci The grooves or indentations found in the cerebral cortex.

Superego In psychoanalytic theory, a personality structure that emerges during the preschool years as a result of identification with parents and the establishment of cultural standards for behavior. The superego includes a conscience and an ego ideal.

Survey approach Data collection procedures that use the direct techniques of interviewing and questionnaires to obtain results.

Symbolic, or fantasy, play The make-believe activities of toddlers and preschoolers that involve the shaping of reality to meet the needs and settle the conflicts of the child's emotional world.

Syntax The way in which a language's words are arranged in terms of phrases and sentences, as well as their variations.

Telegraphic speech The first, abbreviated sentences that very young children create. They contain the minimum numbers of words needed to relate meaning but lack the auxiliary words that adults typically omit from telegram messages.

Temperament A core set of inherited dispositions, which, after modification by experiences, serves as the foundation for later personality.

Teratogens Environmental factors that can affect the development of the fetus.

Transductive reasoning An illogical form of reasoning found in children under the age of 5 or 6.

Unconscious motivation The psychoanalytic principle that people are usually unaware of the processes and factors that motivate their behavior and mental activity.

Unique creativity The type of creativity exhibited by the invention of something totally new and extraordinary.

Univariate statistics Mathematical procedures that are used to analyze the data of only one dependent variable at a time (*see also* Multivariate statistics).

Universal creativity The normal discoveries of infants and children in all human cultures.

Validity The accuracy with which a psychological test measures what it is intended to measure.

Variable A concept that has a property that varies in at least two ways. An independent variable is presumed to be the cause of, or to influence, a dependent variable.

Visual acuity The ability of the perceiver to recognize all of the distinctive components in a visual display.

Visually guided reaching A form of reaching that appears by 4 months of age. The infant uses feedback from the object to make adjustments in his or her successful reach and grasp.

Visually initiated reaching Neonatal reaching that is elicited by a visual stimulus, but the reach does not adjust to the properties of the object.

Zygote A newly fertilized egg cell.

Bibliography

Abramovitch, R. & Grusec, J.E. (1978). Peer imitation in a natural setting. *Child Development, 49*, 60–65.

Abramovitch, R., Pepler, D. & Corter, C. (1982). Patterns of sibling interaction among preschool-age children. In M.E. Lamb & B. Sutton-Smith (Eds.), *Sibling relationships: Their nature and significance across the lifespan.* Hillsdale, NJ: Erlbaum.

Abranavel, E. & Sigafoos, A.D. (1984). Exploring the presence of imitation during early infancy. *Child Development, 55*, 381–392.

Achenbach, T.M. (1978). *Research in developmental psychology: Concepts, strategies, methods.* New York: Free Press.

Ackerman, B.P. (1982). Contextual integration and utterance interpretation: The ability of children and adults to interpret sarcastic utterances. *Child Development, 53*, 1075–1083.

Acredolo, L.P. & Hake, J.L. (1982). Infant perception. In B.B. Wolman (Ed.), *Handbook of developmental psychology.* Englewood Cliffs, NJ: Prentice-Hall.

Action for Children's Television (ACT). Spring 1978, *7* (3).

Adams, R.J. & Maurer, D. (1984). *The use of habituation to study newborns' color vision.* Paper presented at the 4th International Conference on Infant Studies, New York City.

Adams, R.J., Maurer, D. & Davis, M. (1986). Newborns' discrimination of chromatic from achromatic stimuli. *Journal of Experimental Child Psychology, 41*, 267–281.

Ahr, P.R. & Youniss, J. (1970). Reasons for failure on the class inclusion problem. *Child Development, 41*, 131–144.

Ainsworth, M.D.S. (1977). Attachment theory and its utility in cross-cultural research. In P.H. Leiderman, S.R. Tulkin & R. Rosenfeld (Eds.), *Culture and infancy.* New York: Academic Press.

Ainsworth, M.D.S., Bell, S.M. & Stayton, D.J. (1971). Individual differences in strange situation behavior in one-year-olds. In H.R. Schaffer (Ed.), *The origins of human social relations.* London: Academic Press.

Ainsworth, M.D.S., Blehar, M.C., Waters, E. & Wall, S. (1978). *Patterns of attachment: A psychological study of the Strange Situation.* Hillsdale, NJ: Erlbaum.

Aitken, S. & Bower, T.G.R. (1982). Intersensory substitution in the blind. *Journal of Experimental Child Psychology, 33*, 309–323.

Alegria, J.R. & Noirot, E. (1978). Neonate orientation behavior towards the human voice. *International Journal of Behavioral Development, 1*, 291–312.

Algozzine, O. (1977). Perceived attractiveness and classroom interactions. *Journal of Experimental Education, 46*, 63–66.

Allport, G.W. (1961). *Pattern and growth in personality* (2nd ed.). New York: Holt, Rinehart & Winston.

Alwitt, L., Anderson, D., Lorch, E. & Levin, S. (1980). Preschool children's visual attention to television. *Human Communication Research, 7*, 52–67.

American Psychiatric Association. (1980). *Diagnostic and statistical manual of mental disorders* (3rd ed.). Washington, D.C.: APA.

American Psychological Association. (1982). *Ethical principles in the conduct of research with human participants.* Washington, D.C.: Author.

Amsterdam, B.K. (1972). Mirror self-image reactions before age two. *Developmental Psychology, 5*, 297–305.

Anastasi, A. (1958). Heredity, environment and the question "How?" *Psychological Review, 65*, 197–208.

Anastasi, A. (1982). *Psychological testing* (5th ed.). New York: Macmillan.

Anderson, D. & Levin, S. (1976). Young children's attention to Sesame Street. *Child Development, 47*, 806–811.

Anderson, D. & Lorch, E. (1983). Looking at television: Action or reaction. In J. Bryant & D. Anderson (Eds.), *Children's understanding of television: Research on attention and comprehension.* New York: Academic Press.

Anderson, D.R., Lorch, E.P., Field, D.E., Collins, P.A. & Nathan, J.G. (1986). Television viewing at home: Age trends in visual attention and time with TV. *Child Development, 57*, 1024–1033.

Anderson, H.H. (1959). Creativity in perspective. In H.H. Anderson (Ed.), *Creativity and its cultivation.* New York: Harper & Row.

Anderson, J.R. (1983). *The architecture of cognition.* Cambridge, MA: Harvard University Press.

Anderson, J.R. (1985). *Cognitive psychology and its implications* (2nd ed.). New York: Freeman.

Anderson, J.R. & Paulson, R. (1977). Representation and retention of verbatim information. *Journal of Verbal Learning and Verbal Behavior, 16*, 439–451.

Anderson, L., Evertson, C.M. & Brophy, J.E. (1979). An experimental study of effective teaching in first-grade reading groups. *Elementary School Journal, 79*, 193–222.

Antonak, R.F., King, S & Lowy, J.J. (1982). Otis-Lennon Mental Ability Test, Stanford Achievement Test, and three demographic variables as predictors of achievement in grades 2 and 4. *Journal of Educational Research, 75*, 366–373.

Apgar, V. (1953). A proposal for a new method of evaluation of the newborn infant. *Current Researches in Anesthesia and Analgesia, 32*, 260–267.

Appelbaum, M.I. & McCall, R.B. (1983). Design and analysis in developmental psychology. In P.H. Mussen (Ed.), *Handbook of child psychology* (4th ed., vol. 1). New York: Wiley.

Arend, R., Gove, F.L. & Sroufe, L.A. (1979). Continuity of individual adaptation from infancy to kindergarten: A predictive study of ego-resiliency and curiosity in preschoolers. *Child Development, 50*, 950–959.

Aries, P. (1962). *Centuries of childhood.* (Trans. by R. Baldick). New York: Vintage.

Arlin, P.K. (1975). Cognitive development in adulthood: A fifth stage. *Developmental Psychology, 11,* 602–606.

Arlin, P.K. (1984). Adolescent and adult thought: A structural interpretation. In M.L. Commons, F.A. Richards & C. Armon (Eds.), *Beyond formal operations: Late adolescent and adult cognitive development.* New York: Praeger.

Aronfreed, J. (1969). The concept of internalization. In D. Goslin (Ed.), *Handbook of socialization theory and research.* New York: Rand McNally.

Asher, S.R., Hymel, S. & Renshaw, P.D. (1984). Loneliness in children. *Child Development, 55,* 1456–1464.

Asher, S.R., Oden, S.L. & Gottman, J.M. (1977). Children's friendships in school settings. In L.G. Katz et al. (Eds.), *Current topics in early childhood education* (vol. 1). Norwood, NJ: Ablex.

Aslin, R.N. (1977). Development of binocular fixation in human infants. *Journal of Experimental Child Psychology, 23,* 133–150.

Aslin, R.N., Pisoni, D.P. & Jusczyk, P.W. (1983). Auditory development and speech perception in infancy. In P.H. Mussen (Ed.), *Handbook of child psychology* (4th ed., vol. 2). New York: Wiley.

Austin, J.H. (1978). *Chase, chance, and creativity.* New York: Columbia University Press.

Babson, S.G. & Clarke, N.G. (1983). Relationship between infant death and maternal age. *Journal of Pediatrics, 103,* 391–393.

Bacharach, V.R. & Luszcz, M.A. (1979). Communicative competence in young children: The use of implicit linguistic information. *Child Development, 50,* 260–263.

Baer, D.M. & Sherman, J.A. (1964). Reinforcement control of generalized imitation in young children. *Journal of Experimental Child Psychology, 1,* 37–49.

Baillargeon, R., Spelke, E.S. & Wasserman, S. (1985). Object permanence in five-month-old infants. *Cognition, 20,* 191–208.

Bakeman, R. & Brown, J. (1980). Early interaction: Consequences for social and mental development at three years. *Child Development, 51,* 437–447.

Baldwin, J.M. (1897). *Social and ethical interpretations in mental development.* New York: Macmillan.

Bandura, A. (1965). Influence of models' reinforcement contingencies on the acquisition of imitative responses. *Journal of Personality and Social Psychology, 1,* 589–595.

Bandura, A. (1969). Social learning theory of identificatory processes. In D.A. Goslin (Ed.), *Handbook of socialization theory and research.* Chicago: Rand McNally.

Bandura, A. (1971). *Psychological modeling: Conflicting theories.* New York: Lieber-Atherton.

Bandura, A. (1977). *Social learning theory.* Englewood Cliffs, NJ: Prentice-Hall.

Bandura, A. (1986). *Social foundation of thought and action: A social cognitive theory.* Englewood Cliffs, NJ: Prentice-Hall.

Bandura, A., Ross, D. & Ross, S.A. (1963a). A comparative test of the status envy, social power, and secondary reinforcement theories of identificatory learning. *Journal of Abnormal and Social Psychology, 67,* 527–534.

Bandura, A., Ross, D. & Ross, S.A. (1963b). Imitation of film-mediated aggressive models. *Journal of Abnormal and Social Psychology, 66,* 3–11.

Bandura, A., Ross, D. & Ross, S.A. (1963c). Vicarious reinforcement and imitative learning. *Journal of Abnormal and Social Psychology, 67,* 601–607.

Bandura, A. & Walters, R.H. (1963). *Social learning and personality development.* New York: Holt, Rinehart & Winston.

Bane, M.J. (1979). Marital disruption and the lives of children. In G. Levinger & O. Moles (Eds.), *Divorce and separation: Context, causes and consequences.* New York: Basic Books.

Banks, M.S. (1980). The development of visual accommodation during early infancy. *Child Development, 51,* 646–666.

Banks, M.S. & Salapatek, P. (1981). Infant pattern vision: A new approach based on the contrast sensitivity function. *Journal of Experimental Child Psychology, 31,* 1–45.

Banks, M.S. & Salapatek, P. (1983). Infant visual perception. In P.H. Mussen (Ed.), *Handbook of child psychology* (4th ed., vol. 2). New York: Wiley.

Barrera, M.E. & Maurer, D. (1981). The perception of facial expressions by the three-month-old. *Child Development, 52,* 203–206.

Barron, F. & Harrington, D.M. (1981). Creativity, intelligence, and personality. *Annual Review of Psychology, 32,* 439–476.

Baruch, G.K. & Barnett, R.C. (1986). Father's participation in family work and children's sex role attitudes. *Child Development, 57,* 1210–1223.

Bases, R. (1985). Diagnostic ultrasound. *Science, 228,* 648–649.

Bates, E. (1976). *Language and context: The acquisition of pragmatics.* New York: Academic Press.

Bates, J.E., Maslin, C.A. & Frankel, K.A. (1985). Attachment security, mother-child interaction, and temperament as predictors of behavior-problem rating at age three years. In I. Bretherton & E. Waters (Eds.), *Growing points of attachment theory and research. Monographs of the Society for Research in Child Development, 50* (1-2, Serial No. 209).

Bateson, G. (1972). *Steps to an ecology of mind.* New York: Ballantine Books.

Baumrind, D. (1967). Child care practices anteceding three patterns of preschool behavior. *Genetic Psychology Monographs, 75,* 43–88.

Baumrind, D. (1968). Authoritarian vs. authoritative parental control. *Adolescence, 3,* 255–272.

Baumrind, D. (1971). Current patterns of parental authority. *Developmental Psychology Monograph, 4* (1, Pt. 2).

Baumrind, D. (1975). Some thoughts about childbearing. In U. Bronfenbrenner & M.A. Mahoney (Eds.), *Influ-*

ences on human development (2nd ed.). Hinsdale, IL: Dryden Press.

Baumrind, D. (1982). Are androgynous individuals more effective persons and parents? *Child Development, 53,* 44–75.

Baumrind, D. (1986). Sex differences in moral reasoning: Response to Walker's (1984) conclusion that there are none. *Child Development, 57,* 511–521.

Baumrind, D. & Black, A.E. (1967). Socialization practices associated with dimensions of competence in preschool boys and girls. *Child Development, 38,* 291–327.

Bayley, N. (1949). Consistency and variability in the growth of intelligence from birth to eighteen years. *Journal of Genetic Psychology, 75,* 165–196.

Bayley, N. (1968). Cognition in aging. In K.W. Schaie (Ed.), *Theory and methods of research on aging.* Morgantown: West Virginia University Library.

Bayley, N. (1969). *Bayley Scales of Infant Development.* New York: Psychological Corp.

Bayley, N. & Schaefer, E.S. (1964). Correlations of maternal and child behaviors with the development of mental abilities: Data from the Berkeley Growth Study. *Monographs of the Society for Research in Child Development, 29* (Serial No. 97).

Bearison, D.J. & Cassel, T.Z. (1975). Cognitive decentration and social codes: Communicative effectiveness in young children from differing family contexts. *Developmental Psychology, 11,* 29–36.

Beauchamp, G.K., Cowart, B.J. & Moran, M. (1986). Developmental changes in salt acceptability in human infants. *Developmental Psychobiology, 19,* 75–83.

Beauchamp, G.K. & Moran, M. (1985). Acceptance of sweet and salty tastes in 2-year-old children. *Appetite, 5,* 291–305.

Bechtoldt, H.P. & Hutz, C.S. (1979). Stereogasis in young infants and stereopsis in an infant with congenital esotropia. *Journal of Pediatric Opthalmology, 16,* 49–54.

Becker, W.C. (1964). Consequences of different kinds of parental discipline. In M.L. Hoffman & L.W. Hoffman (Eds.), *Review of child development research* (vol. 1). New York: Russell Sage Foundation.

Becker, W.C. & Gersten, R. (1982). A follow-up of follow through: The later effects of the direct instruction model on children in fifth and sixth grades. *American Educational Research Journal, 19,* 75–92.

Beckwith, L. & Parmelee, A.H. (1986). EEG patterns of preterm infants, homes environment, and later IQ. *Child Development, 57,* 777-789.

Bee, H. (1978). *Social issues in developmental psychology* (2nd ed.). New York: Harper & Row.

Beilin, H. (1975). *Studies in the cognitive basis of language acquisition.* New York: Academic Press.

Bell, S.M. & Ainsworth, M.D.S. (1972). Infant crying and maternal responsiveness. *Child Development, 43,* 1171–1190.

Bellugi, U. & Klima, E. (1982). From gesture to sign: Deixis in a visual-gestural language. In R.J. Jarrella & W. Klein (Eds.), *Speech, place and action: Studies in deixis and related topics.* Sussex: Wiley.

Belmont, L. & Marolla, F.A. (1973). Birth order, family size, and intelligence. *Science, 182,* 1096–1101.

Belsky, J., Garduque, L. & Hrncir, E. (1984). Assessing performance, competence and executive capacity in infant play: Relations to home environment and the security of attachment. *Development Psychology, 20,* 406–417.

Belsky, J. & Steinberg, L.D. (1978). The effects of day care: A critical review. *Child Development, 49,* 929–949.

Bem, S.L. (1974). The measurement of psychology androgyny. *Journal of Consulting and Clinical Psychology, 42,* 155–162.

Bem, S.L. (1975). Sex role adaptability: One consequence of psychological androgyny. *Journal of Personality and Social Psychology, 31,* 634–643.

Bem, S.L. (1976). Probing the promise of androgyny. In A.G. Kaplan & J.P. Bean (Eds.), *Beyond sex-role stereotypes: Readings toward a psychology of androgyny.* Boston: Little, Brown.

Benirschke, K., Carpenter, G., Epstein, C., et al. (1976). In R.L. Brent and M.I. Harris (Eds.), *Prevention of embryonic, fetal, and perinatal disease.* (DHEW Publication No. NIH 76-853), Washington, D.C.

Benn, R.K. (1986). Factors promoting secure attachment relationships between employed mothers and their sons. *Child Development, 57,* 1224–1231.

Berk, L.E. (1986). Relationship of elementary school children's private speech to behavioral accompaniment to task, attention, and task performance. *Developmental Psychology, 22,* 671–680.

Berk, R., Bridges, W. & Shih, A. (1981). Does IQ really matter?: A study of the use of IQ scores for tracking of the mentally retarded. *American Sociological Review, 46,* 58–71.

Berko, J. (1958). The child's learning of English morphology. *Word, 14,* 150–177.

Berlyne, D.E. (1969). Laughter, humor, and play. In G. Lindzey & E. Aronson (Eds.), *Handbook of social psychology* (vol. 3). Reading, MA: Addison-Wesley.

Berndt, T.J. (1982a). Fairness and friendship. In K.H. Rubin & H.S. Ross (Eds.), *Peer relationships and social skills in childhood.* New York: Springer-Verlag.

Berndt, T.J. (1982b). The features and effects of friendship in early adolescence. *Child Development, 53,* 1447–1460.

Berndt, T.J. & Bulleit, T.N. (1985). Effects of sibling relationships on preschooler's behavior at home and at school. *Developmental Psychology, 21,* 761–767.

Berndt, T.J., Hawkins, J.A. & Hoyle, S.G. (1986). Changes in friendship during a school year: Effects on children's and adolescents' impressions of friendships and sharing with friends. *Child Development, 57,* 1284–1297.

Bernstein, B. (1971). *Classes, codes and controls.* London: Routledge and Kegan Paul.

Berscheid, E., Walster, E. & Bohrnstedt, G. (1973, November). Body image. *Psychology Today, 7 (6),* 119–131.

Bersoff, D.N. (1981). Testing and the law. *American Psychologist, 36,* 1047–1056.

Berzonsky, M.D. (1981). *Adolescent development*. New York: Macmillan.

Biemer, D.J. (1983). Shyness control: A systematic approach to social anxiety management in children. *School Counselor, 31*, 53–60.

Bierman, K.L. (1986). Process of change during social skills training with preadolescents and its relation to treatment outcome. *Child Development, 57*, 230–240.

Bierman, K.L. & Furman, W.F. (1984). The effects of social skills training and peer involvement in the social development of preadolescents. *Child Development, 55*, 151–162.

Bigelow, B.J. (1977). Children's friendship expectations: A cognitive development study. *Child Development, 48*, 246–253.

Bigelow, B.J. & La Gaipa, J.J. (1975). Children's written descriptions of friendships: A multidimensional analysis. *Developmental Psychology, 11*, 857–858.

Bigner, J.J. (1974). Second borns' discrimination of sibling role concept. *Developmental Psychology, 10*, 564–573.

Bigner, J.J. (1985). *Parent-child relations: An introduction to parenting* (2nd ed.). New York: Macmillan.

Biller, H.B. (1974). *Paternal deprivation*. Lexington, MA: Lexington Books.

Biller, H.B. (1981). The father and sex role development. In M.E. Lamb (Ed.), *The role of the father in child development*. New York: Wiley.

Biller, H.B. (1982). Fatherhood: Implications for child and adult development. In B.B. Wolman (Ed.), *Handbook of developmental psychology*. Englewood Cliffs, NJ: Prentice-Hall.

Birch, L.L. & Billman, J. (1986). Preschool children's food sharing with friends and acquaintances. *Child Development, 57*, 387–395.

Bischof, L.J. (1976). *Adult psychology*. New York: Harper & Row.

Bittman, S. & Zalk, S.R. (1978). *Expectant fathers*. New York: Hawthorn.

Bjorklund, G. (1979). *The effects of toy quantity and qualitative category on toddler's play*. Paper presented at the meeting of the Society for Research in Child Development, San Francisco.

Blake, J. (1974). Can we believe recent data on birth expectation in the United States? *Demography, 11*, 25–44.

Blanchard, R.W. & Biller, H.B. (1971). Father availability and academic performance among third-grade boys. *Developmental Psychology, 81*, 85–88.

Blasi, A. (1980). Bridging moral cognition and moral action: A critical review of the literature. *Psychological Bulletin, 88*, 1–45.

Blasi, A. (1983). Moral cognition and moral action: A theoretical perspective. *Developmental Review, 3*, 178–210.

Blatt, M.J. & Kohlberg, L. (1975). The effects of classroom moral discussion upon children's level of moral judgment. *Journal of Moral Education, 4*, 129–161.

Block, J.H. (1971). *Lives through time*. Berkeley, CA: Bancroft.

Block, J.H. (1976). Issues, problems and pitfalls in assessing sex differences. *Merrill-Palmer Quarterly, 22*, 283–308.

Block, J.H. (1978). Another look at sex differentiation in the socialization behaviors of mothers and fathers. In F.L. Denmark & J.A. Sherman (Eds.), *Psychology of women: Future direction of research*. New York: Psychological Dimensions.

Bloom, A., Wagner, M., Bergman, A., Altshuler, L. & Raskin, L. (1981). Relationship between intellectual status and reading skills for developmentally disabled children. *Perceptual and Motor Skills, 52*, 853–854.

Bloom, B.S. (1964). *Stability and changes in human characteristics*. New York: Wiley.

Bloom, L.P., Lightbown, P. & Hood, L. (1975). Structure and variation in child language. *Monographs of the Society for Research in Child Development, 40* (Serial No. 160).

Blot, W.J. & Miller, R.W. (1973). Mental retardation following in utero exposure to atomic bombs of Hiroshima and Nagasaki. *Radiology, 106*, 617–619.

Boggiano, A.K., Klinger, C.A. & Main, D.S. (1986). Enhancing interest in peer interaction: A developmental analysis. *Child Development, 57*, 852–861.

Bohannan, P. & Erickson, R. (1978, January). Stepping in. *Psychology Today, 11*, 53.

Bonvillian, J.D., Orlansky, M.D., Novack, L.L. & Folven, R.J. (1983). Early sign language acquisition and cognitive development. In D.R. Rogers & J.A. Stoboda (Eds.), *The acquisition of symbolic skills*. New York: Plenum.

Bornstein, M.H. (1976). Infants, recognition memory for hue. *Developmental Psychology, 12*, 185–191.

Bornstein, M.H. (1978). Chromatic vision in infancy. In H.W. Reese and L.P. Lipsitt (Eds.), *Advances in child development and behavior* (vol. 12). New York: Academic Press.

Bossard, M.E. & Galusha, R. (1979). The utility of the Stanford-Binet in predicting WRAT performance. *Psychology in the Schools, 16*, 488–490.

Bower, T.G.R. (1964). Discrimination of depth in premature infants. *Psychonomic Science, 1*, 368.

Bower, T.G.R. (1982). *Development in infancy* (2nd ed.). San Francisco: Freeman.

Bowerman, M. (1978). Systematizing semantic knowledge: Changes over time in the child's organization of word meaning. *Child Development, 49*, 977–987.

Bowlby, J. (1969). *Attachment and loss: Attachment* (vol. 1) New York: Basic Books.

Bowlby, J. (1982). *Attachment and loss: Attachment* (2nd ed. vol. 1). New York: Basic Books.

Brabant, S. & Mooney, L. (1986). Sex role stereotyping in the Sunday comics: Ten years later. *Sex Roles, 14*, 141–148.

Brackbill, Y. (1958). Extinction of the smiling response in infants as a function of reinforcement schedule. *Child Development, 29*, 115–124.

Bradbard, M.R., Martin, C.L., Endsley, R.C. & Halverson, C.F. (1986). Influence of sex stereotypes on children's exploration and memory: A competence versus performance distinction. *Developmental Psychology, 22,* 481–486.

Bradley, R.M. & Stearn, I.B. (1967). The development of the human taste bud during the foetal period. *Journal of Anatomy, 101,* 743–752.

Brainerd, C.J. (1978). *Piaget's theory of intelligence.* Englewood Cliffs, NJ: Prentice-Hall.

Brainerd, C.J. (1979). *The origins of the number concept.* New York: Praeger.

Brainerd, C.J. (1983). Working memory systems and cognitive development. In C.J. Brainerd (Ed.), *Recent advances in cognitive-development theory: Progress in cognitive developmental research.* New York: Springer-Verlag.

Brazelton, T.B. (1984). *Neonatal Behavioral Assessment Scale* (2nd ed.). Philadelphia: Lippincott.

Brenner, J. & Mueller, E. (1982). Shared meaning in boy toddlers' peer relations. *Child Development, 53,* 380–391.

Brittain, C.V. (1963). Adolescent choices and parent-peer cross-pressures. *American Sociological Review, 28,* 385–391.

Brittain, C.V. (1967/1968). An exploration of the bases of peer-compliance and parent-compliance in adolescence. *Adolescence, 2,* 445–458.

Brody, E.B. & Brody, N. (1976). *Intelligence: Nature, determinants, and consequences.* New York: Academic Press.

Bronfenbrenner, U. (1972). *Two worlds of childhood: U.S. and U.S.S.R..* New York: Simon & Schuster.

Bronfenbrenner, U. (1979). *The ecology of human development: Experiments by nature and design.* Cambridge, MA: Harvard University Press.

Brooks-Gunn, J., Petersen, A.C. & Eichorn, D. (1985). The study of maturational timing effects in adolescence. *Journal of Youth and Adolescence, 14,* 149–161.

Brophy, J. (1985). Interactions of male and female students with male and female teachers. In L.C. Wilkinson & C.B. Marrett (Eds.), *Gender influences in classroom interaction.* New York: Academic Press.

Brophy, J.E. (1981). Teacher praise: A functional analysis. *Review of Educational Research, 51,* 5–21.

Brophy, J. & Good, T. (1974). *Teacher-student relationships: Causes and consequences.* New York: Hold, Rinehart & Winston.

Broverman, I.K., Vogel, S.R., Broverman, D.M., Clarkson, F.E. & Rosenkrantz, P.S. (1972). Sex-role stereotypes: A current appraisal. *Journal of Social Issues, 28,* 59–78.

Brown, A.L. & Smiley, S.S. (1978). The development of strategies for studying texts. *Child Development, 49,* 1076–1088.

Brown, G.W., Bhrolchain, M.N. & Harris, T. (1975). Social class and psychiatric disturbance in an urban population. *Sociology, 9,* 225–254.

Brown, G.W. & Harris, T. (1978). *Social origins of depression: A study of psychiatric disorders in women.* New York: Free Press.

Brown, R. (1958). *Words and things.* New York: Free Press.

Brown, R. (1973). *A first language: The early stages.* Cambridge, MA: Harvard University Press.

Brown, R., Cazden, C. & Bellugi, U. (1969). The child's grammar from one to three. In J.P. Hill (Ed.), *Minnesota symposia in child psychology* (vol. 2). Minneapolis: University of Minnesota Press.

Brown, R. & Lenneberg, E.H. (1954). A study in language and cognition. *Journal of Abnormal and Social Psychology, 49,* 454–462.

Brownell, C.A. (1982). *Effects of age and age-mix on toddler peer interaction.* Paper presented at the International Conference on Infant Studies, Austin, TX.

Brownell, C.A. (1986). Convergent developments: Cognitive-developmental correlates of growth in infant/toddler peer skills. *Child Development, 57,* 275–286.

Bruch, H. (1978). *The golden cage.* New York: Vintage.

Bruner, J.S. (1972). The nature and uses of immaturity. *American Psychologist, 27,* 687–708.

Bruner, J.S. (1973). Going beyond the information given. In J.M. Anglin (Ed.), *Beyond the information given.* New York: Norton.

Bruner, J.S. & Goodman, C.C. (1947). Value and need as organizing factors in perception. *Journal of Abnormal and Social Psychology, 42,* 33–44.

Bryant, B.K. (1982). Sibling relationships in middle childhood. In M.E. Lamb & B. Sutton-Smith (Eds.), *Sibling relationships: Their nature and significance across the lifespan.* Hillsdale, NJ: Erlbaum.

Bryant, B.K. & Crockenberg, S. (1980). Correlates and dimensions of prosocial behavior: A study of female siblings with their mothers. *Child Development, 51,* 529–544.

Bryen, D.N. (1974). Special education and the linguistically different child. *Exceptional Children, 40,* 589–599.

Bryen, D.N., Hartman, C. & Tait, P. (1978). *Variant English: An introduction to language variation.* Columbus, OH: Merrill.

Bullock, M. & Gelman, R. (1979). Preschool children's assumptions about cause and effect: Temporal ordering. *Child Development, 50,* 89–96.

Bullock, M., Gelman, R. & Baillargeon, R. (1982). The development of causal reasoning. In W. Friedman (Ed.), *The developmental psychology of time.* New York: Academic Press.

Buss, A.H. & Plomin, R. (1984). *Temperament: Early developing personality traits.* Hillsdale, NJ: Erlbaum.

Buss, A.H. & Plomin, R.A. (1975). *A temperament theory of personality development.* New York: Wiley.

Buss, A.H., Plomin, R. & Willerman, L. (1973). The inheritance of temperaments. *Journal of Personality, 41,* 513–524.

Byrne, D., Ervin, D.H. & Lambreth, J. (1970). Continuity between the experimental study of attraction and real-life computer dating. *Journal of Personality and Social Psychology, 1,* 157–165.

Byrne, J.M. & Horowitz, F.D. (1979). Rocking as a soothing intervention: The influence of direction and type of movement. *Infant Behavior and Development, 2,* 209–214.

Calfee, R.C., Venezky, R.L. & Chapman, R.S. (1969). *Pronunciation of synthetic words with predictable and unpredictable letter-sound correspondences.* Technical Report

No. 71. Wisconsin Research and Development Center for Cognitive Learning.

Campbell, P.B. (1976). Adolescent intellectual decline. *Adolescence, 11,* 629–635.

Campbell, S.D. & Frost, J.L. (1978). *The effects of playground type on the cognitive and social play behaviors of grade two children.* Paper presented at the Seventh World Congress of the International Playground Association, Ottawa.

Campos, J.J., Langer, A. & Crowitz, A. (1970). Cardiac responses on the visual cliff in prelocomotor human infants. *Science, 170,* 196–197.

Caplan, P.J., MacPherson, G.M. & Tobin, P. (1985). Do sex-related differences in spatial abilities exist? A multilevel critique with new data. *American Psychologist, 7,* 786–799.

Caron, A.J., Caron, R.F., Caldwell, R.C. & Weiss, S.J. (1973). Infant perception of the structural properties of the face. *Developmental Psychology, 9,* 385–389.

Caron, R.F., Caron, A.J. & Carlson, V.R. (1979). Infant perception of the invariant shape of objects varying in slant. *Child Development, 50,* 716–721.

Carroll, J.J. & Gibson, E.J. (1981). *Infant's differentiation of an aperture and an obstacle.* Paper presented at the meeting of the Society for Research in Child Development, Boston.

Carroll, J.L. & Rest, J.R. (1982). Moral development. In B.B. Wolman (Ed.), *Handbook of developmental psychology.* Englewood Cliffs, NJ: Prentice-Hall.

Cassidy, J. (1986). The ability to negotiate the environment: An aspect of infant competence as related to quality of attachment. *Child Development, 57,* 331–337.

Cavior, N. & Dokecki, P.R. (1969). *Physical attractiveness and popularity among fifth grade boys.* Paper presented at the meeting of the Southwestern Psychological Association, Austin, TX.

Cavior, N. & Dokecki, P.R. (1970). *Physical attractiveness and popularity among fifth grade boys: A replication with Mexican children.* Paper presented at the meeting of the Southwestern Psychological Association, St. Louis, MO.

Cavior, N. & Dokecki, P.R. (1973). Physical attractiveness, perceived attitude similarity, and academic achievement as contributors to interpersonal attraction among adolescents. *Developmental Psychology, 9,* 43–54.

Cazden, C. (1968). The acquisition of noun and verb inflections. *Child Development, 39,* 433–438.

Cernoch, J.M. & Porter, R.H. (1985). Recognition of maternal axillary odors by infants. *Child Development, 56,* 1593–1598.

Chapman, M., Zahn-Waxler, C., Cooperman, G. & Iannotti, R. (1987). Empathy and responsibility in the motivation for children's helping. *Developmental Psychology, 23,* 140–145.

Charlesworth, W.R. (1972). Developmental psychology: Does it offer anything distinctive? In W.R. Looft (Ed.), *Developmental psychology: A book of readings.* Hinsdale, IL: Dryden Press.

Chase, C.I. (1985). Review of the Torrance Tests of Creative Thinking. In J.V. Mitchell (Ed.), *Ninth Mental Measurements Yearbook.* Lincoln: University of Nebraska Press.

Chasnoff, I.J., Burns, W.J., Schnoll, S.H. & Burns, K. A. (1985). Cocaine use in pregnancy. *New England Journal of Medicine, 313,* 666–669.

Chavez, D. (1985). Perpetuations of gender inequality: A content analysis of comic strips. *Sex Roles, 13,* 93–102.

Chedd, G. (1981). Who shall be born? *Science, 81,* 32–41.

Chomsky, N. (1957). *Syntactic structures.* The Hague: Mouton.

Cialdini, R.B., Baumann, D.J. & Kenrick, D.T. (1981). Insights from sadness: A three-step model of the development of altruism as hedonism. *Developmental Review, 1,* 207–223.

Cicchetti, D. (1984). The emergence of developmental psychopathology. *Child Development, 55,* 1–7.

Clark, H. & Clark, E.V. (1977). *Psychology and language: An introduction to psycholinguistics.* New York: Harcourt Brace Jovanovich.

Clark, E.V. & Sengul, C.J. (1978). Strategies in the acquisition of deixis. *Journal of Child Language, 5,* 457–475.

Clarren, S.K. & Smith, D.W. (1978). The fetal alcohol syndrome. *New England Journal of Medicine, 298,* 1063–1067.

Clifford, E. (1971). Body satisfaction in adolescence. *Perceptual and Motor Skills, 33,* 119–125.

Clifford, M.M. (1975). Physical attractiveness and academic performance. *Child Study Journal, 5,* 201–209.

Clifton, R.K. (1974a). Cardiac conditioning and orienting in the infant. In P.A. Obrist, A.H. Black, J. Brener & L.V. DiCara (Eds.), *Cardiovascular psychophysiology.* Chicago: Aldine.

Clifton, R.K. (1974b). Heart rate conditioning in the newborn infant. *Journal of Experimental Child Psychology, 18,* 9–21.

Clifton, R.K. & Nelson, M.N. (1976). Developmental study of habituation in infants: The importance of paradigm, response system, and state. In T.J. Tighe & R.N. Leaton (Eds.), *Habituation: Perspectives from child development, animal behavior, and neurophysiology.* Hillsdale, NJ: Erlbaum.

Cohen, S.E. (1978). Maternal employment and mother-child interaction. *Merrill-Palmer Quarterly, 24,* 189–197.

Coie, J.D., Dodge, K.A. & Coppotelli, H. (1982). Dimensions and types of social status: A cross-age perspective. *Developmental Psychology, 18,* 557–570.

Coie, J.D. & Krehbiel, G. (1984). Effects of academic tutoring on the social status of low-achieving, socially rejected children. *Child Development, 55,* 1465–1478.

Colby, A., Kohlberg, L., Fenton, E., Speicher-Dubin, B. & Lieberman, M. (1977). Secondary school moral discussion programs led by social studies teachers. *Journal of Moral Education, 6,* 2.

Colby, A., Kohlberg, L., Gibbs, J. & Lieberman, M. (1983). A longitudinal study of moral development.

Monographs of the Society for Research in Child Development, 48 (1-2, Serial No. 200).

Coleman, J.S. (1961). *The adolescent society.* New York: Free Press.

Comstock, G., Chaffee, S., Katzman, N., McCombs, M. & Roberts, D. (1978). *Television and human behavior.* New York: Columbia University Press.

Condon, W.S. & Sander, L.W. (1974). Synchrony demonstrated between movements of the neonate and adult speech. *Child Development, 65,* 456–462.

Congressional Record, October 10, 1978, H–12179.

Conry, R. & Plant, W.T. (1965). WAIS and group test predictions of an academic success criterion: High school and college. *Educational and Psychological Measurement, 25,* 493–500.

Cooley, C.H. (1902). *Human nature and the social order.* New York: Scribner.

Coombs, R.H. & Kenkel, W.F. (1966). Sex differences in dating aspirations and satisfaction with computer-selected partners. *Journal of Marriage and the Family, 28,* 62–66.

Coopersmith, S. (1967). *The antecedents of self-esteem.* San Francisco: Freeman.

Cordua, G.D., McGraw, K.O. & Drabman, K.S. (1979). Doctor or nurse: Children's perceptions of sex typed occupations. *Child Development, 50,* 590–593.

Council for Exceptional Children 1978

Cowan, G. & Hoffman, C.D. (1986). Gender stereotyping in young children: Evidence to support a concept-learning approach. *Sex Roles, 14,* 211–224.

Cowart, B.J. & Beauchamp, G.K. (1986). The importance of sensory context in young children's acceptance of salty tastes. *Child Development, 57,* 1034–1039.

Crain, W.C. (1985). *Theories of development: Concepts and applications* (2nd ed.). Englewood Cliffs, NJ: Prentice-Hall.

Crassini, B. & Broerse, J. (1980). Auditory-visual integration in neonates: A signal detection analysis. *Journal of Experimental Child Psychology, 29,* 144–155.

Cratty, B.J. (1970). *Perceptual and motor development in infants and children* (1st ed.). New York: Macmillan.

Cratty, B.J. (1974). *Psycho-motor behavior in education and sport.* Springfield, IL: Thomas.

Cromer, W. (1970). The difference model: A new exploration for some reading difficulties. *Journal of Education Psychology, 61,* 471–483.

Cronbach, L.J. (1984). *Essentials of psychological testing* (4th ed.). New York: Harper & Row.

Crook, W.G. (1980). Can what a child eats make him dull, stupid, or hyperactive? *Journal of Learning Disabilities, 13,* 281–286.

Cruickshank, W.M. (1972). Some issues facing the field of learning disability. *Journal of Learning Disabilities, 5,* 380–388.

Cultice, J.C., Somerville, S.C. & Wellman, H.M. (1983). Preschoolers' memory monitoring: Feeling of knowing judgements. *Child Development, 54,* 1480–1486.

Cunningham, C.E. & Barkley, R.A. (1979). The interactions of normal and hyperactive children with their mothers in free play and structured tasks. *Child Development, 50,* 217–224.

Cunningham, L., Cadoret, R.J., Loftus, R. & Edwards, J.E. (1975). Studies of adoptees from psychiatrically disturbed biological parents: Psychiatric conditions in childhood and adolescence. *British Journal of Psychiatry, 126,* 534–549.

Curtiss, S. (1977). *Genie: A psycholinguistic study of a modern-day "wild child."* New York: Academic Press.

Dale, P.S. (1976). *Language development: Structure and function* (2nd ed.). New York: Holt, Rinehart & Winston.

Damon, W. (1977). *The social world of the child.* San Francisco: Jossey-Bass.

Damon, W. & Hart, D. (1982). The development of self-understanding from infancy through adolescence. *Child Development, 53,* 841–864.

Daniels, D. & Plomin, R. (1985a). Differential experience of siblings in the same family. *Developmental Psychology, 21,* 747–760.

Daniels, D. & Plomin, R. (1985b). Origins of individual differences in infant shyness. *Developmental Psychology, 21,* 118–121.

Dansky, J.L. (1980). Make-believe: A mediator of the relationship between play and associative fluency. *Child Development, 51,* 576–579.

Dasen, P. (1975). Concrete operational development in three cultures. *Journal of Cross-cultural Psychology, 6,* 156–172.

Dasen, P. & Heron, A. (1981). Cross-cultural tests of Piaget's theory. In H.C. Triandis & A. Heron (Eds.), *Handbook of cross-cultural psychology: Developmental psychology* (vol. 4). Boston: Allyn and Bacon.

Datan, N. & Hughes, F.P. (1985). Burning books and briefcases: Agency, communion and the social context of learning in adulthood. *Academic Psychology Bulletin, 7 (Summer),* 175–186.

Datan, N., Rodeheaver, D. & Hughes, F.P. (1987). Adult development and aging. *Annual Review of Psychology, 38* (In Press).

Davis, G.A. (1975). Care and feeding of creative adolescents. In R.E. Grinder (Ed.), *Studies in adolescence: A book of readings in adolescent development* (3rd ed.). New York: Macmillan.

Day, R.H. & McKenzie, B.E. (1981). Infant perception of the invariant size of approaching and receding objects. *Developmental Psychology, 17,* 670–677.

Deaux, K.V. (1985). Sex and gender. *Annual Review of Psychology, 36,* 49–81.

DeCasper, A.J. & Fifer, W.P. (1980). Of human bonding: Newborns prefer their mothers' voices. *Sciences, 208,* 1174–1176.

DeCasper, A.J. & Prescott, P.A. (1984). Human newborns' perception of male voices: Preference, discrimination and reinforcing value. *Developmental Psychology, 17,* 481–491.

DeLeon, P.H. & VandenBos, G.R. (1985). Public policy and advocacy on behalf of the gifted and talented. In F.D. Horowitz & M. O'Brien (Eds.), *The gifted and talented: Developmental perspectives.* Washington, D.C.: American Psychological Association.

DeLicardie, E.R. & Cravioto, J. (1974). Behavioral responsiveness of survivors of clinically severe malnutrition to cognitive demands. In J. Cravioto et al. Eds.), *Early malnutrition and mental development*, Uppsala, Sweden: Almquist and Wiksell.

DeLoache, J.S., Cassidy, D.J. & Brown, A.L. (1985). Precursors of mnemonic strategies in very young children. *Child Development, 56*, 125–137.

Demorest, A., Meyer, C. & Phelps, E. (1984). Words speak louder than actions: Understanding deliberately false remarks. *Child Development, 55*, 1527–1534.

Dennis, W. (1960). Causes of retardation among institutional children: Iran. *Journal of Genetic Psychology, 96*, 47–59.

Deregowski, J.B. (1980). Perception. In H.C. Triandis & A. Heron (Eds.), *Handbook of cross-cultural psychology: Basic processes* (vol. 3). Boston: Allyn and Bacon.

Desor, J.A., Maller, O. & Andrews, K. (1975). Ingestive responses of human newborns to salty, sour, and bitter stimuli. *Journal of Comparative and Physiological Psychology, 89*, 966–970.

Desor, J.A., Maller, O. & Greene, L.S. (1977). Preference for sweets in humans: Infants, children, and adults. In J. Weiffenbach (Ed.), *Taste and development: The ontogeny of sweet preference*. Washington, D.C.: U.S. Government Printing Office.

Desor, J.A., Maller, O. & Turner, R. (1973). Taste in acceptance of sugars by human infants. *Journal of Comparative and Physiological Psychology, 84*, 496–501.

Dewart, M.H. (1972). Social class and children's understanding of deep structure sentences. *British Journal of Educational Psychology, 42*, 198–203.

de Villiers, J.G. & de Villiers, P.A. (1978). *Language acquisition*. Cambridge, MA: Harvard University Press.

Diamond, N. (1982). Cognitive theory. In B.B. Wolman (Ed.), *Handbook of developmental psychology*. Englewood Cliffs, NJ: Prentice-Hall.

Diaz, R.M. & Berndt, T.J. (1982). Children's knowledge of a best friend: Fact or fancy? *Developmental Psychology, 18*, 787–794.

Di Maria, H., Courpotin, C., Rouzioux, C., Cohen, D., Rio, D. & Boussin, F. (1986). Transplacental transmission of human immunodeficiency virus. *Lancet, 11*, 215–216.

Dion, K.K. (1973). Young children's stereotyping of facial attractiveness. *Developmental Psychology, 9*, 183–198.

Dion, K.K. (1977). The incentive value of physical attractiveness for young children. *Personality and Social Psychology Bulletin, 3*, 67–70.

Dixon, J.C. (1957). Development of self-recognition. *Journal of Genetic Psychology, 91*, 251–256.

Dodd, D.H. (1980). Language development. In R.L. Ault (Ed.), *Developmental perspectives*. Santa Monica, CA: Goodyear.

Dodge, K.A. (1983). Behavioral antecedents of peer social status. *Child Development, 54*, 1386–1399.

Dodge, K.A., Coie, J.D. & Brakke, N.P. (1982). Behavior patterns of socially rejected and neglected preadolescents: The roles of social approach and aggression. *Journal of Abnormal Child Psychology, 10*, 389–410.

Doherty, W.J. & Jacobson, N.S. (1982). Marriage and the family. In B.B. Wolman (Ed.), *Handbook of developmental psychology*. Englewood Cliffs, NJ: Prentice-Hall.

Dominick, J.R. & Greenberg, B.S. (1972). Attitudes toward violence: The interaction of television exposure, family attitudes and social class. In G.A. Comstock & E.A. Rubinstein (Eds.), *Television and social behavior: Television and adolescent aggressiveness* (vol. 3). Washington, D.C.: U.S. Government Printing Office.

Dornbusch, S.M., Carlsmith, J.M., Bushwall, S.J., Ritter, P.L., Leiderman, H., Hastorf, A.H. & Gross, R.T. (1985). Single parents, extended households, and the control of adolescents. *Child Development, 56*, 326–341.

Dornbusch, S.M., Carlsmith, J.M., Gross, R.T., Martin, J.A., Jennings, D., Rosenberg, A. & Duke, P. (1981). Sexual development, age, and dating: A comparison of biological and social influences upon one set of behaviors. *Child Development, 52*, 179–185.

Douvan, E. & Adelson, J. (1966). *The adolescent experience*. New York: Wiley.

Doyle, A.B., Connolly, J. & Rivest, L.P. (1980). The effect of playmate familiarity on the social interactions of young children. *Child Development, 51*, 217–223.

Dubnoff, S.J., Veroff, J. & Kulka, R.A. (1978). *Adjustment to work: 1957–1976*. Paper presented at the meeting of the American Psychological Association, Toronto.

Dubowitz, L.M.S., Dubowitz, V. & Goldberg, C. (1970). Clinical assessment of gestational age in the newborn infant. *Journal of Pediatrics, 77*, 1.

Duncan, P.D., Ritter, P.L., Dornbusch, S.M., Gross, R.T. & Carlsmith, J.M. (1985). The effects of pubertal timing on body image, school behavior, and deviance. *Journal of Youth and Adolescence, 14*, 227–235.

Dunn, J. (1985). *Sisters and brothers*. Cambridge, MA: Harvard University Press.

Dunn, J. & Kendrick, C. (1982). *Siblings: Love, envy, and understanding*. Cambridge, MA: Harvard University Press.

Dunn, J.F., Plomin, R. & Daniels, D. (1986). Consistency and change in mothers' behavior toward young siblings. *Child Development, 57*, 348–356.

Dunn, J. & Wooding, C. (1977). Play in the home and its implications for learning. In B. Tizard & D. Harvey (Eds.), *Biology of play*. London: Heinemann.

Duvall, E. (1977). *Marriage and family development* (5th ed.). New York: Lippincott.

Dweck, C.S. (1977). Learned helplessness and negative evaluation. *ULCA Educator, 19*, 44–49.

Dweck, C.S. (1986). Motivational processes affecting learning. *American Psychologist, 41*, 1040–1048.

Dwyer, J. & Mayer, J. (1968–1969). Psychological effects of variations in physical appearance during adolescence. *Adolescence, 3*, 353–368.

Ebel, R.L. & Frisbie, D.A. (1986). *Essentials of measurement* (4th ed.). Englewood Cliffs, NJ: Prentice-Hall.

Eckerman, C.O. & Stein, M.R. (1982). The toddler's emerging interactive skills. In K.H. Rubin & H.S. Ross (Eds.), *Peer relationships and social skills in childhood*. New York: Springer-Verlag.

Eder, D. & Hallinan, M.T. (1978). Sex differences in children's friendships. *American Sociological Review, 43,* 247–250.

Edwards, C.P. (1981). The comparative study of the development of moral judgment and reasoning. In R.H. Munroe, R.L. Munroe & B.B. Whiting (Eds.), *Handbook of cross-cultural human development.* New York: Garland Press.

Egeland, B. & Farber, E.A. (1984). Infant-mother attachment: Factors related to its development and changes over time. *Child Development, 55,* 743–771.

Ehrhardt, A.A. & Baker, S.W. (1974). Fetal androgens, human central nervous system differentiation, and behavior sex differences. In R.C. Friedman, R.M. Richart & R.L. Vande Wiele (Eds.), *Sex differences in behavior.* New York: Wiley.

Ehrhardt, A.A. & Money, J. (1967). Progestin-induced hermaphroditism: IQ and psychosexual identity in a study of 10 girls. *Journal of Sex Research, 3,* 83–100.

Eichorn, D.H. (1979). Physical development: Current foci of research. In J.D. Osofsky (Ed.), *Handbook of infant development.* New York: Wiley.

Eifferman, R.R. (1971). Social play in childhood. In R.E. Herron & B. Sutton-Smith (Eds.), *Child's play.* New York: Wiley.

Eilers, R.E. & Oller, D. (1976). The role of speech discrimination in developmental sound substitutions. *Journal of Child Language, 3,* 319–330.

Eimas, P.D. (1985). The perception of speech in early infancy. *Scientific American, 252* (1), 46–51.

Eimas, P.D., Siqueland, E.R., Jusczyk, P.W. & Vigorito, J. (1971). Speech perception in infants. *Science, 171,* 303–306.

Eisenberg, N., Lennon, R. & Roth, K. (1983). Prosocial development: A longitudinal study. *Developmental Psychology, 19,* 846–855.

Eitzen, D.A. (1975). Athletics in the status system of male adolescents: A replication of Coleman's *The adolescent society. Adolescence, 10,* 267–276.

Elder, J. & Pederson, D. (1978). Preschool children's use of objects in symbolic play. *Child Development, 49,* 500–504.

Elkind, D. (1981a). *Children and adolescents.* New York: Oxford University Press.

Elkind, D. (1981b). *The hurried child: Growing up too fast too soon.* Reading, MA: Addison-Wesley.

Elkind, D. & Bowen, R. (1979). Imaginary audience behavior in children and adolescents. *Developmental Psychology, 15,* 38–44.

Elliot, A.J. (1981). *Child language.* Cambridge: Cambridge University Press.

Ellis, G.J. (1986). Societal and parental predictors of parent-adolescent conflict. In G.K. Leigh & G.W. Peterson (Eds.), *Adolescents in families.* Cincinnati: South-Western.

Ellis, H.C., Bennett, T.L., Daniel, T.C. & Rickert, E.J. (1979). *Psychology of learning and memory.* Monterey, CA: Brooks/Cole.

Ellis, M.J. (1973). *Why people play.* Englewood Cliffs, NJ: Prentice-Hall.

Emmerich, W., Goldman, K.S., Kirsh, B. & Sharabany, R. (1976). *Development of gender constancy in economically disadvantaged children.* Princeton, NJ: Educational Testing Service.

Emmerich, W., Goldman, K.S., Kirsh, B. & Sharabany, R. (1977). Evidence for a transitional phase in the development of gender constancy. *Child Development, 48,* 930–936.

Engen, T. (1977). Taste and smell. In J.E. Birren & K.W. Schaie (Eds.), *Handbook of the psychology of aging.* New York: Van Nostrand Reinhold.

Engen, T., Lipsitt, L.P. & Peck, M.B. (1974). Ability of newborn infants to discriminate sapid substances. *Developmental Psychology, 10,* 741–746.

Enright, M.K., Rovee-Collier, C.K., Fagen, J.W. & Caniglia, K. (1983). The effects of distributed training on retention of operant conditioning in human infants. *Journal of Experimental Child Psychology, 36,* 209–225.

Epstein, S. (1973). The self-concept revisited, or a theory of a theory. *American Psychologist, 28,* 405–416.

Erikson, E.H. (1963). *Childhood and society* (2nd ed.). New York: Norton.

Erikson, E.H. (1964). *Insight and responsibility.* New York: Norton.

Erikson, E.H. (1968). *Identity, youth, and crisis.* New York: Norton.

Eysenck, H.J. & Kamin, L. (1981). *The intelligence controversy.* New York: Wiley.

Fagot, B.I., Leinbach, M.D. & Hagan, R. (1986). Gender labeling and the adoption of sex-typed behaviors. *Developmental Psychology, 22,* 440–443.

Fakouri, M.E. (1976). "Cognitive development in adulthood: A fifth stage?": A critique. *Developmental Psychology, 12,* 472.

Falbo, T. (1978a). Reasons for having an only child. *Journal of Population, 1,* 181–184.

Falbo, T. (1978b). Only children and interpersonal behavior: An experimental and survey study. *Journal of Applied Social Psychology, 8,* 244–253.

Falbo, T. (1982). Only children in America. In M.E. Lamb & B. Sutton-Smith (Eds.), *Sibling relationships: Their nature and significance across the lifespan.* Hillsdale, NJ: Erlbaum.

Fantz, R.L. (1958). Pattern vision in young infants. *Psychological Record, 8,* 43–47.

Fantz, R.L. (1961). The origin of form perception. *Scientific American, 204,* 66–72.

Fantz, R.L. (1963). Pattern vision in newborn infants. *Science, 140,* 296–297.

Fantz, R.L., Fagan, J.L. & Miranda, S.B. (1975). Early visual selectivity. In L.B. Cohen & P. Salapatek (Eds.), *Infant perception: From sensation to cognition.* New York: Academic Press.

Fantz, R.L. & Nevis, S. (1967). Pattern preferences and perceptual-cognitive development in early infancy. *Merrill-Palmer Quarterly, 13,* 77–108.

Faunce, P.S. & Phipps-Yonas, S. (1979). Women's liberation and human sexual relations. In J.H. Williams (Ed.), *Psychology of women.* New York: Norton.

Faux, M. (1984). *Childless by choice.* New York: Doubleday.

Fein, G.G. (1981). Pretend play in childhood: An integrative review. *Child Development, 52,* 1095–1118.

Feingold, B.F. (1975). *Why your child is hyperactive.* New York: Random House.

Feldman, C. (1971). *The effects of various types of adult responses in the syntactic acquisition of two- to three-year-olds.* Unpublished manuscript, University of Chicago.

Feldman, D. (1974). Universal to unique. In S. Rosner & L.E. Abt (Eds.), *Essays in creativity.* Croton-on-Hudson, NY: North River Press.

Ferreira, A.J. (1960). The pregnant mother's emotional attitude and its reflection upon the newborn. *American Journal of Orthopsychiatry, 30,* 553–561.

Feshbach, N.D. (1979). Empathy training: A field study of affective education. In S. Feshbach and A. Fraazeh (Eds.), *Aggression and behavior change: Biological and social processes.* New York: Praeger.

Feshbach, S. (1970). Aggression. In P.H. Mussen (Ed.), *Carmichael's manual of child psychology* (vol. 2). New York: Wiley.

Feshbach, S. & Weiner, B. (1986). *Personality* (2nd ed.). Lexington, MA: Heath.

Field, J., Muir, D., Pilon, R., Sinclair, M. & Dodwell, P. (1980). Infants' orientation to lateral sounds from birth to three months. *Child Development, 50,* 295–298.

Field, T.M. & Widmayer, S.M. (1982). Motherhood. In B.B. Wolman (Ed.), *Handbook of developmental psychology.* Englewood Cliffs, NJ: Prentice-Hall.

Fine, M.A., Moreland, J.R. & Schwebel, A.I. (1983). Long-term effects of divorce on parent-child relationships. *Developmental Psychology, 19,* 703–713.

Fish, K.D. & Biller, H.B. (1973). Perceived childhood paternal relationships and college females' personal adjustment. *Adolescence, 8,* 415–420.

Flavell, J.H. (1963). *The developmental psychology of Jean Piaget.* New York: Van Nostrand Reinhold.

Flavell, J.H. (1982). Structures, stages, and sequences in cognitive development. In W.A. Collins (Ed.), *Minnesota symposia on child psychology* (vol. 15). Hillsdale, NJ: Erlbaum.

Flavell, J.H. (1985). *Cognitive development* (2nd ed.). Englewood Cliffs, NJ: Prentice-Hall.

Flavell, J.H., Beach, D.R. & Chinsky, J.M. (1966). Spontaneous verbal rehearsal in a memory task as a function of age. *Child Development, 37,* 283–299.

Flavell, J.H., Friedrichs, A.G. & Hoyt, J.D. (1970). Developmental changes in memorization processes. *Cognitive Psychology, 1,* 324–340.

Flavell, J.H. & Wellman, H.M. (1977). Metamemory. In R.V. Kail & J.W. Hagen (Eds.), *Perspectives on the development of memory and cognition.* Hillsdale, NJ: Erlbaum.

Floyd, H.S. & South, D.R. (1972). Dilemma of youth: The choice of parents or peers as a frame of reference for behavior. *Journal of Marriage and the Family, 34,* 627–634.

Fogel, A. (1979). Peer vs. mother-directed behavior in 1- to 3-month-old infants. *Infant Behavior and Development, 2,* 215–216.

Fogel, A. (1984). *Infancy: Infant, family, and society.* St. Paul: West Publishing.

Fox, L.H. & Washington, J. (1985). Programs for the gifted and talented: Past, present, and future. In F.D. Horowitz & M. O'Brien (Eds.), *The gifted and talented: Developmental perspectives.* Washington, D.C.: American Psychological Association.

Fox, N., Kagan, J. & Weiskopf, S. (1979). The growth of memory during infancy. *Genetic Psychology Monographs, 99,* 91–130.

Fraiberg, S. (1977). *Insights from the blind: Comparative studies of blind and sighted infants.* New York: Basic Books.

Frazier, A. & Lisonbee, L.K. (1950). Adolescent concerns with physique. *Social Review, 58,* 397–405.

Freud, A. (1974). *The ego and the mechanisms of defense* (rev. ed.). New York: International Universities Press.

Freud, S. (1930). Civilization and its discontents. *Standard Edition, 21,* 57–145. London: Hogarth.

Freud, S. (1950). Some psychological consequences of the anatomic distinction between the sexes. In *Collected papers* (vol. 5). London: Hogarth.

Freud, S. (1966). Contributions to the psychology of love. In J. Strachey (Ed.), *Complete psychological works of Sigmund Freud* (vol. 22). London: Hogarth.

Freyberg, J. (1973). Increasing the imaginative play of urban disadvantaged kindergarten children through systematic training. In J.L. Singer (Ed.), *The child's world of make-believe.* New York: Academic Press.

Friedrich, L.K. & Stein, A.H. (1973). Aggressive and prosocial television programs and the natural behavior of preschool children. *Monographs of the Society for Research in Child Development, 38* (4, Serial No. 151).

Frodi, A. & Thompson, R. (1985). Infants' affective responses in the Strange Situation: Effects of prematurity and of quality of attachment. *Child Development, 56,* 1280–1290.

Froming, W.J., Allen, L. & Jensen, R. (1985). Altruism, role-taking, and self-awareness: The acquisition of norms governing altruistic behavior. *Child Development, 56,* 1223–1228.

Fuchs, F. (1980). Genetic amniocentesis. *Scientific American, 242,* 47–53.

Furman, W. & Bierman, K. (1983). Developmental changes in young children's conception of friendship. *Child Development, 54,* 549–556.

Furth, H.G. & Wachs, H. (1974). *Thinking goes to school: Piaget's theory in practice.* New York: Oxford University Press.

Furth, H.G. & Youniss, J. (1975). Congenital deafness and the development of thinking. In E.H. Lenneberg & E. Lenneberg (Eds.), *Foundations of language development* (vol. 2). New York: Academic Press.

Galbraith, R.C. (1982). Sibling spacing and intellectual development: A closer look at the confluence model. *Developmental Psychology, 18,* 151–173.

Galler, J.R., Ramsey, F. & Solimano, G. (1985). A follow-up study of the effects of early malnutrition on subsequent development. II. Fine motor skills in adolescence. *Pediatric Research, 19,* 524–527.

Gammon, E.M. (1970). *A syntactical analysis of some first grade readers.* Technical Report No. 155. Stanford University: Institute for Mathematical Studies in the Social Sciences.

Ganon, E.S. & Swartz, K.B. (1980). Perception of internal elements of compound figures by one-month-old infants. *Journal of Experimental Child Psychology, 30,* 159–170.

Garber, J. (1984). Classification of childhood psychopathology: A developmental perspective. *Child Development, 55,* 30–48.

Gardner, H. (1982a). *Art, mind, and brain: A cognitive approach to creativity.* New York: Basic Books.

Gardner, H. (1982b). *Developmental psychology* (2nd ed.). Boston: Little, Brown.

Gardner, R.A. & Gardner, B.T. (1969). Teaching sign language to a chimpanzee. *Science, 165,* 664–672.

Garvey, C. (1977). *Play.* Cambridge, MA: Harvard University Press.

Garvey, C. & Berndt, R. (1977). *Organization of pretend play.* Paper presented at the meeting of the American Psychological Association, Chicago.

Gelman, R. (1972). Logical capacity of very young children: Number invariance rules. *Child Development, 43,* 75–90.

Gelman, R. (1980). What young children knew about numbers. *Educational Psychologist, 15,* 54–68.

Gelman, R. (1982). Basic numerical abilities. In R.J. Sternberg (Ed.), *Advances in the psychology of human intelligence* (vol. 1). Hillsdale, NJ: Erlbaum.

Gelman, R. & Baillargeon, R. (1983). A review of some Piagetian concepts. In P.H. Mussen (Ed.), *Handbook of child psychology* (4th ed., vol. 3). New York: Wiley.

Gelman, R. & Spelke, E. (1981). The development of thoughts about animate and inanimate objects: Implications for research on social cognition. In J.H. Flavell & L. Ross (Eds.), *Social cognitive development: Frontiers and possible futures.* New York: Cambridge University Press.

Gentner, D. (1978). On relational meaning: The acquisition of verb meaning. *Child Development, 49,* 988–998.

Geschwind, N. (1968). Neurological foundations of language. In H.R. Myklebust (Ed.), *Progress in learning disabilities* (vol. 1). New York: Grune & Stratton.

Gewirtz, J.L. (1969). Mechanisms of social learning: Some roles of stimulation and behavior in early human development. In D. Goslin (Ed.), *Handbook of socialization theory and research.* New York: Rand McNally.

Ghiselin, B. (1955). *The creative process.* New York: New American Library.

Gibbs, J.C., Clark, P.M., Joseph, J.A., Green, J.L., Goodrick, T.S. & Makowski, D.G. (1986). Relations between moral judgment, moral courage, and field independence. *Child Development, 57,* 185–193.

Gibson, E.J. (1969). *Principles of perceptual learning and development.* New York: Appleton-Century-Crofts.

Gibson, E.J. & Levin, H. (1975). *The psychology of reading.* Cambridge, MA: MIT Press.

Gibson, E.J. & Spelke, E.S. (1983). The development of perception. In P.H. Mussen (Ed.), *Handbook of child psychology* (4th ed., vol. 3). New York: Wiley.

Gibson, E.J. & Walk, R.D. (1960). The "visual cliff." *Scientific American, 202,* 64–71.

Gibson, J.J. (1979). *The ecological approach to visual perception.* Boston: Houghton Mifflin.

Gibson, J.J. & Gibson, E.J. (1955). Perceptual learning: Differentiation or enrichment? *Psychological Review, 62,* 32–41.

Gilligan, C. (1982). *In a different voice: Psychological theory and women's development.* Cambridge, MA: Harvard University Press.

Ginsburg, H. & Opper, S. (1979). *Piaget's theory of intellectual development* (2nd ed.). Englewood Cliffs, NJ: Prentice-Hall.

Gleason, H.A. (1961). *An introduction to descriptive linguistics.* New York: Holt, Rinehart & Winston.

Gleitman, H. (1986). *Psychology.* New York: Norton.

Glick, P.C. (1977). Updating the life cycle of the family. *Journal of Marriage and the Family, 39,* 5–13.

Glick, P.C. (1984). Marriage, divorce, and living arrangements: Prospective changes. *Journal of Family Issues, 5,* 7–26.

Glucksberg, S., Krauss, R.M. & Higgins, E.T. (1975). The development of referential communication skills. In F.D. Horowitz (Ed.), *Review of child development research.* Chicago: University of Chicago Press.

Gold, D. & Andres, D. (1978a). Developmental comparisons between adolescent children with employed and nonemployed mothers. *Merrill-Palmer Quarterly, 24,* 243–254.

Gold, D. & Andres, D. (1978b). Developmental comparisons between 10-year-old children with employed and nonemployed mothers. *Child Development, 49,* 75–84.

Gold, D. & Andres, D. (1978c). Relations between maternal employment and development of nursery school children. *Canadian Journal of Behavioral Science, 10,* 116–129.

Goldberg, S. (1979). Premature birth: Consequences for the parent-infant relationship. *American Scientist, 67,* 214–220.

Goldberg, S. (1983). Parent-infant bonding: Another look. *Child Development, 54,* 1355–1382.

Goldberg, S. & DiVitto, B.A. (1983). *Born too soon: Preterm birth and early development.* San Francisco: Freeman.

Goldberg, S., Perrotta, M., Minde, K. & Corter, C. (1986). Maternal behavior and attachment in low-birth-weight twins and single twins. *Child Development, 57,* 34–46.

Goldin-Meadow, S. & Mylander, C. (1984). Gestural communication in deaf children: The effects and non-effects of parental input on early language development. *Monographs of the Society for Research in Child Development, 49,* (Serial No. 207).

Goldman, B.D. & Ross, H.S. (1978). Social skills in action: An analysis of early peer games. In J. Glick & K.A. Clarke-Stewart (Eds.), *Studies in social and cognitive development: The development of social understanding* (vol. 1). New York: Gardner Press.

Goldman, W. & Lewis, P. (1977). Beautiful is good: Evidence that the physically attractive are more socially skillful. *Journal of Experimental and Social Psychology, 13,* 125–130.

Goldschmid, M.L., Bentler, P.M., Debus, R.L., Rawlinson, R., Kohustamm, D., Modgil, S., Nicholls, J.C., Reykowski, J., Strupczewska, B. & Warren, N. (1973). A cross-cultural investigation of conservation. *Journal of Cross-cultural Psychology, 4,* 75–88.

Goldsmith, H.H. (1983). Genetic influences on personality from infancy to adulthood. *Child Development, 54,* 331–335.

Goldstein, M.J., Baker, B.L. & Jamison, K.R. (1986). *Abnormal psychology: Experiences, origins, and interventions* (2nd ed.). Boston: Little, Brown.

Goleman, D. (1980, February). 1528 little geniuses and how they grew. *Psychology Today, 13 (9),* 28–43.

Goodman, N. & Marx, G. (1982). *Society today* (4th ed.). New York: Random House.

Gordon, F.R. & Yonas, A. (1976). Sensitivity to binocular depth information in infants. *Journal of Experimental Child Psychology, 22,* 413–422.

Gordon, H. (1923). *Mental and scholastic tests among retarded children.* (Educational Pamphlet, No. 44). London: Board of Education.

Gottesman, I. (1963). Genetic aspect of intelligent behavior. In N. Ellis (Ed.), *Handbook of mental deficiency: Psychological theory and research.* New York: McGraw-Hill.

Gottman, J.M. (1977). Toward a definition of social isolation in children. *Child Development, 48,* 513–517.

Gough, H.G. (1979). A creative personality scale for the adjective check list. *Journal of Personality and Social Psychology, 37,* 1398–1405.

Gould, J.L. (1982). *Ethology.* New York: Norton.

Gould, S.J. (1981). *The mismeasure of man.* New York: Norton.

Gove, W.R. & Geerken, M.R. (1977). The effect of children and employment on the mental health of married men and women. *Social Forces, 56,* 66–76.

Gowan, J.C. (1977). Background and history of the gifted-child movement. In J.C. Stanley, W.C. George & G.H. Solano (Eds.), *The gifted and the creative: A fifty-year perspective.* Baltimore: Johns Hopkins University Press.

Greenfield, P.M. & Smith, J.H. (1976). *The structure of communication in early language development.* New York: Academic Press.

Gresham, F.M. & Nagel, R. (1980). Social skills training with children: Responsiveness to modeling and coaching as a function of peer orientation. *Journal of Consulting and Clinical Psychology, 18,* 718–729.

Gronlund, N.E. (1985). *Measurement and evaluation in teaching* (5th ed.). New York: Macmillan.

Gronlund, N.E. & Anderson, L. (1957). Personality characteristics of socially accepted, socially neglected, and socially rejected junior high school pupils. *Educational Administration and Supervision, 43,* 329–338.

Groos, K. (1901). *The play of man.* New York: Appleton.

Grossman, H.J. (1983). *Classification in mental retardation.* Washington, D.C.: American Association of Mental Deficiency.

Gruber, H.E. (1982). On the hypothesized relation between giftedness and creativity. In D.H. Feldman (Ed.), *Developmental approaches to giftedness and creativity.* San Francisco: Jossey-Bass.

Gruendel, J.M. (1977). Referential extension in early language development. *Child Development, 48,* 1567–1576.

Grusec, J.E. & Abramovitch, R. (1982). Imitation of peers and adults in a natural setting: A functional analysis. *Child Development, 53,* 636–642.

Guardo, C.J. & Bohan, J.B. (1971). Development of the sense of self-identity in children. *Child Development, 42,* 1909–1921.

Guilford, J.P. (1967). *The nature of human intelligence.* New York: McGraw-Hill.

Gunderson, E.K.E. (1965). Body size, self-evaluation, and military effectiveness. Journal of Personality and Social Psychology, 2, 902–906.

Guttmacher, A.F. (1973). *Pregnancy, birth and family planning.* New York: Signet.

Haan, N., Smith, M.B. & Block, J. (1968). Moral reasoning of young adults: Political-social behavior, family background and personality correlates. *Journal of Personality and Social Psychology, 10,* 183–201.

Hagen, J.W. (1971). Some thoughts on how children learn to remember. *Human Development, 14,* 262–271.

Hagen, M.A. & Johnson, M.M. (1977). Hudson pictorial depth perception test: Cultural content and question with a Western sample. *Journal of Social Psychology, 101,* 3–11.

Haith, M.M. (1979). Visual cognition in early infancy. In R.B. Kearsley & I.E. Sigel (Eds.), *Infants at risk: Assessment of cognitive functioning.* Hillsdale, NJ: Erlbaum.

Haith, M.M., Bergman, T. & Moore, M.J. (1977). Eye contact and face scanning in early infancy. *Science, 198,* 853–855.

Hall, E. (1970, May). A conversation with Jean Piaget and Barbel Inhelder. *Psychology Today, 3,* 25–56.

Hall, J.A. & Halberstadt, A.G. (1980). Masculinity and femininity in children: Development of the Children's Personal Attributes Questionnaire. *Developmental Psychology, 16,* 270–280.

Hamil, P.V., Drizd, T.A., Johnson, C.L., Reed, R.B. & Roche, A.F. (1977). *NCHS growth curves for children: Birth-18 years.* (Vital and Health Statistics Series 11. National Health Survey No. 165). Washington, D.C.: U.S. Government Printing Office.

Haney, W. (1981). Validity, vaudeville, and values: A short history of social concerns over standardized testing. *American Psychologist, 36,* 1021–1034.

Hansen, S.L. (1977). Dating choices of high school students. *Family Coordinator, 26,* 13–138.

Hanson, S.W., Streissgirth, A.P. & Smith, D.W. (1978). The effects of moderate alcohol consumption during pregnancy on fetal growth and morphogenesis. *Journal of Pediatrics, 92,* 457–460.

Hantover, J.P. (1978). The Boy Scouts and the validation of masculinity. *Journal of Social Issues, 34,* 184–195.

Harlow, H.F. (1963). The maternal affectional system. In B.M. Foss (Ed.), *Determinants of infant behavior*. London: Methuen.

Harper, L.V. (1975). The scope of offspring effects: From caregiver to culture. *Psychological Bulletin, 82*, 784–801.

Harrington, D.M., Block, J.H. & Block, J. (1983). Predicting creativity in preadolescence from divergent thinking in early childhood. *Journal of Personality and Social Psychology, 45*, 609–623.

Harris, J.A., Jackson, C.M., Patterson, D.G. & Scammon, R.E. (Eds.). (1930). *The measurement of man*. Minneapolis: University of Minnesota Press.

Harris, P. (1984). The hidden face of shyness: A message from the shy for researchers and practitioners. *Human Relations, 37*, 1079–1093.

Harter, S. (1981). A model of intrinsic mastery motivation in children: Individual differences and developmental change. In W.A. Collins (Ed.), *Minnesota symposia on child psychology* (vol. 14). Hillsdale, NJ: Erlbaum.

Harter, S. (1983). Developmental perspectives on the self-system. In P.H. Mussen (Ed.), *Handbook of child psychology* (4th ed., vol. 4). New York: Wiley.

Hartley, R.E. (1959). Sex role pressures in the socialization of the male child. *Psychological Reports, 5*, 457–468.

Hartup, W. (1983). The peer system. In P.H. Mussen (Ed.), *Handbook of child psychology* (4th ed., vol. 4). New York: Wiley.

Hartup, W.W. (1974). Aggression in childhood: Developmental perspectives. *American Psychologist, 29*, 336–341.

Hartup, W.W. (1983). Peer relations. In P.H. Mussen (Ed.), *Handbook of child psychology* (4th ed., vol. 4). New YorK: Wiley.

Hartup, W.W., Glazer, J.A. & Charlesworth, R. (1967). Peer reinforcement and sociometric status. *Child Development, 38*, 1017–1024.

Hatano, G. Mikaye, K. & Tajima, N. (1980). Mother behavior in an unstructured situation and child's acquisition and number conservation. *Child Development, 51*, 379–385.

Havighurst, R.J. (1972). *Developmental tasks and education*. New York: McKay.

Hawkins, J. (1985). Computers and girls: Rethinking the issues. *Sex Roles, 13*, 165–180.

Hay, D.L., Pederson, J. & Nash, A. (1982). Dyadic interaction in the first year of life. In K.H. Rubin & H.S. Ross (Eds.), *Peer relationships and social skills in childhood*. New York: Springer-Verlag.

Hayes, D.S. (1978). Cognitive bases for liking and disliking among preschool children. *Child Development, 49*, 906–909.

Haynes, H., White, B.L. & Held, R. (1965). Visual accommodation in human infants. *Science, 148*, 328–330.

Hazen, N.L. & Durett, M.E. (1982). Relationship of security of attachment to exploration and cognitive mapping abilities in two-year-olds. *Developmental Psychology, 18*, 751–759.

Heath, D. (1972). What meaning effects does fatherhood have for the maturing of professional men? *Merrill-Palmer Quarterly, 24*, 265–278.

Heath, D.H. (1977). *Maturity and competence: A transactional view*. New York: Halsted Press.

Heber, R. & Garber, H. (1970). *An experiment in the prevention of cultural-familial mental retardation*. Paper presented at the Second Congress of the International Association for the Scientific Study of Mental Deficiency, Warsaw, Poland.

Herodotus. (1954). *The histories*. (Trans. by A. de Sélincourt). New York: Penguin Books.

Herrnstein, R.J. (1971). *I. Q. in the meritocracy*. Boston: Little, Brown.

Hetherington, E.M. (1972). Effects of father absence on personality development in adolescent daughters. *Developmental Psychology, 7*, 313–326.

Hetherington, E.M. (1979). Divorce: A child's perspective. *American Psychologist, 34*, 851–858.

Hetherington, E.M., Cox, M. & Cox, R. (1978). The aftermath of divorce. In J.H. Stevens and M. Matthews (Eds.), *Mother-child, father-child relations*. Washington, D.C.: National Association for the Education of Young Children.

Hetherington, E.M., Cox, M. & Cox, R. (1978). *Family interaction and the social, emotional, and cognitive development of children following divorce*. Paper presented at the Symposium on the Family: Setting Priorities, Institute for Pediatric Service, Johnson and Johnson Baby Co., Washington, D.C.

Hicks, D.J. (1965). Imitation and retention of film-mediated aggressive peer and adult models. *Journal of Personality and Social Psychology, 2*, 97–100.

Higgins, E.T. (1976). Social class differences in verbal communicative accuracy: A question of "which question?" *Psychological Bulletin, 83*, 695–714.

Hirschman, R., Melamed, L.E. & Oliver, C.M. (1982). The psychophysiology of infancy. In B.B. Wolman (Ed.), *Handbook of developmental psychology*. Englewood Cliffs, NJ: Prentice-Hall.

Hoar, R.M. (1986). Effects of the environment upon fetal development: Concepts and design. *Biology of Reproduction, 34*, 1–4.

Hockett, C.F. (1954). Chinese vs. English: An exploration of the Whorfian thesis. In H. Hoijer (Ed.), *Language in culture*. Chicago: University of Chicago Press.

Hodapp, R.M. & Mueller, E. (1982). Early social development. In B.B. Wolman (Ed.), *Handbook of developmental psychology*. Englewood Cliffs, NJ: Prentice-Hall.

Hodson, B. (1980). *The assessment of phonological processes*. Danville, IL: Interstate.

Hofer, M.A. (1981). *The roots of human behavior*. San Francisco: Freeman.

Hoff-Ginsberg, E. (1986). Function and structure in maternal speech: Their relation to the child's development of syntax. *Developmental Psychology, 22*, 155–163.

Hoffman, L.W. (1974). Effects of maternal employment on the child: A review of the research. *Developmental Psychology, 10*, 204–228.

Hoffman, L.W. (1979). Maternal employment. *American Psychologist, 34,* 859–865.

Hoffman, L.W. & Hoffman, M. (1973). The value of children to parents. In J.T. Fawcett (Ed.), *Psychological perspectives on population.* New York: Basic Books.

Hoffman, L.W. & Manis, J.D. (1978). Influences of children on marital interaction and parental satisfaction and dissatisfaction. In R.M. Lerner & G.B. Spanier (Eds.), *Child influences on marriage and family interaction.* New York: Academic Press.

Hoffman, M.L. (1970). Moral development. In P.H. Mussen (Ed.), *Carmichael's manual of child psychology.* New York: Wiley.

Hofsten, C., von. (1982). Eye-hand coordination in newborns. *Developmental Psychology, 18,* 450–461.

Hold, E.C.L. (1976). Attention structure and rank specific behavior in preschool children. In M.R.A. Chance & R.R. Larsen (Eds.), *The social structure of attention.* New York: Wiley.

Holmes, D.L., Nagy, J.N., Slaymaker, F., Sosnowski, R.J., Prinz, S.M. & Pasternak, J.F. (1982). Early influences of prematurity, illness, and prolonged hospitalization on infant behavior. *Developmental Psychology, 18,* 744–750.

Holstein, C.B. (1976). Irreversible, stepwise sequence in the development of moral judgment: A longitudinal study of males and females. *Child Development, 47,* 51–61.

Holtzman, W.H. (1982). Cross-cultural comparisons of personality development in Mexico and the United States. In D.A. Wagner & H.W. Stevenson (Eds.), *Cultural perspectives on child development.* San Francisco: Freeman.

Holtzman, W.H., Diaz-Guerrero, R. & Swartz, J.D. (1975). *Personality development in two cultures: A cross-cultural longitudinal study of school children in Mexico and the United States.* Austin: University of Texas Press.

Honzik, M.P., MacFarlane, J.W. & Allen, L. (1948). The stability of mental test performance between two and eighteen years. *Journal of Experimental Education, 18,* 309–324.

Horney, K. (1973). *Feminine psychology.* New York: Norton.

Howes, C. (1983). Patterns of friendship. *Child Development, 54,* 1041–1053.

Huang, M.S. (1983). A developmental study of children's comprehension of embedded sentences with and without semantic constraints. *Journal of Psychology, 114,* 51–56.

Hudson, L. (1966). *Contrary imaginations.* London: Methuen.

Hudson, W. (1960). Pictorial depth perception in subcultural groups in Africa. *Journal of Social Psychology, 52,* 183–208.

Huesmann, L.R., Eron, L.D., Lefkowitz, M.M. & Walder, L.O. (1984). Stability of aggression over time and generations. *Developmental Psychology, 20,* 1120–1134.

Hughes, M. (1978). Sequential analysis of exploration and play. *International Journal of Behavioral Development, 1,* 83–97.

Hughes, M. & Hutt, C. (1979). Heartrate correlates of childhood activities: Play, exploration, problem-solving and day-dreaming. *Biological Psychology, 8,* 253–263.

Humphrey, T. (1978). Function of the nervous system during prenatal life. In U. Stave (Ed.), *Perinatal physiology.* New York: Plenum.

Huston, A.C. (1983). Sex-typing. In P.H. Mussen (Ed.), *Handbook of child psychology* (4th ed., vol. 4). New York: Wiley.

Huston, A., Carpenter, C.J., Atwater, J.B. & Johnson, L.M. (1986). Gender, adult structuring of activities, and social behavior in middle childhood. *Child Development, 57,* 1200–1209.

Huston, A.C., Greer, D., Wright, J.C., Welch, R. & Ross, R. (1984). Child comprehension of televised formal features with masculine and feminine connotations. *Developmental Psychology, 20,* 707–716.

Huston-Stein, A. & Higgins-Trenk, A. (1978). Development of females from childhood through adulthood: Career and feminine observations. In P.B. Baltes (Ed.), *Life-span development and behavior* (vol. 1). New York: Academic Press.

Hutt, C. (1979). Exploration and play. In B. Sutton-Smith (Ed.), *Play and learning.* New York: Gardner Press.

Hutt, C. & Bhavnani, R. (1976). Predictions from play. In J.S. Bruner, A. Jolly & K. Sylva (Eds.), *Play: Its role in development and solution.* New York: Basic Books.

Hyde, J.S. (1981). How large are cognitive differences? A meta-analysis using W^2 and d. *American Psychologist, 36,* 892–901.

Hyde, J.S. (1985). *Half the human experience: The psychology of women* (3rd ed.). Lexington, MA: Heath.

Iannotti, R.J. (1978). Effect of role-taking experiences on role-taking, empathy, altruism, and aggression. *Developmental Psychology, 14,* 119–124.

Ingram, D. (1974). Phonological rules in young children. *Journal of Child Language, 1,* 49–64.

Ingram, D. (1981). *Procedures for the phonological analysis of children's language.* Baltimore: University Park Press.

Inhelder, B. & Piaget, J. (1958). *The growth of logical thinking from childhood to adolescence.* New York: Basic Books.

Inhelder, B. & Piaget, J. (1964). *The early growth of logic in the child.* New York: Norton.

Irwin, D.M. & Bushnell, M.M. (1980). *Observational strategies for child study.* New York: Holt, Rinehart & Winston.

Jacklin, C.N., Maccoby, E.E. & Doering, C.H. (1983). Neonatal sex steroid hormones and timidity in 6-18 month-old boys and girls. *Developmental Psychobiology, 16,* 163–168.

Jacobson, J.L. & Willie, D.E. (1984). Influence of attachment and separation experience on separation distress at 18 months. *Developmental Psychology, 20,* 477–484.

Jacobson, J.L. & Willie, D.E. (1986). The influence of attachment pattern on developmental changes in peer interaction from the toddler to the preschool period. *Child Development, 57,* 338–347.

Jacobson, S.W. (1979). Matching behavior in the young infant. *Child Development, 50,* 425–430.

Jacobson, S.W., Fein, G.G., Jacobson, J.L., Schwartz, P.M. & Dowler, J.K. (1985). The effect of intrauterine PCB exposure on visual recognition memory. *Child Development, 56,* 853–860.

Jacobson, R. (1968). *Child language, aphasia, and phonological universals.* (Trans. by A. Keiler). The Hague: Mouton.

James, W. (1890). *Principles of psychology.* New York: Holt.

James, W. (1968). The self. In C. Gordon & K.J. Gergen (Eds.), *The self in social interaction* (vol. 1). New York: Wiley.

Janos, P.M. & Robinson, N.M. (1985). Psychosocial development in intellectually gifted children. In F.D. Horowitz & M. O'Brien (Eds.), *The gifted and talented: Developmental perspectives.* Washington, D.C.: American Psychological Association.

Jensen, A.R. (1969). How much can we boost IQ and scholastic achievement? *Harvard Educational Review, 39,* 1–123.

Jensen, A.R. (1981). *Straight talk about mental tests.* New York: Free Press.

Jiao, S., Ji, G. & Ching, C.C. (1986). Comparative study of behavioral qualities of only children and sibling children. *Child Development, 57,* 357–361.

Joffe, L.S. & Vaughn, B.E. (1982). Infant-mother attachment: Theory, assessment, and implications for development. In B.B. Wolman (Ed.), *Handbook of developmental psychology.* Englewood Cliffs, NJ: Prentice-Hall.

Johnson, J.E. (1976). Relations of divergent thinking and intelligence test scores with social and non-social make-believe play of preschool children. *Child Development, 47,* 1200–1203.

Johnson, J.E., Christie, J.F. & Yawkey, T.D. (1987). *Play and early childhood development.* Glenview, IL: Scott, Foresman.

Johnson, J.E. & Ershler, J. (1981). Developmental trends in preschool play as a function of classroom setting and gender. *Child Development, 52,* 995–1004.

Johnson, M.M. (1975). Fathers, mothers, and sex typing. *Sociology Inquiry, 45,* 15–26.

Jones, H.E. (1938). The California Adolescent Growth Study. *Journal of Educational Research, 31,* 561–567.

Jones, M.C. (1957). The later careers of boys who were early- or late-maturing. *Child Development, 28,* 113–128.

Jones, M.C. & Bayley, N. (1950). Physical maturing among boys as related to behavior. *Journal of Educational Psychology, 41,* 129–147.

Jones, M.C. & Mussen, P.H. (1958). Self-conceptions, motivations and interpersonal attitudes of early and later maturing girls. *Child Development, 29,* 491–501.

Jones, R.E. (1984). *Human reproduction and sexual behavior.* Englewood Cliffs, NJ: Prentice-Hall.

Jourard, S.M. & Secord, P.L. (1955). Body cathexis and the ideal female figure. *Journal of Abnormal and Social Psychology, 50,* 243–246.

Joyce, L.K. (1977). A study of formal reasoning in elementary education majors. *Science Education, 61,* 153–158.

Kagan, J. & Moss, H.A. (1962). *Birth to maturity.* New York: Wiley.

Kagan, J.S. (1969). Inadequate evidence and illogical conclusions. *Harvard Educational Review, 39,* 2.

Kagan, S. & Madsen, M.C. (1972). Experimental analyses of cooperation and competition of Anglo-American and Mexican children. *Developmental Psychology, 6,* 49–59.

Kail, R. & Hagen, J.W. (1982). Memory in childhood. In B.B. Wolman (Ed.), *Handbook of developmental psychology.* Englewood Cliffs, NJ: Prentice-Hall.

Kalter, H. & Warkany, J. (1983). Congenital malformations: Etiologic factors and their role in prevention. *New England Journal of Medicine, 308,* 424–431.

Kamin, L. (1974). *The science and politics of IQ.* Potomac, MD: Erlbaum.

Kandel, D. & Lesser, G.S. (1969). Parent-adolescent relationships and adolescent independence in the United States and Denmark. *Journal of Marriage and the Family, 31,* 348–358.

Kaplan, E. & Kaplan, G. (1971). The prelinguistic child. In J. Elliot (Ed.), *Human development and cognitive process.* New York: Holt, Rinehart & Winston.

Katchadourian, H. (1977). *The biology of adolescence.* San Francisco: Freeman.

Katz, P.A. (1979). The development of female identity. *Sex Roles, 5,* 155–178.

Kauffman, J.M., Gordon, M.E. & Baker, A. (1978). Being imitated: Persistence of an effect. *Journal of Genetic Psychology, 132,* 319–320.

Kaufmann, R., Maland, J. & Yonas, A. (1981). Sensitivity of 5- and 7-month-old infants to pictorial depth information. *Journal of Experimental Child Psychology, 32,* 162–168.

Kavrell, S.M. & Petersen, A.C. (1986). Patterns of achievement in early adolescence. In M.L. Maehr & M.W. Steinkamp (Eds.), *Women and science.* Greenwich, CT: JAI Press.

Kaye, K. (1982). *The mental and social life of babies: How parents create persons.* Chicago: University of Chicago Press.

Kaye, K. & Marcus, J. (1978). Imitation over a series of trials without feedback: Age six months. *Infant Behavior and Development, 1,* 141–155.

Keasey, C.B. (1972). The lack of sex differences in moral judgments of preadolescents. *Journal of Social Psychology, 86,* 157–158.

Keenan, E.O. (1975). Conversational competence in children. *Journal of Child Language, 2,* 163–183.

Keith, R.W. (1975). Middle ear function in neonates. *Archives of Otolaryngology, 101,* 375–379.

Keller, A., Ford, L.H. & Meacham, J.A. (1978). Dimensions of self-concept in preschool children. *Developmental Psychology, 14,* 483–489.

Kelley, R.K. (1972). The premarital sexual revolution: Comments on research. *Family Coordinator, 21,* 334–336.

Kelly, G.A. (1955). *The psychology of personal constructs.* New York: Norton.

Kelly, J. (1977). The aging male homosexual: Myth and reality. *Gerontologist, 17,* 328.

Kelly, J. (1982). Divorce: The adult perspective. In B.B. Wolman (Ed.), *Handbook of developmental psychology.* Englewood Cliffs, NJ: Prentice-Hall.

Kelly, J.B. & Wallerstein, J.S. (1976). The effects of parental divorce: Experiences of the child in early latency. *American Journal of Orthopsychiatry, 46,* 20–32.

Kelly, M. (1977). Papua, New Guinea, and Piaget. In P. Dasen (Ed.), *Piagetian psychology: Cross-cultural contributions.* New York: Gardner Press.

Kendler, T.S. (1963). Development of mediating responses in children. *Monographs of the Society for Research in Child Development, 28* (2, Serial No. 86).

Kennell, J.H. & Klaus, M.H. (1984). Mother-infant bonding: Weighing the evidence. *Developmental Review, 4,* 275–282.

Kenshalo, D.R. (1977). Age changes in touch, vibration, temperature, kinesthesis, and pain sensitivity. In J.E. Birren & K.W. Schaie (Eds.), *Handbook of the psychology of aging.* New York: Van Nostrand Reinhold.

Kent, S. (1976). How do we age? *Geriatrics, 31,* 128–134.

Kerlinger, F.N. (1973). *Foundations of behavioral research* (2nd ed.). New York: Holt, Rinehart & Winston.

Kessen, W. (1960). Research design in the study of developmental problems. In P.H. Mussen (Ed.), *Handbook of research methods in child development.* New York: Wiley.

Kessen, W. (1965). *The child.* New York: Wiley.

Kessen, W. (1979). The American child and other cultural inventions. *American Psychologist, 34,* 815–820.

Kiminyo, D.M. (1977). A cross-cultural study of the development of conversation of mass, weight, and volume among Kamba children. In P. Dasen (Ed.), *Piagetian psychology: Cross-cultural contributions.* New York: Gardner Press.

King, N.R. (1979). Play: The kindergartner's perspective. *Elementary School Journal, 80,* 81–87.

Klaus, M.H. & Kennell, J.H. (1976). *Maternal-infant bonding: The impact of early separation or loss on family development.* St. Louis: Mosby.

Klaus, M.H. & Kennell, J.H. (1982). *Parent-infant bonding.* St. Louis: Mosby.

Klausmeier, H.J. (1985). *Educational psychology* (5th ed.). New York: Harper & Row.

Kleck, R.E., Richardson, S.A. & Ronald, L. (1974). Physical appearance cues and interpersonal attraction in children. *Child Development, 45,* 305–310.

Klein, A.R. & Young, R.D. (1979). Hyperactive boys in their classroom: Assessment of teacher and peer perceptions, interactions, and classroom behaviors. *Journal of Abnormal Child Psychology, 7,* 425–442.

Klima, E.S. & Bellugi, U. (1973). Teaching apes to communicate. In G. Miller (Ed.), *Communications, language, and meaning.* New York: Basic Books.

Knight, G.P. & Kagan, S. (1977). Acculturation of prosocial and competitive behaviors among second- and third-generation Mexican-American children. *Journal of Cross-cultural Psychology, 8,* 273–284.

Kogan, N. (1973). Creativity and cognitive style: A life-span perspective. In P.B. Baltes & K.W. Schaie (Eds.), *Life-span developmental psychology.* New York: Academic Press.

Kogan, N. (1983). Stylistic variation in childhood and adolescence: Creativity, metaphor and cognitive styles. In P.H. Mussen (Ed.), *Handbook of child psychology* (4th ed., vol. 3). New York: Wiley.

Kohlberg, L. (1966). A cognitive-developmental analysis of children's sex-role concepts and attitudes. In E.E. Maccoby (Ed.), *The development of sex differences.* Stanford, CA: Stanford University Press.

Kohlberg, L. (1969). Stage and sequence: The cognitive-developmental approach to socialization. In D. Gosline (Ed.), *Handbook of socialization and research.* New York: Rand McNally.

Kohlberg, L. (1976). Moral stages and moralization: The cognitive developmental approach. In T. Lickona (Ed.), *Moral development and behavior.* New York: Holt, Rinehart & Winston.

Kohlberg, L. (1977). The implications and moral stages for adult education. *Religious Education, 77,* 183–201.

Kohlberg, L. (1984). Moral stages and moralization: The cognitive developmental approach. In L. Kohlberg (Ed.), *Essays on moral development: The psychology of moral development* (vol. 2). San Francisco: Harper & Row.

Kohlberg, L. & Candee, D. (1984). The relationship of moral judgment to moral action. In L. Kohlberg (Ed.), *Essays on moral development: The psychology of moral development* (vol. 2). San Francisco: Harper & Row.

Kolody, G. (1977). Cognitive development and science teaching. *Journal of Research in Science Teaching, 14,* 21–26.

Kompara, D. (1982). Difficulties in the socialization process of step-parenting. *Family Relations, 29,* 69–73.

Krieger, L.H. & Wells, W.D. (1969). The criteria for friendship. *Journal of Social Psychology, 78,* 109–112.

Kubie, L.S. (1958). *Neurotic distortion of the creative process.* New York: Noonday.

Kuczaj, S.A. (1978). Children's judgments of grammatical and ungrammatical irregular past-tense verbs. *Child Development, 49,* 319–326.

Kuhl, P.K. & Miller, J.D. (1982). Discrimination of auditory target dimensions in the presence or absence of variations in a second dimension by infants. *Perception and Psychophysics, 31,* 279–292.

Kuhn, D., Nash, S.C. & Brucken, L. (1978). Sex role concepts of two- and three-year-olds. *Child Development, 49,* 445–451.

Kuhn, M.H. & McPartland, T. (1954). An empirical investigation of self-attitudes. *American Sociologist Review, 19,* 68–76.

Kunzinger, E.L. (1985). A short-term longitudinal study of memorial development during early grade school. *Developmental Psychology, 21,* 642–646.

Kurdek, L.A. & Krile, D. (1982). A developmental analysis of the relation between peer acceptance and both interpersonal understanding and perceived social self-competence. *Child Development, 53*, 1485–1491.

Labouvie-Vief, G. (1984). Logic and self-regulation from youth to maturity. In M.L. Commons, F.A. Richards & C. Armon (Eds.), *Beyond formal operations: Late adolescent and adult cognitive development*. New York: Praeger.

Labouvie-Vief, G. (1985). Intelligence and cognition. In J.E. Birren & K.W. Schaie (Eds.), *Handbook of the psychology of aging* (2nd ed.). New York: Van Nostrand Reinhold.

Labouvie-Vief, G. (1986a). Modes of knowledge and the organization of development. In M.L. Commons, C. Armon, F.A. Richards & J. Sinnott (Eds.), *Beyond formal operations: The development of adolescent and adult thinking and perception* (vol. 2). New York: Praeger.

Labouvie-Vief, G. (1986b). Towards adult autonomy: A theoretical sketch. In E. Langer & C. Alexander (Eds.), *Adult development*. Cambridge, MA: Oxford University Press.

Labov, W. (1972). *Language in the inner city: Studies in the black English vernacular*. Philadelphia: University of Pennsylvania Press.

Ladd, G.W. (1981). Effectiveness of a social learning method for enhancing children's social interaction and peer acceptance. *Child Development, 52*, 171–178.

La Freniere, P. (1983). *From attachment to peer relations: An analysis of individual differences in preschool peer competence*. Paper presented at the biannual meeting of the Society for Research in Child Development, Detroit.

La Greca, A.M. & Santogrossi, D.A. (1980). Social skills training with elementary school students: A behavioral group approach. *Journal of Consulting and Clinical Psychology, 48*, 220–227.

Lamb, M.E. (1981). Fathers and child development: An integrative overview. In M.E. Lamb (Ed.), *The role of the father in child development* (2nd ed.). New York: Wiley.

Lamb, M.E. & Bornstein, M.H. (1987). *Development in infancy: An introduction* (2nd ed.). New York: Random House.

Lamb, M.E. & Roopnarine, J.L. (1979). Peer influences on sex-role development in preschoolers. *Child Development, 50*, 1219–1222.

Lamb, M.E. & Sutton-Smith, B. (Eds.). (1982). *Sibling relationships: Their nature and significance across the life span*. Hillsdale, NJ: Erlbaum.

Lamb, M.W. & Urberg, K.A. (1978). The development of gender role and gender identity. In M.E. Lamb (Ed.), *Social and personality development*. New York: Holt, Rinehart & Winston.

Lambert, W.E., Yackley, A. & Hein, R.N. (1971). Child training values of English Canadian and French Canadian parents. *Canadian Journal of Behavioral Science, 3*, 217–236.

Langer, J. (1969). *Theories of development*. New York: Holt, Rinehart & Winston.

Langlois, J.H. & Downs, A.C. (1980). Mothers, fathers, and peers as socialization agents of sex-typed play behaviors in young children. *Child Development, 51*, 1237–1247.

Langsdorf, P., Izard, C.E., Rayias, M. & Hembree, E.A. (1983). Interest expression, visual fixation, and heart rate changes in 2- to 8-month old infants. *Developmental Psychology, 19*, 375–386.

Lantz, D. & Steffire, V. (1964). Language and cognition revisited. *Journal of Abnormal and Social Psychology, 69*, 472–481.

Larson, L.E. (1975). The relative influence of parent-adolescent affect in predicting the salience hierarchy among youth. In J.J. Conger (Ed.), *Contemporary issues in adolescent development*. New York: Harper & Row.

Lazar, I., Darlington, R., Murray, H., Royce, J. & Snipper, A. (1982). Lasting effects of early education: A report from the Consortium for Longitudinal Studies. *Monographs of the Society for Research in Child Development, 47*, (2-3, Serial No. 195).

Lazarus, P.J. (1982a). Incidence of shyness in elementary school-age children. *Psychological Reports, 51*, 904–906.

Lazarus, P.J. (1982b). Correlation of shyness and self-esteem for elementary school children. *Perceptual and Motor Skills, 55*, 8–10.

Leboyer, F. (1975). *Birth without violence*. New York: Knopf.

Lecky, P. (1945). *Self-consistency: A theory of personality*. New York: Island Press.

Lefkowitz, M.M., Eron, L.D., Walder, L.O., & Huesmann, L.R. (1972). Television violence and child aggression: A follow-up study. In G.A. Comstock & E.A. Rubinstein (Eds.), *Television and social behavior: Television and adolescent aggressiveness* (vol. 3). Washington, D.C.: U.S. Government Printing Office.

Lefkowitz, M.M., Walder, L.O. & Eron, L.D. (1963). Punishment, identification, and aggression. *Merrill-Palmer Quarterly, 9*, 159–174.

Leiderman, H. (1987, April 13). Interview in *U.S. News & World Report, 102*, 58.

Lenneberg, E.H. (1967). *Biological foundations of language*. New York: Wiley.

Lenney, E. (1979). Androgyny: Some audacious assertions toward its coming of age. *Sex Roles, 5*, 703–719.

Lenz, W. (1962). Thalidomide and congenital deformities. *Lancet, 1 (1)*, 45.

Leung, E.H. & Rheinhold, H.L. (1981). Development of pointing as a social gesture. *Developmental Psychology, 17*, 215–220.

Leventhal, A.S. & Lipsitt, L.P. (1964). Adaptation, pitch discrimination, and sound localization in the neonate. *Child Development, 35*, 759–767.

Lewis, M. & Brooks, J. (1975). Infant's social perception: A constructurist view. In L. Cohen & P. Salapatek (Eds.), *Infant perception*. New York: Academic Press.

Lewis, M. & Brooks-Gunn, J. (1979). *Social cognition and the acquisition of self*. New York: Plenum.

Lieberman, A.F. (1977). Preschoolers' competence with a peer: Relations with attachment and peer experience. *Child Development, 48*, 1277–1287.

Lindow, J., Marrett, C.B. & Wilkinson, L.C. (1985). Overview. In L.C. Wilkinson & C.B. Marrett (Eds.), *Gender influences in classroom interaction*. Orlando: Academic Press.

Linn, P.L. & Howowitz, F.D. (1983). The relationship between infant individual differences and mother-infant interaction during the neonatal period. *Infant Behavior and Development, 6,* 415–428.

Lipsitt, L.P. (1979). Critical conditions in infancy: A psychological perspective. *American Psychologist, 34,* 973–980.

Lipsitt, L.P., Kaye, H. & Bosack, T.N. (1966). Enhancement of neonatal sucking through reinforcement. *Journal of Experimental Child Psychology, 4,* 163–168.

Lockheed, M.E. (1985). Women, girls, and computers. *Sex Roles, 13,* 115–122.

Loeb, R.C., Horst, L. & Horton, P.J. (1980). Family interaction patterns associated with self-esteem in preadolescent girls and boys. *Merrill-Palmer Quarterly, 26,* 203–217.

Loehlin, J.C., Lindzey, G. & Spuhler, J.N. (1975). *Race differences in intelligence*. San Francisco: Freeman.

Loehlin, J.C. & Nichols, R.C. (1976). *Heredity, environment, and personality: A study of 850 twins*. Austin: University of Texas Press.

Logan, L.A. (1976). *Fundamentals of learning and motivation*. Dubuque, IA: William C. Brown.

Logan, R. (1977). Sociocultural change and the emergence of children as burdens. *Child and Family, 16,* 295–304.

Logan, R.D. (1986). A reconceptualization of Erikson's theory: The repetition of existential and instrumental themes. *Human Development, 29,* 125–136.

Longfellow, C. (1979). Divorce in context: Its impact on children. In G. Levinger & O. Moles (Eds.), *Divorce and separation: Context, causes, and consequences*. New York: Basic Books.

Lorenz, K. (1935/1970). *Studies in animal and human behavior*. (Trans. by R. Martin). London: Methuen.

Lowenstein, L.F. (1983). The treatment of extreme shyness in maladjusted children by implosive, counseling, and conditioning approaches. *Interdisciplinaria, 4,* 115–130.

Lowrey, G.H. (1973). *Growth and development of children* (6th ed.). Chicago: Year Book Medical.

Lutey, C. & Copeland, E. (1982). Cognitive assessments of the school-age child. In C.R. Reynolds and T.B. Gutkin (Eds.), *Handbook of school psychology*. New York: Wiley.

Lutkenhaus, P., Grossman, K.E. & Grossman, K. (1985). Infant-mother attachment at twelve months and style of interaction with a stranger at the age of three years. *Child Development, 56,* 1538–1542.

Lykken, D. (1987, April 13). Interview in *U.S. News & World Report, 102 (14),* 59.

Lynn, R. (1977). The intelligence of the Japanese. *Bulletin of the British Psychological Society, 30,* 69–72.

Lynn, R. (1982). IQ in Japan and the United States shows a growing disparity. *Nature, 297,* 222–223.

Maccoby, E.E. (1969). The development of stimulus selection. In J.P. Hill (Ed.), *Minnesota symposia on child psychology* (vol. 3). Minneapolis: University of Minnesota.

Maccoby, E.E. (1980). *Social development*. New York: Harcourt Brace Jovanovich.

Maccoby, E.E. & Jacklin, C.N. (1974). *The psychology of sex differences*. Stanford, CA: Stanford University Press.

Maccoby, E.E. & Jacklin, C.N. (1980). Sex differences in aggression: A rejoinder and reprise. *Child Development, 51,* 964–980.

Maccoby, E.E. & Konrad, K.W. (1966). Age trends in selective listening. *Journal of Experimental Child Psychology, 3,* 113–122.

Maccoby, E.E. & Martin, J.A. (1983). Socialization in the context of the family: Parent-child interaction. In P.H. Mussen (Ed.), *Handbook of child psychology* (4th ed., vol. 4). New York: Wiley.

MacFarlane, A. (1975). Olfaction in the development of social preferences in the human neonate. In *Parent-infant interaction*. Amsterdam: CIBA Foundation.

MacFarlane, J.W. (1963). From infancy to adulthood. *Childhood Education, 39,* 336–342.

Macken, M.A. & Barton, D. (1980). The acquisition of the voicing contrast in English: The study of voice onset time in word-initial stop consonants. *Journal of Child Language, 7,* 41–74.

Maddi, S.R. (1980). *Personality theories: A comparative analysis* (4th ed.). Homewood, IL: Dorsey.

Madsen, C.H., Becker, W.C. & Thomas, D.R. (1968). Rules, praise, and ignoring: Elements of elementary classroom control. *Journal of Applied Behavior Analysis, 1,* 139–150.

Madsen, M.C. (1971). Developmental and cross-cultural differences in the cooperative and competitive behavior of young children. *Journal of Cross-cultural Psychology, 2,* 365–371.

Main, M. (1981). Avoidance in the service of attachment: A working paper. In K. Immelmann, G. Barlow, L. Petrinovich & M. Main (Eds.), *Behavioral development: The Bielefeld Interdisciplinary Project*. New York: Cambridge University Press.

Main, M., Kaplan, N. & Cassidy, J. (1985). Security in infancy, childhood, and adulthood: A move to the level of representation. In I. Bretherton & E. Waters (Eds.), Growing points of attachment theory and research. *Monographs of the Society for Research in Child Development, 50,* (1-2, Serial No. 209).

Mainville, F. & Friedman, R.J. (1976). Peer relations of hyperactive children. *Ontario Psychologist, 8,* 17–20.

Malina, R.M. (1979). Secular changes in size and maturity: Causes and effects. In A.L. Roche (Ed.), secular trends in human growth, maturation, and development. *Monographs of the Society for Research in Child Development, 44* (3-4, Serial No. 179).

Mandler, J.M. (1983). Representation. In P.H. Mussen (Ed.), *Handbook of child psychology* (4th ed., vol. 3). New York: Wiley.

Marcus, D.E. & Overton, W.F. (1978). The development of cognitive gender constancy and sex role preferences. *Child Development, 49,* 434–444.

Marion, R.W., Wiznia, A.A., Hutcheon, R.G. & Rubenstein, A. (1986). Human T-cell lymphotrophic virus type III (HTLV-III) embryopathy. *American Journal of Diseases of Children, 140,* 638–640.

Markman, E.M. (1977). Realizing that you don't understand: A preliminary investigation. *Child Development, 48,* 986–992.

Markus, H. (1977). Self-schemata and processing information about the self. *Journal of Personality and Social Psychology, 35,* 63–78.

Martin, C.L. & Halverson, C.F. (1981). A schematic processing model of sex typing and stereotyping in children. *Child Development, 52,* 1119–1134.

Marx, J.L. (1978). Botulism in infants: A cause of sudden death? *Science, 201,* 799–801.

Mash, E.J. & Johnston, C. (1980). *A behavioral assessment of sibling interactions in hyperactive and normal children.* Paper presented at the meeting of the Association for the Advancement of Behavior Therapy, New York City.

Maslow, A.H. (1964). *Religions, values and peak experiences.* Columbus: Ohio State University Press.

Masters, J.C. & Furman, W. (1981). Popularity, individual friendship selection and specific peer interaction among children. *Developmental Psychology, 17,* 344–350.

Matarazzo, J.D. (1972). *Wechsler's measurement and appraisal of adult intelligence* (5th ed.). Baltimore: Williams & Wilkins.

Matas, L., Arend, A. & Sroufe, L.A. (1978). Continuity of adaptation in the second year: The relationship between quality of attachment and later competence. *Child Development, 49,* 547–556.

Matthews, W.S. (1977). Modes of transformation in the initiation of fantasy play. *Developmental Psychology, 13,* 212–216.

Mauer, D. (1975). Infant visual perception: Methods of study. In L.B. Cohen and P. Salapatek (Eds.), *Infant perception: From sensation to cognition: Basic visual processes* (vol. 1). New York: Academic Press.

Maurer, D. & Barrera, M.E. (1981). Infants' perception of natural and distorted arrangements of a schematic face. *Child Development, 52,* 196–202.

McCall, R.B. (1977a). Challenges to a science of developmental psychology. *Child Development, 48,* 333–344.

McCall, R.B. (1977b). Childhood IQ's as predictors of adult educational and occupational status. *Science, 197,* 482–483.

McCall, R.B. (1981). Nature-nurture and the two realms of development: A proposed integration with respect to mental development. *Child Development, 52,* 1–12.

McCall, R.B. (1983). A developmental psychologist looks at those "other disciplines" in SRCD. *SRCD Newsletter,* Winter, 7–8.

McCall, R.B. (1984). Developmental changes in mental performance: The effect of the birth of a sibling. *Child Development, 55,* 1317–1321.

McCall, R.B., Appelbaum, M.I. & Hogarty, P.S. (1973). Developmental changes in mental performance. *Monographs of the Society for Research in Child Development, 38* (3, Serial No. 150).

McCall, R.B., Parke, R.D. & Kavanaugh, R.D. (1977). Imitation of live and televised models by children one to three years of age. *Monographs of the Society for Research in Child Development, 42* (5, Serial No. 173).

McCauley, E., Kay, T., Ito, J. & Treder, R. (1987). The Turner syndrome: Cognitive deficits, affective discrimination, and behavior problems. *Child Development, 58,* 464–473.

McGhee, P.E. & Frueh, T. (1980). Television viewing and the learning of sex-role stereotypes. *Sex Roles, 6,* 179–188.

McGinnies, E. (1949). Emotionality and perceptual defense. *Psychological Review, 56,* 244–251.

McGraw, M.B. (1935). *Growth: A study of Johnny and Jimmy.* New York: Appleton.

McGraw, M.B. (1945). *The neuromuscular maturation of the human infant.* New York: Hafner Publishing.

McGrew, W.C. (1972). *An ethological study of children's behavior.* London: Academic Press.

McGuire, K.D. & Weisz, J.R. (1982). Social cognition and behavior correlates of preadolescent chumship. *Child Development, 53,* 1478–1484.

McKenzie, B.E., Tootell, H.E. & Day, R.H. (1980). Development of visual size constancy during the first year of human infancy. *Developmental Psychology, 16,* 163–174.

McMichael, P. (1980). Reading difficulties, behavior, and social status. *Journal of Educational Psychology, 72,* 76–86.

McNeill, D. (1966). Developmental psycholinguistics. In F. Smith & G. Miller (Eds.), *The genesis of language.* Cambridge, MA: MIT Press.

Mead, G.H. (1934). *Mind, self, and society.* Chicago: University of Chicago Press.

Mead, M. (1935). *Sex and temperament in three primitive societies.* New York: Morrow.

Mead, M. (1970). *Culture and commitment.* New York: Doubleday.

Mead, M. (1972). *Blackberry winter.* New York: Morrow.

Mead, M. & Newton, N. (1967). Cultural patterning of perinatal behavior. In S.A. Richardson & A.F. Guttmacher (Eds.), *Childbearing: Its social and psychological aspects.* Baltimore: Williams and Wilkins.

Meece, J.L., Eccles-Parsons, J. et al. (1982). Sex differences in math achievement. *Psychological Bulletin, 91,* 324–448.

Mehler, J., Bertoncini, J., Barriere, M. & Jassik-Gerschenfeld, D. (1978). Infant recognition of mother's voice. *Perception, 7,* 491–497.

Meissner, W.W. (1965). Parental interaction of the adolescent boy. *Journal of Genetic Psychology, 107,* 225–233.

Meltzoff, A.N. & Moore, M.K. (1977). Imitation of facial and manual gestures by human neonates. *Science, 198,* 75–78.

Meltzoff, A.N. & Moore, M.K. (1983). Newborn infants imitate adult facial gestures. *Child Development, 54,* 702–709.

Mendelson, M.J. & Haith, M.M. (1976). The relation between audition and vision in the human newborn. *Monographs of the Society for Research in Child Development, 41,* (Whole No. 167).

Menez-Bautista, R., Fikrig, S.M., Pahwa, S., Sarangadharan, M.G. & Stoneburner, R.L. (1986). Monozygotic twins discordant for the acquired immunodeficiency syndrome. *American Journal of Diseases of Children, 140,* 678–679.

Menolascino, F.J. & Egger, M.L. (1978). *Medical dimensions of mental retardation.* Lincoln: University of Nebraska Press.

Menyuk, P. (1982). Language development. In C.B. Kopp & J.B. Krakow (Eds.), *The child: Development in a social context.* Reading, MA: Addison-Wesley.

Milewski, A.E. (1976). Infants' discrimination of internal and external pattern elements. *Journal of Experimental Child Psychology, 22,* 229–246.

Milewski, A.E. (1978). Young infants' visual processing of internal and adjacent shapes. *Infant Behavior and Development, 1,* 359–371.

Milgram, S. (1963). Behavioral study of obedience. *Journal of Abnormal and Social Psychology, 67,* 371–378.

Miller, G.A. (1978). The acquisition of word meaning. *Child Development, 49,* 999–1004.

Miller, G.A. (1981). *Language and speech.* San Francisco: Freeman.

Mills, M. & Melhuish, E. (1974). Recognition of mother's voice in early infancy. *Nature, 252,* 123–124.

Minton, H.L. & Schneider, F.W. (1980). *Differential psychology.* Monterey, CA: Brooks/Cole.

Minuchin, P.P. (1977). *The middle years of childhood.* Monterey, CA: Brooks/Cole.

Molfese, D.L., Molfese, V.J. & Carrell, P.L. (1982). Early language development. In B.B. Wolman (Ed.), *Handbook of development psychology.* Englewood Cliffs, NJ: Prentice-Hall.

Money, J. (1987). Sin, sickness, or status? Homosexual gender identity and psychoneuroendocrinology. *American Psychologist, 42,* 384–399.

Money, J. & Ehrhardt, A.A. (1972). *Man and woman, boy and girl: The differentiation and dimorphism of gender identity from conception to maturity.* Baltimore: Johns Hopkins University Press.

Montague, S.P. & Morais, R. (1976). Football games and rock concerts: The natural enactment. In W. Arens and S.P. Montague (Eds.), *The American dimension: Cultural myths and social realists.* Port Washington, NY: Alfred.

Montemayor, R. & Eisen, M. (1977). The development of self-perceptions from childhood to adolescence. *Developmental Psychology, 13,* 314–319.

Moore, T. (1967). Language and intelligence: A longitudinal study of the first eight years. 1. Patterns of developments in boys and girls. *Human Development, 10,* 88–106.

Moore, T. (1975). Exclusive early mothering and its alternatives: The outcome to adolescence. *Scandinavian Journal of Psychology, 16,* 255–279.

Moriarty, A.E. & Toussieng, D.W. (1976). *Adolescent coping.* New York: Grime & Stratton.

Morrongiello, B.A. & Clifton, R. (1984). Effects of sound frequency on behavioral and cardiac orienting in newborn and five-month-old infants. *Journal of Experimental Child Psychology, 38,* 429–446.

Morrongiello, B.A., Clifton, R.K. & Kulig, J.W. (1982). Newborn cardiac and behavioral orienting responses to sound under varying precedence-effect conditions. *Infant Behavior and Development, 5,* 249–259.

Mueller, E. & Lucas, T.A. (1975). A developmental analysis of peer interaction among toddlers. In M. Lewis & L.A. Rosenblum (Eds.), *Friendship and peer relations.* New York: Wiley.

Mullener, N. & Laird, J.D. (1971). Some developmental changes in the organization of self-evaluations. *Developmental Psychology, 5,* 233–236.

Muller, E., Hollien, H. & Murry, T. (1974). Perceptual responses to infant crying: Identification of cry tapes. *Journal of Child Language, 104,* 135–136.

Munroe, R.H. & Munroe, R.L. (1978). Compliance of socialization and short-term memory in an East African society. *Journal of Social Psychology, 104,* 135–136.

Munroe, R.H., Munroe, R.L. & Whiting, B.B. (Eds.). (1981). *Handbook of cross-cultural development.* New York: Garland Press.

Munroe, R.H., Shimmin, H.S. & Munroe, R.L. (1984). Gender understanding and sex role preference in four cultures. *Developmental Psychology, 20,* 673–682.

Munroe, R.L. & Munroe, R.H. (1977). Land, labor, and the child's cognitive performance among the Logoli. *American Ethnologist, 4,* 309–320.

Murphy, C.M. (1978). Pointing in the context of a shared activity. *Child Development, 49,* 371–380.

Murphy, L., Heider, G.M. & Small, C.T. (1986). Individual differences in infants. *Zero to Three, 7,* 1–8.

Murphy, L.B. & Moriarty, A.E. (1976). *Vulnerability, coping, and growth: From infancy to adolescence.* New Haven, CT: Yale University Press.

Mussen, P. & Eisenberg-Berg, N. (1977). *Roots of caring, sharing, and helping.* San Francisco: Freeman.

Mussen, P.H. & Boutourline-Young, H. (1964). Relationships between rate of physical maturing and personality among boys of Italian descent. *Vita Humana, 7,* 186–200.

Muuss, R.E. (1982). *Theories of adolescence* (4th ed.). New York: Random House.

Myers, B.J. (1984a). Mother-infant bonding: A rejoinder to Kennell and Klaus. *Developmental Review, 4,* 283–288.

Myers, B.J. (1984b). Mother-infant bonding: The status of the critical period hypothesis. *Developmental Review, 4,* 240–274.

Myers, P.I. & Hammill, D.D. (1976). *Methods of learning disorders.* New York: Wiley.

Nadelman, L. & Begun, A. (1982). The effect of the newborn on the older sibling: Mothers' questionnaires. In

M.E. Lamb & B. Sutton-Smith (Eds.), *Sibling relationships: Their nature and significance across the lifespan.* Hillsdale, NJ: Erlbaum.

Naeye, R.L. (1978). Relationship of cigarette smoking to congenital anomalies and perinatal death. *American Journal of Pathology, 90,* 289–294.

Naeye, R.L. (1980). Sudden infant death. *Scientific American, 242,* 56–62.

Naeye, R.L., Ladis, B. & Drage, J.S. (1976). Sudden infant death syndrome: A prospective study. *American Journal of Diseases of Children, 130,* 1207–1210.

Nash, S.C. & Feldman, S.S. (1981). Sex role and sex-related attributions: Constancy or change across the family life cycle? In M.E. Lamb & A.L. Brown (Eds.), *Advances in developmental psychology* (vol. 1). Hillsdale, NJ: Erlbaum.

National Institute of Child Health. (1980). Cesarean childbirth. *Consensus Development Conference Summaries, 3,* 39–53.

Nelson, C.A. & Dolgin, K.G. (1985). The generalized discrimination of facial expressions by seven-month-old infants. *Child Development, 56,* 58–61.

Nelson, K. (1973). Structure and strategy in learning to talk. *Monographs of the Society for Research in Child Development, 38* (1-2, Serial No. 149).

Nelson, K.E. (1971). Accommodation of visual tracking patterns in human infants to object movement patterns. *Journal of Experimental Child Psychology, 12,* 182–196.

Nelson, K., Rescorla, L., Gruendel, J. & Benedict, H. (1978). Early lexicons: What do they mean? *Child Development, 49,* 960–968.

Nelson, M. & Nelson, G.K. (1982). Problems of equity in the reconstituted family: A social exchange analysis. *Family Relations, 31,* 223–231.

Nelson, N.M., Enkin, M.W., Saroj, S., Bennett, K.J., Milner, M. & Sackett, D.L. (1980). A randomized clinical trial of the Leboyer approach to childbirth. *New England Journal of Medicine, 302,* 655–660.

Nerlove, S.B. & Snipper, A.S. (1981). Cognitive consequences of cultural opportunity. In R.H. Munroe, R.L. Munroe & B.B. Whiting (Eds.), *Handbook of cross-cultural human development.* New York: Garland Press.

Nesselroade, J.R. & Baltes, P.B.F. (1974). Adolescent personality development and historical change: 1970–1972. *Monographs of the Society for Research in Child Development, 39* (1, Serial No. 154).

Newport, E.L., Gleitman, H. & Gleitman, L.R. (1977). Mother, I'd rather do it myself: Some effects and noneffects of maternal speech style. In C.E. Snow & C.A. Ferguson (Eds.), *Talking to children.* Cambridge: Cambridge University Press.

Nichols, R. (1964). Parental attitudes of mothers of intelligent adolescents and creativity of their children. *Child Development, 35,* 1041–1049.

Nilsson, L. (1976). *A child is born.* New York: Delacorte Press.

Ninio, A. & Bruner, J. (1978). The achievement and antecedents of labelling. *Journal of Child Language, 5,* 1–15.

Nisbett, R. & Gurwitz, S. (1970). Weight, sex, and the eating behavior of human newborns. *Journal of Comparative and Physiological Psychology, 73,* 245–253.

Noppe, I.C. (1983). A cognitive-developmental perspective on the adolescent self-concept. *Journal of Early Adolescence, 3,* 275–286.

Noppe, I.C. & Noppe, L.D. (1976). *Creativity from a cognitive-developmental perspective.* Paper presented at the Sixth Annual Symposium of the Jean Piaget Society, Philadelphia.

Norton, A.J. & Glick, P.C. (1979). Marital instability in America: Past, present, and future. In G. Levinger & O. Moles (Eds.), *Divorce and separation: Context, causes, and consequences.* New York: Basic Books.

Nye, F.I. (1982). A theoretical perspective on running away. In F.I. Nye (Ed.), *Family relationships: Rewards and costs.* Beverly Hills, CA: Sage.

Nye, F.I. & Edelbrock, C. (1980). Introduction: Some social characteristics of runaways. *Journal of Family Issues, 1-2,* 147–150.

Nyiti, R.M. (1982). The validity of "cultural differences explanations" for cross-cultural variations in the rate of Piagetian cognitive development. In D.A. Wagner & H.W. Stevenson (Eds.), *Cultural perspectives on child development.* San Francisco: Freeman.

Oden, S. & Asher, S.R. (1977). Coaching children in social skills for friendship making. *Child Development, 48,* 495–506.

O'Leary, K.D., Kaufman, K.F., Kass, R.E. & Drabman, R.S. (1970). The effects of loud and soft reprimands on the behavior of disruptive students. *Exceptional Children, 37,* 145–155.

O'Leary, K.D. & O'Leary, S.G. (Eds.) (1977). *Classroom management: The successful use of behavior modification* (2nd ed.). Elmsford, NY: Pergamon.

O'Leary, S.G. & O'Leary, K.D. (1976). Behavior modification in the schools. In H. Leitenberg (Ed.), *Handbook of behavior modification and behavior therapy.* Englewood Cliffs, NJ: Prentice-Hall.

Olsho, L.W. (1984). Infant frequency discrimination. *Infant Behavior and Development, 7,* 27–35.

Olsho, L.W., Schoon, C., Sakai, R., Turpin, R. & Sperduto, V. (1982). Preliminary data on frequency discrimination in infancy. *Journal of the Acoustical Society of America, 71,* 509–511.

Olson, G.M. (1981). The recognition of specific persons. In M.E. Lamb & L.R. Sherrod (Eds.), *Infant social cognition: Empirical and theoretical considerations.* Hillsdale, NJ: Erlbaum.

Olson, G.M. & Sherman, T. (1983). Attention, learning and memory in infants. In P.H. Mussen (Ed.), *Handbook of child psychology* (4th ed., vol. 2). New York: Wiley.

Olweus, D. (1979). Stability and aggression reaction patterns in males: A review. *Psychological Bulletin, 86,* 852–875.

Opper, S. (1977). Concept development in Thai urban and rural children. In P. Dasen (Ed.), *Piagetian psychology: Cross-cultural contributions.* New York: Gardner Press.

Ornstein, P.A., Medlin, R.G., Stone, B.P. & Naus, M.J. (1985). Retrieving for rehearsal: An analysis of active rehearsal in children's memory. *Developmental Psychology, 21,* 633–641.

Ornstein, P.A. & Naus, M.J. (1978). Rehearsal processes in children's memory. In P.A. Ornstein (Ed.), *Memory development in children.* Hillsdale, NJ: Erlbaum.

Ornstein, P.A. & Naus, M.J. (1983). Rehearsing according to artificially generated rehearsal patterns: An analysis of active rehearsal. *Bulletin of the Psychonomic Society, 21,* 419–422.

Osofsky, J.D. (1971). Children's influences upon parental behavior: An attempt to define the relationship using laboratory tasks. *Genetic Psychology Monographs, 83,* 147–169.

Ottinger, D. & Simmons, J. (1964). Behavior of human neonates and prenatal maternal anxiety. *Psychological Reports, 14,* 391–394.

Overton, W.R. & Jackson, J.P. (1973). The representation of imagined objects in action sequences: A developmental study. *Child Development, 44,* 309–314.

Papousek, H. (1967). Experimental studies of appetitional behavior in human newborns and infants. In H.W. Stevenson, E.H. Hess & H.L. Rheingold (Eds.), *Early behavior.* New York: Wiley.

Parke, R.D. & Slaby, R.G. (1983). The development of aggression. In P.H. Mussen (Ed.), *Handbook of child psychology* (4th ed., vol. 4). New York: Wiley.

Parmelee, A.H., Wenner, W.H. & Schulz, H.R. (1964). Infant sleep patterns from birth to 16 weeks of age. *Journal of Pediatrics, 65,* 576–582.

Parsons, J.E. (1980). Psychosexual neutrality: Is anatomy destiny? In J.E. Parsons (Ed.), *The psychobiology of sex differences and sex roles.* Washington, D.C.: Hemisphere Publishing.

Parsons, J.E., Adler, T.F. & Kaczala, C.M. (1982). Socialization of achievement attitudes and beliefs: Parental influences. *Child Development, 53,* 310–321.

Parsons, J.E. Kaczala, C.M. & Meece, J.L. (1982). Socialization of achievement attitudes and beliefs: Classroom influences. *Child Development, 53,* 322–339.

Parten, M.E. (1933). Social play among preschool children. *Journal of Abnormal and Social Psychology, 28,* 136–147.

Passow, A. (1981). The nature of giftedness and talent. *Gifted Child Quarterly, 24,* 5–11.

Patrick, G.T.W. (1916). *The psychology of relaxation.* Boston: Houghton Mifflin.

Pearlin, L.I. & Johnson, J.S. (1977). Marital status, life strains, and depression. *American Sociological Review, 42,* 704–715.

Peck, J. & Goldman, R. (1978). *The behaviors of kindergarten children under selected conditions of the social and physical environment.* Paper presented at the meeting of the American Education Research Association, Toronto.

Pepler, D.J. & Ross, H.S. (1981). The effects of play on convergent and divergent problem-solving. *Child Development, 52,* 1202–1210.

Perry, D.G. & Bussey, K. (1979). The social learning theory of sex differences: Imitation is alive and well. *Journal of Personality and Social Psychology, 37,* 1699–1712.

Peskin, H. (1973). Influence of the developmental schedule of puberty on learning and ego functioning. *Journal of Youth and Adolescence, 2,* 273–290.

Petersen, A.C. & Crockett, L. (1985). Pubertal timing and grade effects on adjustment. *Journal of Youth and Adolescence, 14,* 191–206.

Pfouts, J.H. (1976). The sibling relationship: A forgotten dimension. *Social Work, 21,* 200–204.

Phiffner, L.J., Rosen, L.A. & O'Leary, S.G. (1985). The efficacy of an all-positive approach to classroom management. *Journal of Applied Behavior Analysis, 18,* 257–261.

Piaget, J. (1962). *Play, dreams and imitation in childhood.* New York: Norton.

Piaget, J. (1963). *The origins of intelligence in children.* New York: Norton.

Piaget, J. (1964). Development and learning. In R.E. Ripple & V.N. Rockcastle (Eds.), *Piaget revisited.* Ithaca, NY: Cornell University Press.

Piaget, J. (1965). *The moral judgment of the child.* New York: Free Press.

Piaget, J. (1967). *Six psychological studies.* New York: Vintage.

Piaget, J. (1981). Creativity. In J.M. Gallagher & D.K. Reid (Eds.), *The learning theory of Piaget and Inhelder.* Monterey, CA: Brooks/Cole.

Piaget, J. (1983). Piaget's theory. In P.H. Mussen (Ed.), *Handbook of child psychology* (4th ed., vol. 1). New York: Wiley.

Piaget, J. & Inhelder, B. (1956). *The child's conception of space.* London: Routledge and Kegan Paul.

Piaget, J. & Inhelder, B. (1973). *Memory and intelligence.* New York: Basic Books.

Pipp, S., Fischer, K.W. & Jennings, S. (1987). Acquisition of self- and mother knowledge in infancy. *Developmental Psychology, 23,* 86–96.

Plattner, S. & Minturn, L. (1975). A comparative and longitudinal study of the behavior of communally raised children. *Ethos, 3,* 469–480.

Pleck, J.H. (1976). The male sex role: Definitions, problems, and sources of change. *Journal of Social Issues, 32,* 155–164.

Plomin, R. & Rowe, D.C. (1979). Genetic and environment etiology of social behavior in infancy. *Developmental Psychology, 15,* 62–72.

Polikanina, R.I. (1961). The relation between automatic and somatic components in the development of the conditioned reflex in premature infants. *Pavlov Journal of Higher Nervous Activity, 11,* 51–58.

Porter, R.H., Cernoch, J.M. & McLaughlin, F.J. (1983). Maternal recognition of neonates through olfactory cues. *Physiology and Behavior, 30,* 151–154.

Postman, L., Bruner, J.S. & McGinnies, E. (1948). Personal values as selective factors in perception. *Journal of Abnormal and Social Psychology, 43,* 142–154.

Postman, N. (1982). *The disappearance of childhood.* New York: Delacorte Press.

Pozner, J. & Saltz, E. (1974). Social class, conditional communication, and egocentric speech. *Developmental Psychology, 10,* 764–771.

Premack, D. (1976). *Intelligence in ape and man.* Hillsdale, NJ: Erlbaum.

Price, G.G., Walsh, D.J. & Vilberg, W.R. (1984). The confluence model's good predictions of mental age beg the question. *Psychological Bulletin, 96,* 195–200.

Price-Williams, D. (1981). Concrete and formal operations. In R.H. Munroe, R.L. Munroe, & B.B. Whiting (Eds.), *Handbook of cross-cultural human development.* New York: Garland Press.

Prinz, R.J., Roberts, W.A. & Hartman, E. (1980). Dietary correlates of hyperactive behavior in children. *Journal of Consulting and Clinical Psychology, 48,* 760–769.

Proctor, C.P. (1984). Teacher expectations: A model for school improvement. *Elementary School Journal, 84,* 469–481.

Pueschel, S.M. & Goldstein, A. (1983). Genetic counseling. In J.L. Matson & J.A. Mulick (Eds.), *Handbook of mental retardation.* New York: Pergamon.

Pueschel, S.M. & Thuline, H.C. (1983). Chromosome disorders. In J.L. Matson & J.A. Mulick (Eds.), *Handbook of mental retardation.* New York: Pergamon.

Pulkkinen, L. (1982). Self-control and continuity from childhood to adolescence. In P.B. Baltes & O.G. Brim (Eds.), *Life-span development and behavior* (vol. 4). New York: Academic Press.

Puri, R., Chawla, P., Sharma, M. & Pershad, D. (1984). Impact of an ongoing supplementary feeding programme on the mental abilities of children. *Indian Journal of Pediatrics, 51,* 653–657.

Radin, N. (1972). Father-child interaction and the intellectual functioning of four-year-old boys. *Developmental Psychology, 6,* 353–361.

Radke-Yarrow, M., Zahn-Waxler, C. & Chapman, M. (1983). Children's prosocial disposition and behavior. In P.H. Mussen (Ed.), *Handbook of child psychology* (4th ed., vol. 4). New York: Wiley.

Reed, G.L. & Leiderman, P.H. (1983). Is imprinting an appropriate model for human infant attachment? *International Journal of Behavioral Development, 6,* 51–69.

Reese, H.W. (1976). *Basic learning processes in childhood.* New York: Holt, Rinehart & Winston.

Reich, P.A. (1986). *Language development.* Englewood Cliffs, NJ: Prentice-Hall.

Renner, J.W. (1977). *Analysis of cognitive processes.* Washington, D.C.: National Science Foundation.

Renninger, K.A. & Wozniak, R.H. (1985). Effect of interest on attentional shift, recognition and recall in young children. *Developmental Psychology, 21,* 624–632.

Renzulli, J.S. (1978). What makes giftedness: Reexamining a definition. *Phi Delta Kappan, 60,* 180–184.

Rest, J.R. (1975). Longitudinal study of the Defining Issues Test: A strategy for analyzing developmental change. *Developmental Psychology, 11,* 738–748.

Rest, J.R. (1976). New approaches in the assessment of moral judgment. In J.T. Lickona (Ed.), *Moral development and behavior.* New York: Holt, Rinehart & Winston.

Rest, J.R. (1979). *Development in judging moral issues.* Minneapolis: University of Minnesota Press.

Rest, J.R. (1983). Morality. In P.H. Mussen (Ed.), *Handbook of child psychology* (4th ed., vol. 3). New York: Wiley.

Rest, J.R., Davison, M.L. & Robbins, S. (1978). Age trends in judging moral issues: A review of cross-sectional, longitudinal, and sequential studies of the Defining Issues Test. *Child Development, 49,* 263–279.

Reuter, M.W. & Biller, H.B. (1973). Perceived paternal nurturance-availability and personality adjustment among college males. *Journal of Consulting and Clinical Psychology, 40,* 339–342.

Rheingold, H.L. (1979). *Helping by two-year-old children.* Paper presented at the meeting of the Society for Research in Child Development, San Francisco.

Rheingold, H.L. & Cook, K.V. (1975). The contents of boys' and girls' rooms as an index of parents' behavior. *Child Development, 46,* 459–463.

Rheingold, H.L., Gewirtz, J.L. & Ross, H.W. (1959). Social conditioning of vocalizations in the infant. *Journal of Comparative and Physiological Psychology, 52,* 68–73.

Ricciuti, H. (1974). Fear and development of social attachments in the first year of life. In M. Lewis & L.A. Rosenblum (Eds.), *The origins of human behavior: Fear.* New York: Wiley.

Ricciuti, H. (1980). Developmental consequences of malnutrition in early childhood. From *The uncommon child: Genesis of behavior* (vol. 3). New York: Plenum.

Ricciuti, H.N. (1981). Developmental consequences of malnutrition in early childhood. In E.M. Hetherington & R.D. Parke (Eds.), *Contemporary readings in child psychology* (2nd ed.). New York: McGraw-Hill.

Rice, B. (1979, September). Brave new world of intelligence testing. *Psychology Today, 13 (4),* 26–30.

Rice, F.P. (1984). *The adolescent: Development, relationships, and culture* (4th ed.). Boston: Allyn and Bacon.

Rich, J. (1975). Effects of children's physical attractiveness on teacher's evaluation. *Journal of Educational Psychology, 67,* 599–609.

Richardson, S.A. (1976). The relation of severe malnutrition in infancy to intelligence of school children with differing life histories. *Pediatric Research, 10,* 57–61.

Richmond, V.P. (1985). Shyness and popularity: Children's views. *Western Journal of Speech Communication, 49,* 116–125.

Rierdan, J. & Koff, E. (1980). The psychological impact of menarche: Integrative versus disruptive changes. *Journal of Youth and Adolescence, 9,* 49–58.

Robeck, M.C. (1978). *Infants and children: Their development and learning.* New York: McGraw-Hill.

Roberts, S.O., Crump, E.P., Dickerson, A.E. & Horton, C.P. (1965). *Longitudinal performance of Negro American children at 5 and 10 years on the Stanford-Binet.* Paper presented at the annual meeting of the American Psychological Association, Chicago.

Robinson, C.C. & Morris, J.T. (1986). The gender-stereotyped nature of Christmas toys received by 36-, 48-, and 60-month-old children: A comparison between nonrequested vs. requested toys. *Sex Roles, 15,* 21–32.

Roche, A.F. (Ed.). (1979). Secular trends in human growth, maturation, and development. *Monographs of the Society for Research in Child Development, 44,* (3-4, Serial No. 179).

Rodgers, J.L. (1984). Confluence effects: Not here, not now! *Psychological Bulletin, 96,* 195–200.

Rodgers, J.L. & Rowe, D.C. (1985). Does contiguity breed similarity? A within-family analysis of non-shared sources of IQ differences between siblings. *Developmental Psychology, 21,* 743–746.

Rogers, C.R. (1961). *On becoming a person.* Boston: Houghton Mifflin.

Rogers, D. (1969). *Child psychology.* Monterey, CA: Brooks/Cole.

Rogoff, B. (1981). Schooling and the development of cognitive skills. In H.C. Triandis & A. Heron (Eds.), *Handbook of cross-cultural psychology: Developmental psychology* (vol. 4). Boston: Allyn and Bacon.

Rollins, B.C. & Galligan, R. (1978). The developing child and marital satisfaction of parents. In R.M. Lerner & G.B. Spanier (Eds.), *Child influences on marriage and family interaction.* New York: Academic Press.

Romaine, S. (1984). *The language of children and adolescents.* Oxford: Basic Blackwell.

Romaniuk, J.G. & Romaniuk, M. (1981). Creativity across the life span: A measurement perspective. *Human Development, 24,* 366–381.

Rose, R.J. & Ditto, W.B. (1983). A developmental-genetic analysis of common fears from early adolescence to early adulthood. *Child Development, 54,* 361–368.

Rosenblatt, D. (1977). Developmental trend in infant play. In B. Tizard & D. Harvey (Eds.), *The biology of play.* Philadelphia: Lippincott.

Rosenblith, J.F. & Sims-Knight, J.E. (1985). *In the beginning: Development in the first two years of life.* Monterey, CA: Brooks/Cole.

Rosenthal, R. & Jacobson, L. (1968). *Pygmalion in the classroom.* New York: Holt, Rinehart & Winston.

Ross, G.S. (1980). Categorization in 1- to 2-year-olds. *Developmental Psychology, 16,* 391–396.

Ross, H.S. (1982). Establishment of social games among toddlers. *Developmental Psychology, 18,* 509–518.

Ross, H.S., Lollis, S.P. & Elliott, C. (1982). Toddler-peer communication. In K.H. Rubin & H.S. Ross (Eds.), *Peer relationships and social skills in childhood.* New York: Springer-Verlag.

Ross, J. (1975). The development of paternal identity: A critical review of the interactions and nurturance and generativity in boys and men. *Journal of the American Psychoanalytic Association, 23,* 783–822.

Routh, D.K. (1986). Attention deficit disorder. In R.T. Brown & C.R. Reynolds (Eds.), *Psychological perspectives on childhood exceptionality: A handbook.* New York: Wiley.

Rovee, C.K., Cohen, R.Y. & Shlapack, W. (1975). Lifespan stability in olfactory sensitivity. *Developmental Psychology, 11,* 311–318.

Rovee-Collier, C. (1984). The ontogeny of learning and memory in human infancy. In R.V. Kail, Jr. & N.E. Spear (Eds.), *Comparative perspectives on the development of memory.* Hillsdale, NJ: Erlbaum.

Rubenstein, J. & Howes, C. (1976). The effect of peers on toddlers' interaction with mother and toys. *Child Development, 47,* 597–605.

Rubin, K.H., Fein, G.C. & Vandenberg, B. (1983). Play. In P.H. Mussen (Ed.), *Handbook of child psychology* (4th ed., vol. 4). New York: Wiley.

Rubin, K.H. & Krasnor, L.R. (1980). Changes in the play behaviors of preschoolers: A short-term longitudinal investigation. *Canadian Journal of Behavioral Science, 12,* 278–282.

Rubin, K.H., Maoni, T.L. & Hornung, M. (1976). Free play behaviors in middle and lower class preschoolers: Parten and Piaget revisited. *Child Development, 47,* 414–419.

Rubin, K.H. & Seibel, C. (1981). The effects of ecological setting on the cognitive and social play behaviors of preschoolers. *Proceedings of the Ninth Annual International Interdisciplinary Conference on Piagetian Theory and the Helping Professions*

Rubin, K.H., Watson, K. & Jambor, T. (1978). Free play behaviors in preschool and kindergarten children. *Child Development, 49,* 534–536.

Ruff, H.A. (1984). Infants' manipulative exploration of objects: Effects of age and object characteristics. *Developmental Psychology, 21,* 295–305.

Rumbaugh, D.M. (Ed.) (1977). *Language learning by a chimpanzee: The Lana project.* New York: Academic Press.

Russell, M.J., Mendelson, T. & Peeke, H.V.S. (1983). Mothers' identification of their infants' odors. *Ethology and Sociobiology, 4,* 29–31.

Russo, N.F. (1985). Sex-role stereotyping, socialization, and sexism. In A.G. Sargent (Ed.), *Beyond sex roles* (2nd ed.). St. Paul: West Publishing.

Ryan, J. & Smollar, J. (1978). *A developmental analysis of obligations in parent-child and friend relations.* Unpublished manuscript, Catholic University of America, Washington, D.C.

Ryder, R.G. (1973). Longitudinal data relating marriage satisfaction and having a child. *Journal of Marriage and the Family, 35,* 604–608.

Sagi, A. & Hoffman, M.L. (1976). Empathic distress in the newborn. *Developmental Psychology, 12,* 175–176.

Salapatek, P. (1975). Pattern perception in early infancy. In L.B. Cohen & P. Salapatek (Eds.), *Infant perception: From sensation to cognition.* New York: Academic Press.

Salvia, J., Algozyne, R. & Sheare, J.B. (1977). Attractiveness and school achievement. *Journal of School Psychology, 15,* 60–67.

Sameroff, A.J. (1971). Can conditioned responses be established in the newborn infant? *Developmental Psychology, 4,* 1–12.

Sameroff, A.J. & Cavanaugh, P.J. (1979). Learning in infancy: A developmental perspective. In J. Osofsky (Ed.), *Handbook of infant development.* New York: Wiley.

Sanders, K.M. & Harper, L.V. (1976). Free play fantasy behavior in preschool children: Relations among gender, age, season, and location. *Child Development, 47,* 1181–1185.

Sarnat, H.B. (1978). Olfactory reflexes in the newborn infant. *Journal of Pediatrics, 92,* 624–626.

Sattler, J.M. (1981). *Assessment of children's intelligence.* Philadelphia: Saunders.

Sayre, S.A. & Ball, D.W. (1975). Piagetian cognitive development and achievement in science. *Journal of Research in Science Teaching, 12,* 165–174.

Scarr, S. (1981). *Race, social class, and individual differences in IQ.* Hillsdale, NJ: Erlbaum.

Schaal, B., Montagner, H., Hertling, E., Bolzoni, D., Moyse, A. & Quichon, R. (1980). Les stimulations olfactives dans les relations entre l'enfant et la mere. *Reproduction, Nutrition et Development, 20,* 843–858.

Schacter, D.L. & Moscovitch, M. (1984). Infants amnesics, and dissociable memory systems. In M. Moscovitch (Ed.), *Infant memory.* New York: Plenum.

Schacter, D.L., Moscovitch, M., Tulving, E., McLachlan, D.R. & Freedman, M. (1986). Mnemonic precedence in amnesic patients: An analogue of the AB error in infants? *Child Development, 57,* 816–823.

Schaefer, E.S. (1959). A circumplex model for maternal behavior. *Journal of Abnormal and Social Psychology, 59,* 226–235.

Schaefer, E.S. (1961). Converging conceptual models for maternal behavior and for child behavior. In J.C. Glidewell (Ed.), *Parental attitudes and child behavior.* Springfield, IL: Thomas.

Schaefer, E.S. & Bayley, N. (1963). Maternal behavior, child behavior and their intercorrelations from infancy through adolescence. *Monographs of the Society for Research in Child Development, 28,* 1–27.

Schaffer, H.R. (1971). *The growth of sociability.* Harmondsworth, England: Penguin.

Schaffer, H.R. & Emerson, P.E. (1964). The development of social attachments in infancy. *Monographs of the Society for Research in Child Development, 29,* (Serial No. 94).

Schiff, W., Benasich, A. & Bornstein, M.H. (1986). *Infants' audio-visual integration of information specifying approach and recession.* Unpublished manuscript, New York University (cited in Lamb and Bornstein, 1987).

Schiffman, P.C., Westlake, R.E., Santiago, T.V. & Edelman, N.H. (1980). Ventilatory control in parents of victims of sudden-infant-death syndrome. *New England Journal of Medicine, 302,* 486–491.

Schneider, B., Trehub, S.E. & Bull, D. (1980). High-frequency sensitivity in infants. *Science, 207,* 1003–1004.

Schwartz, S.H., Feldman, R., Brown, M. & Heingartner, A. (1969). Some personality correlates of conduct in two situations of moral conflict. *Journal of Personality, 37,* 41–57.

Schwartzman, H.B. (1979). The sociocultural context of play. In B. Sutton-Smith (Ed.), *Play and learning.* New York: Gardner Press.

Scribner, S. & Cole, M. (1973). Cognitive consequences of formal and informal education. *Science, 182,* 553–559.

Segal, S.A. & Figley, C.R. (1985). Bulimia: Estimate of incidence and relationship to shyness. *Journal of College Student Personnel, 26,* 240–244.

Segall, M.H., Campbell, D.T. & Herskovits, M.J. (1966). *The influence of culture on visual perception.* Indianapolis: Bobbs-Merrill.

Selman, R.L. (1980). *The growth of interpersonal understanding.* New York: Academic Press.

Selman, R.L. & Byrne, D.F. (1974). A structural-developmental analysis of levels of role-taking in middle childhood. *Child Development, 45,* 803–806.

Selman, R.L. & Jacquette, D. (1978). Stability and oscillation in interpersonal awareness: A clinical-development analysis. In C.B. Keasey (Ed.), *The XXV Nebraska Symposium on Motivation.* Lincoln, NE: University of Nebraska Press.

Senn, M.J.E. (1975). Insights on the child development movement in the United States. *Monographs of the Society for Research in Child Development, 40,* (3-4, Serial No. 161).

Serbin, L.A., O'Leary, K.D., Kent, R.N. & Tonick, I.J. (1973). A comparison of teacher response to the pre-academic and problem behavior of boys and girls. *Child Development, 44,* 796–804.

Serralde de Scholz, H.C. & McDougall, R. (1978). Comparison of potential reinforcer ratings between slow learners and regular students. *Behavior Therapy, 9,* 60–64.

Shaheen, S.J. (1984). Neuromaturation of behavior development: The case of childhood lead poisoning. *Developmental Psychology, 20,* 542–550.

Shantz, C.U. (1975). *The development of social cognition.* Chicago: University of Chicago Press.

Shantz, C.U. (1983). Social cognition. In P.H. Mussen (Ed.), *Handbook of child psychology* (4th ed., vol. 3). New York: Wiley.

Shantz, D.W. (1986). Conflict, aggression and peer status: An observational study. *Child Development, 57,* 1322–1331.

Shapera, A. (1976). Developmental differences in competitive behavior of kibbutz and city children in Israel. *Journal of Social Psychology, 98,* 19–26.

Sharabany, R., Gershoni, R. & Hofman, J. (1981). Girlfriend, boyfriend: Age and sex differences in intimate friendship. *Developmental Psychology, 17,* 800–808.

Shatz, M. & Gelman, R. (1973). The development of communication skills: Modifications in the speech of young children as a function of listener. *Monographs of the Society for Research in Child Development, 38,* (5, Serial No. 152).

Shepherd-Look, D.L. (1982). Sex differentiations and the development of sex roles. In B.B. Wolman (Ed.), *Handbook of developmental psychology.* Englewood Cliffs, NJ: Prentice-Hall.

Sherman, J.A. (1967). Problems of sex differences in space perceptions and aspects of intellectual functioning. *Psychological Review, 74,* 290–299.

Sherman, M. & Key, C.B. (1932). The "intelligence" of isolated mountain children. *Child Development, 3,* 279–290.

Sherrod, L.R. (1981). Issues in cognitive perceptual development: The special case of social stimuli. In M.E. Lamb & L.R. Sherrod (Eds.), *Infant social cognition.* Hillsdale, NJ: Erlbaum.

Shields, J. (1962). *Monozygotic twins.* London: Oxford University Press.

Shonkoff, J.P. (1984). The biological substrate and physical health in middle childhood. In W.A. Collins (Ed.), *Development during middle childhood: The years from six to twelve.* Washington, D.C.: National Academy Press.

Shultz, T. & Pilon, R. (1973). Development of ability to detect linguistic ambiguity. *Child Development, 44,* 728–733.

Siegel, L.S. (1983). Correction for prematurity and its consequences for the assessment of the very low birth weight infant. *Child Development, 54,* 1176–1188.

Siegler, R.S. (1986). *Children's thinking.* Englewood Cliffs, NJ: Prentice-Hall.

Simner, M.L. (1971). Newborn's response to the cry of another infant. *Developmental Psychology, 5,* 136–150.

Singer, J.L. (Ed.) (1973). *The child's world of make-believe: Experimental studies of imaginative play.* New York: Academic Press.

Singer, L.M., Brodzinsky, D.M., Ramsay, D., Steir, M. & Waters, E. (1985). Mother-infant attachment in adoptive families. *Child Development, 56,* 1543–1551.

Sinnott, E.W. (1959). The creativeness of life. In H.H. Anderson (Ed.), *Creativity and its cultivation.* New York: Harper & Row.

Siqueland, E.R. (1964). Operant conditioning of head-turning in four-month-old infants. *Psychonomic Science, 1,* 223–224.

Siqueland, E.R. & DeLucia, A. (1969). Visual reinforcement of nonnutritive sucking in human infants. *Science, 65,* 1144–1146.

Skeels, H.M. & Dye, H.B. (1939). A study of the effects of differential stimulation of mentally-retarded children. *Proceedings of the American Association of Mental Deficiency, 44,* 114–136.

Slaby, R.G. & Frey, K.S. (1975). Development of gender constancy and selective attention to same-sex models. *Child Development, 46,* 849–856.

Slade, A. (1987). Quality of attachment and early symbolic play. *Developmental Psychology, 23,* 78–85.

Slobin, D.I. (1971). *Psycholinguistics.* Glenview, IL: Scott, Foresman.

Slobin, D.I. (1973). Cognitive prerequisites for the acquisition of grammar. In C.A. Ferguson & D.I. Slobin (Eds.), *Studies of child language development.* New York: Holt, Rinehart & Winston.

Smetana, J.G. & Letourneau, K.J. (1984). Development of gender constancy and children's sex-typed free play behavior. *Developmental Psychology, 20,* 691–696.

Smiley, S.S. & Brown, A.L. (1979). Conceptual preference for thematic or taxonomic relations: A non-monotonic trend from preschool to old age. *Journal of Experimental Child Psychology, 28,* 249–257.

Smith, D. (1978). Preparation for new life. In D.W. Smith, E.L. Bierman & N.M. Robinson (Eds.), *The biologic ages of man.* Philadelphia: Saunders.

Smith, P.K. & Connolly, K.J. (1972). Social and aggressive behavior in preschool children as a function of crowding. *Social Science Information, 16,* 601–620.

Smith, P.K. & Dutton, S. (1979). Play and training in direct and innovative problem solving. *Child Development, 50,* 830–836.

Smits, G.J. & Cherhoniak, I.M. (1976). Physical attractiveness and friendliness in interpersonal attraction. *Psychological Reports, 39,* 171–174.

Smollar, J. & Youniss, J. (1982). Social development through friendship. In K.H. Rubin & H.S. Ross (Eds.), *Peer relationships and social skills in childhood.* New York: Springer-Verlag.

Snow, C.E. (1972). Mothers' speech to children learning language. *Child Development, 43,* 549–565.

Snow, C.E. (1977). The development of conversation between mothers and babies. *Journal of Child Language, 4,* 1–22.

Snyder, E.E. (1972). High school student perceptions of prestige criteria. *Adolescence, 6,* 129–136.

Sokol, R.J., Miller, S.I. & Reed, G. (1980). Alcohol abuse during pregnancy: An epidemiologic study. *Alcoholism, 4,* 135–145.

Sonnenschein, S. (1986a). Development of referential communication skills: How familiarity with a listener affects a speaker's production of redundant messages. *Developmental Psychology, 22,* 549–552.

Sonnenschein, S. (1986b). Development of referential communication: Deciding that a message is uninformative. *Developmental Psychology, 22,* 164–168.

Sontag, L.W., Baker, C.T. & Nelson, V.L. (1958). Mental growth and personality development: A longitudinal study. *Monographs of the Society for Research in Child Development, 23* (2, Serial No. 68).

Spearman, C. (1927). *The abilities of man.* New York: Macmillan.

Spears, W.C. & Hohle, R.H. (1967). Sensory and perceptual processes in infants. In Y. Brackbill (Ed.), *Infancy and early childhood.* New York: Free Press.

Spelke, E.S. (1979). Perceiving bimodally specified events in infancy. *Developmental Psychology, 15,* 623–636.

Spelke, E.S. (1981). The infant's acquisition of knowledge of bimodally specified events. *Journal of Experimental Child Psychology, 31,* 279–299.

Spelke, E.S. (1985). Perception of unity, persistence, and identity: Thoughts on infants' conceptions of objects. In J.H. Mehler & R. Fox (Eds.), *Neonate cognition: Beyond the blooming, buzzing confusion.* Hillsdale, NJ: Erlbaum.

Spence, J.T. & Helmreich, R.L. (1978). *Masculinity and femininity: Their psychological dimensions, correlates, and antecedents.* Austin: University of Texas Press.

Spencer, H. (1873). *Principles of psychology.* New York: Appleton-Century-Crofts.

Sprigle, J.E. & Schaefer, L. (1985). Longitudinal evaluation of 2 compensatory preschool programs on fourth- through sixth-grade students. *Developmental Psychology, 21,* 702–708.

Sroufe, L.A. & Rutter, M. (1984). The domain of developmental psychopathology. *Child Development, 55,* 17–29.

Staffieri, J.R. (1967). A study of social stereotypes of body image in children. *Journal of Personality and Social Psychology, 7,* 101–104.

Stanton, A.N., Scott, D.J. & Downhan, M.A. (1980). Is overheating a factor in some unexpected infant deaths? *Lancet, 1, (8177),* 1054–1057.

Stechler, G. & Halton, A. (1982). Prenatal influences on human development. In B.B. Wolman (Ed.), *Handbook of developmental psychology.* Englewood Cliffs, NJ: Prentice-Hall.

Stein, Z.H., Susser, M.W., Saenger, G. & Marolla, F. (1975). *Famine and human development: The Dutch hunger winter of 1944–1945.* New York: Oxford University Press.

Steinberg, L.D. (1981). Transformations in family relations at puberty. *Developmental Psychology, 17,* 833–840.

Steiner, J.E. (1979). Human facial expressions in response to taste and smell stimulation. In H.E. Reese & L. Lipsitt (Eds.), *Advances in child development and behavior* (vol. 13). New York: Academic Press.

Steinschneider, A. (1970). Obstetrical medication and infant outcome: Some summary considerations. In W.B. Bowes, Y. Brackbill, E. Conway & A. Steinschneider (Eds.), The effects of obstetrical medication on fetus and infant. *Monographs of the Society for Research in Child Development, 35,* (4, Serial No. 137).

Stern, D.N., Spieker, S. & MacKain, K. (1982). Intonation contours as signals in maternal speech to prelinguistic infants. *Developmental Psychology, 18,* 727–735.

Sternberg, R.J. (1985). *Beyond IQ: A triarchic theory of human intelligence.* New York: Cambridge University Press.

Sternberg, R.J. (1986). *Intelligence applied: Understanding and increasing your intellectual skills.* New York: Harcourt Brace Jovanovich.

Sternglanz, S.H. & Serbin, L.A. (1974). Sex-role stereotyping in children's television programs. *Developmental Psychology, 10,* 710–715.

Steuer, F.B., Applefield, J.M. & Smith, R. (1971). Televised aggression and the interpersonal aggression of preschool children. *Journal of Experimental Child Psychology, 11,* 442–447.

Stevens, R. (1979). *Maternal smoking during pregnancy: Risks to the unborn baby.* Unpublished manuscript, University of Wisconsin-Green Bay.

Stevenson, H.W. (1970). Learning in children. In P.H. Mussen (Ed.), *Carmichael's manual of child psychology* (3rd ed.). New York: Wiley.

Stewart, R.B., Mobley, L.A., Van Tuyl, S.S. & Salvador, M. (1987). The firstborn's adjustment to the birth of a sibling: A longitudinal assessment. *Child Development, 58,* 341–345.

Stoddart, T. & Turiel, E. (1985). Children's concepts of cross-gender activities. *Child Development, 56,* 1241–1252.

Stodolsky, S. & Lesser, G. (1967). Learning patterns in the disadvantaged. *Harvard Educational Review, 37,* 546–593.

Scott, D.H. & Latchford, S.A. (1976). Prenatal antecedents of child health, development, and behavior: An epidemiological report of incidence and association. Journal of the American Academy of Child Psychiatry, 15, 161–191.

Straus, M.A., Geller, R. & Steinmetz, S. (1980). *Behind closed doors.* New York: Doubleday.

Streissguth, A.P., Martin, D.C., Barr, H.M. & Sandman, B.M. (1984). Intrauterine alcohol and nicotine exposure: Attention and reaction time in 4-year-old children. *Developmental Psychology, 20,* 533–541.

Streissguth, A.P., Martin, D.C., Martin, J.C. & Barr, H.M. (1981). The Seattle Longitudinal Prospective Study of Alcohol and Pregnancy. *Neurobehavioral Toxicology and Teratology, 3,* 223–233.

Striegel-Moore, R.H., Silberstein, L.R. & Rodin, J. (1986). Toward an understanding of risk factors for bulimia. *American Psychologist, 41,* 246–263.

Sulik, K.K., Johnston, M.C. & Webb, M.A. (1981). Fetal alcohol syndrome: Embryogenesis in a mouse model. *Science, 214,* 936–938.

Sutton-Smith, B. (1967). The role of play in cognitive development. *Young Children, 22,* 361–370.

Sutton-Smith, B. (1980). Children's play: Some sources of play theorizing. In K.H. Rubin (Ed.), *Children's play.* San Francisco: Jossey-Bass.

Sutton-Smith, B. (1985, October). The child at play. *Psychology Today, 19 (10),* 64–65.

Swanson, R.A. & Henderson, R.W. (1977). Effects of televised modeling and active participation on rule-governed question production among native American preschool children. *Contemporary Educational Psychology, 2,* 345–352.

Sylva, K., Bruner, J.S., & Genova, P. (1976). The role of play in the problem-solving of children 3-5 years old. In J.S. Bruner, A. Jolly & K. Sylva (Eds.), *Play: Its role in development and evolution.* New York: Basic Books.

Taft, L.T. & Cohen, H.J. (1967). Neonatal and infant reflexology. In T. Hellmuth (Ed.), *Exceptional infant* (vol. 1). New York: Brunner/Mazel.

Tamis-LeMonda, C. & Bornstein, M.H. (1986). *Mother-infant interaction: The selectivity of encouraging attention.* Paper presented at the International Conference on Infancy Studies, Los Angeles.

Tanner, J.M. (1962). *Growth at adolescence.* Oxford: Blackwell Scientific.

Tanner, J.M. (1970). Physical growth. In P.H. Mussen (Ed.), *Carmichael's manual of child psychology.* New York: Wiley.

Tanner, J.M. (1973). Growing up. *Scientific American, 229,* 34–43.

Tanner, J.M. (1978). *Fetus into man: Physical growth from conception to maturity.* Cambridge, MA: Harvard University Press.

Tavris, C. & Wade, C. (1984). *The longest war: Sex differences in perspective* (2nd ed.). New York: Harcourt Brace Jovanovich.

Taylor, I.A. (1974). Patterns of creativity and aging. In E. Pfeiffer (Ed.), *Successful aging*. Durham, NC: Duke University Center for the Study of Aging and Human Development.

Terrace, H.S., Pettito, L.A., Sanders, R.J. & Bever, T.G. (1979). Can an ape create a sentence? *Science, 206*, 891–202.

Tessman, L.H. (1978). *Children of parting parents*. New York: Aronson.

Thelen, E. (1984). Learning to walk: Ecological demands and phylogenetic constraints. In L.P. Lipsitt & C. Rovee-Collier (Eds.), *Advances in infancy research* (vol. 3). Norwood, NJ: Ablex.

Thelen, E. (1986). Treadmill-elicited stepping in seven-month-old-infants. *Child Development, 57*, 1498–1506.

Thevenin, D.M., Eilers, R.E., Oller, D.K. & Lavoie, L. (1985). Where's the drift in babbling drift? A cross-linguistic study. *Applied Psycholinguistics, 6*, 3–15.

Thomas, A. & Chess, S. (1977). *Temperament and development*. New York: Brunner/Mazel.

Thomas, A., Chess, S. & Birch, H.G. (1970). The origin of personality. *Scientific American, 223*, 102–109.

Thomas, A., Chess, S., Birch, H.G., Hertiz, M.E. & Korn, S. (1963). *Behavioral individuality in early childhood*. New York: New York University Press.

Thompson, C. (1974). The role of women in this culture. In J. Strouse (Ed.), *Women and analysis: Dialogues on psychoanalytic views of femininity*. New York: Grossman Publishers.

Thompson, R.A., Lamb, M.E. & Estes, D. (1982). Stability of infant-mother attachment and its relationships to changing life circumstances in an unselected middle-class sample. *Child Development, 53*, 144–148.

Thomas, V.D. (1974). Family size: Implicit policies and assumed psychological outcomes. *Journal of Social Issues, 30*, 93–124.

Thurstone, L.L. (1938). Primary mental abilities. *Psychometric Monographs* (No. 1).

Tieger, T. (1980). On the biological basis of sex differences in aggression. *Child Development, 51*, 943–963.

Tizard, B. (1974). *Preschool education in Britain: A research review*. London: Social Science Research Council.

Tobin-Richards, M., Boxer, A. & Petersen, A.C. (1984). The psychological impact of pubertal change: Sex differences in perceptions of self during early adolescence. In J. Brooks-Gunn & A.C. Petersen (Eds.), *Girls at puberty: Biological, psychological and social perspectives*. New York: Plenum.

Torgersen, A.M. & Kringlen, E. (1978). Genetic aspects of temperamental differences in infants: A study of same-sexed twins. *Journal of the American Academy of Child Psychiatry, 17*, 433–444.

Torrance, E.P. (1962). *Gendering creative talent*. Englewood Cliffs, NJ: Prentice-Hall.

Torrance, E.P. (1966). *Torrance Tests of Creative Thinking*. Princeton, NJ: Personnel Press.

Tortora, G.J. & Anagnostakos, N.P. (1984). *Principles of anatomy and physiology* (4th ed.). New York: Harper & Row.

Townsend, J.W., Klein, R.E., Irwin, M.H., Owens, W., Yarbrough, C. & Engle, P.L. (1982). Nutrition and preschool mental development. In D.A. Wagner & H.W. Stevenson (Eds.), *Cultural perspectives on child development*. San Francisco: Freeman.

Traub, G.S. (1983). Correlations of shyness with depression, anxiety, and academic performance. *Psychological Reports, 52*, 849–850.

Treffinger, D.J. (1985). Review of the Torrance Tests of Creative Thinking. In J.V. Mitchell (Ed.), *Ninth Mental Measurements Yearbook*. Lincoln: University of Nebraska Press.

Trehub, S.E. (1973). Infants' sensitivity to vowel and tonal contrasts. *Developmental Psychology, 9*, 91–96.

Trehub, S.E. & Schneider, B. (Eds.). (1985). *Auditory development in infancy*. New York: Plenum.

Trehub, S.E., Schneider, B. & Endman, M. (1980). Developmental changes in infants' sensitivity to octave − + and noises. *Journal of Experimental Child Psychology, 29*, 283–293.

Troll, L.E. (1972). *The salience of members of three-generation families for one another*. Paper presented at the annual meeting of the American Psychological Association, Honolulu.

Troll, L.E. (1982). *Continuations: Adult development and aging*. Monterey, CA: Brooks/Cole.

Troll, L.E. (1984). *Old women: "Poor, dumb, and ugly."* Invited address, Division 35, American Psychological Association, Toronto.

Trotter, R.J. (1986, August). Three heads are better than one. *Psychology Today, 20*, 56–62.

Turiel, E., Edwards, C.P. & Kohlberg, L. (1978). Moral development in Turkish children, adolescents, and young adults. *Journal of Cross-cultural Psychology, 9*, 75–86.

Ullian, D.Z. (1976). The development of conceptions of masculinity and femininity. In B. Lloyd & J. Archer (Eds.), *Exploring sex differences*. New York: Academic Press.

Unger, R.K. (1979). Toward a redefinition of sex and gender. *American Psychologist, 34*, 1085–1094.

U.S. Census Bureau. (1980). *Population and housing*. Washington, D.C.: U.S. Department of Commerce.

Uzgiris, I.C. (1984). Imitation in infancy: Its interpersonal aspects. In M. Perlmutter (Ed.), *The Minnesota symposia on child psychology* (vol. 17). Hillsdale, NJ: Erlbaum.

Vandenberg, B. (1980). Play, problem-solving and creativity. In K.H. Rubin (Ed.), *Children's play: New directions for child development*. San Francisco: Jossey-Bass.

Vandenberg, S.G. & Vogler, G.P. (1985). Genetic determinants of intelligence. In B. Wolman (Ed.), *Handbook of intelligence: Theories, measurements and applications*. New York: Wiley.

Vander Linde, E., Morrongiello, B.A. & Rovee-Collier, C. (1985). Determinants of retention in 8-week-old infants. *Developmental Psychology, 21*, 601–613.

Veevers, J. (1974). Factors in the incidence of childlessness in Canada: An analysis of census data. *Social Biology, 19*, 266–274.

Vernon, P.E. (1979). *Intelligence: Heredity and environment.* San Francisco: Freeman.

Volpe, J. (1976). *The development of children's conceptions of friendship.* Unpublished master's thesis, Catholic University of America, Washington, D.C.

Von Hofsten, C. (1977). Binocular convergence as a determinant of reaching behavior in infancy. *Perception, 6,* 139–144.

Vurpillot, E. (1968). The development of scanning strategies and their relation to visual differentiation. *Journal of Experimental Child Psychology, 6,* 632–650.

Vygotsky, L. (1986). *Thought and language.* (Revised & edited by A. Kozulin). Cambridge, MA: MIT Press.

Waber, D.P. (1979). Cognitive abilities and sex-related variations in the maturation of cerebral cortical functions. In M.A. Wittig and A.C. Petersen (Eds.), *Sex-related differences in cognitive functioning: Developmental issues.* New York: Academic Press.

Waddington, C.H. (1957). *The strategy of the genes.* London: Allen & Son.

Waldrop, M.L. & Halverson, C.L. (1975). Intensive and extensive peer behavior: Longitudinal and cross-sectional analyses. *Child Development, 46,* 19–26.

Walk, R.D. (1981). *Perceptual development.* Monterey, CA: Brooks/Cole.

Walker, L.J. (1984). Sex differences in the development of moral reasoning: A critical review. *Child Development, 55,* 677–691.

Walker, L.J. (1986). Sex differences in the development of moral reasoning: A rejoinder to Baumrind. *Child Development, 57,* 522–526.

Walker, L.J. & deVries, B. (1985). Moral stages/moral orientations: Do the sexes really differ? In C. Blake (Chair), *Gender difference research in moral development.* Symposium conducted at the meeting of the American Psychological Association, Los Angeles.

Walker, L.J. & Richards, B.S. (1979). Stimulating transitions in moral reasoning as a function of stage of cognitive development. *Developmental Psychology, 15,* 95–103.

Wallace, D.B. (1985). Giftedness and the construction of a creative life. In F.D. Horowitz & M. O'Brien (Eds.), *The gifted and talented: Developmental perspectives.* Washington, D.C.: American Psychological Association.

Wallach, M.A. (1985). Creativity testing and giftedness. In F.D. Horowitz & M. O'Brien (Eds.), *The gifted and talented: Developmental perspectives.* Washington, D.C.: American Psychological Association.

Wallach, M.A. & Kogan, N. (1965). *Modes of thinking in young children: A study of the creativity-intelligence distinction.* New York: Holt, Rinehart & Winston.

Wallerstein, J.S. & Kelly, J.B. (1974). The effects of parental divorce: The adolescent experience. In J. Anthony & C. Koupernik (Eds.), *The child in his family: Children at psychiatric risk* (vol. 3). New York: Wiley.

Wallerstein, J.S. & Kelly, J.B. (1975). The effects of parental divorce: Experiences of the preschool child. *Journal of the American Academy of Child Psychiatry, 14,* 600–616.

Wallerstein, J.S. & Kelly, J.B. (1976). The effects of parental divorce: Experiences of the child in early latency. *American Journal of Orthopsychiatry, 46,* 256–267.

Wallerstein, J.S. & Kelly, J.B. (1980). *Surviving the break-up: How children and parents cope with divorce.* New York: Basic Books.

Waters, E., Wippman, J. & Sroufe, L.A. (1979). Attachment, positive affect, and competence in the peer group: Two studies in construct validation. *Child Development, 50,* 821–829.

Watson, J.B. (1925). *Behaviorism.* New York: Norton.

Watson, J.B. & Raynor, R. (1920). Conditioned emotional reactions. *Journal of Experimental Psychology, 3,* 1–14.

Watson, M.M. & Jackowitz, E.R. (1984). Agents and recipient objects in the development of early symbolic play. *Child Development, 55,* 1091–1097.

Watson, R.I. (1978). *The great psychologists* (4th ed.). Philadelphia: Lippincott.

Weatherly, D. (1964). Self-perceived rate of physical maturation and personality in late adolescence. *Child Development, 35,* 1197–1210.

Wechsler, D. (1958). *The measurement and appraisal of adult intelligence* (4th ed.). Baltimore: Williams & Wilkins.

Weill, B.C. (1930). Are you training your child to be happy? p.v. *Lesson material in child management.* Washington, D.C.: U.S. Government Printing Office.

Weisberg, P. (1963). Social and non-social conditioning of infant vocalizations. *Child Development, 34,* 377–388.

Weiss, B., Williams, J.H., Margen, S., Abrams, B., Caan, B., Citron, L.J., Cox, C., McKibben, J., Ogar, D. & Schultz, S. (1980). Behavioral responses to artificial food colors. *Science, 207,* 1487–1489.

Weiss, M.L. & Mann, A.E. (1981). *Human biology and behavior.* Boston: Little, Brown.

Weissberg, J.A. & Paris, S.G. (1986). Young children's remembering in different contexts: A reinterpretation of Istomina's study. *Child Development, 57,* 1123–1129.

Werner, E.E. (1979). *Cross-cultural child development.* Monterey, CA: Wadsworth.

Werner, H. (1957). The concept of development from a comparative and organismic view. In D. Harris (Ed.), *The concept of development.* Minneapolis: University of Minnesota Press.

Werner, P.H. & Burton, E.C. (1979). *Learning through movement: Teaching cognitive content through physical activities.* St. Louis: Mosby.

Wertheimer, M. (1961). Psychomotor coordination of auditory and visual space at birth. *Science, 134,* 1692.

Whalen, C.K., Henker, B. & Dotemoto, S. (1980). Methylphenidate and hyperactivity: Effects on teacher behaviors. *Science, 208,* 1280–1282.

White, B.L. (1971). *Human infants: Experience and psychological development.* Englewood Cliffs, NJ: Prentice-Hall.

White, C.B., Bushnell, N. & Regnemer, J.L. (1978). Moral development in Bahamian school children: A three-year examination of Kohlberg's stages of moral development. *Developmental Psychology, 14,* 58–65.

Whitehurst, G.J. (1982). Language development. In B.B. Wolman (Ed.), *Handbook of developmental psychology*. Englewood Cliffs, NJ: Prentice-Hall.

Whiting, B.B. & Whiting, J.W.M. (1975). *Children of six cultures: A psychocultural analysis*. Cambridge, MA: Harvard University Press.

Whorf, B.L. (1956). *Language, thought, and reality*. New York: Wiley.

Wideman, M.V. & Singer, J.E. (1984). The role of psychological mechanisms in preparation for childbirth. *American Psychologist, 39*, 1357–1371.

Wilkinson, L.C. & Marrett, C.B. (Eds.). (1985). *Gender influences in classroom interaction*. Orlando: Academic Press.

Will, J.A., Self, P.A. & Datan, N. (1976). Maternal behavior and perceived sex of infant. *American Journal of Orthopsychiatry, 46*, 135–139.

Willerman, L. (1975). *Individual and group differences*. New York: Harper's College Press.

Willerman, L. (1979). *The psychology of individual and group differences*. San Francisco: Freeman.

Willerman, L. & Plomin, R. (1973). Activity level in children and their parents. *Child Development, 44*, 854–858.

Williams, J.W. & Stith, M. (1980). *Middle childhood: Behavior and development* (2nd ed.). New York: Macmillan.

Wilson, L., Zurcher, L., McAdams, L. & Curtis, R. (1975). Stepfathers and stepchildren: An exploratory analysis from two national surveys. *Journal of Marriage and the Family, 37*, 526–536.

Winer, G.A. (1980). Class-inclusion reasoning in children: A review of the empirical literature. *Child Development, 51*, 309–328.

Winick, M., Meyer, K. & Harris, R.C. (1975). Malnutrition and environmental enrichment by adoption. *Science, 190*, 1173–1175.

Winick, M. & Russo, P. (1969). Head circumferences and cellular growth of the brain in normal and marasmic children. *Journal of Pediatrics, 74*, 774–778.

Wishart, J.G. (1986). Siblings as models in early infant learning. *Child Development, 57*, 1232–1240.

Wishart, J.G., Bower, T.G.R. & Dunkeld, J. (1978). Reaching in the dark. *Perception, 7*, 507–512.

Wohlwill, J.F. (1973). *The study of behavioral development*. New York: Academic Press.

Wolf, F.M. & Larson, G.L. (1981). On why adolescent formal operators may not be creative thinkers. *Adolescence, 16*, 345–348.

Wolff, P.H. (1963). Observations on the early development of smiling. In B.M. Foss (Ed.), *Determinants of infant behavior* (vol. 2). New York: Wiley.

Wolff, P.H. (1966). The causes, controls, and organization of behavior in the neonate. *Psychological Issues*, vol. 5, no. 1, monograph 17.

Wolff, P.H. (1971). Mother-infant relations at birth. In J.G. Howels (Ed.), *Modern perspectives in international child psychiatry*. New York: Brunner/Mazel.

Woolfolk, A.E. (1987). *Educational psychology* (3rd ed.). Englewood Cliffs, NJ: Prentice-Hall.

Wormith, S.J., Pankhurst, D. & Moffitt, A.R. (1975). Frequency discrimination by young infants. *Child Development, 46*, 272–275.

Wozniak, R.H. (1986). Notes toward a co-constructive theory of the emotion/cognition relationships. In D. Bearison & H. Zimiles (Eds.), *Thought and motion: Developmental perspectives*. Hillsdale, NJ: Erlbaum.

Yankelovich, D. (1969). *Generations apart*. New York: Columbia Broadcasting System.

Yeates, K.O., MacPhee, D., Campbell, L.A. & Ramey, C.T. (1983). Maternal IQ and home environment as determinants of early childhood intellectual competence: A developmental analysis. *Developmental Psychology, 19*, 731–739.

Yonas, A., Bechtold, A.G., Frankel, D., Gordon, F.R., McRoberts, G., Norcia, A. & Sternfels, S. (1977). Development of sensitivity to information on impending collision. *Perception and Psychophysics, 21*, 97–104.

Yonas, A., Cleaves, W. & Pettersen, L. (1978). Development of sensitivity to pictorial depth. *Science, 200*, 77–79.

Yonas, A., Oberg, C. & Norcia, A. (1978). Development of sensitivity to binocular information for the approach of an object. *Developmental Psychology, 14*, 147–152.

Yonas, A., Pettersen, L. & Granrud, C.E. (1982). Infants' sensitivity to familiar size as information for distance. *Child Development, 53*, 1285–1290.

Yonas, A., Pettersen, L., Lockman, J. & Eisenberg, P. (1980). *The perception of impending collision in three-month-old infants*. Paper presented at the International Conference of Infant Studies, New Haven, Connecticut.

Youniss, J. & Smollar, J. (1985). *Adolescent relations with mothers, fathers, and friends*. Chicago: University of Chicago Press.

Yussen, S.R. & Levy, V.M. (1975). Developmental changes in predicting one's own span of short-term memory. *Journal of Experimental Child Psychology, 19*, 502–508.

Zahn-Waxler, C., Friedman, S.L. & Cummings, E.M. (1983). Children's emotions and behaviors in response to infants' cries. *Child Development, 54*, 1522–1528.

Zahn-Waxler, C. & Radke-Yarrow, M. (1982). The development of altruism: Alternative research strategies. In N. Eisenberg-Berg (Ed.), *The development of prosocial behavior*. New York: Academic Press.

Zahn-Waxler, C., Radke-Yarrow, M. & Cummings, E.M. (1983). Children's emotions and behaviors in response to infants' cries. *Child Development, 54*, 1522–1528.

Zajonc, R.B. & Markus, G. (1975). Birth order and intellectual development. *Psychological Review, 82*, 74–88.

Zeits, C.R. & Prince, R.M. (1982). Child effects on parents. In B.B. Wolman (Ed.), *Handbook of developmental psychology*. Englewood Cliffs, NJ: Prentice-Hall.

Zelazo, R.R. (1976). From reflexive to instrumental behavior. In L.P. Lipsett (Ed.), *Developmental psychobiology: The significance of infancy*. New York: Wiley.

Zigler, E. & Lang, M.E. (1986). The "Gourmet Baby" and the "Little Wildflower." *Zero to Three, 7*, 8–12.

Name Index

Subject Index